AMERICAN GOVERNMENT

FREEDOM AND POWER

BRIEF THIRD EDITION

AMERICAN GOVERNMENT

FREEDOM AND POWER

BRIEF THIRD EDITION

THEODORE J. LOWI
CORNELL UNIVERSITY

AND

BENJAMIN GINSBERG
THE JOHNS HOPKINS UNIVERSITY

W. W. NORTON & COMPANY
New York · London

The text of this book is composed in Palatino.
with the display set in Caslon.
Composition by ComCom.
Manufacturing by R. R. Donnelley.
Book design by Suzanne Bennett.

Cover painting: *Stars and Stripes,* by Kari Kaplan/Stockworks.

Library of Congress Cataloging-in-Publication Data

Lowi, Theodore J.
    American government : freedom and power / Theodore J. Lowi
and Benjamin Ginsberg. — Brief 3rd ed.
        p. cm.
    Includes bibliographical references and index.
        1. United States—Politics and government. I. Ginsberg,
Benjamin. II. Title.
JK274.L647   1994b
320.973—dc20   93-14452

ISBN 0-393-96473-6

W. W. Norton & Company, Inc.
500 Fifth Avenue, New York, N.Y. 10110

W. W. Norton & Company Ltd.
10 Coptic Street, London WC1A 1PU

    2 3 4 5 6 7 8 9 0

CONTENTS

Preface xi

PART 1
FOUNDATIONS

Chapter 1
Freedom and Power: An Introduction to the Problem 2

Government and Control 4
Foundations of Government 4
Forms of Government 6
Influencing the Government: Politics 7

From Coercion to Consent 8
Limits and Democratization 8
The Great Transformation: Tying Democracy to Strong Government 11

Freedom and Power: The Problem 12

For Further Reading 13

Chapter 2
Constructing a Government: The Founding and the Constitution 14

The First Founding: Interests and Conflicts 15

Political Strife and the Radicalizing of the Colonists 15
The Declaration of Independence 17
The Articles of Confederation 17

The Second Founding: From Compromise to Constitution 19
International Standing and Balance of Power 19
The Constitutional Convention 20

The Constitution 24
The Legislative Branch 25
The Executive Branch 28
The Judicial Branch 29
National Unity and Power 29
Amending the Constitution 30
Ratifying the Constitution 31
Constitutional Limits on the National Government's Power 31

The Fight for Ratification 33

Reflections on the Founding 34

Chapter Review 36

For Further Reading 37

Chapter 3
The Constitutional Framework: Federalism and the Separation of Powers 38

The First Principle: The Federal Framework 39
Restraining National Power with Dual Federalism, 1789–1937 40
Federalism as a Limitation on the National Government's Power 43
The Continuing Influence of Federalism: State and Local Government Today 46

The Second Principle: The Separation of Powers 50
Checks and Balances 52
Legislative Supremacy 52

Changing the Framework: Constitutional Amendment 56

Amendments: Many Are Called, Few Are Chosen 57
Which Were Chosen? An Analysis of the Twenty-seven 59

Chapter Review 66

For Further Reading 67

Chapter 4
The Constitution and the Individual: The Bill of Rights, Civil Liberties, and Civil Rights 68

Civil Liberties: Nationalizing the Bill of Rights 69
Dual Citizenship 70
The Fourteenth Amendment 71
The Second Constitutional Revolution 73
The Supreme Court—From Warren through Burger to Rehnquist 76

Civil Rights 81
Plessy v. Ferguson: "Separate but Equal" 82
Racial Discrimination after World War II 82
Simple Justice: The Courts, the Constitution, and Civil Rights after Brown v. Board of Education 84
The Politics of Rights: Affirmative Action 89

Chapter Review 93

For Further Reading 94

PART 2
INSTITUTIONS

Chapter 5
Congress: The First Branch 98

Making Law 98
Bicameralism: House and Senate 100

Political Parties: Congress's Oldest
Hierarchy 101
    *Party Leadership in the House and the
    Senate 101*
    Party Discipline 104

The Committee System: The Core of
Congress 111

The Staff System: Staffers and Agencies 112

Informal Organization: The Caucuses 113

Rules of Lawmaking: How a Bill Becomes
a Law 114
    Committee Deliberation 114
    The Calendar 115
    Debate 116
    *Reconciling House and Senate Versions of
    an Act 119*
    The Budget Process 119
    Vetoes 121

Beyond Legislation: Additional
Congressional Powers 121
    Oversight 122
    *Advice and Consent: Special Senate
    Powers 123*
    Direct Committee Government 125
    The Legislative Veto 125
    Direct Patronage 126

Congress and the Future: The Fall and Rise
of Congressional Power 129

Congress: Freedom and Power 134

Chapter Review 137

For Further Reading 138

Chapter 6
The President and the
Executive Branch 140

The Constitutional Basis of the
Presidency 141
    *The President as Head of State: Some
    Imperial Qualities 142*
    *The Domestic Presidency: The President
    as Head of Government 145*

The Rise of Presidential Government 148
    The Legislative Epoch, 1800–1933 149
    The New Deal and the Presidency 151

Presidential Government 152
    *Formal Resources of Presidential
    Power 154*
    Informal Resources 163

Bureaucracy in a Democracy 172
    The President as Chief Executive 173
    Congress and Responsible Bureaucracy 176

Chapter Review 180

For Further Reading 180

Chapter 7
The Federal Courts:
Least Dangerous Branch
or Imperial Judiciary? 182

The Judicial Process 183
    Cases and the Law 183
    Cases in the Courts 185

Federal Jurisdiction 186
    The Lower Federal Courts 186
    The Appellate Courts 188
    The Supreme Court 189

Judicial Review 189
    Judicial Review of Acts of Congress 191
    Judicial Review of State Actions 192
    *Judicial Review and the Administration of
    Justice 192*
    Judicial Review and Lawmaking 194

Influences on Supreme Court Decisions 197
    The Supreme Court Justices 197
    *Controlling the Flow of Cases—The Role
    of the Solicitor General 200*

Judicial Power and Politics 202
    *Traditional Limitations on the Federal
    Courts 202*
    Two Judicial Revolutions 203

Chapter Review 211

For Further Reading 212

PART 3
POLITICS AND POLICY

Chapter 8
Public Opinion and the Media 216

The Marketplace of Ideas 217
  Origins of the Idea Market 217
  The Idea Market Today 219

Shaping Public Opinion 223

The Media 230
  Shaping Events 230
  The Sources of Media Power 230
  Candidates Try to Turn the Tables 234
  The Rise of Investigative Reporting 236

Measuring Public Opinion 240
  Constructing Public Opinion from Surveys 241
  Public Opinion, Political Knowledge, and the Importance of Ignorance 245

Public Opinion and Government Policy 246

Chapter Review 250

For Further Reading 250

Chapter 9
Elections 252

Political Participation 253

Regulating the Electoral Process 253
  Electoral Composition 254
  Translating Voters' Choices into Electoral Outcomes 258
  Insulating Decision-Making Processes 261

How Voters Decide 264
  The Bases of Electoral Choice 264

Electoral Realignments 266
  Realigning Eras 266
  Elections in America Today: Factional Struggle without Realignment 269

The 1992 Election: Shifting Alignments of Political Forces 271
  Republican Disarray 271
  Democratic Opportunity 277
  The Campaign 281
  Democratic Triumph 284
  Congressional Elections 285
  The Consequences of Consent 286

Chapter Review 289

For Further Reading 290

Chapter 10
Political Parties 292

The Two-Party System in America 294
  Similarities and Differences Today 297
  Minor Parties 297

Functions of the Parties 300
  Nominations and Elections 301
  The Parties' Influence on National Government 302
  Facilitation of Mass Electoral Choice 306

Weakening of Party Organization 307
  High-Tech Politics 308
  From Labor-Intensive to Capital-Intensive Politics 313
  Is the Party Over? 316

Chapter Review 322

For Further Reading 323

Chapter 11
Groups and Interests 324

Character of Interest Groups 326
  What Interests Are Represented 326
  Organizational Components 326
  The Characteristics of Members 327

The Proliferation of Groups 328
  Expansion of Government 328
  New Politics Movement and Public Interest Groups 330

Strategies: The Quest for Political
Power 333
  Going Public 333
  Lobbying 336
  Gaining Access 338
  Using the Courts (Litigation) 341
  Electoral Politics 344
Groups and Interests—The Dilemma 349
Chapter Review 352
For Further Reading 352

Chapter 12
Politics and Government: The Problem with the Process 354

Can the Government Govern? 354
The Decline of Voting and the Rise of
Politics by "Other Means" 356
  Politics outside the Electoral Arena 357
  Revelation, Investigation, Prosecution 361
  Divided Government 365
  No More Division? 368
Can Democratic Politics Function without
Voters? 372
Politics and Governance 374
Electoral Mobilization and Governmental
Power 379
  Electoral Mobilization in Contemporary
  Politics 381
Chapter Review 386
For Further Reading 387

Chapter 13
Introduction to Public Policy 388

Techniques of Control 389
  Promotional Techniques 389
  Regulatory Techniques 391

  Redistributive Techniques 397
Substantive Uses of the Policies 399
  The Welfare State as Fiscal and Social
  Policy 399
  Imperfections in the Society: Changing
  the Rules of Inequality 403
  Affirmative Action 406
Chapter Review 413
For Further Reading 414

Chapter 14
Foreign Policy and World Politics 416

The Setting: A World of Nation-States 417
The Values in American Foreign Policy 419
  Legacy of the Traditional System 420
  The Great Leap—Thirty Years Late 421
The Instruments of Modern American
Foreign Policy 421
  Diplomacy 422
  The United Nations 422
  The International Monetary Structure 426
  Economic Aid 427
  Collective Security 430
  Military Deterrence 434
Roles Nations Play 437
  Choosing a Role 437
  Roles for America Today 439
Chapter Review 447
For Further Reading 448

Chapter 15
The State of the Union 450

America the Beacon 450
  Freedom and Power 451
The Conditions for Democracy 453
Freedom or Power? 455
For Further Reading 456

APPENDIX

The Declaration of Independence
A-3

The Constitution of the
United States A-6

Amendments to the Constitution
A-16

The Federalist Papers, No. 10
A-23

The Federalist Papers, No. 51
A-27

Glossary of Terms A-30

Glossary of Court Cases A-44

Acknowledgments A-54

Index A-57

PREFACE
TO THE BRIEF EDITION

*I*n the two years since the publication of the second edition of *American Government: Freedom and Power*, the world has changed in a number of surprising ways. The collapse of the Berlin Wall was followed by the collapse of the Soviet satellite empire, and then by the Soviet Union itself. The Cold War, once a threat to world civilization, seemed to have ended of itself. The war against Iraq, though far from being decisive, nevertheless opened up possibilities for a nonviolent Middle East unimaginable two years ago. Even the hated apartheid system in South Africa was confronting a very probable transformation. The new world is filled with new nations, built on nationalities reborn. Conflicts among them are very probable, but no more probable than peaceful relationships, as for example, the giant steps toward a Western European union. World war seems more remote now than at any either time this century.

Against this backdrop of dramatic political change throughout the world, American domestic politics seems almost to be frozen in time. When we wrote the first and second editions, the United States was plagued by divided government, huge budget deficits, and lack of popular political participation. Today, as we shall see in the third edition, government is no longer divided after Democrat, Bill Clinton's victory in the 1992 presidential election. However, budget deficits are larger than ever and Americans participate less than ever before.

But, in a changing world it is more important than ever to understand the politics of the United States. More than at any other time since the Second World War, the world is looking to America for leadership and for an example of popular government in action. Throughout the world, America—despite its problems and faults—symbolizes the combination of freedom and power to which so many now aspire. This makes the task of our book all the more important.

This *Brief Edition of American Government: Freedom and Power* is designed specifically for use in courses whose length or format requires a more concise text. We preserved as much as possible of the narrative style and historic and comparative analysis of the larger text. Though this is a *Brief Edition,* we have sought to provide a full and detailed discussion of every topic that, in our view, is central to understanding American government and politics. We hope that we have written a book that is physically brief but is not intellectually sketchy.

The collaboration on this book began nearly ten years before its publication, and the book is in every way a product of collaboration in teaching, research, and writing. Each author has taught other courses— for thirty-five and twenty-one years respectively—and has written other books; but we agree that no course has been more challenging than the introductory course, and no book has been more difficult to write. Someone once asked if it is difficult for scholars to "write down" to introductory students. No. It is difficult to "write up" to them. Introductory students, of whatever age or reading level, need more, require more, and expect more of a book.

A good teaching book, like a good novel or play, is written on two levels. One is the level of the narrative, the story line, the characters in action. The second is the level of character development, of the argument of the book or play. We would not be the first to assert that there is much of the theatrical about politics today, but our book may be unusual to the extent that we took that assertion as a guide. We have packed it full of narrative—with characters and with the facts about the complex situations in which they find themselves. We have at the same time been determined not to lose sight of the second level, yet we have tried to avoid making the second level so prominent as to define us as preachers rather than teachers.

The book is only one product of our collaboration. The other important product is about 5,000 Cornell and Johns Hopkins students who took the course out of which this book grew. There is no way to convey adequately our appreciation to those students. Their raw intelligence was not satisfied until the second level could provide a logic linking the disparate parts of what we were asserting was a single system of government. And these linkages had to be made in ordinary language. We hope we brought this to the book.

We hope also that we brought over from our teaching experience a full measure of sympathy for all who teach the introductory course, most particularly those who are obliged to teach the course from departmental necessity rather than voluntarily as a desired part of their career. And we hope our book will help them appreciate the course as we do—as an opportunity to make sense of a whole political system. Much can be learned about the system from a reexamination of the innumerable familiar facts, under the still more challenging condition that the facts be somehow interesting, significant, and, above all, linked.

This points to what must be the most troublesome, sometimes the most embarrassing, problem for this course, for this book, and for political science in general: All Americans are to a great extent familiar with the politics and government of their own country. No fact is intrinsically difficult to grasp, and in such an open society, facts abound. In America, many facts are commonplace that are suppressed elsewhere. The ubiquity of political commonplaces is indeed a problem, but it can be turned into a virtue. These very commonplaces give us a vocabulary that is widely shared, and such a vocabulary enables us to communicate effectively at the first level of the book, avoiding abstract concepts and professional language (jargon). Reaching beyond the commonplaces to the second level also identifies what is to us the single most important task of the teacher of political science—to confront the million facts and to choose from among them the small number of really significant ones.

We have tried to provide a framework to help the teacher make choices among facts and to help the students make some of the choices for themselves. This is good political science, and it is good citizenship, which means more than mere obedience and voting; it means participation through constructive criticism, being able to pierce through the information explosion to the core of enduring political reality.

Our framework is freedom and power. To most Americans that means freedom *versus* governmental power, because Americans have been raised to believe that every expansion of the government's power involves a contraction of personal freedom. Up to a point we agree with this traditional view. The institutions of American government are in fact built on a contradiction: Popular freedom and governmental power *are* contradictory, and it is the purpose of our Constitution to build a means of coping with that contradiction. But as Supreme Court justices sometimes say to their colleagues, "We concur, dissenting in part." For in truth, freedom and power are related to each other as husband and wife—each with some conflicting requirements, but neither able to produce, as a family, without the other.

Just as freedom and power are in conflict, so are they complementary. *There can be little freedom, if any, without governmental power.* Freedom of any one individual depends fundamentally on the restraints of everyone else in his or her vicinity. Most of these restraints are self-imposed. We call that *civility,* respect for others born of our awareness that it is a condition of their respect for us. Other restraints vital to personal freedom are imposed spontaneously by society. Europeans call those restraints *civil society;* sociologists call them *institutions.* Institutions exist as society's means of maintaining order and predictability through routines, customs, shared values. But even in the most stable society, the restraints of civility and of civil society are incomplete and insufficient; there remains a sphere of deliberate restraint that calls for the exercise of public control (public power). Where society falls down, or where new events and new technologies produce new stresses, or where even the most civil of human beings find their basic needs in conflict with others, there will be an exercise of public control, or public power. Private property, that great bastion of personal freedom in the Western world, would disappear without elaborate government controls.

If freedom were only a matter of the absence of control, there would be no need for a book like ours. In fact, there would be little need for political science at all. But politics, however far away in the national or the state capital, is a matter of life and death. It can be as fascinating as any good novel or adventure film if the key political question is one's own survival or the survival of one's society. We have tried to write each chapter of this book in such a way that the reader is tempted to ask what that government institution, that agency, this committee or that election, this group or that amendment has to do with *me* and *us,* and how has it come to be that way? That's what freedom and power are all about—my freedom and your restraint, my restraint and your freedom.

Having chosen a framework for the book there was also a need for a method. The method must be loyal to the framework; it must facilitate the effort to choose which facts are essential, and it must assist in evaluating those facts in ways that not only enlighten students but enable them to engage in analysis and evaluation for themselves. Although we are not bound exclusively to a single method in any scientific or philosophic sense, the method most consistently employed is one of history, or history as development: First, we present the state of affairs, describing the legislature, the party, the agency, or policy, with as many of the facts as are necessary to tell the story and to enable us to reach the broader question of freedom versus governmental power. Next, we ask how we have gotten to where we are. By what series of steps, and when by choice, and when by accident? To what extent was the history of Congress or of the parties or the presidency a fulfillment of constitutional principle, and when were the developments a series of dogged responses to economic necessity? History is our method because it helps choose which facts are significant. History also helps those who would like to try to explain why we are where we are. But more important even than explanation, history helps us make judgments. In other words, we look less to causes and more to consequences. Political

science cannot be satisfied with objective description, analysis, and explanation. Political science would be a failure if it did not have a vision about the ideal as well as the real. What is a good and proper balance between freedom and governmental power? What can a constitution do about it? What can enlightened people do about it?

Evaluation makes political science worth doing but also more difficult to do. Academics make a distinction between the hard sciences and the soft sciences, implying that hard science is the only real science: laboratory, people in white coats, precision instruments making measurements to several decimal points, testing hypotheses with "hard data." But as medical scientist Jared Diamond observes, that is a recent and narrow view, considering that science in Latin means knowledge and careful observation. Diamond suggests, and we agree, that a better distinction is between hard (i.e., difficult) science and easy science, with political science fitting into the hard category, precisely because many of the most significant phenomena in the world cannot be put in a test tube and measured to several decimal points. We must nevertheless be scientific about them. And more: unlike physical scientists, social scientists have an obligation to judge whether the reality could be better. In trying to meet that obligation, we hope to demonstrate how interesting and challenging political science can be.

The Design of the Book

The objective we have taken upon ourselves in writing this book is thus to advance our understanding of freedom and power by exploring in the fullest possible detail the way Americans have tried to balance the two through careful crafting of the rules, through constructing balanced institutions, and by maintaining moderate forms of organized politics. The book is divided into four parts, reflecting the historical process by which freedom and governmental power are (or are not) kept in balance. Part I, "Foundations," comprises the chapters concerned with the writing of the rules of the contract. The founding of 1787–1789 put it all together, but that was actually a second effort after a first failure. The original contract, the Articles of Confederation, did not achieve an acceptable balance—too much freedom, and not enough power. The second founding, the Constitution ratified in 1789, was itself an imperfect effort to establish the rules, and within two years new terms were added—the first ten amendments, called the Bill of Rights. And for the next century and a half following their ratification in 1791, the courts played umpire and translator in the struggle to interpret those terms. Chapter 1 introduces our theme. Chapter 2 concentrates on the founding itself. Chapters 3 and 4 chronicle the long struggle to establish what was meant by the three great principles of limited government, *federalism, separation of powers,* and *individual liberties and rights.*

Part II, "Institutions," includes the chapters sometimes referred to as the "nuts and bolts." But none of these particles of government mean anything except in the larger context of the goals governments must meet and the limits that have been imposed upon them. Chapter 5 is an introduction to the fundamental problem of *representative government* as this has been institutionalized in Congress. Congress, with all its problems, is the most creative legislative body in the world. But how well does Congress provide a meeting ground between consent and governing? How are society's demands taken into account in debates on the floor of

Congress and deliberations by its committees? What interests turn out to be most effectively "represented" in Congress? What is the modern Congress's constituency?

Chapter 6 explores the same questions for the presidency and the government bureaucracy. Although Article II of the Constitution provides that the president should see that the laws made by Congress are "faithfully executed," the presidency was always part of our theory of representative government, and the modern presidency has increasingly become a law *maker* rather than merely a law implementor. What, then, does a strong presidency with a large executive branch do to the conduct and the consequences of representative government?

Chapter 7 on the judiciary should not be lost in the shuffle. Referred to by Hamilton as "the least dangerous branch," the judiciary truly has become a co-equal branch, to such an extent that if Hamilton were alive today he would probably eat his words.

Part III we entitle "Politics and Policy." Politics encompasses all the efforts by any and all individuals and groups inside as well as outside the government to determine what government will do and on whose behalf it will be done. Our chapters take the order of our conception of how politics developed since the Age of Revolution and how politics works today: Chapter 8, "Public Opinion and the Media"; Chapter 9, "Elections"; Chapter 10, "Political Parties"; and Chapter 11, "Groups and Interests." But we recognize that, although there may be a pattern to American politics, it is not readily predictable. One need only contemplate the year-long nomination of presidential candidates to recognize how much confusion, downright disorder, there is in what we political scientists blithely call "political process." Chapter 12 is an evaluation of that process. We ask whether our contemporary political process is consistent with good government. Unfortunately, the answer is not entirely positive.

The last chapters are primarily about public policies, which are the most deliberate and goal-oriented aspects of the still-larger phenomenon of "government in action." Chapter 13 is virtually a handbook of public policy. Since most Americans know far less about policies than they do about institutions and politics, we felt it was necessary to provide a usable, common vocabulary of public policy. Since public policies are most often defined by the goals that the government establishes in broad rhetorical terms and since there can be an uncountable number of goals, we have tried to get beyond and behind goals by looking at the "techniques of control" that any public policy goal must embody if the goal is even partially to be fulfilled. Chapter 14, "Foreign Policy and World Politics," turns to the international realm and America's place in it. Our concern here is to understand American foreign policies and why we have adopted the policies that we have. Given the traditional American fear of "the state" and the genuine danger of international involvements to domestic democracy, a chapter on foreign policies is essential to a book on American government and also reveals a great deal about America as a culture.

Chapter 15 is a summation. We are not debaters, and we are not lawyers writing a brief for the defense of freedom or power. Our brief is for the balance. It is not, as some popular authors would put it, "that delicate balance." It is for us a very "*in*delicate balance." Nearly 160 years ago, Alexis de Tocqueville wrote that Americans would eventually permit their government to become so powerful that elections and representative processes would come to be ironic interludes providing citizens with little more than the opportunity to wave the chains by which the government had bound them. Can we have both popular freedom and governmental power in a nation of 250 million people making up a nation-state with historic obligations and historic vulnerabilities to 200 other nation-states? To what extent can we continue to depend upon and benefit from governmental power while retaining our liberties? These are the questions every generation must ask for itself—if it is fortunate enough to be able to do so.

Acknowledgments

Our students at Cornell and Johns Hopkins have already been identified as an essential factor in the writing of this book. They have been our most immediate intellectual community, a hospitable one indeed. Another part of our community, perhaps a large suburb, is the discipline of political science itself. Our debt to the scholarship of our colleagues is scientifically measurable, probably to several decimal points, in the footnotes of each chapter. Despite many complaints that the field is too scientific or not scientific enough, political science is alive and well in the United States. It is an aspect of democracy itself, and it has grown and changed in response to the developments of government and politics that we have chronicled in our book. If we did a "time line" on the history of political science as we have done for each chapter of the book, it would show a close association with developments in "the American state." Sometimes the discipline has been out of phase and critical; at other times, it has been in phase and perhaps apologetic. But political science has never been at a loss for relevant literature, and without it, our job would have been impossible.

There have, of course, been individuals on whom we have relied in particular. Of all writers, living and dead, we find ourselves most in debt to the writing of two—James Madison and Alexis de Tocqueville. Many other great authors have shaped us as they have shaped all political scientists. But Madison and Tocqueville have stood for us not only as the bridge to all timeless political problems; they represent the ideal of political science itself—that political science must be steadfastly scientific in the search for what is, yet must keep alive a strong sense of what ought to be, recognizing that democracy is neither natural nor invariably good, and must be fiercely dedicated to constant critical analysis of all political institutions in order to contribute to the maintenance of a favorable balance between individual freedom and public power.

We are pleased to acknowledge our debt to the many colleagues who had a direct and active role in criticism and preparation of the manuscript. The first edition was read and reviewed by: Gary Bryner, Brigham Young University; James F. Herndon, Virginia Polytechnic Institute and State University; James W. Riddlesperger, Jr., Texas Christian University; John Schwarz, University of Arizona; Toni-Michelle Travis, George Mason University; and Lois Vietri, University of Maryland. Their comments were enormously helpful. For subsequent editions, we relied heavily on the thoughtful manuscript reviews we received from Russell Hanson, University of Indiana; William Keech, University of North Carolina; Donald Kettl, University of Wisconsin; William McLauchlan, Purdue University; J. Roger Baker, Wittenburg University; James Lennertz, Lafayette College; and Allan McBride, Grambling State University. The advice we received from these colleagues was especially welcome because all had used the book in their own classrooms. Other colleagues who offered helpful comments based upon their own experience with the text included Douglas Costain, University of Colorado; Robert Hoffert, Colorado State University; Mark Silverstein, Boston University; and Norman Thomas, University of Cincinnati.

We also want to reiterate our thanks to the four colleagues who allowed us the privilege of testing a trial edition of our book by using it as the major text in their introductory American Government courses. Their reactions, and those of their students, played an important role in our first edition. We are very grateful to Gary Bryner, Brigham Young University; Allan J. Cigler, University of Kansas; Burnet V. Davis, Alma College; and Erwin A. Jaffe, California State University-Stanislaus.

We owe a special debt to Robert J. Spitzer, State University of New York—College at Cortland, for preparing most of the essays profiling important individuals that appear throughout the book. By linking concepts and events to real people, these essays help to make this a more lively and interesting book and thus one that students will be more likely to read and remember. Professor Spitzer also helped develop the new "Debating the Issues" boxes, in which core concepts are debated by political thinkers.

We also are grateful for the talents and hard work of several research assistants, whose contribution can never be adequately compensated: Douglas Dow and John Forren prepared the test bank. Brenda Holzinger helped to develop the study questions. Steve McGovern prepared the film guide and the annotated bibliographies. Others who gave us significant help with the book are Melody Butler, Rebecca Fisher, Michael Harvey, Nancy Johnson, David Lytell, Dennis Merryfield, Rachel Reiss, Nandini Sathe,

Noah Silverman, Rob Speel, Jennifer Waterston, and Daniel Wirls (now a member of the Politics faculty at the University of California at Santa Cruz).

Jacqueline Discenza not only typed several drafts of the manuscript, but also helped to hold the project together. We thank her for her hard work and dedication.

Theodore Lowi would like to express his gratitude to the French-American Foundation and the Gannett Foundation whose timely invitations helped him prepare for his part of this enterprise.

Perhaps above all, we wish to thank all those who kept the production and all the loose ends of the book coherent and in focus. Roby Harrington has been an extremely talented editor. Through three editions, Roby has kept careful track of all the details while maintaining a clear vision of the text as a whole. Margie Brassil, as our project editor, kept us from making too many mistakes. Nancy Yanchus devoted the better part of a year to the third and brief editions. Stephen Dunn and Sandra Smith helped out on many editorial and marketing questions. Ruth Dworkin was our efficient production manager. We also want to reiterate our thanks to Amy Cherry and Sandy Lifland for their marvelous work on the first edition. Finally, our thanks to Donald Lamm, Norton's president, for his continuing commitment to the project.

We are, however, more than happy to absolve all of these contributors from any flaws, errors, and misjudgments that will inevitably be discovered. We wish the book could be free of all production errors, grammatical errors, misspellings, misquotes, missed citations, etc. From that standpoint, a book ought to try to be perfect. But substantively we have not tried to write a flawless book; we have not tried to write a book to please everyone. We have again tried to write an effective book, a book that cannot be taken lightly. Our goal was not to make every reader a political scientist. Our goal was to restore politics as a subject matter of vigorous and enjoyable discourse, recapturing it from the bondage of the thirty-second news bite and the thirty-page technical briefing. Every person can be knowledgeable because everything about politics is accessible. One does not have to be an anchor person to profit from political events. One does not have to be a philosopher to argue about the requisites of democracy, a lawyer to dispute constitutional interpretations, an economist to debate a public policy. We would be very proud if our book contributes in a small way to the restoration of the ancient art of political controversy.

Theodore J. Lowi
Benjamin Ginsberg
August 1993

PART 1

FOUNDATIONS

1

FREEDOM AND POWER: AN INTRODUCTION TO THE PROBLEM

A story often told by politicians concerns a voter from the Midwest who, upon returning home from military service in Korea, took advantage of his federal education benefits under the G.I. Bill to complete college. After graduation, this individual was able to obtain a government loan from the Small Business Administration (SBA) to help him start a business, and a mortgage subsidized by the Federal Housing Administration (FHA) to purchase a home. Subsequently, he received medical care in a Veteran's Administration Hospital, including treatment with drugs developed by the National Institutes of Health. This voter drove to work every day on a four-lane highway built under the federal interstate highway program, frequently used Amtrak to travel to a nearby city and, though he was somewhat nervous about air travel, relied on the Federal Aviation Administration (FAA) to make certain that the aircraft he depended on for business and vacation trips were safe. When this voter's children reached college age, they obtained federal student loans to help pay their expenses. At the same time, his aging parents were happy to begin receiving monthly Social Security checks and, when his father unexpectedly required major surgery, financial disaster was averted because the federal government's Medicare program paid the bulk of the cost.

What was our midwestern friend's response to all of this? Well, in both 1980 and 1984, he strongly supported Ronald Reagan's presidential candidacy because of Reagan's promise to get the federal government off people's backs. In 1988, our friend voted for George Bush because he believed that Bush would continue Reagan's efforts to hold the line on federal domestic spending. In 1992, disgruntled by Bush's failure to adhere to his pledge not to raise taxes, this midwesterner supported Ross Perot. During this entire period, meanwhile he also voted for the re-election of his congressman, a staunch Democrat, who steadfastly opposed any cuts in the government's domestic programs. This is an example of the love-hate relationship between Americans and their government.

Government has become a powerful and pervasive force in the United States. In 1789, 1889, and even in 1929, America's national government was limited in size, scope, and influence, while states provided most of the important functions of government. By 1933, however, the influence of the government expanded to meet the crises created by the stock market crash of 1929, the ensuing Great Depression, and the run on the banks of 1933. Congress passed legislation that brought the government into the business of home mortgages, farm mortgages, credit, and relief of personal distress. Today, the national government is an enormous institution with programs and policies reaching into every corner of American life. It oversees the nation's economy; it is the nation's largest employer; it provides citizens with a host of services; it controls a formidable military establishment; and it regulates a wide range of social and commercial activities. The founding fathers never dreamed the government could take on such obligations; we today can hardly dream of a time when the government was such an important part of our lives.

The growth of government in the United States has been accompanied by a change in the way Americans look at government. In the nineteenth century, Americans generally were wary of government, especially the remote national government. Government meant control, and control meant fewer individual liberties. The best government, as Thomas Jefferson put it, was the one that governed least. Many Americans today continue to pay lip service to this early view, but a new theory of democratic government has gradually come to dominate political thought. This new theory states that if government could be made less of a threat and less remote by the development of elections and other forms of popular control, then a more powerful government would be one with greater capacity to serve the people. In other words, government control of the people would be more acceptable if people, in turn, controlled the government.[1]

Today, there is a broad consensus favoring a large and active government. Ronald Reagan, our most conservative president in more than half a century, began his successful 1980 presidential campaign not by promising to curtail government activity, but rather by vowing to "restore to the federal government the capacity to do the people's work." In his first inaugural address, President Reagan pledged to curb the growth of the federal establishment but at the same time declared, "Now so there will be no misunderstanding, it is not my intention to do away with government. It is,

---

[1] For examples, see Richard Wollheim, "A Paradox of the Theory of Democracy," in *Philosophy, Politics and Society*, ed. Peter Laslett and W. G. Runciman (Oxford: Blackwell, 1962).

rather, to make it work."[2] Reagan repeated this sentiment in his 1985 inaugural. In 1992, in his speech accepting the Democratic presidential nomination, Bill Clinton noted correctly that "the Republicans have campaigned against big government for a generation. . . . But have you noticed? They've run this big government for a generation and they haven't changed a thing.[3]

Americans want to keep the political and economic benefits they believe they derive from government (see Table 1.1). According to polls, many Americans would be willing to pay higher taxes to maintain government services and programs. How did government come to play such an important role in our lives? How did Americans come to lose some of their fear of remote government and to look at government as a valuable servant rather than a threat to freedom?

To answer these questions, this chapter will first assess the meaning and character of government in general, describing some of the alternative forms government can take and the key differences among them. Second, we will examine the factors that led to one particular form of government—representative democracy—in Western Europe and the United States. Finally, we will begin to address the question central not only to our book but also to the most fundamental and enduring problem of democratic politics—the relationship between government and freedom.

Government and Control

Government is the term generally used to describe the formal institutions through which a land and its people are ruled. To govern is to rule. *Government is composed of institutions and processes that rulers establish to strengthen and perpetuate their power or control over a territory and its inhabitants.* A government may be as simple as a tribal council that meets occasionally to advise the chief, or as complex as our own vast establishment with its forms, rules, and bureaucracies.

Foundations of Government

Groups aspire to govern for a variety of reasons. Some have the most high-minded aims, while others are little more than ambitious robbers. But whatever their motives and character, those who aspire to rule must be able to secure obedience and fend off rivals as well as collect the revenues needed to accomplish these tasks.[4] That is why, whatever their makeup, governments historically have included two basic components: a means of coercion, such as an army or police force, and a means of collecting revenue. Some governments, including many in the Third World of less-developed nations today, have consisted of little more than an army and a tax-collecting agency. Other governments, especially those in the developed nations such as our own, attempt to provide services as well as to collect taxes in order to secure popular consent for control. For some, power is an end in itself. For most, power is necessary to maintain public order.

---

[2]"President Reagan's Inaugural Address," *New York Times*, 21 January 1981, p. B1.

[3]E. J. Dionne, "Beneath the Rhetoric, an Old Question," *Washington Post*, 31 August 1992, p. 1.

[4]For an excellent discussion, see Charles Tilly, "Reflections on the History of European State-Making," in *The Formation of Nation States of Western Europe*, ed. Charles Tilly (Princeton: Princeton University Press, 1975), pp. 3–83. See also Charles Tilly, "War Making and State Making as Organized Crime," in *Bringing the State Back In*, ed. Peter Evans, Dietrich Rueschemeyer, and Theda Skocpol (New York: Cambridge University Press, 1985), pp. 169–91.

TABLE 1.1
SOME ACTIVITIES OF THE U.S. GOVERNMENT IN 1993

Beneficiary and Program	Cost	Beneficiary and Program	Cost
Business		**Farmers**	
Department of Energy, *Energy Supply, Research & Dev. Activities*	2,576,000,000	Department of Agriculture, *Commodity Credit Corporation*	9,745,000,000
Export-Import Bank of U.S.	2,236,385,000	Department of Agriculture, *Farmers Home Administration, Agriculture Credit Insurance Fund*	4,043,000,000
Needy Children			
Department of Agriculture, Food & Nutrition Science, *Child Nutrition Program*	5,577,000,000	**Homeowners**	
		HUD, Federal Housing Administration Fund	1,937,300,000
Department of Health & Human Services, *Health Resources & Human Services*	1,862,000,000	**Labor Unions**	
		Department of Labor, Training & Employment Services	4,079,000,000
College Students and Universities		**The Sick and Disabled**	
Department of Education, Office of Postsecondary Education, *Pell Grants*	6,715,000,000	Department of Education, Office of Special Education & Rehabilitation Services, Education for the Handicapped	2,467,000,000
Department of Education, Office of Postsecondary Education, Guaranteed Student Loans	1,956,402,000	HHS,National HIV Program	1,760,000,000
		HSS, Supplemental Security Income Program	14,234,000,000
The Elderly		HHS, Social Security, Federal Disability Insurance	29,158,000,000
HSS, *Supplemental Security Income Program*	14,234,000,000	**Veterans**	
HHS, *Federal Old-Age & Survivors Insurance*	285,487,968,000	*Veterans Administration, Compensation*	16,397,000,000
		VA, Pensions	3,981,000,000
Law Enforcement		*VA, Medical Care*	12,335,000,000
FBI	1,699,000,000		
Drug Enforcement Administration	696,000,000		

Source: Executive Office of the President, Office of Management and Budget, *Budget of the United States, Fiscal Year 1993* (Washington, DC: Government Printing Office, 1992).

THE MEANS OF COERCION. Government must have the power to order people around, to get people to obey its laws, and to punish them if they do not. Coercion takes many different forms, and each year millions of Americans are subject to one form of government coercion or another. One aspect of coercion is *conscription,* whereby government requires certain involuntary services of citizens. The best-known example of conscription is military conscription, which is called "the draft." Although there has been no draft since 1974, there were drafts during the Civil War, World War I, World War II and the postwar period, and the wars in Korea and Vietnam. With these drafts, our government compelled millions of men to serve in the armed forces; one-half million of these soldiers made the ultimate contribution by giving their lives in their nation's service. If the need arose, military conscription would undoubtedly be reinstituted. Eighteen-year-old males are required to register today, just in case. We can also, by law, be compelled to serve on juries, to appear before legal tribunals when summoned, to file a great variety of official reports, including income tax returns, and to attend school or to send our children to school.

THE MEANS OF COLLECTING REVENUE. Each year American governments on every level collect enormous sums from their citizens to support their institutions and programs. Taxation has grown steadily over the years. In 1989, the national government alone collected $516 billion in individual income taxes, $117 billion in corporate income taxes, $341 billion in social insurance taxes, $26 billion in excise taxes, and another $18 billion in miscellaneous revenue. The grand total amounted to more than one trillion dollars or more than $4,000 from every living soul in the United States. But not everyone benefits equally from programs paid for by their tax dollars. One of the perennial issues in American politics is the distribution of tax burdens versus the distribution of program benefits. Every group would like more of the benefits while passing more of the burdens of taxation onto others.

Forms of Government

Governments vary in their institutional structure, in their size, and in the way they operate. Two questions are of special importance in determining how governments differ from one another: Who governs? How much government control is permitted?

In some nations, a single individual—a king or dictator—governs. This is called *autocracy.* Where a small group of landowners, military officers, or wealthy merchants control most of the governing decisions, that government is an *oligarchy.* If many people participate, and if the populace is deemed to have some influence over their actions, that government is tending toward *democracy.*

Governments also vary considerably in how they govern. In the United States and a small number of other nations, governments are severely limited by law as to *what* they are permitted to control (substantive limits), as well as *how* they go about it (procedural limits). Governments that are so limited are called *constitutional,* or liberal governments. In other nations, including many in Europe, South America, Asia, and Africa, political and social institutions that the government is unable to control—such as an organized church, organized business groups, or organized labor unions—may help keep the government in check, but the law imposes few real limits. Such governments are generally called *authoritarian.* In a third group of nations, including the Soviet Union under Joseph Stalin, governments not only are free of legal limits but seek to

---

In Brief Box

CONSTITUTIONAL, AUTHORITARIAN, AND TOTALITARIAN GOVERNMENTS SCOPE AND LIMITS OF POWER

Constitutional Governments
Scope: power prescribed by a constitution
Limits: society can challenge government when it oversteps constitutional boundaries
Examples: United States, France, Canada

Authoritarian Governments
Scope: answer only to a small number of powerful groups
Limits: recognize no obligations to limit actions, whether or not such obligations exist
Examples: Spain (under General Francisco Franco) and Portugal (under Prime Minister Antonio Salazar)

Totalitarian Governments
Scope: government encompasses all important social institutions
Limits: rivals for power are not tolerated
Examples: Germany's Third Reich in the 1930s and 1940s (under Adolf Hitler) and the Soviet Union from the 1930s through the 1950s (under Marshall Joseph Stalin)

---

eliminate those organized social groupings or institutions that might challenge or limit their authority. Because these governments typically attempt to dominate or control every sphere of political, economic, and social life, they are called **totalitarian**.

Influencing the Government: Politics

In its broadest sense, the term "politics" refers to conflicts over the character, membership, and policies of any organizations to which people belong. As Harold Lasswell, a famous political scientist, once put it, politics is the struggle over "who gets what, when, how."[5] Although politics is a phe-

nomenon that can be found in any organization, our concern in this book is more narrow. Here, politics will refer only to conflicts and struggles over the leadership, structure, and policies of *governments*. The goal of politics, as we define it, is to have a share or a say in the composition of the government's leadership, how the government is organized, and what its policies are going to be. Having a share is called **power** or **influence**.

As we shall see throughout the book, not only does politics influence government, but the character and actions of government also influence a nation's politics. A constitutional government tries to gain more popular consent by opening channels for political expression. People accept these channels in the hope that they can make the government more responsive to their demands.

[5]Harold Lasswell, *Politics: Who Gets What, When, How* (New York: Meridian Books, 1958).

From Coercion to Consent

Americans have the good fortune to live in a constitutional democracy, with its legal limits on what government can do and how it does it. But such democracies are relatively rare in today's world—it is estimated that only 20 or so of the world's nearly 200 governments could be included in this category. And constitutional democracies were unheard of before the modern era. Prior to the eighteenth and nineteenth centuries, governments seldom sought—and rarely received—the support of their ordinary subjects. History strongly suggests that the ordinary people had little love for the government or for the social order. After all, they had no stake in it. They equated government with the police officer, the bailiff, and the tax collector.[6]

Beginning in the seventeenth century, in a handful of Western nations, two important changes began to take place in the character and conduct of government. First, governments began to acknowledge formal limits on their power. Second, a small number of governments began to provide the ordinary citizen with a formal voice in public affairs through the vote.

Limits and Democratization

Obviously, the desirability of limits on government and the expansion of popular influence on government were at the heart of the American Revolution of 1776. "No taxation without representation," as we shall see in Chapter 2, was hotly debated, beginning with the American Revolution and continuing through the founding in 1789. But even before the American Revolution, there was a tradition of limiting government and expanding participation in the political process all over western Europe. Thus, to understand how the relationship between rulers and the ruled was transformed, we must broaden our focus to take into account events in Europe as well as those in America. We will divide the transformation into its two separate parts. The first is the effort to put limits on government. The second is the effort to expand the influence of the people through politics.

LIMITING GOVERNMENT. The key force behind the imposition of limits on government power was a new social class, the "bourgeoisie." *Bourgeois* is a French word for freeman of the city, or bourg. Being part of the bourgeoisie later became associated with being "middle class" and with being in commerce or industry. In order to gain a share of control of government—to join the kings, aristocrats, and gentry who had dominated governments for centuries—the bourgeoisie sought to change existing institutions—especially parliaments—into instruments of real political participation. Parliaments had existed for centuries, controlling from the top, and not allowing influence from below. The bourgeoisie embraced parliament as the means by which they could use their greater numbers and growing economic advantage against their aristocratic rivals.

Although motivated primarily by self-interest, the bourgeoisie advanced many of the principles that became the central underpinnings of individual freedom for *all* citizens—freedom of speech, of assembly, of conscience, and freedom from arbitrary search and seizure. It is important to note here that the bourgeoisie generally did not favor democracy as such. They were advocates of electoral and representative institu-

---

[6]See Eugen Weber, *Peasants into Frenchmen* (Stanford, CA: Stanford University Press, 1976), Chapter 5.

tions, but they favored property requirements and other restrictions so as to limit participation to the middle classes. Yet, once the right to engage in politics was established, it was difficult to limit it just to the bourgeoisie. We will see time after time that principles first stated to justify a selfish interest can take on a life of their own, extending to those for whom the principles were not at first designed.

THE EXPANSION OF DEMOCRATIC POLITICS. Along with limits on government came an expansion of democratic government. Three factors explain why rulers were forced to give ordinary citizens a greater voice in public affairs: internal conflict, external threat, and national unity and development.

First, during the eighteenth and nineteenth centuries, every nation was faced with intense conflict among the landed gentry, the bourgeoisie, lower-middle-class shopkeepers and artisans, the urban working class, and farmers. Many governments came to the conclusion that if they did not deal with basic class conflicts in some constructive way, disorder and revolution would result. One of the best ways of dealing with such conflict was to extend the rights of political participation, especially voting, to each new group as it grew more powerful. Such a liberalization was sometimes followed by suppression, as rulers began to fear that their calculated risk was not paying off.

This was true even in the United States. The Federalists, who were securely in control of the government after 1787, began to fear the emergence of a vulgar and dangerous democratic party led by Thomas Jefferson. The Federalist majority in Congress adopted an infamous law, the Alien and Sedition Acts of 1798, which, among other things, declared any opposition to or criticism of the government to be a crime. Alexander Hamilton and other Federalist leaders went so far as to urge that the opposition be eliminated by force, if necessary. The Federalists failed to suppress their Republican opposition, in large measure because they lacked the military and political means of doing so. Their inability to crush the opposition eventually led to acceptance of the principle of the "Loyal Opposition."[7]

Another form of internal threat is social disorder. Thanks to the Industrial Revolution, societies had become much more interdependent and therefore much more vulnerable to disorder. As that occurred, and as more people moved from rural areas to cities, disorder had to be managed, and one important approach to that management was to give the masses a bigger stake in the system itself. As one supporter of electoral reform put it, the alternative to voting was "the spoliation of property and the dissolution of social order."[8] In the modern world, social disorder helped to compel East European regimes and the republics of the former Soviet Union to take steps toward democratic reform.

The second factor that helped expand democratic government was external threat. The main external threat to governments' power is the existence of other nation-states. During the past three centuries, more and more tribes and nations—people tied together by a common culture and language—have formed into separate principalities, or "nation-states," in order to defend their populations more effectively. But

---

[7] See Richard Hofstadter, *The Idea of a Party System* (Berkeley: University of California Press, 1969).

[8] Quoted in John Cannon, *Parliamentary Reform, 1640–1832* (Cambridge, England: Cambridge University Press, 1973), p. 216.

DEBATING THE ISSUES

Freedom and Power: The Enduring Debate

Striking the right balance between freedom and power is the essential paradox of governing. One could select any point in American history and find a vigorous debate between those who want a stronger government and those who believe that individual freedom is endangered by an encroaching state. This debate was a central feature of the early struggle to establish a permanent, stable, yet limited national government in America.

Thomas Jefferson was an eloquent spokesman for a government of sharply limited powers. He laid his trust in majority will and personal freedom. In fact, he considered regular revolts by the people to be healthy for a democracy, not unlike the way the physicians of his time viewed bloodletting. "The tree of liberty must be refreshed from time to time, with the blood of patriots and tyrants."

Opposing him was Alexander Hamilton, an avowed elitist, who recognized the failings of weak government (such as the country had experienced under the Articles of Confederation). Hamilton argued that the national government had to possess the power to enforce its decisions in order to ensure the political and economic well-being of its citizenry.

Jefferson

I own, I am not a friend to a very energetic government. It is always oppressive. It places the governors indeed more at their ease, at the expense of the people. The late rebellion in Massachusetts [Shays's Rebellion] has given more alarm, than I think it should have done. Calculate that one rebellion in thirteen States in the course of eleven years, is but one for each

---

as more nation-states formed, the more likely it was that external conflicts would arise. War and preparation for war became constant rather than intermittent facts of national life, and the size and expense of military forces increased dramatically with the size of the nation-state and the size and number of its adversaries.

The cost of defense forced rulers to seek popular support to maintain military power. It was easier to raise huge permanent armies of citizen-soldiers and induce them to fight more vigorously and to make greater sacrifices if they were imbued with enthusiasm for cause and country. The turning point was the French Revolution in 1789.

The unprecedented size and commitment and the military success of the French citizen-army convinced the rulers of all European nations that military power was forevermore closely linked with mass support. The expansion of participation and representation in government were key tactics used by the European regimes to raise that support. Throughout the nineteenth century, war and the expansion of the suffrage went hand in hand.

The third factor often associated with the expansion of democratic politics was the promotion of national unity and development. In some instances, governments seek to subvert local or regional loyalties by link-

State in a century and a half. No country should be so long without one. Nor will any degree of power in the hands of government, prevent insurrections. . . . And say . . . whether peace is best preserved by giving energy to the government, or information to the people. This last is the most certain, and the most legitimate engine of government. Educate and inform the whole mass of the people. Enable them to see that it is their interest to preserve peace and order, and they will preserve them. And it requires no very high degree of education to convince them of this. They are the only sure reliance for the preservation of our liberty. After all, it is my principle that the will of the majority should prevail.[1]

Hamilton

If it be possible at any rate to construct a federal government capable of regulating the common concerns, and preserving the general tranquillity, it must be founded . . . upon the reverse of the principle contended for by the opponents of the proposed Constitution [that is, a confederacy]. It must carry its agency to the persons of the citizens. It must stand in need of no intermediate legislations, but must itself be empowered to employ the arm of the ordinary magistrate to execute its own resolutions. The majesty of the national authority must be manifested through the medium of the courts of justice. The government of the Union, like that of each State, must be able to address itself immediately to the hopes and fears of individuals; and to attract to its support those passions which have the strongest influence upon the human heart. It must, in short, possess all the means, and have a right to resort to all the methods, of executing the powers with which it is entrusted, that are possessed and exercised by the governments of the particular States.[2]

[1]Thomas Jefferson, Letter to James Madison, December 20, 1787, in *Jefferson's Letters,* arr. by Willson Whitman (Eau Claire, WI: E. M. Hale, 1950), p. 85.
[2]Clinton Rossiter, ed., *The Federalist Papers* (New York: New American Library, 1961), No. 16, p. 116.

ing citizens directly to the central government via the ballot box. America's founding fathers saw direct popular election of members of the House of Representatives as a means through which the new federal government could compete with the states for popular allegiance.

The Great Transformation: Tying Democracy to Strong Government

The expansion of democratic politics had two historic consequences. First, democracies opened up the possibility that citizens might use government for their own benefit rather than simply watching it being used for the benefit of others. This consequence is widely understood. But the second is not so well understood: Once citizens perceived that governments could operate in response to their demands, they *became increasingly willing to support the expansion of government.* The public's belief in its capacity to control the government's action is only one of the many factors responsible for the growth of government. But at the very least, this linkage of democracy and strong government set into motion a wave of governmental growth in the West that began in the middle of the nineteenth century and has continued to this day.

Freedom and Power: The Problem

Ultimately, the growth of governmental power poses the most fundamental threat to the liberties that Americans have so long enjoyed. Because ours is a limited government subject to democratic control, we often see government as simply a powerful servant. But the growth of governmental power continues to raise profound questions about the future.

First, expansion of governmental powers inevitably reduces popular influence over policy making. The enormous scope of national programs in the twentieth century has required an elaborate bureaucracy and the transfer of considerable decision-making power from politically responsive bodies like Congress to administrative agencies. As a result, today's public policies are increasingly dominated by bureaucratic institutions, rules, and procedures that voters cannot easily affect. Can citizens use the power of the bureaucracies we have created, or are we doomed simply to become their subjects?

Second, as government has grown in size and power, the need for citizen cooperation has diminished. In the eighteenth and nineteenth centuries, rulers became responsive to mass opinion because their power was so fragile. Without popular support, rulers lacked the means to curb disorder, collect taxes, and maintain their military power. In an important sense, the eighteenth and nineteenth centuries in the West represented a "window of opportunity" for popular opinion. A conjunction of political and social circumstances compelled those in power to respond to public opinion to shore up their power. Westerners tend to assume that this commitment on the part of eight-

eenth- and nineteenth-century rulers forever binds their successors to serve public opinion.

It is true that the links between government and opinion—elections, representative bodies, and so on—developed during the eighteenth and nineteenth centuries have flourished for nearly 200 years. What has generally gone unnoticed is that the underlying conditions—the windows of opportunity—that produced these institutions have, in many respects, closed behind them. Many Western states today may now have sufficiently powerful administrative, military, and police agencies that they *could* curb disorder, collect taxes, and keep their foes in check without necessarily depending upon popular support and approval. Will government continue to bow to the will of the people even though favorable public opinion may not be as crucial as it once was?

Finally, because Americans view government as a servant, they believe that they can have both the blessings of freedom and the benefits of a strong government. Even the most self-proclaimed conservatives have learned to live with Big Brother. In today's America, agencies of the government have considerable control over who may enter occupations, what may be eaten, what may be seen and heard over the airwaves, what forms of education are socially desirable, what types of philanthropy serve the public interest, what sorts of business practices are acceptable, as well as citizens' marital plans, vacation plans, child-rearing practices, and medical care. Is this government still a servant?

Of course, we continue to exert our influence through elections, representation, and, occasionally, direct popular referenda. But do even these processes mean that we can *control* the government? One hundred fifty years ago, Alexis de Tocqueville predicted that Americans would eventually permit their government to become so powerful that elections, representative processes, and so on would come to be ironic interludes providing citizens little more than the opportunity to wave the chains by which the government had bound them. Can we have both freedom and government? To what extent can we continue to depend upon and benefit from government's power while still retaining our liberties? These are questions every generation of Americans must ask.

For Further Reading

Bendix, Reinhard. *Kings or People: Power and the Mandate to Rule.* Berkeley: University of California Press, 1978.

Bendix, Reinhard. *Nation-Building and Citizenship.* New York: Wiley, 1964.

Binder, Leonard, et al., eds. *Crises and Sequences in Political Development.* Princeton: Princeton University Press, 1971.

Dahl, Robert A. *Polyarchy: Participation and Opposition.* New Haven: Yale University Press, 1971.

Grant, Ruth W. *John Locke's Liberalism.* Chicago: University of Chicago Press, 1987.

Hartz, Louis. *The Liberal Tradition in America.* New York: Harcourt, Brace, 1955.

Higgs, Robert. *Crisis and Leviathan: Critical Episodes in the Growth of American Government.* New York: Oxford University Press, 1987.

Huntington, Samuel P. *American Politics: The Promise of Disharmony.* Cambridge: Harvard University Press, 1981.

Keller, Morton. *Affairs of State: Public Life in Late Nineteenth Century America.* Cambridge: Harvard University Press, 1977.

Moore, Barrington. *Social Origins of Dictatorship and Democracy.* Boston: Beacon Press, 1966.

Schumpeter, Joseph A. *Capitalism, Socialism and Democracy.* New York: Harper, 1942.

Skocpol, Theda. *States and Social Revolutions.* New York: Cambridge University Press, 1979.

Strayer, Joseph R. *On the Medieval Origins of the Modern State.* Princeton: Princeton University Press, 1970.

Tilly, Charles, ed. *The Formation of Nation-States in Western Europe.* Princeton: Princeton University Press, 1975.

Tocqueville, Alexis de. *Democracy in America.* Translated by Phillips Bradley. New York: Knopf, Vintage Books, 1945; orig. published 1835.

Weber, Max. *The Theory of Social and Economic Organization.* Translated by Talcott Parsons. New York: Oxford University Press, 1947.

2

CONSTRUCTING A GOVERNMENT: THE FOUNDING AND THE CONSTITUTION

"*N*o taxation without representation" were words that stirred a generation of Americans long before they even dreamed of calling themselves Americans rather than Englishmen. Among the new English attempts to extract tax revenues to pay for the troops that were being sent to defend the colonial frontier was the infamous Stamp Act of 1765. This act created revenue stamps and required that they be affixed to all printed and legal documents, including newspapers, pamphlets, advertisements, notes and bonds, leases, deeds, and licenses. Protests erupted throughout the colonies against the act. The colonists conducted mass meetings, parades, bonfires, and other demonstrations throughout the spring and summer of 1765. In Boston, for example, a stamp agent was hanged and burned in effigy. Later, the home of the lieutenant-governor was sacked, leading to his resignation and that of all of his colonial commission and stamp agents. By November 1765, business proceeded and newspapers were published without the stamp; in March 1766, Parliament repealed the detested law. Through their protest, the colonists took the first steps that ultimately would lead to war and a new nation.

To most contemporary Americans, the revolutionary period represents a heroic struggle by a determined and united group of colonists against British oppression. The Boston Tea Party, the battles of Lexington and Concord, the winter at Valley Forge—these are the events that we emphasize in our history. Similarly, the American Constitution—the document establishing the system of government that ultimately emerged from this struggle—is often seen as an inspired, if not divine, work, expressing timeless principles of democratic government.

To really understand the character of the American founding and the meaning of the American Constitution, however, it is essential to look beyond the myths and rhetoric and explore the conflicting interests and forces at work during the revolutionary and constitutional periods. Thus, we will first assess the political backdrop of the American Revolution, and then we will examine the Constitution that ultimately emerged as the basis for America's government.

The First Founding: Interests and Conflicts

Competing ideals and principles often reflect competing interests, and so it was in revolutionary America. The American Revolution and the American Constitution were outgrowths of a struggle among economic and political forces within the colonies. Five sectors of society had interests that were important in colonial politics: (1) the New England merchants; (2) the southern planters; (3) the "royalists"—holders of royal lands, offices, and patents (licenses to engage in a profession or business activity); (4) shopkeepers, artisans, and laborers; and (5) small farmers. Throughout the eighteenth century, these groups were in conflict over issues of taxation, trade, and commerce. For the most part, however, the southern planters, the New England merchants, and the royal office and patent holders— groups that together made up the colonial elite—were able to maintain a political alliance that held in check the more radical forces representing shopkeepers, laborers, and small farmers. After 1750, however, British tax and trade policies split the colonial elite, permitting radical forces to expand their political influence, and setting into motion a chain of events that culminated in the American Revolution (see Box 2.1).[1]

Political Strife and the Radicalizing of the Colonists

The political strife within the colonies was the background for the events of 1773–1774. In 1773, the British government granted the politically powerful East India Company a monopoly on the export of tea from Britain, eliminating a lucrative form of trade for colonial merchants. Together with their southern allies, the merchants called upon their radical adversaries—shopkeepers, artisans, laborers, and small farmers—for support. The most dramatic result was the Boston Tea Party of 1773, led by Samuel Adams.

This event was of decisive importance in American history. The merchants had hoped to force the British government to rescind the Tea Act, but they did not support any demands beyond this one. They

[1] The social makeup of colonial America and some of the social conflicts that divided colonial society are discussed in Jackson Turner Main, *The Social Structure of Revolutionary America* (Princeton: Princeton University Press, 1965).

BOX 2.1
The Road to Revolution

*T*he road that led the American colonies to break with England was long, indirect, and by no means inevitable. Most rebel leaders hoped for reform; few spoke openly of revolution. Yet dissatisfaction, misunderstanding, and violence spread, yielding what in many ways was an eighteenth-century American guerrilla war against the world's superpower of the day.

The first American casualties of the Revolution came on a frosty March day in 1770. Massachusetts had been a hotbed of dissent against various British actions, including impressment (forced military conscription) and various economic measures. Boston was the center of colonial smuggling that proliferated as Americans sought to avoid what they considered unfair and oppressive levies and taxes. Among the many repugnant economic measures were the Townshend Acts, enacted in 1767, which levied duties on colonial imports and created a Board of Customs Commission in Boston to oversee the collection of revenue.

In 1769, the British stationed 2,000 soldiers in Boston to quell the rising tide of disturbances. The presence of the troops, however, merely provided a focal point for local discontent. Moreover, the British soldiers began to take the jobs of local people at a time when jobs were scarce, driving up unemployment.

On March 5, a crowd that included ropemakers who had lost their jobs to British soldiers gathered in front of the Boston Customhouse (where the hated customs commissioners did their work). At the head of the crowd was a runaway slave named Crispus Attucks, who had worked for several years on ships out of Boston. The crowd taunted the sentry on duty, who called for help. Nine other soldiers appeared, and they soon found themselves being taunted and pelted with snowballs, clamshells, and sticks by the growing crowd. In the fear and confusion of the moment, one soldier was knocked to the ground. He rose and fired. The other soldiers then fired into the belligerent but unarmed crowd. When the smoke cleared, five were dead, and eight wounded. The first to be shot and mortally wounded was Attucks. Thus it was that the first casualty of the Revolutionary War was a black man.

The resistance cause had its first real martyrs, and resistance leaders lost no time in capitalizing on the propaganda value of the incident. After the "Boston Massacre," as it was dubbed by pamphleteers, the Massachusetts governor ordered the troops withdrawn from Boston to avoid further incidents. Six British soldiers were tried for murder. Four were acquitted, and two were punished by having their thumbs branded and being discharged from the army.

Despite a subsequent lull in direct confrontations, anti-British sentiment escalated, as did the cycle of violence. As with many revolutions to follow, few anticipated where the cycle of repression and violence would lead. But leaders were quick to seize as symbols those actions deemed unjust and pernicious. Indeed, the facts of the day were in a real sense less important than the symbols they generated.

Source: Robert A. Divine, et al., *American Past and Present* (Glenview, IL: Scott, Foresman, 1984).

certainly did not seek independence from Britain. Samuel Adams and the other radicals, however, hoped to induce the British government to take actions that would alienate its colonial supporters and pave the way for a rebellion. This was precisely the purpose of the Boston Tea Party, and it succeeded. By dumping the East India Company's tea into Boston Harbor, Adams and his followers goaded the British into enacting a number of harsh reprisals. The House of Commons closed the port of Boston to commerce, changed the provincial government of Massachusetts, provided for the removal of accused persons to England for trial, and, most important, restricted movement to the West—further alienating the southern planters who depended upon access to new western lands. These acts of retaliation confirmed the worst criticisms of England and helped radicalize Americans.

Thus, the Boston Tea Party set into motion a cycle of provocation and retaliation that in 1774 resulted in the convening of the First Continental Congress—an assembly consisting of delegates from all parts of the country—that called for a total boycott of British goods and, under the prodding of the radicals, began to consider the possibility of independence from British rule. The eventual result was the Declaration of Independence.

The Declaration of Independence

In 1776, the Second Continental Congress appointed a committee consisting of Thomas Jefferson of Virginia, Benjamin Franklin of Pennsylvania, Roger Sherman of Connecticut, and Robert Livingston of New York to draft a statement of American independence from British rule. The Declaration of Independence, written by Jefferson

and adopted by the Second Continental Congress, was an extraordinary document both in philosophical and political terms. Philosophically, the Declaration was remarkable for its assertion that certain rights, called "unalienable rights"—including life, liberty, and the pursuit of happiness—could not be abridged by governments. In the world of 1776, a world in which some kings still claimed to rule by divine right, this was a dramatic statement. The Declaration was remarkable as a political document because it identified and focused on problems, grievances, aspirations, and principles that might unify the various colonial groups. The Declaration was an attempt to identify and articulate a history and set of principles that might help to forge national unity.[2]

The Articles of Confederation

Having declared their independence, the colonies needed to establish a governmental structure. In November 1777, the Continental Congress adopted the Articles of Confederation and Perpetual Union—the United States's first written constitution. Although it was not ratified by all the states until 1781, it served as the country's constitution for almost twelve years, until March 1789.

The Articles of Confederation was concerned primarily with limiting the powers of the central government. There was no executive branch. Congress constituted the central government, but it had little power. Execution of its laws was to be left to the individual states. Its members were not much more than delegates or messengers

[2]See Carl Becker, *The Declaration of Independence* (New York: Vintage, 1942).

Samuel Adams
Career Politician

Samuel Adams
(1722–1803)

*U*nlike other revolutionary political leaders, Samuel Adams resembled many of the career politicians we see today. Born in Boston in 1722 and educated at Harvard, he quickly established his propensity for politics over other occupations. His family's brewery business failed shortly after he took it over, and he secured an appointment as a tax collector in Boston in 1756.

Adams thrived on public life. He developed his early constituency in the taverns, clubs, and fire companies of eighteenth-century Boston and became the epitome of an early republican. He was adept at manipulating information and not at all averse to engaging in extralegal acts to attain his goals when he thought his actions would be supported by public opinion. He was elected to the Massachusetts House of Representatives in 1762. As a member of that body, he was instrumental in securing a colony-wide boycott of British goods after the British Parliament passed a new series of taxes, the Townshend Acts. This boycott was so successful that Parliament repealed these acts altogether in 1770. Adams subsequently chaired the Boston committee of correspondence, which proved a highly effective means of mobilizing popular support to protest British attempts to control commerce in the colonies. He is best remembered for organizing and managing the Boston Tea Party in 1773 in response to Parliament's restrictions on the tea trade in the colonies. Adams participated in the Continental Congress and signed the Declaration of Independence.

After the Revolutionary War, he remained active in Massachusetts politics, serving as both lieutenant governor and governor. He was well into his sixties by that time, and his views on national politics were becoming dated. Receding into the background, he remained a political observer until his death in 1803.

from the state legislatures. They were chosen by the state legislatures, their salaries were paid out of the state treasuries, and they were subject to immediate recall by state authorities. In addition, each state, regardless of its size, had only a single vote.

Congress was given the power to declare war and make peace, to make treaties and alliances, to coin or borrow money, and to regulate trade with the Native Americans. It could also appoint the senior officers of the United States Army. But it could not levy taxes or regulate commerce among the states. Moreover, the army officers it appointed had no army to serve in because the nation's armed forces were composed of the state militias. Probably the most unfortunate part of the Articles of Confederation was that the central government could not prevent one state from discriminating against other states in the quest for foreign commerce.

In brief, the relationship between Congress and the states under the Articles of Confederation was much like the contemporary relationship between the United Nations and its member states, a relationship in which virtually all governmental powers are retained by the states. It was called a "confederation" because, as provided under Article II, "each state retains its sovereignty, freedom and independence, and every power, jurisdiction, and right, which is not by this confederation expressly delegated to the United States, in Congress assembled." Not only was there no executive, there was also no judicial authority and no other means of enforcing Congress's will. If there was to be any enforcement at all, it would have to be done for Congress by the states.[3]

The Second Founding: From Compromise to Constitution

The Declaration of Independence and the Articles of Confederation were not sufficient to hold the nation together as an independent and effective nation-state. From almost the moment of armistice with the British in 1783, moves were afoot to reform and strengthen the Articles of Confederation.

[3]See Merrill Jensen, *The Articles of Confederation* (Madison: University of Wisconsin Press, 1963).

International Standing and Balance of Power

There was a special concern for the country's international position. Competition among the states for foreign commerce allowed the European powers to play the states off against one another, which created confusion on both sides of the Atlantic. At one point during the winter of 1786–1787, John Adams of Massachusetts, a leader in the independence struggle, was sent to negotiate a new treaty with the British, one that would cover disputes left over from the war. The British government responded that, since the United States under the Articles of Confederation was unable to enforce existing treaties, it would negotiate with each of the thirteen states separately.

At the same time, well-to-do Americans—in particular the New England merchants and southern planters—were troubled by the influence that "radical" forces exercised in the Continental Congress and in the governments of several of the states. The colonists' victory in the Revolutionary War had not only meant the end of British rule, but it had also significantly changed the balance of political power within the new states. As a result of the Revolution, one key segment of the colonial elite—the royal land, office, and patent holders—was stripped of its economic and political privileges. In fact, many of these individuals, along with tens of thousands of other colonists who considered themselves loyal British subjects, left for Canada after the British surrender. And while the elite was weakened, the radicals were now better organized than ever before. They controlled forces in such states as Pennsylvania and Rhode Island, where they pursued economic and political policies that struck terror into the hearts of the pre-revolutionary political establishment. The central government under the Articles of Confederation was powerless to intervene.

The new nation's weak international position and domestic turmoil led many Americans to consider whether a new version of the Articles might be necessary. Delegates from five states met in Annapolis, Maryland, in the fall of 1786 and called on Congress to send commissioners to Philadelphia at a later time to devise adjustments to the Constitution. Their resolution took on force as a result of an event that occurred the following winter in Massachusetts: Shays's Rebellion. Daniel Shays led a mob of farmers, who were protesting foreclosures on their land, in a rebellion against the state government. The state militia dispersed the mob within a few days, but the threat posed by the rebels scared Congress into action. The states were asked to send delegates to Philadelphia to discuss constitutional revision, and eventually delegates were sent from every state but Rhode Island.

The Constitutional Convention

Fifty-five delegates selected by the state governments convened in Philadelphia in May 1787, with political strife, international embarrassment, national weakness, and local rebellion fixed in their minds. Recognizing that these issues were symptoms of fundamental flaws in the Articles of Confederation, the delegates soon abandoned the plan to revise the Articles and committed themselves to a second founding—a second, and ultimately successful, attempt to create a legitimate and effective national system. This effort occupied the convention for the next five months.

THE GREAT COMPROMISE. The proponents of a new government fired their opening shot on May 29, 1787, when Edmund Randolph of Virginia offered a resolution that proposed corrections and enlargements in the Articles of Confederation. The proposal was not a simple motion. It provided for virtually every aspect of a new government. Randolph later admitted it was intended to be an alternative draft constitution, and it did in fact serve as the framework for what ultimately became the Constitution. (There is no verbatim record of the delegates, but James Madison, a Virginia delegate, was present during virtually all of the deliberations and kept full notes on them.)[4]

The portion of Randolph's motion that became most controversial was the "Virginia Plan." This plan provided for a system of representation in the national legislature based upon the population of each state or the proportion of each state's revenue contribution, or both. (Randolph also proposed a second branch of the legislature, but it was to be elected by the members of the first branch.) Since the states varied enormously in size and wealth, the Virginia Plan was thought to be heavily biased in favor of the large states.

While the convention was debating the Virginia Plan, additional delegates were arriving in Philadelphia and were beginning to mount opposition to it. In particular, delegates from the less populous states, which included Delaware, New Jersey, Connecticut, and New York, asserted that the more populous states, such as Virginia, Pennsylvania, North Carolina, Massachusetts, and

[4]Madison's notes along with the somewhat less complete records kept by several other participants in the convention are available in a four-volume set. See Max Farrand, *The Records of the Federal Convention of 1787*, 4 vols., rev. ed. (New Haven: Yale University Press, 1966).

Abigail Adams
The First Feminist

Abigail Adams
(1744-1818)

Known mostly as the wife of colonial leader and the second president, John Adams, and the mother of the sixth president, John Quincy Adams, Abigail Adams was not a woman to be content with singlehandedly raising a large family and managing the family farm in Braintree, Massachusetts, while her husband attended to affairs of state. A vivacious, intelligent, witty woman, Abigail tirelessly involved herself in many causes, especially the promotion of women's rights.

In a celebrated letter to husband John, written in March of 1776 (four months before the completion of the Declaration of Independence), she urged her husband to extend legal protections to half the country's population: ". . . in the new code of laws which I suppose it will be necessary for you to make, I desire you would remember the ladies, and be more generous to them than your ancestors. Do not put such unlimited power in the hands of husbands. Remember, all men would be tyrants if they could."

Her entreaties fell on unsympathetic ears. Thomas Jefferson wrote in the Declaration of Independence that "all men are created equal," and his meaning was clarified later when he stated that women would be "too wise to wrinkle their foreheads with politics."

Ironically, women who owned property often voted before the Revolution. After the Revolution, women were specifically barred from voting in every state except New Jersey, where women were formally excluded in 1807.

Despite this and other legal inequities

(for example, married women forfeited control of their own property to their husbands), women assumed a heavy burden during the war with Britain and in establishing the new postwar nation. In 1870, for example, Esther DeBerdt Reed founded a women's organization in Philadelphia that raised over $300,000 for the colonial army. Other women participated in more strictly revolutionary activities, from taking up arms against the British to enacting an all-female equivalent of the Boston Tea Party, wherein a group of women seized a wealthy merchant's coffee for distribution to American troops.

Abigail Adams continued to champion political and social causes, particularly as an ardent spokesperson for the rights of women. During her husband's difficult presidential administration (1797-1801), she was a center of Washington social life and a skillful political hostess. She is considered one of the nation's most influential First Ladies.

Source: Lester J. Cappon, ed., *The Adams-Jefferson Letters* (Chapel Hill, NC: University of North Carolina Press, 1959); Howard Zinn, *A People's History of the United States* (New York: Harper & Row, 1980)

DEBATING THE ISSUES

The Constitution:
Property versus Pragmatism

T *hroughout the second half of the nineteenth century, the prevailing attitude toward the country's founders was increasingly that of veneration, even worship. Like Moses receiving the Ten Commandments, the founders came to be viewed as messengers from God who had received the Constitution intact and whole rather than creating it through a messy political process. Historian Charles Beard helped shatter this myth in the early twentieth century when he argued that the founders were members of the social and economic elite, little interested in democracy and more motivated by a desire to protect their property and wealth, and that the Constitution was their instrument to achieve this end.*

Many have examined Beard's work, and found fault with his arguments and facts. Notably, political scientist John P. Roche, writing in the 1960s, argued that the founders, even if they were elite, were excellent politicians who were simply trying to forge a government that would be more effective than the Articles of Confederation. Still, Beard's impact was great, in that he helped move constitutional analysis away from uncritical worship and much closer to viewing the political realities of the late eighteenth century.

Beard

The Constitution was essentially an economic document based upon the concept that the fundamental private rights of property are anterior to government and morally beyond the reach of popular majorities.

The major portion of the members of the [Constitutional] Convention are on record as recognizing the claim of property to a special and defensive position in the Constitution.

In the ratification of the Constitution, about three-fourths of the adult males failed to vote on the question, having abstained from the elections at which delegates to the state conventions were chosen, either on account of their indifference or their disfranchisement by property qualifications.

Georgia, would dominate the new government if representation were to be determined by population. The smaller states argued that each state should be equally represented in the new regime regardless of its population. The proposal, called the "New Jersey Plan" (after its sponsor, William Patterson of New Jersey), focused on revising the Articles rather than replacing them. Their opposition to the Virginia Plan's system of representation was suffi-

cient to send the proposals back to committee for reworking into a common document.

The outcome was the Connecticut Compromise, also known as the Great Compromise. Under the terms of this compromise, in the first branch of Congress—the House of Representatives—the representatives would be apportioned according to the number of inhabitants in each state. This, of course, was what delegates from the large states had sought. But in the second

The Constitution was ratified by a vote of probably not more than one-sixth of the adult males.

It is questionable whether a majority of the voters participating in the elections for the state [ratifying] conventions in New York, Massachusetts, New Hampshire, Virginia, and South Carolina, actually approved the ratification of the Constitution....

In the ratification, it became manifest that the line of cleavage for and against the Constitution was between substantial personalty interests on the one hand and the small farming and debtor interests on the other.

The Constitution was not created by 'the whole people' as the jurists have said; neither was it created by 'the states' as Southern nullifiers long contended; but it was the work of a consolidated group whose interests knew no state boundaries and were truly national in their scope.[1]

Roche

The Constitution ... was not an apotheosis of 'constitutionalism,' a triumph of architectonic genius; it was a patch-work sewn together under the pressure of both time and events by a group of extremely talented democratic politicians. They refused to attempt the establishment of a strong, centralized sovereignty on the principle of legislative supremacy for the excellent reason that the people would not accept it. They risked their political fortunes by opposing the established doctrines of state sovereignty because they were convinced that the existing system was leading to national impotence and probably foreign domination. For two years, they worked to get a convention established. For over three months, in what must have seemed to the faithful participants an endless process of give-and-take, they reasoned, cajoled, threatened, and bargained amongst themselves. The result was a Constitution which the people, in fact, by democratic processes, did accept, and a new and far better national government was established.[2]

[1]Charles Beard, *An Economic Interpretation of the Constitution of the United States* (New York: Macmillan, 1935), pp. 324–25.
[2]John P. Roche, "The Founding Fathers: A Reform Caucus in Action," *American Political Science Review* 55 (December 1961), pp. 815–16.

branch—the Senate—each state would have an equal vote regardless of its size; this was to deal with the concerns of the small states. This compromise was not immediately satisfactory to all the delegates. In the end, however, both sets of forces preferred compromise to the breakup of the union, and the plan was accepted.

THE QUESTION OF SLAVERY: THE "THREE-FIFTHS" COMPROMISE. The story so far is too neat, too easy, and too anticlimactic. After all, the notion of a bicameral (two-chambered) legislature was very much in the air in 1787. Some of the states had had this for years. The Philadelphia delegates might well have gone straight to the adoption of two chambers based on two different principles of representation even without the dramatic interplay of conflict and compromise. But a far more fundamental issue had to be confronted before the Great Compromise could take place: the issue of slavery.

Many of the conflicts that emerged during the Constitutional Convention were reflections of the fundamental differences between the slave and the nonslave states—differences that pitted the southern planters and the New England merchants against one another. This was the first premonition of a conflict that was almost to destroy the Republic in later years. In the midst of debate over large versus small states, Madison observed, "The great danger to our general government is the great southern and northern interests of the continent, being opposed to each other. Look to the votes in Congress, and most of them stand divided by the geography of the country, not according to the size of the states."[5]

Over 90 percent of all slaves resided in five states—Georgia, Maryland, North Carolina, South Carolina, and Virginia—where they accounted for 30 percent of the total population. In some places, slaves outnumbered nonslaves by as much as ten to one. Were they to be counted in determining how many congressional seats a state should have? Northerners and southerners eventually reached agreement through the "Three-fifths Compromise." The seats in the House of Representatives would be apportioned according to a "population" in which five slaves would count as three persons. The slaves would not be allowed to vote, of course, but the number of representatives would be apportioned accordingly. This arrangement was supported by the slave states, which included some of the biggest and some of the smallest states at that time. It was also accepted by delegates from nonslave states who strongly supported the principle of property representation, whether that property was expressed in slaves or in land, money, or stocks.

The concern exhibited by most delegates was over how much slaves would count toward a state's representation rather than whether the institution of slavery would continue. The Three-fifths Compromise, in the words of political scientist Donald Robinson, "gave Constitutional sanction to the fact that the United States was composed of some persons who were 'free' and others who were not, and it established the principle, new in republican theory, that a man who lives among slaves had a greater share in the election of representatives than the man who did not. Although the Three-fifths Compromise acknowledged slavery and rewarded slave owners, nonetheless, it probably kept the South from unanimously rejecting the Constitution."[6]

The Constitution

The political significance of the Great Compromise and Three-fifths Compromise was to reinforce the unity of those who sought the creation of a new government. The Great Compromise reassured those who feared that the importance of their own local or regional influence would be reduced by the new governmental framework. The Three-fifths Compromise temporarily defused the rivalry between the merchants and planters. Their unity secured, members of the alliance supporting the establishment of a new government moved to fashion a constitutional framework for this government that would be congruent with their economic and political interests.

[5]Ibid., vol. 1, p. 476.

[6]Donald Robinson, *Slavery in the Structure of American Politics, 1765–1820* (New York: Harcourt Brace Jovanovich, 1971), p. 201.

In particular, the framers sought a new government that, first, would be strong enough to promote commerce and protect property from radical state legislatures such as Rhode Island's. This became the basis for the establishment in the Constitution of national control over commerce and finance, as well as the establishment of national judicial supremacy, and a strong presidency. Second, the framers sought to prevent what they saw as the threat posed by the "excessive democracy" of the state and national governments under the Articles of Confederation. This led to such constitutional principles as bicameralism (division of the Congress into two chambers), checks and balances, staggered terms in office, and indirect election (selection of the president by an electoral college rather than voters directly).

Third, hoping to secure support from the states or the public-at-large for the new form of government they proposed, the framers provided for direct popular election of representatives and, subsequently, for the addition of the Bill of Rights. Finally, to prevent the new government from abusing its power, the framers incorporated principles such as the separation of powers and federalism into the Constitution. Let us assess the major provisions of the Constitution's seven articles to see how each relates to these broad objectives.

The Legislative Branch

The Constitution provided in the first seven sections of Article I for a Congress consisting of two chambers—a House of Representatives and a Senate. Members of the House of Representatives were given two-year terms in office and were to be subject to direct popular election—though generally only white males had the right to vote.

State legislatures were to appoint members of the Senate (this was changed in 1913 by the Seventeenth Amendment, providing for direct election of senators) for six-year terms. These terms, moreover, were staggered so that the appointments of one-third of the senators would expire every two years. The Constitution assigned somewhat different tasks to the House and Senate. Though the approval of each body was required for the enactment of a law, the Senate alone was given the power to ratify treaties and approve presidential appointments. The House, on the other hand, was given the sole power to originate revenue bills.

The character of the legislative branch was directly related to the framers' major goals. The House of Representatives was designed to be directly responsible to the people in order to encourage popular consent for the new Constitution and, as we saw in Chapter 1, to help enhance the power of the new government. At the same time, to guard against "excessive democracy," the power of the House of Representatives was checked by the Senate, whose members were to be appointed for long terms rather than elected directly by the people for short terms.

Staggered terms of service in the Senate were intended to make that body even more resistant to popular pressure. Since only one-third of the senators would be selected at any given time, the composition of the institution would be protected from changes in popular preferences transmitted by the state legislatures. Thus, the structure of the legislative branch was designed to contribute to governmental power, to promote popular consent for the new government, and at the same time to place limits on the popular political currents that many of the framers saw as a radical threat to the economic and social order.

THE POWERS OF CONGRESS AND THE
STATES. The issues of power and consent
were important throughout the Constitution. Section 8 of Article I specifically listed
the powers of Congress, which include the
authority to collect taxes, to borrow money,
to regulate commerce, to declare war, and
to maintain an army and navy. By granting
it these powers, the framers indicated very
clearly that they intended the new government to be far more influential than its
predecessor. At the same time, by giving
these important powers to Congress, the
framers sought to reassure citizens that their
views would be fully represented whenever
the government exercised its new powers.

As a further guarantee to the people that
the new government would pose no threat
to them, the Constitution implied that any
powers *not* listed were not granted at all.
This is the doctrine of *expressed power.*The
Constitution grants only those powers specifically *expressed* in its text. But the framers
intended to create an active and powerful
government, and so they included the "necessary and proper clause," sometimes
known as the *elastic clause,*which signified
that the enumerated powers were meant to
be a source of strength to the national government, not a limitation on it. Each power
could be used with the utmost vigor, but no
new powers could be seized upon by the
national government without a constitutional amendment. Any power not enumerated was conceived to be "reserved" to the
states (or the people).

If there had been any doubt at all about
the scope of the necessary and proper
clause, it was settled by Chief Justice John
Marshall in one of the most important constitutional cases in American history,
McCulloch v. *Maryland,* which dealt with the
question of whether states could tax the

federally chartered Bank of the United
States.[7] This bank was largely under the
control of the Federalist party and was extremely unpopular in the West and South.
A number of states, including Maryland,
imposed stiff taxes on the bank's operations,
hoping to weaken or destroy it. When the
bank's Baltimore branch refused to pay
state taxes, the state brought a suit that was
eventually heard by the U.S. Supreme Court
(see also Chapter 3).

Writing for the Court, Chief Justice John
Marshall ruled that states had no power to
tax national agencies. Moreover, Marshall
took the opportunity to give an expansive
interpretation of the "necessary and
proper" clause of the Constitution by asserting that Congress clearly possessed the
power to charter a bank even though this
was not explicitly mentioned in the Constitution. Marshall argued that so long as Congress was passing acts pursuant to one of
the enumerated powers, then any of the
means convenient to such an end were also
legitimate. As he put it, any government
"entrusted with such ample powers . . .
must also be entrusted with ample means
for their execution." It was through this avenue that the national government could
grow in power without necessarily taking
on any powers that were not already enumerated.

LIMITS ON THE NATIONAL GOVERNMENT
AND THE STATES. The Constitution listed
in Section 9 a number of important limitations on the national government, which are
in the nature of a mini bill of rights. These
included the right of *habeas corpus,* which
means, in effect, that the government cannot
deprive a person of liberty without explain-

---

[7]McCulloch v. Maryland, 4 Wheaton 316 (1819).

In Brief Box

THE SEVEN ARTICLES OF THE CONSTITUTION

1. The Legislative Branch

House: two-year terms, elected directly by the people.

Senate: six-year terms (staggered so that only one-third of the Senate changes in any given election), appointed by state legislature (changed in 1913 to direct election).

Expressed powers of the national government: include collecting taxes, borrowing money, regulating commerce, declaring war, and maintaining an army and a navy; all other power belongs to the states, unless deemed otherwise by the elastic ("necessary and proper") clause.

Exclusive powers of the national government: states are expressly forbidden to issue their own paper money, tax imports and exports, regulate trade outside their own borders, and impair the obligation of contracts; these powers are the exclusive domain of the national government.

2. The Executive Branch

Presidency: four-year terms (maximum of two terms), elected indirectly by the electoral college.

Powers: can recognize other countries, negotiate treaties, grant reprieves and pardons, convene Congress in special sessions, and veto congressional enactments.

3. The Judicial Branch

Supreme Court: lifetime terms, appointed by the president with the approval of the Senate.

Powers: include resolving conflicts between federal and state laws, determining whether power belongs to national government or the states, and settling controversies between citizens of different states.

4. National Unity and Power

Reciprocity among states: establishes that each state must give "full faith and credit" to official acts of other states, and guarantees citizens of any state the "privileges and immunities" of every other state.

5. Amending the Constitution

Procedures: requires two-thirds approval in Congress, and three-fourths adoption by the states.

6. National Supremacy

The Constitution and national law are the supreme law of the land and cannot be overruled by state law.

7. Ratification

The Constitution became effective when approved by nine states.

ing the reason to a court. These limitations are part of the reason that most delegates at the Constitutional Convention felt no urgent need to add a full-scale bill of rights to the Constitution. Some provisions were clearly designed to prevent the federal government from threatening important property interests. For example, Congress was prohibited from giving preference to the ports of one state over those of another. Furthermore, neither Congress nor the state legislatures could require American vessels to pay duty as they entered the ports of any state, thereby preventing the states from charging tribute. All this was part of the delegates' effort to clear away major obstructions to national commerce.

The framers also included restrictions on the states because of their fear of the capacity of the state legislatures to engage in radical action against property and creditors. There are few absolutes in the Constitution, and most of them are found in Article I, Section 10, among the limitations on state powers in matters of commerce. The states were explicitly and absolutely denied the power to tax imports and exports and to place any regulations or other burdens on commerce outside their own borders. They were also explicitly prohibited from issuing paper money or providing on their own for the payment of debts in any form except gold and silver coin.

Finally, and of greatest importance, the states were not allowed to impair the obligation of contracts. This was almost sufficient by itself to reassure commercial interests because it meant that state legislatures would not be able to cancel their contracts to purchase goods and services. Nor would they be able to pass any laws that would seriously alter the terms of contracts between private parties. All the powers that the states were in effect forbidden to exercise

came to be known as the "exclusive powers" of the national government.

The Executive Branch

The Constitution provided for the establishment of the presidency in Article II. As Alexander Hamilton put it, the presidential article sought "energy in the Executive." It did so in an effort to overcome the natural stalemate that was built into the bicameral legislature as well as into the separation of powers among the legislative, executive, and judicial branches. The Constitution afforded the president a measure of independence from the people and from the other branches of government—particularly the Congress.

In line with the framers' goal of increased power to the national government, the president was granted the unconditional power to accept ambassadors from other countries; this amounted to the power to "recognize" other countries. He was also given the power to negotiate treaties, although their acceptance required the approval of the Senate. The president was given the unconditional right to grant reprieves and pardons, except in cases of impeachment. And he was provided with the power to appoint major departmental personnel, to convene Congress in special session, and to veto congressional enactments. (The veto power is formidable. But it is not absolute, since Congress can override it by a two-thirds vote.)

At the same time, the framers sought to help the president withstand (excessively) democratic pressures by making him subject to indirect rather than direct election (through his selection by a separate electoral college). The extent to which the framers' hopes were actually realized will be the topic of Chapter 6.

The Judicial Branch

Article III establishes the judicial branch. This provision reflects the framers' concern with giving more power to the national government and checking radical democratic impulses, while guarding against abuse of liberty and property by the new national government itself.

The framers created a court that was to be literally a supreme court of the United States, and not merely the highest court of the national government. The Supreme Court was given the power to resolve any conflicts that might emerge between federal and state laws and to determine to which level of government a power belonged. In addition, the Supreme Court was assigned jurisdiction over controversies between citizens of different states. The long-term significance of this was that as the country developed a national economy, it came to rely increasingly on the federal judiciary rather than on the state courts for resolution of disputes.

Judges were given lifetime appointments in order to protect them from popular politics and from interference by the other branches. But they would not be totally immune to politics or to the other branches, for the president was to appoint the judges, and the Senate to approve the appointments. Congress would also have the power to create inferior (lower) courts, to change the jurisdiction of the federal courts, to add or subtract federal judges, even to change the size of the Supreme Court.

No direct mention is made in the Constitution of *judicial review* —the power of the courts to render the final decision when there is a conflict of interpretation of the Constitution or of laws. This conflict could be between the courts and Congress, the courts and the executive branch, or the courts and the states. Scholars generally feel that judicial review is implicit in the very existence of a written Constitution and in the power given directly to the federal courts over "all Cases . . . arising under this Constitution, the Laws of the United States and Treaties made, or which shall be made, under their Authority" (Article III, Section 2). The Supreme Court eventually assumed the power of judicial review. Its assumption of power, as we shall see in Chapter 7, was based not on the Constitution itself but on the politics of later decades and the membership of the Court.

National Unity and Power

Various provisions in the Constitution addressed the framers' concern with national unity and power. Article IV's provisions for comity (reciprocity) among states and among citizens of all states were extremely important, for without them there would have been little prospect of unobstructed national movement of persons and goods. Both "comity clauses," the *full faith and credit* clause and the *privileges and immunities* clause, were taken directly from the Articles of Confederation. The first clause provided that each state had to give "full faith and credit" to the official acts of all other states. The second provided that the citizens of any state were guaranteed the "privileges and immunities" of every other state, as though they were citizens of that state. Each state was also prohibited from discriminating against the citizens of other states in favor of its own citizens, with the Supreme Court being the arbiter in each case.

The Constitution also contained the infamous provision that obliged persons living in free states to capture escaped slaves and return them to their owners. This provision, repealed in 1865 by the Thirteenth Amendment, was a promise to the South that it would not have to consider itself an economy isolated from the rest of the country.

The Constitution provided for the admission of new states to the union and guaranteed existing states that no territory would be taken from any of them without their consent. The Constitution provided that the United States "shall guarantee to every State . . . a Republican Form of Government." But this is not an open invitation to the national government to intervene in the affairs of any of the states. A clause states that the federal government can intervene in matters of domestic violence only when invited to by a state legislature or the state executive when the legislature is not in session or when necessary to enforce a federal court order. This has left the question of national intervention in local disorders almost completely to the discretion of local and state officials.

The framers' concern with national supremacy was also expressed in Article VI, in the "supremacy clause," which provided that national laws and treaties "shall be the supreme law of the land." This meant that all laws made under the "authority of the United States" would be superior to all laws adopted by any state or any other subdivision, and the states would be expected to respect all treaties made under that authority. This was a direct effort to keep the states from dealing separately with foreign nations or businesses. The supremacy clause also bound the officials of all state and local as well as federal governments to take an oath of office to support the national Constitution. This meant that every action taken by the United States Congress would have to be applied within each state as though the action were in fact state law.

To found the nation on a solid economic base, the Constitution also provided that all debts entered into under the Articles of Confederation were to be continued as valid debts under the new Constitution. The first Congress acted to assume all debts incurred by the states during the Revolution. This action secured the allegiance of the mercantile class within the country, because most of the debts incurred by the national and state governments during and after the Revolution were held by wealthy Americans concerned about the dependability of their government. It was one of the most important assurances to the commercial interests that the Constitution favored commerce. It also assured foreign countries, especially France and England, that the United States could be trusted in matters of trade, treaties, defense, and credit. Repudiation of debts at the very outset would have endangered the country's sovereignty, since sovereignty depends on the credibility a nation enjoys in the eyes of other nations.

Amending the Constitution

The Constitution established procedures for its own revision in Article V. Its provisions are so difficult that Americans have succeeded in the amending process only seventeen times since 1791, when the first ten amendments were adopted. Many other amendments have been proposed in Congress, but fewer than forty of them have even come close to fulfilling the Constitution's requirement of a two-thirds vote in Congress, and only a fraction have gotten anywhere near adoption by three-fourths of the states. The Constitution could also be amended by a constitutional convention. Occasionally, proponents of particular measures, such as a "balanced-budget amendment," have called for a constitutional convention to consider their proposals. Whatever the purpose for which it was called, however, such a convention would presumably have the authority to revise America's entire system of government. (A breakdown of these figures and further discussion of amending the Constitution appear in Chapter 3.)

Ratifying the Constitution

The rules for the ratification of the Constitution of 1787 made up Article VII of the Constitution. This provision actually violated the lawful procedure for constitutional change incorporated in the Articles of Confederation. For one thing, it adopted a nine-state rule in place of the unanimity among the states required by the Articles of Confederation. For another, it provided that ratification would occur in special state conventions called for that purpose rather than in the state legislatures. All the states except Rhode Island eventually did set up state conventions to ratify the Constitution, and none seemed to protest very loudly the extralegal character of the procedure.

Constitutional Limits on the National Government's Power

As we have indicated, though the framers sought to create a powerful national government, they also wanted to guard against possible misuse of that power. To that end, the framers incorporated two key principles into the Constitution—the *separation of powers* and *federalism* (see Chapter 3). A third set of limitations, in the form of a *bill of rights,* was added to the Constitution to help secure its ratification when opponents of the document charged that it paid insufficient attention to citizens' rights.

THE SEPARATION OF POWERS. No principle of politics was more widely shared at the time of the 1787 founding than the principle that power must be used to balance power. The French political theorist Montesquieu (1689–1755) believed that this balance was an indispensable defense against tyranny, and his writings, especially his major work, *The Spirit of the Laws,* "were taken as political gospel" at the Philadelphia Convention.[8] This principle is not stated explicitly in the Constitution, but it is clearly built on Articles I, II, and III, which provide for:

1. Three separate and distinct branches of government.
2. Different methods of selecting the top personnel, so that each branch is responsible to a different constituency. This is supposed to produce a "mixed regime," in which the personnel of each department will develop very different interests and outlooks on how to govern, and different groups in society will be assured some access to governmental decision making.
3. "Checks and balances," a system under which each of the branches is given some power over the others. Familiar examples are the presidential veto power over legislation and the power of the Senate to approve presidential appointments.

One clever formulation conceives of this system not as separated powers but as "separated institutions sharing power,"[9] and thus diminishing the chance that power will be misused.

FEDERALISM. Federalism was actually a step toward greater centralization of power. The delegates agreed that they needed to place more power at the national governmental level, without completely undermining the power of the state governments. Thus, they

[8]Max Farrand, *The Framing of the Constitution of the United States* (New Haven: Yale University Press, 1962), p. 49.

[9]Richard E. Neustadt, *Presidential Power* (New York: Wiley, 1960), p. 33.

James Madison and George Clinton
A Federalist and an Antifederalist Who Built a Nation

James Madison is best known as the man who, more than any other, shaped the U.S. Constitution, forged in Philadelphia in 1787. George Clinton, who served as a popular New York governor from 1777 to 1795 and again from 1801 to 1804, is little remembered by history except for his opposition to the Constitution. Yet Clinton's contribution as an Antifederalist was nearly as significant to the new government as Madison's.

As a member of Congress under the Articles of Confederation, Madison was convinced that a new system of government was necessary. At the Constitutional Convention, he was the primary architect of the Virginia Plan, the original constitutional blueprint, and even though some of Madison's most cherished ideas were defeated by the convention (such as the idea that Congress should have an absolute veto over all state laws), he is credited with being the "father" of the Constitution. After the convention, Madison worked tirelessly for the document's ratification; with Alexander Hamilton and John Jay, he wrote *The Federalist* essays, which were published in newspapers around the country to persuade the nation to accept the Constitution.

George Clinton was among the prominent figures who opposed Madison's efforts. Like many Antifederalists, Clinton was suspicious of the enhanced powers of this new central government, fearing that a single government ruling a large population would be too quick to deprive the people of their

James Madison

devised a system of two sovereigns—the states and the nation—with the hope that competition between the two would be an effective limitation on the power of both.

THE BILL OF RIGHTS. Late in the Philadelphia Convention, a motion was made to include a bill of rights in the Constitution.

After a brief debate in which hardly a word was said in its favor and only one speech was made against it, the motion to include it was almost unanimously turned down. Most delegates sincerely believed that since the federal government was already limited to its expressed powers, further protection of citizens was not needed. The delegates

liberties. Unlike Madison, who opposed too much government by the people, Clinton believed that government should be founded on the consent of the governed. His opinions on direct representation based on geographically small districts buttressed arguments on behalf of retaining a "popular house" in Congress—that is, the House of Representatives.

When the new Constitution was sent to the states for ratification, it met a chilly reception in New York, a hotbed of Antifederalist sentiment. When the state's ratification convention met in the summer of 1788, Antifederalists outnumbered Federalists 2 to 1. The convention selected Governor Clinton to preside, but in doing so, silenced his eloquent voice (since he had to concern himself with conducting the meetings). Led by Alexander Hamilton, the Federalists decided to stall the proceedings in the hope that other key states would ratify the new document in the meantime, thereby increasing the pressure on New York. News of Virginia's ratification—the tenth state to do so—forced the collapse of Antifederalist resistance, and New York ratified by the closest vote of any state, 30 to 27.

Despite Clinton's silence at the state convention, once the Constitution was approved, his was a leading voice on behalf of the addition of a Bill of Rights to safeguard individual liberties against governmental encroachment. In 1791, the first ten amendments were added to the Constitution, thanks in part to the key guidance of Congressman James Madison. Despite enduring personal animosities, when Madison became president, in 1808, he chose George Clinton for his vice-president.

Source: Stephen L. Schechter, ed., *The Reluctant Piller* (Troy, NY: Russell Sage College, 1985).

George Clinton

argued that the states should adopt bills of rights because their powers needed more limitations than those of the federal government. But almost immediately after the Constitution was ratified, there was a movement to adopt a national bill of rights. This is why the Bill of Rights, adopted in 1791, comprises the first ten amendments to the Constitution rather than being part of the body of it. We will have a good deal more to say about the Bill of Rights in Chapter 3.

The Fight for Ratification

The first hurdle faced by the new Constitution was ratification by state conventions of delegates elected by white, propertied males of each state. This struggle for ratification was carried out in thirteen separate campaigns. Each involved different individuals, moved at a different pace, and was influenced by local as well as national considerations. Two sides faced off throughout all the states, however, taking the names of Federalists and Antifederalists. The Federalists supported the Constitution and preferred a strong national government. The Antifederalists opposed the Constitution and preferred a more decentralized federal system of government; they took on their name by default, in reaction to their better-organized opponents. The Federalists were united in their support of the Constitution. The Antifederalists, although opposing this plan, were divided as to what they believed the alternative shoud be.

Under the name of "Publius," Alexander Hamilton, James Madison, and John Jay wrote eighty-five articles in the New York papers supporting ratification of the Constitution. These *Federalist Papers,* as they are collectively known today, defended the principles of the Constitution and sought to dispel the fears of a national authority. The Antifederalists, however, such as Richard Henry Lee and Patrick Henry of Virginia, and George Clinton of New York, argued that the New Constitution betrayed the Revolution and was a step toward monarchy. They accused the Philadelphia Convention of being a "Dark Conclave," which had worked under a "thick veil of secrecy" to overthrow the law and spirit of the Articles of Confederation.

By the end of 1787 and the beginning of 1788, five states had ratified the Constitution. Delaware, New Jersey, and Georgia ratified it unanimously; Connecticut and Pennsylvania ratified by wide margins. Opposition was overcome in Massachusetts by the inclusion of nine recommended amendments to the Constitution to protect human rights. Ratification by Maryland and South Carolina followed. In June 1788, New Hampshire became the ninth state to ratify. That put the Constitution into effect, but for the new national government to have real power, the approval of both Virginia and New York would be needed. After impassioned debate and a great number of recommendations for future amendment of the Constitution, especially for a bill of rights, the Federalists mustered enough votes for approval of the Constitution in June (Virginia) and July (New York) of 1788. North Carolina joined the new government in 1789, after a bill of rights actually was submitted to the states by Congress, and Rhode Island held out until 1790 before finally voting to become part of the new union.

Reflections on the Founding

The final product of the Constitutional Convention would have to be considered an extraordinary victory for those who wanted a new system of government to replace the Articles of Confederation. The new Constitution laid the groundwork for a government that would be sufficiently powerful to promote trade, to protect property, and to check the activities of radical state legislatures. Moreover, this new government was so constructed through internal checks and balances, indirect selection of officeholders, lifetime judicial appointments, and other similar provisions to preclude the "excessive" democracy feared by many of the founding fathers. Some of the framers favored going even further in limiting popular influence, but the general consensus at the convention was that a thoroughly undemocratic document would never receive the popular approval needed to be ratified by the states.[10]

Yet, while the Constitution sought to lay the groundwork for a powerful government, the framers were very concerned to reconcile government power with freedom. The framers surrounded the powerful institutions of the new regime with a variety of safeguards—a continual array of checks and balances—designed to make certain that the power of the national government could not be used to undermine the states' power and their citizens' freedoms. Thus, the framers were the first Americans to confront head-on the dilemma of freedom and power. Whether their solutions to this dilemma were successful is, of course, the topic of the remainder of our story.

[10]See Farrand, *The Records of the Federal Convention*, vol. 1, p. 132.

Time Line on the Founding

EVENTS		INSTITUTIONAL DEVELOPMENTS
	1750	Albany Congress calls for colonial unity (1754)
French defeated in North America (1760)		Stamp Act Congress attended by delegates from all colonies (1765)
Stamp Act enacted (1765)		
Townshend duties enacted (1767)		
Boston Massacre (1770)	**1770**	
Tea Act; Boston Tea Party (1773)		
British adopt Coercive Acts to punish colonies (1774)		First Continental Congress adopts Declaration of American Rights (1774)
Battles of Lexington and Concord (1775)		Second Continental Congress assumes role of revolutionary government (1775); adopts Declaration of Independence (1776)
		New state constitutions adopted (1776–1784)
		Second Continental Congress adopts Articles of Confederation (1777)
British surrender at Yorktown (1781)	**1780**	

EVENTS		INSTITUTIONAL DEVELOPMENTS
Shays's Rebellion (1786)		Annapolis Convention calls for consideration of government revision (1786)
		Constitutional Convention drafts blueprint for new government (1787)
Federalist Papers (1788)	**1790**	Constitution ratified by states (1788–1790)

Chapter Review

Political conflicts between the colonies and England, and among competing groups within the colonies, led to the first founding as expressed by the Declaration of Independence. The first constitution, the Articles of Confederation, was adopted one year later (1777). Under this document, the states retained their sovereignty. The central government, composed solely of Congress, had few powers and no means of enforcing its will. The national government's weakness soon led to the second founding as expressed by the Constitution of 1787.

In this second founding the framers sought, first, to fashion a new government sufficiently powerful to promote commerce and protect property from radical state legislatures. Second, they sought to bring an end to the "excessive democracy" of the state and national governments under the Articles of Confederation. Third, they sought to introduce mechanisms that would secure popular consent for the new government. Finally, the framers sought to make certain that their new government would not itself pose a threat to liberty and property.

The Constitution consists of seven articles. Article I provides for a Congress of two chambers (Sections 1–7), defines the powers of the national government (Section 8), interprets the national government's powers as a source of strength rather than a limitation (necessary and proper clause), places specific restrictions on the national government (Section 9), and limits state powers (Section 10). Article II describes the presidency and establishes it as a separate branch of government. Article III is the judiciary article. While there is no direct mention of judicial review in this article, the Supreme Court eventually assumed that power. The main provisions of Article IV, the full faith and credit clause and the privileges and immunities clause, provide for reciprocity among the states. Article V describes the procedures for amending the Constitution. Article VI establishes that national laws and treaties are "the supreme law of the land." And finally, Article VII specifies the procedure for ratifying the Constitution of 1787.

For Further Reading

Bailyn, Bernard. *The Ideological Origins of the American Revolution.* Cambridge: Harvard University, 1967.

Beard, Charles. *An Economic Interpretation of the Constitution of the United States.* New York: Macmillan, 1913.

Becker, Carl L. *The Declaration of Independence.* New York: Vintage, 1942.

Cohler, Anne M. *Montesquieu's Comparative Politics and the Spirit of American Constitutionalism.* Lawrence: University Press of Kansas, 1988.

Farrand, Max, ed. *The Records of the Federal Convention of 1787.* New Haven: Yale University Press, 1966.

McDonald, Forrest. *The Formation of the American Republic.* New York: Penguin, 1967.

Palmer, R. R. *The Age of the Democratic Revolution.* Princeton: Princeton University Press, 1964.

Storing, Herbert, ed. *The Complete Anti-Federalist.* Chicago: University of Chicago Press, 1980.

Walker, Samuel. *In Defense of American Liberties—A History of the ACLU.* New York: Oxford University Press, 1990.

Wills, Garry. *Explaining America.* New York: Penguin, 1982.

Wood, Gordon S. *The Creation of the American Republic.* New York: W. W. Norton, 1982.

3

THE CONSTITUTIONAL FRAMEWORK: FEDERALISM AND THE SEPARATION OF POWERS

*T*he failings of the Articles of Confederation frustrated the newly emerging economic interests in the United States seeking larger national and international markets. Their frustration fueled a movement to reform the Articles. This "reform movement" was powerful enough to create a revolutionary new constitution that gave the national government far more authority. (See Chapter 2.)

But the political power of the new economic interests alone would never have been sufficient to push through an entirely new constitution. These interests had to be translated into higher *principles* in order to gain the loyalty and support from other powerful interests as well as from the American people. In fact, loyal support for any government depends on the powerful and the powerless alike accepting the principles of government as *legitimate*.

Legitimacy can be defined as *the next best thing to being good*. Legitimacy is not synonymous with popularity. A government can be considered legitimate when its actions appear to be consistent with the highest principles that people already hold. In most countries, governments have attempted to derive their legitimacy from *religion* or from a common past of shared experiences and sacrifices that are called *tradition*. Some governments, or their rulers, have tried to derive their legitimacy from the *need for defense against a common enemy.* The American approach to legitimacy contained parts of all of these factors but with a unique addition: *contract.* A contract is an exchange, a deal. The contract we call the American Constitution was simply this: *the people would give their consent to a strong national government if that government would in turn accept certain strict limitations on its powers.* In other words, power in return for limits.

Three fundamental limitations were the principles involved in the contract between the American people and the framers of the Constitution: *federalism,* the *separation of powers,* and *individual rights.* Nowhere in the Constitution are these mentioned by name, but we know from the debates and writings that they were to be the primary framework within which constitutional power would be exercised.

The principle of *federalism* sought to limit the national government by creating a second layer of state governments in opposition to it. American federalism recognized two sovereigns in the original Constitution and reinforced the principle in the Bill of Rights by granting a few "expressed powers" to the national government and reserving all the rest to the states.

The principle of the *separation of powers* sought to limit the power of the national government by dividing it against itself—by giving the legislative, executive, and judicial branches separate functions, thus forcing them to share power.

The principle of *individual rights* sought to limit government by defining the people as separate from it—granting to each individual an identity in opposition to the government itself. Individuals are given rights, which are claims to identity, to property, and to personal satisfaction or "the pursuit

of happiness," that cannot be denied except by extraordinary procedures that demonstrate beyond doubt that the need of the government or the "public interest" is more compelling than the claim of the citizen. The principle of individual rights implies also the principle of *representation.* If there is to be a separate private sphere, there must be a set of procedures, separate from judicial review of individual rights, that somehow takes into account the preferences of citizens before the government acts.

This chapter will be concerned with the first two principles—federalism and the separation of powers. The purpose here is to look at the evolution of each principle in order to understand how we got to where we are and what the significance of each principle in operation is. After that we will look briefly at how and why the constitutional framework can be changed through the process of constitutional amendment. The third key principle, individual rights, will be the topic of the next chapter. But all of this is for introductory purposes only. All three principles form the background and the context for every other chapter in the book.

The First Principle: The Federal Framework

Few will disagree that the Constitution has had its most fundamental influence on American life through federalism. **Federalism** can be defined with misleading ease and simplicity as the division of powers and functions between the national government and the state governments. Tracing out the influence of federalism is not so simple, but we can make the task easier by breaking it down into three distinctive forms.

First, federalism sought to limit national power by creating two sovereigns—the national government and the state governments. It was called "dual federalism." At the time of our nation's founding, the states already existed as former colonies and, for nearly thirteen years, as virtually autonomous units under the Articles of Confederation. The Constitution imposed a stronger national government upon the states. But even after the ratification of the Constitution, the states continued to be more important than the national government. For nearly a century and a half, virtually all of the fundamental policies governing the lives of American citizens were made by the state legislatures, not by Congress.

The novelty of this arrangement can be appreciated by noting that all of the major European countries at that time had *unitary* governments: a single national government with national ministries; a national police force; and a single, national code of laws for crimes, commerce, public works, education, and all other areas.

Second, that same federalism specifically restrained the power of the national government over the economy. The Supreme Court's definition of "interstate commerce" was so restrictive that Congress could only legislate as to the actual flow of goods across state lines; local conditions were protected from Congress by the contrary doctrine called "intrastate" commerce. As we shall see later in this chapter and again in Chapter 13, the federalism of strong states and weak national government reigned until 1937, when the Supreme Court redefined "interstate commerce" to permit the national government to regulate local economic conditions.

Third, since federalism freed the states to make so many important policies according to the wishes of their own citizens, states were therefore also free to be different from one another. Federalism allowed a great deal of variation from state to state in the rights enjoyed by citizens, in the roles played by governments, and in definitions of crime and its punishment. During the past half century, we have moved toward greater national uniformity in state laws and in the rights enjoyed by citizens. Nevertheless, as we shall see, federalism continues even today to permit significant differences among the states.

Each of these consequences of federalism will be considered in its turn. The first two—the creating of two sovereigns and the restraining of the economic power of the national government—will be treated in this chapter, along with an assessment of their continuing influence. The third, even though it is an aspect of federalism, will be an important part of the next chapter, because it relates to the framework of individual rights and liberties.

Restraining National Power with Dual Federalism, 1789–1937

As we have noted, the Constitution created two layers of government: the national government and the state governments. This two-layer system is called dual federalism or dual sovereignty. The consequences of this dual sovereignty are fundamental to the American system of government in theory and in practice; they have meant that states have done most of the fundamental governing in this country. For evidence, look at Table 3.1. It lists the major types of public policies by which Americans were governed for the first century and a half under the Constitution. We call it the "traditional system" because it prevailed for three-quarters of our history and because it closely approximates the intentions of the framers

TABLE 3.1
THE FEDERAL SYSTEM: SPECIALIZATION OF GOVERNMENTAL FUNCTIONS IN THE TRADITIONAL SYSTEM (1800-1933)

National Government Policies (Domestic)	State Government Policies	Local Government Policies
Internal improvements	Property laws (including	Adaptation of state laws to
Subsidies	slavery)	local conditions
Tariffs	Estate and inheritance laws	("variances")
Public lands disposal	Commerce laws	Public works
Patents	Banking and credit laws	Contracts for public works
Currency	Corporate laws	Licensing of public
	Insurance laws	accommodations
	Family laws	Assessible improvements
	Morals laws	Basic public services
	Public health laws	
	Education laws	
	General penal laws	
	Eminent domain laws	
	Construction codes	
	Land-use laws	
	Water and mineral laws	
	Criminal procedure laws	
	Electoral and political	
	parties laws	
	Local government laws	
	Civil service laws	
	Occupations and	
	professions laws	

of the Constitution.

Under the traditional system, the national government was quite small by comparison both to the state governments and to the governments of other Western nations. Not only was it smaller than most governments of that time; it was actually very narrowly specialized in the functions it performed. Our national government built or sponsored the construction of roads, canals, and bridges ("internal improvements"). It provided cash subsidies to shippers and ship builders and free or low-priced public land to encourage western settlement and business ventures. It placed relatively heavy taxes on imported goods (tariffs), not only to raise revenues but to protect "infant industries" from competition from the more advanced European enterprises. It protected patents and provided for a common currency, also to encourage and facilitate enterprises and to expand markets.

What do these functions of the national government reveal? First, virtually all its functions were aimed at assisting commerce. It is quite appropriate to refer to the traditional American system as a "commercial republic." Second, virtually none of the national government's policies directly coerced citizens. The emphasis of governmental programs was on assistance, promotion, and encouragement—the allocation of land or capital where they were insufficiently available for economic development.

Meanwhile, state legislatures were actively involved in economic regulation during the nineteenth century. In the United States, then and now, private property exists only in state laws and state court decisions regarding property, trespass, and real estate. American capitalism as we know it took its form from state property and trespass laws, as well as state laws and court decisions regarding contracts, markets, credit, banking, incorporation, and insurance. Laws concerning slavery were a subdivision of property law in states where slavery existed. The practice of important professions such as law and medicine was and is illegal, except as provided for by state law. The birth or adoption of a child, marriage, and divorce have always been regulated by state law. To educate or not to educate a child has been a decision governed more by state laws than by parents, and not at all by national law. It is important to note also that virtually all the criminal laws—regarding everything from trespass to murder—have been state laws. Most of the criminal laws adopted by Congress are concerned with the District of Columbia and other federal territories.

All this (and more, as shown in column 2 of Table 3.1) demonstrates without any question that most of the fundamental governing in this country was done by the states. The contrast between national and state policies, as shown by the table, demonstrates the difference in the power vested in each. The list of items in column 2 could actually have been made longer. Moreover,

each item on the list is a category of law that fills many volumes of statutes and court decisions.

This contrast between national and state governments is all the more impressive because it is basically what the framers of the Constitution intended. There is probably no better example in world history of consistency between formal intentions and political reality. Since the 1930s, the national government has expanded into local and intrastate matters, far beyond what anyone would have foreseen in 1890 or even in 1914. But this significant expansion of the national government did not alter the basic framework. The national government has become much larger, but the states have continued to be central to the American system of government.

Here lies probably the most important point of all: The fundamental impact of federalism on the way the United States is governed comes not from any particular provision of the Constitution but from the framework itself, which has determined the flow of government functions and, through that, the political developments of the country. By allowing state governments to do most of the fundamental governing, the Constitution saved the national government from many policy decisions that might have proven too divisive for this large and very young country. There is no doubt that if the Constitution had provided for a unitary rather than a federal system, the war over slavery would have come in 1789 or 1809 rather than 1860; and if it had come that early, the South might very well have seceded and established a separate and permanent slaveholding nation.

In helping the national government remain small and aloof from the most divisive issues of the day, federalism contributed significantly to the political stability of the nation, even as the social, economic, and political systems of many of the states and regions of the country were undergoing tremendous and profound, and sometimes violent, change.[1] As we shall see, some important aspects of federalism have changed, but the federal framework has survived two centuries and a devastating civil war.

Federalism as a Limitation on the National Government's Power

Having created the national government, and recognizing the potential for abuse of power, the states sought through federalism to constrain the national government. The "traditional system" of a weak national government prevailed for over a century despite economic forces favoring its expansion and despite Supreme Court cases giving a pro-national interpretation to Article I, Section 8, of the Constitution.

That article delegates to Congress the power "to regulate commerce with foreign nations, and among the several States and with the Indian tribes," and this clause was consistently interpreted *in favor* of national power by the Supreme Court for most of the nineteenth century. The first and most important case favoring national power over the economy was *McCulloch* v. *Maryland* (1819).[2] The case involved the question of whether Congress had the power to charter a national bank, since such an explicit grant of power was nowhere to be found in Article I, Section 8. Chief Justice John Marshall answered that the power could be "implied" from other powers that were expressly delegated to Congress such as the "powers to lay and collect taxes; to borrow money; to regulate commerce; and to declare and conduct a war."

The constitutional authority for the implied powers doctrine is a clause in Article I, Section 8, which enables Congress "to make all laws which shall be necessary and proper for carrying into Execution the foregoing powers." By allowing Congress to use the "necessary and proper" clause to interpret its delegated powers expansively, the Supreme Court created the potential for an unprecedented increase in national government power. Marshall also concluded that whenever a state law conflicted with a federal law (as in the case of *McCulloch* v. *Maryland*), the state law would be deemed invalid since the Constitution states that "the laws of the United States . . . 'shall be the supreme law of the land.'" Both parts of this great case are "pro-national," yet Congress did not immediately seek to expand the policies of the national government.

Another major case, *Gibbons* v. *Ogden* in 1824, reinforced this nationalistic interpretation of the Constitution. The important but relatively narrow issue was whether the state of New York could grant a monopoly to Robert Fulton's steamboat company to operate an exclusive service between New York and New Jersey. Chief Justice Marshall argued that the state of New York did not have the power to grant this particular monopoly. In order to reach this decision, it was necessary for Marshall to define what Article I, Section 8, meant by "commerce among the several states." He insisted that the definition was "comprehensive," extending to "every species of commercial intercourse." He did say that this comprehensiveness was limited "to that commerce which concerns more states than one," giving rise to what later came to be called "in-

---

[1] For a good treatment of the contrast between national political stability and social instability, see Samuel P. Huntington, *Political Order in Changing Societies* (New Haven: Yale University Press, 1968), Chapter 2.

[2] McCulloch v. Maryland, 4 Wheaton 316 (1819). See also Chapter 2.

terstate commerce." *Gibbons* is important because it established the supremacy of the national government in all matters affecting interstate commerce.[3] But what would remain uncertain during several decades of constitutional discourse was the precise meaning of interstate commerce.

Article I, Section 8, backed by the "implied powers" decision in *McCulloch* and by the broad definition of "interstate commerce" in *Gibbons,* was a source of power for the national government as long as Congress sought to facilitate commerce through subsidies, services, and land grants. But later in the nineteenth century, when the national government sought to use those powers to *regulate* the economy rather than merely to promote economic development, federalism and the concept of interstate commerce began to operate as a restraint on, rather than a source of, national power.

Any effort of the national government to regulate commerce in such areas as fraud, the production of impure goods, the use of child labor, or the existence of dangerous working conditions or long hours was declared unconstitutional by the Supreme Court as a violation of the concept of interstate commerce. Such legislation meant that the federal government was entering the factory and workplace—local areas—and was attempting to regulate goods that had not passed into commerce. To enter these local workplaces was to exercise police power—the power reserved to the states for the protection of the health, safety, and morals of their citizens. No one questioned the power of the national government to regulate businesses that intrinsically involved interstate commerce, such as railroads, gas pipelines, and waterway transportation.

[3] Gibbons v. Ogden, 9 Wheaton 1 (1824).

But well into the twentieth century, the Supreme Court used the concept of interstate commerce as a barrier against most efforts by Congress to regulate local conditions.

This aspect of federalism was alive and well during an epoch of tremendous economic development, the period between the Civil War and the 1930s. It gave the American economy a freedom from federal government control that closely approximated the ideal of "free enterprise." The economy was, of course, never entirely free; in fact, entrepreneurs themselves did not want complete freedom from government. They needed law and order. They needed a stable currency. They needed courts and police to enforce contracts and prevent trespass. They needed roads, canals, and railroads. But federalism, as interpreted by the Supreme Court for seventy years after the Civil War, made it possible for business to have its cake and eat it too. Entrepreneurs enjoyed the benefits of national policies facilitating commerce and were protected by the Courts from policies regulating commerce.[4]

All this changed after 1937, when the Supreme Court responded to New Deal legislation by throwing out the old distinction of interstate and intrastate commerce and starting with a clean slate. The Court permitted Congress to adopt a whole series of policies regulating commerce: laws protecting the rights of employees to organize and engage in collective bargaining, laws regu-

[4] The Sherman Antitrust Act, adopted in 1890, for example, was enacted, not to restrict commerce, but rather to protect it from monopolies, or trusts, so as to prevent unfair trade practices, and to enable the market again to become *self-regulating.* Moreover, the Supreme Court sought to uphold liberty of contract to protect businesses. For example, in Lochner v. New York, 198 U.S. 45 (1905), the Court invalidated a New York law regulating the sanitary conditions and hours of labor of bakers on the grounds that the law interfered with liberty of contract.

PROCESS BOX 3.1

**How the National Government Actually Governs—
There Is More to American Government than Federalism**

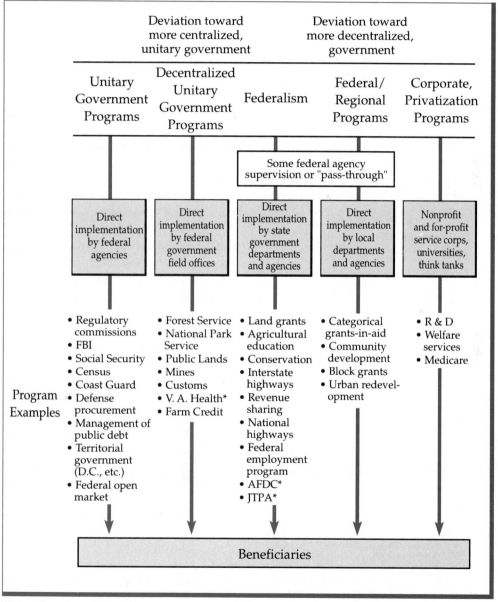

* V.A. = Veterans Administration; AFDC = Aid to Family with Dependent Children; JTPA = Job Training Partnership Act

Source: My thanks to Randall Ripley, Gary Bryner, and Donald Kettl for help in adapting a General Accounting Office diagram. See also Randall Ripley and Grace Franklin, *Policy Implementation and Bureaucracy* (Homewood, IL: Dorsey Press, 1986), p. 69.

lating the amount of farm land in cultivation, laws extending low-interest credit to small businesses and farmers, laws restricting the activities of corporations dealing in the stock market, and a bundle of laws, taken together, constructing the "welfare state." Although the Court has not abdicated its power to review acts of Congress, it will probably never again use "interstate commerce" as a means of limiting national power. In effect, the Supreme Court converted the commerce clause from a source of limitations to a source of power. This has been referred to as the First Constitutional Revolution.[5] (A Second Constitutional Revolution will be identified and discussed in Chapter 4.)

The Continuing Influence of Federalism: State and Local Government Today

STATE GOVERNMENT. Expansion of the power of the national government has not left the states powerless. We cannot repeat too often that the state governments continue to make most of the fundamental laws

and that the national government did not expand at the expense of the states. Growth of the national government has been an addition, not a redistribution, of power from the states. No better demonstration of the continuing influence of the federal framework can be offered than the fact that Column 2 of Table 3.1 is still a fairly accurate characterization of state government today.

LOCAL GOVERNMENT AND THE CONSTITUTION. Local government occupies a peculiar but very important place in the American system. In fact, the status of American local government is probably unique in world experience. First, it must be pointed out that local government has no status in the American Constitution. The policies listed in column 3 of Table 3.1 are there because state legislatures created local governments, and state constitutions and laws permitted local governments to take on some of the responsibilities of the state governments. Most states amended their own constitutions to give their larger cities *home rule* —a guarantee of non-interference in various areas of local affairs. But local governments enjoy no such recognition in the U.S. Constitution. Local governments have always been mere conveniences of the states.[6]

Local governments became administratively important in the early years of the Republic because the states possessed little administrative capability. They relied on lo-

---

[5]The key case in the First Constitutional Revolution is generally considered to be NLRB v. Jones & Laughlin Steel Corporation, 301 U.S. 1 (1937), in which the Supreme Court approved federal regulation of the workplace and thereby virtually eliminated interstate commerce as a limit on national government power. Equally important was the Supreme Court's approval of the welfare state and of the national power of taxation to redistribute wealth, in Steward Machine Co. v. Davis, 301 U.S. 548 (1937). Since at least the 1960s, "interstate commerce" has become a source of congressional power rather than restraint, especially in national efforts to improve the status of blacks and other minorities. The Court held valid provisions of the Civil Rights Act of 1964 regulating racial discrimination in restaurants, motels, and other public accommodations even when these accommodations were not directly in the stream of interstate commerce. See, for example, Heart of Atlanta Motel v. U.S., 379 U.S. 241 (1964); and Katzenbach v. McClung, 379 U.S. 294 (1964). See also Chapter 4.

[6]A good discussion of the constitutional position of local governments is in York Willbern, *The Withering Away of the City* (Bloomington: Indiana University Press, 1971). For more on the structure and theory of federalism, see Thomas R. Dye, *American Federalism: Competition among the States* (Lexington, MA: Lexington Books, 1990), Chapter 1; and Martha Derthick, "Up-to-Date in Kansas City: Reflections on American Federalism" (the 1992 John Gaus Lecture), *PS: Political Science & Politics* 25 (December 1992), pp. 671–75.

TABLE 3.2

82,341 GOVERNMENTS IN THE UNITED STATES

Type	Number
National	1
State	50
County	3,041
Municipal	19,076
Townships	16,734
School districts	14,851
Other special districts	28,588

Source: *Statistical Abstract of The United States,* 1986 (Washington, DC: Government Printing Office, 1986).

cal governments—cities and counties—to implement the laws of the state. Local government was an alternative to a statewide bureaucracy. (See Table 3.2.)

UPDATING FEDERALISM. Paradoxically, as the national government has expanded, state and local governments have become stronger, not weaker. Since 1937, the national government has exerted more and more influence over the states and localities; but, thanks to American federalism, the form of some of that influence has contributed to state and local power. One type of federal influence is direct, imposed by law and administrative control—for example, in occupational health and safety regulations, air pollution control laws, and voting rights. Most of the influence of the national government, however, is through *grants-in-aid.* A grant-in-aid is really a kind of bribe—Congress gives money to state and local governments, but on the condition that the money will be spent for a particular purpose as designed by Congress. Thus, Congress is using grants-in-aid because it recognizes that it does not usually have the political or constitutional power to command the cities to do its bidding directly.

The principle of grants-in-aid goes back to the nineteenth-century land grants to states for the improvement of agriculture and farm-related education. Since farms were not in "interstate commerce," it was unclear whether the Constitution would permit the national government to provide direct assistance to agriculture. Grants-in-aid to the states, earmarked to go to the farmers, presented a way of avoiding the constitutional problem while pursuing what was recognized in Congress as a national goal.

This same approach was applied to cities beginning in the late 1930s. Congress set national goals such as public housing and assistance to the unemployed and provided grants-in-aid to meet these goals. The value of these grants increased from $2.3 billion in 1950, to $7 billion in 1960, $24 billion in 1970, $94.8 billion in 1981, to more than $120 billion in 1989 (see Table 3.3). Sometimes Congress requires the state or local government to match the national contribution dollar for dollar; but for some programs, such as the interstate highway system, the congressional grant-in-aid provides 90 percent of the cost of the program.

On more than one occasion, the number of grants-in-aid and the amount of money involved have come under criticism, by

TABLE 3.3

HISTORICAL TREND OF FEDERAL GRANTS-IN-AID
(FISCAL YEARS; DOLLAR AMOUNTS IN BILLIONS)

Fiscal year	Amount of grants-in-aid	Total*	Domestic programs†	State and local expenditures‡	Gross National Product‡
Five-year intervals:					
1950	$2.3	5.3%	11.6%	10.4%	0.8%
1955	3.2	4.7	17.2	10.1	0.8
1960	7.0	7.6	20.6	14.6	1.4
1965	10.9	9.2	20.3	15.2	1.6
1970	24.1	12.3	25.3	19.2	2.4
1975	49.8	15.0	23.1	22.7	3.3
Annually:					
1980	91.5	15.5	23.3	25.8	3.4
1981	94.8	14.0	21.6	24.6	3.2
1982	88.2	11.8	19.0	21.6	2.8
1983	92.5	11.4	18.6	21.3	2.8
1984	97.6	11.5	19.6	20.9	2.6
1985	105.9	11.2	19.3	20.9	2.7
1986	112.4	11.3	19.8	20.5	2.7
1987	108.4	10.8	19.0	18.3	2.4
1988	115.4	10.8	19.0	NA	2.4
1989	122.0	10.7	18.7	NA	2.4
1990	136.9	10.9	17.0	18.0	2.5
1991 estimate	158.6	11.2	17.0	NA	2.8
1992 estimate	171.0	11.8	18.0	NA	2.9
1993 estimate	184.1	12.7	19.0	NA	2.9
1994 estimate	162.0	11.6	17.1	NA	2.2
1995 estimate	169.2	11.5	NA	NA	2.2

*Federal grants as percentage of federal outlays. Includes off-budget outlays; all grants are on-budget.
†As a percentage of federal outlays for domestic programs. Excludes outlays for national defense, international affairs, and net interest.
‡As a percentage of state and local expenditures, and as a percentage of GNP.
NA=Not available.
Source: Executive Office of the President, Office of Management and Budget, *Budget of the United States Government, Fiscal Year 1991* (Washington, DC: Government Printing Office, 1991), p. A321.

Democrats as well as Republicans, ultra-liberals as well as ultra-conservatives. But there is general agreement that grants-in-aid helped to reduce disparities of wealth between rich states and poor states. And although some critics have asserted that grants encouraged state and local governments to initiate programs merely because

FIGURE 3.1
The Rise and Decline of Federal Aid

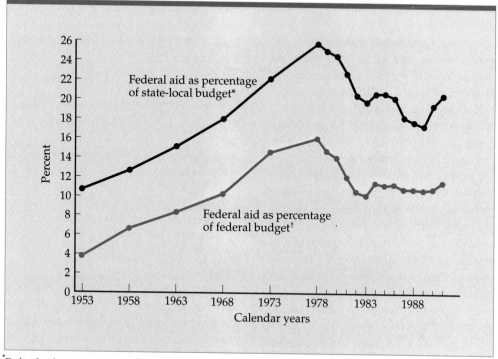

*Federal aid as a percentage of state-local expenditures after transfers.
†Federal aid as a percentage of federal expenditures from own funds.
Source: Advisory Commission on Intergovernmental Relations, *Significant Features of Fiscal Federalism 1982–1983* (Washington, DC: Government Printing Office, January 1984).

"free money from Washington" was available, the fact is that when federal grants were reduced by the Reagan administration, most states and localities continued funding the same programs with their own revenues.

Federalism has not stood still. If the traditional system of two separate sovereigns performing highly different functions could be called dual federalism, historians of federalism suggest that the system since the New Deal era could be called *cooperative federalism,* through which grants-in-aid have been used strategically to encourage states and localities (without commanding them) to pursue nationally defined goals. The most important student of the history of federalism, Morton Grodzins, characterized this as a move from "layer cake federalism" to "marble cake federalism,"[7] in which intergovernmental cooperation and sharing have blurred the line between where the national government ends and the state and local governments begin. Figure 3.1 demonstrates the financial basis of the marble cake idea. At the high point of

[7]Morton Grodzins, "The Federal System," in *Goals for Americans* (Englewood Cliffs, NJ: Prentice-Hall, 1960), p. 265. In a marble cake, the white cake is distinguishable from the chocolate cake, but the two are streaked rather than in distinct layers.

grant-in-aid policies, in 1977–1978, federal aid contributed an average of 25 percent of the operating budgets of all the state and local governments in the country.

A third development, presumably going beyond marble cake federalism, was called *creative federalism* by the Johnson administration. During the 1960s, the federal government used grants-in-aid more as a stick than as a carrot, threatening to withhold money unless state and local governments conformed to national civil rights and poverty program standards. President Nixon changed this with his "new federalism," actually an effort to turn back toward the traditional form. Nixon cut the number of grants-in-aid, and he replaced as many as possible with *revenue sharing,* a scheme to allocate national revenues to the states according to a population and income formula and to leave the states more discretion in how to use the grant money.

The Reagan administration introduced its own version of "new federalism," which included an immediate cut in funding levels from the maximum reached in 1981 of $94.8 billion down to $88.2 billion in grants-in-aid for 1982. But the number of grants was reduced through consolidation of large numbers of specified grants into single "block grants," to give states and localities more discretion over the use of funds.

Although President Reagan succeeded in reducing national appropriations for grants-in-aid during his first term, he could not prevent increases during his second term. Both he and Bush were only able to hold the line sufficiently to keep the outlays from increasing faster than the overall increase in the national budget. Note on Figure 3.1 that federal aid as a percentage of total federal outlays has been close to constant since 1984.

But the increases are no measure of increased national dominance. Federalism re-

mains a vital part of the American system of government, even as the national government grows larger. States and cities clamor (and lobby) for a larger share of the national budget, but they hold on jealously to their freedom of action.

The Second Principle: The Separation of Powers

James Madison is best qualified to speak to Americans of the separation of powers:

> There can be no liberty where the legislative and executive powers are united in the same person . . . [or] if the power of judging be not separated from the legislative and executive powers.[8]

Using this same reasoning, many of Madison's contemporaries argued that there was not *enough* separation among the three branches, and Madison had to do some backtracking to insist that the principle did not require complete separation:

> . . . unless these departments [branches] be so far connected and blended as to give each a constitutional control over the others, the degree of separation which the maxim requires, as essential to a free government, can never in practice be duly maintained.[9]

This is the secret of how we have made the separation of powers effective: We made the principle self-enforcing by giving each branch of government the means to participate in and partially or temporarily to obstruct the workings of the other branches.

[8]Clinton Rossiter, ed., *The Federalist Papers* (New York: New American Library, 1961), No. 47, p. 302.

[9]Ibid., No. 48, p. 308.

Dred Scott
When Persons Were Property

Dred Scott
(1795?–1858)

Slave life for Dred Scott was not as gruelling as it was for most. Born in Virginia about 1795, Scott was originally owned by the Blow family. In 1833, he was sold to an army surgeon living in St. Louis, Dr. John Emerson. In 1834, Scott was taken along as a personal servant to Rock Island, Illinois, and then to Fort Snelling in the Wisconsin Territory (what is now Minnesota), returning to St. Louis in 1838.

When Dr. Emerson died in 1843, Scott attempted to buy his freedom. But instead, he was transferred to Emerson's widow, who then moved to New York, leaving Scott in the care of his previous owners, the Blow family. At least one member of the Blow family felt some sympathy for Scott. Opposed to the extension of slavery into the West, Henry Blow (who later helped found the anti-slavery Free Soil party) provided financial support to Scott to test in court whether his residence on free soil in Illinois and the Wisconsin territory would provide a basis for declaring Scott a free man.

A suit was brought in Missouri in 1846 on this basis, where a jury ruled in Scott's favor. On appeal to the state supreme court, this verdict was overturned. The Missouri court ruled in 1852 that under state law Scott continued to be a slave. The case eventually made its way to the Supreme Court.

In a 7-to-2 ruling handed down in 1857, the Court ruled against Scott. Speaking for the majority, Chief Justice Roger Taney said that blacks such as Scott were not meant to be considered citizens as the term was used in the Con-

stitution, and that blacks "were never thought of or spoken of except as property." This was, without doubt, a crushing defeat for Scott and other blacks. Yet, the Court went even further in its pronouncement than the law or the particulars of the case required, and by doing so, it unintentionally hastened the bloody war that marked the demise of slavery.

At the urging of President James Buchanan, Justice Taney attempted to carve out a broad Court ruling that he hoped would resolve the issue of slavery by providing clear protection for it. In particular, he ruled that Congress lacked the constitutional authority to bar slavery in the territories. For the first time since *Marbury* v. *Madison,* the Court declared an act of Congress—the Missouri Compromise—unconstitutional. These bold steps enraged much of the country.

As for Scott himself, his life had been marked by frail health. His owners freed him a few weeks after the Court decision, but Scott died in St. Louis on September 17, 1858, of tuberculosis. His funeral expenses were paid by Henry Blow.

Source: Bruce Catton, "The Dred Scott Case," in *Quarrels That Have Shaped the Constitution,* ed. John A. Garraty (New York: Harper & Row, 1964). Dred Scott v. Sandford, 19 How. 393 (1857).

Checks and Balances

The means by which each branch of government is able to participate in each other branch are known informally as "checks and balances." The best-known examples are shown in the In Brief Box. The framers sought to guarantee that the three branches would in fact use these checks and balances as weapons against one another by giving each branch a different political constituency and therefore a different perspective on what the government ought to do: direct, popular election for the members of the House; indirect election of senators (until the Seventeenth Amendment, adopted in 1913); indirect election of the president through the electoral college; and appointment of federal judges for life. All things considered, the best characterization of the separation of powers principle in action is, as we said in Chapter 2, "separated institutions sharing power."[10]

Legislative Supremacy

Although each branch was to be given adequate means to compete with the other branches, it is also clear that within the system of separated powers the framers provided for *legislative supremacy.* Legislative supremacy made the provision of checks and balances in the other two branches all the more important.

The most important indications of the intentions of the framers were the provisions in Article I, the legislative article, to treat the powers of the national government as powers of Congress and their decision to give Congress the sole power over appropriations.

Legislative supremacy became a fact and not just theory soon after the founding decade. National politics centered on Congress. Undistinguished presidents followed one another in a dreary succession. Even Madison—so brilliant as a constitutional theorist, so loyal as a constitutional record keeper, and so effective in the struggle for the founding—was a weak president. Jackson and Lincoln are the only two who stand out in the entire nineteenth century, and their successors dropped back out of sight; except for these two, the other presidents operated within the accepted framework of legislative supremacy (see Chapter 6).

The development of political parties, and in particular the emergence in 1832 of the national party convention as a way of nominating presidential candidates, saved the presidency from complete absorption into the orbit of legislative power by giving the president a base of power independent of Congress. But although this development preserved the presidency and salvaged the separation of powers, it did so only in a negative sense. That is to say, presidents were more likely after 1832 to veto congressional enactments than before, or to engage in a military action, but they were not more likely to present programs for positive legislation or to attempt to lead Congress in the enactment of legislation.[11] Given the importance that we are today confronting *presidential* supremacy—it is difficult to grasp at first the extent of legislative supremacy in the nineteenth century.

The role of the judicial branch in the separation of powers has depended upon the power of judicial review, a power not pro-

---

[10]Richard E. Neustadt, *Presidential Power* (New York: Wiley, 1960), p. 33.

[11]For a good review of the uses of the veto, see Raymond Tatalovich and Byron Daynes, *Presidential Power in the United States* (Monterey, CA: Brooks/Cole, 1984), pp. 148–51; and Robert Spitzer, *The Presidential Veto: Touchstone of the American Presidency* (Albany: SUNY Press, 1988).

In Brief Box

CHECKS AND BALANCES

Legislative Branch
Checks executive:
Controls appropriations. (Neither the executive branch nor the judicial branch can spend any money without an act of Congress appropriating it. Includes salaries, except Congress cannot reduce compensation of president or judges during their term.)
Controls by statute. (Except for a narrow sphere of national security and emergency operations, under executive order of the president, no agency in the executive branch has any authority to act except as provided by statutes delegating such authority to the agency or to the department in which the agency is housed.)
Checks judicial:
Controls appropriations (see above).
Can create inferior courts. (All federal district courts and courts of appeal were created by Congress; so were the tax court and the court of claims and the U.S. customs court.)
Can add new judges. (Congress can add new judges by expanding the number of judgeships for existing courts, including the Supreme Court, and it can add judges whenever it creates a new court.)

Executive Branch
Checks legislative:
Can commence a special session. (The president may call Congress into special session "on extraordinary occasions" to take care of unfinished or new legislative business—e.g., to pass a law without which the president feels he cannot carry out his promises or responsibilities.)
Power to veto legislation.
Checks judicial:
Appoints federal judges.

Judicial Branch
Checks legislative:
Judicial review of legislation. (Any and all legislation can come before the federal courts when there is a dispute over the interpretation of the law or over its constitutionality. It is rare, however, that courts will declare the law unconstitutional, although that is always a possibility.)
Checks executive:
Can issue or refuse to issue warrants. (The police or any other executive officers cannot engage in any searches or arrests without a warrant from a judge showing "probable cause" and specifying the place to be searched and the persons or things to be seized.)

Is the Separation of Powers Obsolete?

*T*he separation of governmental powers among three branches of government is a cornerstone of the political system constructed by the Constitution's framers in 1787. In recent years, however, the separation of powers has come under increasing attack by many who feel that this political arrangement is a root cause of many of the difficulties of modern governing. Political gridlock, governmental paralysis, and a seeming inability of government to create a coherent policy are all problems seen as resulting from the separation of powers.

In 1987, a distinguished group of academics and former government officials issued a report calling for extensive changes in a system they believe is no longer suited to resolving pressing American problems. The historian Arthur M. Schlesinger, Jr., among others, argues that the virtues of the separation of powers continue to outweigh its drawbacks.

Committee on the Constitutional System

The separation of powers, as a principle of constitutional structure, has served us well in preventing tyranny and the abuse of high office, but it has done so by encouraging confrontation, indecision and deadlock, and by diffusing accountability for the results. . . . Because the separation of powers encourages conflict between the branches and because the [political] parties are weak, the capacity of the federal government to fashion, enact and administer coherent public policy has diminished and the ability of elected officials to avoid accountability for governmental failures has grown. More specifically, the problems include: Brief Honeymoons. Only the first few months of each four-year presidential term provide an opportunity for decisive action on domestic problems. . . . Divided Government. We have had divided government (one party winning the White House and the other a majority in one or both houses of Congress). . . . Lack of Party Cohesion in Congress. Even in times of united government, disunity persists between the branches. . . . Loss of Accountability. Divided government and party disunity also lead to diffused accountability. . . . Lack of a Mechanism for Replacing Failed or Deadlocked Government. Presently there is no way between our fixed election dates to resolve basic disagreements between the President and

vided for in the Constitution but asserted by Chief Justice Marshall in 1803:

> If a law be in opposition to the Constitution; if both the law and the Constitution apply to a particular case, so that the Court must either decide that case conformable to the law, disregarding the Constitution, or conformable to the Constitution, disregarding the law; the Court must determine

which of these conflicting rules governs the case: This is of the very essence of judicial duty.[12]

The Supreme Court has exercised the power of judicial review with caution, as though to protect its power by using it sparingly. For example, in the fifty years since

[12]Marbury v. Madison, 1 Cranch 137 (1803).

Congress by referring them to the electorate.[1]

Schlesinger

Is the difficulty we encounter these days in meeting our problems really the consequence of defects in the structure of our government? After all, we have had the separation of powers from the beginning of the republic. This has not prevented competent presidents from acting with decision and dispatch. The separation of powers did not notably disable Jefferson or Jackson or Lincoln or Wilson or the Roosevelts. . . . Why are things presumed to be so much worse today?

It cannot be that . . . we face tougher problems than our forefathers. Tougher problems than slavery? the Civil War? the Great Depression? World War II? . . .

The real difference is that the presidents who operated the system successfully *knew what they thought should be done*—and were able to persuade Congress and the nation to give the remedies a try. . . . Our problem is not at all that we know what to do and are impeded from doing it by some structural logjam in the system. Our problem—let us face it—is that we do not know what to do. . . .

If we don't know what ought to be done, efficient enactment of a poor program is a dubious accomplishment. . . . What is the great advantage of acting with decision and dispatch when you don't know what you are doing? . . .

When the country is not sure what ought to be done, it may be that delay, debate and further consideration are not a bad idea. . . .

I believe that in the main our Constitution has worked pretty well. It has ensured discussion when we have lacked consensus and has permitted action when a majority can be convinced that the action is right. . . .

My concern is that this agitation about constitutional reform is a form of escapism. Constitution-tinkering is a flight from the hard question, which is the search for remedy.[2]

[1]Committee on the Constitutional System, *A Bicentennial Analysis of the American Political Structure: Report and Recommendations of the Committee on the Constitutional System*, (January 1987), pp. 3–7.

[2]Arthur M. Schlesinger, Jr., "Leave the Constitution Alone," in *Reforming American Government: The Bicentennial Papers of the Committee on the Constitutional System*, ed. Donald L. Robinson (Boulder, CO: Westview Press, 1985), pp. 53–54.

the rise of big government and strong presidents, no important congressional enactment has been invalidated on constitutional grounds. During the same period, there have been only two important judicial confrontations with the president.[13]

[13]Youngstown Sheet & Tube Co. v. Sawyer, 343 U.S. 579 (1952); and U.S. v. Nixon, 418 U.S. 683 (1974). For details on these cases, see Chapters 6 and 7.

All in all, the separation of powers has had an uneven history. Although "presidential government" seemed to supplant legislative supremacy after 1937, the relative power position of the three branches has varied. The power play between the president and Congress is especially intense when one party controls the White House and another controls Capitol Hill, as has been the case almost solidly since 1969.

Since Watergate, Congress has tried to get back some of the power it had delegated to the president (see Chapter 6). One of the methods it seized upon was the Ethics in Government Act of 1978, which established a "special prosecutor" (later called "independent counsel") with the authority to investigate allegations of wrongdoing by executive branch officials. The statute provides for a special panel of federal judges to appoint an independent counsel. To guard against any conflict of interest on the part of the attorney general, the act also provided that the independent counsel could be removed by the attorney general only for causes specified in the statute.

In 1988 the Court of Appeals declared the act unconstitutional on the grounds that it violated the separation of powers, because it gave law enforcement powers to an officer not appointed by the president. Had it been upheld by the Supreme Court, the investigations of many of the key figures in the Iran-Contra affair would have been terminated. A reversal might well have been expected, because seven of the nine justices were Republican appointees, and Rehnquist had received his promotion to chief justice from Reagan. It surprised many when an unusual majority of seven to one rejected the Justice Department's argument that the executive should control all administrative matters. The Supreme Court reversed the Court of Appeals decision and restored to Congress the power to provide for the investigation of the executive branch.[14]

[14]Morrison v. Olson, 108 S.Ct. 2597 (1988). For a lively account of this case and the issues involved in it, see David G. Savage, *Turning Right—The Making of the Rehnquist Supreme Court* (New York: Wiley, 1992), pp. 194–203. See also Louis Fisher, *American Constitutional Law* (New York: McGraw-Hill, 1990), p. 225 and pp. 263–271.

Some will argue that the lower court was correct in its argument that Congress was violating the separation of powers by infringing on executive hierarchy and administrative responsibility to the president. Others could argue that the Supreme Court decision was the one that strengthened the separation of powers, by restoring to Congress a weapon for use in its competition with presidential power. Either way, the very effort of Congress to provide by law for competition with the executive branch suggests that the separation of powers is still very much alive. And the judiciary is very much a part of the continuing vitality of the separation of powers.

Although the federal courts rarely question the constitutionality of a statute, they are constantly involved in judicial review of statutes and administrative orders, because federal agencies have to get court orders to enforce their decisions. This gives the judiciary a regular opportunity to influence executive as well as legislative actions (see the In Brief Box on page 53). In other words, in order for the government to be able to apply a statute, the court has to first interpret it; and to interpret a statute is to have the power to change it. (See also Chapter 7.) This offers more evidence of the continuing vitality of the separation of powers.

Changing the Framework: Constitutional Amendment

The Constitution has endured for two centuries as the framework of government. But it has not endured without change. Without change, the Constitution might have become merely a sacred text, stored under glass.

Amendments: Many Are Called, Few Are Chosen

The framers of the Constitution recognized the need for change. The provisions for amendment incorporated into Article V were thought to be "an easy, regular and Constitutional way" to make changes, which would occasionally be necessary because members of Congress "may abuse their power and refuse their consent on that very account . . . to admit to amendments to correct the source of the abuse."[15] James Madison, again writing in *The Federalist*, made a more balanced defense of the amendment procedures: "It guards equally against that extreme facility, which would render the Constitution too mutable; and that extreme difficulty, which might perpetuate its discovered faults."[16]

Experience since 1789 raises questions even about Madison's more modest claim. The Constitution has proven to be extremely difficult to amend. In the history of efforts to amend the Constitution, the most appropriate characterization is "many are called, few are chosen." Between 1789 and 1993, 9,746 amendments were formally offered in Congress. Of these, Congress officially proposed only twenty-nine, and only twenty-seven of these were eventually ratified by the states. But the record is even more severe than that. Since 1791, when the first ten amendments, the Bill of Rights, were added, only seventeen amendments have been adopted. And two of them—pro-hibition of alcohol (Eighteenth) and its repealer (Twenty-first)—cancel each other out, so that for all practical purposes, only fifteen amendments have been added to the Constitution since 1791. Despite the vast changes in American society and its economy, only twelve amendments have been adopted since the Civil War amendments (Thirteenth, Fourteenth, and Fifteenth) in 1868.

One amendment is noteworthy for its history alone. On May, 7, 1992, Michigan and New Jersey became the thirty-eighth and thirty-ninth states to ratify the Twenty-seventh Amendment, which bans pay raises for Congress "until an election of Representatives shall have intervened." The first state to ratify it was Maryland, on December 19, 1789. It had been proposed by James Madison as one of the twelve original amendments, of which ten were immediately ratified to become the Bill of Rights. Six states ratified this amendment at that time, but since Congress at that time made no provision for a deadline or terminal date, the Madison amendment did not die. The proposed amendment was revived in 1978 by Wyoming's ratification, and then a trickle of other states followed during the mid-1980s. Once the thirty-eighth state came in, the U.S. archivist had no choice but to certify the amendment and to publish it in the *Federal Register*, making it official. Speaker of the House Tom Foley somewhat begrudgingly accepted it: "I think as a practical matter, it will be considered a part of the Constitution."[17]

---

[15] Observation by Colonel George Mason, delegate from Virginia, early during the convention period, quoted in Max Farrand, *The Records of the Federal Convention of 1787*, vol. 1, rev. ed. (New Haven: Yale University Press, 1966), pp. 202–3.

[16] *The Federalist*, No. 43, p. 278, in Rossiter edition.

[17] "Madison's 1789 Pay Raise Amendment Is Approved," *Congressional Quarterly Guide to Current American Government* (Washington: Congressional Quarterly Inc., 1992), pp. 2–3. Thanks also to Peter Belej of Rochester Institute of Technology.

How the Constitution Is Amended: Four Possible Routes

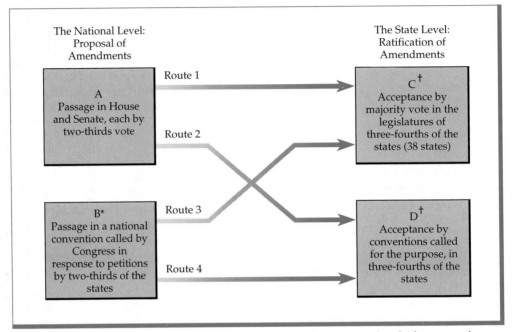

* This method of proposal has never been employed. Thus amendment routes 3 and 4 have never been attempted.

† Congress chooses the method of ratification. In each amendment proposal Congress has the power to provide for the method of ratification, the time limit for consideration by the states, and other conditions of ratification.

As Process Box 3.2 illustrates, four methods of amendment are provided for in Article V:

1. Passage in House and Senate by two-thirds vote; then ratification by majority vote of the legislature of three-fourths (thirty-eight) of the states.

2. Passage in House and Senate by two-thirds vote; then ratification by conventions called for the purpose in three-fourths of the states.

3. Passage in a national convention called by Congress in response to petitions by two-thirds of the states; ratification by majority vote of the legislatures of three-fourths of the states.

4. Passage in a national convention, as in (3); then ratification by conventions called for the purpose in three-fourths of the states.

Since no amendment has ever been proposed by national convention, however, methods (3) and (4) have never been employed. And method (2) has only been employed once (the Twenty-first Amendment, which repealed the Eighteenth, or Prohibition, Amendment). Thus, method (1) has been used for all the others.

It is now clear why it has been so difficult to amend the Constitution. The main reason is the requirement of a two-thirds vote in the

House and the Senate, which means that any proposal for an amendment in Congress can be killed by only 34 senators *or* 136 members of the House. What is more, if the necessary two-thirds vote is obtained, the amendment can still be killed by the refusal or inability of only thirteen state legislatures to ratify it. Since each state has an equal vote regardless of its population, the thirteen hold-out states may represent a small fraction of the total American population. In the 1970s, the Equal Rights Amendment (ERA), granting protection from denial of rights on account of sex, got the necessary two-thirds vote in Congress but failed by three states to get the necessary three-fourths votes of the states, even after a three-year extension on ratification.[18]

If the ERA was a defeat for liberal forces, conservatives have done no better. Constitutional amendments were high on the agenda of the Republican party from the beginning of their presidential victories in the 1980s, and had the blessings of Presidents Reagan and Bush. The school prayer amendment sought to restore power to the states to require selected religious observances, thereby reversing a whole series of earlier Supreme Court decisions.[19] The pro-life amendment sought to reverse *Roe* v.

Wade in order to restore to the states the power to outlaw abortions.

Two other efforts of less social but of great economic significance were the amendment proposed to require a balanced budget and the amendment proposed to give the president the "line-item veto" power. A more recent proposal was for an amendment to protect the flag, to outlaw flag burning or other flag desecration. President Bush had supported such a law in the 1988 election campaign and went on to become the leading supporter of the constitutional amendment for the same purpose. None of these efforts got close to being adopted by Congress for submission to the states for ratification. No genuinely serious effort was made by the Left or by the Right between 1989 and 1993 to amend the Constitution.

Which Were Chosen? An Analysis of the Twenty-seven

There is, however, more to the amending difficulties than the politics of getting votes. It would appear that only a limited number of changes needed by society can actually be made through the Constitution. Most efforts to amend the Constitution fail because they are simply attempts to use the Constitution as an alternative to legislation for dealing directly with a public problem. The school prayer amendment is an example. A review of the successful amendments will provide two insights: First, it will give us some understanding of the condition underlying successful amendments; and second, it will reveal a great deal about what constitutionalism means.

The purpose of the ten amendments in the Bill of Rights was basically *to give each of the three branches clearer and more restricted*

---

[18]Marcia Lee, "The Equal Rights Amendment—Public Policy by Means of a Constitutional Amendment," in *The Politics of Policy Making in America,* ed. David Caputo (San Francisco: W. H. Freeman, 1977); Gilbert Steiner, *Constitutional Inequality: The Political Fortunes of ERA* (Washington, DC: Brookings Institution, 1985); and Jane Mansbridge, *Why We Lost the ERA* (Chicago: University of Chicago Press, 1986).

[19]For judicial action see Engel v. Vitale, 370 U.S. 421 (1926). For the efforts of states to get around the Supreme Court requirement that public schools be secular, see John A. Murley, "School Prayer: Free Exercise of Religion or Establishment of Religion?" in *Social Regulatory Policy,* ed. Raymond Tatalovich and Byron Daynes (Boulder, CO: Westview Press, 1988), pp. 5–40.

TABLE 3.4
THE BILL OF RIGHTS: ANALYSIS OF ITS PROVISIONS

Amendment	Purpose
I	*Limits on Congress:* Congress is not to make any law establishing a religion or abridging speech, press, assembly, or petition freedoms.
II, III, IV	*Limits on Executive:* The executive branch is not to infringe on the right of people to keep arms (II), is not to arbitrarily take houses for a militia (III), and is not to engage in the search or seizure of evidence without a court warrant swearing to belief in the probable existence of a crime (IV).
V, VI, VII, VIII	*Limits on Courts:* The courts are not to hold trials for serious offenses without provision for a grand jury (V), a petit (trial) jury (VII), a speedy trial (VI), presentation of charges, confrontation of hostile witnesses (VI), immunity from testimony against oneself (VI), and immunity from trial more than once for the same offense (V). Neither bail nor punishment can be excessive (VIII), and no property can be taken without just compensation (V).
IX, X	*Limits on National Government:* All rights not enumerated are reserved to the states or the people.

boundaries (see Table 3.4). The First Amendment clarified Congress's turf. Although the powers of Congress under Article I, Section 8, would not have justified laws regulating religion, speech, and the like, the First Amendment made this limitation explicit: "Congress shall make no law. . . ." The Second, Third, and Fourth Amendments similarly spelled out limits on the executive branch, a necessity given the abuses of executive power Americans had endured under British rule.

The Fifth, Sixth, Seventh, and Eighth Amendments contain some of the most important safeguards for individual citizens against the arbitrary exercise of government power. And these amendments sought to accomplish their goal by defining the judicial branch more concretely and clearly than had been done in Article III of the Constitution.

Five amendments adopted since 1791 are directly concerned with expansion of the electorate (see Table 3.5). The founders were unable to establish a national electorate with uniform voting qualifications. They decided to evade the issue by providing in the final draft of Article I, Section 2, that eligibility to vote in a national election would be the same as "the Qualification requisite for Elector of the most numerous branch of the state Legislature." Article I, Section 4, added that Congress could alter state regulations as to the "Times, Places and Manner of holding Elections for Senators and Representatives," but this meant that any important *expansion* of the American electorate would almost certainly require a constitutional amendment.

Six more are also electoral in nature, although not concerned directly with voting rights and the expansion of the electorate. These six amendments are concerned with the elective offices themselves or with the relationship between elective offices and the electorate (see Table 3.6).

TABLE 3.5
AMENDING THE CONSTITUTION TO EXPAND THE ELECTORATE

Amendment	Purpose	Year Proposed	Year Adopted
XV	Extended voting rights to all races	1869	1870
XIX	Extended voting rights to women	1919	1920
XXIII	Extended voting rights to residents of the District of Columbia	1960	1961
XXIV	Extended voting rights to all classes by abolition of poll taxes	1962	1964
XXVI	Extended voting rights to citizens aged 18 and over	1971	1971*

*The Twenty-sixth Amendment holds the record for speed of adoption. It was proposed on April 23, 1971, and adopted on July 5, 1971. The only other adoption time that comes close is the Prohibition repealer (XXI), proposed February 20, 1933, and adopted December 5, 1933.

Another five have sought to expand or to delimit the powers of the national and state governments (see Table 3.7).[20] The Eleventh Amendment protected the states from suits by private individuals and took away from the federal courts any power to take suits by private individuals of one state (or a foreign country) against another state. The other

TABLE 3.6
AMENDING THE CONSTITUTION TO CHANGE THE RELATIONSHIP BETWEEN ELECTED OFFICES AND THE ELECTORATE

Amendment	Purpose	Year Proposed	Year Adopted
XII	Separate ballot for vice-president in the electoral college	1803	1804
XIV	(Part 1) Provided a national definition of citizenship*	1866	1868
XVII	Provided direct election of senators	1912	1913
XX	Eliminated "lame duck" session of Congress	1932	1933
XXII	Limited presidential term	1947	1951
XXV	Provided presidential succession in case of disability	1965	1967

*In defining *citizenship*, the Fourteenth Amendment actually provided the constitutional basis for expanding the electorate to include all races, women, and residents of the District of Columbia. Only the "eighteen-year-olds' amendment" should have been necessary, since it changed the definition of citizenship. The fact that additional amendments were required following the Fourteenth suggests that voting is not considered an inherent right of U.S. citizenship. Instead it is viewed as a privilege.

[20]The Fourteenth Amendment is included in this table as well as in Table 3.6 because it seeks not only to define citizenship but seems to intend also that this definition of citizenship included, along with the right to vote, all the rights of the Bill of Rights, regardless of the state in which the citizen resided. A great deal more will be said about this in the next chapter.

Phyllis Schlafly and Gloria Steinem
The Battle over Equal Rights

Phyllis Schlafly and Gloria Steinem have carved out leadership roles on opposing sides of many issues that have dominated the American political scene in recent decades, including abortion, family values, sexuality, and equal rights. The fight to ratify the Equal Rights Amendment was among their most public struggles.

Phyllis Schlafly has long been active in Republican and conservative politics, even running for Congress herself three times (unsuccessfully). She attracted national attention for defending the presidential candidacy of Barry Goldwater in 1964 in a book called *A Choice Not an Echo*. Schlafly is best known, however, for her opposition to the proposed Equal Rights Amendment (ERA).

As head of the Eagle Forum and Stop-ERA, she has argued that efforts such as the ERA are not only unnecessary but even harmful to women. Women are "extremely well treated," she has asserted. "The women's liberationist is imprisoned by her own negative view of herself and of her place in the world around her." Schlafly's alternative is "the Positive Woman," who "rejoices in the creative capability within her body and . . . understands that men and women are different, and that those very differences provide the key to her success as a person and fulfillment as a woman."

As a prominent conservative Republican, Schlafly has exerted pressure within the party to maintain traditional values. In 1992, for example, she successfully fought for wording in the Republican party platform that called for a ban on all abortions, even including instances in which the woman's life is in danger.

Gloria Steinem, credited with being one of

Phyllis Schlafly

three amendments in Table 3.7 are obviously designed to reduce state power (Thirteenth), to reduce state power and expand national power (Fourteenth), and to expand national power (Sixteenth). The Twenty-seventh put a moderate limit on Congress's ability to raise its own salary.

The one missing amendment underscores the meaning of the rest: the Eighteenth, or Prohibition, Amendment. This is the only amendment that the country used to try to *legislate*. In other words, it is the only amendment that was designed to deal directly with some substantive social prob-

the founders of the modern women's movement, is the granddaughter of a pioneering feminist. After graduating *magna cum laude* from Smith College, she became a journalist and helped found the National Organization for Women (NOW) and *Ms.* magazine. Steinem believes that women's contributions to society have been undervalued; that popular images of women perpetuate stereotypes harmful to women; and that historical patterns of sexism and discrimination against women require remedies such as the ERA and legislation to protect a woman's rights.

The text of the ERA says that "equality of rights under the law shall not be denied or abridged by the United States or by any state on account of sex." The initial efforts of Steinem and her allies to get the amendment ratified were very successful. ERA easily passed Congress in 1972 and was quickly ratified by twenty-eight states, thanks to coordinated state-by-state campaigns designed to sway state legislatures. But Schlafly (sometimes labeled "the Gloria Steinem of the Right") and her allies mounted a comparable state-by-state counterattack, and although the ratification deadline was extended to 1982, it fell three states short of the necessary thirty-eight for ratification. Charges from Schlafly and others that the ERA would require the drafting of women into military service and legitimize homosexual marriages had helped defeat it.

Despite periodic calls to revive the ERA, most proponents consider it a dead issue for the immediate future. Instead, Steinem and her allies have increased pressure on state governments, the national government, and the courts to realize ERA-type protections. For example, congressional passage of a family leave bill, and the Clinton administration's decision to allow women to fly military combat missions, both enacted in 1993, represented important changes consistent with the goals of ERA.

Sources: Phyllis Schlafly, *The Power of the Positive Woman* (New Rochelle, NY: Arlington House, 1977); Gloria Steinem, *Outrageous Acts and Everyday Rebellions* (New York: Signet, 1986).

Gloria Steinem

lem. And it was the only amendment ever to have been repealed. Two other amendments—the Thirteenth, which abolished slavery, and the Sixteenth, which established the power to levy an income tax—can be said to have had the effect of legislation. But the purpose of the Thirteenth was to restrict the power of the states by forever forbidding them to treat any human being as property. As for the Sixteenth, it is certainly true that income tax legislation followed immediately; nevertheless, the amendment concerns itself strictly with establishing the power of Congress to enact such legislation.

TABLE 3.7
AMENDING THE CONSTITUTION TO EXPAND OR LIMIT
THE POWER OF GOVERNMENT

Amendment	Purpose	Year Proposed	Year Adopted
XI	Limited jurisdiction of federal courts over suits involving the states	1794	1798
XIII	Eliminated slavery and eliminated the right of states to allow property in persons	1865*	1865
XIV	(Part 2) Applied due process of Bill of Rights to the states	1866	1868
XVI	Established national power to tax incomes	1909	1913
XXVII	Limited Congress's power to raise its own salary	1789	1992

*The Thirteenth Amendment was proposed January 31, 1865, and adopted less than a year later, on December 18, 1865.

The legislation came later; and if down the line a majority in Congress had wanted to abolish the income tax, they could also have done this by legislation rather than through the arduous path of a constitutional amendment repealing the income tax.

All of this points to the principle underlying the twenty-five amendments in force: All are concerned with the structure or composition of the government. This is consistent with the concept of a constitution as "higher law," because the whole point and purpose of a higher law is to establish *a framework within which government and the process of making ordinary law can take place.* Even those who would have preferred more changes in the Constitution would have to agree that there is great wisdom in this principle. A constitution ought to *enable* legislation and public policies to take place, but it should not attempt to *determine* what that legislation or those policies ought to be.

For those whose hopes for social change center on the Constitution, it must be emphasized that the amendment route is and always will be extremely limited. Through a constitution it is possible to establish a working structure of government; and through a constitution it is possible to establish basic rights of citizens by placing limitations and obligations on the powers of that government. Once these things have been accomplished, the real problem is how to extend rights that exist in theory to those people who do not already enjoy them in practice. Of course, the Constitution cannot enforce itself. But it can and does have a real influence on everyday life because a right or an obligation set forth in the Constitution can become a *cause of action* in the hands of an otherwise powerless person. Whether that person's cause of action will have any beneficial effect will still depend upon the ordinary workings of legislatures and courts rather than on any further changes in the Constitution itself.

A constitution is good if it produces the *cause of action* that leads to good legislation, good case law, appropriate police behavior. A constitution cannot eliminate power. But its principles can be a citizen's dependable defense against the abuse of power.

Time Line On Federalism

EVENTS		INSTITUTIONAL DEVELOPMENTS
National Bank established; national excise tax on whiskey enacted (1791); Jay's Treaty with Great Britain approved by Senate (1795)		Congress establishes national economic power, power to tax, power over foreign policy (1791–1795)
	1800	Epoch of Dual Federalism: Congress promotes commerce; states possess unchallenged police power (1800–1937)
Hartford Convention—New England states threaten secession from Union (1814)		Secession from Union first threatened by some states (1814)
States attempt to resist national economic power (early 1800s)		*McCulloch* v. *Maryland* (1819) and *Gibbons* v. *Ogden* (1824) reaffirm national supremacy
President Andrew Jackson decisively deals with South Carolina's threat to the Union (1833)		Supremacy of the Union is upheld during the Nullification Crisis (1833)
Attempt to use U.S. Bill of Rights to restrict state power (1830s)		*Barron* v. *Baltimore*—State power not subject to the U.S. Bill of Rights (1833)
Territorial expansion; slaves taken into territories (1800s)		
	1850	*Dred Scott* v. *Sandford*—Congress may not regulate slavery in the territories (1857)
Secession of southern states (1860–1861)		Union destroyed (1860–1861)
Civil War (1861–1865)		
Reconstruction of South (1867–1877)		Union restored (1865)
	1870	Constitution amended: XIII (1865), XIV (1868), XV (1870) Amendments
Compromise of 1877—self-government restored to former Confederate states (1877)		Reestablishment of South's full place in the Union (1877)
Consolidation of great national industrial corporations (U.S. Steel, AT&T, Standard Oil) (1880s and 1890s)		Interstate Commerce Act (1887) and Sherman Antitrust Act (1890) provide first national regulation of monopoly practices
	1930	Supreme Court upholds expanded powers of president in *U.S.* v. *Curtiss-Wright* (1936); and of Congress in *Stewart Machine* v. *Davis* (1937) and *NLRB* v. *Jones & Laughlin Steel* (1937)
Franklin D. Roosevelt's first New Deal programs for national economic recovery enacted by Congress (1933)		

EVENTS		INSTITUTIONAL DEVELOPMENTS
	1950	
Blacks reject segregation after World War II (1950s)		Supreme Court holds that segregation is "inherently unequal" in *Brown* v. *Board of Ed.* (1954)
Registration drive to register southern blacks to vote (1965)		Voting Rights Act (1965)
Black protests against segregation in South (1950s and 1960s)		National power expanded to reach discrimination, poverty, education, and poor health (1960s)
Republicans take control of the White House (1968)	**1970**	Revenue sharing under Nixon to strengthen state governments (1972)
Election of Ronald Reagan (1980)		States' rights reaffirmed by Reagan and Bush administrations (1980–1990s)
Election of George Bush (1988)	**1990**	
		Americans with Disabilities Act (1990)
Election of Bill Clinton; Democrats control Congress and executive (1992)		Civil Rights Act (1991)

Chapter Review

In this chapter we have had two objectives. The first was to trace out the development of two of the three basic principles of the U.S. Constitution—federalism and the separation of powers. Federalism involves a division between two layers of government, national and state. The separation of powers involves the division of the national government into three branches. These principles are limitations on the powers of government; Americans specified these principles as a condition of giving their consent to be governed. And these principles became the framework within which the government operates. The persistence of local government and of reliance of the national government on grants-in-aid to coerce local governments into following national goals demonstrates the continuing vitality of the federal framework. The intense competition among the president, Congress, and the courts dramatizes the continuing vitality of the separation of powers.

The second goal was to gain an appreciation of constitutionalism itself. In addition to describing how the Constitution is formally amended, we analyzed the twenty-seven amendments in order to determine what they had in common, in contrast to the hundreds of amendments that were offered but never adopted. With the exception of the Prohibition Amendment, the amendments were oriented toward some change in the framework or structure of government. The Prohibition Amendment was the only adopted amendment that sought to legislate by constitutional means.

Our conclusion was that the purpose of a constitution is to organize the makeup or the composition of the government, the *framework within which* government and politics, including actual legislation, can take place. A country does not require fed-

eralism and the separation of powers to have a real constitutional government. And the country does not have to approach individual rights in the same manner as the American Constitution. But to be a true constitutional government, a government must have some kind of framework, which consists of a few principles that cannot be manipulated by people in power merely for their own convenience. This is the essence of constitutionalism—principles that are above the reach of everyday legislatures, executives, bureaucrats, and politicians, yet that are not so far above their reach that they cannot under some conditions be adapted to changing conditions.

For Further Reading

Anton, Thomas. *American Federalism and Public Policy.* Philadelphia: Temple University Press, 1989.

Bensel, Richard. *Sectionalism and American Political Development: 1880–1980.* Madison: University of Wisconsin Press, 1984.

Berger, Raoul. *Executive Privilege: A Constitutional Myth.* Cambridge: Harvard University Press, 1974.

Bowman, Ann O'M., and Richard Kearny. *The Resurgence of the States.* Englewood Cliffs, NJ: Prentice-Hall, 1986.

Crovitz, L. Gordon, and Jeremy Rabkin, eds. *The Fettered Presidency: Legal Constraints on the Executive Branch.* Washington, DC: American Enterprise Institute, 1989.

Dye, Thomas R. *American Federalism: Competition among Governments.* Lexington, MA: Lexington Books, 1990.

Elazar, Daniel. *American Federalism: A View from the States.* New York: Harper & Row, 1984.

Ginsberg, Benjamin, and Martin Shefter. *Politics by Other Means: Institutional Conflict and the Declining Significance of Elections in America.* New York: Basic Books, 1990.

Grodzins, Morton. *The American System.* Chicago: Rand McNally, 1974.

Kelley, E. Wood. *Policy and Politics in the United States: The Limits of Localism.* Philadelphia: Temple University Press, 1987.

Kettl, Donald. *The Regulation of American Federalism.* Baltimore: Johns Hopkins University Press, 1987.

Palley, Marian Lief, and Howard Palley. *Urban America and Public Policies.* Lexington, MA: D.C. Heath, 1981.

Peterson, Paul, Barry Rabe, and Kenneth K. Wong. *When Federalism Works.* Washington, DC: Brookings Institution, 1986.

Robinson, Donald L. *To the Best of My Ability.* New York: W. W. Norton, 1986.

Wright, Deil S. *Understanding Intergovernmental Relations.* Monterey, CA: Brooks/Cole, 1982.

4

THE CONSTITUTION AND THE INDIVIDUAL: THE BILL OF RIGHTS, CIVIL LIBERTIES, AND CIVIL RIGHTS

When Americans think of liberties and rights, they think of written guarantees, like the Bill of Rights—the first ten amendments to the Constitution, adopted in 1791 to provide a framework for the defense and protection of the individual. The words of those first ten amendments have remained unchanged for 200 years, and they have inspired people of all nations. But they have also generated controversy. The Bill of Rights is as lively a topic today as it was two centuries ago.

The Bill of Rights—its history and controversy of interpretation surrounding it—can be usefully subdivided into two categories: civil liberties and civil rights. This chapter will be divided accordingly. *Civil liberties* are defined as protections of citizens from improper government action. When adopted in 1791, the Bill of Rights was seen as marking out a private sphere of personal liberty or freedom from governmental restrictions.[1] As Jefferson had put it, a bill of rights "is what people are entitled to *against every government on earth.*"

---

[1] Lest there be confusion in our interchangeable use of the words "liberty" and "freedom," treat them as synonymous. "Freedom" is from the German, *Freiheit*. "Liberty" is from the French, *liberté*. Both have to do with the absence of restraints on individual choices of action.

Note the emphasis—citizen against government. In this sense, we could call the Bill of Rights a "bill of liberties" because the amendments focus on what government must *not* do. For example (with emphasis added):

1. "Congress shall make *no* law. . . ." (I)
2. "The right to . . . bear Arms, shall *not* be infringed." (II)
3. "No soldier shall . . . be quartered . . ." (III)
4. "*No* warrants shall issue, but upon probable cause . . ." (IV)
5. "*No* person shall be held to answer . . . unless on presentment or indictment of a Grand Jury . . ." (V)
6. "Excessive bail shall *not* be required . . . *nor* cruel and unusual punishments inflicted." (VIII)

Thus, the Bill of Rights is a series of "thou shalt nots"—restraints addressed to government. Some of these restraints are **substantive,** putting limits on *what* the government shall and shall not have power to do—such as establishing a religion, quartering troops in private homes without consent, or seizing private property without just compensation. Other restraints are **procedural,** dealing with *how* the government is supposed to act. For instance, the Sixth Amendment requires the government to provide the accused with a "speedy and public trial, by an impartial jury."

While civil liberties are phrased as negatives, *civil rights* are obligations imposed on government to take *positive (or affirmative) action to protect citizens from the illegal actions of other private citizens and other government agencies.* Civil rights did not become part of the Constitution until 1868 with the adoption of the Fourteenth Amendment, which addressed the issue of who was a citizen and provided for each citizen "the equal protection of the laws." From that point on, we can see more clearly the distinction between civil liberties and civil rights, because civil liberties issues arise under the "due process of law" clause, and civil rights issues arise under the "equal protection of the laws" clause.[2]

Civil Liberties: Nationalizing The Bill of Rights

The First Amendment provides that "Congress shall make no law respecting an establishment of religion . . . or abridging freedom of speech, or of the press; or the right of [assembly and petition]." But this is the only amendment in the Bill of Rights that addresses itself exclusively to the national government. For example, the Second Amendment provides that "the right of the people to keep and bear Arms shall not be infringed." The Fifth Amendment says, among other things, that "*no person* shall . . . be twice put in jeopardy of life or limb" for the same crime; that *no person* "shall be compelled in any Criminal Case to be a witness against himself"; that *no person* shall "be deprived of life, liberty, or property, without due process of law"; and that private property cannot be taken "without just compensation."[3]

---

[2]For some recent scholarship on the Bill of Rights and its development, see Geoffrey Stone, Richard Epstein, and Cass Sunstein, eds., *The Bill of Rights and the Modern State* (Chicago: University of Chicago Press, 1992); and Michael J. Meyer and William A. Parent, eds., *The Constitution of Rights* (Ithaca: Cornell University Press, 1992).

[3]It would be useful at this point to review all the provisions of the Bill of Rights (in the Appendix) to confirm this disctinction between the wording of the First Amendment and the rest. Emphasis in the example quotations was not in the original. For a spirited and enlightening essay on the extent to which the entire Bill of Rights was about equality, see Martha Minow, "Equality and the Bill of Rights," in Mayer and Parent, *The Constitution of Rights*, pp. 118–28.

In Brief Box

THE BILL OF RIGHTS

Amendment I: Limits on Congress
Congress cannot make any law establishing a religion or abridging freedoms of religious exercise, speech, assembly, or petition.

Amendments II, III, IV: Limits on the Executive
The executive branch cannot infringe on the right of people to keep arms (II), cannot arbitrarily take houses for a militia (III), and cannot search for or seize evidence without a court warrant swearing to the probable existence of a crime (IV).

Amendments V, VI, VII, VIII: Limits on the Judiciary
The courts cannot hold trials for serious offenses without provision for a grand jury (V), a trial jury (VII), a speedy trial (VI), presentation of charges and confrontation by the accused of hostile witnesses (VI), immunity from testimony against oneself and immunity from trial more than once for the same offense (V). Furthermore, neither bail nor punishment can be excessive (VIII), and no property can be taken without "just compensation" (V).

Amendments IX, X: Limits on the National Government
Any rights not enumerated are reserved to the states or the people (X), but the enumeration of certain rights in the Constitution should not be interpreted to mean that those are the only rights the people have.

Dual Citizenship

Since the First Amendment is the only part of the Bill of Rights that is explicit in its intention to put limits on the national government, a fundamental question inevitably arises: *Do the remaining amendments of the Bill of Rights put limits on state governments or only on the national government?* This question was settled in 1833 in a way that seems odd to Americans today. The case was *Barron* v. *Baltimore*, and the facts were simple. In paving its streets, the city of Baltimore had disposed of so much sand and gravel in the water near Barron's wharf that the value of the wharf for commercial purposes was virtually destroyed. Barron brought the city into court on the grounds that it had, under the Fifth Amendment, unconstitutionally deprived him of his property without just compensation. Barron had to take his case all the way to the Supreme Court. There Chief Justice Marshall, in one of the most significant Supreme Court decisions ever handed down, disagreed with Barron:

> The Constitution was ordained and established by the people of the United States for themselves, for their own government, and not for the government of the individual States. Each State established a constitution for itself, and in that constitution provided such limitations and restrictions on the powers of its particular government as its judgment dictated. ... If these propositions be correct, *the fifth amendment must be understood as restraining the power of the general government, not as applicable to the States.*[4]

---

[4]Barron v. Baltimore, 7 Peters 243 (1833), p. 246. [Emphasis added.]

In other words, if an agency of the *national* government had deprived Barron of his property, there would have been little doubt about Barron's winning his case. But if the constitution of the state of Maryland contained no such provision protecting citizens of Maryland from such action, then Barron had no legal leg to stand on against Baltimore, an agency of the state of Maryland.

Barron v. *Baltimore* confirmed "dual citizenship"—that is, that each American was a citizen of the national government and *separately* a citizen of one of the states. This meant that the Bill of Rights did not apply to decisions or procedures of state (or local) governments. Even slavery could continue, because the Bill of Rights could not protect anyone from state laws treating people as property. In fact, the Bill of Rights did not become a vital instrument for the extension of civil liberties for anyone until after a bloody Civil War and a revolutionary Fourteenth Amendment intervened. And even so, as we shall see, nearly a second century would pass before the Bill of Rights would truly come into its own.

The Fourteenth Amendment

From a constitutional standpoint, the defeat of the South in the Civil War settled one question and raised another. It probably settled forever the question of whether secession was an option for any state. After 1865 there was more "united" than "states" to the United States. But this left unanswered just how much the states were obliged to obey the Constitution, in particular, the Bill of Rights. Just reading the words of the Fourteenth Amendment, anyone might think it was almost perfectly designed to impose the Bill of Rights on the states and thereby to reverse *Barron* v. *Baltimore*. The very first words of the Fourteenth Amendment point in that direction.

> All persons born or naturalized in the United States, and subject to the jurisdiction thereof, are citizens of the United States and of the State wherein they reside.

This provides for a *single national citizenship,* and at a minimum that means that civil liberties should not vary drastically from state to state. That would seem to be the spirit of the Fourteenth Amendment: *to nationalize the Bill of Rights by nationalizing the definition of citizenship.*

This interpretation of the Fourteenth Amendment is reinforced by the next clause of the Amendment:

> *No state* shall make or enforce any law which shall abridge the privileges or immunities of citizens of the United States; nor shall any state deprive any person of life, liberty, or property, without due process of law. [Emphasis added.]

All of this sounds like an effort to extend the Bill of Rights in its *entirety* to citizens *wherever* they might reside.[5] But this was not to be the Supreme Court's interpretation for nearly a hundred years. Within five years of ratification of the Fourteenth Amendment, the Court was making decisions as though it had never been adopted.[6] The shadow of

---

[5] The Fourteenth Amendment also seems designed to introduce civil rights. The final clause of the all-important Section 1 provides that no state can "deny to any person within its jurisdiction the equal protection of the laws." It is not unreasonable to conclude that the purpose of this provision was to obligate the state governments as well as the national government to take *positive* actions to protect citizens from arbitrary and discriminatory actions, at least those based on race. This will be explored in the second half of the chapter.

[6] The Slaughterhouse Cases, 16 Wallace 36 (1883); The Civil Rights Cases, 109 U.S. 3 (1833).

TABLE 4.1
INCORPORATION OF THE BILL OF RIGHTS INTO THE FOURTEENTH AMENDMENT

Selected Provisions and Amendments	Year "Incorporated"	Key Case
Eminent domain (V)	1897	*Chicago, Burlington and Quincy Railroad v. Chicago*
Freedom of speech (I)	1925	*Gitlow* v. *New York*
Freedom of press (I)	1931	*Near* v. *Minnesota*
Freedom of assembly (I)	1939	*Hague* v. *CIO*
Freedom from warrantless search and seizure (IV) ("exclusionary rule")	1961	*Mapp* v. *Ohio*
Right to counsel in any criminal trial (VI)	1963	*Gideon* v. *Wainwright*
Right against self-incrimination and forced confessions (V)	1964	*Malloy* v. *Hogan* *Escobedo* v. *Illinois*
Right to counsel and to remain silent (VI)	1966	*Miranda* v. *Arizona*
Right against double jeopardy (V)	1969	*Benton* v. *Maryland*
Right to privacy (III, IV & V)	1973	*Roe* v. *Wade* *Doe* v. *Bolton*

Barron grew longer and longer. Table 4.1 outlines the major developments in the history of the Fourteenth Amendment against the backdrop of *Barron,* citing the particular provisions of the Bill of Rights as they were incorporated by Supreme Court decisions into the Fourteenth Amendment as limitations on all the states. This is a measure of the degree of "nationalization" of civil liberties.

The only change in civil liberties during the first sixty years following the adoption of the Fourteenth Amendment came in 1897, when the Supreme Court held that the due process clause of the Fourteenth Amendment did in fact prohibit states from taking property for a public use without just compensation.[7] This effectively overruled the specific holding in *Barron;* henceforth a citi-

zen of Maryland or any state was protected from a "public taking" of property (eminent domain) even if the state constitution did not provide such protection. But in a broader sense, *Barron* still cast a shadow, because the Supreme Court had "incorporated" into the Fourteenth Amendment *only* the property protection provision of the Fifth Amendment, despite the fact that the "due process" clause applied to the taking of life and liberty as well as property.

No further expansion of civil liberties through incorporation occurred until 1925, when the Supreme Court held that freedom of speech is "among the fundamental personal rights and 'liberties' protected by the due process clause of the Fourteenth Amendment from impairment by the states."[8] In 1931, the Court added freedom

[7]Chicago, Burlington and Quincy Railroad Company v. Chicago, 166 U.S. 266 (1897).

[8]Gitlow v. New York, 268 U.S. 652 (1925).

of the press to that short list of civil rights protected by the Bill of Rights from state action; in 1939, it added freedom of assembly.[9] But that was as far as the Court was willing to go for the next two decades.

The shadow of *Barron* extended into its second century, despite adoption of the Fourteenth Amendment. At the time of World War II, the Constitution, as interpreted by the Supreme Court, left standing the framework in which the states had the power to determine their own law on a number of fundamental issues. It left states with the power to pass laws segregating the races. It also left states with the power to engage in search and seizures without a warrant, to indict accused persons without benefit of a grand jury, to deprive persons of trial by jury, to deprive persons of their right not to have to testify against themselves, to deprive accused persons of their right to confront adverse witnesses, and to prosecute accused persons more than once for the same crime.[10] Few states exercised these powers, but the power was there for any state whose legislative majority chose to use it.

The Second Constitutional Revolution

Signs of change in the constitutional framework could be detected beginning after World War II, and virtually everyone could see the writing on the wall after 1954, in *Brown* v. *Board of Education*, which found state segregation laws for schools unconstitutional. *Brown* indicated that the Supreme Court under Chief Justice Earl Warren was

going to be expansive about civil liberties. In retrospect, one could say that the Second Constitutional Revolution began with or soon after *Brown* v. *Board of Education* (1954). This can be seen in Table 4.1 by the number of civil liberties incorporated after 1954.

The First Constitutional Revolution, as we saw in Chapter 3, began when the Supreme Court in 1937 interpreted "interstate commerce" in favor of federal government regulation.[11] Both revolutions, then, were movements toward nationalization, but they required opposite motions on the part of the Supreme Court. In the area of commerce (the first revolution), the Court had to decide to assume a *passive* role by not trying to interfere as Congress expanded the meaning of the commerce clause of Article I, Section 8. This expansion has been so extensive that the national government can now constitutionally reach a single farmer growing twenty acres of wheat or a small neighborhood restaurant selling barbecues to local "whites only" without being anywhere near interstate commerce routes. In the second revolution—involving the Bill of Rights and particularly the Fourteenth Amendment—the Court had to assume an *active* role. It required close review of the laws of state legislatures and decisions of state courts, in order to apply a single national Fourteenth Amendment standard to the rights and liberties of all citizens.

Until 1961, only the First Amendment and one clause of the Fifth Amendment clearly incorporated into the Fourteenth Amendment.[12] After 1961, several other im-

---

[9]Near v. Minnesota, 283 U.S. 697 (1931); Hague v. C.I.O., 307 U.S. 496 (1939).

[10]All of these were implicitly identified in Palko v. Connecticut, 302 U.S. 319 (1937) as "not incorporated" into the Fourteenth Amendment as a limitation on the powers of the states.

[11]NLRB v. Jones & Laughlin Steel Corp. (1937).

[12]The one exception was the right to public trial (Sixth Amendment), but a 1948 case (In re Oliver, 33, U.S. 257) did not actually mention the right to public trial as such; but it was cited in a 1968 case (Duncan v. Louisiana, 391, U.S. 145) as a case establishing the right to public trial as part of the Fourteenth Amendment.

Dennis Banks
America's First Americans

Even though the Indian Wars ended long ago, Native Americans continue to struggle for their rights as they face poverty, discrimination, alcoholism, and widespread hopelessness on their reservations. Native American activist Dennis Banks has struggled for over twenty years to dramatize these problems and improve the lives of his people.

A member of the Chippewa, or Ojibwa, Banks was born in Minnesota but was sent to boarding schools in North and South Dakota run by the Bureau of Indian Affairs (BIA), where the students were forbidden to speak their native language. In 1968 he co-founded the American Indian Movement (AIM). AIM first made national headlines in 1969 when two hundred Indians, including Banks, took over the abandoned federal prison, Alcatraz, just off the coast of California, saying they were reclaiming it for the Indians. The occupation lasted over eighteen months, but in the end accomplished nothing. In 1972, the group staged a march on Washington, called the Trail of Broken Treaties, which converged on the offices of the BIA. After a scuffle with police, some of the marchers took over the building, occupying it for five days. The occupation resulted in a leadership shakeup at BIA, but again no real policy changes.

In a move that garnered considerable national attention, Banks and other AIM members took over the town of Wounded Knee in 1971, the site of the last major battle and massacre of Indians in 1890. Periodic gunfire was exchanged between the Indians and federal agents during the seventy-one-day standoff. The occupation finally ended by negotiation, with promises from the federal government to investigate Indian com-

Dennis Banks
(b. 1932)

plaints. Banks and other leaders were convicted for their involvement in the takeover. Later investigations revealed that the government had falsified evidence against Banks and another activist, Russell Means, and the charges were eventually dropped. Still facing prison time for another crime, Banks fled to California, where he served for a time as chancellor of D-Q University, in Davis, California, a two-year college for Indian students. In 1984, however, Banks gave himself up to South Dakota officials and served a year in prison.

Returning to a South Dakota reservation, Banks switched to less confrontational and more local activities, working as an alcohol counselor. He also persuaded Honeywell and other companies to locate plants in the area, which provided hundreds of jobs to formerly unemployed Indians. He has continued to serve as a leader and spokesman for Indian causes.

Banks and other AIM members have turned away from the militancy of the 1970s. Yet that militancy, and the extensive press coverage, especially of the Alcatraz and Wounded Knee incidents, served to focus national attention on the plight of America's first Americans.

Source: Dee A. Brown, *Bury My Heart at Wounded Knee* (New York: Pocket Books, 1981).

PROCESS BOX 4.1

Free Speech: Protection by the First Amendement

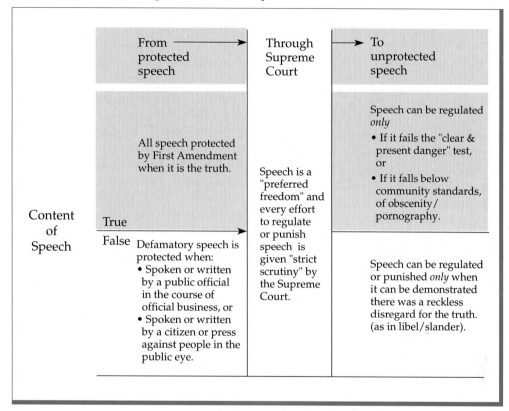

		From → protected speech	Through Supreme Court	→ To unprotected speech
Content of Speech	True	All speech protected by First Amendment when it is the truth.	Speech is a "preferred freedom" and every effort to regulate or punish speech is given "strict scrutiny" by the Supreme Court.	Speech can be regulated *only* • If it fails the "clear & present danger" test, or • If it falls below community standards, of obscenity/ pornography.
	False	Defamatory speech is protected when: • Spoken or written by a public official in the course of official business, or • Spoken or written by a citizen or press against people in the public eye.		Speech can be regulated or punished *only* when it can be demonstrated there was a reckless disregard for the truth. (as in libel/slander).

portant provisions of the Bill of Rights were incorporated. Then, as one important study of constitutional history put it, "the final step in nationalizing the Bill of Rights was taken by Congress. In the Civil Rights Act of 1968 it extended the guarantees of the first eight amendments to Indians living under tribal authority on reservations. Thus, all governments in the United States—federal, state, local and Indian tribal—were restricted by the Bill of Rights."[13] The first

eight amendments really are the true Bill of Rights. The Ninth Amendment confirms that the enumeration of rights in the Constitution is not supposed to mean that other rights cannot be added later. The Tenth Amendment reassures the states that the powers not delegated to the national government (and not explicitly prohibited to the states) are reserved to the states or the people.

Even today, however, the spirit of *Barron v. Baltimore* has not been entirely put to rest. Many have urged the Supreme Court to take the final step by declaring as a matter of constitutional law that the Fourteenth

[13]Alfred Kelly et al., *The American Constitution: Its Origins and Development,* 6th ed. (New York: W. W. Norton, 1983), p. 647.

Amendment incorporates the *entire* Bill of Rights. But the Court has not been willing to do so. In fact, a court with the power to expand the Bill of Rights has the power to contract it.[14]

The Supreme Court—From Warren through Burger to Rehnquist

Chief Justice Earl Warren forcefully led the Court through the fifteen years that finally made the Fourteenth Amendment an active part of the constitutional framework. Table 4.1 is virtually a history of the Warren Court.

When Warren retired in 1969, he was replaced by Chief Justice Warren Burger, a conservative. President Nixon and others pinned their hopes for a more traditional interpretation, or "strict construction," of the Constitution on Burger. Those hopes were strengthened by President Nixon's opportunity to appoint three additional justices—Harry Blackmun, Lewis Powell, and William Rehnquist. Nevertheless, the directions set by the Warren Court and the Second Constitutional Revolution *were not reversed*. But the Burger Court did chart its own course in two broad areas of civil liberties. The first was a conservative redirection of the Warren Court's liberal emphasis on protecting the procedural rights of criminal defendants; the Burger Court instead strengthened the hands of state and local police and prosecutors. In the second area, the Burger Court actually *extended* Warren Court rulings regarding women, their power over their own bodies, and the general right to privacy. Each of these areas deserves closer examination.

CIVIL LIBERTIES AND THE POLICE—BURGER CONSERVATISM. Two of the most important decisions handed down by the Warren Court, *Mapp* and *Miranda*,[15] put severe restrictions on the ability of local police and prosecutors to deal with suspects, prisoners, and all persons accused of crimes. In *Mapp*, the Court held that evidence obtained in violation of the Fourth Amendment ban on unreasonable searches and seizures would be excluded from trial. This "exclusionary rule" was particularly irksome to the police and prosecutors because it meant that patently guilty defendants sometimes go free because the evidence that clearly damned them could not be used. In *Miranda*, the Court's ruling required that arrested persons be informed of the right to remain silent and to have counsel present during interrogation. This is the basis of the "Miranda rule" of reading persons their rights.

Decisions like these gave rise to the "law and order" movement that helped elect Richard Nixon in 1968. Yet, the Burger Court, which could have been called the Nixon Court, disappointed the law and order forces, as most courts disappoint their political supporters. The Burger Court refused to reverse either the *Mapp* or *Miranda* decisions or, for that matter, any of the major civil liberties decisions. At the same time, however, the Burger Court did give those decisions a more conservative interpretation. In *U.S.* v. *Harris*,[16] Chief Justice Burger, writing for the majority, argued that mere technical violations of search and seizure ought not to be used to free known criminals.

Several other cases also strengthened the

---

[14] For a lively treatment of the possibilities of restricting provisions of the Bill of Rights without actually reversing Warren Court decisions, see David N. Savage, *Turning Right—The Making of the Rehnquist Court* (New York: Wiley, 1992).

[15] Mapp v. Ohio, 367 U.S. 643 (1961); Miranda v. Arizona, 384 U.S. 436 (1966).

[16] U.S. v. Harris, 403 U.S. 924 (1971).

position of the police. For example, the Burger Court held that the professional judgment of police ought to be sufficient for warrants, that warrantless searches can under certain circumstances be accepted, and that illegally seized evidence might be presented to a grand jury even when it was not presentable to the trial jury.[17] The Burger Court revised *Miranda* by holding that although a statement was inadmissible in court if the Miranda warning wasn't given, the prosecutor could nonetheless use it to impeach the defendant's testimony if the defendant took the stand.[18] Yet, this same Burger Court *extended* the liberal position toward right to counsel in one respect by requiring counsel not only for those accused of felonies but also for those accused of misdemeanors.[19]

WOMEN AND THE "RIGHT TO PRIVACY"—BURGER LIBERALISM. To the surprise of many, the Burger Court significantly expanded (and nationalized) an important area of civil liberties with its decisions on a new right, the right of privacy. Nowhere can such a right of privacy be found in the Bill of Rights or the Fourteenth Amendment. But from early in the Warren era, the Court had been developing a concept of a "right of privacy" that went well beyond mere incorporation of clauses in the first eight amendments. The Court concluded that there was in particular a right of privacy (that is, to be left alone) that could be derived from a combination of other more specific constitutional provisions. In 1958, the Supreme Court recognized "privacy in one's association" in its argument protecting the NAACP

from the use of its membership list by the state of Alabama.[20] In 1965, the Court held that the privacy right included the right of marital privacy in regard to married persons' use of contraceptives and the circulation of birth control information.[21] In 1972, the Court extended that right to unmarried women.[22]

This right of privacy was confirmed and extended in the most important of all the privacy cases, *Roe* v. *Wade* (1973), to support the Court's ruling that the states had no constitutional power to make abortion a criminal act.[23] Note again that the essence of civil liberties involves rights to be free of government interference. And note also that the preference for privacy and for its extension to include the rights of women to control their own bodies was not something invented by the Supreme Court in a political vacuum. Over half of the states in existence at the time did not regulate abortion until the second half of the nineteenth century, and the state legislatures began to "decriminalize" and "deregulate" abortion well before the 1973 Supreme Court decision. In the wake of the Court's 1989 decision in the case of *Webster* v. *Reproductive Health Services,* however, a number of states moved to reinstate restrictive statues.[24]

Like any important principle, once privacy was established as an aspect of civil liberties that was protected by the Bill of

---

[17] An excellent treatment of these cases will be found in Kelly et al., *The American Constitution,* pp. 718–19.

[18] Harris v. New York, 401 U.S. 222 (1971).

[19] Argersinger v. Hamlin, 407 U.S. 25 (1972).

[20] NAACP v. Alabama ex rel. Patterson, 357 U.S. 449 (1958).

[21] Griswold v. Connecticut, 381 U.S. 479 (1965).

[22] Eisenstadt v. Baird, 405 U.S. 438 (1972).

[23] Roe v. Wade, 410 U.S. 113 (1973).

[24] Webster v. Reproductive Health Services, 109 S. Ct. 3040 (1989). In this 5-to-4 decision, written by Chief Justice Rehnquist, the Court upheld a Missouri law that restricted the use of public medical facilities for abortion, thus opening the way for other states to limit the availability of abortions.

Norma McCorvey and Randall Terry
From *Roe v. Wade* to *"Operation Rescue"*

Abortion is perhaps the most potent and explosive issue of the last two decades. Norma McCorvey (known to most as Jane Roe) and Randall Terry demonstrates the power of this issue to bring average people into the political fray in a highly personal way. Each in their own ways, both McCorvey and Terry have sought to redefine the constitutional interpretation surrounding abortion.

In 1969, Norma McCorvey was a twenty-one-year-old carnival worker, divorced with a five-year-old daughter, and living on the edge of poverty. She was in Texas with the carnival when she discovered she was pregnant. Seeking an abortion, McCorvey found she was in a state that only allowed abortions to save the life of the woman. In her words, "I found one doctor who offered to abort me for $500. Only he didn't have a license, and I was scared to turn my body over to him. So there I was—pregnant, . . . alone and stuck."

McCorvey bore her child and gave it up for adoption, but in the process she met two recent law school graduates, Sarah Weddington and Linda Coffey. These three women decided to challenge the Texas abortion law in court. In order to avoid personal stigma, McCorvey's name was changed to Jane Roe. The defendant was Henry Wade, a district attorney for Dallas County, Texas. The result of the challenge was the controversial landmark Supreme Court case *Roe* v. *Wade* (1973), in which a seven-member majority of the court affirmed a constitutional right to abortion under most circumstances.

That case stunned and mobilized abortion opponents, including Randall Terry, a used-car salesman. A native of upstate New York, Terry and his wife settled in Binghamton,

Norma McCorvey

Rights through the Fourteenth Amendment, it took on a life all its own. In a number of important decisions, the Supreme Court and the lower federal courts sought to protect rights that could not be found in the text of the Constitution but could be discovered through the study of the philosophic sources of fundamental rights. Through this line of reasoning, the federal courts ruled to protect sexual autonomy, lifestyle choices, sexual preferences, procreational choice, and various forms of intimate association.

where they began to stand in front of abortion clinics to try to talk women out of getting abortions. By 1988, Terry quit his job and devoted his full-time energies to his organization Operation Rescue. Led by Terry, the group has sought to close down doctors' offices, clinics, and other places where abortion is discussed or practiced. His means have been highly controversial. At the Southern Tier Women's Services office near Binghamton, for example, Terry was arrested for the first of many times for spreading nails in the office's parking lot and for gluing the office doors shut.

Terry has led large-scale protests in such cities as Wichita, Kansas, and Buffalo, New York, where his followers have attempted to forcibly block entrances, harass physicians as well as clients, and otherwise disrupt abortion-related activities. Terry has been repeatedly cited and tried for trespass, destruction of property, harassment, and other violations. During the Democratic National Party Convention in 1992, an associate of Terry's attempted to present Democratic presidential nominee Bill Clinton with an aborted fetus. Terry's motivation for the action was his belief that "to vote for Bill Clinton is to sin against God." He also accused Clinton of "actively promoting rebellion against the Ten Commandments."

To the members of Operation Rescue, such illegal activities are justifiable as a means to discourage abortions. Yet the extreme tactics of Operation Rescue, while receiving much publicity, have served to alienate many Americans. In the midst of this charged political atmosphere, the Supreme Court (dominated by Reagan and Bush appointees) ruled in the 1992 case of *Planned Parenthood v. Casey* that the constitutional right to privacy continued to support the "essence" of the right to abortion as established in *Roe.*

Source: Marian Faux, *Roe v. Wade* (New York: Dutton, 1989).

Randall Terry

Criticism mounted with every extension of this line of reasoning. The federal courts were accused of creating an uncontrollable expansion of rights demands. The Supreme Court, the critics argued, had displaced the judgments of legislatures and state courts with its own judgment of what is reasonable, without regard to public preferences and without regard to specific constitutional provisions. This is virtually the definition of what came to be called "judicial activism" in the 1980s, and it was the basis for a more critical label, "the imperial judiciary."[25]

REHNQUIST: A DE-NATIONALIZING TREND? Controversy over judicial power will extend well into the 1990s. Burger's successor is a guarantee of that. As an associate justice, William Rehnquist was the leading critic of "judicial activism" as it bore on privacy and other new rights, such as the right to be represented in districts of numerically equal size[26] and the right not to be required to participate in prayers in school.[27]

Although it is difficult to determine just how much influence Rehnquist has had as Chief Justice, the Court has in fact been moving in a more conservative, de-nationalizing direction. Constitutional scholar David O'Brien has made the following comparison: Between 1961 and 1969, more than 76 percent of the Warren Court's rulings from term to term tended to be liberal—that is, tending toward nationalizing the Bill of Rights to protect individuals and minorities mainly against the actions of state government. During the Burger years, 1969–1986, the liberal tendency dropped on the average below 50 percent. During the first four years of the Rehnquist Court (the extent of O'Brien's research), the average liberal "score" dropped to less than 35 percent.[28]

For example, O'Brien reports that in the 1990 term the Court ruled against prisoners' claims in twenty-three out of thirty-one cases, leaving more power over prisoners in state and local hands. The direction was equally conservative on the burning issue of abortion and freedom of choice. The Court actually upheld *Roe* v. *Wade* in a 5-to-4 decision in July 1992 but, in so doing, nevertheless refused to invalidate a Pennsylvania law that significantly restricts freedom of choice. The majority of the Court was willing to recognize a woman's right to choose an abortion, but defined it as a "limited or qualified" right subject to regulation by the states as long as the regulation does not impose an "undue burden." As one constitutional authority concluded from this case, "Until there is a Freedom of Choice Act, and/or a U.S. Supreme Court able to wean *Roe* from its respirator, state legislatures will have significant discretion over the access that women will have to legalized abortions."[29]

---

[25] A good discussion will be found in Paul Brest and Sanford Levinson, *Processes of Constitutional Decisionmaking: Cases and Materials*, 2nd ed. (Boston: Little, Brown, 1983), p. 660. See also Chapter 7.

[26] Baker v. Carr, 369 U.S. 186 (1962).

[27] Engel v. Vitale, 370 U.S. 421 (1962), on the Court's striking down a state-composed prayer for recitation in the schools. Of course, a whole line of cases followed *Engel*, as states and cities tried various ways and means of getting around the Court's principle that any organized prayer in the public schools violated the First Amendment rights of the individual.

[28] David M. O'Brien, *Supreme Court Watch—1991*, Annual Supplement to *Constitutional Law and Politics* (New York: W. W. Norton, 1991), p. 6 and Chapter 4.

[29] Gayle Binion, "Undue Burden? Government Now Has Wide Latitude to Restrict Abortions," *Santa Barbara News-Press*, 5 July 1992, p. A13. The case being referred to is Planned Parenthood of Southeastern Pennsylvania v. Casey 112 S.Ct. 2791 (1992). A case three years earlier had already significantly narrowed the scope of the *Roe v. Wade* precedent: Webster v. Reproductive Health Services 109 S.Ct. 3040 (1989). In this 5-to-4 decision, written by Rehnquist, the Court upheld a Missouri law that restricted the use of public medical facilities for abortion, thus opening the way for other states to limit the availability of abortions. The first to act was the Pennsylvania legislature, which adopted in late 1989 a law banning all abortions after pregnancy had passed twenty-four weeks, except to save the life of the pregnant woman or to prevent irreversible impairment of her health. In 1990, the pace of state legislative action increased, with new statutes being passed in South Carolina, Ohio, and Minnesota. The governors of some states vetoed state legislation on the grounds that it would be declared unconstitutional by the Supreme Court. However in 1991 the Louisiana legislature adopted the

But the question remains: Will a Supreme Court, even with a majority of conservatives, reverse the nationalization of the Bill of Rights? Possibly, but not necessarily. First of all, the Rehnquist Court has not actually reversed any of the decisions made by the Warren or Burger Courts nationalizing most of the clauses of the Bill of Rights. As we have seen, the Rehnquist Court has given narrower and more restrictive interpretations of some earlier decisions, but it has not literally reversed any, not even *Roe v. Wade*. Second, with the appointment of Ruth Bader Ginsburg to replace the retiring Justice Byron White in 1993, and the probable retirement of Justice Harry Blackmun, the oldest sitting justice, President Clinton will have a chance to affect the balance of the Court, and possibly alter the direction of the Rehnquist Court. Unquestionably, the expansion or contraction of the Bill of Rights and the Fourteenth Amendment will be in the forefront of political debate for a long time to come.

Civil Rights

The very simplicity of the "civil rights clause" of the Fourteenth Amendment left it open to interpretation:

> No State shall make or enforce any law which shall . . . deny to any person within its jurisdiction the equal protection of the laws.

But in the very first Fourteenth Amendment case to come before the Supreme Court, in 1873, the majority gave it a distinct meaning:

> . . . it is not difficult to give meaning to this clause ["the equal protection of the laws"]. The existence of laws in the States . . . which discriminated with gross injustice and hardship against [Negroes] as a class, was the evil to be remedied by this clause, and by it such laws are forbidden.[30]

The Court at the time understood well that private persons offering accommodations or places of amusement to the public had an obligation to offer them to one and all.[31] That put the government under the obligation to take positive actions extending to each citizen the opportunities and resources necessary to enjoyment of their freedom.

Discrimination is the use of unreasonable and unjust exclusion. Of course, all laws discriminate, including some people while excluding others; but some discrimination is considered unreasonable. Now, for example, it is considered reasonable to enforce twenty-one as the legal drinking age; thus the age criterion is considered reasonable discrimination. But is age a reasonable distinction when seventy (or sixty-five or sixty) is selected as the age for compulsory retirement? In the mid-1970s, Congress answered this question by making old age a new civil right; compulsory retirement at seventy is now an unlawful, unreasonable discriminatory use of age.[32]

---

[30] The Slaughterhouse Cases, 16 Wallace 36 (1873).

[31] See Civil Rights Cases, 109 U.S. 3 (1883), where the Supreme Court affirmed this position even as it was holding against the black plaintiffs by declaring the Civil Rights Act of 1875 unconstitutional.

[32] A superb discussion of age discrimination is found in Lawrence Friedman, *Your Time Will Come—The Law of Age Discrimination and Mandatory Retirement* (New York: Russell Sage, 1984).

---

strictest law yet over the governor's veto. The Louisiana law would prohibit all abortions except when the mother's life is threatened or when rape or incest victims report those crimes immediately.

Plessy *v.* Ferguson: *"Separate but Equal"*

Following its initial decision making "equal protection" a right, the Supreme Court turned conservative, no more ready to enforce the civil rights aspects of the Fourteenth Amendment than it was to enforce the civil liberties provisions. The Court declared the Civil Rights Act of 1875 unconstitutional on the ground that it sought to protect blacks against discrimination by *private* businesses, while the Fourteenth Amendment, according to the Court's interpretation, was intended to protect individuals only against discrimination by *public* officials of state and local governments.

In 1896, the Court went still further, in the infamous case of *Plessy* v. *Ferguson,* by upholding a Louisiana statue that *required* segregation of the races on trolleys and other public carriers (and by implication in all public facilities, including schools). The Supreme Court held that the Fourteenth Amendment's "equal protection of the laws" was not violated by racial distinction as long as the facilities were equal.[33] People generally pretended they were equal as long as some accommodation existed. What the Court was saying in effect was that it was not unreasonable to use race as a basis of exclusion in public matters. This was the origin of the "separate but equal" doctrine that was not reversed until 1954.

Racial Discrimination after World War II

The shame of discrimination against black military personnel during World War II, plus revelation of Nazi racial atrocities, moved President Harry S. Truman finally to bring the problem to the White House and national attention, with the appointment in 1946 of a President's Committee on Civil Rights. In 1948, the committee submitted its report, *To Secure These Rights,* which laid bare the extent of the problem of racial discrimination and its consequences.

The Supreme Court had begun to change its position regarding racial discrimination just before World War II by being stricter about what the states would have to do to provide equal facilities under the "separate but equal" rule. In 1938, the Court rejected Missouri's policy of paying the tuition of qualified blacks to out-of-state law schools rather than admitting them to the University of Missouri Law School.[34] After the war, modest progress resumed. In 1950, the Court rejected Texas's claim that its new law school for Negroes afforded education equal to that of the all-white University of Texas Law School; without confronting the "separate but equal" principle itself, the Court's decision anticipated *Brown* v. *Board* by opening the question of whether *any* segregated facility could be truly equal.[35]

As the Supreme Court was ordering the admission of blacks to all-white state law schools, it was also striking down the southern practice of "white primaries," which legally excluded blacks from participation in the nominating process.[36] The most important pre-1954 decision was probably *Shelley* v. *Kraemer,*[37] in which the Court ruled against the practice of "restrictive convenants," whereby the seller of a home added a clause to the sales contract requiring the buyer to agree not to resell the home to a non-Caucasian, non-Christian, etc.

Although none of those cases confronted "separate but equal" and the principle of

---

[33]Plessy v. Ferguson, 163 U.S. 537 (1896).

[34]Missouri ex rel. Gaines v. Canada, 305 U.S. 337 (1938).

[35]Sweatt v. Painter, 339 U.S. 629 (1950).

[36]Smith v. Allwright, 321 U.S. 649 (1944). See Chapter 10.

[37]Shelley v. Kraemer, 334 U.S. 1 (1948).

Cause and Effect in the Civil Rights Movement
Interaction Between Government Action and Political Action

Judicial and Legal Action	Political Action
1954 *Brown* v. *Board of Education*	
1955 *Brown* II—Implementation of *Brown* I	**1955** Montgomery Bus Boycott
1956 Federal courts order school integration, especially one ordering Autherine Lucy admitted to University of Alabama, with Governor Wallace officially protesting	
1957 Civil Rights Act creating Civil Rights Commission; President Eisenhower sends paratroops to Little Rock, Arkansas, to enforce integration of Central High School	**1957** Southern Christian Leadership Conference (SCLC) formed, with King as president
1960 First substantive Civil Rights Act, primarily voting rights	**1960** Student Nonviolent Coordinating Committee formed to organize protests, sit-ins, freedom rides
1961 Interstate Commerce Commission orders desegregation on all buses, trains, and in terminals	
1961 JFK favors executive action over civil rights legislation	
1963 JFK shifts, supports strong civil rights law; assassination; LBJ asserts strong support for civil rights	**1963** Nonviolent demonstrations in Birmingham, Alabama, lead to King's arrest and his "Letter from the Birmingham Jail"
	1963 March on Washington
1964 Congress passes historic Civil Rights Act covering voting, employment, public accommodations, education	
1965 Voting Rights Act	**1965** King announces drive to register 3 million blacks in the South
1966 War on Poverty in full swing	Movement dissipates: part toward litigation, part toward Community Action Programs, part toward war protest, part toward more militant "Black Power" actions

racial discrimination as such, they were extremely significant to black leaders, giving them encouragement enough to believe that there was at last an opportunity and enough legal precedent to change the constitutional framework itself. By the fall of 1952, the Court had on its docket cases from Kansas, South Carolina, Virginia, Delaware, and the District of Columbia challenging the constitutionality of school segregation. Of these, the Kansas case became the chosen one. It seemed to be ahead of the pack in its district court, and it had the special advantage of being located in a state outside the Deep South.[38]

Oliver Brown, the father of three girls, lived "across the tracks" in a low-income, racially mixed Topeka neighborhood. Every school-day morning, Linda Brown took the school bus to Monroe School for colored children about a mile away. In September 1950, Oliver Brown took Linda to the all-white Sumner School, which was actually closer to home, to enter her into the third grade in defiance of state law and local segregation rules. When they were refused, Brown took his case to the NAACP, and soon thereafter Brown v. Board of Education of Topeka was born.

In deciding the case, the Court, to the surprise of many, rejected as inconclusive all the learned arguments about the intent and the history of the Fourteenth Amendment and committed itself to considering only the consequences of segregation:

> Does segregation of children in public schools solely on the basis of race, even though the physical facilities and other "tangible" factors may be equal, deprive the children of the minority group of equal educational opportunities? We believe that it does. . . . We conclude that in the field of public education the doctrine of "separate but equal" has no place. Separate educational facilities are inherently unequal.[39]

The *Brown* decision altered the constitutional framework in two fundamental respects. First, after *Brown*, the states would no longer have the power to use race as a basis of discrimination in law. Second, the national government would from then on have the power (and eventually the obligation) to intervene with strict regulatory policies against the discriminatory actions of state or local governments, school boards, employers, and many others in the private sector (see Chapter 13).

Simple Justice: *The Courts, the Constitution, and Civil Rights after* Brown v. Board of Education

Although *Brown* v. *Board of Education* withdrew all constitutional authority to use race as a criterion of exclusion, this historic decision was merely a small opening move.[40] First, most states refused to cooperate until sued, and many ingenious schemes were employed to delay obedience (such as paying the tuition for white students to attend newly created "private" academies). Second, even as southern school boards began to cooperate by eliminating their legally enforced (*de jure*) school segregation, there remained extensive actual (*de facto*) school

---

[38]The District of Columbia case came up too, but since the District of Columbia is not a state, it did not directly involve the Fourteenth Amendment and its "equal protection" clause. It confronted the Court on the same grounds, however, that segregation is inherently unequal. Its victory in effect was "incorporation in reverse," with equal protection moving from the Fourteenth amendment to become part of the Bill of Rights (Bolling v. Sharpe, 347 U.S. 497 [1954]).

[39]Brown v. Board of Education of Topeka, Kansas, 347 U.S. 483 (1954).

[40]The heading for this section is drawn from the title of Richard Kluger's important book, *Simple Justice* (New York: Vintage, 1975).

segregation in the North as well as the South. *Brown* could not affect *de facto* segregation, which was not legislated but happened as a result of racially segregated housing. Third, *Brown* did not directly touch discrimination in employment, public accommodations, juries, voting, and other areas of social and economic activity.

A decade of frustration following *Brown* made it fairly obvious to all that the goal of "equal protection" required positive, or affirmative, action by Congress and by administrative agencies. And given massive southern resistance and a generally negative national public opinion toward racial integration, progress would not be made through courts, Congress, *or* agencies without intense, well-organized support.

SCHOOL DESEGREGATION. Although the District of Columbia and some of the school districts in the border states began to respond almost immediately to court-ordered desegregation, the states of the Deep South responded with a well-planned delaying tactic. Southern legislatures passed laws ordering school districts to maintain segregated schools and state superintendents to withhold state funding from racially mixed classrooms. Some southern states centralized public school authority in order to give them power to close the schools that might tend to obey the Court and to provide alternative private schooling.

Most of these plans of "massive resistance" were tested in the federal courts and were struck down as unconstitutional.[41] But southern resistance was not confined to leg-

islation. For example, in Arkansas in 1957, Governor Orval Faubus ordered the National Guard to prevent enforcement of a federal court order to integrate Central High School of Little Rock. President Eisenhower was forced to deploy U.S. troops and literally place the city under martial law. The Supreme Court handed down a unanimous decision requiring desegregation in Little Rock.[42] The end of massive resistance, however, became simply the beginning of still another southern strategy. "Pupil placement" laws authorized school districts to place each pupil in a school according to a whole variety of academic, personal, and psychological considerations, never mentioning race at all. This put the burden of transferring to an all-white school on the nonwhite children and their parents. It was thus almost impossible for a single court order to cover a whole district, let alone a whole state. This delayed desegregation a while longer.[43]

As new devices were invented by the southern states to avoid desegregation, it was becoming unmistakably clear that the federal courts could not do the job alone.[44] The first modern effort to legislate in the field of civil rights was made in 1957; but the

---

[41] The two most important cases were Cooper v. Aaron, 358 U.S. 1 (1958), which required Little Rock, Arkansas, to desegregate; and Griffin v. Prince Edward County School Board, 377 U.S. 218 (1964), which forced all the schools of that county to reopen after five years of closing to avoid desegregation.

[42] In Cooper v. Aaron, the Supreme Court ordered immediate compliance with the lower court's desegregation order and went beyond that with a stern warning that it is "emphatically the province and duty of the judicial department to say what the law is." The justices also took the unprecedented action of personally signing the decisions.

[43] Shuttlesworth v. Birmingham Board of Education, 358 U.S. 101 (1958). This decision upheld a "pupil placement" plan purporting to assign pupils on various bases, with no mention of race. This case interpreted Brown v. Board of Education to mean that school districts must stop explicit racial discrimination but were under no obligation to take positive steps to desegregate. For a while black parents were doomed to case-by-case approaches.

[44] For good treatments of that long stretch of the struggle of the federal courts to integrate the schools, see Paul Brest and Sanford Levinson, *Processes of Constitutional Decision-making*, pp. 471–80; and Kelly et al., *The American Constitution*, pp. 610–16.

Martin Luther King, Jr.
"A Drum Major for Justice"

Martin Luther King, Jr.
(1929–1968)

No advocate for civil rights could lay greater claim to having advanced the standards of justice and equality for blacks than this highly educated, charismatic minister from Georgia.

Martin Luther King, Jr., received his Ph.D. in theology from Boston University in 1955. His studies of philosophy and religion shaped his approach to the struggle for civil rights. In his words, "From my Christian background I gained my ideals, and from [Mohandas K.] Gandhi my operational technique."

King first received national attention for his leadership of the Montgomery Improvement Association, an organization formed in 1955 to integrate the Alabama city's segregated bus system. During the 382-day boycott, King's home was firebombed and he was arrested for the first of many times. Yet he urged positive, nonviolent action, a strategy borrowed from Gandhi's successful effort to free India from British rule, and Christian forgiveness of one's enemies. The strategy worked in Montgomery, and throughout the South.

In 1957, King co-founded the Southern Christian Leadership Conference, becoming president and leader of efforts to eliminate racial discrimination in transportation facilities, public accommodations, hiring practices, and voting. In 1957 alone, King traveled 780,000 miles and delivered 208 speeches. In succeeding years, King met with presidents, world leaders, and fellow Americans to advance the rights and dignity of all people. Repeatedly beaten, arrested, and threatened with death, King and his followers continued to use the tactics of civil disobedience and passive resistance in the face of guns, fire hoses, and police dogs.

King galvanized national opinion as a leader of the March on Washington in August 1963. Addressing the more than 250,000 participants from the steps of the Lincoln Memorial, he delivered his prophetic and moving "I Have a Dream" speech. The following year, King was awarded the Nobel Peace Prize, becoming at thirty-five its youngest recipient. His efforts stirred the nation's conscience, contributing directly to the enactment of landmark civil rights legislation in the 1960s.

Despite rising violence in the mid-1960s, King continued to urge nonviolence. But the cycle of violence eventually snared the Georgia preacher, as he was shot and killed by an assassin's bullet outside of a Memphis, Tennessee, motel on April 4, 1968. The previous February, when asked what he would want as a eulogy, King had responded, "Say that I was a drum major for justice. Say that I was a drum major for peace. Say that I was a drum major for righteousness."

Source: Juan Williams, *Eyes on the Prize* (New York: Penguin, 1988).

law contained only a federal guarantee of voting rights, without any powers of enforcement, although it did create the Civil Rights Commission to study abuses. Much more important legislation for civil rights followed during the 1960s, especially the Civil Rights Act of 1964. These acts will be discussed in Chapter 13.

Further progress in the desegregation of schools came in the form of busing[45] and redistricting, but it was slow and is likely to continue to be slow unless the Supreme Court decides to permit federal action against *de facto* segregation and against the varieties of private schools and academies that have sprung up for the purpose of avoiding integration.[46] A Supreme Court decision handed down January 15, 1991, dimmed the prospects for further school integration. The opinion, written by Chief Justice Rehnquist, held that lower federal courts could end supervision of local school boards if those boards could show compliance "in good faith" with court orders to desegregate and could show that "vestiges of past discrimination" had been eliminated "to the extent practicable."[47] It will not be easy for a school board to prove that the new standards have been met, but this is the first time since *Brown* and the 1964 Civil Rights Act that the Court has opened the door at all to retreat.

OUTLAWING DISCRIMINATION IN EMPLOYMENT. Despite the agonizingly slow progress of school desegregation, there was some progress in other areas of civil rights during the 1960s and 1970s. Voting rights were established and fairly quickly began to revolutionize southern politics. Service on juries was no longer denied to minorities. But progress in the right to participate in politics and government dramatized the relative lack of economic progress. This became the new frontier in the civil rights struggle, and with it came the historic joining of women's rights to the civil rights cause.

The federal courts and the Justice Department entered this area through Title VII of the Civil Rights Act of 1964. Title VII outlawed job discrimination by all private and public employers, including governmental agencies (such as fire and police departments), that employed more than fifteen workers. We have already seen that the Supreme Court gave "interstate commerce" such a broad definition that Congress had the constitutional authority to outlaw discrimination by virtually any local employer.[48] Title VII made it unlawful to discriminate in employment on the basis of color, religion, sex, and national origin, as well as race.

[45]Swann v. Charlotte-Mecklenberg Board of Education, 402 U.S. 1 (1971). See also Bernard Schwartz, *Swann's Way: The School Busing Case and the Supreme Court* (New York: Oxford University Press, 1986).

[46]For a good evaluation, see Gary Orfield, *Must We Bus? Segregated Schools and National Policy* (Washington: The Brookings Institution, 1978), pp. 144–46. See also Bob Woodward and Scott Armstrong, *The Brethren: Inside the Supreme Court* (New York: Simon and Schuster, 1979), pp. 426–27; and J. Anthony Lukas, *Common Ground* (New York: Random House, 1986).

[47]Board of Education of Oklahoma City v. Dowell, U.S. 111 S.Ct. 630, 112 L. Ed. 2d. 715.

[48]See especially Katzenbach v. McClung, 379 U.S. 294 (1964). Almost immediately after passage of the Civil Rights Act of 1964, a case was brought challenging the validity of Title II, which covered discrimination in public accommodations. Ollie's Barbecue was a neighborhood restaurant in Birmingham, Alabama, located eleven blocks away from an interstate highway and even farther from railroad and bus stations. Its table service was for whites only; there was only a take-out service for blacks. The Supreme Court agreed that Ollie's was strictly an intrastate restaurant, but since a substantial proportion of its food and other supplies were bought from companies outside the state of Alabama, there was a sufficient connection to interstate commerce; therefore, racial discrimination at such restaurants would "impose commercial burdens of national magnitude upon interstate commerce." Although this case involved Title II, it had direct bearing on the constitutionality of Title VII.

DEBATING THE ISSUES

Affirmative Action

The principle of equality has long been a bedrock value of the American political system. Yet the devotion to equality has contrasted sharply with the fact that Americans have not all been treated equally. Women, African Americans, Latinos, Native Americans, and other groups rightly claim that they have suffered historical patterns of discrimination that have deprived them of basic rights. African Americans in particular believe that hundreds of years of slavery and savage treatment cannot simply be wiped away by the proclamation that all are now equal.

This belief has prompted the government to promote affirmative-action programs designed to provide an added advantage for minorities in areas such as college admissions and employment, based on the principle that past discrimination against African Americans and others can be rectified only by tilting the scales more in their favor now. Advocates of affirmative action, such as Supreme Court Justice Thurgood Marshall, have argued that equal treatment of unequals merely perpetuates inequality. Opponents to such programs, such as law professor Stephen L. Carter, contend that such preferential treatment is inconsistent with American values and may actually harm those it tries to help.

Marshall

Three hundred and fifty years ago, the Negro was dragged to this country in chains to be sold into slavery. Uprooted from his homeland and thrust into bondage for forced labor, the slave was deprived of all legal rights. It was unlawful to teach him to read; he could be sold away from his family and friends at the whim of his master; and killing or maiming him was not a crime. The system of slavery brutalized and dehumanized both master and slave.

The denial of human rights was etched into the American colonies' first attempts at establishing self-government. . . . The self-evident truths and the unalienable rights were intended . . . only to apply to white men. . . . The implicit protection of slavery embodied in the Declaration of Independence was made explicit in the Constitution. . . . The status of the Negro as property was officially erased by his emancipation at the end of the Civil War. But

One problem with Title VII was that the complaining party had to show that deliberate discrimination was the cause of the failure to get the job or the training opportunity. Rarely does an employer explicitly admit discrimination on the basis of race, sex, or any other illegal reason. For a time, courts allowed the complaining parties to make their case if they could show that an employer's hiring practices, whether intentional or not, had the *effect* of exclusion. Employers, in effect, had to justify their actions.[49]

[49]Griggs v. Duke Power Company, 401 U. S. 24 (1971).

the long awaited emancipation, while freeing the Negro from slavery, did not bring him citizenship or equality in any meaningful way. Despite the passage of the Thirteenth, Fourteenth, and Fifteenth Amendments, the Negro was systematically denied the rights those amendments were supposed to secure. . . . In light of the sorry history of discrimination and its devastating impact on the lives of Negroes, bringing the Negro into the mainstream of American life should be a state interest of the highest order. To fail to do so is to ensure that America will forever remain a divided society. . . . We now must permit the institutions of this society to give consideration to race in making decisions about who will hold the positions of influence, affluence and prestige in America. For far too long, the doors to those positions have been shut to Negroes.[1]

Carter

If we as a people were not defeated by slavery and Jim Crow, we will not be defeated by the demise of affirmative action. Before there were any racial preferences, before there was a federal antidiscrimination law with any teeth, our achievements were already on the rise: our middle class was growing, as was our rate of college matriculation—both of them at higher rates than in the years since. Black professionals, in short, should not do much worse without affirmative action than we are doing with it, and thrown on our own resources and knowing that we have no choice but to meet the same tests as everybody else, we may do better.

We must be about the business of defining a future in which we can be fair to ourselves and demand opportunities without falling into the trap of letting others tell us that our horizons are limited, that we cannot make it without assistance. . . . The likely demise, or severe restriction, of racial preferences will also present for us a new stage of struggle, and we should treat it as an opportunity, not a burden. It is our chance to make ourselves free of the assumptions that too often underlie affirmative action, assumptions about our intellectual incapacity and other competitive deficiencies. It is our chance to prove to a doubting, indifferent world that our future as a people is in our hands.[2]

[1]Regents of the University of California v. Bakke, 438 U.S. 265, 387 (1978).
[2]Stephen L. Carter, *Reflections of an Affirmative Action Baby* (New York: Basic Books, 1991), as excerpted in George McKenna and Stanley Feingold, eds., *Taking Sides: Clashing Views on Controversial Political Issues*, 8th ed. (Guilford, CT: Dushkin, 1993), pp. 192–93.

The Politics of Rights: Affirmative Action

The relatively narrow goal of equalizing opportunity by eliminating discriminatory barriers had been developing toward the far broader goal of *affirmative action*—compensatory action to overcome the consequences of past discrimination. An affirmative action policy tends to involve two novel approaches: (1) positive or benign discrimination in which race or some other status is actually taken into account, but for compensatory action rather than mistreatment; and (2) compensatory action to favor members of the disadvantaged group who themselves may never have been the victims of discrimination. (Quotas may be, but are not necessarily, involved in affirmative action policies.)

President Johnson inaugurated affirmative action by ordering a policy of minority employment in the federal civil service and in companies doing business with the national government. As the movement spread in the 1970s, it also began to divide civil rights activists and their supporters. Must more highly qualified white candidates have to give way to less qualified minority candidates? Wasn't this a case of "reverse discrimination"? The whole issue was addressed formally in the case of Allan Bakke. Bakke, a white male with no minority affiliation, brought suit against the University of California at Davis Medical School on the ground that in denying him admission the school had discriminated against him on the basis of his race (that year the school had reserved 16 of 100 available seats for minority applicants). He argued that his grades and test scores had ranked him well above many black or Hispanic students who had been accepted.

In 1978, Bakke won his case before the Supreme Court and was admitted to the medical school, but he did not succeed in getting affirmative action declared unconstitutional. The Court rejected the procedures at the University of California because its medical school had used both a quota *and* a separate admissions system for minorities. The Court held that the method of a rigid quota of student slots assigned on the basis of race was incompatible with the equal protection clause. Thus, the Court permitted universities (and presumably other schools, training programs, and hiring authorities) to continue to take minority status into consideration but restricted the

use of quotas to situations in which (1) previous discrimination had been shown, and (2) it was used more as a *guideline* for social diversity than as a mathematically defined ratio.[50]

For nearly a decade after *Bakke*, the Supreme Court was tentative and permissive about efforts by corporations and governments to experiment with affirmative action programs in employment.[51] But in 1989, the Court returned to the *Bakke* position that any "rigid numerical quota" is suspect. In *Wards Cove* v. *Atonio*, the Court backed away further from affirmative action by easing the way for employers to prefer white males, holding that the burden of proof of unlawful discrimination should be shifted from the defendant (the employer) to the plaintiff (the person claiming to be the victim of discrimination).[52] This decision virtually overruled the Court's prior holding in *Griggs*. That same year the Court ruled that any affirmative action program already approved by federal courts could be subsequently challenged by white males who alleged that the program discriminated against them.[53]

In 1991, Congress strengthened affirmative action with the Civil Rights Act of 1991, which put the burden of proof back on the employer to show that educational and other standards for employment that fa-

[50]Regents of the University of California v. Bakke, 438 U.S. 265 (1978).

[51]United Steelworkers v. Weber, 443 U.S. 193 (1979); and Fullilove v. Klutznick, 100 S.Ct. 2758 (1980).

[52]City of Richmond v. J.A. Croson Co., 109 S.Ct. 706 (1989); Ward's Cove v. Atonio, 109 S.Ct. 2115 (1989).

[53]Martin v. Wilks, 109 S.Ct. 2180 (1989). In this case, Chief Justice Rehnquist held that white fire fighters in Birmingham could challenge the legality of a consent decree mandating goals for hiring and promoting blacks, even though they had not been parties to the original litigation.

vored whites or males were "essential to the job." Despite Congress's actions, however, the federal judiciary will have the last word when cases under the new law reach the courts. In fact, in a 5-to-4 decision in 1993, the Court ruled that employees had to prove their employers intended discrimination, once again placing the burden of proof on employees.[54]

Until the 1992 election, there had been little reason to expect that the federal courts would be sympathetic to Congress's efforts. But that could now change. President Clinton began his term with nearly fifty federal judgeships to appoint, Congress will almost certainly expand the number of federal judicial posts, and other vacancies will occur at all levels, including that of the Supreme Court, where Clinton has already had the opportunity to fill one vacancy. (See also Chapter 7.)

The conservatives' disagreements with affirmative action can be reduced to two major points. The first is that rights in the American tradition are innately individual, and affirmative action violates this concept by concerning itself with "group rights," an idea that they say is alien to the American tradition. The second point has to do with quotas. Conservatives would argue that the Constitution is "color-blind," and that any

discrimination, even if it is called positive or benign discrimination, ultimately violates the equal protection clause and the American way.

The liberal side agrees that rights ultimately come down to individuals. But the essence of discrimination is the use of unreasonable and unjust exclusion to deprive *an entire group* access to something valuable in society. Thus, discrimination itself has to be attacked on a group basis. Liberals can also use Court history to support their side. The first definitive interpretation of the Fourteenth Amendment by the Supreme Court in 1873 stated explicitly,

> The existence of laws in the state where the newly emancipated Negroes resided, which discriminated with gross injustice and hardship against them *as a class,* was the evil to be remedied by this clause.[55]

Although the problems of rights in America are agonizing, they can be looked at optimistically. The United States has a long way to go before it constructs a truly just, "equally protected" society. But it also has come very far in a relatively short time. All explicit *de jure* (legal) barriers to minorities have been dismantled. Many *de facto* barriers have also been dismantled, and thousands upon thousands of new opportunities have been opened.

---

[54] St. Mary's Honor Center v. Hicks.

[55] Slaughterhouse Cases, 16 Wallace 36 (1873). [Emphasis added.]

Time Line On Civil Liberties And Civil Rights

EVENTS		INSTITUTIONAL DEVELOPMENTS
Bill of Rights sent to states for ratification (1789)		States ratify U.S. Bill of Rights (1791)
Undeclared naval war with France (1798–1800); passage of Alien and Sedition Acts (1798)	**1800**	Alien and Sedition Acts, limiting free speech, press, and aliens, disregarded and not renewed (1801)
Maine admitted to Union as free state (1820); Missouri admitted as slave state (1821)		Missouri Compromise regulates expansion of slavery into territories (1820)
		Barron v. *Baltimore* confirms dual citizenship (1833)
Slaves taken into territories (1800s)		*Dred Scott* v. *Sandford* invalidates Missouri Compromise; perpetuates slavery (1857)
Civil War (1861–1865)	**1860**	
		Emancipation Proclamation (1863); Thirteenth Amendment prohibits slavery in the U.S. (1865)
Southern blacks now vote but Black Codes in South impose special restraints (1865)		Civil Rights Act (1866)
Reconstruction (1867–1877)		Fourteenth Amendment ratified (1868)
"Jim Crow" laws spread throughout the South (1890s)		*Plessy* v. *Ferguson* upholds doctrine of "separate but equal" (1896)
World War I (1914–1919)	**1920**	*Gitlow* v. *N.Y.* (1925) and *Near* v. *Minnesota* (1931) apply First Amendment to states
Postwar pacifist and anarchist agitation and suppression (1920s and 1930s)		
U.S. enters World War II (1941–1945)		
Civil rights movement, e.g., Montgomery bus boycott (1955); lunch counter sit-ins (1960); freedom riders (1961)	**1950**	*Brown* v. *Board of Education* overturns *Plessy,* invalidates segregation (1954); federal use of troops to enforce court order to integrate schools (1957)
March on Washington, largest civil rights demonstration in American history (1963)		Civil Rights Act outlaws segregation (1964)

EVENTS		INSTITUTIONAL DEVELOPMENTS
		Katzenbach v. *McClung* upholds use of commerce clause to bar segregation (1964)
Spread of movement politics—students, women, environment, right to life (1970s)	**1970**	*Roe* v. *Wade* prohibits states from outlawing abortion (1973)
Affirmative action plans enacted in universities and corporations (1970s and 1980s)		Court orders to end malapportionment and segregation (1970s and 1980s)
		Georgia law upheld in *Bowers* v. *Hardwick* allowing states to regulate homosexual activity (1986)
Challenges to affirmative action plans continue (1980s–1990s)		Court accepts affirmative action on a limited basis—*Regents of Univ. of Calif.* v. *Bakke* (1978), *Wards Cove* v. *Atonio* (1989), *Martin* v. *Wilks* (1989)
		Missouri law restricting abortion upheld in *Webster* v. *Reproductive Health Services* (1989)
States adopt restrictive abortion laws (1990–1991)	**1990**	
Bush signs civil rights bill favoring suits against employment discrimination (1991)		Court permits school boards to terminate busing (1991)
		Roe upheld; prisoner rights expanded (1992)
		Clinton's positions on abortion and gay rights revives civil rights activity (1993)

Chapter Review

Civil liberties and *civil rights* are two quite different phenomena and have to be treated legally and constitutionally in two quite different ways. We have defined civil liberties as that sphere of individual freedom of choice created by restraints on governmental power. The Bill of Rights explicitly placed a whole series of restraints on government. Some of these were *substantive,* regarding *what* government could do; some of these restraints were *procedural,* regarding *how* the government was permitted to act. The rights in the Bill of Rights we call civil liberties because they are rights to be free from arbitrary government interference.

But *which* government? This was settled in the *Barron* case in 1833 when the Supreme Court held that the restraints in the Bill of Rights were applicable only to the national government, and not to the states. The Court was recognizing "dual citizenship." At the time of its adoption in 1868, the Fourteenth Amendment was considered by many as a deliberate effort to reverse *Barron,* to put an end to dual citizenship, and to nationalize the Bill of Rights, applying its restrictions to state governments as well as to the national government. But the post–Civil War Supreme Court interpreted the Fourteenth Amendment otherwise. Dual citizenship remained almost as it had been before the Civil War, and the shadow of *Barron* extended across the rest of the nineteenth century and well into the twentieth century.

The slow process of nationalizing the Bill of Rights began in the 1920s, when the Supreme Court recognized that at least the restraints of the First Amendment had been "incorporated" into the Fourteenth Amendment as restraints on the state governments. But it was not until the 1960s that most of the civil liberties in the Bill of Rights were incorporated into the Fourteenth Amendment.

The second aspect of protection of the individual, *civil rights,* stresses the expansion of governmental power rather than restraints upon it. If the constitutional base of civil liberties is the "due process" clause of the Fourteenth Amendment, the constitutional base of civil rights is the "equal protection" clause. This clause imposes a positive obligation on government to advance civil rights, and its original motivation seems to have been to eliminate the gross injustices suffered by "the newly emancipated Negroes . . . as a class." But as with civil liberties, there was little advancement in the interpretation or application of the "equal protection" clause until after World War II. The major breakthrough came in 1954 with *Brown* v. *Board of Education of Topeka,* and advancements came in fits and starts during the succeeding ten years.

After 1964, Congress finally supported the federal courts with effective civil rights legislation. From that point, civil rights developed in two ways. First, the definition of civil rights was expanded to include victims of discrimination other than blacks. Second, the definition of civil rights became increasingly positive through affirmative action policies. Judicial decisions, congressional statutes, and administrative agency actions have all moved beyond the original goal of eliminating discrimination toward creating new opportunities for minorities and, in some areas, compensating present minority individuals for the consequences of discriminatory actions against members of their group in the past. This kind of compensatory civil rights action has sometimes relied upon quotas, which has given rise to intense debate over the constitutionality as well as the desirability of affirmative action.

The story has no end and is not likely to. The politics of rights will remain an important part of American political discourse.

For Further Reading

Abraham, Henry. *Freedom and the Court: Civil Rights and Liberties in the United States.* 4th ed. New York: Oxford University Press, 1982.

Baer, Judith A. *Equality under the Constitution: Reclaiming the Fourteenth Amendment.* Ithaca: Cornell University Press, 1983.

Brigham, John. *Civil Liberties and American Democracy*. Washington, DC: Congressional Quarterly Press, 1984.

Eisenstein, Zillah. *The Female Body and the Law*. Berkeley: University of California Press, 1988.

Forer, Lois G. *A Chilling Effect: The Mounting Threat of Libel and Invasion of Privacy Actions to the First Amendment*. New York: W. W. Norton, 1987.

Friendly, Fred W. *Minnesota Rag: The Dramatic Story of the Landmark Supreme Court Case that Gave New Meaning to Freedom of the Press*. New York: Vintage, 1982.

Garrow, David J. *Bearing the Cross: Martin Luther King and the Southern Christian Leadership Conference: A Personal Portrait*. New York: William Morrow, 1986.

Hentoff, Nat. *The First Freedom: The Tumultuous History of Free Speech in America*. New York: Delacorte, 1980.

Kelly, Alfred, Winfred A. Harbison, and Herrman Beltz. *The American Constitution: Its Origins and Development*. 7th ed. New York: W. W. Norton, 1991.

Levy, Leonard. *Freedom of Speech and Press in Early America: Legacy of Suppression*. New York: Harper & Row, 1963.

Lewis, Anthony. *Gideon's Trumpet*. New York: Vintage, 1964.

Minnow, Martha. *Making All the Difference—Inclusion, Exclusion, and American Law* (Ithaca: Cornell University Press, 1990).

Randall, Richard S. *Censorship of the Movies*. Madison: University of Wisconsin Press, 1970.

Silberman, Charles. *Criminal Violence, Criminal Justice*. New York: Random House, 1978.

Silverstein, Mark. *Constitutional Faiths*. Ithaca: Cornell University Press, 1984.

Sunstein, Cass. *After the Rights Revolution*. Cambridge: Harvard University Press, 1990.

Thernstrom, Abigail M. *Whose Votes Count? Affirmative Action and Minority Voting Rights*. Cambridge: Harvard University Press, 1987.

Thurow, Sarah, ed. *E Pluribus Unum: Constitutional Principles and the Institutions of Government*. Washington, DC: University Press of America, 1988.

PART 2

INSTITUTIONS

5

CONGRESS: THE FIRST BRANCH

*T*he U.S. Congress is the "first branch" of government under Article I of our Constitution. Prior to the twentieth century, the Congress, not the executive, was the central policy-making institution in the United States. Congressional leaders were the dominant political figures of their time and often treated mere presidents with disdain. But during the twentieth century, congressional influence waned relative to that of the executive branch. The presidency became the central institution of American government. Members of Congress may support or oppose, but they are seldom free to ignore presidential leadership. Moreover, the bureaucracies of the executive branch have—often with the encouragement of Congress—seized a good deal of legislative power.

Congress has not taken the diminishment of its influence lightly. From time to time it stands up to the White House and flexes its legislative muscles. And the future may well bring a resurgence of congressional influence, as we will see in the last section of this chapter. First, however, we will examine closely how Congress exercises its most important power—making laws. Then we will take a look at some congressional powers that go beyond legislation.

Making Law

In 1992, Americans elected the largest group of new senators and representatives to enter Congress since 1948. Taking the House and Senate together, the 103rd Congress included 122 new members. This Congress is also the most diverse ever elected. Thirty-eight African Americans were elected to serve in the House and one in the Senate (the 102nd Congress had only twenty-five African American representatives). At the same time, forty-two women were elected to the House and six to the Senate. This was a substantial increase over the 102nd Congress, where twenty-nine women had served in the House and only two in the Senate. Indeed, California became the first state to be represented by two women in the Senate when it elected Diane Feinstein and Barbara Boxer, both Democrats.

Many observers hailed the emergence of a more representative Congress and expressed confidence that this Congress would rapidly enact important new programs and policies. Others were more cautious about predicting any sort of quick action on its part.

It is extraordinarily difficult for a large representative assembly to formulate, enact, and implement laws. The internal complexities of conducting business within Congress—the legislative process—make things complicated. In addition, there are many individuals and institutions that have the capacity to influence the legislative process. For example, legislation to raise the salaries of members of the House of Representatives received input from congressional leaders of both parties, special legislative task forces, the president, the national chairmen of the two major parties, public interest lobbyists, the news media, and the mass public before it became law in 1989. Since successful legislation requires the confluence of so many distinct factors, it is little wonder that most of the thousands of bills considered by Congress each year are defeated long before they reach the president.

Before an idea or proposal can become a law, it must pass through a complex set of organizations and procedures in Congress. Collectively, these are called the policy-making process, or the legislative process. Understanding this process is central to understanding why some ideas and proposals eventually become the law of the land while most do not. Although the supporters of legislative proposals often feel that the formal rules of the congressional process are deliberately designed to prevent their own deserving proposals from ever seeing the light of day, these rules allow Congress to play an important role in lawmaking. If it wants to be more than simply a rubber stamp for the executive branch, like so many other representative assemblies around the world, a national legislature like the Congress must develop a division of labor, set an agenda, maintain order through rules and procedures, and place limits on discussion. Equality among the members of Congress must give way to hierarchy—ranking people according to their function within the institution.

To exercise its power to make the law, Congress must first bring about something close to an organizational miracle. In this chapter, we will examine the organization of Congress and the legislative process. In particular, we will be concerned with the basic building blocks of congressional organization: bicameralism, political parties, the committee system, congressional staff, the caucuses, and the parliamentary rules of the House and Senate. Each of these factors plays a key role in the organization of Congress and in the process through which Congress formulates and enacts laws. We will also look at other powers Congress has in addition to lawmaking, and we will explore the future role of Congress in relation to the powers of the executive.

Bicameralism: House and Senate

The framers of the Constitution provided for a **bicameral legislature**—that is, a legislative body consisting of two chambers. As we saw in Chapter 2, the framers intended each of these chambers, the House and Senate, to serve a different constituency. Members of the Senate, appointed by state legislatures for six-year terms, were to represent the elite members of society and to be more attuned to the interests of property than to those of population. Today, members of the House and Senate are both elected directly by the people. The 435 members of the House are elected from districts apportioned according to population; the 100 members of the Senate are elected by state, with 2 senators from each. Senators continue to have much longer terms in office and usually represent much larger and more diverse constituencies than do their counterparts in the House (Table 5.1).

The House and Senate play different roles in the legislative process. In essence, the Senate is the more deliberative of the two bodies—the forum in which any and all ideas can receive a thorough public airing. The House is the more centralized and organized of the two bodies—better equipped to play a routine role in the governmental process. In part, this difference stems from the different rules governing the two bodies. These rules give House leaders more control over the legislative process and provide for House members to specialize in certain legislative areas. The rules of the much smaller Senate give the leadership relatively little power and discourage specialization.

Both formal and informal factors contribute to differences between the two chambers of Congress. Differences in the length of terms and requirements for holding office specified by the Constitution in turn generate differences in how members of each body develop their constituency and exercise their powers of office. The result is that members of the House most effectively and frequently serve as the agents of well-organized local interests with specific legislative agendas—for instance, used car dealers seeking relief from regulation, labor unions seeking more favorable legislation, farmers looking for higher subsidies. The small size and relative homogeneity of their constituencies and the frequency with which they must seek re-election make House members

TABLE 5.1
DIFFERENCES BETWEEN THE HOUSE AND THE SENATE

	House	Senate
Minimum age of member	25 years	30 years
U.S. citizenship	at least 7 years	at least 9 years
Length of term	2 years	6 years
Number per state	Depends on population 1 per 30,000 in 1789 now 1 per 550,000	2 per state
Constituency	Tends to be local	Both local and national

more attuned to these well-organized local interests with individual legislative needs.

Senators, on the other hand, serve larger and more heterogeneous constituencies. As a result, they are somewhat better able than members of the House to serve as the agents for groups and interests organized on a statewide or national basis. Moreover, with longer terms in office, senators have the luxury of considering "new ideas" or seeking to bring together new coalitions of interests, rather than simply serving existing ones.

Thus, the House and Senate represent somewhat different forces in American political life. The House is more likely to represent entrenched local interests; the Senate is better able to serve new or emergent national forces. In recent years, as a result, it has been the Senate that has been most friendly to new social movements, such as feminism and gay rights.

Political Parties: Congress's Oldest Hierarchy

The Constitution makes only one provision for the organization of business in Congress. In Article I, it gives each chamber a presiding officer. In the Senate, this officer is known as the president, and the office is held ex officio by the vice-president of the United States. The Constitution also allows the Senate to elect a president pro tempore—a temporary president—to serve in the absence of the vice-president. In the House of Representatives, the presiding officer is known as the Speaker and is elected by the entire House membership.

Article I of the Constitution gives little guidance for how to conduct congressional business. Even during the first Congress (1789–1791), it was the political parties that provided the organization needed by the House and Senate. For the first century or more of the Republic, America had literally a party government in Congress.[1]

Party Leadership in the House and the Senate

Every two years, at the beginning of a new Congress, the members of each party gather to elect their House leaders. This gathering is traditionally called the *caucus*, or *conference*.

The elected leader of the majority party is later proposed to the whole House and is automatically elected to the position of Speaker, with voting along straight party lines. The House majority caucus then also elects a majority leader. The minority party goes through the same process and selects the minority leader. Both parties also elect whips to line up party members on important votes and relay voting information to the leaders. In December 1992, prior to the opening of the 103rd Congress, Democrats designated Thomas Foley of Washington to continue as Speaker, Richard Gephardt of Missouri to remain the majority leader, and David Bonior of Michigan to continue as whip.

Republicans re-elected Robert Michel of Illinois to the position of minority leader and Newt Gingrich of Georgia to that of minority whip. In a victory for the GOP's conservative wing, House Republicans unseated the Republican conference chair, Jerry Lewis of California, and replaced him with Richard Armey of Texas. Armey, like Gingrich, is an advocate of confrontational politics. His selection to the House Republican leadership put Democrats on notice that

[1] *Origins and Development of Congress* (Washington, DC: Congressional Quarterly Press, 1982).

Tom Foley and Newt Gingrich
The Traditional and Modern Styles of Congress

*T*he careers and styles of congressional leaders Tom Foley and Newt Gingrich closely mirror the opposing forces that shape the modern Congress.

Tom Foley was first elected to the House of Representatives as a Democrat from Washington state in 1964. Quiet, hard-working, known for his fairness and integrity, Foley rose in the ranks of his party rapidly. In 1972, he was chosen to chair the Democratic Study Group, a policy oriented group of House Democrats. After the 1974 elections, Foley was selected to chair the Agriculture Committee after the Democratic Caucus pushed aside the committee's aged chair, Robert Poage. Although the chairing of a committee is normally a highly sought-after privilege, Foley had actually backed Poage.

After the 1980 elections, House Speaker Tip O'Neill and Majority Leader Jim Wright chose Foley to serve as majority whip. (Foley was the last to obtain this post by leader appointment; thereafter, the position became elective.) When O'Neill retired in 1986, Foley moved up to majority leader; when the new Speaker, Jim Wright, resigned his seat in the wake of ethics violations charges in 1989, Foley became the Speaker. Without question, the rise of this highly respected leader would not have occurred had competition for the whip position been opened up to all House Democrats, as is now the case. Yet Foley's calm, conciliatory, almost non-partisan style raised questions in 1993 about whether he could be tough and ruthless enough to impose the discipline necessary to win enactment of President Clinton's ambitious legislative program. Responding to these criticisms, Foley said "You don't get support for these programs by routine arm-twisting. It's mythical to think members can be forced to do something they don't want to do."

In contrast, the rise of Georgia's Newt Gin-

Tom Foley

Republican opposition was likely to become more vocal and more intense than ever.

Next in line of importance for each party after the Speaker and majority or minority leader is its Committee on Committees (called the Steering and Policy Committee by the Democrats), whose tasks are to assign new legislators to committees and to deal

grich reflects the more wide-open, competitive process increasingly seen in Congress in recent years. First elected to the House in 1978, this conservative Republican quickly became known for his brash, contentious, abrasive style. In an environment in which collegiality, respect, and deference were considered necessary to win advancement, Gingrich waged what was labeled "guerrilla warfare against the Democrats." For example, he and fellow conservative Republicans used C-SPAN (the televised proceedings of Congress) to harshly criticize the Democrats and even some Republican party leaders in a manner designed to be highly public and therefore highly embarrassing. Gingrich was among the first to criticize Speaker Wright for alleged ethics problems. Gingrich himself summed up his tactics as, "conflict equals exposure equals power."

In 1989, a sudden vacancy for the position of House minority whip opened up. Despite an unimpressive legislative record and lack of service in a leadership role either on a committee or for the party, Gingrich won a narrow vote among House Republicans and became the Republican Whip. Gingrich's surprise victory underscored the discontent of many Republicans who were no longer satisfied with accepting the Republicans' seemingly permanent status as minority party (the Republicans have not held a majority in the House since 1954). In Gingrich's words, "We had a choice of being attack dogs or lapdogs. We decided attack dogs are more useful."

Many feared that Gingrich's aggressive style would only further reduce Republican influence in the House. But Gingrich toned down his rhetoric and began to practice the kind of congressional leadership skills so ably employed by Speaker Foley. Still, on some issues, such as the 1990 deficit-reduction package, Gingrich has been a strident and vocal critic of the Democrats and some Republican leaders. Gingrich's "conflict" style maintains a certain appeal, but it is also clear that the low-key, bargaining style epitomized by Foley is still vital to an effective Congress.

Source: Roger H. Davidson and Walter J. Oleszek, 3rd ed., *Congress and Its Members* (Washington, DC: Congressional Quarterly Press, 1990).

Newt Gingrich

with the requests of incumbent members for transfers from one committee to another. The Speaker serves as chair of the Democratic Steering and Policy Committee, while the minority leader chairs the Republican Committee on Committees. (The Republicans have a separate Policy Committee, now chaired by Henry Hyde of Illinois.) At one time, party leaders strictly controlled committee assignments, using them to enforce party discipline. Today, in principle, representatives receive the assignments they want. But assignments on the most important committees are often sought by several individuals, which gives the leadership an opportunity to cement alliances (and, perhaps, make enemies) as it resolves conflicting requests.

Generally, representatives seek assignments that will allow them to influence decisions of special importance to their districts. Representatives from farm districts, for example, may request seats on the Agriculture Committee.[2] Seats on powerful committees such as Ways and Means, which is responsible for tax legislation, and Appropriations are especially popular. In order to integrate the extraordinarily large freshman class elected in 1992 into the congressional process, and to win their loyalty, the House Democratic leadership made a special effort to give them significant committee appointments. As a result, Democratic freshmen received coveted appointments to Appropriations, Ways and Means, and other key committees at the start of the 103rd Congress.

Most freshmen had campaigned on platforms calling for congressional reform, and many had entered Congress pledging to cut congressional expenditures, to reduce the perquisites of office, and, in general, to make Congress a more open and democratic body. Partly as a result of the leadership's efforts, however, even the most reform-minded Democratic freshmen gradually accepted the rules and traditions of the Congress. Some Democratic freshmen did not want to make demands that might impede

the passage of President Clinton's program. Others, particularly representatives from districts with heavy Democratic majorities, quickly recognized that the congressional seniority system would eventually make them influential figures in the Congress. This recognition reduced their enthusiasm for reforms that might someday reduce their own power.[3]

Within the Senate the president pro tempore exercises mainly ceremonial leadership. Usually, the majority party designates a member with the greatest seniority to serve in this capacity. Real power is in the hands of the majority leader and minority leader, each elected by party caucus. Currently, George Mitchell of Maine is majority leader and Robert Dole of Kansas is minority leader. Together they control the Senate's calendar or agenda for legislation. In addition, the senators from each party elect a whip. Each party also selects a Policy Committee, which advises the leadership on legislative priorities. The majority party structures for the House and Senate are shown in Figures 5.1 and 5.2.

Party Discipline

In both the House and Senate, party leaders have a good deal of influence over the behavior of their party members. This influence, sometimes called "party discipline," was once so powerful that it dominated the lawmaking process. At the turn of the century, because of their control of patronage and the nominating process, party leaders could often command the allegiance of more than 90 percent of their members. A vote on which 90 percent or more of the

[2]Richard Fenno, Jr., *Home Style: House Members in Their Districts* (Boston: Little, Brown, 1978).

[3]See Clifford Krauss, "Leaders Blunt Lances of Quixotic Freshmen," *New York Times*, 4 April 1993, p. 26.

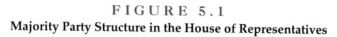

FIGURE 5.1
Majority Party Structure in the House of Representatives

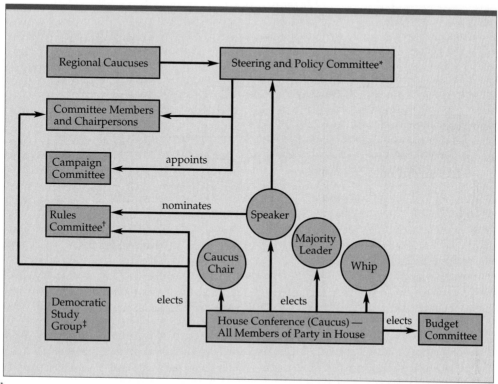

[*]Includes Speaker (chairperson), majority leader, chief and deputy whips, caucus chairperson, four members appointed by Speaker, and twelve members elected by regional caucuses. Created by caucus to assist party leaders in making committee assignments, ordering legislation, and developing policy.
[†]Speaker nominates members, ratified by caucus, elected by House. Official committee for determining the order of business in the House.
[‡]Similar to Republicans' Wednesday Club. Both serve as self-conscious, policy-oriented voting blocs. The Democratic Study Group is the larger and is thought to be the more effective of the two.

members of one party take a particular position while at least 90 percent of the members of the other party take the opposing position is called a *party vote.* At the beginning of the twentieth century, nearly half of all roll-call votes in the House of Representatives were party votes. Today, primary elections have deprived party leaders of the power to decide who receives the party's official nomination. The patronage resources available to the leadership, moreover, have become quite limited. As a result, party-line voting happens less often. It is, however, fairly common to find at least a majority of Democrats opposing a majority of Republicans on any given issue. This dis-

FIGURE 5.2

Majority Party Structure in the Senate

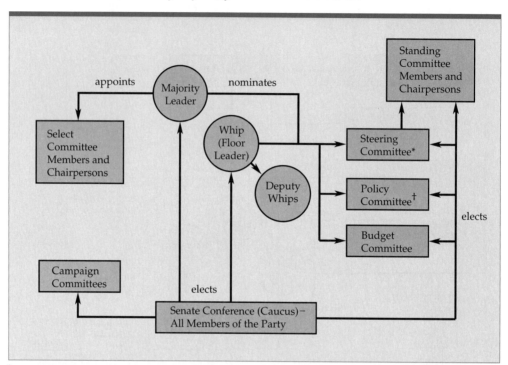

*Chaired by majority leader. Members nominated by majority leader and whip to reflect a geographical and philosophical balance.
†Schedules legislative activity.

play of party unity has increased in recent sessions of Congress as a consequence of the intense partisan struggles during the Reagan and Bush years (see Figure 5.3).

During the first session of the 103rd Congress, party-line voting reemerged briefly in the House of Representatives. House Democrats were almost unanimous in their support of a number of President Clinton's policy proposals. For their part, House Republicans were united in their opposition to Clinton. In the March 18, 1993, House vote on Clinton's proposed tax increases and spending cuts, the president was supported by 96 percent of the Democratic

members and opposed by 100 percent of the Republicans. The next day, Clinton's economic stimulus package was supported by 91 percent of the Democrats and opposed by 98 percent of the Republicans.

Most political observers attributed this high level of party unity to the fervent desire of congressional Democrats to contribute to the success of the first Democratic administration in twelve years. Many Democrats, particularly members of the large group of congressional newcomers, considered their own political futures to be tied, at least in part, to Clinton's success or failure.

FIGURE 5.3
Party Unity Scores by Chamber*

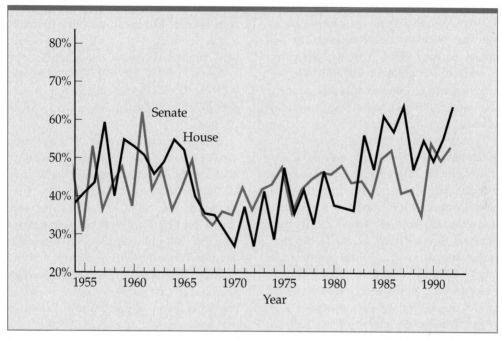

*The percentage of times that members voted with the majority of their party, based on recorded votes on which a majority of one party voted against the majority of the other party.
Source: *Congressional Quarterly Weekly Report*, 19 December 1992, p. 3849. Used by permission.

Republicans were equally determined to make certain that any future blame for Clinton's programs should fall entirely upon the shoulders of the Democrats. Republicans also deeply resented what they saw as Democratic "steamroller" tactics that completely ignored the views of GOP legislators. "For two months they acted like we weren't even around," complained one Republican aide.[4]

Given the many long-term factors working against party discipline in the United States, few observers expected this situation to continue for long. The early show of

Democratic party unity was achieved only after an intense debate within the Democratic camp.[5] Conservative Democrats, led by Congressman Charles Stenholm of Texas, supported Clinton's economic package only after insisting on $55 billion in spending cuts beyond the president's request. To maintain the support of western Democratic senators for his economic package, Clinton was forced to give in to demands that he drop his proposal to charge higher fees for the use of public lands by

[4]David Broder, "Republicans Turn Democrats' Hardball Tactics into Rallying Point," *Washington Post*, 3 April 1993, p. 1.

[5]David Broder, "Hill Democrats Vote as One: New Era of Unity or Short-term Honeymoon?" *Washington Post*, 14 March 1993, p. A1. See also Adam Clymer, "All Aboard: Clinton's Plan Gets Moving," *New York Times*, 21 March 1993, sec. 4, p. 1.

western ranchers and mining interests.[6] By the summer, Democratic unity in the House had once again diminished. In June, thirty-eight conservative Democrats broke ranks with the president and voted against his budget package. Eleven of the defectors chaired subcommittees, and loyal Democrats demanded they be stripped of their positions. The House leadership, however, balked at such a divisive step.

Typically, party unity is greater in the House than in the Senate. House rules grant greater procedural control of business to the majority party leaders, giving them more influence over their members. In the Senate, the leadership has few sanctions over its members. Senator Tom Daschle (Democrat–South Dakota), co-chair of the Democratic Policy Committee, observed that a Senate leader seeking to influence other senators has "a bushel full of carrots and a few twigs."[7] Even so, during President Clinton's spring 1993 "honeymoon" with Congress, Senate Democrats also gave him almost u-nanimous support, producing extraordinary, straight party-line voting. The one exception was Senator Richard Shelby of Alabama, who strongly opposed the president's economic program and responded to its introduction by saying, "The taxman cometh."[8] Democratic unity eroded still further in June, when the president's economic package came up for a vote. Six Democrats joined the Republicans to vote against it, leaving Gore to cast the necessary tie-breaking vote. In August 1993, Republicans in both the House and Senate again voted

unanimously in opposition to President Clinton's budget proposals. Clinton was supported by a solid core of Democrats in both houses, but because of defections by conservative Democrats, his victory margin was razor thin. Clinton won in the House by a mere two votes, 218-to-216. In the Senate, Vice-President Gore again cast a tie-breaking vote to give the Clinton budget a 51-to-50 edge.

To some extent, party unity is based on ideology and background. Republican members of Congress are more likely than Democrats to be drawn from rural or suburban areas. Democrats are likely to be more liberal on economic and social questions than their Republican colleagues. These differences certainly help to explain roll-call divisions between the two parties. Ideology and background, however, are only part of the explanation of party unity. The other part has to do with party organization and leadership.

Although party organization has weakened since the turn of the century, today's party leaders still have some resources at their disposal: (1) committee assignments, (2) access to the floor, (3) the whip system, (4) logrolling, and (5) the presidency. These resources are regularly used and are often effective in securing the support of party members.

COMMITTEE ASSIGNMENTS. Leaders can create debts among members by helping them get favorable committee assignments. These assignments are made early in the congressional careers of most members and cannot be taken from them if they later balk at party discipline. Nevertheless, if the leadership goes out of its way to get the right assignment for a member, this effort is likely to create a bond of obligation that can be called upon without any other payments or favors.

[6]Adam Clymer, "Single-Minded President," *New York Times*, 3 April 1993, p. 1.

[7]Holly Idelson, "Signs Point to Greater Loyalty on Both Sides of the Aisle," *Congressional Quarterly Weekly Report*, 19 December 1992, p. 3849.

[8]Lloyd Grove, "Rebel Senator Faces White House Wrath," *Washington Post*, 4 April 1993, p. 1.

Patty Murray
"Just a Mom in Tennis Shoes"

Patty Murray
(b. 1951)

The political experts and pundits gave Patty Murray, Washington state mother and housewife, no chance to win election to the U.S. Senate in 1992. That verdict did not deter Murray, however.

Murray launched her campaign against incumbent Democratic senator Brock Adams in the fall of 1991. The motivation for her race began in 1980, when Democrat Murray went to Washington's state capital, Olympia, to lobby against proposed budget cuts for the state's community colleges. One male member of the state legislature dismissed Murray by saying, "You can't do anything; you're just a mom in tennis shoes." A community college teacher by training, Murray then became involved in various neighborhood political groups, served on the local school board, and won election to the Washington state senate.

The "mom in tennis shoes" theme became the basis of her U.S. Senate campaign; one of her political advertisments even featured a re-enactment of the incident, and one of her campaign gimmicks included handing out sets of shoelaces with her name on them. Murray won the open senatorial primary in September 1992, outpolling the Democratic and Republican contenders. (Washington holds blanket primaries, where candidates from both parties compete on the same ballot.) By this time, Adams had decided to withdraw from the race, in the wake of accusations of sexual misconduct against him.

Murray's campaign avoided labels like "feminist" or "liberal" and emphasized her average middle-class roots and outsider status. Yet she took strong stands on issues during the campaign, including support for abortion rights, the environment, and an array of educational and family issues. Even during the campaign, she continued to take care of her elderly parents and her two children, for whom she still prepared meals several times a week. In Murray's words, "What I am is a different role model. This mom in tennis shoes is really what I am." Referring to the event that drove many women into politics in 1992, she added, "I didn't see anything like me during the Clarence Thomas hearings."

Murray won a solid victory over a better-financed conservative Republican congressman. Her win was built on support from both rural and urban areas around the state. She relied heavily for campaign finance support from a national organization specializing in financing women candidates called Emily's List. Harriet Woods, head of the National Women's Political Caucus, explained Murray's success this way: "Here is a woman who has none of the lofty credentials, but she represents just what the voters are looking for: an outsider, who is close to them and understands their lives."

Source: Gary Jacobson, *The Politics of Congressional Elections* (New York: HarperCollins, 1992).

This is one reason the leadership worked so hard to give freshmen favorable assignments in the 103rd Congress.

ACCESS TO THE FLOOR. The most important everyday resource available to the parties is control over access to the floor. With thousands of bills awaiting passage and most members clamoring for access in order to influence a bill or to publicize themselves, floor time is precious. In the Senate, the leadership allows ranking committee members to influence the allocation of floor time—who will speak for how long; in the House, the Speaker, as head of the majority party (in consultation with the minority leader), allocates large blocks of floor time. Thus, floor time is allocated in both houses of Congress by the majority and minority leaders. More important, the Speaker of the House and the majority leader in the Senate possess the power of recognition. Although this power may not appear to be substantial, it is a formidable authority, and it can be used to block a piece of legislation completely or to frustrate a member's attempts to speak on a particular issue. Because the power is significant, members of Congress usually attempt to stay on good terms with the Speaker and the majority leader in order to ensure that they will continue to be recognized.

Some House members, Republicans in particular, have also taken advantage of "special orders," under which members can address the floor after the close of business. These addresses are typically made to an empty chamber, but carried live by C-Span, a cable channel. Democrats control the House floor and tend to have ample time to present their positions during the day. Republicans, however, have often used "special orders" to present their views effectively to national audiences. Representative Newt Gingrich launched a televised after-hours attack on House Speaker Jim Wright in 1988 that ultimately led to Wright's resignation.[9]

THE WHIP SYSTEM. Some influence accrues to party leaders through the whip system, which is primarily a communications network. Between twelve and twenty assistant and regional whips are selected by zones to operate at the direction of the majority or minority leader and the whip. They take polls of all the members in order to learn their intentions on specific bills. This enables the leaders to know if they have enough support to allow a vote as well as whether the vote is so close that they need to put pressure on a few swing votes. Leaders also use the whip system to convey their wishes and plans to the members, but only in very close votes do they actually exert pressure on a member. In those instances, the Speaker or a lieutenant will go to a few party members who have indicated they will switch if their vote is essential. The whip system helps the leaders limit pressuring members to a few times per session.

The whip system helps maintain party unity in both houses of Congress, but it is particularly critical in the House of Representatives because of the large number of legislators whose positions and votes must be accounted for. The majority and minority whips and their assistants must be adept at inducing compromise among legislators who hold widely differing viewpoints. The whips' personal styles and their perception of their function significantly affect the development of legislative coalitions and influence the compromises that emerge.

---

[9]See Beth Donovan, "Busy Democrats Skirt Fights to Get House in Order," *Congressional Quarterly Weekly Report*, 12 December 1992, p. 3778.

LOGROLLING. An agreement between two or more members of Congress who have nothing in common except the need for support is called logrolling. The agreement states, in effect, "You support me on bill *X* and I'll support you on another bill of your choice." Since party leaders are the center of the communications networks in the two chambers, they can help members create large logrolling coalitions. Hundreds of logrolling deals are made each year, and while there are no official record-keeping books, it would be a poor party leader whose whips did not know who owed what to whom.

THE PRESIDENCY. Of all the influences that maintain the clarity of party lines in Congress, the influence of the presidency is probably the most important. Indeed, it is a touchstone of party discipline in Congress. Since the late 1940s, under President Truman, presidents each year have identified a number of bills to be considered part of the administration's program. By the mid-1950s, both parties in Congress began to look to the president for these proposals, which became the most significant part of Congress's agenda. The president's support is a criterion for party loyalty, and party leaders in Congress are able to use it to rally some members.

The Committee System: The Core of Congress

The committee system provides Congress with its second organizational structure, but it is more a division of labor than a hierarchy of power. Committee and subcommittee chairs have a number of important powers, but their capacity to discipline committee members is limited. Ultimately, committee members are hired and fired by the voters, not by the leadership. Committee chairs just have to put up with members whose views they might find distasteful.

Six fundamental characteristics define the congressional committee system:

1. *Each committee is a standing committee.* It is given a permanent status by the official rules with a fixed membership, officers, rules, staff, offices, and, above all, a jurisdiction that is recognized by all other committees and usually the leadership as well.

2. *The jurisdiction of each standing committee is defined according to the subject matter of basic legislation.* Except for the House Rules Committee, all the important committees are organized to receive proposals for legislation and to process them into official bills. The House Rules Committee decides the order in which bills come up for a vote and determines the specific rules that govern the length of debate and the opportunity for amendments. Rules can be used to help or hinder particular proposals.

3. *Committees' jurisdictions usually parallel those of the major departments or agencies in the executive branch.* There are important exceptions—Appropriations (House and Senate) and Rules (House), for example—but by and large, the division of labor is self-consciously designed to parallel executive branch organization.

4. *Bills are assigned to committees on the basis of subject matter, but the Speaker of the House and the Senate's presiding officer have some discretion in the allocation of bills to committees.* Most bills "die in committee"—that is, they are not reported out favorably. Ordinarily this ends a bill's life. There is only one way for a legislative proposal to escape committee processing: A bill passed in one chamber may be permitted to go directly on to the calendar of the other chamber. Even here, however, the bill has received the full

committee treatment before passage in the first chamber.

5. *Each committee is unique.* No effort is made to compose the membership of any committee to be representative of the total House or Senate membership. Members with a special interest in the subject matter of a committee are expected to seek membership on it. In both the House and the Senate, each party has established a Committee on Committees, which determines the committee assignments of new members and of established members who wish to change committees. Ordinarily, members can keep their committee assignments as long as they like.

6. *Each committee's hierarchy is based on seniority.* Seniority is determined by years of continuous service on a particular committee, not by years of service in the House or Senate. In general, each committee is chaired by the most senior member of the majority party. Although the power of committee chairs is limited, they play an important role in scheduling hearings, selecting subcommittee members, and appointing committee staff. Because Congress has a large number of subcommittees and has given each representative a larger staff, the power of committee chairs has been diluted. Democrats elect committee chairs by secret ballot, rather than permit seniority to determine the outcome automatically. However, seniority has been followed in all but a handful of cases in recent years.

At the opening of the 103rd Congress, House Democrats partially reversed the decentralizing reforms of the 1970s by opting to abolish 16 of the 137 subcommittees. Under the rubric of congressional cost savings, four select committees were also eliminated. These dealt with hunger, children, the el-

derly, and illegal drugs. The Democrats also establish a party policy council to set a legislative agenda. This twenty-member group was selected by the Speaker, with half of its members coming from the Steering and Policy Committee. With these reforms, Democrats increased the power of the House leadership, paving the way for the more efficient enactment of new programs and policies.

For their part, House Republicans chose to weaken seniority by limiting their members to six consecutive years in any committee's top position. Under the new rule, there would be a complete turnover of every committee's ranking Republican spot in 1996. The major purpose of the rule was to embarrass the Democrats, who had declined to adopt term limits for committee chairs. Most observers predicted that the Republicans would rescind the rule before it took effect in 1996.

The Staff System: Staffers and Agencies

A congressional institution second in importance only to the committee system is the staff system. Every member of Congress employs a large number of staff members, whose tasks include handling constituency requests and, to a large and growing extent, dealing with legislative details and overseeing the activities of administrative agencies. Increasingly, staffers bear the primary responsibility for formulating and drafting proposals, organizing hearings, dealing with administrative agencies, and negotiating with lobbyists. Indeed, legislators typically deal with one another through staff, rather than through direct, personal contact. Representatives and senators together employ nearly eleven thousand staffers in their

Washington and home offices. Today, staffers even develop policy ideas, draft legislation, and, in some instances, have a good deal of influence over the legislative process.

In addition to the personal staffs of individual senators and representatives, Congress also employs roughly three thousand committee staffers. These individuals comprise the permanent staff, who stay regardless of turnover in Congress, attached to every House and Senate committee, and who are responsible for organizing and administering the committee's work, including research, scheduling, organizing hearings, and drafting legislation. Congressional staffers can come to play key roles in the legislative process. For example, according to informal accounts, important pieces of legislation such as the Clean Air Act of 1963, the Mass Transportation Act of 1964, and the Budget and Impoundment Act of 1974 were actually shaped by congressional staffers with only cursory supervision from their bosses.[10] In some cases, staffers have enormous influence over the behavior and thinking of the senators and representatives for whom they work. For example, Senator Warren Magnuson (Democrat-Washington) served as chair of the Senate Commerce Committee for twenty-three years (1955–1978). During this period, under the influence of staffers Gerald Grinstein and Michael Pertschuk, Magnuson shifted from a conservative political stance to become a liberal activist on such national issues as consumer affairs.[11] The influence of con-

gressional staff was summarized by Senator Robert Morgan (Democrat-North Carolina), who said, "This country is basically run by the legislative staffs of the Senate and House of Representatives."[12]

Not only does Congress employ personal and committee staff, but the Congress has also established four staff agencies designed to provide the legislative branch with resources and expertise independent of the executive branch. Thus they enhance Congress's capacity to oversee administrative agencies and to evaluate presidential programs and proposals. These staff agencies are the Congressional Research Service, which performs research for legislators who wish to know the facts and competing arguments relevant to policy proposals or other legislative business; the General Accounting Office, through which Congress can investigate the financial and administrative affairs of any government agency or program; the Office of Technology Assessment, which provides Congress with analyses of any scientific or technical issues that may be relevant to national programs; and the Congressional Budget Office, which assesses the economic implications and likely costs of proposed federal programs.

Informal Organization: The Caucuses

In addition to the formal organization of Congress, there also exists an informal organizational structure—the caucuses. Caucuses are groups of senators or repre-

---

[10]See Harrison W. Fox and Susan W. Hammond, *Congressional Staffs: The Invisible Force in American Lawmaking* (New York: Free Press, 1977).

[11]Michael W. Malbin, *Unelected Representatives* (New York: Basic Books, 1980), pp. 29–30.

[12]*Congressional Record*, 8 September 1976, S15432. Quoted in Fox and Hammond, *Congressional Staffs*, p. 3.

sentatives who share certain opinions, interests, or social characteristics. There are ideological caucuses such as the liberal Democratic Study Group, the conservative Democratic Forum (popularly known as the "boll weevils") and the moderate Republican Wednesday Group. At the same time, there are a large number of caucuses composed of legislators representing particular economic or policy interests such as the Travel and Tourism Caucus, the Steel Caucus, the Mushroom Caucus, and the Concerned Senators for the Arts. Legislators who share common backgrounds or social characteristics have organized caucuses such as the Congressional Black Caucus, the Congressional Caucus for Women's Issues, and the Hispanic Caucus.

All these caucuses seek to advance the interests of the groups they represent by promoting legislation, encouraging Congress to hold hearings, and pressing administrative agencies for favorable treatment. The Congressional Black Caucus, for example, which now includes thirty-eight representatives and one senator, is expected to increase its role in the 103rd Congress. Representative Kweisi Mfume of Maryland, elected to chair the caucus, has become an important and effective congressional advocate for economic development in the African American community.[13] The policy-making role of the caucuses has become important enough to make them a "third force," rivaling, though not equaling, committees and parties.

[13]See Jeffrey Katz, "Mfume to Chair Caucus," *Congressional Quarterly Weekly Report*, 12 December 1992, p. 3780.

Rules of Lawmaking: How a Bill Becomes a Law

The institutional structure of Congress is one key factor that helps to shape the legislative process. A second and equally important factor is the rules of congressional procedures (see In Brief Box on pages 116–117). These rules govern everything from the introduction of a bill through its submission to the president for signing. Not only do these regulations influence the fate of each and every bill; they also help to determine the distribution of power in the Congress.

Committee Deliberation

Even if a member of Congress, the White House, or a federal agency has spent months developing and drafting a piece of legislation, it does not become a bill until it is submitted officially by a senator or representative to the clerk of the House or Senate and referred to the appropriate committee for deliberation. No floor action on any bill can take place until the committee with jurisdiction over it has taken all the time it needs to deliberate. During the course of its deliberations, the committee typically refers the bill to one of its subcommittees, which may hold hearings, listen to expert testimony, and amend the proposed legislation before referring it to the full committee for its consideration. The full committee may accept the recommendation of the subcommittee or hold its own hearings and prepare its own amendments. Or, even more frequently, the committee and subcommittee may do little or nothing with a bill that has been submitted to them. Many bills are simply allowed to "die in committee" with little or no serious consideration ever given to them. Often, members of Congress introduce legislation, which they neither expect nor desire to see enacted into law, merely to please a constituency group. These bills die a quick and painless death. Other pieces of legislation have ardent supporters and die in committee only after a long battle. But in either case, most bills are never reported out of the committees to which they are assigned. In a typical congressional session, 95 percent of the roughly eight thousand bills introduced die in committee—an indication of the power of the congressional committee system.

The relative handful of bills that are reported out of the committee to which they were originally referred must, in the House, pass one additional hurdle within the committee system—the Rules Committee. This powerful committee determines the rules that will govern action on the bill on the House floor. In particular, the Rules Committee allots the time for debate and decides to what extent amendments to the bill can be proposed from the floor. A bill's supporters generally prefer what is called a "closed rule," which puts severe limits on floor debate and amendments. Opponents of a bill usually prefer an "open rule," which permits potentially damaging floor debate and makes it easier to add amendments that may cripple the bill or weaken its chances for passage. Thus, the outcome of the Rules Committee's deliberations can be extremely important and the committee's hearings can be an occasion for sharp conflicts.

In 1988, House Republicans lashed out at the Rules Committee, claiming that restrictive rules barring floor amendments had seriously weakened their power. Since House committees are currently controlled by the Democrats, bills reported out of committees generally reflect a Democratic bias, and Republicans consider themselves disadvantaged when they cannot propose amendments on the floor. At least one Republican charged that the Rules Committee had relegated Republicans to second-class status. In the last decade under Democratic control, the number of bills issuing from committees with "open" rules has dropped from 88 percent to 56 percent.

The Calendar

Once reported out of a "subject matter" committee and the Rules Committee, a bill must be placed on a calendar—Congress's name for its agenda. There are several calendars, each of which indicates the status as well as the stature of a bill. The House has five legislative calendars: the *Union Calendar* for revenue, appropriations, and other public bills to be considered by the whole House; the *House Calendar* for public bills not included in the Union Calendar; the *Consent Calendar* for noncontroversial bills likely to be passed without objections or debate; the *Private Calendar* for all private bills; and the *Discharge Calendar* for motions to discharge bills from committees. The Senate has only two calendars: the *Executive Calendar* for treaties and nominations, and the *Calendar of Business* for all legislation.

Some bills, even if favorably reported by a committee, may stay on a calendar through one or both sessions of Congress, while others go on the calendar and off to the floor for debate after only a brief wait. In both chambers, each week's business is drawn from the calendar according to decisions made by majority and minority party leaders who have consulted with appropriate committee chairs, the White House, and leaders from the other chamber. Usually, a program of floor activities is posted on Fri-

In Brief Box

A SELECTION OF IMPORTANT CONGRESSIONAL RULES

Rules Governing Deliberation	*Comments*
1. Most of the rules of each chamber, especially since 1946, define the jurisdictions of the standing committees, one rule for each.	1. The Speaker's power over committees is limited since there is little discretion on where to assign bills.
2. All proposals are read once and referred immediately to committee.	2. A committee can be bypassed only when a bill has already been passed by the other chamber.
3. Public bills cannot go to calendar (be put on the agenda) until reported out of committee.	3. Again, the only exception is when the bill has already been passed by the other chamber.
4. Committees may be given the power to subpoena witnesses and compel testimony, as a type of grand jury.	4. A limitation on this rule is that the committee questions must have a legislative purpose when citizens other than administrators of agencies and departments are subpoenaed.
5. Bills remain in committee until the committee is ready to report them out.	5. This power of life and death over bills is mainly a result of the great difficulty of discharging bills from committee.
6. Discharge and Calendar Wednesday are the only two meaningful exceptions to the power of a committee to retain and deliberate on bills as long as it chooses.	6. In the House, a discharge petition must be signed by an absolute majority (218). Then the bill goes on calendar, after which it can be debated only on the second or fourth Monday of each month. In the Senate, a discharge motion requires only a simple majority but is subject to debate and therefore to the cloture rule. Calendar Wednesday is even more limited.

day for the following week so members can plan accordingly.

Debate

Party control of the agenda is reinforced by the rule giving the Speaker of the House and the president of the Senate the power of recognition during debate on a bill. Usually the chair knows the purpose for which a member intends to speak well in advance of the occasion. Spontaneous efforts to gain recognition are often foiled. For example, the speaker may ask, "For what purpose does the member rise?" before deciding whether to grant recognition.

Virtually all of the time allotted by the Rules Committee for debate on a given bill is controlled by the bill's sponsor and by its leading opponent. In almost every case, these two people are the committee chair and the ranking minority member of the

Rules Governing Debate	*Comments*
1. Rule and tradition give unlimited power of recognition to the presiding officer, especially the Speaker of the House.	1. Senate presiding officers try to play down this power, attempting to work through agreements between majority and minority committee leaders.
2. While in session, Congress must meet every day except Sunday.	2. There rarely are weekend sessions. Occasionally, the leadership threatens such sessions to discourage casual attendance or diversionary tactics.
3. To encourage talk, House rules allow the House to adjourn into the "Committee of the Whole House on the State of the Union."	3. A quorum is 100 instead of 218, and rules governing debate are less strict than formal House rules.
4. In both House and Senate, actual debate time is controlled by the committee responsible for handling the bill.	4. The "floor managers" are the chairperson and the top ranking minority member of the committee whose bill is up for debate. They can designate another committee member as floor manager.
5. House rules severely limit the power of a member to offer amendments to bills. These limits are policed by the Rules Committee and chairpersons. The Senate sets no serious limit on the right of senators to offer amendments and to speak for them.	5. Even in the Senate, there is a long distance between offering an amendment and getting it adopted as part of a bill. Amendments not agreed to in advance by the bill's sponsors have a low probability of acceptance.
6. When the House sits as the House again, it hears the Report of the Committee of the Whole. Amendments rejected by the Committee of the Whole cannot be reconsidered, and debate on the bill is usually closed very quickly. The Senate allows amendments at any time.	6. A Senate rule requires germaneness, but unless someone makes a point of order that the rule is being violated, it is not seriously observed.

committee that processed the bill—or those they designate. These two participants are, by rule and tradition, granted the power to allocate most of the debate time in small amounts to members who are seeking to speak for or against the measure. Preference in the allocation of time goes to the members of the committee whose jurisdiction covers the bill.

In the Senate, the leadership has much less control over floor debate. Indeed, the Senate is unique among the world's legislative bodies for its commitment to unlimited debate. Once given the floor, a senator may speak as long as he or she wishes. On a number of memorable occassions, senators have used this right to prevent action on legislation that they opposed. Through this tactic, called the *filibuster,* small minorities or even one individual in the Senate can force the majority to give in to their demands. During the 1950s and 1960s, for ex-

PROCESS BOX 5.1
How a Bill Becomes a Law

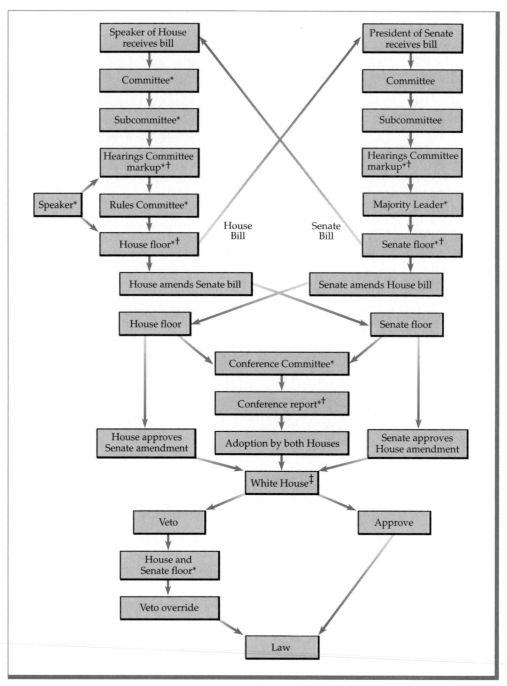

* Points at which bill can be amended.

† Points at which bill can die.

‡ If the president neither signs nor vetoes the bill within ten days, it automatically becomes law.

ample, opponents of civil rights legislation often sought to block its passage by adopting the tactic of filibuster. The votes of three-fifths of the Senate, or sixty votes, are needed to end a filibuster. This procedure is called cloture.

In April 1993, Senate Republicans, joined by one Democrat, Senator Richard Shelby of Alabama, were able to use the filibuster to block the adoption of President Clinton's proposal to spend more than $16 billion on public works and other programs the president said were needed to create jobs and stimulate the economy. Republicans claimed that the spending program consisted mainly of wasteful pork-barrel projects. The Democrats held only a 57-to-43 majority in the Senate. Thus, so long as the Republicans remained unified, the Democrats had no hope of mustering the sixty votes needed to end debate on the bill and bring it to a vote. Republicans calculated that their filibuster would force the Clinton administration to modify its economic stimulus package and, even more important, to negotiate with the GOP on future legislative proposals.[14]

Reconciling House and Senate Versions of an Act

Getting a bill out of committee and through one of the houses of Congress is no guarantee that a bill will eventually be enacted into law. Frequently, bills that began with similar provisions in both chambers emerge with little resemblance to each other. Alternatively, a bill may be passed by one cham-

ber but undergo substantial revision in the other chamber. In such cases, a conference committee composed of the senior members of the committees or subcommittees that initiated the bills may be required to iron out differences between the two pieces of legislation. Sometimes members or leaders will let objectionable provisions pass on the floor with the idea that they will get the change they want in conference. Usually, conference committees meet behind closed doors. Agreement requires a majority of each of the two delegations.

Legislation that emerges from a conference committee is more often a compromise than a clear victory of one set of forces over another. For example, in 1989 the House and Senate passed conflicting versions of a bill authorizing funds for building a B-2 or "stealth" bomber. The House bill was less generous than the Senate bill because a substantial bloc in the House wanted to scrap the plane altogether. Negotiations between the House and Senate conferees produced a bill that allowed for more funds than the original House bill and less funds than the original Senate bill. In 1993, House and Senate negotiators had considerable difficulty reconciling their differing versions of President Clinton's economic plan. The Senate version eliminated the energy tax, which had been approved in the House version. It also left less money for expanding domestic social programs than had been allocated in the House version.

The Budget Process

The budget is handled a bit differently from other pieces of legislation. The budget process is designed to allow Congress to consider the overall relationship between anticipated revenues and expenditures during

---

[14]Ruth Marcus and Helen Dewar, "Partisan Strategy on Stimulus Was Clinton Gamble," *Washington Post,* 4 April 1993, p. 1. See also Michael Wines, "Truly Modern Filibuster," *New York Times,* 4 March 1993, p. 26.

BOX 5.1
The Filibuster

Slavery, Civil War, Reconstruction, and blacks' voting rights were all sparks for frequent and contentious filibusters during the nineteenth century. Opponents had no weapon against them; proposed rules to restrict debate were repeatedly rejected. The majority's only recourse was to win unanimous consent for a time limit on considering a bill, on a case-by-case basis.

Minor curbs were adopted early in the twentieth century. But they did not hinder Republican filibusters from killing two of President Wilson's proposals to put the nation on a war footing—a 1915 ship-purchase bill and a 1917 bill to arm merchant ships. Public revulsion, however, forced the Senate to yield. On March 8, 1917, it finally adopted a cloture rule, allowing for a vote of two-thirds of the senators present to end a filibuster.

The rule's framers predicted it would be little used, and for years that was the case. The first successful motion, in 1919, ended debate on the Treaty of Versailles. Nine more motions were voted on through 1927, and three were successful. Over the next 35 years, until 1962, only 16 were voted on and not one was adopted.

In large part, that reflected the politics of civil rights. Southern Democrats successfully filibustered legislation against the poll tax, literacy tests, lynching and employment discrimination, by building an anti-cloture coalition that included westerners and some Republicans. In return for their allies' votes against cloture on civil-rights filibusters, the southerners supported westerners' highway and water projects and Republicans' fights against labor legislation.

Slowly, the anti-cloture coalition began to dissolve. A signal of its demise was the 1962 vote to end a filibuster against a proposed communications satellite—the first successful cloture vote since 1927. Then in 1964, the Senate for the first time invoked cloture on a civil rights bill. During seventy-four days of debate, the longest filibuster in Senate history, West Virginia Democrat Robert C. Byrd gave one of the longest speeches by an individual—14 hours, 13 minutes.

A year later, cloture was approved for another civil rights measure, the Voting Rights Act. And in 1968, a thirty-four-day filibuster of an open-housing bill was stopped.

By the 1970's, the liberals' victories on civil rights had cooled their ardor for cloture reform. Moreover, they had become the ones doing much of the filibustering—against President Nixon's Vietnam policies, weapons systems, and anti-busing proposals.

In 1973, for the first time in years, the Senate did not fight over the cloture rule. But in 1975, the liberals tried again—and won. Now three-fifths of the Senate, or 60 votes, could shut off a filibuster instead of up to 67, two-thirds of those present and voting.

Source: Modified from Jacqueline Calmes, "Dilatory Debate: A Tactic as Old as the Senate," *Congressional Quarterly,* September 5, 1987, p. 2119. Used by permission.

any given year. The first step in the process is the adoption of a budget resolution by the House and Senate. This resolution stipulates the amount of money that will be spent and the amount of revenue that will be raised each year.

Subsequently, the House and Senate appropriations committees work to develop a plan for discretionary spending whose total level—enacted into law in a series of thirteen appropriations bills (one for each of thirteen functional areas, such as defense, commerce, and transportation)—may not exceed the overall limit stated by the budget resolution.

At the same time, congressional authorization and tax-writing committees must produce legislation to meet the revenue targets and any savings goals embodied in the budget resolution. Such legislation includes changes in tax policy and, where necessary, adjustments in entitlement programs. All such changes are ultimately bundled together in a reconciliation bill. In the Senate, the reconciliation bill is considered under special rules that make it immune to filibusters. This is designed to prevent senators from blocking the entire bill while they seek to compel the enactment (or deletion) of a specific item. In addition, nongermane amendments are prohibited to prevent "killer amendments"—provisions added deliberately to reduce a bill's chance of passage.

In 1993, President Clinton and his allies in Congress secured the enactment of the federal budget providing for spending cuts and substantial tax increases. Clinton said his budget would trim the nation's budget deficit by nearly $500 billion over a five-year period. Republicans argued that Clinton's estimates were based on optimistic projections and the president should have cut spending more and raised taxes less.

Vetoes

Once adopted by the House and Senate, a bill goes to the president, who may choose to sign the bill into law or veto it. To veto a bill, the president returns it within ten days to the house of Congress in which it originated, along with his objections to the bill. If Congress adjourns during the ten-day period, and the president has taken no action, the bill is also considered to be vetoed. This latter method is known as the "pocket veto." The veto is the president's constitutional power to reject a piece of legislation. The possibility of a presidential veto affects how willing members of Congress are to push for different pieces of legislation at different times. If they think a proposal is likely to be vetoed they might shelve it for a later time.

A presidential veto may be overridden by a two-thirds vote in both the House and Senate. A veto override says much about the support that a president can expect from Congress, and it can deliver a stinging blow to the executive branch. Bush used his veto power on forty-six occasions during his four years in office and, in all but one instance, was able to defeat or avoid a congressional override of his action. Bush's frequent resort to the veto power was one indicator of the struggle between the White House and the Congress over domestic and foreign policy that took place during his term.

Beyond Legislation: Additional Congressional Powers

In addition to the power to make the law, Congress has at its disposal an array of other instruments through which to influence the process of government. The Constitution

TABLE 5.2
CONGRESSIONAL WEAPONS OF CONTROL

Statutes	Public laws: Authorization acts Public laws: Revenue acts Public laws: Appropriations acts Private legislation
Oversight of administration	Hearings Investigation Supervision (congressional lobbying)
Oversight of citizens (committee as grand jury) Advice and consent (Senate) Debate Direct committee government (public works) Legislative veto	Hearings Investigation

gives the Senate the power to approve treaties and appointments. And Congress has drawn to itself a number of other powers through which it can share with the other branches the capacity to administer the laws. The powers of Congress can be called "weapons of control" to emphasize the fact of Congress's power to govern and to call attention to what governmental power means. Table 5.2 is an outline of Congress's weapons of control.

Oversight

Oversight, as applied to Congress, refers not to something neglected but to the effort to oversee or to supervise. Congress sometimes finds it difficult to pass statutes that are clear in wording and intent. That is why the lawmaking branch relied increasingly on legislative oversight of administrators.

Individual senators and members of the House can engage in a form of oversight simply by calling or visiting administrators, sending out questionnaires, or talking to constituents about programs. But in a more formal sense, oversight is carried out by committees or subcommittees of the Senate or House, which conduct hearings and investigations. Congress delegates to these committees or subcommittees the power to subpoena witnesses, take oaths, cross-examine, compel testimony, and bring criminal charges for contempt (refusing to cooperate) and perjury (lying).

Hearings and investigations resemble each other in many ways, but they differ on one fundamental point. A hearing is usually held on a specific bill, and the questions asked there are usually intended to build a record with regard to that bill. In an investigation, the committee or subcommittee does not begin with a particular bill, but examines a broad area or problem and then concludes its investigation with one or more proposed bills. An example of an investigation is the congressional inquiry into the Reagan administration's shipment of arms to the government of Iran.

Committees and subcommittees can subpoena any government official or any other citizen as a witness to testify on the behavior of individual administrators or as an expert to analyze and evaluate agencies and the effectiveness of their programs. The purpose may be to locate inefficiencies, to explore the relationship between what an agency does and what a law intended, or to change or abolish a program. Most programs and agencies are subject to some oversight every year during the course of hearings on appropriations, the funding of agencies and government programs. Both the House and Senate have an appropriations committee, which is divided into subcommittees to cover one or more departments and major agencies. Regular standing committees also have opportunities to engage in oversight of past agency behavior, even while considering bills proposing new agency responsibilities. Thus, for example, the House and Senate Intelligence Committees seek to monitor the actions of the Central Intelligence Agency (CIA) and other U.S. intelligence agencies on an ongoing basis.

Investigating committees occasionally run into trouble when they start subpoenaing ordinary citizens rather than administrative officials. No one would deny Congress the ability to subpoena citizens as witnesses in evaluating a specific agency or bill or in defining or evaluating a general problem in an investigation. But when a committee seeks to investigate individual wrongdoing, it has converted itself into a combination grand jury and trial court. In that role, it can easily jeopardize the rights of citizens involved in its investigation, as often happened with the infamous House Un-American Activities Committee (HUAC) during the 1950s. To address this problem, the Supreme Court has required that each question the committee asks in such a situation be shown to serve a "legislative purpose" before the witness must respond to it.[15]

Advice and Consent: Special Senate Powers

The Constitution has given the Senate a special power, one that is not based on lawmaking. The president has the power to make treaties and to appoint top executive officers, ambassadors, and federal judges—but only "with the Advice and Consent of the Senate" (Article II, Section 2). For treaties, two-thirds of those present must concur; for appointments, a majority is required.

The power to approve or reject presidential requests also involves the power to set conditions. The Senate only occasionally exercises its power to reject treaties and appointments, and usually that is when opposite parties control the Senate and White House. During the final two years of President Reagan's term, Senate Democrats rejected Judge Robert Bork's Supreme Court nomination and gave clear indications that they would reject a second Reagan nominee, Judge Douglas Ginsburg, who withdrew his nomination before the Senate could act. During the first year of the Bush administration, the Senate rejected President Bush's nominee for defense secretary, John Tower. These instances, however, actually underscore the restraint with which the Senate usually uses its power to reject presidential requests. For example, only nine judicial nominees have been rejected by the Senate during the past century, while hundreds have been approved.

Most presidents make every effort to take potential Senate opposition into account in

---

[15]McGrain v. Dougherty, 273 U.S. 135 (1927).

Carol Moseley-Braun
Breaking Into the Club

Carol Moseley-Braun
(b. 1947)

One of the most distinctive milestones of the 1992 elections was the election of the first African American woman to the United States Senate.

Carol Moseley-Braun grew up on Chicago's South Side, graduated from the University of Illinois, and received her law degree from the University of Chicago. She began her career as an assistant attorney general and then won election to the Illinois state legislature, where she served for ten years. She was serving as recorder of deeds for Cook County in 1991 when, along with millions of other TV viewers, she became outraged at what she saw as the unfair treatment of Anita Hill by the all-white, all-male Senate Judiciary Committee during the Clarence Thomas nomination hearings. That outrage focused on Illinois's senior senator, Democrat Alan Dixon, who voted in favor of Thomas's confirmation.

Moseley-Braun entered the March Democratic primary against Dixon, despite the fact that the two-term senator had proven himself one of the state's biggest vote-getters; even the Republicans considered a challenge to Dixon all but futile. Despite the fact that she began with no budget, organization, or political backing, she launched a grass-roots campaign aimed at tapping into popular disaffection with a Senate viewed by many as, in Moseley-Braun's words, "an elitist club made up of mostly white male millionaires over fifty." In a stunning upset, the unknown Moseley-Braun defeated Dixon and another challenger by capitalizing on the nation's anti-incumbent disposition and by criticizing Dixon for his key support for Thomas. The primary victory catapulted Moseley-Braun into the national spotlight.

Moseley-Braun's candidacy was in keeping with the feeling that 1992 was the year of the outsider. She became an instant national celebrity and dominated the fall campaign, raising $5 million to finance her efforts and attracting large crowds in appearances around the state. She was careful to broaden her appeal in order to reach beyond the ethnic constituencies of Chicago, spending much of her time in predominantly white suburbs. Moseley-Braun's appeal was especially strong to women in a campaign year dubbed "the year of the woman."

Yet Moseley-Braun's campaign stumbled in early October when she was accused of mishandling a large sum of money that her ailing mother had received from the sale of some land. Moseley-Braun's Republican opponent, former Reagan administration aide Richard Williamson, sought to exploit the issues of ethics and credibility. Despite losing some support, Moseley-Braun won a decisive victory in November. Moseley-Braun promised to remain responsive to her constituents: "Elected officials have to be very clear that they are not leaders, but servants of the people."

Source: R. Darcy, Susan Welch, and Janet Clark, *Women, Elections, and Representation* (New York: Longman, 1987).

treaty negotiations and will frequently resort to "executive agreements" with foreign powers instead of treaties. The Supreme Court has held that such agreements are equivalent to treaties, but they do not need Senate approval.[16] In the past, presidents sometimes concluded secret agreements without informing Congress of the agreements' contents, or even their existence. American involvement in the Vietnam War grew in part out of a series of secret arrangements made between American presidents and the South Vietnamese during the 1950s and 1960s. Congress did not even learn of the existence of these agreements until 1969.

In 1972, Congress passed the Case Act, which required that the president inform Congress of any executive agreement within sixty days of its having been reached. This provides Congress with the opportunity to cancel agreements that it opposes. In addition, Congress can limit the president's ability to conduct foreign policy through executive agreement by refusing to appropriate the funds needed to implement an agreement. In this way, for example, executive agreements to provide American economic or military assistance to foreign governments can be modified or even canceled by Congress.

Direct Committee Government

Direct committee government refers to the practice of delegating certain congressional powers from the whole Congress to one of its committees. Each chamber can grant a committee the power to approve a proposed agency project without having to return to Congress for authorization and appropria-

tion. This device was widely used during the 1950s and early 1960s, when a great deal of money was spent on public works facilities for defense and space exploration. It was Congress's way of guaranteeing itself a role in handing out some choice projects to favored constituents.

The Legislative Veto

The legislative veto is a technique through which Congress grants the president the authority to act, but reserves the right to reject or override his actions if it is not satisfied with what he does. In 1932 and 1933, Congress granted the president the power to reorganize administrative agencies and departments. The president was required to submit a reorganization plan to Congress, and if it took no action within sixty days, the plan would go into effect. The law granting this power of overriding presidential action expired in 1973, but it was revived early in the Carter administration. Subsequently, the legislative veto was incorporated in a number of other statutes. In the 1983 case of *Immigration and Naturalization Service* v. *Chadha,* however, the Supreme Court held that the legislative veto was unconstitutional, primarily because it seemed to reverse the usual relationship between the president and Congress. That is, Congress was vetoing the executive branch rather than the other way around.[17]

Despite this Supreme Court decision, Congress has continued to enact—and the president to sign—statutes incorporating a modified legislative veto, the "committee veto," where presidential actions must be approved by a congressional committee. Be-

---

[16]U.S. v. Pink, 315 U.S. 203 (1942). For a good discussion of the problem, see James W. Davis, *The American Presidency* (New York: Harper & Row, 1987), Chapter 8.

[17]Immigration and Naturalization Services v. Chadha, 462 U.S. 919 (1983).

PROCESS BOX 5.2

How Members of Congress Represent Their Districts

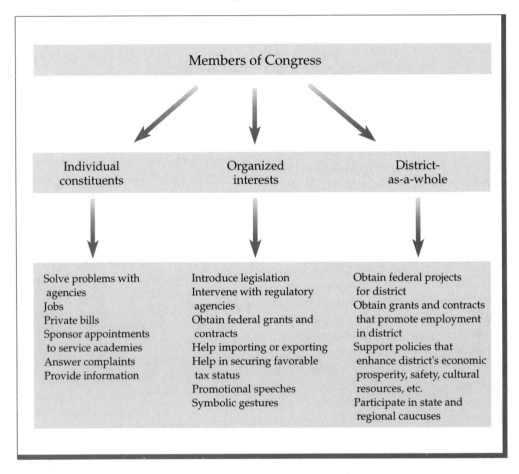

cause Congress sees the legislative veto as an important source of power, and the executive branch is willing to accept statutes containing the veto so long as the statute also delegates to the executive powers it seeks, Congress and the president have essentially ignored the Supreme Court on this question.

Direct Patronage

Another instrument of congressional power is direct patronage. Members of Congress often have an opportunity to provide direct benefits for their constituents. The most important of these opportunities for direct patronage is in legislation that has been described half-jokingly as the pork barrel. This type of legislation specifies the projects or other authorizations and the location within a particular district. Many observers of Congress argue that pork-barrel bills are the only ones that some members take seriously because they boost the members' reelection prospects. Often, congressional leaders will use pork-barrel projects in exchange for votes on other matters, and other members seek immortality through pork. The Mark Hatfield Marine Science Center in Oregon was built with funds obtained by Oregon's Senator Mark Hatfield. The Mildred and Claude Pepper fountain is the centerpiece of a Miami park project that had been strongly supported by the late Representative Claude Pepper. Federal dollars secured by Pennsylvania Representative Bud Shuster helped to build the Bud Shuster Byway, a four-lane highway serving Everett, Pennsylvania. The most important rule of pork-barreling is that any member of Congress whose district receives a project as part of a bill must support all the other projects on the bill. This cuts across party and ideological lines (see Box 5.2).

Another form of direct patronage is intervening with federal administrative agencies on behalf of constituents and supporters. Members of the House and Senate spend a great deal of time on the telephone and in administrative offices seeking to get them favorable treatment. A small but related form of patronage is getting an appointment to one of the military academies for the child of a constituent. Traditionally, these appointments are allocated one to a district.

Sometimes patronage can go too far. The case of the so-called Keating Five raised serious questions about the extent to which members of Congress could properly and legitimately seek to intervene with regulating agencies on a constituent's or a supporter's behalf. In this case, five senators— Alan Cranston (Democrat-California), Dennis DeConcini (Democrat-Arizona), John Glenn (Democrat-Ohio), John McCain (Republican-Arizona), and Donald Riegle (Democrat-Michigan)—came under scrutiny of the Senate Ethics Committee because of charges that they sought to pressure a federal regulatory agency to give lenient treatment to a savings and loan bank headed by Charles Keating, a generous political contributor. The bank later failed, at a cost to the government of more than $2 billion. Keating was charged with improperly using $1.1 billion in deposits for personal purposes and for company contributions. The Senate Ethics Committee recommended that the Senate censure Cranston for his role in the Keating affair, and he retired from the Senate when his term ended in 1992. The four other senators received only mild rebukes. Critics of the Senate process charged that the Ethics Committee had not gone nearly far enough in its investigations or recommendations for punishment.[18]

A different form of patronage is the private bill—a proposal to grant some kind of relief, special privilege, or exemption to the person named in the bill. The private bill is a type of legislation, but it should be distinguished from a public bill, which is supposed to deal with general rules and categories of behavior, people, and institutions.

As many as 75 percent of all private bills introduced (and one-third of the ones that pass) are concerned with providing relief for foreign nationals who cannot get permanent visas to the United States because the immigration quota for their country is filled or because of something unusual about their situation. Most of the other private bills are introduced to give money to individual citizens for injuries allegedly received from a public action or for a good deed that would have otherwise gone unrewarded. About 20 percent of those bills become law.[19]

[18] *Congressional Quarterly Weekly Report,* 27 January 1990, pp. 211–16.

[19] Congressional Quarterly, *Guide to the Congress of the United States,* 2nd. ed., pp. 229–310.

BOX 5.2
The Federal Pork Barrel

Public Law 101-101
101st Congress

An Act

Making appropriations for energy and water development for the fiscal year ending September 30, 1990, and for other purposes.

Be it enacted by the Senate and House of Representatives of the United States of America in Congress assembled, That the following sums are appropriated, out of any money in the Treasury not otherwise appropriated, for the fiscal year ending September 30, 1990, for energy and water development, and for other purposes, namely:

For the prosecution of river and harbor, flood control, shore protection, alteration and removal of obstructive bridges, and related projects authorized by laws; and detailed studies, and plans and specifications, of projects (including those for development with participation or under consideration for participation by States, local governments, or private groups) authorized or made eligible for selection by law (but such studies shall not constitute a commitment of the Government to construction), $997,400,000, of which such sums as are necessary pursuant to Public Law 99-662 shall be derived from the Inland Waterways Trust Fund, to remain available until expended: *Provided,* That with funds herein appropriated the Secretary of the Army, acting through the Chief of Engineers, is directed to undertake the following projects in fiscal year 1990 in the amounts specified:

Beaver Lake, Arkansas (Water Quality Enhancement), $1,100,000;
Red River Emergency Bank Protection, Arkansas and Louisiana, $2,000,000;
Westwego to Harvey Canal, Louisiana, Hurricane Protection, $1,100,000;
Atlantic Coast of Maryland, Maryland, $8,200,000;
Cape Girardeau-Jackson, Missouri, $500,000;
Missouri National Recreation River, Nebraska and South Dakota, $620,000;
Papillion Creek and Tributaries, Nebraska, $2,500,000;
Great Egg Harbor Inlet and Peck Beach, New Jersey, $250,000;
Shinnecock Inlet, New York, $5,300,000;
Roanoke River Upper Basin, Virginia, $200,000;
Kissimmee River, Florida, $4,000,000;
Sarasota County, Florida, $2,000,000;
Roseau River (Duxby Levee), Minnesota, $200,000;
Trimble Wildlife Area, Smithville Lake, Little Platte River, Missouri, $1,570,000;
Acequias Irrigation System, New Mexico, $2,000,000;
Grays Harbor, Washington, $13,000,000;
Small Boat Harbor, Buffalo Harbor, New York, $1,000,000.

[And many other projects.]

Private legislation is a congressional privilege that is often abused, but it is impossible to imagine members of Congress giving it up completely. It is one of the easiest, cheapest, and most effective forms of patronage available to each member.

The Fall and Rise of Congressional Power

Since Franklin D. Roosevelt expanded the power of the presidency at the time of the Depression, scholars have been proclaiming the era of presidential government and the demise of congressional power. Indeed, in 1965 one influential political scientist suggested that Congress consider abandoning its legislative efforts altogether, to focus more fully on constituency service and oversight.[20] Subsequent events, however, have shown that obituaries for congressional power were premature. Congress has been more than able to cope with presidential efforts to dominate the governmental process.

From the 1930s through the administration of Lyndon Johnson, the presidency seemed to be the dominant institution in American politics and government. Events that took place during the 1960s and 1970s, however, set the stage for a reassertion of congressional power. In this period, a number of new groups and forces emerged in American society and sought to change the focus and direction of American foreign and domestic policy. These groups, which formed "public interest" lobbies, included

blacks, women, upper-middle-class professionals (dubbed "yuppies" by the media and the "new class" by conservative sociologists). On such issues as the Vietnam War, civil rights, and women's rights, as well as environmental and consumer affairs, these new groups were intensely opposed to the policies and aims of the older coalition of forces—including organized labor, heavy industry, organized agriculture, and urban political machines—that had been closely linked to the presidency since the 1930s.

To counter their foes' links with the executive branch, the new forces of the 1960s and 1970s sought to use Congress as an institutional base. The Senate, in particular, proved to be receptive to these forces. Senators saw civil rights, antiwar, environmental, and consumer groups as potentially important sources of support for their own re-election efforts—and, perhaps, presidential bids. A number of senators became prominent spokespersons for these groups. Senate hearings on the Vietnam War, on threats to the environment, and on other issues gave the new political forces a forum in which to assert their claims.

As Congress began to serve these forces, they in turn became supporters of congressional power, ready to defend the powers of Congress—"their branch" of government—against executive encroachments. This development greatly enhanced the potential power of Congress, and as Congress continued to serve its new constituencies, it came into sharp conflict with the presidency and those groups in American society that supported presidential programs.

During the course of this conflict, which began during the Johnson administration and continues to this day, Congress sought to reassert some of the authority it lost to the

---

[20]Samuel Huntington, "Congressional Responses to the Twentieth Century," in *The Congress and America's Future*, ed. David Truman (Englewood Cliffs, NJ: Prentice-Hall, 1965), pp. 5–31.

executive branch during the previous thirty years.[21] The most dramatic illustration of this reassertion of power was, of course, the congressional investigation that led to President Nixon's resignation from office. Congress also enacted legislation and adopted practices designed to enhance its role in government and to diminish the power of the executive. For example, Congress adopted the War Powers Resolution (1973), intended to limit the president's ability to make unilateral foreign and military policy decisions by giving Congress a broader formal role in these areas. At the same time, Congress began writing laws that gave the executive branch very little discretion in its exercise of power. For example, the Endangered Species Act, the Campaign Finance Act (1974), and the various environmental and consumer safety acts adopted by Congress during the 1970s contain clear and specific instructions to the executive branch and leave little room for administrators to act on their own.

Congress also sought to strengthen its budgetary powers. The budget is always a central arena of conflict between Congress and the executive branch. Several presidents, most notably President Nixon, refused to spend money appropriated by Congress for programs they opposed—a tactic called *impoundment.* Congress responded with the Budget and Impoundment Control Act of 1974. This act was designed not only to inhibit the practice of impoundment but also to expand congressional budgetary powers more generally. The act limited the use of impoundment by requiring the president to spend any funds appropriated by Congress unless that body specifically agreed to cancel the expenditure.

The 1974 act also established two budget committees, one in the House and one in the Senate. The function of these committees was to allow Congress to coordinate the appropriations recommendations made by the other standing committees and to assess the relationship between expenditures and revenues. Prior to 1974, appropriations had been the domain of the appropriations committees, while revenue came under the supervision of the House Ways and Means and Senate Finance committees. By coordinating these functions, Congress hoped to acquire more control over the budget and more influence over presidential budget requests.

Finally, the 1974 act created the Congressional Budget Office (CBO) to give Congress expertise in economic analysis and forecasts. Before 1974, the Office of Management and Budget (OMB) in the executive branch had given the president a virtual monopoly over "the facts" upon which economic policy decisions were based. Under the terms of the Budget and Impoundment Control Act, Congress established a new, two-part budgetary process. First, each budget committee was to set target figures for taxing and spending. Second, the sum of the appropriations enacted by all other congressional committees was to be reconciled with the initial targets. Through this process, Congress sought to force itself to deal with national priorities in a coordinated way rather than merely succumbing to the pleas of an array of constituents.

As its creators had intended, this budget process gave Congress more power. Indeed, Congress, rather than the president, was the dominant budgetary actor during the Ford and Carter administrations. In the area of budgets, however, as in a number of other

[21]See James L. Sundquist, *The Decline and Resurgence of Congress* (Washington, DC: Brookings Institution, 1981).

areas, the Reagan administration was initially able to block the reassertion of congressional power and to force Congress back on the defensive. Reagan's enormous budget deficits made it impossible for Congress to propose new spending programs, and his promise to veto any tax increases made it impossible to enact new tax programs. In essence, congressional control of the budget became meaningless. At the same time, the Reagan administration undermined Congress's new foreign policy powers through *faits accomplis* such as the invasion of Grenada and the bombing of Libya. Not only was Congress ignored but it could not even oppose the president, because his actions turned out to be enormously popular. At the beginning of the Reagan era, the balance of power shifted back toward the executive branch.

But presidential power began to wane dramatically as Congress investigated the 1986 Iran-Contra affair, in which the Reagan administration had sold weapons to Iran in exchange for the promised release of several American hostages held in Lebanon. The profits from this sale were then illegally funneled to the Nicaraguan Contra rebels whom the administration supported in their campaign against the leftist Sandinista government in Nicaragua.

Over the next several years, Lawrence E. Walsh, the independent counsel appointed by the attorney general to investigate the administration's dealings with Iran, was able to secure indictments against a number of important Reagan administration officials, charging them with withholding information from Congress. However, all were pardoned by President Bush in December 1992, just before he left office. Undaunted, Walsh vowed that he would continue to focus his investigation on charges that, while serving as Reagan's vice-president, Bush had participated in discussions of the arms sales to Iran and then lied to Congress about his involvement. Thus, six years later, the Iran-Contra investigation continued to remind officials in the executive branch that the days of their unquestioned supremacy in the area of foreign policy were long past.

On the domestic front, when George Bush entered the White House in 1989, he inherited a massive deficit and a weakening economy, and Congress appeared to be in the driver's seat. In the fall of 1990, Bush and the congressional Democratic leadership engaged in a pitched battle over the 1991 federal budget. In the end, Bush was forced to renege on his campaign pledge of no new taxes—a pledge that had been a cornerstone of the Republican electoral strategy. The budget adopted for 1991 included tax increases that especially affected wealthier taxpayers, which permitted congressional Democrats to present themselves as friends of the common people and to depict the Republicans as protectors of millionaires. The budget compromise represented virtually a total victory for Congress and a major defeat for the president.

Following on the heels of its budget victory, Congress sought to challenge President Bush's Persian Gulf policies. Most members of Congress had initially expressed support for the president's decision to dispatch massive American forces to the Persian Gulf following Iraq's invasion of Kuwait in August 1990. By the end of the year, however, congressional leaders sought to constrain the president's ability to use these forces in combat, urging him instead to rely on diplomacy and economic sanctions to compel Iraq to withdraw from Kuwait. Congressional criticism, especially televised Senate hearings in December 1990, helped erode Bush's popular standing, al-

---

Congressional Term Limits: Remedy or Snake Oil?

*T*he idea of limiting by law or constitutional amendment the number of terms that a member of Congress may serve is not new, but in the 1990s it gained considerable momentum. In the 1992 elections, for example, fourteen states enacted some kind of measure to limit the terms of their national representatives.

Editorial-page writer John H. Fund argues that term limits will break the hold of political professionals and curtail the power of incumbency. Political scientist Charles R. Kesler asserts that such a move will only serve to make new members of Congress even more dependent on Washington professionals and will divert attention away from the real problems of Washington governance.

Fund

Not since Proposition 13 created a national tidal wave of tax protest has a political idea caught on with such speed. Polls show that over 70 percent of Americans back a limit on terms for elected officials. . . .

Term limits will encourage different people to run for office and pave the way for passage of other reforms—including rules to make legislative districts more competitive and reduce incumbent advantages in campaign financing. . . .

Franking privileges, huge staffs, liberal travel funds, easy access to the news media, and unfair campaign finance laws have all provided incumbents with a grossly unfair advantage. . . . The playing field must be made more level than it is now.

A limit on elected congressional and state legislative tenure would reduce the incentive for such abuses of power by eliminating congressional careerism. No longer would those political offices be held by longtime incumbents. They would be held by citizen-legislators, who would be more disposed to represent the will of the people and rein in the out-of-control bureaucracy that now substitutes for a federal government.

The idea of citizen-representatives serving a relatively short time is not new or radical. Although the writers of the Constitution did not see fit to include a term limitation, perhaps

---

most undermining the president's power to act in the crisis.

In January 1991, however, President Bush sought and received congressional approval for the use of military force against Iraq if it failed to honor the United Nations deadline of January 15 for an Iraqi withdrawal from Kuwait. This approval came by a very narrow margin in the Senate and a

somewhat more comfortable margin in the House, as enough moderate and conservative Democrats deserted their party's leadership to pass resolutions authorizing the use of force.

The complete success of the American military effort led to a surge of public support for President Bush. In the immediate aftermath of the war the president's popu-

that was because the public-service norm of those days did not include careerist senators and representatives. Instead, the attitude of that time can be seen in the decision of George Washington to voluntarily serve only two terms as president.

Term limitation is a traditional and uniquely American concept. Now it must be made mandatory instead of voluntary because the spirit of voluntary service limitation has obviously been lost.[1]

Kesler

Limiting congressional terms to 12 years will do little or nothing to remedy the situation [of problems with Congress]. Any new faces that are brought to Washington as the result of such an amendment will find themselves up against the same old incentives. They will still be eligible for reelection five times. How will they ensure their continued political prosperity without seeing to constituents' administrative needs? If anything, these new congressmen will find themselves confronting bureaucrats rendered more powerful by the representatives' own ignorance of the bureaucracy; for in the administrative state, knowledge is power. It is likely, therefore, that the new congressmen will initially be at a disadvantage relative to the agencies. To counter this they will seek staff members and advisers who are veterans of the Hill, and perhaps larger and more district-oriented staffs to help ward off challengers who would try to take advantage of their inexperience. Is it wise to increase the already expansive power of bureaucrats and congressional staff for the sake of a new congressman in the district every half-generation or so?

. . . [Term limits] could deprive the country of the experience and wisdom gained by an incumbent, perhaps just when that experience is needed most. This is particularly true for senators, whose terms would be limited even though Senate races are frequently quite competitive. . . . The pursuit of a constitutional amendment to limit congressional terms would act as a colossal distraction from the serious work of politics that needs to be done.[2]

[1] John H. Fund, "Term Limitation: An Idea Whose Time Has Come," Policy Analysis No. 141, Cato Institute, reprinted in Gerald Benjamin and Michael J. Malbin, eds., *Limiting Legislative Terms* (Washington, DC: Congressional Quarterly Press, 1992), pp. 225, 235–37.

[2] Charles R. Kesler, "Bad Housekeeping: The Case against Congressional Term Limits," *Policy Review* (Summer 1990), reprinted in Benjamin and Malbin, eds., *Limiting Legislative Terms*, pp. 247–49.

larity topped the 90 percent mark. Most members of Congress were compelled to declare their support for the president's war policies. Those who had opposed Bush before the war were left to explain their actions to suddenly hawkish constituents.

By the end of April, however, congressional Democrats began to turn public attention away from the Persian Gulf and back to domestic issues, such as health care and civil rights. Congress rejected the president's budgetary proposals and demanded higher levels of spending for domestic social programs. As the 102nd Congress resumed its work in the spring of 1991, Congress and the president continued to be locked in a struggle over control of the government. Congress had succeeded in stalemating presidential power without, however, developing a set of responses of its own to the nation's problems. Although Congress defeated President Bush on the 1991 budget, it really did nothing to solve the nation's deficit problem. The 1991 budget deficit grew to about $250 billion, and the 1992 deficit exceeded $300 billion.

After Bill Clinton's victory in 1992, congressional Democrats hoped that they would finally be in a position to enact programs and policies that would strengthen the Congress, their party, and the nation as a whole. Of course, congressional leaders were not prepared to permit an activist president—even a fellow Democrat—to run roughshod over them. The House and Senate leadership greeted Bill Clinton's request for the line-item veto, which would permit the president to veto portions of bills rather than accept or reject the entire bill, with the same lack of enthusiasm they had shown when Bush and Reagan made the same request.

Nevertheless, at the start of the Clinton administration, Congress seemed prepared to cooperate with the White House. For his part, Clinton signaled that he wanted to work closely with members of Congress by appointing Senator Lloyd Bentsen of Texas as treasury secretary, Representative Mike Espy of Mississippi as agriculture secretary, Representative Leon Panetta of California as director of the Office of Management and Budget, and Representative Les Aspin of Wisconsin as defense secretary. These appointments represented Clinton's strongest possible acknowledgment that support on Capitol Hill would be critical to the success of his administration.

Thus, at the beginning of a new Congress and a new presidency, members of both institutions seemed ready for a truce in their long struggle. Given the governmental framework created by the nation's founders, however, we should not expect this truce to last very long.

Congress: Freedom and Power

The struggle between Congress and the White House is one more illustration of the dilemma that lies at the heart of the American system of government. The framers of the Constitution checked and balanced a powerful Congress with a powerful executive. This was seen as a way of limiting the potential for abuse of governmental power and of protecting freedom. No doubt, it has this effect. Certainly, a vigilant Congress was able to curb presidential abuse of power during the Nixon era. Similarly, the executive branch under the leadership of President Eisenhower played a role in curbing congressional witch hunts ostensibly aimed at uncovering communist agents in the federal government, conducted by Senator Joseph McCarthy (Republican-Wisconsin) during the 1950s.

At the same time, however, the constant struggle between Congress and the president can hinder stable and effective governance. Over the past quarter century, in particular, Republican presidents and Democratic Congresses often seemed to be more interested in undermining one another than in promoting the larger public interest. On issues of social policy, economic policy, and foreign policy, Congress and the president have been at each other's throats while the nation suffered. As noted above, for example, this struggle between the White House and Capitol Hill is one reason that the United States presently faces a deficit crisis of unprecedented magnitude. We shall return to this point in Chapter 12.

Thus, we face a fundamental dilemma. A political arrangement designed to preserve freedom can undermine the government's power. Indeed, it can undermine the government's very capacity to govern. Must we always choose between freedom and power? Can we not have both? Let us turn now to the second branch of American government, the presidency, to view this dilemma from a somewhat different angle.

Time Line on Congress

EVENTS		INSTITUTIONAL DEVELOPMENTS
New Congress of U.S. meets for first time (1789)		Creation of House Ways and Means Committee (1789)
Jeffersonian party born in Congress (1792)		House committees develop. First procedural rules adopted—Jefferson's Rules (1790s)
	1800	Congressional party caucuses control presidential nominations (1804–1828)
		Congressional committees take control of legislative process. Rise of congressional government (1820s)
		Presidential nominating conventions replace caucuses (1831–1832)
Andrew Jackson renominated for president by Democratic party convention (1832)		
Whigs and Democrats struggle for power (1840s)		
Abraham Lincoln elected president (1860)	**1850**	
South secedes. Its delegation leaves Washington (1860–1861) period of Republican leadership (1860s)		No longer blocked by southerners, Congress adopts protective tariff, transcontinental railroad, Homestead Act, National Banking Act, Contract Labor Act (1861–1864)
Congress impeaches but does not convict Andrew Johnson (1868)		
		Filibuster develops as a tactic in the Senate (1880s)
Long era of Republican ascendancy begins (1897)	**1900**	House revolt against power of Speaker; rise of seniority system in House (1910)
Theodore Roosevelt makes U.S. a world power (1901–1909)		

EVENTS		INSTITUTIONAL DEVELOPMENTS
Democratic interlude with election of Woodrow Wilson (1913)		Seventeenth Amendment ratified; authorizes direct election of senators (1913)
Democrats take charge; Franklin Delano Roosevelt elected president (1932)		Rise of presidential government as Congress passes legislation putting into effect FDR's New Deal (1930s)
		Legislative Reorganization Act (1946)
		Regulation of lobbyists (1949)
	1950	Democratic Congresses pass laws expanding coverage of Social Security and federal expenditures for public health (1954–1959)
McCarthy hearings (1950s)		
		Use of legislative investigations as congressional weapon against executive (1950–1980s)
		Growing importance of incumbency (1960s–1980s)
	1970	
		Code of ethics adopted (1971)
Watergate hearings (1973–1974)		Campaign Finance Act (1974)
Richard Nixon resigns presidency (1974)		Congress given more power through Budget and Impoundment Act (1974)
		Filibuster reform (1975)
		Enactment of statutory limits on presidential power—War Powers Resolution (1973); Budget and Impoundment Control Act (1974); Amendments to Freedom of Information Act (1974); Ethics in Government Act (1978)
		Revival of party caucus and weakening of seniority rules (1970s–1980s)
Ronald Reagan elected president; begins conflict with Congress (1980)	**1980**	Gramm-Rudman Hollings Act (1985)

EVENTS		INSTITUTIONAL DEVELOPMENTS
Republicans temporarily take control of Senate (1980–1986)		Deficits impose budgetary limits on Congress (1980s and 1990s)
Iran-Contra hearings damage Reagan administration (1987)		
George Bush elected president (1988)		Intense conflict between president and Congress resulting from divided government (1980s and 1990s)
Democrats retain control of Congress (1990)	**1990**	
Congress defeats Bush in budget crisis (1990)		
Congress authorizes military action against Iraq (1991)		
		Pledges of new cooperation between Congress and White House; Congress considers giving president modified line-item veto (1993)
Democrats control Congress and White House for first time in 12 years; Republicans rely on Senate filibuster threat to influence Clinton program (1993)		Congress enacts new tax and deficit reduction programs (1993)

Chapter Review

The legislative process must provide the order necessary for legislation to take place amid competing interests. It is dependent on a hierarchical organizational structure within Congress. Six basic dimensions of Congress affect the legislative process: (1) the parties, (2) the committees, (3) the staff, (4) the caucuses, (5) the rules, and (6) the presidency.

Since the Constitution provides only for a presiding officer in each house, some method had to be devised for conducting business. Parties quickly assumed the responsibility for this. In the House, the majority party elects a leader every two years. This individual becomes Speaker. In addition, a majority leader and a minority leader

(from the minority party) and party whips are elected. Each party has a committee whose job it is to make committee assignments. Party structure in the Senate is similar, except that the vice-president of the United States is the Senate president.

While party voting regularity remains strong, party discipline has declined. Still, parties do have several means of maintaining discipline: (1) Favorable committee assignments create obligations. (2) Floor time in the debate on one bill can be allocated in exchange for a specific vote on another. (3) The whip system allows party leaders to assess support for a bill and convey their wishes to members. (4) Party leaders can help members create large logrolling coalitions. (5) The president, by identifying pieces of legislation as his own, can muster support along party lines. In most cases,party leaders accept constituency obligations as a valid reason for voting against the party position.

The committee system surpasses the party system in its importance in Congress. In the early nineteenth century, standing committees became a fundamental aspect of Congress. They have, for the most part, evolved to correspond to executive branch departments or programs and thus reflect and maintain the separation of powers.

The Senate has a tradition of unlimited debate, on which the various cloture rules it has passed have had little effect. Filibusters still occur. The rules of the House restrict talk and support committees; deliberation is recognized as committee business. The House Rules Committee has the power to control debate and floor amendments. The rules prescribe the formal procedure through which bills become law. Generally, the parties control scheduling and agenda, but the committees determine action on the floor. Committees, seniority, and rules all limit the ability of members to represent their constituents. Yet, these factors enable Congress to maintain its role as a major participant in government.

This power of the post–New Deal presidency does not necessarily signify the decline of Congress and representative government. During the 1970s Congress again became the "first branch" of government. During the early years of the Reagan administration, some of the congressional gains of the previous decade were diminished, but in the last two years of Reagan's second term, and in President Bush's term, Congress reasserted its role. At the start of the Clinton administration, congressional leaders promised to cooperate with the White House, rather than confront it.

For Further Reading

Arnold, R. Douglas. *Congress and the Bureaucracy.* New Haven: Yale University Press, 1979.

Arnold, R. Douglas. *The Logic of Congressional Action,* New Haven: Yale University Press, 1990.

Baker, Ross K. *House and Senate.* New York: W. W. Norton, 1989.

Burnham, James. *Congress and the American Tradition.* Chicago: Henry Regnery, 1965.

Clem, Alan L. *Congress: Powers, Processes and Politics.* Pacific Grove, CA: Brooks/Cole, 1989.

Congressional Quarterly. *Origins and Development of Congress.* Washington, DC: Congressional Quarterly Press, 1982.

Congressional Quarterly. *Powers of Congress.* Washington, DC: Congressional Quarterly Press, 1976.

Davidson, Roger, ed. *The Postreform Congress.* New York: St. Martin's Press, 1991.

Dodd, Lawrence, and Bruce J. Oppenheimer, eds. *Congress Reconsidered.* Washington, DC: Congressional Quarterly Press, 1988.

Fenno, Richard F. *Congressmen in Committees.* Boston: Little, Brown, 1973.

Fenno, Richard. *Homestyle: House Members in Their Districts.* Boston: Little, Brown, 1978.

Fiorina, Morris. *Congress: Keystone of the Washington Establishment.* New Haven: Yale University Press, 1977.

Fisher, Louis. *The Politics of Shared Power: Congress and the Executive.* Washington, DC: Congressional Quarterly Press, 1981.

Foreman, Christopher. *Signals from the Hill: Congressional Oversight and the Challenge of Social Regulation.* New Haven: Yale University Press, 1988.

Fowler, Linda, and Robert McClure. *Political Ambition: Who Decides to Run for Congress?* New Haven: Yale University Press, 1989.

Jacobson, Gary. *The Politics of Congressional Elections.* Boston: Little, Brown, 1983.

Leloup, Lance T. *Budgetary Politics.* Brunswick, OH: King's Court, 1986.

Light, Paul. *Forging Legislation.* New York: W. W. Norton, 1991.

Malbin, Michael. *Unelected Representatives: Congressional Staff and the Future of Representative Government.* New York: Basic Books, 1970.

Mayhew, David R. *Congress: The Electoral Connection.* New Haven: Yale University Press, 1974.

Oleszek, Walter J. *Congressional Procedures and the Policy Process.* Washington, DC: Congressional Quarterly Press, 1983.

Ornstein, Norman, and Shirley Elder. *Interest Groups, Lobbying and Policymaking.* Washington, DC: Congressional Quarterly Press, 1978.

Ornstein, Norman, et al. *Vital Statistics on Congress.* Washington, DC: Congressional Quarterly Press, 1987.

Peabody, Robert L. *Leadership in Congress.* Boston: Little, Brown, 1976.

Price, David. *Who Makes the Laws?: Creativity and Power in Senate Committees.* Cambridge: Schenkman, 1972.

Rieselbach, Leroy. *Congressional Reform.* Washington, DC: Congressional Quarterly Press, 1986.

Ripley, Randall. *Congress: Process and Policy.* New York: W. W. Norton, 1988.

Schick, Allen, ed. *Making Economic Policy in Congress.* Washington, DC: American Enterprise Institute, 1983.

Sinclair, Barbara. *Majority Leadership in the U.S. House.* Baltimore: Johns Hopkins University Press, 1983.

Sinclair, Barbara. *The Transformation of the U.S. Senate.* Baltimore: Johns Hopkins University Press, 1989.

Smith, Steven S., and Christopher Deering. *Committees in Congress.* Washington, DC: Congressional Quarterly Press, 1984.

Strahan, Randall. *New Ways and Means: Reform and Change in a Congressional Committee.* Chapel Hill: University of North Carolina Press, 1990.

Sundquist, James L. *The Decline and Resurgence of Congress.* Washington, DC: Brookings Institution, 1981.

6

THE PRESIDENT AND THE EXECUTIVE BRANCH

*G*eorge Bush spent eight years in the vice-presidency as a "yes man" to President Reagan. When campaigning for president in 1988, he was plagued by suspicions and allegations that he was a wimp. Even his most memorable 1988 campaign pledge, "Read my lips, no new taxes," seemed to be no more than a commitment to continue the policies of the Reagan administration. Yet, as soon as he was inaugurated in January 1989, President Bush became a strong chief executive. And he continued to be a strong president even through his seventy-nine days as a "lame duck" following his defeat on November 3, 1992. He committed over 25,000 U.S. troops to Somalia and brought along with him U.N. sponsorship and the contributions of the troops, supplies, and political support of thirty-four other countries. Bush, the wimp of the 1980s, did not become a strong president through an assertiveness-training program. Bush became a strong president, and remained strong despite declining polls and electoral defeat, because the presidency is strong. And President Clinton inherited this strong presidency in 1993. A strong presidency no longer depends on its occupant; its strength has become institutionalized.

Presidential supremacy, or "presidential government," dates only from the late 1930s. How presidential supremacy developed, its sources, and its problems will be the focus of this chapter. We will divide the discussion into three sections. First, we will review the constitutional origins of the presidency, especially the constitutional basis for the president's foreign and domestic roles. Second, we will review the history of the American presidency to see how the office has evolved from its original status under the Constitution. We will look particularly at the way in which Congress has added to the president's constitutional powers by deliberately delegating to the presidency some of its own responsibilities. Third, we will assess both the formal and the informal means that presidents seek to enhance their own ability to govern, including their efforts to build popular support. We will close the chapter with a look at how the presidency and the American system of government have tried to adapt the vast apparatus of the national government to the requirements of a representative democracy.

The Constitutional Basis of the Presidency

Although Article II of the Constitution, which establishes the presidency, has been called "the most loosely drawn chapter of the Constitution,"[1] the framers were neither indecisive nor confused. They held profoundly conflicting views of the executive branch, and Article II was probably the best compromise they could make. The formulation the framers agreed upon is magnificent in its ambiguity: "The executive power shall be vested in a President of the United States of America" (Article II, Section 1, first sentence). The meaning of "executive power," however, is defined only indirectly in the

very last sentence of Section 3, which provides that the president "shall take Care that the Laws be faithfully executed."[2]

One very important conclusion can be drawn from these two provisions. The office of the president was to be an office of *delegated powers.* Since, as we have already seen, the Constitution defines all of the powers of the national government as powers of Congress, then "executive power" must be understood as the power to execute faithfully the laws *as they are adopted by Congress.* This does not doom the presidency to weakness. Presumably, Congress can pass laws delegating almost any of its powers to the president. But presidents are not free to discover sources of executive power completely independent of the laws passed by Congress. In the 1890 case of *In re Neagle,* the Supreme Court did hold that the president could be bold and expansive in his view of the Constitution as to "the rights, duties and obligations" of the presidency; but the powers of the president would have to come from the Constitution and laws and not from some independent or absolute idea of executive power.[3]

Immediately following the first sentence of Section 1, Article II defines the manner in which the president is to be chosen. This is

---

[1] E. S. Corwin, *The President: Office and Powers,* 3d rev. ed. (New York: New York University Press, 1957), p. 2.

[2] There is a Section 4, but all it does is to define impeachment.

[3] In re Neagle, 135 U.S. 1 (1890). Neagle, a deputy U.S. marshal, had been authorized by the president to protect a Supreme Court justice whose life had been threatened by an angry litigant. When the litigant attempted to carry out his threat, Neagle shot and killed him. Neagle was then arrested by the local authorities and tried for murder. His defense was that his act was "done in pursuance of a law of the United States." Although the law was not an act of Congress, the Supreme Court declared that it was an executive order of the president, and the protection of a federal judge was a reasonable extension of the president's power to "take care that the laws be faithfully executed." See Chapter 7 for a more detailed account of the bizarre facts underlying *In re Neagle.*

a very odd sequence, but it does say something about the struggle the delegates were having over how to give power to the executive and at the same time to balance that power with limitations. The struggle was between those delegates who wanted the president to be selected by Congress, and thus responsible to it, and those delegates who preferred that the president be elected directly by the people. Direct popular elections would create a more independent and more powerful presidency. The framers finally agreed on a scheme of indirect election through an electoral college in which the electors would be selected by the state legislatures (and close elections would be resolved in the House of Representatives). In this way the framers hoped to achieve a "republican" solution: a strong president responsible to state and national legislators rather than directly to the electorate.

The heart of presidential power as defined by the Constitution is found in Sections 2 and 3, where several clauses define the presidency in two dimensions: the president as head of state and the president as head of government. Although these will be given separate treatment, the presidency can be understood only by the combination of the two.

The President as Head of State: Some Imperial Qualities

The position of the president as head of state is defined by three constitutional provisions, which are the source of some of the most important powers on which presidents can draw. The areas covered by these provisions can be classified as:

1. *Military.* Article II, Section 2, provides for the power as "Commander in Chief of the Army and Navy of the United States, and of the Militia of the several States,

when called in to the actual Service of the United States."

2. *Judicial.* Article II, Section 2, also provides the power to "grant reprieves and pardons for Offenses against the United States, except in Cases of impeachment."

3. *Diplomatic.* Article II, Section 3, provides the power to "receive Ambassadors and other public ministers."

MILITARY. The position of commander in chief makes the president the highest military officer in the United States, giving him control of the entire military establishment. The preference for civilian control of the military is so strong in America, however, that no president would dare put on a military uniform for a state function—not even a former general like Eisenhower. The president is also the head of the secret intelligence hierarchy, which includes not only the Central Intelligence Agency (CIA) but also the National Security Council (NSC), the National Security Agency, the Federal Bureau of Investigation (FBI), and a host of less well-known but very powerful international and domestic security agencies.

JUDICIAL. The presidential power to grant reprieves, pardons, and amnesties involves the power of life and death over all individuals who may be a threat to the security of the United States. Presidents may use this power on behalf of a particular individual, as did Gerald Ford when he pardoned Richard Nixon in 1974 "for all offenses against the United States which he . . . has committed or may have committed." Or they may use it on a large scale, as did President Andrew Johnson in 1868, when he gave full amnesty to all southerners who had participated in the "Late Rebellion," and President Carter in 1977, when he declared an amnesty for all the draft evaders of the Vietnam War. President Bush used this power before

Andrew Jackson
"King Andrew the First"

If the Constitution that took effect in 1789 provided the forms of democracy, many of the realities of democracy were not realized until forty years later with the election of the seventh president. Andrew Jackson did not set out to remake American politics, yet that is what he did.

Born in the South Carolina backwoods, the son of Irish immigrants, Jackson fought in a Revolutionary War battle at the young age of twelve. Jackson won election to the House of Representatives when Tennessee was admitted as a state in 1796. The following year, he served briefly in the Senate. He established his military reputation by successfully defending New Orleans from British assault during the War of 1812 (although the battle was fought after the war had ended).

Jackson then turned his ambitions to national politics. In the election of 1824, he outpolled his three rivals, but since no candidate received a majority of electoral college votes, the election was thrown into the House of Representatives where the election swung to John Quincy Adams. Four years later, Jackson swept into office as the first non-aristocrat from a state other than Massachusetts or Virginia by arousing mass sentiment against the Washington cabals and thus quadrupling his popular vote. During the next four years, Jackson and his allies persuaded the states to eliminate property qualifications for voting, establishing universal white male suffrage.

In addition to the extension of voting rights, the spread of "Jacksonian democracy" was marked by adoption of the more open political party nominating convention, by which Jackson was

Andrew Jackson
(1767-1845)

renominated in 1832 (eliminating the more elitist caucus method of nomination). He succeeded in dismantling the Bank of the United States, regarded by common people as an institution to serve the privileged. He challenged the ascendence of Congress and waged political war by using his veto to block the bank and internal improvement projects.

Jackson's actions caused an uproar in Washington but fanned his popularity in the country. Viewing the election of 1832 as a referendum on his policies, Jackson won handily, carrying the electoral votes of 17 of 24 states. In 1834, the Senate formally voted to censure Jackson for actions taken to dismantle the bank. Yet, Jackson continued to challenge congressional control over executive agencies and national policy, winning him the sarcastic nickname "King Andrew the First." Jackson successfully used his popularity as a lever to expand the power of the presidential office, establishing precedents that would open the door to the modern strong presidency. Jackson retired from office in 1836, and died in 1845.

Source: Arthur M. Schlesinger, Jr., *The Age of Jackson* (Boston: Little, Brown, 1945).

his retirement in mid-December 1992, when he pardoned former Secretary of Defense Caspar Weinberger and five other participants in the Iran-Contra affair. This power of life and death over others has helped elevate the president to the level of earlier conquerors and kings by establishing him as the person before whom supplicants might come to make their pleas for mercy.

DIPLOMATIC. When President George Washington received Edmond Genêt ("Citizen Genêt") as the formal emissary of the revolutionary government of France in 1793, he transformed the power to "receive Ambassadors and other public ministers" into the power to "recognize" other countries. That power gives the president the almost unconditional authority to review the claims of any new ruling groups to determine if they indeed control the territory and population of their country, so that they can commit it to treaties and other agreements. Critics questioned the wisdom of President Franklin Roosevelt's exchange of ambassadors with the Soviet Union fifteen years after the Russian Revolution in 1917.

They also questioned the wisdom of President Nixon's recognition of the People's Republic of China and of President Carter's recognition of the Sandinista government in Nicaragua. But they did not question the president's authority to make such decisions. Because the breakup of the Soviet bloc countries was generally perceived as a positive event, no one criticized Bush for his quick recognition of the several former Soviet and Yugoslav republics as soon as they declared themselves independent states. And few would not approve of President Clinton recognizing the two new republics that came into being in January 1993 when Czechoslovakia divided into the Czech Republic and Slovakia.

Have presidents used these three constitutional powers—military, judicial, and diplomatic—to make the presidency too powerful, indeed "imperial"?[4] Debate over the answer to this question has produced an unusual lineup, with presidents and the Supreme Court on one side and Congress on the other. The Supreme Court supported the expansive view of the presidency in three historically significant cases. The first was *In re Neagle,* discussed above. The second was the 1956 *Curtiss-Wright* case in which the Court held that Congress may delegate a degree of discretion to the president in foreign affairs.[5] In the third case, *U.S. v. Pink,* the Supreme Court upheld the president's power to use executive agreements to conduct foreign policy.[6] An *executive agreement* is exactly like a treaty because it is a contract between two countries; but an executive agreement does not require a two-thirds vote of approval by the Senate. Ordinarily, executive agreements are used to carry out commitments already made in

[4] Arthur M. Schlesinger, Jr., *The Imperial Presidency* (Boston: Houghton Mifflin, 1973).

[5] U.S. v. Curtiss-Wright Export Corp., 299 U.S. 304 (1936). In 1934, Congress passed a joint resolution authorizing the president to prohibit the sale of military supplies to Bolivia and Paraguay, who were at war, if the president determined that the prohibition would contribute to peace between the two countries. When prosecuted for violating the embargo order by President Roosevelt, the defendants argued that Congress could not constitutionally delegate such broad discretion to the president. The Supreme Court disagreed. Previously, however, the Court had rejected the National Industrial Recovery Act precisely because Congress had delegated too much discretion to the president in a domestic policy, see Schechter Poultry Corp. v. U.S., 295 U.S. 495 (1936).

[6] In United States v. Pink, 315 U.S. 203 (1942), the Supreme Court confirmed that an executive agreement is the legal equivalent of a treaty, despite the absence of Senate approval. This case approved the executive agreement that was used to establish diplomatic relations with the Soviet Union in 1933. An executive agreement was used in 1940 to exchange "fifty over-age destroyers" for ninety-nine-year leases on some important military bases.

treaties, or to arrange for matters well below the level of policy. But when presidents have found it expedient to use an executive agreement in place of a treaty, the Court has gone along. This verges on an imperial power.

The Domestic Presidency: The President as Head of Government

The constitutional basis of the domestic presidency also has three parts. Here again, although real power grows out of the combination of the parts, the analysis is greatly aided by examining the parts separately:

1. *Executive.* The "executive power" is vested in the president by Article II, Section 1, to see that all the laws are faithfully executed (Section 3), and under Article II, Section 2, to appoint and supervise all executive officers and to appoint all federal judges.

2. *Military.* This power is derived from Article IV, Section 4, which stipulates that the president has the power to protect every state "against Invasion . . . and against domestic Violence."

3. *Legislative.* The president is given the power under various provisions to participate effectively and authoritatively in the legislative process.

EXECUTIVE POWER. The most important basis of the president's power as chief executive is to be found in the sections of Article II which stipulate that the president must see that all the laws are faithfully executed, and which provide that the president will appoint all executive officers and all federal judges. In this manner, the Constitution focuses executive power and legal responsibility upon the president. The famous sign on President Truman's desk, "The buck stops here," was not a mere assertion of President Truman's personal sense of re-

sponsibility. It acknowledged his acceptance of the constitutional imposition of that responsibility upon the president. The president is subject to some limitations, because the appointment of all the top officers, including ambassadors and ministers and federal judges, is subject to a majority approval by the Senate. But these appointments are at the discretion of the president. Although the Constitution is silent on the power of the president to remove such officers, the federal courts have filled this silence with a series of decisions that grant the president this power.[7]

MILITARY SOURCES OF DOMESTIC PRESIDENTIAL POWER. Although Article IV, Section 4, provides that the "United States shall protect every State . . . against Invasion and . . . domestic Violence," Congress has made this an explicit presidential power through statutes directing the president as commander-in-chief to discharge these obligations.[8] The Constitution restrains the president's use of domestic force by providing that a state legislature (or governor when the legislature is not in session) must request federal troops before the president can send them into the state to provide public order. Yet, this proviso is not absolute. First, presidents are not obligated to deploy national troops merely because the state legislature or governor makes such a request. And more important, presidents may deploy troops in a state or city without a spe-

---

[7] Myers v. U.S., 272 U.S. 114 (1926); modified by Humphrey's Executor v. U.S., 295 U.S. 602 (1935), Wiener v. U.S., 357 U.S. 349 (1958), Bowsher v. Synar, 478 U.S. 714 (1986), and Morrison v. Olson, 108 S.Ct. 2579 (1988). See also Michael Nelson, ed., "The Removal Power," in *Congressional Quarterly's Guide to the Presidency* (Washington, DC: Congressional Quarterly Press, 1989), pp. 414–15.

[8] These statutes are contained mainly in Title 10 of the United States Code, Sections 331, 332, and 333.

cific request if they consider it necessary to maintain an essential national service, to enforce a federal judicial order, or to protect federally guaranteed civil rights.

A famous example of the unilateral use of presidential power to protect the states against domestic disorder occurred in 1957 under President Eisenhower. He decided to send troops into Little Rock, Arkansas, literally against the wishes of the state of Arkansas, to enforce court orders to integrate Little Rock's Central High School. Arkansas Governor Orval Faubus had actually posted National Guardsmen at the entrance of the school to prevent the court-ordered admission of nine black students. After an effort to negotiate with Governor Faubus failed, President Eisenhower reluctantly sent a thousand paratroopers to Little Rock, who stood watch while the black students took their places in the all-white classrooms. This case makes quite clear that the president does not have to wait for a decision of a state legislature or governor before acting as domestic commander in chief.[9] However, in most instances of domestic disorder—whether from human or from natural causes—presidents tend to exercise unilateral power justified by declaring a "state of emergency," thereby making available federal grants, insurance, and direct assistance as well as troops. In 1992, in the aftermath of the riots in Los Angeles and the devastating storms in Florida, American troops were very much in evidence—but in the role more of Good Samaritan than of military police.

THE PRESIDENT'S LEGISLATIVE POWER. The president plays a role not only in the administration of government but also in the legislative process. Two constitutional provisions are the primary sources of the president's power in the legislative arena. Article II, Section 3, provides that the president "shall from time to time give to the Congress Information of the State of the Union, and recommend to their consideration such measures as he shall judge necessary and expedient." The second of the president's legislative powers is the "veto power" assigned the president by Article I, Section 7.[10]

The first of these has been important only since Franklin Delano Roosevelt began to use the provision to initiate proposals for legislative action in Congress. Roosevelt established the presidency as the primary initiator of legislation. The second, the veto power, alone makes the president the most important single legislative leader. No bill vetoed by the president can become law unless both the House and the Senate override the veto by a two-thirds vote. Taking these two sources of power together—the president's constitutional duty to address Congress on the state of the union and rec-

---

[9]The best study covering all aspects of the domestic use of the military is that of Adam Yarmolinsky, *The Military Establishment* (New York: Harper & Row, 1971).

[10]There is a third source of presidential power implied from the provision for "faithful execution of the laws." This is the president's power to impound funds—that is, to refuse to spend money Congress has appropriated for certain purposes. One author referred to this as a "retroactive veto power." (Robert E. Goosetree, "The Power of the President to Impound Appropriated Funds," *American University Law Review,* January 1962.) This impoundment power was used freely and to considerable effect by many modern presidents, and Congress occasionally delegated such power to the president by statute. But reacting to the Watergate scandal, Congress adopted the Budget and Impoundment Control Act of 1974 and designed this act to circumscribe the president's ability to impound funds by requiring that the president must spend all appropriated funds unless both Houses of Congress consent to an impoundment within forty-five days of a presidential request. Therefore, since 1974, the use of impoundment has declined significantly. Presidents have either had to bite their tongues and accept unwanted appropriations or to revert to the older and more dependable but politically limited method of vetoing the entire bill.

The Veto
How a Bill Is Born, Dies, Is Reborn, Becomes Law (or Not)

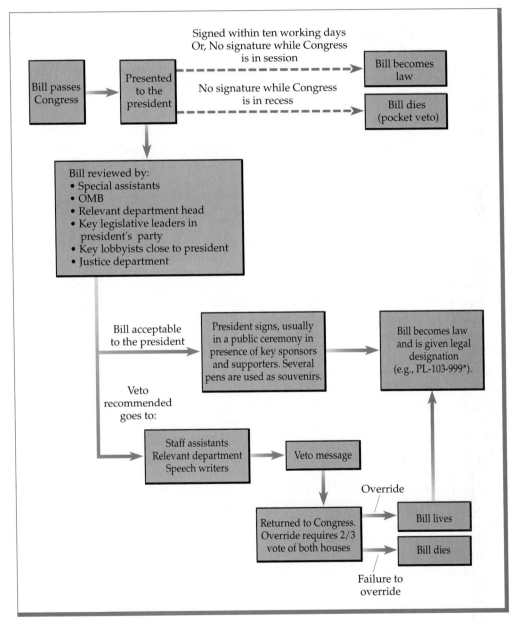

*PL = Public Law; 103 = Number of Congress (103rd is 1993 – 94); 999 = the actual law.

DEBATING THE ISSUES

Presidential Power: Broad or Narrow?

*P*residents and pundits have debated the proper scope of presidential power since the founding of
the Republic. Some have argued that the Constitution provides broad latitude for presidents to
act as they think best; others have asserted that presidents must be mindful of constitutional and
political limitations in a three-branch system of government. In the twentieth century, the argument
for a strong presidency has carried more weight. Yet in the face of such abuses of presidential power
as Watergate and Iran-Contra, some have argued for a return to a more limited view of the presidency.

 *The first elected president of this century, Theodore Roosevelt, described in his autobiography his
support for expansive presidential authority. Roosevelt's successor, William Howard Taft, summarized the arguments for presidential restraint. Their views are as timely today as a century ago.*

Roosevelt

My view was that every executive officer, and above all every executive officer in high
position, was a steward of the people bound actively and affirmatively to do all he could for
the people, and not to content himself with the negative merit of keeping his talents
undamaged in a napkin. I declined to adopt the view that what was imperatively necessary
for the nation could not be done by the president unless he could find some specific
authorization to do it. My belief was that it was not only his right but his duty to do anything

---

ommend action and the president's veto
power—it is remarkable that it took so long
(well over a century) for these constitutional
powers to be fully realized. Let us see how
this happened as well as why it took so long.

The Rise of Presidential Government

Most of the real power of the modern presidency comes from the powers granted by
the Constitution and the laws made by Congress.[11] Thus, any person properly elected
and sworn in as president will possess all of

the power held by the strongest presidents
in American history. That is true regardless
of how large or small a margin of victory a
president has. *The popular base of the presidency is important less because it gives the president power than because it gives him consent to
use all the powers already vested by the Constitution in the office.* Anyone installed in the
office could exercise most of its powers.

 The presidency is a democratic institution. Although the office is not free from the
influence of powerful interests in society,
neither is it a product or a captive of any one
set of interests. Its broad popular base is a
great resource for presidential power. *But
resources are not power.* They must be converted to power, and as in physics, energy
is expended in the conversion. It took more
than a century, perhaps as much as a cen-

---

[11]This very useful distinction between pow*er* and pow*ers* is
inspired by Richard Neustadt, *Presidential Power* (New York:
Wiley, 1960), p. 28.

that the needs of the nation demanded unless such action was forbidden by the Constitution or by the laws. Under this interpretation of executive power I did and caused to be done many things not previously done by the president and the heads of the departments. I did not usurp power, but I did greatly broaden the use of executive power. In other words, I acted for the public welfare, I acted for the common well-being of all our people, whenever and in whatever manner was necessary, unless prevented by direct constitutional or legislative prohibition.[1]

Taft

The true view of the executive functions is, as I conceive it, that the president can exercise no power which cannot be fairly and reasonably traced to some specific grant of power or justly implied and included within such express grant as proper and necessary to its exercise. Such specific grant must be either in the federal Constitution or in an act of Congress passed in pursuance thereof. There is no undefined residuum of power which he can exercise because it seems to him to be in the public interest, and there is nothing in the . . . law of the United States, or in other precedents, warranting such an inference. The grants of executive power are necessarily in general terms in order not to embarrass the executive within the field of action plainly marked for him, but his jurisdiction must be justified and vindicated by affirmative constitutional or statutory provision, or it does not exist.[2]

[1]*The Autobiography of Theodore Roosevelt* (New York: Scribner's, 1958), pp. 197–200.
[2]William Howard Taft, *Our Chief Magistrate and His Powers* (New York: Columbia University Press, 1916), pp. 138–45.

tury and a half, before presidential government came to replace congressional government. A bit of historical review will be helpful in understanding how presidential government arose.

The Legislative Epoch, 1800–1933

In 1885, political science professor Woodrow Wilson entitled his general textbook *Congressional Government* because American government was just that, "congressional government" (see Chapter 5). This characterization seemed to fly in the face of the separation of powers principle that three separate branches were and ought to be equal. Nevertheless, the clear intent of the Constitution was for *legislative supremacy*. As we saw in Chapter 3, the strongest evidence of this original intent is the fact that the powers of the national government were listed in Article I, the legislative article. Madison had laid it out explicitly in *The Federalist*, No. 51: "In republican government, the legislative authority necessarily predominates."

The first decade of our government was unique precisely because it was first; everything was precedent making, and nothing was secure. It was a state-building decade in which relations between president and Congress were more cooperative than they were going to be at any time thereafter. Before the Republic was a decade old, Congress began to develop a strong organization, including its own elected leadership, the first standing committees, and the party hierarchies. Consequently, by the second term of President Jefferson (1805), the executive branch was beginning to play the secondary role anticipated by the Constitution. The quality of presidential performance and then of presidential personality and character declined accordingly. The president was seen by some observers as little more than America's "chief clerk." Of President James Madison, who had been the principal author of the Constitution, it was said that he knew everything about government except how to govern. Indeed, after Jefferson and until the beginning of this century, most historians agree that Presidents Jackson and Lincoln were the only exceptions to what was the rule of weak presidents; and those two exceptions can be explained, since one was a war hero and founder of the Democratic party and the other was a wartime president and first leader of the newly founded Republican party.

One reason that so few great men became presidents in the nineteenth century is that there was only occasional room for greatness in such a weak office.[12] As Chapter 3 indicated, the national government of that period was not particularly powerful. Another reason is that during this period the presidency was not closely linked to major national political and social forces. Federalism had taken very good care of this by fragmenting political interests and diverting the energies of interest groups toward the state and local levels of government, where most key decisions were being made.

The presidency was strengthened somewhat in the 1830s with the introduction of the national convention system of nominating presidential candidates. Until then,

presidential candidates had been nominated by their party's congressional delegates. This was the "caucus" system of nominating candidates, and it was derisively called "King Caucus" because any candidate for president had to defer to his party's leaders in Congress if he was to succeed in getting the party's nomination and the support of the party's congressional delegation in the election. The national nominating convention arose outside Congress in order to provide some representation for a party's voters who lived in districts where they weren't numerous enough to elect a member of Congress. The political party in each state made its own provisions for selecting delegates to attend the presidential nominating convention, and in virtually all states the selection was dominated by the party leaders (called "bosses" by the opposition party). Only in recent decades have state laws intervened to regularize the selection process and provide (in all but a few instances) for open election of delegates.

In the nineteenth century, the national nominating convention was seen as a victory for democracy against the congressional elite. And the national convention gave the presidency a base of power independent of Congress. Eventually, though more slowly, the presidential selection process began to be further democratized, with the adoption of primary elections through which millions of ordinary citizens were given an opportunity to take part in the presidential nominating process by popular selection of convention delegates.

This independence did not immediately transform the presidency into the office we recognize today, because Congress was able to keep tight reins on the president's power. The real turning point came during the administration of Franklin Delano Roosevelt.

---

[12]For a related appraisal, see Jeffrey Tulis, *The Rhetorical Presidency* (Princeton: Princeton University Press, 1988).

The New Deal was a response to the political forces that had been gathering national strength and focus for fifty years. What is remarkable is not that they gathered but that they were so long gaining influence in Washington.

The New Deal and the Presidency

The "First Hundred Days" of the Roosevelt administration in 1933 had no parallel in U.S. history. But this period was only the beginning. The policies proposed by President Roosevelt and adopted by Congress during the first thousand days so changed the size and character of the national government that they constitute a moment in American history equivalent to the founding or to the Civil War. The president's constitutional obligation to see "that the laws be faithfully executed" became virtually a responsibility to *shape* the laws before executing them.

NEW PROGRAMS EXPAND THE ROLE OF NATIONAL GOVERNMENT. Many of the New Deal programs were extensions of the traditional national government approach, which was described in Chapter 3 (see especially Table 3.1). But the New Deal also adopted policies never before tried on a large scale by the national government. It began intervening into economic life in ways that had hitherto been reserved to the states. In other words, the national government discovered that it, too, had "police power" and could directly regulate individuals as well as provide roads and other services.

The new programs were such dramatic departures from the traditional policies of the national government that their constitutionality was in doubt. The turning point came in 1937 with *National Labor Relations*

Board v. *Jones & Laughlin Steel Corporation*. At issue was the National Labor Relations Act, or Wagner Act, which prohibited corporations from interfering with the efforts of employees to engage in union activities. The newly formed National Labor Relations Board (NLRB) had ordered Jones & Laughlin to reinstate workers fired because of their union activities. The appeal reached the Supreme Court because Jones & Laughlin had made a constitutional issue over the fact that its manufacturing activities were local and therefore beyond the national government's reach. The Supreme Court rejected this argument with the response that a big company with subsidiaries and suppliers in many states was innately in interstate commerce.[13] Since the end of the New Deal, the Supreme Court has never again questioned the constitutionality of an important act of Congress authorizing the executive branch to intervene into the economy or society.[14]

---

[13]NLRB v. Jones & Laughlin Steel Corporation, 301 U.S. 1 (1937). Congress had attempted to regulate the economy before 1933, as with the Interstate Commerce Act and Sherman Antitrust Act of the late nineteenth century and with the Federal Trade Act and the Federal Reserve in the Wilson period. But these were rare attempts, and each, very carefully, was restricted to a narrow and acceptable definition of "interstate commerce." The big break did not come until after 1933.

[14]Some will argue that there are at least two exceptions to this statement. One was the 1976 case declaring unconstitutional Congress's effort to supply national minimum wage standards to state and local government employees (National League of Cities v. Usery, 426 U.S. 833 [1976]). But the Court reversed itself nine years later, in 1985 (Garcia v. San Antonio Metropolitan Transit Authority, 469 U.S. 528 [1985]). The second was the 1986 case declaring unconstitutional the part of the Gramm-Rudman law authorizing the Comptroller General to make "across the board" budget cuts when total appropriations exceeded legally established ceilings (Bowsher v. Synar, 92 L. Ed. 583 [1986]). But cases such as these are few and far between, and they only touch on part of a law, not the constitutionality of the entire program.

DELEGATION OF POWER. The most important constitutional effect of Congress's actions and the Supreme Court's approval of those actions during the New Deal was the enhancement of *presidential power*. Most major acts of Congress in this period involved significant exercises of control over the economy. But few programs specified the actual controls to be used. Instead, Congress authorized the president or, in some cases, a new agency to determine what the controls would be. Some of the new agencies were independent commissions responsible to Congress. But most of the new agencies and programs of the New Deal were placed in the executive branch directly under presidential authority.

This form of congressional act is called the "delegation of power." In theory, the delegation of power works as follows: (1) Congress recognizes a problem; (2) Congress acknowledges that it has neither the time nor the expertise to deal with the problem; and (3) Congress therefore sets the basic policies and then delegates to an agency the power to "fill in the details." But in practice, Congress was delegating not merely the power to "fill in the details," but actual and real *policy-making powers,* that is, real legislative powers, to the executive branch.

No modern government can avoid the delegation of significant legislative powers to the executive branch. But the fact remains that these delegations of power cumulatively produced a fundamental shift in the American constitutional framework. *During the 1930s, the growth of the national government through acts delegating legislative power tilted the American national structure away from a Congress-centered government toward a president-centered government.* Congress continues to be the constitutional source of pol-

icy, and Congress can rescind these delegations of power or restrict them with later amendments, committee oversight, or budget cuts. But since Congress has continued to enact large new programs involving very broad delegations of legislative power to the executive branch, and since the Court has gone along with such actions,[15] we can say that presidential government has become an established fact of American life.

Presidential Government

There was no great mystery in the shift from Congress-centered government to president-centered government. Congress simply delegated its own powers to the executive branch. Congressional delegations of power, however, are not the only resources available to the president. Presidents have at their disposal a variety of other formal and informal resources that enable them to govern. Indeed, without these other resources, presidents would lack the tools needed to make much use of the power and responsibility given to them by Congress. Let us first consider the president's formal or official resources (see Figure 6.1). Then, in the section following, we will turn to the more informal resources that affect a president's capacity to govern, in particular the president's base of popular support.

---

[15]The Supreme Court did in fact *dis*approve broad delegations of legislative power by declaring the National Industrial Recovery Act of 1933 unconstitutional on the grounds that Congress did not accompany the broad delegations with sufficient standards or guidelines for presidential discretion (Panama Refining Co. v. Ryan, 293 U.S. 388 [1935], and Schechter Poultry Corp. v. United States, 295 U.S. 495 [1935]). The Supreme Court has never reversed those two decisions, but it has also never really followed them. Thus, broad delegations of legislative power from Congress to the executive branch can be presumed to be constitutional.

FIGURE 6.1

The Institutional Presidency*

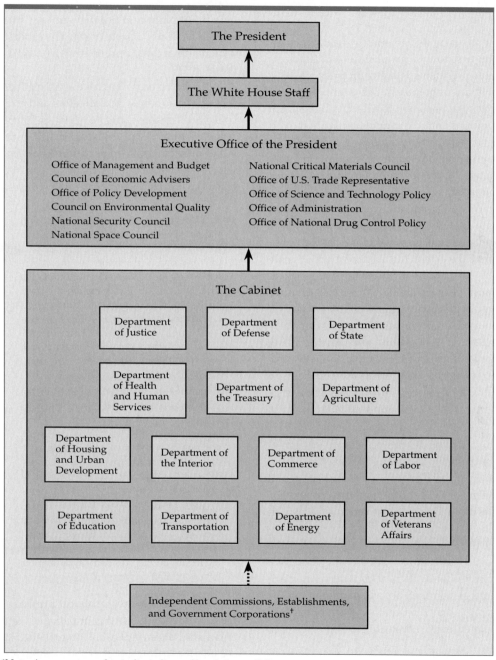

*Note: Arrows are used to indicate lines of legal responsibility.

†There are fifty-six independent regulatory commissions in the executive branch, but they are legally responsible to Congress, not directly to the president.

Source: *U.S. Government Organization Manual, 1985–1986* (Washington, DC: Government Printing Office, 1986), p. 827.

Formal Resources of Presidential Power

PATRONAGE AS A TOOL OF MANAGEMENT.
The first tool of management available to most presidents is the choice of high-level political appointees. These appointments allow the president to fill top management positions with individuals committed to his agenda and, at the same time, to build links to powerful political and economic interests by giving them representation in the administration.

When President Clinton took office, he had, literally, at his disposal about 4,000 appointments he could make "at the pleasure of the president." At the top are roughly 700 cabinet and high White House positions. Next are about 800 Senior Executive Service (SES) positions that can be appointed from outside the career service.[16] Although 4,000 plums were far too many appointments for President Clinton to make personally, as one committed to being a "strong president," he did supervise a large percentage of these appointments.

THE CABINET. In the American system of government, the *cabinet* is the traditional but informal designation for the heads of all the major federal government departments. The cabinet has no constitutional status. Unlike that of England and many other parliamentary countries, where the cabinet *is* the government, the American cabinet is not a collective body. It meets but makes no decisions as a group. Each appointment must be approved by the Senate, but the person appointed is not responsible to the Senate or to

Congress at large. Cabinet appointments help build party and popular support, but the cabinet is not a party organ. The cabinet is made up of directors but is not a board of directors.

Why can't a president have a real cabinet that serves as a board of directors and as a collective lightning rod to share political responsibilities? The explanation lies deep in the American system of national politics, which catches the cabinet and each member of it in a web of three basic interacting forces:

1. Each presidential candidate must build a winning electoral coalition, state by state. Expectations come to focus *personally* on the candidate. He is under too much personal pressure once he gets the nomination to stop and create a viable cabinet. In fact, by the time a president is inaugurated, it is already too late to create a cabinet government. Presidents don't even know personally some of their appointees, and many of them don't know each other.

2. Cabinet members have their own constituencies and are usually selected by the president because of the support they can bring him. But these constituencies do not automatically transfer to the president, and they may continue to be at odds with him. For the same reason, it is extremely difficult to remove a cabinet member or other high-level official.

3. Each cabinet member heads a department that is composed of a large bureaucracy with a momentum of its own. Cabinet members often face a choice between giving loyalty to the president or gaining the loyalty of their department.

Aware of this web of forces, the president tends to develop a burning impatience with and a mild distrust of cabinet members. He seeks to make the cabinet a rubber stamp for actions already decided on; and he demands results, or the appearance of results, more immediately and more frequently than most department heads can provide.

---

[16]For a complete directory of these exempt positions see Committee on Post Office and Civil Service, House of Representatives, *United States Government, Policy and Supporting Positions* (Washington, DC: Government Printing Office, 1992).

Since cabinet appointees generally come from differing careers, the formation of an effective, governing group out of this motley collection of appointments is very unlikely.

President Clinton's insistence on a cabinet diverse enough to resemble American society itself could be considered an act of political wisdom. On the other hand, it virtually guarantees that few of his appointees would ever have spent any time working together or would know the policy positions or beliefs of the other appointees. Columnist David Broder reported on the basis of his interviews in early 1993 that, although Clinton's top appointees were to be commended for "intellectual firepower," the pattern of appointments indicated that Clinton "wants this to be a very personal and very powerful presidency [with] the policy reins firmly in his own hands."[17]

Some presidents have relied heavily on an "inner cabinet," the National Security Council (NSC). The NSC, established by law in 1947, is composed of the president, the vice-president, the secretaries of state, defense, and the treasury, the attorney general, and other officials invited by the president. It has its own staff of foreign policy specialists run by the special assistant to the president for national security affairs. A counterpart, the Domestic Council, was created by law in 1970, but no specific departments were designated for it. President Clinton hit upon his own version of the Domestic Council, entitled the National Economic Council, which may or may not end up with a status higher than the Domestic Council's. But it will operate in competition with the Council of Economic Advisers.

Table 6.1 presents the pattern of appoint-

ments to the four most important cabinet posts, showing a distinct preference among presidents for outsiders. Few of the top presidential appointees were former cabinet members or had lengthy experience in national governmental affairs either as part of the inner circle of the party of the president or as career politicians.

President Clinton's early pattern of top-level appointees is a bit of a hybrid. Three of his four inner-cabinet appointees are genuine insiders, with long experience in national government and in the Democratic party. Secretary of the Treasury Bentsen brought to the cabinet his long experience in the Senate as the most powerful figure in matters of finance and taxation. Secretary of State Warren Christopher was so influential and valuable in the preceding Democratic administration that President Carter often referred to him as his "secret weapon." Secretary of Defense Les Aspin is a "policy wonk," much like President Clinton himself, and worked himself into the inside by spending his entire professional life in the House, most recently as chairman of the Armed Services Committee. Although Attorney General Janet Reno is the exception, inasmuch as she had no significant national public experience, she did spend her entire career as a government official, in local law enforcement in Miami. But Clinton also balanced that government service pattern with a "national unity pattern" more like that of President Kennedy, by staffing the outer circle of the cabinet as well as the inner White House with millionaires and prominent interest group representatives.

Presidents have obviously been uneven and unpredictable in their reliance on the NSC and other subcabinet bodies, because executive management is inherently a personal matter. However, despite all the personal variations, one generalization can be

[17]David Broder, "Clinton's Eclectic Cabinet," *Washington Post National Weekly Edition*, 4–10 January 1993, p. 13.

TABLE 6.1
Backgrounds of Appointees to Inner Cabinet* (1961–1989)

Republicans	Democrats
Secretary of State	
William Rogers (RMN) Law practice, att. gen.	Dean Rusk (JFK-LBJ) Foreign service, foundation executive
Henry Kissinger (RMN-GF) Professor	
Alexander Haig (RR) General, assistant to the president, NATO command	Cyrus Vance (JC) International law, department of defense official
George Shultz (RR) Professor, secretary of treasury (RMN), corporate executive	Edmund Muskie (JC) Senator
	Warren M. Christopher (WC)
James Baker (GB) Texas corporate law, chief of staff, secretary of treasury (RR)	Corporate law, Department of State official
Secretary of the Treasury	
David Kennedy (RMN) Banking and finance	Douglas Dillon (JFK-LBJ) Securities and finance, state department
John Connally (RMN) Governor, law practice	
George Shultz (RMN) Professor	Henry Fowler (LBJ) Banking, law practice
William Simon (RMN-GF) Securities and investments	Joseph Barr (LBJ) Mayor, state government official
	Michael Blumenthal (JC) Corporate executive
Donald Regan (RR) Securities executive	William Miller (JC) Corporate executive, Federal Reserve Board
James Baker (RR) Texas corporate law, chief of staff	
Nicholas Brady (RR-GB) Investment banker	Lloyd M. Bensten (WC) Financier, senator
Secretary of Defense	
Melvin Laird (RMN) Congressman	Robert McNamara (JFK-LBJ) Corporate executive
Elliot Richardson (RMN) State lieutenant governor, secretary of HEW	Clark Clifford (LBJ) Law practice
James Schlesinger (RMN-GF) Professor, science administrator, head of CIA, head of OMB	Harold Brown (JC) Air Force secretary, college president
Donald Rumsfeld (GF) Congressman, NATO official	Les Aspin (WC) Chair, House Armed Services Committee
Caspar Weinberger (RR) Secretary of HEW (RMN), head of OMB, corporate official	
Frank Carlucci (RR) Career government official	
Richard Cheney (GB) Wyoming congressman, White House chief of staff (GF)	
Attorney General	
John Mitchell (RMN) Law practice, securities adviser	Robert Kennedy (JFK-LBJ) Counsel for Senate investigatory committee
Richard Kleindienst (RMN) Law practice	Nicholas Katzenbach (LBJ) Professor
Elliot Richardson (RMN) State official, lieutenant governor, secretary of defense (RMN)	Ramsey Clark (LBJ) Law practice
	Griffin Bell (JC) Law practice
William Saxbe (RMN-GF) Senator, state att. gen.	Benjamin Civiletti (JC) Law practice
Edward Levi (GF) Law professor, college president	Janet Reno (WC) Dade County (Miami) prosecutor
William French Smith (RR) Lawyer, adviser to president	
Edwin Meese (RR) Lawyer, aide to president	
Richard Thornburgh (RR-GB) Governor, lawyer	

*These are the four cabinet posts that legally compose the National Security Council. JFK=John F. Kennedy; LBJ= Lyndon B. Johnson; RMN=Richard M. Nixon; GF= Gerald Ford; JC=Jimmy Carter; RR=Ronald Reagan; GB=George Bush; WC=William Clinton.

Sources: *Congress and the Nation,* vol. 4 (Washington, DC: Congressional Quarterly, 1977), pp. 1107–11; *Who's Who in American Politics* (New York: Bowker, 1973, 1977); and *Who's Who in America* (Chicago: Marquis, various years).

made: Presidents have increasingly preferred the White House staff to the cabinet as their means of managing the gigantic executive branch.

THE WHITE HOUSE STAFF.[18] It is not accidental that journalists have come to popularize the staff of each president with such names as the "Irish Mafia" (Kennedy), the "Georgia Mafia" (Carter), and the "California Mafia" (Reagan). One White House watcher characterized President Bush's inner staff as less a "mafia" and more a "club," composed of "comradery, humor, and male bonding."[19] President Clinton's inner staff is a lot like Bush's. Several, including Chief of Staff Thomas McLarty, served with Clinton in Arkansas and go back virtually to childhood bonding. They were joined by a few more recent "friends of Bill," who worked closely for Clinton in the 1992 campaign. Every president gathers around him a few people he can trust, some of whom are strongly enough bonded to the president to be able to give him bad news.

The *White House staff* is composed mainly of analysts and advisers. Although many of the top White House staffers are given the title "special assistant" for a particular task or sector, the types of judgments they are expected to make and the kinds of advice they are supposed to give are a good deal broader and more generally political than that which comes from the cabinet department or the Executive Office of the President. For example, the special assistant to the president for intergovernmental affairs will advise the president on the functioning of the various branches of government.

From an informal group of fewer than a dozen people (popularly called the "Kitchen Cabinet"), and no more than four dozen at the height of the domestic Roosevelt presidency in 1937, the White House staff has grown substantially with each successive president (see Table 6.2).[20] Richard Nixon employed 550 staffers in 1972. President Carter, who found so many of the requirements of presidential power distasteful, and who publicly vowed to keep his staff small and decentralized, built an even larger and more centralized staff.

President Clinton promised during the campaign to reduce the White House staff by 25 percent and announced in February 1993 that he was proceeding to carry out his promise. It is highly probable, however, that the staff will eventually expand back to earlier levels, because a large White House staff has become essential.

The biggest variation among presidential management practices lies not in the size of the White House staff but in its organization. President Reagan went to the extreme in delegating important management powers to his chief of staff, and he elevated his budget director to an unprecedented level of power in *policy making* rather than merely *budget* making. President Bush went to still more staff centralization under his chief of staff, John Sununu. At the same time, President Bush continued to deal directly with his cabinet heads, the press, and key members of Congress. President Clinton showed a definite preference for competition among

---

[18] A substantial portion of this segment is taken from Theodore J. Lowi, *The Personal President* (Ithaca: Cornell University Press, 1985), pp. 141–50.

[19] Ann Reilly Dowd, "How Bush Manages the Presidency," *Fortune*, August 27, 1990, p. 74.

[20] All the figures since 1967, and probably 1957, are understated, because there are additional White House staff members who are on detached service from the military and other departments and are not counted here because they are not on the White House payroll.

TABLE 6.2
THE EXPANDING WHITE HOUSE STAFF

Year	President	Full-time employees	Year	President	Full-Time employees
1937	Franklin D. Roosevelt	45	1975	Gerald R. Ford	533
1947	Harry S. Truman	190	1980	Jimmy Carter	488
1957	Dwight D. Eisenhower	364	1984	Ronald Reagan	575*
1967	Lyndon B. Johnson	251	1992	George Bush	605**
1972	Richard M. Nixon	550	1993	Bill Clinton	543**

*The vice-president employs over 20 staffers, and there are at least 100 on the staff of the National Security Council. These work in and around the White House and Executive Office but are not included in the above totals.

**The figures for 1992 and 1993 are made up of the Office of the President, the Executive Residences, and the Office of the Vice-President, according to OMB. They also don't include the 50 to 75 employees temporarily detailed to the White House from outside agencies. While not precisely comparable to previous years, they convey a sense of scale.

Sources: Thomas E. Cronin, "The Swelling of the Presidency: Can Anyone Reverse the Tide?" in Peter Woll, ed., *American Government: Readings and Cases,* 8th ed. (Boston: Little Brown, 1984), p. 347. Copyright © 1984 by Thomas E. Cronin. Reproduced with the permission of the author. For 1990: U.S. Office of Personnel Management, *Federal Civilian Workforce Statistics, Employment and Trends as of January 1990* (Washington, DC: Government Printing Office, 1990), p.29. For 1992 and 1993: Office of Management and Budget and the White House.

equals in the cabinet and among senior White House officials, obviously liking the competition and conflict among staff members, for which FDR was also famous. But rather than making President Carter's mistake "micromanaging" his administration, President Clinton had to ultimately settle on some degree of hierarchy. Politics by pluralism is one thing. Government by pluralism is quite another matter.

THE EXECUTIVE OFFICE OF THE PRESIDENT. The development of the White House staff can be appreciated only in its relation to the still larger Executive Office of the President (EOP). Created in 1939, the EOP is what is often called the "institutional presidency"—

the permanent agencies that perform defined management tasks for the president (see Figure 6.2). Somewhere between fifteen hundred and two thousand highly specialized people work for EOP agencies.[21]

The numbers in parentheses on Figure 6.2 are the official numbers of employees in each agency. The importance of each agency in EOP varies according to the personal orientations of each president. For example, the NSC staff was of immense importance under President Nixon, especially because it served essentially as the personal staff of

---

[21] The actual number is difficult to estimate because some EOP personnel, especially in national security work, are detached to EOP from outside agencies.

FIGURE 6.2

Executive Office of the President

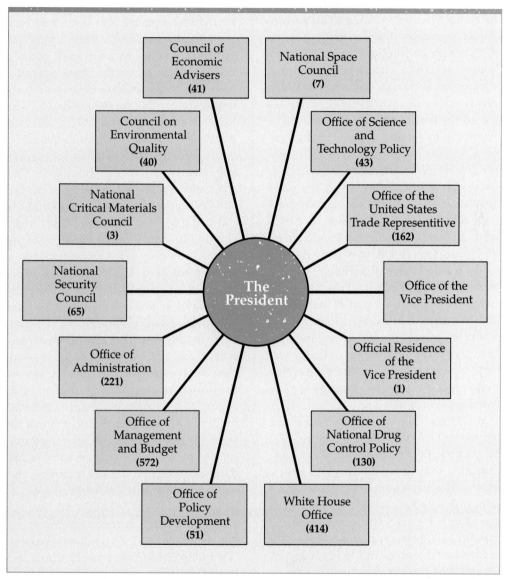

Source: *The United States Government Manual 1991–1992* (Washington, DC: Government Printing Office, 1991), p. 88.

presidential assistant Henry Kissinger. But it was of less importance to President Bush, who looked outside the EOP altogether for military policy matters, much more to the Joint Chiefs of Staff and its chairman, General Colin Powell.

The status and power of the Office of Management and Budget (OMB) within the

EOP has grown in importance from president to president. Under President Reagan, the budget director was granted literal cabinet status. Presidents Bush and Clinton continued to increase the director's role, but even if they had not chosen to make the budget director a virtual prime minister, circumstances would have imposed the choice upon them. In 1974, Congress passed the Budget and Impoundment Act, to impose upon itself a more rational approach to the budget. Up until 1974, congressional budget decisions were decentralized, with budget decisions made by the appropriations committees and subcommittees in the House and Senate, and with revenue decisions made independently by the House Ways and Means Committee and by the Senate Finance Committee. The primary purpose of the 1974 act was to impose enough discipline on congressional budget decision making to enable Congress as a whole to confront the presidency more effectively. This centralization of Congress's budget process also centralized the executive budget process, concentrating it more than ever in the OMB.

By 1985, confronting the very deficits and fragmented decision making that the 1974 act and the Reagan presidency had been dedicated to controlling, Congress adopted the Gramm-Rudman-Hollings Act.[22] (Hollings's name is usually dropped from everyday reference.) This act requires the president and budget director to meet with congressional leaders and to reach spending and taxing agreements that are virtually

like treaties in their legal weight. Gramm-Rudman required that the budget be set in such a way that the annual deficits would be reduced year by year until they were wiped out entirely and a "balanced budget" achieved. If in any year the deficit goal was not met, an across-the-board spending cut—known as sequestration—had to be imposed, such that the FBI and the IRS were to be cut equally with the Mining and Mineral Resources Research Institute. (Social Security and some other mandatory programs were exempted.)

Gramm-Rudman requirements boosted still further the role of OMB and its director. But in 1986, the Supreme Court ruled Gramm-Rudman's enforcement provisions unconstitutional, on the grounds that since the General Accounting Office (GAO) was an agent of Congress, it could not be given the power to make the Gramm-Rudman cuts and to decide when and how to sequester funds, because these are executive functions.[23] The 1987 revision of Gramm-Rudman met the constitutional issue created by the Court by transferring responsibility from GAO to OMB, and it gave OMB still more power by giving the director (for the president) more discretion regarding the estimates on which the cuts are to be based, more discretion on the kinds of programs and commitments whose expenditures can be exempted from the budget calculations, and more discretion about whether to sequester funds at all. The still newer provisions adopted by Congress in 1990 provided that OMB look beyond the overall budget deficit to a bill-by-bill evaluation of appropriations.

Budgeting is no longer "bottom up," with expenditure and program requests passing from the lowest bureaus through

---

[22] The official title of the Gramm-Rudman-Hollings Act is the Balanced Budget and Emergency Deficit Control Act of 1985. A good account of the transition from 1981 to the Gramm-Rudman era will be found in David Price, "The House: A Report from the Field," in *Congress Reconsidered*, ed. Lawrence Dodd and Bruce Oppenheimer (Washington, DC: Congressional Quarterly Press, 1989), pp. 413–41.

[23] Bowsher v. Synar, 92 L. Ed. 583 (1986).

PROCESS BOX 6.2
The Budget and Deficit Process Set by Law for 1992–1995

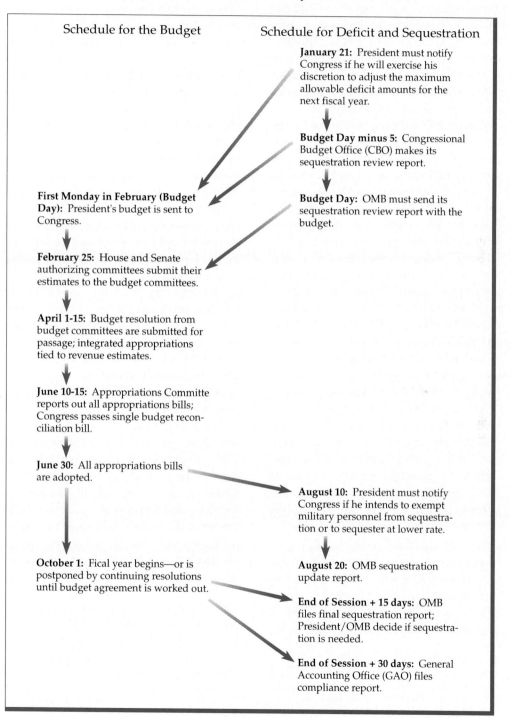

Schedule for the Budget

Schedule for Deficit and Sequestration

January 21: President must notify Congress if he will exercise his discretion to adjust the maximum allowable deficit amounts for the next fiscal year.

Budget Day minus 5: Congressional Budget Office (CBO) makes its sequestration review report.

First Monday in February (Budget Day): President's budget is sent to Congress.

Budget Day: OMB must send its sequestration review report with the budget.

February 25: House and Senate authorizing committees submit their estimates to the budget committees.

April 1-15: Budget resolution from budget committees are submitted for passage; integrated appropriations tied to revenue estimates.

June 10-15: Appropriations Committe reports out all appropriations bills; Congress passes single budget reconciliation bill.

June 30: All appropriations bills are adopted.

August 10: President must notify Congress if he intends to exempt military personnel from sequestration or to sequester at lower rate.

August 20: OMB sequestration update report.

October 1: Fical year begins—or is postponed by continuing resolutions until budget agreement is worked out.

End of Session + 15 days: OMB files final sequestration report; President/OMB decide if sequestration is needed.

End of Session + 30 days: General Accounting Office (GAO) files compliance report.

the departments to "clearance" in OMB and hence to Congress, where each agency could be called in to reveal what its "original request" had been before OMB got hold of it. The process became one of "top down," with OMB setting the budget guidelines for agencies as well as for Congress.

Bush and Richard Darman formed a particularly powerful budget duo. Since President Bush had few commitments to new domestic policies, he could make demands on Congress and then threaten to use his veto power. Darman gave Bush added leverage with his complete command of budgetary details and the effectiveness of his warnings about the contribution of new programs to greater deficits. President Clinton and his budget director, Leon Panetta, have had a more difficult time from the start, despite Democratic control of both House and Senate, because Clinton's program requires more statutes and therefore needs more positive congressional cooperation. For Bush, a veto was a kind of success and "divided government" was virtually an advantage, given his genuine commitment to "smaller government." For President Clinton, a veto would be a sign of failure, and Panetta's knowledge of budgetary details has to serve a more delicate balance between fighting the deficit and stimulating the economy.

THE VICE-PRESIDENCY. The vice-presidency was created along with the presidency by the Constitution and exists for two purposes only: to succeed the president in the case of a vacancy[24] and to preside over the Senate and cast the tie-breaking vote when necessary.[25] The main value of the vice-presidency as a political resource for the president is electoral. Traditionally, a presidential candidate's most important rule for the choice of a running mate is that he or she bring the support of at least one state (preferably a large one) not otherwise likely to support the ticket. Another rule holds that the vice-presidential nominee should come from a region and, where possible, from an ideological or ethnic subsection of the party differing from the presidential nominee's. It is very doubtful that John Kennedy would have won in 1960 without his vice-presidential candidate, Lyndon Johnson, and the contribution Johnson made to carrying Texas. It is equally doubtful that southerner Jimmy Carter would have been elected if his running mate had not been someone like Walter Mondale from Minnesota. It was for virtually the same reason that Walter Mondale designated Geraldine Ferraro, a representative from New York, as his running mate.

The emphasis has recently shifted away from geographical to ideological balance. In 1980, Ronald Reagan probably could have carried Texas without George Bush, a Texan, as his running mate. But he needed someone like Bush from the moderate mainstream of the party to help unite the party. Bush's second-place finish in the primaries also made him an attractive candidate who

---

[24]This provision was clarified by the Twenty-fifth Amendment (1967), which provides that the president (with majority confirmation of House and Senate) must appoint someone to fill the office of vice-president if the vice-president should die or should fill a vacancy in the presidency. This procedure has been invoked twice—once in 1973 when President Nixon nominated Gerald Ford, and the second time in 1974 when President Ford, having automatically succeeded the resigned President Nixon, filled the vice-presidential vacancy with Nelson Rockefeller.

[25]Article I, Section 3, provides that the vice-president "shall be President of the Senate, but shall have no Vote, unless they be equally divided."

would help Reagan reunify the party. In 1988, both presidential candidates went for ideological balance. Democrat Michael Dukakis, a Massachusetts liberal, selected as his running mate Lloyd Bentsen, whose record put him at the conservative end of the party spectrum. Since the conservative wing of his party did not fully embrace George Bush, despite his eight loyal years of service to President Reagan, he chose arch-conservative Indiana Senator J. Danforth Quayle as his running mate. Quayle's youth and Midwest location may have helped marginally, but ideological balance was the key to Bush's choice. Bill Clinton combined considerations of region and ideology in his selection of a vice-presidential running mate. The choice of Al Gore signaled that Bill Clinton was solidly on the right wing of the Democratic party and would remain steadfastly a southerner. Democratic strategists had become convinced that Clinton could not win without carrying a substantial number of southern states.

Presidents have constantly promised to give their vice-presidents more responsibility, but they almost always break their promise. No one can explain exactly why. Perhaps it is just too much trouble to share responsibility. But management style is certainly a key factor. George Bush, as vice-president, was "kept within the loop" of decision making because President Reagan delegated so much power. A copy of everything made for Reagan was made for Bush, especially during the first term when Bush's close friend James Baker was chief of staff. But, as one observer put it, that situation "can hardly be compared with that of the Bush White House, from which a torrent of notes and phone calls to world figures and people around the country routinely goes forth. Keeping Vice-President Quayle in the loop just wouldn't be possible."[26]

Vice-President Gore shows promise of enjoying relatively enhanced status, considering that President Clinton kept him ostentatiously present at all public appearances during the transition and during the vital public and private efforts to present and campaign for the president's program early in 1993. However, this laying on of hands during the early part of an administration guarantees nothing about the status or power of the office later on.

Informal Resources

ELECTIONS AS A RESOURCE. Although we emphasized earlier that even an ordinary citizen, legitimately placed in office, would be a very powerful president, there is no denying that a decisive presidential election translates into a more effective presidency. Some presidents claim that a landslide election gives them a "mandate," by which they mean that the electorate approved the programs offered in the campaign and that Congress ought to therefore go along. And Congress is not unmoved by such an appeal. The Johnson and Reagan landslides of 1964 and 1980 gave them real strength during their honeymoon year. In contrast, the close elections of Kennedy in 1960, Nixon in 1968, and Carter in 1976 seriously hampered their effectiveness.

Although Bush was elected decisively in 1988, he had no legislative commitments that would have profited from any claim to an electoral mandate. President Clinton, a much more action-oriented president, was nevertheless seriously hampered by having been elected by a minority of the popular

[26] John Newhouse, "Profiles," *New Yorker*, May 7, 1990, p. 70.

Dan Quayle and Al Gore
Is the Vice-Presidency the "Most Insignificant Office"?

*T*he office of vice-president has long been a dead-end, powerless, thankless job. Yet the office has been highly sought after in recent decades, and recent vice-presidents, including Dan Quayle and Al Gore, have played key roles in their administrations.

Indiana native Dan Quayle grew up in a prosperous publishing family that owned a chain of newspapers. After graduating from college and law school, Quayle worked as an associate publisher of the *Huntington Herald-Press,* which stimulated his interest in politics. In 1976, he stunned the experts by winning a seat in Congress against a nine-term incumbent. Four years later, he again surprised doubters by winning a Senate seat. In 1988, Republican presidential nominee George Bush picked the then-unknown senator for his running mate, hoping to strengthen and "balance" his ticket by choosing a young conservative from the Midwest. (Bush claimed Texas as his home state.) Despite some political embarrassments during the campaign, such as revelations that his family connections had helped Quayle gain entrance to law school and avoid military service in Vietnam, the Bush-Quayle ticket defeated Democratic rivals Michael Dukakis and Lloyd Bentsen.

As vice-president, Quayle was a part of Bush's inner decision-making circle, playing an active role in such key issues as America's response to the military revolt in the Philippines and the Persian Gulf War of 1991. A staunch conservative, Quayle also served as a key administration liaison to Christian fundamentalists and other conservative constituencies. He rallied conservative sympathies but outraged other constituencies during the 1992 presidential campaign when he argued that the fictional television character, Murphy Brown, offered a poor role model to Americans when she bore a child out of wedlock. Conservatives hailed the criticism as a just rebuke to those who opposed what they

Dan Quayle

vote, a mere 43 percent. He was further burdened by the 19.7 million votes (19 percent) cast for Ross Perot, in fact, so much so that he adopted a substantial portion of Perot's program. In the days following announcement of his dramatic economic program on February 7, 1993, President Clinton, along with Vice-President Gore and

labeled "family values." Liberals responded that Quayle's attack of a fictional character (who had decided against the abortion option) revealed the poverty of the Bush administration's commitment to assistance for single mothers.

Al Gore grew up in a political family: his father, Al Gore, Sr., was a three-term senator from Tennessee. Both Gore and his father had opposed the Vietnam War, yet, following his graduation from college, he felt a strong duty to serve his country (he was also concerned about harming his father's reputation if he avoided service). Gore entered the military and served a tour of duty in Vietnam, finishing in 1971. After leaving the service, Gore wrote for a Tennessee newspaper and then entered divinity school.

In 1976, Gore decided almost on impulse to pursue the family business, seeking and winning a Tennessee congressional seat. In 1984, he captured a vacant Senate seat. Gore's first foray into national politics came four years later when he unsuccessfully sought the Democratic presidential nomination. In 1992, Bill Clinton picked Gore as his running mate, hoping to strengthen his ticket with Gore's experience and knowledge of foreign policy and environmental issues. This decision was criticized, not because of questions about Gore's credentials, but because the two were so much alike—young southerners, considered liberal on domestic social policy and conservative on defense. Despite violating the unwritten rule that a running mate should be selected to "balance" the ticket by region or ideology, the two proved to be highly compatible and a strong campaign team.

As vice-president, Gore continued to play an active role in Clinton's inner circle. His expertise on nuclear and military strategy and environmental and family issues placed him in a leadership position in the administration. Like his most recent predecessor, Gore's vice-presidency has been active in both policy formulation and political advocacy.

John Adams once labeled the vice-presidency "the most insignificant office that ever the invention of man contrived." Quayle and Gore may have made this dictum obsolete.

Sources: Richard F. Fenno, Jr., *The Making of a Senator: Dan Quayle* (Washington, DC: Congressional Quarterly Press, 1989); Al Gore, *Earth in the Balance* (New York: Houghton Mifflin, 1992).

Al Gore

most of the members of his cabinet, traveled around the country to build the base of public support that had not been captured adequately in the November 1992 election.

INITIATIVE AS A RESOURCE. "To initiate" means to originate, and in government that can mean power. The president as an individual is able to initiate decisive action, while Congress as a relatively large assembly must deliberate and debate before it can act.

Over the years, Congress has sometimes deliberately and sometimes inadvertently enhanced the president's power to seize the initiative. Curiously, the most important congressional gift to the president seems the most mundane, namely, the Office of Management and Budget (OMB), known until 1974 as the Bureau of the Budget.

In 1921, Congress provided for an "executive budget," and turned over to a new Bureau of the Budget in the executive branch the responsibility for maintaining the nation's accounts. In 1939, this bureau was moved from the Treasury Department to the newly created Executive Office of the President. The purpose of this move was to enable the president to make better use of the budgeting process as a management tool. In addition, Congress provided for a process called *legislative clearance,* which enables the president to require all agencies of the executive branch to submit to him through the budget director all requests for new legislation along with estimates of their budgetary needs.[27] Thus, heads of agencies must submit budget requests to the White House so that the requests of all the competing agencies can be balanced. Although there are many violations of this rule, it is usually observed.

At first, legislative clearance was a defensive weapon, used mainly to allow the president to avoid the embarrassment of having to oppose or veto legislation origi-

nating in his own administration. But eventually, legislative clearance became far more important. It became the starting point for the development of comprehensive presidential programs.[28] As noted earlier, recent presidents have also used the budget process as a method of gaining tighter "top down" management control. Professed anti-government Republicans, such as Reagan and Bush, as well as allegedly pro-government Democrats, such as Clinton, are alike in their commitment to central management control and program planning. This is precisely why all three recent presidents have given the budget directorship cabinet status.

PRESIDENTIAL USE OF THE MEDIA. The president is able to take full advantage of his access to the communications media mainly because of the legal and constitutional bases of initiative. Virtually all the media look to the White House as the chief source of news, and they tend to assign their most important and skillful reporters to the White House "beat." Since news is money, they need the president as much as he needs them to meet their mutual need to make news. Presidents have successfully gotten from Congress significant additions to their staff to take care of press releases and other forms of communications.

Presidential personalities affect how the media are used by each president. Although Franklin Roosevelt gave several press conferences a month, they were not recorded or broadcast "live"; direct quotes were not per-

---

[27]Sometimes in appropriations hearings before committees, a member of Congress will attempt to reverse the OMB effort to hold down requests by asking an executive branch witness to reveal "what was your original request." But generally the rule of clearance through OMB and the White House has been observed. The clearance function was formalized in 1940 in the Office of Legislative Reference in the Budget Bureau.

[28]Although dated in some respects, the best description and evaluation of budgeting as a management tool and as a tool of program planning is still found in Richard E. Neustadt's two classic articles, "Presidency and Legislation: Planning the President's Program" and "Presidency and Legislation: The Growth of Central Clearance," in *American Political Science Review,* September 1954 and December 1955.

mitted. The model we know today got its start with Eisenhower and was put into final form by Kennedy. Since 1961, the presidential press conference has been a distinctive institution, available to every president when he wants to dominate the news. About 400 reporters attend and file their accounts within minutes of the concluding words, "Thank you, Mr. President."

But despite the importance of the press conference, its value to each president has varied. Its use declines notably when presidents are in political trouble. Although the average from Kennedy through Carter was about two press conferences a month, Johnson dropped virtually out of sight for almost half of 1965 when Vietnam was warming up, and so did Nixon for over five months in 1973 during the Watergate hearings. President Reagan was not comfortable with the give and take of press conferences. He single-handedly brought the average down by holding only seven press conferences during his first year in office and only sporadically thereafter.

In great contrast, President Bush held more news conferences during his first seventeen months than Reagan did in eight years. Moreover, Bush shifted them from elaborate primetime affairs in the ornate East Room to less formal gatherings in the White House briefing room. Fewer reporters and more time for follow-up questions permitted media representatives to "concentrate on information for their stories, rather than getting attention for themselves."[29]

President Clinton has tended to take both Reagan and Bush approaches, combining Reagan's high profile—elaborate press conferences and prime-time broadcasts—with the more personal one-on-one approach generally preferred by Bush. But, thanks to Ross Perot, there is now a third approach, for which President Clinton has shown a certain amount of aptitude—the informal and basically nonpolitical talk shows, such as those of Larry King, Arsenio Hall, MTV, and Oprah Winfrey. Low-key, laid back, no time pressure, no concerted message. Just the personal touch.

Of course, in addition to the presidential press conference there are other routes from the White House to news prominence.[30] For example, President Nixon preferred direct television addresses, and President Carter tried to make the initiatives more homey with a television adaptation of President Roosevelt's "fireside chats." President Reagan made unusually good use of prime-time television addresses and his more informal but regular Saturday afternoon radio broadcasts.

PARTY AS A PRESIDENTIAL RESOURCE. Although on the decline, the president's party is far from insignificant as a political resource for him, as Figure 6.3 dramatically demonstrates. The figure gives a thirty-five-year history of the "presidential batting average" in Congress—the percentage of winning roll-call votes in Congress on bills publicly supported by the president. Note, for example, that President Eisenhower's "batting average" started out with a very impressive .900 but declined to .700 by the end of his first term and to little more than half his starting point by the end of his administration. The single most important explanation of this decline was President

[29]David Broder, "Some Newsworthy Presidential CPR," *Washington Post National Weekly Edition*, June 4–10, 1990, p. 4.

[30]See George Edwards III, *At the Margins—Presidential Leadership of Congress* (New Haven: Yale University Press, 1989), Chapter 7; and Robert Locander, "The President and the News Media," in *Dimensions of the Modern Presidency*, ed. Edward Kearny (St. Louis: Forum Press, 1981), pp. 49–52.

FIGURE 6.3

The Presidential Batting Average: Presidential Success on Congressional Votes*
(1953-1992)

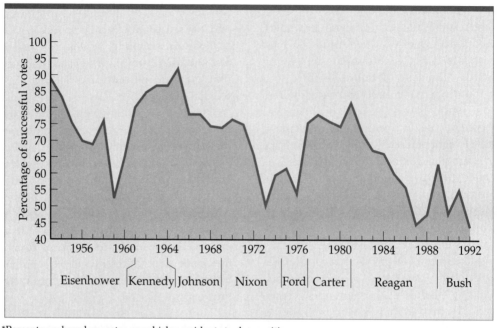

*Percentages based on votes on which presidents took a position.
Source: *Congressional Quarterly Weekly Report,* 19 December 1992; p. 3842.

Eisenhower's loss of a Republican party majority in Congress after 1954, the recapture of some seats in 1956, and then a significant loss of seats to the Democrats after the election of 1958.

The presidential batting average went back up and stayed consistently higher through the Kennedy and Johnson years, mainly because these two presidents enjoyed Democratic party majorities in the Senate and in the House. Even so, Johnson's batting average in the House dropped significantly during his last two years, following a very large loss of Democratic seats in the 1966 election. Note how much higher Carter's success rate was than that of Ford or of Nixon during his last two years in office; this was clearly attributable to the *party* factor—the substantial Democratic party majorities in the two chambers of Congress.

At the same time, party has its limitations as a resource. The more unified the president's party is behind his legislative requests, the more unified the opposition party is also likely to be. Unless the president's party majority is very large, he must also appeal to the opposition to make up for the inevitable defectors within the ranks of his own party. Consequently, the president often poses as being above partisanship in order to win "bipartisan" support in Congress. Thus, even though President Clinton enjoys Democratic majorities in the House and the Senate, he must still be cautious with Republicans because the defection of just four or five Democrats in a close Senate vote can endanger important but controversial legislation. It may feel like walking on a tightrope. To the extent that the president pursues a bipartisan strategy, he cannot afford to throw himself fully into building his own party discipline, and vice versa.

GROUPS AS A PRESIDENTIAL RESOURCE. The classic case in modern times of groups as a resource for the presidency is the New Deal coalition that supported President Franklin Roosevelt.[31] The New Deal coalition was composed of an inconsistent, indeed contradictory, set of interests. Some of these interests were not organized interest groups, but were regional or ethnic interests, such as southern whites, or residents of large cities in the industrial Northeast and Midwest, or blacks who later succeeded in organizing as an interest group. In addition, there were several large, self-consciously organized interest groups, including organized labor, agriculture, and the financial community.[32] All of the parts were held together by a judicious use of patronage—not merely in jobs but also in policies. Many of the groups virtually were permitted to write their own legislation. In exchange, the groups supported President Roosevelt and

his Democratic successors in their battles with opposing politicians.

Republicans have had their group coalition base, too, including not only their traditional segments of organized business, upper-income groups, and certain ethnic groups but also a very large share of traditionally Democratic southern whites and northern blue-collar workers. This coalition began to loosen toward the end of the Bush administration, and the astute Bill Clinton was quick to sense it. His 1992 campaign succeeded in large part because he was able to bring back together many of the original interests that made up the New Deal coalition. And he attempted to go beyond these interests by holding an unprecedented "economic summit" in Little Rock, Arkansas, less than a month after his election. It was a very public meeting of some three hundred bankers, corporate executives, and other interest group representatives, with Clinton himself presiding for almost the entire forty-eight hours. It was indeed an extraordinary effort to expand the president's coalition base.

MASS POPULARITY AS A RESOURCE (AND A LIABILITY). As presidential government grew, a presidency developed whose power is linked directly to the people.[33] Successful presidents have to be able to mobilize mass opinion. But as we shall see, each president tends to *use up* his mass resources as he *uses* them. Virtually everyone is aware that presidents are constantly making appeals to the public over the heads of Congress and the Washington community. But the mass public does *not* turn out to be made up of fools. The American people generally react

[31] A wider range of group phenomena will be covered in Chapter 11. In that chapter the focus is on the influence of groups *upon* the government and its policy-making processes. Here our concern is more with the relationship of groups to the presidency and the extent to which groups and coalitions of groups become a dependable resource for presidential government.

[32] For updates on the group basis of presidential politics, see Thomas Ferguson, "Money and Politics," in *Handbooks to the Modern World—The United States,* vol. 2, ed. Godfrey Hodgson (New York: Facts on File, 1992), pp. 1060–84; and Lucius J. Barker, ed., "Black Electoral Politics," *National Political Science Review,* vol. 2 (New Brunswick, NJ: Transaction Publishers, 1990).

[33] For a book-length treatment of this shift, see Theodore Lowi, *The Personal President.* For an analysis of the character of mass democracy, see Benjamin Ginsberg, *The Captive Public* (New York: Basic Books, 1986).

FIGURE 6.4

Presidential Performance Ratings from Truman to Reagan
Nationwide responses to the question "Do you approve of the way the
president is handling his job?"*

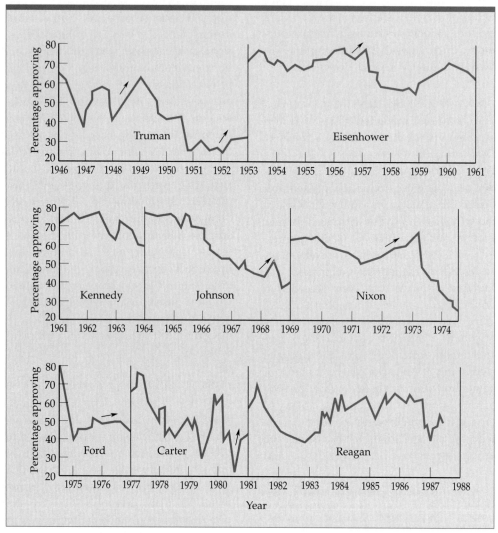

* Note: Arrows indicate pre-election upswings.
Source: Data from the Gallup poll and the Harris survey through regular press releases.
Courtesy of the Gallup Organization and Louis Harris & Associates.

to presidential *actions* rather than mere speeches or other image-making devices.

The public's sensitivity to presidential actions can be seen in the tendency of all presidents since Kennedy *to lose* popular support over the course of their time in office (Figure 6.4). The general downward tendency is to be expected if the American voters are rational, since almost any action taken by the president is bound to please some voters and displease others. Public disapproval of specific actions has a cumulative effect on the president's overall performance rating.

All presidents are faced with the problem of keeping up their approval rating. And the public generally reacts favorably to presidential actions in foreign policy or, more precisely, to international events associated with the president. Analysts call this the "rallying effect." However, the rallying effect turns out to be a momentary reversal of the more general tendency of presidents to lose popular support.

Because the public rallies behind the president when there is an international crisis, presidents are under pressure to use foreign events as a means of shoring up domestic political support. President Bush offers a significant example. (See Figure 6.5.) No president has enjoyed such high ratings, and they remained unprecedentedly high for the first fifteen months, when they should have been dropping. Even Reagan's high ratings dropped during his first fifteen months. But note the remarkable flow of international events. During his first weeks in office, which should have been the honeymoon for passage of key domestic legislation, Bush was abroad meeting heads of state. By the time the honeymoon should have been over, with the expected decline in

FIGURE 6.5
A Profile of Bush's Presidential Popularity, 1989–1992

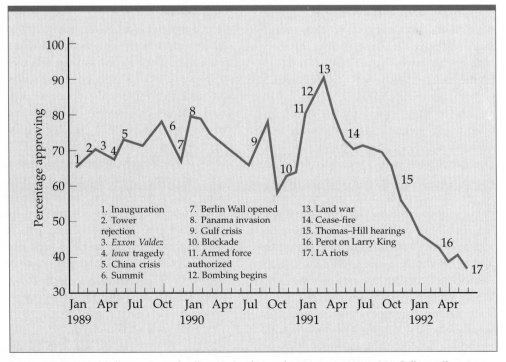

1. Inauguration
2. Tower rejection
3. *Exxon Valdez*
4. *Iowa* tragedy
5. China crisis
6. Summit
7. Berlin Wall opened
8. Panama invasion
9. Gulf crisis
10. Blockade
11. Armed force authorized
12. Bombing begins
13. Land war
14. Cease-fire
15. Thomas–Hill hearings
16. Perot on Larry King
17. LA riots

Source: NBC News/*Wall Street Journal* poll, in *National Journal,* 19 January 1991, p. 184; Gallup poll, various years.

approval ratings, the Chinese revolution/counterrevolution initiated what was to become the most remarkable series of international events since World War II. From the presidential perspective, these were a "political jackpot," as Republican Chairman Lee Atwater said of still another jackpot, the brief invasion of Panama and the capture of General Manuel Noriega.

The readiness of President Reagan and of President Bush to "go it alone" and to take dramatic actions and to make dramatic pronouncements produced immense benefits in public opinion ratings. Not only did Bush's approval ratings move steadily upward to new record highs; they continued at record levels all through 1990. The two highpoints in his first two years came in January 1990 (81 percent approval) following the culmination of the collapse of the Soviet empire, the destruction of the Berlin Wall, and the initiation of the reunification of Germany; and September 1990, the first poll following Iraq's invasion of Kuwait and Bush's decisive response to that invasion with the dispatch of over 200,000 military personnel to Saudi Arabia and the Persian Gulf (91 percent approval).

The "rallying effect" in the American public may well be a sign of mass citizen rationality. But is it a healthy situation for a president to have to decide *between* popularity and diplomacy? There is no easy answer to this question, because the president's popularity is not merely an ego trip; it is a major political resource and something he needs not only to conduct foreign affairs but also to effectively manage the five million members of the U.S. federal bureaucracy. While foreign affairs often grab the headlines, the functioning of the bureaucracy is the essence of our system of government. How the president deals with this massive operation is our next topic.

Bureaucracy in a Democracy

Despite widespread and consistent complaints about how bureaucracy is out of control and how difficult it is to supervise over five million civilian and military personnel working for the executive branch, most Americans ultimately recognize that maintaining order in a large society is impossible without a large governmental apparatus of some sort.[34] When we approve of what government is doing, we tend to give the phenomenon a positive name, administration; when we disapprove of what government is doing, we call the same phenomenon *bureaucracy*.

The In Brief Box on the facing page defines bureaucracy by identifying its six basic characteristics. These characteristics enable us to look more clearly at the bureaucratic phenomenon. The size of the federal service is less imposing when placed against the context of the total work force and the number of state and local government employees. The ratio of federal service employment to the total work force has been relatively steady since 1950; in fact, the ratio has actually declined slightly in the past fifteen years. Moreover, between 1950 and 1990, during which the federal civil service employment remained at around 3 percent of the total work force, public employment in state and local governments moved from about 6.5 percent of the country's work force to nearly 15 percent. All in all, we can say that the growth of the national government bureaucracy has merely kept pace with the growth of the national economy. The national government is indeed very large, but so is the American economy and

---

[34]The title of this section was inspired by an important book by Charles Hyneman, *Bureaucracy in a Democracy* (New York: Harper, 1950).

In Brief Box

SIX PRIMARY CHARACTERISTICS OF BUREAUCRACY

Division of Labor
In order to increase productivity, workers are specialized.
Each develops a skill in a particular job and then performs that job routinely.

Allocation of Functions
Each worker depends on the output of other workers.
No worker makes an entire product alone.

Allocation of Responsibility
A task becomes a personal and contractual responsibility.

Supervision
An unbroken chain of command ties superiors to subordinates from top to bottom
   to ensure orderly communication between workers and levels of the organization.
Each superior is assigned a limited number of subordinates to supervise—this is
   the span of control.

Purchase of Full-time Employment
The organization controls all the time the worker is on the job, so each worker can
   be assigned and held to a task.

Identification of Career within Organization
Paths of seniority along with pension rights and promotions are all designed to encourage workers to identify with an organization.

---

society. The question is not one of size, but whether government and society relate to each other in a productive way.

In the balance of this chapter, we explore how the American system of government has tried to adapt the vast apparatus of the national government to the requirements of representative democracy. The title of this section, "Bureaucracy in a Democracy," conveys the sense that the two are contradictory. We cannot live without bureaucracy, because bureaucracy is the most efficient way to organize people and technology to get a large collective job done. But we can't live comfortably with bureaucracy either, because hierarchy, appointed authority, and professional expertise make bureaucracy the natural enemy of representation, discussion, reciprocity, and individualism. Our task is neither to retreat nor to attack but to try constantly to take advantage of the strengths of bureaucracy while trying to make it more accountable to democratic processes. We look first to the role of the president in the struggle for accountability, and then to Congress.

The President as Chief Executive

In 1939, President Roosevelt, through his President's Committee on Administrative Management, made the plea that "the presi-

---

In Brief Box

GOVERNMENT: EXPANSION AND RESPONSE

Period of Government Expansion	*Response of Presidency to Expansion*
Wilson (1914–18): World War I; budget rises from $800 million to over $18 billion in 1919; agencies expanded	Budget and Accounting Act, 1921; executive branch forms Bureau of the Budget; General Accounting Office (GAO) becomes agent of Congress
Roosevelt (1933–36): New Deal period; budget growth; new agencies formed resulting in the "alphabetocracy"	Reorganization of powers including Budget Bureau as part of Executive Office of President in 1939
Roosevelt (1940–44): World War II; total mobilization	Council of Economic Advisers formed, 1946; Secretary of Defense, National Security Council; Joint Chiefs of Staff in 1947
Truman (1947–51): post-World War II; Korean War mobilization	Emergence of "president's program," 1948+; White House Staff, 1950+
Eisenhower (1953–60): Cold War; reaction against domestic government	Formalizing of White House staff; enhancement of National Security Council; effort to control social agencies; Hoover Commission
Kennedy (1961–63): Increased taxing power; direct pressure to control wages and prices	Specialized White House staff applied central budgeting to Defense Department (Planning Programming Budgeting System, PPBS); upgraded Council of Economic Advisers

---

dent needs help." This is the story of the modern presidency. It can be told largely as a series of responses to the rise of big government: *Each expansion of the national government in the twentieth century has been accompanied by a parallel expansion of presidential management authority.* The In Brief Box on this page provides a sketch of this pattern over most of this century.

FROM CABINET TO WHITE HOUSE STAFF. We have already observed that the president's cabinet does not perform as a board of directors. The cabinet is not a constitutionally or historically recognized, collective decision-making body, and only a minority of the members of the cabinet are sufficiently in command of their own respective departments to be able to contribute much to the president's need to be an actual chief executive officer. The vacuum

Johnson (1964–66): Expansion of domestic and social programs like Medicare and Medicaid and civil rights agencies; expansion of war powers	Applied PPBS to domestic agencies; created Organization for Economic Opportunity (OEO) to coordinate welfare programs; established HUD and Department of Transportation
Nixon (1969–73): Increased Social Security benefits; expansion of diplomacy; price controls; new regulatory programs	Centralization and further specialization of White House staff; Office of Management and Budget (OMB) created; decentralization of urban and welfare programs; formation of cabinet-level coordinating councils on wages and prices and domestic policy; "indexing" of Social Security to eliminate annual legislative adjustments; enhanced use of FBI surveillance of administrators
Carter (1977–80): post-Watergate	New Departments of Energy and Education; civil service reformed; zero-base budgeting; intense effort to reduce paperwork of the bureaucracy; first to impose cost-benefit analysis on regulation; first major effort to "deregulate" government
Reagan (1980–85): Dramatic expansion of defense budget; growth of national trade deficit	Director of OMB promoted to cabinet status; expansion of OMB power of regulatory review; formation of cabinet councils; expanded cost-benefit test for regulations

created by the absence of cabinet management has been filled to a certain extent by the White House staff.

Within the White House staff, in the past thirty years, the "special assistants to the president" have been given specialized jurisdictions over one or more executive departments. These staffers have additional power and credibility beyond their access to the president because they also have access to the CIA for international intelligence and to the FBI and the Treasury for knowledge about the agencies themselves. With this information they can go beyond what the agencies themselves report and gain a great deal of leverage over the departments.

OMB AS A MANAGEMENT AGENCY. It was not accidental that the Bureau of the Budget, established in 1921 and brought into the EOP in 1939, was reorganized and given a new name (OMB) in 1970. President Nixon was deeply committed to making the existing bureaucracy, a product of eight years of growth and commitment under the Democrats, more responsive to Republican programs. The Office of Management and Budget was his instrument of choice, and the management power of the director of OMB seems to have increased with each president since Nixon. Some management authority had always been lodged with the director of the budget, but greater emphasis was placed on planning and budgetary allocations. From President Nixon onward, questions of management became central to the operation of the executive branch.

A decade after the establishment of OMB, President Reagan gave the director cabinet status, appointing David Stockman, who had been a member of Congress and had been instrumental in developing the ideology and program of the Reagan administration.

President Bush's director, Richard Darman, had even more formidable credentials than David Stockman; he combined Stockman's budgetary prowess with long and deep experience in administrative management, extending back to the Nixon administration. If Stockman was given cabinet status, Darman was made virtually the president's prime minister.

President Clinton projected his approach to management in his 1993 Man of the Year interview with *Time* magazine:

> [O]ne of the things that struck me since I won this election is that there are a huge number of people who work for the Federal Government . . . devoted people who ought to be given a chance to hook into this

future we are trying to build. . . . I believe that if you look at the most successful organizations in this country, that's what they do.[35]

In other words, more of actual management should, in his view, be delegated to the responsible administrators "on the line."

Responsible bureaucracy, however, will never come simply from more presidential power, more administrative staff, or more management control. All this was, for example, inadequate to the task of keeping the National Security Staff from seizing the initiative to run its own policies toward Iran and Nicaragua for at least two years (1985–1986) after Congress had explicitly restricted activities with Nicaragua and the president had formally forbidden negotiations with Iran. This served to expose the fact that each White House management innovation, from one president to the next, reveals plainly the inadequacy of the previous innovations. As the White House staff grows, and the executive offices of the president grow, the management bureaucracy itself becomes a management problem. Congress may be part of the solution, but Congress is also part of the problem.

Congress and Responsible Bureaucracy

Congress is constitutionally essential to responsible bureaucracy because, in "a government of laws," legislation is the key to bureaucratic responsibility. When a law is adopted and its intent is clear, the president knows what to "faithfully execute," and the agency understands its guidelines. But when Congress enacts vague legislation, everybody, from president to agency to courts to interest groups, gets involved in

---

[35]*Time*, 4 January 1993, p. 37.

the interpretation of legislation. In that event, to whom is the agency responsible?

Congress's answer has not been to clarify its legislative intent but to try to supervise agency actions and interpretations through *oversight* (see also Chapter 5). The more legislative power Congress delegates to the executive, the more it seeks to get back into the game of government through committee and subcommittee oversight of the agencies. The standing committee system of Congress is well-suited for oversight, inasmuch as most congressional committees and subcommittees have jurisdictions roughly parallel to one or more executive departments or agencies. Appropriations committees and authorization committees have oversight powers—and delegate their respective oversight powers to their subcommittees. In addition, there is a committee on government operations in the House and in the Senate, and these committees have oversight powers not limited by departmental jurisdiction.

Committees and subcommittees oversee agencies through public hearings. Representatives from each agency, the White House, major interest groups, and other concerned citizens are called as witnesses to present testimony at these hearings. These are printed in large volumes and are widely circulated. Detailed records of the recent activities and expenditures of each and every agency can be found in these volumes. The number of hearings and equivalent public meetings (sometimes called investigations) has increased fairly dramatically during the past forty years, largely because there is more government to oversee.[36]

Another form of legislative oversight is conducted by individual members of Congress. This is all part of Congress's "case work," and much of legislative oversight is for individual constituents seeking everything from honest information to favoritism. Some legislation and other good results may come from these acts of oversight by individual representatives and senators, but the greater influence of case work is to particularize the process, bringing the focus of administration away from good policy and responsible management to individual interests.

Obviously the best approach is for Congress to spend more of its time clarifying its legislative intent and less of its time on committee or individual oversight. If the intent of the law were clear, Congress could then count on the president to maintain a higher level of bureaucratic responsibility, because bureaucrats are more responsive to clear legislative guidance than to anything else. Nevertheless, this is not a neat and sure solution, because Congress and the president can still be at odds, and when they are at odds, bureaucrats have an opportunity to evade responsibility by playing one branch off against the other.

Bureaucracy is here to stay, and there is no ultimate solution to the problem of bureaucracy in a democracy. The national bureaucracy will not suddenly become smaller. Congress will not suddenly change its practice of loose and vague legislative draftsmanship. Presidents will not suddenly discover new reserves of power or vision to draw more tightly the reins of responsible

---

[36]For figures on the frequency and character of oversight, see Lawrence Dodd and Richard Schott, *Congress and the Administrative State* (New York: Wiley, 1979), p. 169. See

also Norman Ornstein et al., *Vital Statistics on Congress, 1987–88* (Washington, DC: Congressional Quarterly Press, 1987), pp. 161–62. For a valuable and skeptical assessment of legislative oversight of administration, see James W. Fesler and Donald F. Kettl, *The Politics of the Administrative Process* (Chatham, NJ: Chatham House, 1991), Chapter 11.

management. As in all complex social and political problems, the solution lies in being aware of the nature of the problem and not in attempting quick fixes.

Time Line on the Presidency

EVENTS		INSTITUTIONAL DEVELOPMENTS
George Washington elected first president (1789)	**1800**	President establishes powers in relation to Congress (1789)
Thomas Jefferson elected president (1800)		Orderly transfer of power from Federalists to Jeffersonian Republicans (1801)
"Midnight judicial appointments" by John Adams before he leaves office (1801)		*Marbury v. Madison holds that Congress and the president are subject to judicial review (1803)*
Republican caucus nominates James Madison, who is elected president (1808)		Congress dominates presidential nominations through "King Caucus" (1804–1831)
Andrew Jackson elected president (1828)		Strengthening of presidency; nominating conventions introduced; broaden president's base of support (1830s)
Period of weak presidents (Martin Van Buren, William Harrison, James Polk, Zachary Taylor, Franklin Pierce, James Buchanan) (1837–1860)	**1860**	
Abraham Lincoln elected president (1860)		"Constitutional dictatorship" during Civil War and after (1861–1865)
Impeachment of President Andrew Johnson (1868)		Congress takes back initiative for action (1868–1933)
Industrialization, big railroads, big corporations (1860s–1890s)		*In re Neagle*—Court holds to expansive inference from Constitution on rights, duties, and obligations of president (1890)
World War I (1914–1919)	**1920**	
Congress fails to approve Wilson's League of Nations (1919–1920)		Budget and Accounting Act; Congress provides for an executive budget (1921)

EVENTS		INSTITUTIONAL DEVELOPMENTS
FDR proposes New Deal programs to achieve economic recovery from the Depression U.S. enters World War II (1941–1945)		Congress adopts first New Deal programs; epoch of presidential government (1930's) *U.S. v. Pink*—Court confirms legality of executive agreements in foreign relations (1942)
Korean War without declaration (1950–1953)	**1950**	*Steel Seizure* case holds that president's power must be authorized by statute and is not inherent in the presidency (1952)
Gulf of Tonkin Resolution (1964); U.S. troop buildup begins in Vietnam (1965)		Great Society program enacted; president sends troops to Vietnam without consulting Congress (1965)
Watergate affair (1972); Watergate cover-up revealed (1973–1974)	**1970**	Congressional resurgence begins—War Powers Act (1973); Budget and Impoundment Act (1974)
Nixon becomes first president to resign; Gerald Ford succeeds after Nixon's resignation (1974)		
Reagan's election begins new Republican era of "supply side" economics, deregulation, and military buildup (1980–1988)		*INS v. Chadha*—Court holds legislative veto to be unconstitutional (1983)
Iran-Contra affair (1986–1987)		Gramm-Rudman Act seeks to contain deficit spending (1985)
Bush elected on "no new taxes" pledge (1988)		
End of Cold War puts new emphasis on foreign policy (1989)	**1990**	With unprecedented use of veto power Bush checks Democratic agenda, amid charges of gridlock (1989–1990) Congress approves Iraq War; Bush gets U.N. sponsorship for 29-nation effort (1991)
Clinton elected, with help of voter support for Perot (1992)		Clinton bets his administration's success on deficit reduction with large tax increases (1993)

Chapter Review

The foundations for presidential government were set down in the Constitution by providing for a unitary executive and making the president head of state as well as head of government. The first section of this chapter reviewed the powers of each: the head of state with its military, judicial, and diplomatic powers, and the head of government with its executive, military, and legislative powers. But the presidency was subordinated to congressional government during the nineteenth century and part of the twentieth, as the national government took part in few domestic functions and was inactive or sporadic in foreign affairs.

The second section of the chapter showed the rise of modern presidential government following the long period of congressional government. There is no mystery in the shift to government centered on the presidency. Congress built the modern presidency essentially in the 1930s by delegating to it not only the power to implement the vast new programs of the New Deal but also by delegating its own legislative power to make policy. The cabinet, the other top presidential appointments, the White House staff, and the Executive Office of the President are some of the impressive formal resources of presidential power.

The third section focused on the president's impressive informal resources, in particular his political party, the supportive group coalitions, his access to the media, and, through that, his access to the millions of Americans who make up the general public. These resources are not cost-free or risk-free. The president's relationship with the public is his most potent modern resource, but the polls reveal that the public's rating of presidential performance tends to go down. Only international actions or events can boost presidential performance ratings, and then only briefly. This means that presidents may be tempted to use foreign policy for domestic purposes, which is not a good foundation for the task of taming the federal bureaucracy. For the president, the bureaucracy is a problem second only to foreign affairs.

The chapter concluded with an assessment of how well the two political branches (the executive and the legislative) make the bureaucracy accountable to the people it serves and controls. The president attempts to maintain accountability through management—largely through the cabinet, the White House staff, and the OMB. But each president's failure to achieve a satisfactory level of political accountability is marked by the willingness of Congress to give the next president more management help. Congress has basically two tools to meet its own responsibilities for maintaining bureaucratic accountability: clear legislation and legislative oversight. Legislative oversight breaks down into committee oversight and individual oversight. The ideal approach to bureaucratic accountability is statutes with clear legislative intent and presidents who respect that intent and see that it is imposed through management staff in the agencies themselves. "Bureaucracy in a democracy" was the theme of this section of the chapter not because we have succeeded in democratizing bureaucracies but because it is the never-ending task of politics in a democracy.

For Further Reading

Arnold, Peri E. *Making the Managerial Presidency: Comprehensive Organization Planning.* Princeton: Princeton University Press, 1986.

Bryner, Gary. *Bureaucratic Discretion.* New York: Pergamon Press, 1987.

Corwin, Edward S. *The Presidency: Office and*

Powers. 3rd ed. New York: New York University Press, 1957.

Edwards, George C. III. *The Public Presidency: The Pursuit of Popular Support.* New York: St. Martin's Press, 1983.

Fesler, James W., and Donald F. Kettl. *The Politics of the Administrative Process.* Chatham, NJ: Chatham House, 1991.

Frederickson, H. George, ed. *Ethics and Public Administration.* Armonk, NY: M. E. Sharpe, 1993.

Fry, Bryan R. *Mastering Public Administration—From Max Weber to Dwight Waldo.* Chatham, NJ: Chatham House, 1987.

Heclo, Hugh. *A Government of Strangers.* Washington, DC: Brookings Institution, 1977.

Hill, Larry B., ed. *The State of Public Bureaucracy.* Armonk, NY: M. E. Sharpe, 1991.

Kearns, Doris. *Lyndon Johnson and the American Dream.* New York: Harper & Row, 1965.

Lowi, Theodore J. *The Personal President: Power Invested, Promise Unfulfilled.* Ithaca: Cornell University Press, 1985.

Lynn, Naomi B., and Aaron Wildavsky. *Public Administration—The State of the Discipline.* Chatham, NJ: Chatham House, 1990.

McKay, David. *Domestic Policy and Ideology:*

Presidents and the American State, 1964–1987. New York: Cambridge University Press, 1989.

Mosher, Frederic C., *Democracy and the Public Service.* New York: Oxford University Press, 1968.

Nathan, Richard. *The Plot That Failed: Nixon's Administrative Presidency.* New York: Wiley, 1975.

Neustadt, Richard E. *Presidential Power: The Politics of Leadership from Roosevelt to Reagan,* rev. ed. New York: Free Press, 1990.

Pfiffner, James P., ed. *The Managerial Presidency.* Pacific Grove, CA: Brooks/Cole, 1991.

Polsby, Nelson, and Aaron Wildavsky. *Presidential Elections.* New York: Free Press, 1988.

Ripley, Randall B., and Grace A. Franklin. *Congress, the Bureaucracy and Public Policy.* Homewood, IL: Dorsey Press, 1991.

Rubin, Irene S. *The Politics of Public Budgeting.* Second Edition. Chatham, NJ: Chatham House, 1993.

Wildavsky, Aaron. *The New Politics of the Budget Process.* Second Edition. New York: HarperCollins, 1992.

Wilson, James Q. *Bureaucracy: What Government Agencies Do and Why They Do It.* New York: Basic Books, 1989.

7

THE FEDERAL COURTS: LEAST DANGEROUS BRANCH OR IMPERIAL JUDICIARY?

*E*very year nearly 25 million cases are tried in American courts and one American in every nine is directly involved in litigation. Cases can arise from disputes between citizens, from efforts by government agencies to punish wrongdoing, or from citizens' efforts to prove that a right provided them by law has been infringed upon as a result of government action—or inaction. Many critics of the American legal system assert that we have become much too ready to use the courts for all purposes, and perhaps we have. But the heavy use that Americans make of the courts is also an indication of the extent of conflict in American society. And given the existence of social conflict, it is far better that Americans seek to settle their differences through the courts rather than by fighting or feuding.

In this chapter, we will first examine the judicial process, including the types of cases that the federal courts consider. Second, we will assess the organization and structure of the federal court system as well as the flow of cases through the courts. Third, we will consider judicial review and how it makes the Supreme Court a "law-making body." Fourth, we will examine various influences on the Supreme Court. Finally, we will analyze the role and power of the federal courts in the American political process, looking in particular at the growth of judicial power in the United States. The framers of the American Constitution called the Court the "least dangerous branch" of American government. Today, it is not unusual to hear friends and foes of the Court alike refer to it as the "imperial judiciary."[1] Before we can understand this transformation and its consequences, however, we must look in some detail at America's judicial process.

The Judicial Process

Originally, a "court" was the place where a sovereign ruled—where the king and his entourage governed. Settling disputes between citizens was part of governing. According to the Bible, King Solomon had to settle the dispute between two women over which of them was the mother of the child both claimed. Judging is the settling of disputes, a function that was slowly separated from the king and the king's court and made into a separate institution of government. Courts have taken over from kings the power to settle controversies by hearing the facts on both sides and deciding which side possesses the greater merit. But since judges are not kings, they must have a basis for their authority. That basis in the United States is the Constitution and the law. Courts decide cases by hearing the facts on both sides of a dispute and applying the relevant law or principle to the facts. (See the In Brief Box on page 184 for the various types of laws and disputes.)

Cases and the Law

Most cases in the United States arise under common law and civil law, types of law that overlap. *Common law* has no statutory basis. It is established by judges, who apply previous case decisions to present cases. The previous cases are called *precedents;* they are applied under the doctrine of *stare decisis* ("let the decision stand"). Common law cases are always state and local cases; there is no federal common law. Lawyers representing each side in a dispute attempt to show, to their own clients' advantage, that a previous case is or is not a binding precedent for the case at hand. For example, did Smith's failure to deliver the goods on time constitute a breach of contract, or did certain circumstances relieve Smith of the obligation? Was Jones's injury in Johnson's swimming pool due to Johnson's negligence (*tort*), or did Jones contribute to it by drinking or horseplay (*contributory negligence*)? The one who brings a complaint is the *plaintiff;* the one against whom the complaint is brought is the *defendant.* In the twentieth century, more of these "civil" (noncriminal) cases have risen under laws adopted by legislatures rather than under common law. These legislative enactments are known as *civil law.*

The second category of law is *criminal law.* The government is the plaintiff and alleges that someone has committed a crime. Most of these cases arise in state courts. But there is a large body of federal criminal law and a growing number of federal criminal cases in such areas as tax evasion, mail fraud, false advertising, and sale of narcotics.

---

[1]See Richard Neely, *How Courts Govern America* (New Haven: Yale University Press, 1981).

In Brief Box

TYPES OF LAWS AND DISPUTES

Type of Law	Type of Case or Dispute	Form of Case
Judge-made law		
Common law	Previous decisions (precedents) applied by judges to current cases. Basis of large proportion of disputes between private citizens over contracts, property, divorce, injuries, and so on.	*Smith* v. *Jones*
Equity	Cases where applicable precedents are considered too rigid or inadequate	*Smith* v. *Jones*
Statutory law		
Civil law	Cases involving disputes between citizens or between government and citizen where no crime is alleged. Two general types are contract and tort. *Contract cases* are disputes that arise over voluntary actions. *Tort cases* are disputes that arise out of obligations inherent in social life. Negligence and slander are examples of torts.	*Smith* v. *Jones* *New York* v. *Jones* *U.S.* v. *Jones* *Jones* v. *New York*
Criminal law	Cases arising out of actions that violate laws protecting the health, safety, and morals of the community. The government is always the plaintiff.	*U.S. (or state)* v. *Jones* *Jones* v. *U.S (or state)*, if Jones lost and is appealing
Public law	All cases where the powers of government or the rights of citizens are involved. The government is the defendant. *Constitutional law* involves judicial review of the basis of a government's action in relation to specific clauses of the Constitution as interpreted in Supreme Court cases. *Administrative law* involves disputes over the statutory authority, jurisdiction, or procedures of administrative	*Jones* v. *U.S. (or state)* *In re Jones* *Smith* v. *Jones*, if a license or statute is at issue in their private dispute

A case becomes a matter of the third category, *public law*, if a plaintiff or a defendant can show that it involves questions of the government's authority to take action. For example, one vitally important public law case was *Berman* v. *Parker*, decided by the U.S. Supreme Court in 1954.[2] This case involved a government effort to clear slum properties in the nation's capital to make way for new housing. The Court held that the government had a very broad constitutional sanction, under the concept of "eminent domain," to declare that the public interest required the taking of land from a private owner. *Eminent domain* is a right of the government to seize private property for public purposes. In these cases, the government is, in a sense, always the defendant, because the court has to be convinced that the government does have the constitutional power or that the agency does have the statutory authority to take the action it seeks against a citizen. Public law cases include those in which a citizen claims that a government action violates his or her civil rights, as well as instances in which citizens charge that administrative agencies are conducting their activities in a manner inconsistent with the law—failing to file an environmental impact statement for a proposed project, for example.

Another kind of case is an *equity case*. This is a proceeding in court where the applicable law is either too rigid or too limited to provide a just as well as a legal remedy. For example, a common law principle or a statute may provide for monetary compensation for damage or injury, but a court may consider this compensation insufficient if the case involves damage to a family heirloom of great sentimental value. An equity case may also seek to prevent damage rather than to provide compensation after the damage is done.

Cases in the Courts

Courts of original jurisdiction are the courts that are responsible for discovering the facts in a controversy and creating the record upon which a judgment is based. Although the Constitution gives the Supreme Court original jurisdiction in several types of cases, such as those affecting ambassadors and those in which a state is one of the parties, most original jurisdiction goes to the lowest courts—the trial courts. (In courts that have appellate jurisdiction, judges receive cases after factual record is determined by the trial court. Ordinarily, new facts cannot be presented before appellate courts.)

THE ROLE OF JURIES. In courts of original jurisdiction, judges may be provided with juries to help them make their decisions. The Constitution requires juries for all criminal prosecutions (unless the defendant waives the right to a jury) and the right of trial by jury for all civil actions where the value in controversy exceeds $20. The jury brings community values to bear in the trial, and it helps weigh evidence and decide who gets the money or who is culpable and to what degree. The jury's role in the legal process, however, is quite circumscribed and heavily dependent upon the judge. The judge defines what the facts are, which of them are admissible, and which are relevant. The judge also defines the alternative verdicts open for a jury to reach. Jury decisions may also be reversed or altered by appeals courts when an error of procedure

[2]Berman v. Parker, 348 U.S. 26 (1954).

BOX 7.1
Federal Laws and Federal Cases

S ince all common law and most statutory laws in the American federal system are of state and local origin, it is not surprising that over 99 percent of all cases are tried in state and local courts. The relatively few federal cases can be grouped into three categories:

1. *Civil cases involving "diversity of citizenship."* The Constitution provides for federal jurisdiction whenever a citizen of one state brings suit against a citizen of another state. Congressional legislation requires that the amount at issue be more than $10,000. Otherwise the case is handled by a regular state court in the state where the grievance occurs.
2. *Civil cases where an agency of the federal government is seeking to enforce federal laws that provide for civil, not criminal, penalties.* These laws can range from bankruptcy laws to admiralty and maritime laws to occupational and consumer safety laws, environmental protection laws, and energy conservation and development laws.
3. *Cases where federal criminal statutes are involved or where issues of public law have been made of state criminal cases.* State prisoner petitions alleging mistreatment, unfair trial, or abridgement of civil rights represent the largest source of criminal cases coming before the federal appellate courts.

---

is deemed to have been made, even when the appeals court sympathizes with the original verdict.

Federal Jurisdiction

The overwhelming majority of court cases are tried not in federal courts but in state and local courts under state common law, state statutes, and local ordinances. Of all cases heard in the United States in 1990, federal district courts (the lowest federal level) received 266,000 (see Box 7.1). Although this number is up substantially from the 87,000 cases heard in 1961, it still constitutes under 1 percent of the judiciary's business. The federal courts of appeal listened to 40,898 cases in 1990, and the U.S. Supreme Court reviewed 6,316 in its 1990 term. Only 125 cases were given full-dress Supreme Court

review (the nine justices actually sitting *en banc*—in full court—and hearing the lawyers argue the case).[3]

The Lower Federal Courts

Most of the approximately 200,000 annual cases of original federal jurisdiction are handled by the federal district courts (see Figure 7.1 for the organization of all the U.S. courts). The federal district courts are trial

---

[3]Data were drawn from the National Court Statistical Project, Department of Justice, Law Enforcement Assistance Administration, *State Court Caseload Studies; Annual Report 1977* (Washington, DC: Government Printing Office, 1979); Administrative Office of the U.S. Courts, 1979 (Washington, DC: Government Printing Office, 1980); and Administrative Office of the U.S. Courts, *Annual Report of the Director 1979* (Washington, DC: Government Printing Office, 1980); Bureau of the Census, *Statistical Abstract of the United States* (Washington, DC: Government Printing Office, 1992).

FIGURE 7.1
Organization of the Courts

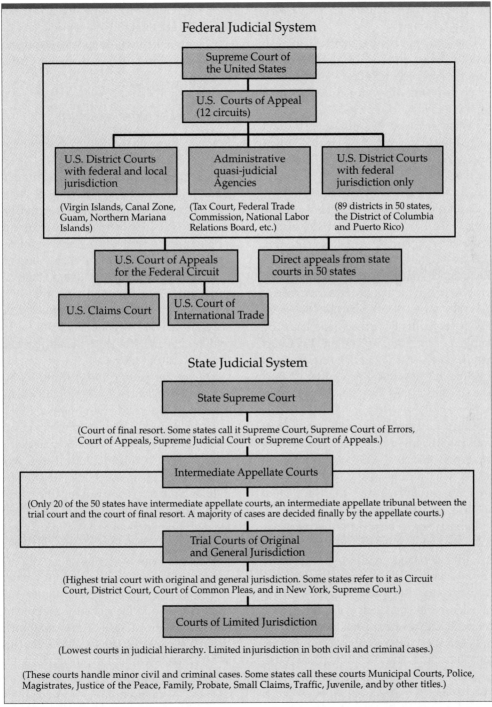

Federal Judicial System

Supreme Court of
the United States

U.S. Courts of Appeal
(12 circuits)

U.S. District Courts
with federal and local
jurisdiction

Administrative
quasi-judicial
Agencies

U.S. District Courts
with federal
jurisdiction only

(Virgin Islands, Canal Zone,
Guam, Northern Mariana
Islands)

(Tax Court, Federal Trade
Commission, National Labor
Relations Board, etc.)

(89 districts in 50 states,
the District of Columbia
and Puerto Rico)

U.S. Court of Appeals
for the Federal Circuit

Direct appeals from state
courts in 50 states

U.S. Claims Court

U.S. Court of
International Trade

State Judicial System

State Supreme Court

(Court of final resort. Some states call it Supreme Court, Supreme Court of Errors,
Court of Appeals, Supreme Judicial Court or Supreme Court of Appeals.)

Intermediate Appellate Courts

(Only 20 of the 50 states have intermediate appellate courts, an intermediate appellate tribunal between the
trial court and the court of final resort. A majority of cases are decided finally by the appellate courts.)

Trial Courts of Original
and General Jurisdiction

(Highest trial court with original and general jurisdiction. Some states refer to it as Circuit
Court, District Court, Court of Common Pleas, and in New York, Supreme Court.)

Courts of Limited Jurisdiction

(Lowest courts in judicial hierarchy. Limited in jurisdiction in both civil and criminal cases.)

(These courts handle minor civil and criminal cases. Some states call these courts Municipal Courts, Police,
Magistrates, Justice of the Peace, Family, Probate, Small Claims, Traffic, Juvenile, and by other titles.)

Source: Congressional Quarterly, *Guide to the Congress of the United States*, 3rd ed. (Washington, DC:
Congressional Quarterly, Inc., 1982). Used by permission.

courts of general jurisdiction and their cases are, in form, indistinguishable from cases in the state trial courts.

There are eighty-nine district courts in the fifty states, plus one in the District of Columbia and one in Puerto Rico, and four territorial courts. In an effort to deal with the greatly increased court workload, in 1978 Congress increased the number of district judgeships from 400 to 517. District judges are assigned to district courts according to the workload; the busiest of these courts may have as many as twenty-seven judges.

Besides the district courts, there are also some federal courts with original jurisdiction over specific classes of cases. The U.S. Court of Claims has jurisdiction over disputes about compensation when property has been taken for a public use, cases alleging that a government agency has not properly observed its contracts, and claims by employees for back pay. The U.S. Tax Court handles cases arising out of enforcement of the Internal Revenue (income tax) Code. The Customs Court also handles tax cases, but mainly those involving tariffs. The disputes are most often over the value that ought to be put on imported merchandise for tariff purposes. Original jurisdiction over patent infringement cases is given to an administrative agency, the U.S. Patent and Trademark Office.

Indeed, many administrative agencies enjoy the status of federal district courts in that their decisions go directly to a court of appeals and are not further tried by the district courts. Regulatory agencies whose decisions are appealed over the district courts directly to the appeals courts include the Securities and Exchange Commission, the National Labor Relations Board, the Federal Trade Commission, and the Interstate Commerce Commission. In 1990, the various U.S. appeals courts handled 40,898

cases. Of this total, 38,323 came directly from the U.S. district courts, and 2,578 came from the administrative agencies, boards, and commissions whose appeals go directly to the appeals courts, bypassing the district courts.

The Appellate Courts

Roughly 10 percent of all lower court and agency cases are accepted for review by the federal appeals courts and by the Supreme Court in its capacity as an appellate court. The country is divided into eleven judicial circuits, each of which has a U.S. Court of Appeals. Prior to the establishment of the appellate courts in 1891, each Supreme Court justice, in addition to his duties in Washington, was expected to act as the presiding judge of a circuit. This involved the arduous task of traveling from city to city within a circuit to review all cases appealed from the district courts.

One of the more colorful stories of Supreme Court justices "riding circuit" in the nineteenth century derives from the case of *In re Neagle* (1890). While sitting as a circuit justice in California, Justice Stephen Field ruled against a litigant, Mrs. Terry, who thereby lost a claim involving title to over a million dollars. Dismayed by the result, Mrs. Terry and her husband accused Justice Field of corruption and vowed to kill him if he should ever return to California. The next time Justice Field was obligated to ride circuit in California, he was assigned a bodyguard, Neagle, by the U.S. attorney general. Undaunted and determined to execute his murderous threat, Mr. Terry confronted Justice Field in a restaurant one day. But just as Mr. Terry was about to pull out his knife, Neagle shot and killed him. Neagle was arrested for murder, but he was acquitted. The Supreme Court held that he had acted on the basis of a valid executive order. (See Chapter 6 for a discussion of the broader constitutional issues raised by the case.) In 1891, Congress enacted a law creating a network of appellate courts to relieve Justice Field and other Supreme Court justices of having to ride circuit. Each justice is still chief of a circuit but is no longer required to be present as its presiding judge.

Except for cases selected for review by the Supreme Court, decisions made by the appeals courts are final. Because of this finality, certain safeguards have been built into the system. The most important is the provision of more than one judge for every appeals case. Each court of appeals has from three to fifteen permanent judgeships, depending on the workload of the circuit. Although normally three judges hear appealed cases, in some instances a larger number of judges sit together *en banc.*

Another safeguard is provided by the assignment of a Supreme Court justice as the circuit justice for each of the elven circuits. Since the creation of the appeals court in 1891, the circuit justice's primary duty has been to review appeals arising in the circuit in order to expedite Supreme Court action. The most frequent and best-known action of circuit justices is that of reviewing requests for stays of execution when the full Court is unable to do so—mainly during the summer, when the Court is in recess.

The Supreme Court

The Supreme Court is without question the apex of the entire U.S. judiciary—local, state, and federal. Article III of the Constitution vests "the judicial power of the United States" in the Supreme Court, and this court is supreme in fact as well as form. It has the power of judicial review—the power and the obligation to review any lower court decision where a substantial issue of public law is involved. The disputes can be over the constitutionality of federal or state laws, over the propriety or constitutionality of the court procedures followed, and over whether public officers are exceeding their authority. (See Box 7.2.)

Congress and the state legislatures do have the power virtually to overturn Court decisions by remedial legislation. Congress sought to overturn a series of 1989 Supreme Court decisions that limited the ability of members of minority groups to prove that they had been victims of employment discrimination. Although President Bush had vetoed a similar bill in 1990, Congress succeeded with the Civil Rights Act of 1991, which put the "burden of proof" to show discrimination back on the employer. Most of the time, however, state legislators and members of Congress have found it extremely difficult to summon up the majorities necessary to react against a Supreme Court decision. As Justice Robert Jackson once put it, "The Court is not final because it is infallible; the Court is infallible because it is final."[4]

Judicial Review

The Supreme Court's power of judicial review has come to mean review not only of lower court decisions but also of state legislation and acts of Congress. For this reason, if for no other, the Supreme Court is more than a judicial agency—it is also a major lawmaking body.

The Supreme Court's power of judicial review over lower court decisions has never been at issue. Nor has there been any serious quibble over the power of the federal courts

---

[4]Brown v. Allen, 344 U.S. 443 (1952).

BOX 7.2
Access to the Courts: The Rules of Standing

Over the years, in order to manage the many cases that come before it, the Supreme Court has developed rules governing which cases it can and cannot properly hear. The rules of access can be broken down into three major categories: (1) case or controversy, (2) standing, and (3) mootness.

(1) *Case or controversy:* The Constitution provides the judiciary with the power to decide various "cases" and "controversies," and the Supreme Court has from the very first taken this language to mean that it does not have the power to render advisory opinions. In *Muskrat* v. *United States* (1911), the Court extended the rule to eliminate feigned controversy. The case before the court must be a real controversy, with two truly adversarial parties: Even after a law is enacted, the courts will generally refuse to consider its constitutionality until it is actually applied. The major exception to this rule is the so-called declaratory judgement, in which a statute is deemed to be unconstitutional on its face. In the case of *Ada* v. *Guam Society of Obstetricians and Gynecologists,* for example, a federal appeals court in San Francisco struck down a 1990 Guam statute that made performing an abortion a felony.[*] The statute was challenged immediately after its enactment, and before it could actually be enforced, by Guam physicians who feared prosecution if they performed abortions. The federal appeals court declared that the statute, on its face, represented a violation of the constitutional protection of the right to abortion established in *Roe* v. *Wade.* In November 1992, the U.S. Supreme Court, with three justices dissenting, refused to give the case further consideration.

(2) *Standing:* To have standing is to be the proper person to bring a suit, and the basic requirement for standing is to show injury to oneself. In order for a group or class of people to have standing (as in class action suits), each member must show injury. The Court's definition of injury has changed over the years; it has expanded from the narrow reading of the term—personal and/or economic harm—to include such values as "aesthetic and environmental well-being" (*Sierra Club* v. *Morton* [1972]).

(3) *Mootness:* There are two time-factor requirements that must be met for the Court to hear a case. One is the question of ripeness. The Court must feel that the issue is ready to be heard—that the issue is still not too abstract, that all other possible remedies have been exhausted, that the matter has been absorbed into the national consciousness. Conversely, it is necessary that the case not be moot—that the particular problem not already have been resolved by other means. The Court began to relax its rules on mootness in cases where the situation was likely to come up again. For example, under the original definition of mootness, it was usually impossible to challenge election rules since the election was almost sure to be over by the time the case reached the appellate courts. But the Court began to hear some such cases if the issue was likely to be repeated in later elections (*Moore* v. *Ogilvie* [1969]). And as the Court pointed out in *Roe* v. *Wade* (1973), the major abortion case, questions relating to pregnancy could never be appealed if the older standards of mootness were to be applied, since the case would surely take longer than the pregnancy.

[*]See *Congressional Weekly Report*, 5 December 1992, p. 3751.

to review administrative agencies in order to determine whether their actions and decisions are within the powers delegated to them by Congress. There has, however, been a great deal of controversy occasioned by the Supreme Court's efforts to review acts of Congress and the decisions of state courts and legislatures.

Judicial Review of Acts of Congress

Since the Constitution does not give the Supreme Court the power of judicial review of congressional enactments, the Court's exercise of it is something of a usurpation.

Though Congress and the president have often been at odds with the Court, its legal power to review acts of Congress has not been seriously questioned since 1803 (see Box 7.3). One reason is that judicial power has been accepted as natural even though not specifically intended by the framers of the Constitution. Another reason is that the Supreme Court has rarely reviewed the constitutionality of the acts of Congress, especially in the past fifty years. When such acts do come up for review, the Court makes a self-conscious effort to give them an interpretation that will make them constitutional.

BOX 7.3
Marbury v. Madison

The 1803 Supreme Court decision handed down in *Marbury* v. *Madison* established the power of the Court to review acts of Congress. The case arose over a suit filed by William Marbury and seven other people against Secretary of State James Madison to require him to approve their appointments as justices of the peace. These had been last-minute ("midnight judges") appointments of outgoing President John Adams. Chief Justice John Marshall held that although Marbury and the others were entitled to their appointments, the Supreme Court had no power to order Madison to deliver them.

Marshall reasoned that constitutions are framed to serve as the "fundamental and paramount law of the nation." Thus, he argued, with respect to the legislative action of Congress, the Constitution is a "superior. . . . law, unchangeable by ordinary means." He concluded that an act of Congress that contradicts the Constitution must be judged void.

As to the question of whether the Court was empowered to rule on the constitutionality of legislative action, Marshall responded emphatically that it is "the province and duty of the judicial department to say what the law is." Since the Constitution is the supreme law of the land, he reasoned, it is clearly within the realm of the Court's responsibility to rule on the constitutionality of legislative acts and treaties. This principle has held sway ever since.

Sources: Gerald Gunther, *Constitutional Law* (Mineola, N.Y.: Fountain Press, 1980), pp. 9–11; and Marbury v. Madison, 1 Cr. 137 (1803).

Judicial Review of State Actions

The power of the Supreme Court to review state legislation or other state action and to determine its constitutionality is neither granted by the Constitution nor inherent in the federal system. But the logic of the "supremacy clause" of Article VI of the Constitution, which declares it and laws made under its authority to be the supreme law of the land, is very strong. Furthermore, in the Judiciary Act of 1789, Congress conferred on the Supreme Court the power to reverse state constitutions and laws whenever they are clearly in conflict with the U.S. Constitution, federal laws, or treaties.[5] This power gives the Supreme Court jurisdiction over all of the millions of cases handled by American courts each year.

The supremacy clause of the Constitution not only established the federal Constitution, statutes, and treaties as the "supreme law of the land," but also provided that "the Judges in every State shall be bound thereby, any Thing in the Constitution or Laws of the State to the Contrary notwithstanding." Under this authority, the Supreme Court has frequently overturned state constitutional provisions or statutes and state court decisions that it feels are counter to rights or privileges guaranteed under the Constitution or federal statutes.

Judicial Review and the Administration of Justice

Given the millions of disputes that arise every year, the job of the Supreme Court would be impossible if it were not able to control the flow of cases and its own case load (see Process Box 7.1). Its original jurisdiction is only a minor problem. The original jurisdiction includes: (1) cases between the United States and one of the fifty states, (2) cases between two or more states, (3) cases involving foreign ambassadors or other ministers, and (4) cases brought by one state against citizens of another state or against a foreign country. The most important of these cases are disputes between states over land, water, or old debts. Generally, the Supreme Court deals with these cases by appointing a "special master," usually a retired judge, to hear the case and present a report. The Supreme Court then allows the states involved in the dispute to present arguments for or against the master's opinion.[6]

The Supreme Court's major problem is the same as that of the head of any large organization—keeping most decisions at the lower level and bringing to the top only the few disputes that involve high-level policy. To do this, the Court must keep tight control over the number and type of cases it accepts for review.

Decisions handed down by lower courts can today reach the Supreme Court in one of two ways: through a writ of *certiorari,* or, in the case of convicted state prisoners, through a writ of *habeas corpus.* A writ is a court document conveying an order of some sort. In recent years, an effort has been made to give the Court more discretion regarding the cases it chooses to hear. Before 1988, the Supreme Court was obligated to review cases on what was called a writ of appeal. This has since been eliminated, and the

---

[5] This review power was affirmed by the Supreme Court in Martin v. Hunter's Lessee, 1 Wheaton 304 (1816).

[6] Walter F. Murphy, "The Supreme Court of the United States," in *Encyclopedia of the American Judicial System,* ed. Robert J. Janosik (New York: Scribners, 1987).

PROCESS BOX 7.1

How Cases Reach the Supreme Court

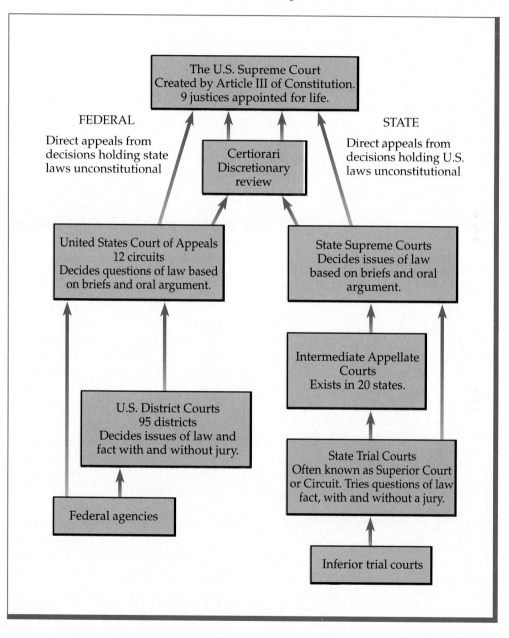

FEDERAL

Direct appeals from decisions holding state laws unconstitutional

STATE

Direct appeals from decisions holding U.S. laws unconstitutional

The U.S. Supreme Court
Created by Article III of Constitution.
9 justices appointed for life.

Certiorari
Discretionary
review

United States Court of Appeals
12 circuits
Decides questions of law based
on briefs and oral argument.

State Supreme Courts
Decides issues of law
based on briefs and oral
argument.

Intermediate Appellate
Courts
Exists in 20 states.

U.S. District Courts
95 districts
Decides issues of law and
fact with and without jury.

State Trial Courts
Often known as Superior Court
or Circuit. Tries questions of law
fact, with and without a jury.

Federal agencies

Inferior trial courts

Court now has virtually complete discretion over what cases it will hear.

Most cases reach the Supreme Court through the *writ of certiorari*, which is granted whenever four of the nine justices agree to review a case. The Supreme Court was once so inundated with appeals that in 1925 Congress enacted laws giving it some control over its case load with the power to issue writs of *certiorari*. Rule 10 of the Supreme Court's own rules of procedure defines *certiorari* as "not a matter of right, but of sound judicial discretion . . . granted only where there are special and important reasons therefor." The reasons provided for in Rule 10 are:

1. Where a state court has made a decision that conflicts with previous Supreme Court decisions.

2. Where a state court has come up with an entirely new federal question.

3. Where one court of appeals has rendered a decision in conflict with another.

4. Where there are other inconsistent rulings between two or more courts or states.

5. Where a single court of appeals has sanctioned too great a departure by a lower court from normal judicial proceedings (a reason rarely given).

The *writ of habeas corpus* is a fundamental safeguard of individual rights. Its historical purpose is to enable an accused person to challenge arbitrary detention and to force an open trial before a judge. But in 1867, Congress's distrust of southern courts led it to confer on federal courts the authority to issue writs of habeas corpus to prisoners already tried or being tried in state courts of proper jurisdiction, where the constitutional rights of the prisoner were possibly being violated. This writ gives state prisoners a second channel toward Supreme Court review in case their direct appeal from the highest state court fails. The writ of habeas corpus is discretionary; that is, the Court can decide which cases to review.

Judicial Review and Lawmaking

When courts of original jurisdiction apply existing statutes or past cases directly to citizens, the effect is the same as legislation. Lawyers study judicial decisions in order to discover underlying principles, and they advise their clients accordingly. Often the process is nothing more than reasoning by analogy; the facts in a particular case are so close to those in one or more previous cases that the same decision should be handed down.

The appellate courts, however, are in another realm. When a court of appeals hands down its decision, it accomplishes two things. First, of course, it decides who wins—the person who won in the lower court or the person who lost in the lower court. But at the same time, it expresses its decision in a manner that provides guidance to the lower courts for handling future cases in the same area. Appellate judges try to give their reasons and rulings in writing so the "administration of justice" can take place most of the time at the lowest judicial level. They try to make their ruling or reasoning clear, so as to avoid confusion, which can produce a surge of litigation at the lower levels. These rulings can be considered laws, but they are laws governing the behavior only of the judiciary. Decisions by appellate courts affect citizens by giving them a cause of action or by taking it away from them. That is, they open or close access to the courts.

In Brief Box

JUDICIAL REVIEW

Appellate courts are courts that exist solely to hear cases on appeal and, therefore, have no original jurisdiction. The exception to this rule is the Supreme Court, the highest appellate court in the country, which has original jurisdiction over cases between the states and cases involving foreign ambassadors and foreign countries. Most cases begin at the inferior trial courts or lower level courts, and then reach the Supreme Court in one of three ways:

Writ of Appeal	*Writ of Certiorari*	*Writ of Habeas Corpus*
A right available to all litigants	Not considered a right to all litigants	A fundamental safeguard of individual rights designed to enable an accused person to challenge arbitrary detention and to force an open trial before a judge
The Supreme Court accepts cases on appeal when it believes that it must do so	Cases heard when: state court decision conflicts with previous Supreme Court decisions; a new federal question has been raised; and if there have been inconsistent rulings between two or more states or courts of appeals	Cases appealed on a writ of *habeas corpus* are left to judicial discretion
Such cases are those in which a state law directly conflicts with the Constitution or a federal law, or where the United States is party to a civil suit	Most cases reach the Supreme Court on a writ of *certiorari*	
These situations occur rarely. The Court often remands the cases to a lower court rather than fully reviewing them	Cases appealed this way are left to judicial discretion where four of the nine justices must agree to hear the case	

BOX 7.4
Miranda v. Arizona

Throughout the 1950s and 1960s, increasingly vocal critics decried what they viewed as an alarming rise in "judicial activism" on the part of the Supreme Court. In a series of controversial rulings, the Court, led by Chief Justice Earl Warren, handed down sweeping rulings in controversial areas such as racial discrimination, school prayer, reapportionment, and rights of the accused. Few cases aroused more ire than that of the 1966 case of *Miranda* v. *Arizona*.

Ernesto Miranda was a poorly educated indigent of limited mental capabilities who had confessed to kidnapping and raping an eighteen-year-old woman. Miranda's confession provided key evidence of his complicity, but his conviction was challenged on the grounds that he had not been informed of his constitutional rights to remain silent and to have counsel during police questioning, as stated in the Fifth and Sixth Amendments, respectively.

By a 5-to-4 vote, the Supreme Court overturned Miranda's conviction, ruling that his confession was inadmissible in the absence of prior warnings from the police. "Prior to any questioning," the Court said, "the person must be warned that he has a right to remain silent, that any statement he does make may be used against him, and that he has a right to the presence of an attorney, either retained or appointed." The decision was based on the understanding that custodial interrogation of suspects not allowed to have lawyers present made it extremely difficult for a suspect to assert the right to avoid self-incrimination.

Critics raged that these new rules amounted to judicial invasion of local police houses, that they tied the hands of law enforcement officials, and balanced the scales of justice too heavily in favor of criminals. But the Supreme Court and others noted that the FBI had followed these procedures for years without a problem. Indeed, suspects often waived their rights and confessed. Studies of police behavior and criminal prosecutions after *Miranda* indicated that police were not prevented from doing their jobs.

Still, the *Miranda* decision did not sit well with many who felt that an individual who probably belonged in jail could be freed on a "technicality." President Richard Nixon won election in 1968 in part on a campaign of "law and order" that was based partially on Court rulings like *Miranda*. In the same year, Congress passed the Omnibus Crime Control and Safe Streets Act, Title II of which was aimed at curtailing suspect rights by allowing submission of confessions and other incriminating evidence if offered voluntarily but without Miranda warnings.

Despite protracted controversy and the appointment to the Supreme Court of more conservative justices, the Miranda principle has become an integral part of the law enforcement process, and an essential means for protecting basic rights, including the presumption of innocence, for all suspects. What some labeled derisively as legal "technicalities" are basic procedural safeguards that provide protection from the exercise of arbitrary government power.

Source: Liva Baker, *Miranda: Crime, Law and Politics* (New York: Atheneum, 1983).

Influences on Supreme Court Decisions

The judiciary is conservative in its procedures, but its impact on society can be radical. That impact depends on a variety of influences, three of which stand out above the rest. The first influence is the individual members of the Supreme Court, their attitudes, and their relationships with each other. The second is the Justice Department, especially the solicitor general, who regulates the flow of cases involving public law issues. The third is the pattern of cases.

The Supreme Court Justices

If any individual judges in the country influence the federal judiciary, they are the Supreme Court justices. Often in American history, presidents have sought to gain influence over the Court through the justices they appoint and, just as often, have been disappointed.

Both Republican presidents Ronald Reagan and George Bush assigned a high priority to the creation of a judiciary more sympathetic to conservative ideas and interests. Influenced by their five appointees, the Court grew more conservative over the past decade, modifying many high-court decisions of the previous thirty years in the areas of civil rights, criminal procedures, and abortion.

In 1993, the Library of Congress made public the papers of the late Justice Thurgood Marshall, long a champion of civil rights. The papers reveal not only his disappointment with the conservative direction of the Court, but also the key role played by Reagan's appointees in bringing about that change. For one, the papers reveal how close the Court came to overturning *Roe* in its *Webster* decision. Chief Justice Rehnquist's earliest drafts would have overturned *Roe*,

but he had only the support of three other justices, Scalia, Kennedy, and White, and needed O'Connor for a majority. She ultimately decided not to overturn *Roe,* and Rehnquist was forced to write a narrower ruling in the *Webster* case.[7]

A number of recent cases, in fact, suggest the development of a moderate bloc on the Court, consisting of Justices O'Connor, Kennedy, and Souter, thus defeating the Republican efforts to reshape the judiciary. Although all three were seen as conservatives at the time of their appointments, they have opposed the views of the political Right, particularly in the areas of school prayer and abortion.

In the 1992 case of *Lee* v. *Weisman,* the Court, by a 5-to-4 vote, held that the use of a prayer at a high school graduation was impermissible.[8] As to abortion, in the important 1992 case of *Planned Parenthood of Southeastern Pennsylvania* v. *Casey,* while the Court upheld state regulations requiring that women wait twenty-four hours after being provided with abortion information and requiring parental consent for minors, it reaffirmed the constitutional right to an abortion established by *Roe.* Indeed, in their unusual joint opinion, Justices O'Connor, Kennedy, and Souter expressed irritation at the White House for its ceaseless pressure on the Court to strike down *Roe* v. *Wade.*[9]

---

[7] See Joan Biskupic, "The Marshall Files: How an Era Ended in Civil Rights Law," *Washington Post,* 24 May 1993, p. 1; and Benjamin Weiser and Bob Woodward, "Roe's Eleventh-Hour Reprieve: 89 Drafts Show Court Poised to Strike Down Abortion Ruling," *Washington Post,* 23 May 1993, p. 1.

[8] Lee v. Weisman, 112 S.Ct. 2649 (1992).

[9] Planned Parenthood of Southeastern Pennsylvania v. Casey, 112 S.Ct. 2791 (1992). See also Joan Biskupic, "New Term Poses Test for Alliance at Center of Conservative Court," *Wall Street Journal,* 4 October 1992, p. A12; and Paul M. Barrett, "David Souter Emerges as Reflective Moderate on the Supreme Court," *Wall Street Journal,* 2 February 1993, p. 1.

John Marshall
The Great Chief Justice

John Marshall
(1755-1835)

John Marshall was sworn in as chief justice of the Supreme Court on February 4, 1801. Appointed in the waning days of the administration of John Adams, Marshall was a diehard Federalist at a time when that party was losing power. Adams's successor, Thomas Jefferson, was an archenemy, and the two were often at opposite ends of political quarrels. Moreover, Marshall came to the Court with marginal legal credentials. His formal education consisted of attending a few months' worth of lectures at the College of William and Mary. In short, Marshall's appointment resembled little more than the elevation of a political hack to the nation's highest court.

Yet, in his thirty-four years on the Supreme Court, John Marshall would win the admiration of friends and foes alike. He would help elevate the status of the judiciary to its rightful position among the three branches of government, and he would craft some of the most important decisions in the Court's history.

Although his formal training was limited, Marshall was admitted to the bar in 1780, and practiced law in western Virginia, his native state. Marshall earned a reputation as brilliant in constructing arguments, and became one of his state's most renowned lawyers. Marshall was a delegate to the Virginia Ratifying Convention, convened in 1788 to consider the new Constitution, where he staunchly defended the document.

Marshall viewed the Constitution as the central instrument of national unity and federal power. He considered the Constitution to be a precise document articulating specific powers, yet also as a living document open to broad interpretation for the purpose of affirming appropriate federal authority. He established for posterity the right of the Court to rule on the constitutionality of federal and state laws in the landmark case of *Marbury* v. *Madison*. In the *Dartmouth College* case and many others, he elevated the inviolability of contract and property rights. He gave teeth to the federal government's interstate commerce power in *Gibbons* v. *Ogden* by affirming that the federal government alone could regulate trade, travel, and navigation between the states.

In these and many other cases, Marshall exhibited an extraordinarily adept sense not only of law but also of the political and the possible. He recognized early that the courts had very limited power resources (neither purse nor sword). They would thus have to rely on procedure, precedent, respect for the law, and the avoidance of direct political confrontations. The shroud of constitutional legitimacy that today envelops the courts is the product more of John Marshall than of any other jurist.

Source: Robert McCloskey, *The American Supreme Court* (Chicago: University of Chicago Press, 1960).

TABLE 7.1

SUPREME COURT JUSTICES, 1994 (IN ORDER OF SENIORITY)

Name	Year of Birth	Prior Experience	Appointed By	Year of Appointment
William H. Rehnquist Chief Justice	1924	Assistant Attorney General	Nixon*	1972
Harry A. Blackmun	1908	Federal Judge	Nixon	1970
John Paul Stevens	1916	Federal Judge	Ford	1975
Sandra Day O'Connor	1930	State Judge	Reagan	1981
Antonin Scalia	1936	Law Professor, Federal Judge	Reagan	1986
Anthony Kennedy	1937	Federal Judge	Reagan	1988
David Souter	1940	Federal Judge	Bush	1990
Clarence Thomas	1948	Federal Judge	Bush	1991
Ruth Bader Ginsburg	1923	Federal Judge	Clinton	1993

*Appointed chief justice by Reagan in 1986.

They felt that this pressure posed a threat to the institutional integrity of the Supreme Court.

Bill Clinton's election in 1992 reduced the possibility of any further rightward drift on the part of the Court, for a time at least. During Clinton's first year in office, Justice Byron White, the conservative bloc's lone Democrat, announced his desire to retire from the bench. After a long search, the president nominated a Federal Appeals Court judge, Ruth Bader Ginsburg, to succeed White. Ginsburg was known as a moderate liberal. She had a long record of support for abortion rights and women's rights. However, as a federal appeals court judge, she often sided with the government in criminal cases and did not hesitate to vote against affirmative action plans she deemed to be too broad. Most observers viewed Ginsburg as a probable addition to Kennedy, Souter, and O'Connor in the Court's moderate bloc.[10]

OPINION WRITING. When the Court reaches a decision on a case, it renders an "opinion"; the Court issues both a majority opinion and a minority, or dissenting, opinion. The assignment to write the majority opinion in an important constitutional case is an opportunity for the chosen justice to exercise great influence on the Court. The assignment is made by the chief justice, or by the senior associate justice in the majority when the chief justice is a dissenter. But it is not a simple procedure. Serious thought has to be

[10]See Richard L. Berke, "Clinton Names Ruth Ginsburg, Advocate for Women, To Court: Centrist Role Cited," *New York Times*, 15 June 1993, p. 1. See also Joan Biskupic, "Judge Ruth Ginsburg Named to High Court: Nominee's Philosophy Seen Strengthening the Center," *Washington Post*, 15 June 1993, p. 1.

given to the impression the case will make on lawyers and on the public and to the probability that one justice's opinion will be more widely accepted than another's.

One of the more dramatic instances of this tactical consideration occurred in 1944, when Chief Justice Harlan F. Stone chose Justice Felix Frankfurter to write the opinion in the "white primary" case, *Smith* v. *Allwright*. The chief justice believed that this sensitive case, which overturned the southern practice of prohibiting black participation in nominating primaries, required the efforts of the most brilliant and scholarly jurist on the Court. But, the day after Stone made the assignment, Justice Robert H. Jackson wrote a letter to Stone urging a change of assignment. In it Jackson argued that Frankfurter, a foreign-born Jew from New England, would not win the South with his opinion, regardless of its brilliance. Stone accepted the advice and substituted Justice Stanley Reed, an American-born Protestant from Kentucky, who was a southern Democrat in good standing.[11]

DISSENT. Ironically, the most dependable way an individual justice can exercise a direct and clear influence on the Court is to write a dissenting opinion. Because there is no need to please a majority, dissenting opinions can be more eloquent and less guarded than majority opinions (see Box 7.5). Indeed, some of the greatest writing in the history of the Court is found in dissents, and some of the most famous justices, such as Oliver Wendell Holmes and Louis D. Brandeis earlier in this century, and liberal Justice William O. Douglas in more recent years, were notable dissenters. In the single 1952–1953 Court term, Douglas wrote dis-

senting opinions in thirty-five cases. In the 1958–1959 term, he wrote eleven dissents. During the latter term, Justices Frankfurter and Harlan wrote thirteen and nine dissents, respectively.

Dissent plays a special role in the work and impact of the Court because it amounts to an appeal to lawyers all over the country to keep bringing cases of the sort at issue. Therefore, an effective dissent influences the flow of cases through the Court as well as the arguments that will be used by lawyers in later cases. Even more important, dissent emphasizes the fact that, although the Court speaks with a single opinion, it is the opinion only of the majority—and one day the majority might go the other way.

Individual Supreme Court justices thus have a certain amount of influence by virtue of their participation in choosing cases and in constituting a majority—or a dissenting minority—on the decisions. Since four justices must vote to grant *certiorari*, however, there are only three ways a single justice can significantly influence the judicial process: (1) by writing an eloquent dissenting opinion, (2) by issuing a stay of execution pending full Court review, and (3) by issuing a writ of habeas corpus, temporarily removing a criminal case from state jurisdiction until the Court can determine its merits. The latter two powers lead to temporary stoppages pending review by the full Court.

Controlling the Flow of Cases—The Role of the Solicitor General

If any single person has greater influence than the individual justices over the work of the Supreme Court, it is the solicitor general of the United States. The solicitor general is third in status in the Justice Department (below the attorney general and the deputy

---

[11]*Smith v. Allwright*, 321 U.S. 649 (1944).

BOX 7.5
Dissenting Opinion

D issenting opinions differ significantly in form from majority opinions. A dissenting opinion points out the fallacies in the majority's reasoning and attempts to lay the groundwork for limiting or overruling the majority opinion in the future. Because a dissenting judge need not hold together a majority of the Court, such an opinion is often quite direct in its criticism of the majority. For example, in *New York* v. *Quarles* (1984), Justice Marshall began his dissent with the observation that "[t]he majority's treatment of the legal issues presented in this case is no less troubling than its abuse of the facts."

In *Bowers* v. *Hardwick* (1986), the Supreme Court was asked to decide whether a Georgia statute prohibiting sodomy violated a constitutional right to privacy. Hardwick, a Georgia male, had been cited for violating the statute by engaging in consensual sexual activity with another male in Hardwick's home. The majority of the Court upheld the Georgia statute, ruling that the constitutional right of privacy protected the traditional family unit and did not protect conduct between homosexuals when that conduct offended "traditional Judeo-Christian values." The following passage is excerpted from the dissenting opinion of Justice Blackmun:

> This case is no more about "a fundamental right to engage in homosexual sodomy," as the Court purports to declare . . . than *Stanley* v. *Georgia* was about a fundamental right to watch obscene movies, or *Katz* v. *United States* was about a fundamental right to place interstate bets from a telephone booth. Rather, this case is about "the most comprehensive of rights and the right most valued by civilized men," namely, "the right to be let alone" (*Olmstead* v. *United States*).

* * *

> Like Justice Holmes, I believe that "[i]t is revolting to have no better reason for a rule of law than that it was laid down in the time of Henry IV. It is still more revolting if the grounds upon which it was laid down have vanished long since, and the rule simply persists from blind imitation of the past" (Holmes, *The Path of the Law*). I believe we must analyze respondent's claim in the light of the values that underlie the constitutional right to privacy. If that right means anything, it means that, before Georgia can prosecute its citizens for making choices about the most intimate aspects of their lives, it must do more than assert that the choice they have made is an "abominable crime not fit to be named among Christians" (*Herring* v. *State*).

* * *

> I can only hope that . . . the Court soon will reconsider its analysis and conclude that depriving individuals of the right to choose for themselves how to conduct their intimate relationships poses a far greater threat to the values most deeply rooted in our Nation's history than tolerance of nonconformity could ever do. Because I think the Court today betrays those values, I dissent.

attorney general, who serve as the government's chief prosecutors) but is the top government defense lawyer in almost all cases before the appellate courts where the government is a party. Although others can regulate the flow of cases, the solicitor general has the greatest control, with no review of his actions by any higher authority in the executive branch. More than half the Supreme Court's total work load consists of cases under his direct charge. Even the bland description in the *U.S. Government Manual* cannot mask the extraordinary importance of the solicitor general:

> The Solicitor General is in charge of representing the Government in the Supreme Court. He decides what cases the Government should ask the Supreme Court to review and what position the Government should take in cases before the Court; he supervises the preparation of the Government's Supreme Court briefs and other legal documents and the conduct of the oral arguments in the Court and argues most of the important cases himself. The Solicitor General's duties also include deciding whether the United States should appeal in all cases it loses before the lower courts.[12]

The influence of the solicitor general is especially strong because he screens cases long before they approach the Supreme Court, and the justices rely on him to "screen out undeserving litigation and furnish them with an agenda to government cases that deserve serious consideration."[13] Agency heads may lobby the president or

otherwise try to circumvent the solicitor general, and a few of the independent agencies have a statutory right to make direct appeals, but these are almost inevitably doomed to *per curiam* rejection—rejection through a brief, unsigned opinion by the whole Court—if the solicitor general refuses to participate.

The solicitor general can enter a case even when the federal government is not a direct litigant by writing an *amicus curiae* ("friend of the court") brief. A "friend of the court" is not a direct party to a case but has a vital interest in its outcome. Thus, when the government has such an interest, the solicitor general can file as *amicus curiae,* or the Court can invite him to file a brief because it wants his opinion in writing. The solicitor general also has the power to invite others to enter cases as *amici curiae.*

Judicial Power and Politics

One of the most important institutional changes to occur in the United States during the past half century has been the striking transformation of the role and power of the federal courts, those of the Supreme Court in particular. Understanding how this transformation came about is the key to understanding the contemporary role of the courts in America.

Traditional Limitations on the Federal Courts

For much of American history, the power of the federal courts was subject to five limitations.[14] First, courts were constrained by ju-

---

[12]*United States Government Organization Manual* (Washington, DC: Government Printing Office, 1985).

[13]Robert Scigliano, *The Supreme Court and the Presidency* (New York: Free Press, 1971), p. 162. For an interesting critique of the solicitor general's role during the Reagan administration, see Lincoln Caplan, "Annals of the Law," *New Yorker,* 17 August 1987, pp. 30–62.

[14]For limits on judicial power, see Alexander Bickel, *The Least Dangerous Branch* (Indianapolis: Bobbs-Merrill, 1962).

dicial rules of standing that limited access to the bench. Claimants who simply disagreed with governmental action or inaction could not obtain access. Access to the courts was limited to individuals who could show that they were directly affected by the government's behavior in some area. This limitation on access to the courts diminished the judiciary's capacity to forge links with important political and social forces. Second, courts were traditionally limited in the kind of relief they could provide. In general, courts acted only to offer relief or assistance to individuals and not to broad social classes, again inhibiting the formation of alliances between the courts and important social forces.

Third, courts lacked enforcement powers of their own and were compelled to rely upon executive or state agencies to ensure compliance with their edicts. And if the executive or state agencies were unwilling to assist the courts, judicial enactments could go unheeded, as was illustrated when President Andrew Jackson declined to enforce Chief Justice John Marshall's 1832 order to the state of Georgia to release two missionaries it had arrested on Cherokee lands. Marshall asserted that the state had no right to enter the lands of the Cherokees without their assent.[15] Jackson is reputed to have said, "John Marshall has made his decision, now let *him* enforce it."

Fourth, federal judges are appointed by the president (with the consent of the Senate). As a result, the president and Congress can shape the composition of the federal courts and ultimately, perhaps, the character of judicial decisions. Finally, Congress has the power to change both the size and the jurisdiction of the Supreme Court and

other federal courts. In many areas, federal courts obtain their jurisdiction not from the Constitution but from congressional statutes.

On a number of occasions, Congress has threatened to take matters out of the Court's hands when it was unhappy with the Court's rulings on certain cases.[16] For example, on one memorable occasion, presidential and congressional threats to expand the size of the Supreme Court—Franklin Roosevelt's "court packing" plan—encouraged the justices to drop their opposition to New Deal programs. As a result of these five limitations on judicial power, through much of their history the chief function of the federal courts was to provide judicial support for executive agencies and to legitimate acts of Congress by declaring them to be consistent with constitutional principles. Only on rare occasions did the federal courts actually dare to challenge Congress or the executive.[17]

Two Judicial Revolutions

Since the Second World War, however, the role of the federal judiciary has been strengthened and expanded. There have actually been two judicial revolutions in the United States since World War II. The first and most visible of these was the substantive revolution in judicial policy. In policy areas, including school desegregation, legislative apportionment, and criminal procedure, as well as regarding obscenity, abortion, and voting rights, the Supreme Court was at the forefront of a series of sweeping changes in the role of the U.S. government

---

[15]Worcester v. Georgia, 6 Peters 515 (1832).

[16]See Walter Murphy, *Congress and the Court* (Chicago: University of Chicago Press, 1962).

[17]Robert Dahl, "The Supreme Court and National Policy Making," *Journal of Public Law* 6 (1958), p. 279.

DEBATING THE ISSUES

Interpreting the Constitution and Original Intent

*J*udges bear the responsibility of interpreting the meaning and applicability of the Constitution, written over two hundred years ago, to modern society. The application of constitutional principles to modern problems is inherently difficult because of disagreements over what the founders intended and over how the Constitution's words ought to apply to issues and problems unimagined in the eighteenth century.

Former federal judge Robert H. Bork argues in favor of the "original intent" approach, urging judges to stick as closely to the Constitution's text and original meaning as possible. Constitutional scholar Leonard W. Levy counters that original intent, even if it could be divined, is an inadequate and inappropriate way to deal with constitutional interpretation.

Bork

What was once the dominant view of constitutional law—that a judge is to apply the Constitution according to the principles intended by those who ratified the document—is now very much out of favor among the theorists of the field. . . .

In truth, only the approach of original understanding meets the criteria that any theory of constitutional adjudication must meet in order to possess democratic legitimacy. Only that approach is consonant with the design of the American Republic. . . .

. . . The original understanding is . . . manifested in the words used and in secondary materials, such as debates at the conventions, public discussion, newspaper articles, dictionaries in use at the time, and the like.

The search for the intent of the lawmaker is the everyday procedure of lawyers and judges when they apply a statute, a contract, a will, or the opinion of a court. . . . Lawyers and judges should seek in the Constitution what they seek in other legal texts: the original meaning of the words. . . .

A judge, no matter on what court he sits, may never create new constitutional rights or destroy old ones. Any time he does so, he violates the limits of his own authority and, for that reason, also violates the rights of the legislature and the people. . . .

---

and, ultimately, in the character of American society.[18]

But at the same time that the courts were introducing important policy innovations, they were also bringing about a second, less

visible revolution. During the 1960s and 1970s, the Supreme Court and other federal courts instituted a series of changes in judicial procedures that fundamentally expanded the power of the courts in the United States. First, the federal courts liberalized the concept of standing to permit almost any group to bring its case before the federal bench.

Second, the federal courts broadened the

[18]Martin Shapiro, "The Supreme Court: From Warren to Burger," in *The New American Political System,* ed. Anthony King (Washington, DC: American Enterprise Institute, 1978).

The role of a judge committed to the philosophy of original understanding is not to "choose a level of abstraction." Rather, it is to find the meaning of a text—a process which includes finding its degree of generality, which is part of its meaning—and to apply that text to a particular situation. . . . The equal-protection clause [for example] was adopted in order to protect freed slaves, but its language, being general, applies to all persons.[1]

Levy

James Madison, Father of the Constitution and of the Bill of Rights, rejected the doctrine that the original intent of those who framed the Constitution should be accepted as an authoritative guide to its meaning. "As a guide in expounding and applying the provisions of the Constitution . . . . the debates and incidental decisions of the Convention can have no authoritative character." . . . We tend to forget the astounding fact that Madison's Notes were first published in 1840, fifty-three years after the Constitutional Convention had met. . . . What mattered to them [the founders] was the text of the Constitution, construed in the light of conventional rules of interpretation, the ratification debates, and other contemporary expositions. . . . Original intent is an unreliable concept because it assumes the existence of one intent. . . . The entity we call "the Framers" did not have a collective mind. . . . In fact, they disagreed on many crucial matters. . . .

Fifty years ago . . . Jacobus tenBroek asserted, rightly, that "the intent theory . . . inverts the judicial process." . . . Original intent . . . makes the judge "a mindless robot whose task is the utterly mechanical function" of using original intent as a measure of constitutionality. In the entire history of the Supreme Court . . . no Justice employing the intent theory has ever written a convincing and reliable study.

The Court has the responsibility of helping regenerate and fulfill the noblest aspirations for which the nation stands. It must keep constitutional law constantly rooted in the great ideals of the past yet in a state of evolution in order to realize them. . . . Chief Justice Earl Warren . . . declared, "We serve only the public interest as we see it, guided only by the Constitution and our own consciences." That, not the original intent of the Framers, is our reality.[2]

[1]Robert H. Bork, "The Case against Political Judging," *National Review,* 8 December 1989, pp. 23–28.
[2]Leonard W. Levy, *Original Intent and the Framers' Constitution* (New York: Macmillan, 1988), pp. 1–2, 294, 388, 396, 398.

scope of relief to permit action on behalf of broad categories or classes of persons in "class action" cases, rather than just on behalf of individuals.[19] A class action suit permits large numbers of persons with common interests to join together under a representative party to bring or defend a lawsuit.

Third, the federal courts began to employ so-called structural remedies, in effect retaining jurisdiction of cases until the court's mandate had actually been implemented to its satisfaction.[20] The best-known of these instances was Federal Judge W. Arthur Garrity's effort to operate the Boston School

[19]See "Developments in the Law—Class Actions," *Harvard Law Review* 89 (1976), p. 1318.

[20]See Donald Horowitz, *The Courts and Social Policy* (Washington, DC: Brookings Institution, 1977).

Thurgood Marshall and Clarence Thomas From Helping Others to Self-Help

A s the first and second African Americans to serve on the Supreme Court, Thurgood Marshall and Clarence Thomas both claimed humble origins rooted in America's troubled racial past. Marshall was the great-grandson of a slave; Thomas was a sharecropper's grandson. Yet their public careers represent diametrically opposed views on how the law should treat disadvantaged citizens.

Born and raised in a Baltimore family of modest means but grand ambitions, Marshall graduated from Howard Law School and began a legal practice specializing in cases defending blacks mistreated by the legal system. In 1938, he became head of Legal Services for the National Association for the Advancement of Colored People (NAACP). In the 1940s and 1950s, he spearheaded legal efforts to end discrimination, arguing thirty-two cases before the Supreme Court (including *Brown* v. *Board of Education*). After Marshall had served on the U.S. Court of Appeals and as President Lyndon Johnson's solicitor general, he was elevated by Johnson to the Supreme Court in 1967.

Clarence Thomas's appointment to the high court by President George Bush in 1991 reinforced the Court's more conservative tendencies. His early education in a Catholic seminary had instilled in Thomas the belief that hard work and individual initiative could overcome racial discrimination and other adversities. Ironically, Thomas won admission to Yale Law School on a program aimed at recruiting blacks and others from disadvantaged backgrounds. His rapid rise included service in the Missouri attorney general's office. In his early work, Thomas carefully avoided race-related issues, but the Reagan

Thurgood Marshall

system from his bench in order to ensure its desegregation. Between 1974 and 1985, Judge Garrity issued fourteen decisions relating to different aspects of the Boston school desegregation plan that had been developed under his authority and put into effect under his supervision.[21] In its 5-to-4 decision in the 1990 case of *Missouri* v. *Jenkins*, the Supreme Court held that federal

---

[21]Moran v. McDonough, 540 F. 2nd 527 (1 Cir., 1976; *cert denied* 429 U.S. 1042 [1977]).

administration named him head of the Equal Employment Opportunity Commission, the agency that enforces laws against discrimination. Thomas then served briefly on the court of appeals before his ascension to the Supreme Court.

In his many opinions from the bench, Marshall championed government efforts to eliminate discrimination through such means as busing to achieve racial balance in schools and the implementation of affirmative action programs designed to provide educational and employment opportunities for those who had been historically closed out of certain areas. Thomas has been a strong critic of such programs. In a 1987 law journal article, for example, Thomas criticized the landmark *Brown* case; later he sharply attacked Marshall himself, saying that it was wrong for Marshall to dwell on slavery during the commemoration of the Constitution's bicentennial.

Thomas himself ran afoul of the nation's heightened sensitivity to discrimination and fair treatment when a former employee, law school professor Anita Hill, leveled charges of sexual harassment against him that riveted the nation's attention.

On the Court, Thomas's conservative philosophy has stood in stark contrast to Marshall's liberal philosophy. Unlike the man he succeeded, Thomas favors the death penalty (including limiting death penalty appeals) and limiting the rights of the accused, opposes abortion rights, and in general has sided with the conservative activist wing of the Court.

Justice Marshall sought to focus the powers of government to assist those who have benefited least from the American system. Justice Thomas argues that self-help and limited government interference provide the most appropriate remedy for injustice. Both of these arguments will continue to find support in American courts.

Source: Richard Kluger, *Simple Justice* (New York: Vintage Books, 1975).

Clarence Thomas

judges could actually order local governments to increase taxes to remedy such violations of the Constitution as school segregation.[22] This decision upheld an order by

the federal district judge, Russel G. Clark, to the Kansas City, Missouri, school board to adopt a "magnet" school plan that would lessen segregation in the schools. Potentially, this decision claims for the judiciary the power to levy taxes—a power normally

[22]*Missouri v. Jenkins*, 110 S.Ct. 1651 (1990).

seen as belonging to elected legislatures.

Through these three judicial mechanisms, the federal courts paved the way for an unprecedented expansion of national judicial power. In essence, liberalization of the rules of standing and expansion of the scope of judicial relief drew the federal courts into linkages with important social interests and classes, while the introduction of structural remedies enhanced the courts' abilities to serve these constituencies. Thus, during the 1960s and 1970s, the power of the federal courts expanded in the same way that the power of the executive expanded during the 1930s—through links with constituencies, such as civil rights, consumer, environmental, and feminist groups, that staunchly defended the Supreme Court in its battle with Congress, the executive, or other interest groups.

The Reagan and Bush administrations, of course, sought to end this relationship between the Court and liberal political forces. As we have seen, the conservative judges appointed by these Republican presidents modified the Court's position in areas such as abortion, affirmative action, and judicial procedure—though not as completely as some conservatives had hoped. Interestingly, however, the Court has not been eager to surrender the expanded powers carved out by its liberal predecessors. In a number of decisions during the 1980s and 1990s, the Court was willing to make use of its expanded powers on behalf of interests it favored.[23]

In the important 1992 case of *Lujan* v. *Defenders of Wildlife,* the Court seemed to retreat to a conception of standing more restrictive than that affirmed by liberal activist jurists.[24] Rather than an example of judicial restraint, however, the *Lujan* case was actually a direct judicial challenge to congressional power. The case involved an effort by an environmental group, the Defenders of Wildlife, to make use of the 1973 Endangered Species Act to block the expenditure of federal funds being used by the governments of Egypt and Sri Lanka for public works projects. Environmentalists charged that the projects threatened the habitats of several endangered species of birds and, therefore, that the expenditure of federal funds to support the projects violated the 1973 act. The Interior Department claimed that the act affected only domestic projects.[25]

The Endangered Species Act, like a number of other pieces of liberal environmental and consumer legislation enacted by Congress, encourages citizen suits—suits by activist groups not directly harmed by the action in question—to challenge government policies they deem to be inconsistent with the act. Justice Scalia, however, writing for the Court's majority, reasserted a more traditional conception of standing, requiring those bringing suit against a government policy to show that the policy is likely to cause *them* direct and imminent injury.

Had Scalia stopped at this point, the case might have been seen as an example of judicial restraint. Scalia, however, went on to question the validity of any statutory provision for citizen suits. Such legislative provisions, according to Justice Scalia, violate Article III of the Constitution, which limits the federal courts to consideration of actual "cases" and "controversies." This interpre-

---

[23]Mark Silverstein and Benjamin Ginsberg, "The Supreme Court and the New Politics of Judicial Power," *Political Science Quarterly* 102 (Fall 1987), pp. 371–88.

[24]Lujan v. Defenders of Wildlife, 112 S.Ct. (1992).

[25]Linda Greenhouse, "Court Limits Legal Standing in Suits," *New York Times,* 13 June 1992, p. 12.

tation would strip Congress of its capacity to promote the enforcement of regulatory statutes by encouraging activist groups not directly affected or injured to be on the lookout for violations that could provide the basis for lawsuits. This enforcement mechanism—which conservatives liken to bounty hunting—was an extremely important congressional instrument and played a prominent part in the enforcement of such pieces of legislation as the 1990 Americans with Disabilities Act (see Chapter 11). Thus, the *Lujan* case offers an example of judicial activism rather than of judicial restraint.

But it also remains to be seen what effect a Democratic president will have on the composition of the Court. If President Clinton has his way, in a few years, conservatives may be complaining again about judicial liberalism.

Time Line on the Judiciary

EVENTS		INSTITUTIONAL DEVELOPMENTS
George Washington appoints John Jay chief justice (1789–1795)	**1800**	Judiciary Act creates federal court system (1789)
John Marshall appointed chief justice (1801)		*Marbury* v. *Madison* provides for judicial review (1803)
States attempt to tax the second Bank of the U.S. (1818)		*McCulloch* v. *Maryland*—Court upholds supremacy clause, broad construction of necessary and proper clause; denies right of states to tax federal agencies (1819)
Andrew Jackson appoints Roger Taney chief justice; Taney Court expands power of states (1835)		*Barron* v. *Baltimore*—Court rules that only the federal government and not the states are limited by the U.S. Bill of Rights (1833)
Period of westward expansion; continuing conflict and congressional compromises over slavery in the territories (1830s–1850s)	**1850**	*Dred Scott* v. *Sandford*—Court rules that federal government cannot exclude slavery from the territories (1857)
Civil War (1861–1865)		*Slaughterhouse Cases*—Court limits scope of Fourteenth Amendment to newly freed slaves; states retain right to regulate state businesses (1873)
Reconstruction (1866–1877)		
Self-government restored to former Confederate states (1877)		

EVENTS		INSTITUTIONAL DEVELOPMENTS
"Jim Crow" laws spread throughout southern states (1890s)	**1890**	*Plessy* v. *Ferguson*—Court upholds doctrine of "separate but equal" (1896)
World War I; wartime pacifist agitation in U.S. (1914–1919)		*Abrams* v. *U.S.* (1919) to *Gitlow* v. *N.Y.* (1925) apply First Amendment to states and limit free speech by "clear and present danger" test
Red Scare; postwar anarchist agitation (1919–1920)		
FDR's New Deal (1930s)	**1930**	Court invalidates many New Deal laws, e.g., *Schechter Poultry Co.* v. *U.S.* (1935)
Court-packing crisis—proposal to increase the number of Supreme Court justices defeated by Congress (1937)		Court reverses position, upholds most of New Deal, e.g., *NLRB* v. *Jones & Laughlin Steel* (1937)
U.S. enters World War II (1941–1945)		*Korematsu* v. *U.S.*—Court approves sending Japanese-Americans to internment camps (1944)
Korean War (1950–1953)	**1950**	*Youngstown Sheet & Tube Co.* v. *Sawyer*—Court rules that president's steel seizure must be authorized by statute (1952)
Earl Warren appointed chief justice (1953)		
Civil rights movement (1950s and 1960s)		*Brown* v. *Board of Ed.*—Court holds that school segregation is unconstitutional (1954)
		Court begins nationalization of the Bill of Rights—*Baker* v. *Carr* (1962); *Gideon* v. *Wainwright* (1963); *Escobedo* v. *Ill.* (1964); *Miranda* v. *Arizona* (1966), etc.
Consumer, environmental, feminist, and antinuclear movements (1960s–1990s)		*Flast* v. *Cohen*—Court permits class action suits (1968)
Warren Burger appointed chief justice (1969)		

EVENTS		INSTITUTIONAL DEVELOPMENTS
Right-to-life movement (1970s and 1990s)	**1970**	*Roe* v. *Wade*—Court strikes down state laws making abortion illegal (1973)
Affirmative action programs (1970s–1990s)		*Univ. of Calif.* v. *Bakke*—Court holds that race may be taken into account but limits use of quotas (1978)
Court arbitrates conflicts between Congress and president (1970s and 1980s)		*U.S.* v. *Nixon*—Court limits executive privilege (1974); *Bowsher* v. *Synar*—Court invalidates portion of Gramm-Rudman Act (1986);
William Rehnquist appointed chief justice (1986)		*Morrison* v. *Olson*—Court upholds constitutionality of special prosecutor (1988)
Bush appoints David Souter to the Supreme Court (1990)	**1990**	Reagan and Bush appointees create a Republican Court (1980–1991)
Bush appoints Clarence Thomas to the Supreme Court (1991)		
Clinton appoints Ruth Bader Ginsburg to the Supreme Court (1993)		Souter, O'Connor, and Kennedy form a moderate bloc (1992)

Chapter Review

Millions of cases come to trial every year in the United States. The great majority—nearly 99 percent—are tried in state and local courts. The types of law are common law, civil law, criminal law, and public law. In addition, equity proceedings permit courts to take into account special situations and conditions when rigid literal adherence to precedents and statutes would not serve the interests of justice.

There are three kinds of federal cases: (1) civil cases involving diversity of citizenship, (2) civil cases where a federal agency is seeking to enforce federal laws that provide for civil penalties, and (3) cases involving federal criminal statutes or where state criminal cases have been made issues of public law.

Juries help define the American judicial process. In courts of original jurisdiction, juries are constitutionally required in all criminal prosecutions and, when requested by the defendants, in all civil actions where the value in controversy exceeds $20.

Judge-made law is like a statute in that it articulates the law as it relates to future controversies. It differs from a statute in that it is intended to guide judges rather than the citizenry in general.

The organization of the federal judiciary provides for original jurisdiction in the federal district courts, the U.S. Court of Claims, the U.S. Tax Court, the Customs Court, and federal regulatory agencies.

Each district court is in one of the eleven appellate districts, called circuits, presided over by a court of appeals. Appellate courts admit no new evidence; their rulings are based solely on the records of the court proceedings or agency hearings that led to the original decision. Appeals court rulings are final unless the Supreme Court chooses to review them.

The Supreme Court has some original jurisdiction, but its major job is to review lower court decisions involving substantial issues of public law. Supreme Court decisions can be reversed by Congress and the state legislatures, but this seldom happens. There is no explicit constitutional authority for the Supreme Court to review acts of Congress. Nonetheless, the 1803 case of *Marbury* v. *Madison* established the Court's right to review congressional acts. The supremacy clause of Article VI and the Judiciary Act of 1789 give the Court the power to review state constitutions and laws.

Cases reach the Court mainly through the writ of *certiorari*. The Supreme Court controls its case load by issuing few writs and by handing down clear leading opinions that enable lower courts to resolve future cases without further review.

The judiciary as a whole is subject to three major influences: (1) the individual members of the Supreme Court, who have lifetime tenure; (2) the Justice Department—particularly the solicitor general, who regulates the flow of cases; and (3) the pattern of cases.

The influence of the individual member of the Supreme Court is limited when the Court is polarized, and close votes in a polarized Court impair the value of the decision rendered. Writing the majority opinion for a case gives a justice an opportunity to influence the judiciary. But the need to frame an opinion in such a way as to develop majority support on the Court may limit such opportunities. Dissenting opinions can have more impact than the majority opinion; they stimulate a continued flow of cases around that issue. The solicitor general is the most important single influence outside the Court itself because he controls the flow of cases brought by the Justice Department; he also shapes the argument in those cases.

In recent years, the importance of the federal judiciary—the Supreme Court in particular—has increased substantially as the courts have developed new tools of judicial power and forged alliances with important forces in American society.

For Further Reading

Abraham, Henry. *The Judicial Process.* New York: Oxford University Press, 1986.

Bickel, Alexander. *The Least Dangerous Branch.* Indianapolis: Bobbs-Merrill, 1962.

Blasi, Vincent. *The Burger Court: The Counter-Revolution That Wasn't.* New Haven: Yale University Press, 1983.

Bryner, Gary, and Dennis L. Thompson. *The Constitution and the Regulation of Society.* Provo, UT: Brigham Young University, 1988.

Carp, Robert, and Ronald Stidham, *The Federal Courts.* Washington, DC: Congressional Quarterly Press, 1985.

Davis, Sue. *Justice Rehnquist and the Constitution.* Princeton: Princeton University Press, 1989.

Faulkner, Robert K. *The Jurisprudence of John Marshall.* Princeton: Princeton University Press, 1968.

Goldman, Sheldon, and Thomas P. Jahnige, *The Federal Courts as a Political System.* New York: Harper & Row, 1985.

Graber, Mark A. *Transforming Free Speech: The Ambiguous Legacy of Civil Libertarianism.* Berkeley: University of California Press, 1991.

Hamilton, Charles V. *The Bench and the Ballot: Southern Federal Judges and Black Voters.* New York: Oxford University Press, 1973.

Haskins, George L., and Herbert A. Johnson. *History of the Supreme Court of the United States.* New York: Macmillan, 1981.

Maveety, Nancy. *Representation Rights and the Burger Years.* Ann Arbor: University of Michigan Press, 1991.

Melnick, R. Shep. *Regulation and the Courts: The Case of the Clean Air Act.* Washington, DC: Brookings Institution, 1983.

Mezey, Susan G. *No Longer Disabled: The Federal Courts and the Politics of Social Security Disability.* New York: Greenwood Press, 1988.

Nardulli, Peter F., James Eisenstein, and Roy B. Fleming. *The Tenor of Justice: Criminal Courts and the Guilty Plea.* Urbana: University of Illinois Press, 1988.

Neely, Richard. *How Courts Govern America.* New Haven: Yale University Press, 1981.

O'Brien, David, M. *Storm Center: The Supreme Court in American Politics,* 2nd ed. New York: W. W. Norton, 1990.

Rosenberg, Gerald. *The Hollow Hope: Can Courts Bring about Social Change?* Chicago: University of Chicago Press, 1991.

Rubin, Eva. *Abortion, Politics and the Courts.* Westport, CT: Greenwood Press, 1982.

Scigliano, Robert. *The Supreme Court and the Presidency.* New York: Free Press, 1971.

Stimson, Shannon C. *The American Revolution in the Law: Anglo-American Jurisprudence before John Marshall.* Princeton, NJ: Princeton University Press, 1990.

Tribe, Lawrence. *Constitutional Choices.* Cambridge: Harvard University Press, 1985.

Wolfe, Christopher. *The Rise of Modern Judicial Review.* New York: Basic Books, 1986.

PART 3

POLITICS AND POLICY

8

PUBLIC OPINION AND THE MEDIA

*I*n January 1991, after American-led coalition forces
achieved a swift victory over Iraq, President George
Bush's level of public approval soared to an
unprecedented 91 percent. Many commentators assumed
that Bush would be re-anointed, rather than merely
re-elected, in 1992. Indeed, several leading Democratic
presidential aspirants decided there would be no point in
challenging Bush in the coming presidential race. Only a
year later, however, Bush's poll standing had fallen below
50 percent. By the late summer of 1992, the Democratic
presidential candidate, Bill Clinton, had opened a
commanding lead in the polls over Bush, who by then
could barely muster a 40 percent popular approval rating.

After his election to the presidency, Clinton, too, found
that public opinion could be quite fickle. By May 1993, only
one hundred days after his inauguration, Clinton's
approval ratings had fallen sharply. According to a May
4–6 New York Times/CBS News poll, 50 percent of
Americans disapproved of the way Clinton was handling
the economy while only 38 percent approved. Only a
month earlier, nearly half of all respondents to the same
poll had approved of Clinton's economic performance,
while only 37 percent had disapproved.[1]

---

[1]Gwen Ifill, "As Ratings Stall, Clinton Tries Tune-Up," *New York Times*, 10 May
1993, p. A16.

Consistent with the pattern discussed in Chapter 6, Clinton's public approval rating briefly increased by 11 points, to nearly 50 percent, in June 1993 after he ordered a cruise missile attack on Iraqi intelligence headquarters. The attack was in retaliation for an alleged Iraqi plot to assassinate former president George Bush. Clinton attributed his improved poll standing not to the missile attack but to what he termed better public understanding of his economic program. Within a few days, however, Clinton's approval rating dropped back to its previous 38 percent level.

Commentators and social scientists, of course, carefully plotted these massive changes in public opinion and pondered their causes. Significantly, however, no analyst charting these shifts in popular sentiment was so bold as to ask whether public opinion was right or wrong—whether it made sense or nonsense. Rather, public opinion was viewed as a sort of natural force that, like the weather, affected everything but was itself impervious to human intervention and immune to criticism.

Public opinion has become the ultimate standard against which the conduct of contemporary governments is measured. In the democracies, especially in the United States, both the value of government programs and the virtue of public officials are typically judged by the magnitude of their popularity. Twentieth-century dictatorships, for their part, are careful at least to give lip service to the idea of popular sovereignty in their countries, if only to bolster public support at home and to maintain a favorable image abroad.

In this chapter, we will examine the role of public opinion in American politics. First, we will look at the institutions and processes that help to shape public opinion in the United States, most notably the "marketplace of ideas," where opinions compete for acceptance, and the news media. Second, we will assess the government's role in shaping American public opinion. Third, we will address the problem of measuring opinion. Finally, we will consider the issue of governmental responsiveness to citizens' opinions.

The Marketplace of Ideas

Opinions are products of individuals' personalities, social characteristics, and interests. But opinions are also shaped by institutional, political, and governmental forces that make it more likely that citizens will hold some beliefs and less likely that they will hold others. In the United States and the other Western democracies, opinions and beliefs compete for acceptance in what is sometimes called the "marketplace of ideas." In America, it is mainly the hidden force of the market that determines which opinions and beliefs will flourish and which will fall by the wayside. Thus, to understand public opinion in the United States, it is important to understand the origins and operations of this "idea market."

Origins of the Idea Market

Prior to the nineteenth century, each of the various regional, religious, ethnic, linguistic, and economic strata generally possessed their own ideas and beliefs based upon their own experiences and life circumstances. The members of different groups generally had little contact with one another, and they knew remarkably little about the history, customs, or character—much less the opinions—of their fellow citizens.

In every European nation and in America, city was separated from countryside and region from region by the lack of usable roads, or effective communications media, and, in many nations in Europe, by the absence of even a common national language. Language barriers could be formidable. Equally significant was the matter of class. The members of the different social classes, even when living near each other, existed in very different worlds. Often, each class spoke its own language, adhered to its own religious beliefs, maintained its own cultural orientations, and saw the political and social universe very differently.

The autonomy of the various regions, groups, and classes began to diminish in the nineteenth century. During this period, every European regime initiated the construction of a national forum in which the views of all strata would be exchanged. Westerners often equate freedom of opinion and expression with the absence of state interference. Western freedom of opinion, however, is not the unbridled freedom of some state of nature. It is, rather, the structured freedom of a public forum constructed and maintained by the state. The creation and maintenance of this forum, this "marketplace of ideas," has required nearly two centuries of extensive governmental effort in the areas of education, communication, and jurisprudence.

First, in the nineteenth century, most Western nations engaged in intense efforts to impose a single national language upon their citizens. In the United States, massive waves of immigration during the nineteenth century meant that millions of residents spoke no English. In response, the American national government, as well as state and local governments, made vigorous efforts to impose the English language upon these newcomers. Schools were established

to provide adults with language skills. At the same time, English was the only language of instruction permitted in the public elementary and secondary schools. Knowledge of English became a prerequisite for American citizenship.

Second, and closely related to the problem of a common language, was the matter of literacy. Prior to the nineteenth century, few people were able to read or write. Possession of these skills was, for the most part, limited to the upper strata. Communication depended upon word of mouth, a situation hardly conducive to the spread of ideas across regional, class, or even village or neighborhood boundaries. During the nineteenth and twentieth centuries, all Western governments actively sought to expand popular literacy. With the advent of universal, compulsory education, children were taught to read and write the national language. Together with literacy programs for adults, including extensive efforts by the various national military services to instruct uneducated recruits, this educational process led to the gradual reduction of illiteracy in the industrial West.

A third facet of the construction of the marketplace of ideas was the development of communications mechanisms. During the early nineteenth century, governments built hundreds of thousands of miles of roads, opening lines of communication among the various regions and between cities and countryside. Road building was followed later in the century by governmental promotion of the construction of rail and telegraph lines, further facilitating the exchange of goods, persons, and, not least important, ideas and information among previously disparate and often isolated areas. Such internal improvements constituted the single most important activity undertaken by the

American central government both before and after the Civil War. During the twentieth century, all Western regimes promoted the development of radio, telephone, television, and the complex satellite-based communications networks that today link the world.

The final key component of the construction of a free market of ideas was, and is, legal protection for free expression of ideas. This last factor is, of course, what most clearly distinguished the construction of the West's idea market from the efforts of authoritarian regimes. The cumulative result of all these governmental efforts was the gradual destruction of internal barriers to communication in every Western nation, and the construction of a forum in which the views of all groups and strata could easily be exchanged.

The Idea Market Today

The operation of the idea market in the United States today has meant that individuals are continually exposed to concepts and information that originate outside their own region, class, or ethnic community. It is this steady exposure over time that leads members of every social group to acquire at least some of the ideas and perspectives embraced by the others. Given continual exposure to the ideas of other strata, it is virtually impossible for any group to resist some modification of its own beliefs.

COMMON FUNDAMENTAL VALUES. Today most Americans share a common set of political beliefs and opinions. First, Americans generally believe in *equality of opportunity*. That is, they assume that all individuals should be allowed to seek personal and material success. Moreover, Americans

generally believe that such success should be linked to personal effort and ability rather than family, "connections," or other forms of special privilege. Second, Americans strongly believe in *individual freedom*. They typically support the notion that governmental interference with individuals' lives and property should be kept to the minimum consistent with the general welfare (although in recent years Americans have grown accustomed to greater levels of governmental intervention than would have been deemed appropriate by the founding fathers of liberal theory). Third, most Americans believe in *democracy*. They presume that every person should have the opportunity to take part in the nation's governmental and policy-making processes and to have some "say" in determining how they are governed.[2]

One indication of the extent to which Americans of all political stripes share these fundamental values is shown by a comparison of the acceptance speeches delivered by Bill Clinton and George Bush upon receiving their parties' presidential nominations in 1992. Clinton and Bush differed on many specific issues and policies. Yet, the political visions they presented reveal an underlying similarity. The fundamental emphasis of both candidates was on equality of opportunity. Clinton, in his speech, declared:

> Somewhere at this very moment another child is born in America. . . . Let it be our cause to see that child has the chance to live to the fullest of her God-given capacities. Let it be our cause to see that child grow

[2]For a discussion of the political beliefs of Americans, see Harry Holloway and John George, *Public Opinion* (New York: St. Martin's Press, 1986). See also Paul R. Abramson, *Political Attitudes in America* (San Francisco: W. H. Freeman, 1983).

up strong and secure, braced by her challenges but never struggling alone; with
family and friends and a faith that in
America, no one is left out; no one is left
behind.

And George Bush concluded his acceptance
speech by proclaiming:

> And the world changes for which we've
> sacrificed for a generation have finally
> come to pass, and with them a rare and
> unprecedented opportunity to pass the
> sweet cup of prosperity around our
> American table. . . . As I travel our land I
> meet veterans who once worked the tur-
> rets of a tank and can now master the
> keyboards of a high-tech economy. . . .

Agreement on fundamental political values, though certainly not absolute, is probably more widespread in the United States
than anywhere else in the Western world.
During the course of Western political history, competing economic, social, and political groups put forward a variety of radi-
cally divergent views, opinions, and
political philosophies. America was never
socially or economically homogeneous. But
two forces that were extremely powerful
and important sources of ideas and beliefs
elsewhere in the world were relatively weak
or absent in the United States.

First, the United States never had the
feudal aristocracy like the one that dominated during so much of European history.
Second, for reasons including America's
prosperity and the early availability of political rights, no Socialist movements comparable to those that developed in nineteenth-century Europe were ever able to
establish themselves in the United States. As
a result, during the course of American history, there existed neither an aristocracy to
assert the virtues of inequality, special privi-

lege, and a rigid class structure, nor a powerful American Communist or Socialist
party to seriously challenge the desirability
of limited government and individualism.[3]

AGREEMENT AND DISAGREEMENT ON IS-
SUES. Agreement on fundamentals, however, by no means implies that Americans
do not differ with one another on a wide
variety of issues. American political life is
characterized by vigorous debate on economic, foreign policy, and social policy issues; race relations; environmental affairs;
and a host of other matters. Differences of
political opinion are to some extent linked
to divergences in various groups' economic
and political positions and to their histories
and experiences. Thus, factors such as income, education, and occupation, which influence individuals' economic interests,
have a great deal of influence upon their
opinions. Similarly, factors such as race,
gender, ethnicity, age, religion, and region,
which not only influence individuals' interests but also shape their experiences and
upbringing, have enormous influence upon
their beliefs and opinions.

For example, individuals whose incomes
differ substantially have different views on
the desirability of a number of important
economic and social programs. In general,
the poor—who are the chief beneficiaries of
these programs—support them more
strongly than the well-to-do Americans
whose taxes pay for the programs. Similarly, blacks and whites have rather different views on questions of civil rights and
civil liberties—presumably reflecting differences of interest and historical experi-

---

[3]See Louis Hartz, *The Liberal Tradition in America* (New York:
Harcourt, Brace, 1955).

ence. In recent years, many observers have begun to take note of a number of differences between the views expressed by men and those supported by women, especially on foreign policy questions, where women appear to be much more concerned with the dangers of war, and on social welfare issues, where women show more concern than men for the problems of the poor and unfortunate. Quite conceivably these differences—known collectively as the "gender gap"—reflect the results of differences in the childhood experiences and socialization of men and women in America.

LIBERALISM AND CONSERVATISM. Many Americans describe themselves as either liberal or conservative in political orientation. Historically these terms were defined somewhat differently than they are today. As recently as the nineteenth century, a liberal was an individual who favored freedom from state control, while a conservative was someone who supported the use of governmental power and favored continuation of the influence of church and aristocracy in national life.

Today, the term *liberal* has come to imply support for political and social reform; support for extensive governmental intervention in the economy; the expansion of federal social services; more vigorous efforts on behalf of the poor, minorities, and women; and greater concern for consumers and the environment. In social and cultural areas, liberals generally support abortion rights, are concerned with the rights of persons accused of crime, support decriminalization of drug use, and oppose state involvement with religious institutions and religious expression. In international affairs, liberal positions are usually seen as including support for arms control, opposi-

tion to the development and testing of nuclear weapons, support for aid to poor nations, opposition to the use of American troops to influence the domestic affairs of Third World nations, opposition to South Africa's system of apartheid, and support for international organizations such as the United Nations.

To say that individuals' opinions are related or linked to their economic interests or social characteristics is not to say that it is always easy or even possible to predict opinions from these factors. Some individuals resolutely hold views that seem to run counter to their obvious economic interests. Wealthy Socialists are an example. Moreover, the same set of interests or social characteristics can reasonably give rise to any number of opinions and viewpoints, depending upon the circumstances of the time. Opinions are formed from the interaction of individual interests, personalities, and experiences with the particular issues, events, and problems of the day. Thus, the views of "the rich," "women," or "young people" are hardly fixed and immutable attributes of these groups but instead depend upon and often change as the interests and experiences of these groups interact with changing economic, social, and political realities.

By contrast, the term *conservative* today is used to describe those who generally support the social and economic status quo and are suspicious of efforts to introduce new political formulae and economic arrangements. Conservatives believe strongly that a large and powerful government poses a threat to citizens' freedom. Thus, in the domestic arena, conservatives generally oppose the expansion of governmental activity, asserting that solutions to social and economic problems can be developed in the private sector. Conservatives particularly oppose efforts to impose government regulation on business, pointing out that such regulation is frequently economically inefficient and costly and can ultimately lower the entire nation's standard of living. As to social and cultural positions, many conservatives oppose abortion, support school prayer, are more concerned for the victims than the perpetrators of crimes, oppose school busing, and support traditional family arrangements. In international affairs, conservatism has come to mean support for the maintenance of American military power.

Often political observers search for logical connections among the various positions identified with liberalism or with conservatism, and they are disappointed or puzzled when they are unable to find a set of coherent philosophical principles that define and unite the several elements of either of these sets of beliefs. On the liberal side, for example, what is the logical connection between opposition to U.S. intervention in Asia and Africa and demands that the United States seek to force South Africa to end apartheid? Surely the latter is a call for the sort of intervention that liberals claim to deplore. On the conservative side, what is the logical relationship between opposition to governmental regulation of business and support for a ban on abortion? Indeed, the latter would seem to be just the sort of regulation of private conduct that conservatives claim to abhor.

Frequently, the relationships among the various elements of liberalism or the several aspects of conservatism are *political* rather than *logical.* One underlying basis of liberal views is that all or most represent criticisms of or attacks on the foreign and domestic policies and cultural values of the business and commercial strata that have been prominent in the United States for the past century. In some measure, the tenets of contemporary conservatism represent this elite's defense of its positions against its enemies, who include organized labor, minority groups, and some intellectuals and professionals. Thus, liberals attack business and commercial elites by advocating more governmental regulation, including consumer protection and environmental regulation, opposition to military weapons programs, and support for expensive social programs. Conservatives counterattack by asserting that governmental regulation of the economy is ruinous and that military weapons are needed in a changing world, and they seek to stigmatize their opponents for showing no concern for the rights of "unborn" Americans.[4]

Of course, it is important to note that many people who call themselves liberals or conservatives accept only part of the liberal or conservative ideology. During the 1980s many political commentators asserted that Americans were becoming increasingly conservative in their political orientations. Indeed, it was partly in response to this view that the Democrats in 1992 selected a presidential candidate drawn from the party's moderate wing. Although it appears that Americans have adopted more conservative outlooks on some issues, their views in most areas have remained largely unchanged or even become more liberal in recent years (see Table 8.1). Thus, there are many individuals who are liberal on social issues but conservative on economic issues.

[4]For a discussion of this conflict, see Benjamin Ginsberg and Martin Shefter, "A Critical Realignment? The New Politics, the Reconstituted Right, and the Election of 1984," in *The Elections of 1984,* ed. Michael Nelson (Washington, DC: Congressional Quarterly Press, 1985), pp. 1–26.

TABLE 8.1
HAVE AMERICANS BECOME MORE CONSERVATIVE?

	1972	1978	1980	1982	1984	1986	1988
Percentage responding "yes" to the following questions:							
Should the government help minority groups?	30%	25%	16%	21%	27%	26%	13%
Should the government see to it that everyone has a job and a guaranteed standard of living?	27	17	22	25	28	25	24
Should abortion never be permitted?							
Should the government provide fewer services and reduce spending?	NA	NA	27	32	28	24	25

NA = Not asked
Source: Center for Political Studies of the Institute for Social Research, University of Michigan. Data were made available through the Inter-University Consortium for Political and Social Research.

There is nothing illogical about these mixed positions. They indicate the relatively open and fluid character of American political debate.

The idea market has created a common ground for Americans in which discussion of issues is encouraged and based on common understandings. Despite the many and often sharp divisions that exist in the twentieth century—between liberals and conservatives, different income groups, different regional groups—most Americans see the world through similar lenses.

Shaping Public Opinion

In many areas of the world, governments determine which opinions their citizens may or may not express. People who assert views that their rulers do not approve of may be subject to imprisonment—or worse. Americans and the citizens of the other Western democracies are fortunate to live in nations where freedom of opinion and expression are generally taken for granted.

Freedom of opinion, however, does not mean that all ideas and opinions flourish. Both private groups and the government itself today attempt to influence which opinions do take hold in the public imagination.

Few ideas spread spontaneously. Usually, whether they are matters of fashion, science, or politics, ideas must be vigorously promoted to become widely known and accepted. For example, the clothing, sports, and entertainment fads that occasionally seem to appear from nowhere and sweep the country before being replaced by some new trend are almost always the product of careful marketing campaigns by some commercial interest, rather than spontaneous phenomena. Even in the sciences, generally considered *the* bastions of objectivity, new theories, procedures, and findings are not always accepted simply and immediately on their own merit. Often, the proponents of a new scientific principle or practice must campaign within the scientific community on behalf of their views. Like their counterparts in fashion and science, successful—or at least widely held—political ideas are usually the products of carefully orchestrated campaigns by government or by organized groups and interests, rather than the results of spontaneous popular enthusiasm.

GOVERNMENT MANAGEMENT OF ISSUES. All governments attempt, to a greater or lesser extent, to influence, manipulate, or manage their citizens' beliefs. In the United States, some efforts have been made by every administration since the nation's founding to influence public sentiment. But efforts to shape opinion did not become a routine and formal official function until World War I when the Wilson administration created a censorship board, enacted sedition and espionage legislation, and attempted to suppress groups that opposed the war, like the International Workers of the World (IWW) and the Socialist party. Eugene Debs, a prominent Socialist and presidential candidate, was arrested and convicted of having violated the Espionage Law, and he was sentenced to ten years in prison for delivering a speech that defended the IWW.

At the same time, however, World War I was the first modern industrial war requiring a total mobilization of popular effort on the home front for military production. The war effort required the government to persuade the civilian population to bear the costs and make the sacrifices needed to achieve industrial and agricultural, as well as military, success. The Committee on Public Information (CPI), chaired by journalist and publicist George Creel, organized a massive public relations and news management program aimed at promoting popular enthusiasm for the war effort. This program included the dissemination of favorable news, the publication of patriotic pamphlets, films, photos, cartoons, bulletins, and periodicals, and the organization of "war expositions" and speakers' tours. Special labor programs were aimed at maintaining the loyalty and productivity of the work force. Many of the CPI's staff were drawn from the major public relations firms of the time.[5]

The extent to which public opinion is actually affected by governmental public relations efforts is probably limited. The government—despite its size and power—is only one source of information and evaluation in the United States. Very often, governmental claims are disputed by the media, by interest groups, and, at times, by opposing forces within the government itself. Thus, for example, efforts by Presidents Reagan and Bush to convince Americans that we should provide support for anti-Communist forces in Nicaragua, Afghanistan, and Mozambique have been countered by the public relations efforts of a variety of political and religious groups, as well as by the publicity campaigns mounted by Reagan's and Bush's opponents in the Congress.

Often, too, governmental efforts to manipulate public opinion backfire when the public is made aware of the government's tactics. Thus, in 1971, the United States government's efforts to build popular support for the Vietnam War were hurt when CBS News aired its documentary "The Selling of the Pentagon," to reveal the extent and char-

[5]See George Creel, *How We Advertised America* (New York: Harper and Brothers, 1920).

acter of governmental efforts to sway popular sentiment. In this documentary, CBS demonstrated the techniques, including planted news stories and faked film footage, the government had used to misrepresent its activities in Vietnam. The revelations, of course, had the effect of undermining popular trust in all governmental claims. During the 1991 Persian Gulf War, the U.S. military was very careful about the accuracy of its assertions.

At the start of his new administration in 1993, President Clinton made a major effort to shape popular opinion in support of his programs and initiatives. The president had the Democratic National Committee (DNC) hire a "campaign manager" to coordinate a nationwide grassroots effort to mobilize public support for Clinton's health care reform plan.[6] Clinton also turned to the DNC to hire a telemarketing firm to arrange a cascade of phone calls and letters to members of Congress, the media, and pollsters in support of his economic program. He wanted to make certain that there would be an outpouring of popular support for the plan presented in his February 17, 1993, State of the Union address.[7] Clinton, Vice-President Al Gore, and other key members of the administration also engaged in extensive media campaigning and public appearances to muster support for their programs.

Indeed, a hallmark of the Clinton administration has been the steady use of campaign techniques like those used in election campaigns to bolster popular enthusiasm for White House initiatives. The president established a "political war room" in the Executive Office Building similar to the one that operated in his campaign headquarters. Representatives from all departments meet in the war room every day to discuss and coordinate the president's public relations efforts. Many of the same consultants and pollsters who directed the successful Clinton campaign have been employed in the selling of the president's programs.[8]

PRIVATE GROUPS AND SHAPING PUBLIC OPINION. The success of a political idea is often determined by the marketing efforts of organized interests. Two examples of successful political ideas—ideas that have attracted millions of adherents—are *right to life*, the notion that abortions should be severely curtailed or outlawed altogether, and *nuclear freeze*, the argument that the United States should halt the development and production of nuclear weapons either unilaterally or through the negotiation of agreements with other nations with nuclear weapons. These ideas obviously differ in substance and certainly appeal to very distinct subgroups of the population. The notion of the right to life is most popular among Protestant and Catholic social conservatives, while the appeal of the nuclear freeze argument is strongest among liberal urban professionals. But despite their dissimilarity in subject matter and adherents, these two political ideas are similar in one important respect. Both were developed and successfully promoted by well-financed and well-organized groups using sophisticated public relations techniques. Though each of these ideas can and should

[6]Dana Priest, "White House to Stump for Health Plan," *Washington Post*, 6 February 1993, p. 1.

[7]Ruth Marcus and Ann Devroy, "Asking Americans to Face Facts, Clinton Presents Plan to Raise Taxes, Cut Deficit," *Washington Post*, 19 February 1993, p. 1.

[8]Gerald F. Seib and Michael K. Frisby, "Selling Sacrifice," *Wall Street Journal*, 5 February 1993, p. 1.

be debated on its own merits, it is also important to understand their political origins and implications.

The right-to-life issue was heavily promoted by conservative politicians who saw the issue of abortion as a potential means of uniting Catholic and Protestant conservatives and linking both groups to the Republican coalition, at that time led by President Reagan. These politicians convinced Catholic and evangelical Protestant leaders that they shared similar views on the question of abortion, and they worked with religious leaders to focus public attention on the negative issues in the abortion debate. To advance their cause, leaders of the movement sponsored well-publicized Senate hearings, where testimony, photographs, and other exhibits were presented to illustrate the violent effects of abortion procedures.

At the same time, publicists for the movement produced leaflets, articles, books, and films such as *The Silent Scream* to highlight the agony and pain ostensibly felt by the unborn when they were being aborted. Finally, Catholic and evangelical Protestant religious leaders were organized to denounce abortion from their church pulpits and, increasingly from their electronic pulpits on the Christian Broadcasting Network (CBN) and the various other television forums available for religious programming. Religious leaders also organized demonstrations, pickets, and disruptions at abortion clinics throughout the nation.[9]

Like the right-to-life issue, the idea of a nuclear freeze was developed and promoted by organized political forces seeking to further their political interests. In particular, liberal activists conceived the idea of a nuclear freeze in the early 1980s as a means of reviving and galvanizing the liberal antiwar coalition that had been such an important force in American politics during the Vietnam era.

To promote their cause, advocates of the nuclear freeze employed the full gamut of public relations mechanisms. Liberal senators introduced a resolution supporting the concept of a freeze and conducted well-publicized hearings on the topic. Rallies were held throughout the nation on behalf of the freeze, including a gigantic New York City rally in 1982 that attracted several hundred thousand participants. Local organizations were formed, generally on college and university campuses, to foster local antinuclear activities and to enlist potential student activists. Scientists, entertainers, physicians, politicians, and educators gave speeches and held press conferences throughout the country on the dangers of nuclear war. Finally, nuclear freeze advocates helped to promote films that depicted the dangers of nuclear war, such as *Testament* and, most notably, the television film *The Day After*, viewed by tens of millions of Americans. The result of these efforts was a substantial increase in popular concern with issues of war and peace and, in particular, heightened public fear of nuclear war.[10]

In general, the notions that are most successful in the marketplace of ideas are precisely those advocated and promoted by the nation's more important political and economic forces. Ideas are best marketed by groups with access to financial resources,

[9]See Gillian Peele, *Revival and Reaction* (Oxford, England: Clarendon Press, 1985). Also see Connie Paige, *The Right to Lifers* (New York: Summit, 1983).

[10]See Adam Garfinkle, *The Politics of the Nuclear Freeze* (Philadelphia: Foreign Policy Research Institute, 1983). Also see Fox Butterfield, "Autonomy of the Nuclear Protest," *New York Times Magazine*, 11 July 1982, pp. 14–39.

public or private institutional support, and sufficient skill or education to select, develop, and draft ideas that will attract interest and support. Thus, the development and promotion of conservative themes and ideas in recent years has been greatly facilitated by the millions of dollars that conservative corporations and business organizations such as the Chamber of Commerce and the Public Affairs Council spend each year on public information and what is now called in corporate circles "issues management." In addition, conservative businessmen have contributed millions of dollars to such conservative institutions as the Heritage Foundation, the Hoover Institution, and the American Enterprise Institute.[11] Many of the ideas that helped those on the Right influence political debate were first developed and articulated by scholars associated with these institutions.

Although they do not usually have access to financial assets that match those available to their conservative opponents, liberal intellectuals and professionals have ample organizational skills, access to the media, and practice in creating, communicating, and using ideas. During the past three decades, the chief vehicle through which liberal intellectuals and professionals advanced their ideas has been the "public interest group," an institution that relies heavily upon voluntary contributions of time, effort, and interest on the part of its members. Through groups like Common Cause, the National Organization for Women, the Sierra Club, Friends of the Earth, and Physicians for Social Responsibility, intellectuals and professionals have been able to use their organizational skills

and educational resources to develop and promote ideas like the nuclear freeze.[12]

As journalist and author Joe Queenan put it, though political ideas can erupt spontaneously, they almost never do. Instead,

> issues are usually manufactured by tenured professors and obscure employees of think tanks. . . . It is inconceivable that the American people, all by themselves, could independently arrive at the conclusion that the depletion of the ozone layer poses a dire threat to our national well-being, or that an immediate, across-the-board cut in the capital-gains tax is the only thing that stands between us and the economic abyss. The American people do not have that kind of sophistication. *They have to have help.*[13]

One interesting recent case in which a politician seemed willing to provide the American people with quite a bit of "help" in arriving at an idea was the 1992 independent presidential candidacy of Ross Perot. After withdrawing from the race in July 1992, Perot announced in September that he would be willing to reenter the contest, but only if his supporters across the nation asked him to do so. Indeed, Perot contrasted his own campaign organization, United We Stand America, which he described as "driven from the bottom up," with the efforts of other politicians, which were "driven from the top down by a handful of powerful people."[14] Ostensibly to learn how his supporters felt about a re-

[11]See David Vogel, "The Power of Business in America: A Reappraisal," *British Journal of Political Science* 13 (January 1983), pp. 19–44.

[12]See David Vogel, "The Public Interest Movement and the American Reform Tradition," *Political Science Quarterly* 96 (Winter 1980), pp. 607–27.

[13]Joe Queenan, "Birth of a Notion," *Washington Post,* 20 September 1992, p. C1.

[14]Steven Holmes, "Grass-Roots Drive Shows Hand of Oz," *New York Times,* 30 September 1992, p. A20.

James Carville and Mary Matalin
All's Fair in Love, War, and Politics

*T*he tumultuous 1992 presidential campaign contained many dramatic elements, including George Bush's surprising drop in the polls following the Persian Gulf War, and Bill Clinton's phoenix-like rise in the polls in the summer and fall before the election. The candidates' campaign managers labored unceasingly throughout the campaign to swing public sentiment their way. Yet, like a made-for-television movie, this pitched political battle between the Bush and Clinton camps included a melodramatic quality: the real-life romance between Clinton's top strategist, James Carville, and Bush's political director, Mary Matalin.

James Carville began his political career in his home state of Louisiana. A mediocre student at Louisiana State University, Carville completed his undergraduate degree in seven years (interrupted by service in the Marines) and acquired a law degree in 1973. After working on several state political campaigns, Carville struck out on his own as a political consultant in 1982, working for state Democratic candidates around the country. Carville acquired a national reputation in 1991 when he engineered the come-from-behind Pennsylvania Senate victory of unknown Democrat Harris Wofford against former attorney general Richard Thornburgh.

The Clinton campaign posed a similar challenge in that Clinton was little known and given little chance of winning. Carville brought to the campaign two key principles: the campaign should respond immediately to any charges or attacks and the campaign should stay focused on its own core message and not allow itself to be forced on the defensive. These tactics were crucial to Clinton's winning effort.

Mary Matalin is also considered a rising young star in the world of campaign management. Brought up on the South Side of Chicago, the daughter of a steel mill worker, Matalin also took seven years to complete her

James Carville

newal of his presidential bid, Perot established an 800-number and invited citizens to call with their advice. During the first week in October, Perot announced his deci-

sion to reenter the presidential race—purely in response to the demands of the American people.

Whatever the actual merits of the Perot

undergraduate degree and then had early experience in Illinois political campaigns. In the 1980s, she did political work with the Republican National Committee in Washington, D.C. Her big break came when she was credited with designing Bush's winning strategy in the important Michigan caucuses during the 1988 Republican nominating season. Matalin acknowledges having learned much from Republican campaign wizard Lee Atwater, who was credited with successfully guiding the Reagan and Bush campaigns of the 1980s.

In the race against Clinton, Matalin was considered among the toughest and most loyal campaign leaders in the Bush camp. Despite taking some flak for saying that the Clinton campaign had to control its "bimbo eruptions" (a reference to allegations of womanizing by Clinton), Matalin was one of Bush's most effective campaign operatives. Unlike the Clinton campaign, however, the Bush campaign faced organizational problems, including indecisiveness about which direction the campaign should take.

Both Carville and Matalin are considered tough, quick-witted, plain-speaking, hard-working partisans. Their romantic relationship began after meeting at a Washington dinner party in 1991. In public, both agreed to suspend their relationship during the campaign. Yet gossip columnists reported that they continued to see each other throughout the campaign. When asked if they fought about politics, Matalin responded "In terms of intense disagreements that we've had, politics ranks pretty much in the middle." When Matalin was criticized for the "bimbo" remark, Carville expressed public sympathy for her plight.

After the campaign, the two left for an extended European vacation. On returning, they signed a joint book agreement to publish their campaign memoirs. Love notwithstanding, Carville picked up where he left off, working for the re-election of New Jersey Democratic governor Jim Florio, and Matalin resumed her work for the Republican party.

Source: Gerald M. Pomper, et al., *The Election of 1992* (Chatham, NJ: Chatham House, 1993).

Mary Matalin

candidacy, one thing is clear: The American people had considerable help in deciding that it was a good idea. According to Federal Election Commission (FEC) records, after nominally withdrawing from the presidential race in July 1992, Perot spent several million dollars making certain that his name would be on the presidential ballot in all fifty states. At the same time, according to the FEC and a number of Perot volunteers, United We Stand volunteer coordinators in several key states were replaced by paid political professionals during the months of August and September, when Perot was presumably not a candidate.[15] Moreover, many individuals who called Perot's 800-number to urge him *not* to enter the presidential race were surprised to learn that *any* call to the number was automatically recorded as favoring Perot's candidacy. Obviously, Perot forces did not want to risk the possibility that ideas "driven from the bottom up" would fail to coincide with their own.

The Media

Among the most important forces shaping public opinion are the national news media. The content and character of news and public affairs programming—what the media choose to present and how they present it—can have the most far-reaching political consequences. Media disclosures can greatly enhance—or fatally damage—the careers of public officials. Media coverage can rally support for—or intensify opposition to—national policies. The media can shape and modify, if not fully form, public perceptions of events, issues, and institutions.

Shaping Events

In recent American political history, the media have played a central role in at least three major events. First, the media were critically important factors in the civil rights movement of the 1950s and 1960s. Television pictures showing peaceful civil rights marchers attacked by club-swinging police helped to generate sympathy among northern whites for the civil rights struggle and greatly increased the pressure on Congress to bring an end to segregation.[16]

Second, the media were instrumental in compelling the Johnson and Nixon administrations to negotiate an end to the Vietnam War. Beginning in 1967, the national media portrayed the war as misguided and unwinnable and, as a result, helped to turn popular sentiment against continued American involvement.[17]

Third, the media were central actors in the Watergate affair, which ultimately forced President Richard Nixon, landslide victor in the 1972 presidential election, to resign from office in disgrace. It was the relentless series of investigations launched by the *Washington Post*, the *New York Times*, and the television networks that led to the disclosures of the various abuses of which Nixon was guilty and ultimately forced Nixon to choose between resignation and almost certain impeachment.

The Sources of Media Power

The power of the media stems from several sources. First, the media help to set the agenda for political discussion. Groups and forces that wish to bring their ideas before the public in order to generate support for

---

[15]Ibid.

[16]David Garrow, *Protest at Selma* (New Haven: Yale University Press, 1978).

[17]See Todd Gitlin, *The Whole World Is Watching* (Berkeley: University of California Press, 1980).

policy proposals or political candidacies must somehow secure media coverage. If the media are persuaded that an idea is newsworthy, then they may declare it an "issue" that must be resolved or a "problem" to be solved, thus clearing the first hurdle in the policy-making process. On the other hand, if an idea lacks or loses media appeal, its chance of resulting in new programs or policies is diminished. Some ideas seem to surface, gain media support for a time, lose media appeal, and then resurface. Examples include repair of the "infrastructure," a topic that surfaced in the early 1980s, disappeared after 1983, and then re-emerged in the press in the 1992 presidential campaign. Similarly, national health insurance excited media attention in the 1970s, all but disappeared during the 1980s, and became a major topic after 1992.

The single most amusing example of an issue created and then dropped by the media remains Lincoln Steffens's "crime wave." Steffens, who later became a famous and influential journalist, began his career as a police reporter for the *New York Post* in the early 1900s. One quiet summer, Steffens began reading the police daily crime file and reporting all the crimes he found there. To compete, the reporters for all the other city papers began to follow suit. Soon, all the papers proclaimed that the city was in the grip of a crime wave of monstrous proportions and demanded that city officials take immediate action. Interestingly enough, during this "crime wave," the actual incidence of crime in the city was at a low point—only the number of newspaper stories about crime had increased. Police Commissioner (and later U.S. President) Theodore Roosevelt ended the crime wave by blocking newspaper access to the police files. With their source of crime news re-

moved, the reporters moved on to other topics.[18]

A second source of the media's power is their influence as interpreters and evaluators of events and political results. For example, media interpretations may often determine how people perceive an election outcome. In 1968, despite the growing strength of the opposition to his Vietnam War policies, incumbent President Lyndon Johnson won two-thirds of the votes cast in New Hampshire's Democratic presidential primary. His rival Senator Eugene McCarthy received less than one-third. The broadcast media, however, declared the outcome to have been a great victory for McCarthy, who was said to have done much better than "expected" (or at least expected by the media). His "defeat" in New Hampshire was one of the factors that persuaded Johnson to withdraw from the 1968 presidential race.

During the 1992 campaign, while being interviewed on "60 Minutes," Ross Perot ascribed his earlier decision to withdraw from the presidential campaign to his fear of a Republican "dirty tricks" campaign directed against him. Most media commentators reacted to Perot's assertion with incredulity and cited it as evidence that the Texan lacked the emotional stability needed by a president. Following that episode, they perceived that Perot's campaign was losing "momentum." Though Perot still received approximately 19 percent of the popular vote, the "60 Minutes" broadcast and the subsequent media reaction probably lost him substantial support in the electorate.

Finally, the media have a good deal of power to shape popular perceptions of

---

[18]Lincoln Steffens, *The Autobiography of Lincoln Steffens* (New York: Literary Guild, 1931), Chapter 14.

DEBATING THE ISSUES

The Media: How Influential Are They?

*I*n recent years there has emerged an important political argument over the real or imagined political
power of the media. Commentators, politicians, and others routinely attribute vast influence to the
American media; yet many who study the matter argue that claims about media power are exaggerated.

Newspaper editor Michael J. O'Neill summarizes the thinking of many critics as he describes the
media's reach and influence. On the basis of his study of media coverage of Congress, media analyst
Stephen Hess argues that the media's actual power is less than most assume.

O'Neill

The extraordinary powers of the media, most convincingly displayed by network television
and the national press, have been mobilized to influence major public issues and national
elections, to help diffuse the authority of Congress and to disassemble the political parties—
even to make Presidents or to break them. Indeed, the media now weigh so heavily on the
scales of power that some political scientists claim we are upsetting the historic checks and
balances invented by our forefathers. . . . This is flattering, of course, because all newspaper-
men dream of being movers and shakers and the thought that we may actually be threatening
the national government is inspirational. In several respects, it is also true. . . .

No longer are we just the messengers, observers on the sidelines, witch's mirrors faithfully
telling society how it looks. Now we are deeply imbedded in the democratic process itself,
as principal actors rather than bit players or mere audience. . . . Thanks mainly to television,
we are often partners in the creation of news—unwilling and unwitting partners, perhaps,
but partners nonetheless. . . .

In ways that Jefferson and Hamilton never intended nor could even imagine, Americans

---

political leaders. Most citizens will never
meet George Bush or Bill Clinton or Al Gore.
Popular perceptions and evaluations of
these individuals are based upon their media images. Obviously, through public relations and other techniques, politicians seek
to cultivate favorable media images. But the
media have a good deal of discretion over
how individuals are portrayed, or how they
are allowed to portray themselves.

In the case of political candidates, the
media have considerable influence over

whether or not a particular individual will
receive public attention, whether or not a
particular individual will be taken seriously
as a viable contender, and whether the public will perceive a candidate's performance
favorably. Thus, if the media find a candidate interesting they may treat him or her as
a serious contender even though the facts of
the matter seem to suggest otherwise. For
example, in 1992, the broadcast media
found Ross Perot to be an incredible novelty. Here was a self-made billionaire with

now have the whole world delivered to them every day, in pulsating, living color—all of life swept inside their personal horizon.[1]

Hess

There is no shortage of claims for the power of the press on Capitol Hill. . . . So many knowledgeable people, including senators, tell us that this is so that surely it must be so.

The most obvious reason why influence is attributed to the media is that the members of Congress, and especially their staffs, are incorrigible news junkies. . . .

The problem is that cause and effect are so difficult to match up. . . .

During the year I spent as an observer at the Senate, I did not see any cause and effect. I saw a lot of reporters writing stories. I saw a lot of bills being voted up or down. The stories often helped explain the votes, but I do not think the stories caused the votes. . . .

Ultimately, a lot more people and groups have an interest in noting the power of the press than in showing that media power sometimes may be akin to that of the Wizard of Oz. . . . There are also certain participants in the governmental process who must find it useful to blame "media power" for their own failures or frustrations. Books about the power that is will always sell better than those about the power that is not. And finally, there are media researchers whose entitlements in the world of conference going and journal articles . . . will be in direct proportion to our colleagues' sense that we are writing about one of the real power players in public policy. This then becomes a collective bias of which readers should be aware. Beware.[2]

[1]Michael J. O'Neill, "The Power of the Press." A presidential address to the American Society of Newspaper Editors, 1982, reprinted in *The Mass Media: Opposing Viewpoints* (St. Paul, MN: Greenhaven Press, 1988), pp. 150–51.
[2]Stephen Hess, *The Ultimate Insiders: U.S. Senators and the National Media* (Washington, DC: Brookings Institution, 1986), pp. 100–112.

oversized ears who was determined to challenge the American political establishment. Some members of the press depicted Perot as a potential Mussolini, while others portrayed him as a wealthy Harry Truman. Nevertheless, from the beginning, Perot received enormous media attention, which helped to make his quixotic candidacy a serious threat to the two major parties.[19]

[19]See Carl Bernstein, "The Idiot Culture," *New Republic*, 8 June 1992, pp. 22–28.

In a similar vein, the media may declare that a candidate has "momentum," a mythical property that the media confer upon candidates they admire. Momentum has no substantive meaning—it is simply a media prediction that a particular candidate will do even better in the future than in the past. Such media prophecies can become self-fulfilling as contributors and supporters jump on the bandwagon of the fortunate candidate.

In 1992, for example, when Bill Clinton's

poll standings surged in the wake of the Democratic National Convention (see Chapter 9), the media determined that Clinton had enormous momentum. In fact, nothing that happened during the remainder of the race led the media to change its collective judgment. Even when George Bush's poll standing began to improve, many news stories pointed to Bush's inability to gain momentum. While there is no way to ascertain what impact this coverage had on the race, at the very least, Republican contributors and activists must have been discouraged by the constant portrayal of their candidate as lacking—and the opposition as possessing—this magical "momentum."

Of course, what the media confer they can also take away. Soon after his "momentum" carried Bill Clinton to victory in the 1992 election, the new president became the target of fierce attacks by prominent members of the national media. After a series of miscues during his first month in office, previously friendly commentators described Clinton as "incredibly inept," as "stumbling," and as a man with the "common sense of a gnat." Clinton went, according to one prominent journalist, "from Time's 'Man of the Year' to punching bag of the week." Some analysts suggested that the media were trying to compensate for their earlier enthusiastic support for Clinton.[20]

Media power to shape images is not absolute. Other image-makers compete with and indeed do manipulate the media by planting stories and rumors and staging news events. Some politicians are so adept at communicating with the public and shaping their own images that the media seem to have little effect upon them. For example, for six years Ronald Reagan appeared to have the ability to project such a positive image to millions of Americans that media criticism had little or no effect upon his popularity. The media came to refer to Reagan as the "Teflon-coated" president—criticisms never seemed to "stick" (although eventually even Reagan's Teflon coating chipped and cracked).

While the power of the media to shape perceptions is not unlimited, it is substantial. Media portrayals of "bumbling" Jerry Ford, "tricky" Dick Nixon, and "cry baby" Ed Muskie helped to shape our images of these individuals and to shorten their political careers. Similarly, media investigations of Richard Nixon, 1984 Democratic vice-presidential candidate Geraldine Ferraro, Vice-President Spiro Agnew, and others sealed their political fates. Equally important media interpretation of events can actually overpower and recreate reality, as in the "victorious" North Vietnamese Tet offensive and in Lyndon Johnson's "loss" in the 1968 New Hampshire primary.

Candidates Try to Turn the Tables

During the 1992 presidential campaign, as we saw in the last chapter, candidates developed a number of techniques designed to take control of the image-making process away from journalists and media executives. Among the most important of these techniques were the many town meetings and television talk and entertainment show appearances that all the major candidates made. Frequent exposure on such programs as "Larry King Live," "Today," and even "Arsenio Hall" gave candidates an oppor-

---

[20]Howard Kurtz, "Media Pounce on Troubles as Pendulum Swings Again," *Washington Post*, 1 February 1993, p. 1.

tunity to shape and focus their own media images and to overwhelm any negative image that might be projected by the media. This strategy worked especially well for the independent candidate Ross Perot. By the end of the 1992 campaign, many journalists were depicting Perot as more than a bit of a kook. Nevertheless, Perot's numerous appearances on talk shows, in addition to his lengthy "infomercials," allowed him to maintain some—though not total—control over his media image.

Members of the national news media responded by aggressively investigating and refuting many of the candidates' claims. Each of the major television networks, for example, aired regular critical analyses of the candidates' speeches, television commercials, and talk show appearances. "NBC Nightly News" frequently featured "Campaign Close-up" and "Ad Watch." Similarly, almost every night during the latter stages of the presidential campaign, "CBS Evening News" featured "Campaign 92 Reality Check." The PBS "MacNeil-Lehrer Newshour" regularly used its "Fact or Fiction" segment to probe candidates' assertions. Even the most innocuous photo opportunities came under media fire.

Thus, when George Bush appeared in Texas to witness American, Mexican, and Canadian representatives initial the North American Free Trade Agreement (NAFTA), NBC commentators dismissed the trip as election-year politics. CBS also told viewers that the trip was purely political and added a segment featuring a group of American workers who feared that the NAFTA agreement would threaten their jobs. CNN investigated and refuted a Clinton television commercial claiming that Bush's labor Secretary, Lynn Martin, had called job growth in Arkansas during Clinton's tenure as gov-

ernor, "enormous." This was a claim that Clinton repeated during the presidential debates. CNN reporter Brooks Jackson revealed that what Martin actually said was Arkansas had low wages and dead-end jobs; she then went on to say, "If you say Arkansas's growth is enormous, if you are working from a low base, it's true."[21]

This type of political coverage serves the public interest by subjecting candidates' claims to scrutiny and refuting errors and distortions. At the same time, such critical coverage serves the interests of the news media by enhancing their own control over political imagery and perceptions and, thus, the power of the media vis-à-vis other political actors and institutions in the United States. We shall examine this topic next, as we consider the development and significance of investigative reporting.

After his election, President Clinton returned to the town meeting format that had served him well during the campaign as a way of reaching the public without media intervention. The national media, however, were not prepared to accept the president's efforts to circumvent them and moved to reassert their own political "spin" control. For example, following Clinton's February 10, 1993, nationally televised town meeting on the economy, many major newspapers were sharply critical of the president's responses to questions posed by members of a Michigan studio audience and a group of callers from across the country. Clinton was accused both of giving inadequate answers to questions and of screening participants to exclude hostile questioners. Some media commentators challenged the validity of the

[21] Alan Otten, "TV News Drops Kid-Glove Coverage of Election, Trading Staged Sound Bites for Hard Analysis," *Wall Street Journal,* 12 October 1992, p. A12.

entire town meeting format, claiming that members of the general public—as distinguished from journalists—were not adequately prepared to confront the president. Commentators called for more events dominated by the media, such as press conferences, and fewer events like town meetings in which the role of the media was reduced.[22]

The Rise of Investigative Reporting

The political power of the news media has been greatly increased in recent years through the growing prominence of "investigative reporting"—a form of journalism in which the media adopt an adversary posture toward the government and public officials.

During the nineteenth century, American newspapers were completely subordinate to the political parties. Newspapers depended upon official patronage—legal notices and party subsidies—for their financial survival and were controlled by party leaders. (A vestige of that era survived into the twentieth century in such newspaper names as the *Springfield Republican* and the *St. Louis Globe-Democrat*.) At the turn of the century, with the development of commercial advertising, newspapers became financially independent. This made possible the emergence of a formally nonpartisan press.

Presidents were the first national officials to see the opportunities in this development. By communicating directly to the electorate through newspapers and maga-

zines, Theodore Roosevelt and Woodrow Wilson established political constituencies for themselves independent of party organizations and strengthened their own power relative to Congress. President Franklin Roosevelt used the radio, most notably in his famous fireside chats, to reach out to voters throughout the nation and to make himself the center of American politics (see Box 8.1). FDR was also adept at developing close personal relationships with reporters that enabled him to obtain favorable news coverage despite the fact that in his day a majority of newspaper owners and publishers were staunch conservatives. Following Roosevelt's example, subsequent presidents have all sought to use the media to enhance their popularity and power. For example, through televised news conferences, President John F. Kennedy mobilized public support for his domestic and foreign policy initiatives.

During the 1950s and 1960s, a few members of Congress also made successful use of the media—especially television—to mobilize national support for their causes. Senator Estes Kefauver of Tennessee became a major contender for the presidency and won a place on the 1956 Democratic national ticket as a result of his dramatic televised hearings on organized crime. Senator Joseph McCarthy of Wisconsin made himself a powerful national figure through his well-publicized investigations of alleged Communist infiltration of key American institutions. These senators, however, were more exceptional than typical. Through the mid-1960s, the executive branch continued to generate the bulk of news coverage, and the media served as a cornerstone of presidential power.

The Vietnam War shattered this relationship between the press and the presidency.

[22]See Ann Devroy, "TV Public Puts Clinton on Defensive," *Washington Post*, 11 February 1993, p. 1. See also Howard Kurtz, "Inaugurating a Talk Show Presidency," *Washington Post*, 12 February 1993, p. A4.

BOX 8.1
The First Fireside Chat
March 12, 1933

I want to talk for a few minutes with the people of the United States about banking—with the comparatively few who understand the mechanics of banking but more particularly with the overwhelming majority who use banks for the making of deposits and the drawing of checks. I want to tell you what has been done in the last few days, why it was done, and what the next steps are going to be. I recognize that the many proclamations from State capitols and from Washington, the legislation, the treasury regulations, etc., couched for the most part in banking and legal terms, should be explained for the benefit of the average citizen. I owe this in particular because of the fortitude and good temper with which everybody has accepted the inconvenience and hardships of the banking holiday. I know that when you understand what we in Washington have been about I shall continue to have your cooperation as fully as I have had your sympathy and help during the past week. . . .

After all, there is an element in the readjustment of our financial system more important than currency, more important than gold, and that is the confidence of the people. Confidence and courage are the essentials of success in carrying out our plan. You people must have faith; you must not be stampeded by rumors or guesses. Let us unite in banishing fear. We have provided the machinery to restore our financial system; it is up to you to support and make it work.

It is your problem no less than it is mine. Together we cannot fail.

During the early stages of U.S. involvement, American officials in Vietnam who disapproved of the way the war was being conducted leaked information critical of administrative policy to reporters. Publication of this material infuriated the White House, which pressured publishers to block its release—on one occasion, President Kennedy went so far as to ask the *New York Times* to reassign its Saigon correspondent. The national print and broadcast media—the network news divisions, the national news weeklies, the *Washington Post* and the *New York Times*—discovered, however, that there was an audience for critical coverage among segments of the public skeptical of administration policy.

As the Vietnam conflict dragged on, critical media coverage fanned antiwar sentiment. Moreover, growing opposition to the war among liberals encouraged some members of Congress, most notably Senator J. William Fulbright, chairman of the Senate Foreign Relations Committee, to break with the president. In turn, these shifts in popular and congressional sentiment emboldened journalists and publishers to continue to present critical news reports. Through this process, journalists developed a commitment to "investigative reporting," while a constituency emerged that would rally to the defense of the media when it came under White House attack.

This pattern endured through the 1970s and into the 1980s. Political forces opposed to presidential policies, many members of Congress, and the national news media began to find that their interests often overlapped. Liberal opponents of the Nixon, Carter, Reagan, and Bush administrations welcomed news accounts critical of the conduct of executive agencies and officials in foreign affairs and in such domestic areas as race relations, the environment, and regulatory policy. In addition, many senators and representatives found it politically advantageous to champion causes favored by the antiwar, consumer, or environmental movements because, by conducting televised hearings on such issues, they were able to mobilize national constituencies, to become national figures, and in a number of instances to become serious contenders for their party's presidential nomination. Senator Sam Nunn of Georgia had this in mind when he held televised hearings in late 1990 to criticize President Bush's policies in the Persian Gulf. Virtually every witness Nunn called explained why Bush's policies were incorrect or dangerous. The success of Bush's diplomatic and military strategy in 1991, however, undercut Nunn's efforts.

For their part, aggressive use of the techniques of investigation, publicity, and exposure has allowed the national media to enhance their autonomy and carve out a prominent place for themselves in American government and politics. Increasingly, media coverage has come to influence politicians' careers, the mobilization of political constituencies, and the fate of issues and

causes. Inasmuch as members of Congress and groups opposed to presidential policies in the 1970s and 1980s benefited from the growing influence of the press, they were prepared to rush to its defense when it came under attack. This constituency could be counted upon to denounce any move by the White House or its supporters to curb media influence as an illegitimate offer to manage the news, chill free speech, and undermine the First Amendment. It was the emergence of these overlapping interests, more than an ideological bias, that has often led to an alliance between liberal political forces and the national news media.

This confluence of interests was in evidence during the 1992 presidential campaign. Most journalists endeavored to be evenhanded in their coverage of the candidates. As we saw above, the media subjected all the major campaigns to regular scrutiny and criticism. However, as several studies have since indicated, during the course of the campaign the media tended to be more critical of Bush and more supportive of Clinton.[23] This was an almost inevitable outgrowth of the *de facto* alliance that developed over a number of years between the media and liberal forces. Like any longstanding relationship, this one tends to shape the attitudes and perceptions of the participants. Without any need for overt bias or sinister conspiracy, journalists tend naturally to provide more favorable coverage to liberal politicians and causes.

Thus, for example, writing in the *Washington Post*, noted print and television jour-

---

[23] See, for example, Howard Kurtz, "Networks Stressed the Negative in Comments about Bush, Study Finds," *Washington Post*, 15 November 1992, p. A7. See also Howard Kurtz, "Republicans and Some Journalists Say Media Tend to Boost Clinton, Bash Bush," *Washington Post*, 1 September 1992, p. A7.

PROCESS BOX 8.1
How a News Story Is Prepared

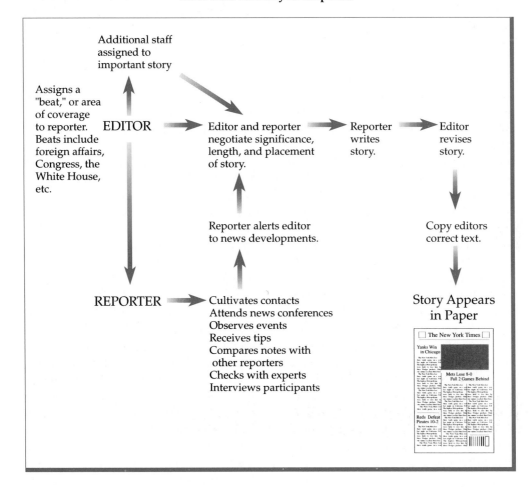

nalist Michael Kinsley angrily rejected charges that the media showed a liberal bias during the 1992 campaign. Kinsley admitted that the views of most journalists, including his own, were liberal. However, said Kinsley, this was not a bias. These views were merely "the sort of views a reasonable, intelligent person would hold."[24]

[24]Michael Kinsley, "Bias and Baloney," *Washington Post,* 26 November 1992, p. A29.

Thus, overlapping interests and perceptions, not conspiracies or overt biases, have tended to link substantial segments of the media to liberal political groups in the United States. This linkage is by no means necessarily permanent or absolute. It has, however, helped liberal forces in their political struggles over the past several decades. We shall return to the role of the media in politics in the next chapter.

At the same time, the increasing decay of party organizations (see Chapter 10) has made politicians ever more dependent upon favorable media coverage. National political leaders and journalists have had symbiotic relationships, at least since FDR's presidency, but initially politicians were the senior partners. They benefited from media publicity, but they were not totally dependent upon it as long as they could still rely on party organizations to mobilize votes. Journalists, on the other hand, depended upon their relationships with politicians for access to information, and would hesitate to report stories that might antagonize valuable sources. Newsmen feared exclusion from the flow of information in retaliation. Thus, for example, reporters did not publicize potentially embarrassing information, widely known in Washington, about the personal lives of such figures as Franklin Roosevelt and John F. Kennedy.

With the decline of party, the balance of power between politicians and journalists has been reversed. Now that politicians have become heavily dependent upon the media to reach their constituents, journalists no longer need fear that their access to information can be restricted in retaliation for negative coverage.

By the early 1990s, many commentators were beginning to wonder whether the media had become too critical and adversarial in their coverage of public figures and events. Media critics pointed to a February 1993 admission by "NBC News" that it had used staged footage in a broadcast designed to demonstrate that some General Motors trucks were likely to explode in crashes as evidence that the news media were more concerned with sensationalism than with truth. Defenders of the media, of course, called this an isolated incident. In Chapter 12, we shall look again at the role the media play in contemporary American politics and consider some of its more—and less—positive implications.

Measuring Public Opinion

As recently as fifty years ago, American political leaders gauged public opinion by people's applause or cheers and by the presence of crowds in meeting places. This direct exposure to the people's views did not necessarily produce accurate knowledge of public opinion. It did, however, give political leaders confidence in their public support—and therefore confidence in their ability to govern by consent.

Abraham Lincoln and Stephen Douglas confronted each other seven times in the summer and autumn of 1858, two years before they became presidential nominees. Their debates took place before audiences in parched cornfields and courthouse squares. A century later, the presidential debates, although seen by millions, take place before a few reporters and technicians in television studios that might as well have been on the moon. The public's response cannot be experienced directly. This distance between leaders and followers is one of the agonizing problems of modern democracy. The media send information to millions of people, but they are not yet as efficient at getting information back to leaders. Is government by consent possible where the scale of communication is so large and impersonal? In order to compensate for the decline in their ability to experience public opinion for themselves, leaders have turned to science, in particular to the science of opinion polling.

It is no secret that politicians and public officials make extensive use of public opinion polls to help them decide whether to run for office, what policies to support, how to

PROCESS BOX 8.2
How a Poll Is Conducted

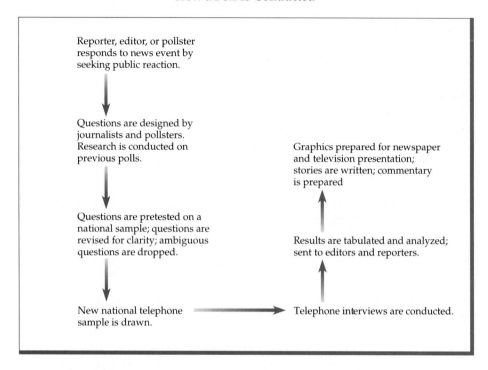

Reporter, editor, or pollster responds to news event by seeking public reaction.

↓

Questions are designed by journalists and pollsters. Research is conducted on previous polls.

↓

Questions are pretested on a national sample; questions are revised for clarity; ambiguous questions are dropped.

↓

New national telephone sample is drawn. ⟶ Telephone interviews are conducted.

↑

Results are tabulated and analyzed; sent to editors and reporters.

↑

Graphics prepared for newspaper and television presentation; stories are written; commentary is prepared

vote on important legislation, and what types of appeals to make in their campaigns. President Lyndon Johnson was famous for carrying the latest Gallup and Roper poll results in his hip pocket, and it is widely believed that he began to withdraw from politics as the polls reported losses in public support. All recent presidents and other major political figures have worked closely with polls and pollsters.

Constructing Public Opinion from Surveys

The population in which pollsters are interested is usually quite large. To conduct their polls they choose a sample of the total population. The selection of this sample is important. Above all, it must be representative; the views of those in the sample must accurately and proportionately reflect the views of the whole. To a large extent, the validity of the poll's results depends on the sampling procedure used, several of which are described in the In Brief Box.

The degree of reliability in polling is a function of sample size. The same sample is needed to represent a small population as to represent a large population. The typical size of a sample ranges from 450 to 1,500 respondents. This number, however, reflects a trade-off between cost and degree of

---

In Brief Box

METHODS OF MEASURING PUBLIC OPINION

Interpreting Mass Opinion from Mass Behavior and Mass Attributes

Consumer behavior: predicts that people tend to vote against the party in power during a downslide in the economy

Group demographics: can predict party affiliation and voting by measuring income, race, and type of community (urban or rural)

Getting Public Opinion Directly from the Prople

Person-to-person: form impressions based on conversations with acquaintances, aides, and associates

Selective polling: form impressions based on intervies with a few representative members of a group or groups

Bellwether districts: form impressions based on an entire community that has a reputation for being a good predictor of the entire nation's attitudes

Constructing Public Opinion from Surveys

Quota sampling: respondents are chosen because they match a general population along several significant dimensions, such as geographic region, sex, age, and race

Probability sampling: respondents are chosen without prior screening, based entirely on a lottery system

Area sampling: respondents are chosen as part of a systematic breakdown of larger homogenous units into smaller representative areas

Haphazard sampling: respondents are chosen by pure chance with no systematic method

Systematically biased sampling: respondents are chosen with a hidden or undetected bias towards a given demographic group

---

precision desired. The degree of accuracy that can be achieved with a small sample can be seen from the polls' success in predicting election outcomes.

Table 8.2 shows how accurate the major national polling organizations have been in predicting the outcomes of presidential elections. In only three instances between 1952 and 1992 did the final October polls predict the wrong outcome; and in all three instances—Roper in 1960, Harris in 1968, and Gallup in 1976—the actual election was

extremely close and the prediction was off by no more than two percentage points.

Even with reliable sampling procedures, problems can occur. Validity can be adversely affected by poor question format, faulty ordering of questions, inappropriate vocabulary, ambiguity of questions, or questions with built-in biases. Often, apparently minor differences in the wording of a question can convey vastly different meanings to respondents and, thus, produce quite different response patterns. For exam-

TABLE 8.2
THE POLLSTERS AND THEIR RECORD (1948–1992)

	Harris	Gallup	Actual Outcome
1992			
Clinton	44%	44%	43%
Bush	38	37	38
Perot	17	14	19
1988			
Bush	51%	53%	54%
Dukakis	47	42	46
1984			
Reagan	56%	59%	59%
Mondale	44	41	41
1980			
Reagan	48%	47%	51%
Carter	43	44	41
Anderson		8	
1976			
Carter	48%	48%	51%
Ford	45	49	48
1972			
Nixon	59%	62%	61%
McGovern	35	38	38
1968			
Nixon	40%	43%	43%
Humphrey	43	42	43
G. Wallace	13	15	14
1964			
Johnson	62%	64%	61%
Goldwater	33	36	39
1960			
Kennedy	49%	51%	50%
Nixon	41	49	49
1956			
Eisenhower	NA	59.5%	58%
Stevenson		40.5	42
1952			
Eisenhower	47%	51%	55%
Stevenson	42	49	44
1948			
Truman	NA	44.5%	49.6%
Dewey		49.5	45.1

All figures except those for 1948 are rounded. NA = Not asked.

*Polling done in August rather than in October.

Sources: Data from the Gallup Poll, the Harris Survey (New York: Chicago Tribune-New York News Syndicate, various press releases 1964-1992). Courtesy of the Gallup Organization, and Louis Harris & Associates.

ple, prior to World War II, a poll asked Americans if they supported "collaboration" with Great Britain to combat Germany. The overwhelming majority of those surveyed said they were opposed. But when the same poll asked Americans if they supported "cooperation" with Britain against Germany, an equally overwhelming majority of respondents indicated their support.[25]

Similarly, for many years the University of Chicago's National Opinion Research Center (NORC) has asked respondents whether they think the federal government is spending too much, too little, or about the right amount of money on "assistance for the poor." Answering the question posed this way, about two-thirds of all respondents seem to believe that the government is spending too little. However, the same survey also asks whether the government spends too much, too little, or about the right amount for "welfare." When the word "welfare" is substituted for "assistance for the poor," about half of all respondents indicate that too much is being spent by the government.[26]

In the early days of a political campaign when voters are asked which candidates they do, or do not, support, the answer they give often has little significance, because the choice is not yet salient to them. Their preference may change many times before the actual election. This is part of the explanation for the phenomenon of the post-convention "bounce" in the popularity of presidential candidates, which was observed after the 1992 Democratic and Republican national conventions.[27] Respondents' preferences reflected the amount of attention the candidates received during the conventions rather than strongly held views.

Salient interests are interests that stand out beyond others, that are of more than ordinary concern to respondents in a survey or to voters in the electorate. Politicians, social scientists, journalists, or pollsters who assume something is important to the public, when in fact it is not, are creating an illusion of saliency. This illusion can be created and fostered by polls despite careful controls over sampling, interviewing, and data analysis. In fact, the illusion is strengthened by the credibility that science gives survey results.

The problem of saliency has become especially acute as a result of the proliferation of media polls. The television networks and major national newspapers all make heavy use of opinion polls. Increasingly, polls are being commissioned by local television stations and local and regional newspapers as well.[28] On the positive side, polls allow journalists to make independent assessments of political realities—assessments not influenced by the partisan claims of politicians.

At the same time, however, media polls can allow journalists to make news when none really exists. Polling diminishes journalists' dependence upon news makers. A poll commissioned by a news agency can provide the basis for a good story even when candidates, politicians, and other news makers refuse to cooperate by engaging in newsworthy activities. Thus, on days

[25]Burns W. Roper, "Are Polls Accurate?" *Annals of the American Academy of Political and Social Science,* no. 472 (March 1984), p. 32.

[26]Michael Kagay and Janet Elder, "Numbers Are No Problem for Pollsters. Words Are," *New York Times,* 9 August 1992, p. E6.

[27]See Richard Morin, "Is Bush's Bounce a Boom or a Bust?" *Washington Post National Weekly Edition,* 31 August–6 September 1992, p. 37.

[28]See Thomas E. Mann and Gary Orren, eds., *Media Polls in American Politics* (Washington, DC: Brookings Institution, 1992).

when little or nothing is actually taking place in a political campaign, poll results, especially apparent changes in candidate margins, can provide voters exciting news. Several times during the 1992 presidential campaign, for example, small changes in the relative standing of the Democratic and Republican candidates produced banner headlines around the country. Stories about what the candidates actually did or said often took second place to reporting the "horse race."

Interestingly, because rapid and dramatic shifts in candidate margins tend to take place when voters' preferences are least fully formed, horse race news is most likely to make the headlines when it is actually least significant.[29] In other words, media interest in poll results is inversely related to the actual salience of voters' opinions and the significance of the polls' findings. However, by influencing perceptions, especially those of major contributors, media polls can influence political realities.

The most noted, but least serious, of polling problems is the bandwagon effect, which occurs when polling results influence people to support the candidate marked as the probable victor. Some scholars argue that this bandwagon effect can be offset by an "underdog effect" in favor of the candidate who is trailing in the polls.[30] However, a candidate who demonstrates a lead in the polls usually finds it considerably easier to raise campaign funds than a candidate whose poll standing is poor. With additional funds, poll leaders can often afford to

pay for television time and other campaign activities that will cement their advantage. For example, Bill Clinton's substantial lead in the polls during much of the summer of 1992 helped the Democrats raise far more money than in any previous campaign, primarily from interests hoping to buy access to a future President Clinton. For once, the Democrats were able to outspend the usually better-heeled Republicans. Thus, the appearance of a lead, provided by the polls, helped make Clinton's lead a reality.

Public Opinion, Political Knowledge, and the Importance of Ignorance

Many people are distressed to find public opinion polls not only unable to discover public opinion but unable to avoid producing unintentional distortions of their own. No matter how hard they try, no matter how mature the science of opinion polling becomes, politicians forever may remain substantially ignorant of public opinion.

Although knowledge is good for its own sake, and knowledge of public opinion may sometimes produce better government, ignorance also has its uses. It can, for example, operate as a restraint on the use of power. Leaders who think they know what the public wants are often autocratic rulers. Leaders who realize that they are always partially in the dark about the public are likely to be more modest in their claims, less intense in their demands, and more uncertain in their uses of government power. Their uncertainty may make them more accountable to their constituencies because they will be more likely to continue searching for consent.

One of the most valuable benefits of survey research is actually "negative knowledge"—knowledge that pierces through ir-

---

[29]For an excellent and reflective discussion by a journalist, see Richard Morin, "Clinton Slide in Survey Shows Perils of Polling," *Washington Post*, 29 August 1992, p. A6.

[30]See Michael Traugott, "The Impact of Media Polls on the Public," in Mann and Orren, eds., *Media Polls in American Politics*, pp. 125–49.

responsible claims about the breadth of opinion or the solidarity of group or mass support. Because this sort of knowledge reveals the complexity and uncertainty of public opinion, it can help make citizens less gullible, group leaders less strident, and politicians less deceitful. This alone gives public opinion research, despite its great limitations, an important place in the future of American politics.[31]

Public Opinion and Government Policy

In democratic nations leaders should pay attention to public opinion, and the evidence suggests that they do. There are many instances in which public policy and public opinion do not coincide, but in general the government's actions are consistent with citizens' preferences. One recent study, for example, found that between 1935 and 1979, in about two-thirds of all cases, significant changes in public opinion were followed within one year by changes in government policy consistent with the shift in the popular mood.[32] Other studies have come to similar conclusions.

Despite the evidence of broad agreement between opinion and policy, there are always areas of disagreement. For example, the majority of Americans for years have favored stricter governmental control of handguns—without much result. Similarly,

most Americans—blacks as well as whites—oppose school busing to achieve racial balance, which nevertheless continues to be used extensively throughout the nation. Most Americans are far less concerned with the rights of the accused than the federal courts seem to be. Most Americans oppose U.S. military intervention in other nations' affairs, yet such interventions continue to take place and often win public approval after the fact.

Several factors can contribute to a lack of consistency between opinion and governmental policy. First, the nominal majority on a particular issue may not be as intensely committed to its preference as the adherents of the minority viewpoint. An intensely committed minority may often be more willing to commit its time, energy, efforts, and resources to the affirmation of its opinions than an apathetic, even if large, majority. In the case of firearms, for example, although the proponents of gun control are in the majority by a wide margin, most do not regard the issue as one of critical importance to themselves and are not willing to commit much effort to advancing their cause. The opponents of gun control, by contrast, are intensely committed, well organized, and well financed, and as a result are usually able to carry the day.

A second important reason that public policy and public opinion may not coincide has to do with the character and structure of the American system of government. The framers of the American Constitution, as we saw in Chapter 2, sought to create a system of government that was based upon popular consent but that did not invariably and automatically translate shifting popular sentiments into public policies. As a result, the American governmental process includes arrangements such as an appointed

---

[31] For a fuller discussion of the uses of polling and the role of public opinion in American politics, see Benjamin Ginsberg, *The Captive Public* (New York: Basic Books, 1986).

[32] Benjamin I. Page and Robert Y. Shapiro, "Effects of Public Opinion on Policy," *American Political Science Review* 77 (March 1983), pp. 175–90.

judiciary that can produce policy decisions that may run contrary to prevailing popular sentiment—at least for a time.

When, however, all is said and done, there can be little doubt that in general the actions of the American government do not remain out of line with popular sentiment for very long. A major reason for this is, of course, the electoral process, to which we shall now turn.

Time Line on Public Opinion and the Media

EVENTS		INSTITUTIONAL DEVELOPMENTS
Alien and Sedition Acts attempt to silence opposition press (1798)	**1800**	Newspapers and pamphlets serve leaders (early 1800s)
New printing presses introduced, allowing cheaper printing of more newspapers (1820s–1840s)		Expansion of popular press; circulation of more newspapers, magazines, and books (1840s)
First transmission of telegraph message between cities (from Baltimore to Washington) (1844)		Nation begins to be linked by telegraph communications network (1840s)
Creation of Associated Press (AP) (1848)	**1850**	
Completion of telegraph connections across country to San Francisco (1861)		Birth of advertising industry— scientific manipulation of public opinion (1880s)
Democrats denounce polling as a Republican plot (1896)		Advertising industry makes press financially free of parties; beginnings of an independent, nonpartisan press (1880s)
Publisher William R. Hearst sparks Spanish-American War (1898)		Circulation war between Hearst's *N.Y. Journal* and Pulitzer's *N.Y. World* leads to "yellow journalism"—sensationalized reporting (1890s)
Rise of large corporations and municipal corruption spark Progressive reform efforts (1880s–1890s)		Beginning of "muckraking"— exposure of social evils by journalists (1890s)
First radio news bulletins transmitted over radio; regular radio programs introduced (1920)	**1920**	Beginning of radio broadcasting (1920s)

EVENTS		INSTITUTIONAL DEVELOPMENTS
NBC links radio stations into network(1926)		Regulation of broadcast industry begins with Federal Radio Commission (1927)
Great Depression (1929–1933)		*Near* v. *Minnesota*—Supreme Court holds that government cannot exercise prior restraint (1931)
Literary Digest poll predicts Hoover will defeat Roosevelt (1932)		Federal Communications Act creates Federal Communications Commission (FCC) (1934)
Franklin D. Roosevelt uses radio "fireside chats" to assure the nation and restore confidence (1930s)		
Gallup poll (1936)		Growth of national polls (1930s–1950s)
		Television is introduced (late 1940s–1950s)
Televised Senate hearings (1950s)	**1950**	Computer analysis of polls (1959)
Televised Kennedy-Nixon debate (1960)		Fairness doctrine governing TV coverage (1960s)
John F. Kennedy uses televised news conferences to mobilize public support for his policies (1961–1963)		Beginning of extended national television news coverage (1963)
		Emergence of exit polls (1960s)
"Daisy Girl" commercial helps defeat Goldwater and elect Lyndon Johnson president (1964)		*N.Y. Times* v. *Sullivan* asserts "actual malice" standard in libel cases involving public officials (1964)
Vietnam War; American officials in Vietnam leak information to the press (1960s–early 1970s)	**1970**	Vietnam War first war to receive extended television coverage, which contributes to expansion of opposition to the war (1965–1973)
		TV spot ads become candidates' major weapons (1960s–1990s)
		Red Lion Broadcasting v. *U.S.* establishes "right of rebuttal" (1969)

EVENTS		INSTITUTIONAL DEVELOPMENTS
		Media attack governmental opinion manipulation (1960s–1970s)
		Era of investigative reporting and critical journalistic coverage of government (1960s–1990s)
Pentagon Papers on Vietnam War published by *N.Y. Times* and *Washington Post* (1971)		*N.Y. Times* v. *U.S.*—*Supreme Court* rules against prior restraint in Pentagon Papers case (1971)
Televised Watergate hearings (1973–1974)		
Exit polls used to predict presidential elections before polls close on West Coast (1976–1988)		
Unsuccessful libel suits by Israeli General Ariel Sharon against Time magazine (1984) and by General William Westmoreland against CBS News (1985)	**1980**	FCC stops enforcing fairness doctrine (1985)
Televised Iran-Contra hearings (1987)		
Live coverage of Persian Gulf War (1991)	**1990**	Military controlled media access throughout Persian Gulf conflict (1990–1991)
Candidates use talk show appearances in 1992 campaign; Ross Perot pioneers the "infomercial"; televised town meetings (1992)		Politicians create new media formats to pitch themselves and their programs; era of permanent campaign (1992)
President Clinton uses town meetings and media appeals to bolster popular support for programs; Congress lobbies by mobilizing popular pressure (1993)		Members of presidential campaign staffs become part of White House staff to bolster public support for programs (1993)

Chapter Review

All governments claim to obey public opinion, and in the democracies politicians and political leaders actually try to do so.

The American government does not directly regulate opinions and beliefs in the sense that dictatorial regimes often seek to do. Opinion is regulated by an institution that the government constructed and that it maintains—the marketplace of ideas. In this marketplace, opinions and ideas compete for support. In general, opinions supported by upper-class groups have a better chance of succeeding than those views that are mainly advanced by the lower classes.

Americans share a number of values and viewpoints but often classify themselves as liberal or conservative in their basic orientations. The meaning of these terms has changed greatly over the past century. Once liberalism meant opposition to big government. Today liberals favor an expanded role for the government. Once conservatism meant support for state power and aristocratic rule. Today conservatives oppose almost all government regulation.

Although the United States relies mainly on market mechanisms to regulate opinion, even our government intervenes to some extent, seeking both to influence particular opinions and, more important, the general climate of political opinion, often by trying to influence media coverage of events.

Another important force shaping public opinion is the media, which help to determine the agenda or focus of political debate and to shape popular understanding of political events. The power of the media stems from their having the freedom to present information and opinion critical of government, political leaders, and policies. Free media are essential ingredients of popular government.

The scientific approach to learning public opinion is random sample polling. Through polling, elections can be accurately predicted; polls also provide information on the bases and conditions of voting decisions and make it possible to assess trends in attitudes and the influence of ideology on attitudes.

For Further Reading

Asher, Herbert. *Polling and the Public: What Every Citizen Should Know.* Washington, DC: Congressional Quarterly Press, 1988.

Bennett, W. Lance. *Public Opinion in American Politics.* New York: Harcourt Brace Jovanovich, 1980.

Braestrup, Peter. *Big Story: How the American Press and Television Reported and Interpreted the Crisis of Tet 1968 in Vietnam and Washington.* Boulder, CO: Westview Press, 1977.

Cook, Timothy. *Making Laws and Making News: Media Strategies in the House of Representatives.* Washington, DC: Brookings Institution, 1989.

Erikson, Robert S., Norman Luttbeg, and Kent Tedin. *American Public Opinion: Its Origins, Content and Impact.* New York: Wiley, 1980.

Gallup, George. *The Pulse of Democracy.* New York: Simon and Schuster, 1940.

Ginsberg, Benjamin. *The Captive Public: How Mass Opinion Promotes State Power.* New York: Basic Books, 1986.

Graber, Doris. *Mass Media and American Politics.* Washington, DC: Congressional Quarterly Press, 1989.

Hess, Stephen. *Live From Capitol Hill: Studies of Congress and the Media.* Washington, DC: Brookings Institution, 1991.

Holloway, Harry, and John George. *Public Opinion: Coalitions, Elites and Masses.* New York: St. Martin's Press, 1986.

Joslyn, Richard A. *Mass Media and Elections.* Reading, MA: Addison-Wesley, 1984.

Lippmann, Walter. *Public Opinion.* New York: Harcourt, Brace, 1922.

Lipset, Seymour M., and William Schneider. *The Confidence Gap: Business, Labor and Government in the Public Mind.* Rev. ed. Baltimore: Johns Hopkins University Press, 1987.

Margolis, Michael, and Gary A. Mauser. *Manipulating Public Opinion.* Pacific Grove, CA: Brooks/Cole, 1989.

Nacos, Brigitte L. *The Press, Presidents and Crises.* New York: Columbia University Press, 1990.

Neuman, W. Russell. *The Paradox of Mass Politics: Knowledge and Opinion in the American Electorate.* Cambridge: Harvard University Press, 1986.

Owen, Diana. *Media Messages in American Presidential Elections.* Westport, CT: Greenwood, 1991.

Sullivan, John L., James Piereson, and George E. Marcus. *Political Tolerance and American Democracy.* Chicago: University of Chicago Press, 1982.

Winfield, Betty Houchin. *FDR and the News Media.* Urbana, IL: University of Illinois, 1990.

9

ELECTIONS

*T*he peaceful participation of ordinary people in politics is one of the great accomplishments of the United States and the other Western democracies. Its importance cannot be overstated, although it can be misunderstood. Most Americans, including many who seldom vote, are committed to two propositions about elections. First, we believe that elections promote *accountability*. That is, we believe that elections force those in power to conduct themselves in a responsible manner and to take account of popular interests when they make their decisions. Second, Americans feel that elections facilitate popular *influence*, that the chance to select some public officials is also an opportunity to make choices about the policies, programs, and future directions of government action. Accountability and influence are the two key principles underlying the electoral process.

In this chapter, we will look first at what distinguishes voting from other forms of political activity. Second, we will examine the formal structure and setting of American elections. Third, we will see how—and what—voters decide when they take part in elections. Fourth, we will discuss the consequences of elections, especially electoral realignment, to try to make sense of contemporary American electoral politics. Fifth, we will focus on recent national elections. Finally, we will assess the place of elections in the American political process.

Political Participation

In the twentieth century, voting is viewed as the normal form of mass political activity. Yet, ordinary people took part in politics long before the introduction of the election or any other formal mechanism of popular involvement in political life. If there is any natural or spontaneous form of mass political participation, it is the riot rather than the election. Indeed, the urban riot and the rural uprising were a major part of life in western Europe prior to the nineteenth century and to eastern Europe until the twentieth. In eighteenth-century London, for example, one of the most notorious forms of popular political action was the "illumination." Mobs would march up and down the street demanding that householders express support for their cause by placing a candle or lantern in a front window. Those who refused to illuminate in this way risked having their homes put to the torch by the angry crowd. This eighteenth-century form of civil disorder may well be the origin of the expression "to shed light upon" an issue.

The fundamental difference between voting and rioting is that voting is a socialized and institutionalized form of mass political action.[1] When, where, how, and which individuals participate in elections are matters of public policy rather than questions of spontaneous individual choice. With the advent of the election, control over the agenda for political action passed at least in part from the citizen to the government.

In an important study of participation in the United States, Sidney Verba and Norman Nie define political participation as consisting of "activities 'within the system'—ways of influencing politics that are generally recognized as legal and legitimate."[2] Governments try very hard to channel and limit political participation to actions "within the system." Even with that constraint, however, the right to political participation is a tremendous advancement in the status of citizens on two levels. At one level, it increases the probability that they will regularly affect the decisions that governments make. On the other level, it reinforces the concept of the individual as independent from the state.

Those holding power are willing to concede the right to participate in the hope that it will encourage citizens to give their consent to being governed. This is a calculated risk for citizens. They give up their right to revolt in return for the right to participate regularly. They can participate, but only in ways prescribed by the government. Outside the established channels, their participation can be suppressed or disregarded. It is also a calculated risk for the politician, who may be forced into certain policy decisions or forced out of office altogether by citizens exercising their right to participate. This risk is usually worth taking, since in return, governments acquire consent, and through consent citizens become supporters of government action.[3]

Regulating the Electoral Process

The compromise between rulers and ruled that is at the heart of the voting process is, perhaps, best illustrated by the rule governing electoral institutions. While elections al-

---

[1] For a fuller discussion, see Benjamin Ginsberg, *The Consequences of Consent* (New York: Random House, 1982).

[2] Sidney Verba and Norman Nie, *Participation in America* (New York: Harper & Row, 1972), pp. 2–3.

[3] See Ginsberg, *Consequences of Consent.*

low citizens a chance to participate in politics, they also allow the government a chance to exert a good deal of control over when, where, how, and which of its citizens will participate. Electoral processes are governed by a variety of rules and procedures that allow government an excellent opportunity to regulate and control popular involvement. Three general forms of regulation have played especially important roles in the electoral history of the Western democracies. First, governments often attempt to regulate who can vote in order to diminish the influence of groups they deem to be undesirable. Second, governments frequently seek to manipulate the translation of voters' choices into electoral outcomes. Third, virtually all governments attempt to insulate the policy-making process from electoral intervention through regulation of the relationship between the ballot box and the organization of government.

Electoral Composition

Perhaps the oldest and most obvious device used to regulate voting and its consequences is manipulation of the electorate's composition. In the first elections in western Europe, for example, the suffrage was generally limited to property owners and others who could be trusted to vote in a manner acceptable to those in power. Property qualifications in France prior to 1848 limited the electorate to 240,000 of some 7 million men over the age of twenty-one.[4] No women were permitted to vote. During the same era, other nations manipulated the electorate's composition by assigning unequal electoral weights to different classes of voters. The 1831 Belgian constitution, for example, assigned individuals anywhere from one to three votes depending upon their property holdings, education, and position.[5] But even in the context of America's ostensibly universal and equal suffrage in the twentieth century, the composition of the electorate is still subject to manipulation. Until recent years, some states manipulated the vote by the discriminatory use of poll taxes and literacy tests or by such practices as the placement of polls and the scheduling of voting hours to depress participation by one or another group. Today the most important example of the regulation of the American electorate's composition is our unique personal registration requirements.

Levels of voter participation in twentieth-century American elections are quite low by comparison to those of the other Western democracies.[6] Indeed, voter participation in presidential elections in the United States has barely averaged 50 percent recently. During the nineteenth century, by contrast, voter turnout in the United States was extremely high. Records, in fact, indicate that in some counties as many as 105 percent of those eligible voted in presidential elections. Some proportion of this total obviously was artificial—a result of the widespread corruption that characterized American voting practices during that period. Nevertheless, it seems clear that the proportion of eligible voters actually going to the polls was considerably larger in nineteenth-century America than it is today.

As Figure 9.1 indicates, the critical years

---

[4]Stein Rokkan, *Citizens, Elections, Parties* (New York: David McKay, 1970), p. 149.

[5]John A. Hawgood, *Modern Constitutions since 1787* (New York: D. Van Nostrand, 1939), p. 148.

[6]See Walter Dean Burnham, "The Changing Shape of the American Political Universe," *American Political Science Review* 59 (1965), pp. 7–28.

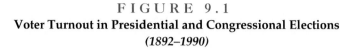

FIGURE 9.1

Voter Turnout in Presidential and Congressional Elections
(1892–1990)

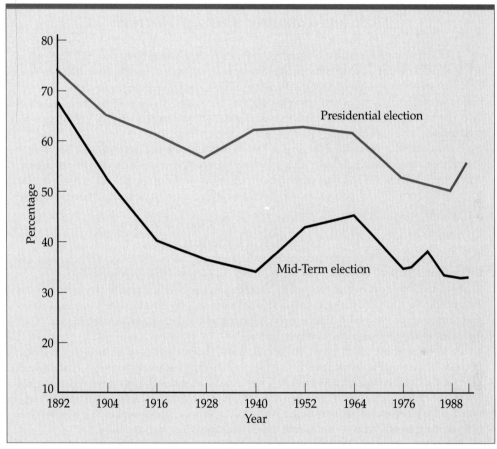

Sources: For 1890 to 1958, Erik Austin and Jerome Clubb, *Political Facts of the United States since 1789* (New York: Columbia University Press, 1986), pp. 378–79; for 1960–1992, Bureau of the Census, *Statistical Abstract of the United States* (Washington, DC: Government Printing Office, 1992).

during which voter turnout declined across the United States were between 1890 and 1910. These years coincide with the adoption of laws across much of the nation requiring eligible citizens to appear personally at a registrar's office to register to vote some time prior to the actual date of an election. Personal registration was one of several "Progressive" reforms initiated at the turn of the century. The ostensible purpose of registration was to discourage fraud and corruption. But to many Progressive reformers, "corruption" was a code word, referring to the type of politics practiced in

---

Do Elections and Voting Matter?

*M*ost Americans take pride in the country's annual election rituals, pointing out that few nations of the world have mechanisms for transferring power in such a smooth and peaceful fashion. Critics of American elections argue, however, that the differences between the candidates and political parties are marginal, if not nonexistent; that elections and campaigns are more spectacle and show than about real power; and that elections pacify the electorate more than they encourage true citizenship.

Political scientists Gerald M. Pomper and Susan S. Lederman argue that elections in fact do meet the criteria for meaningful political exercises. Political scientist Howard L. Reiter, on the other hand, argues that voting is at best a poor method for translating preferences into policies and, worse, that voting tends to channel citizens toward a relatively harmless political act and away from other more effective methods of political expression.

Pomper and Lederman

The first necessity for meaningful elections is an organized party system. . . . Without a choice between at least two competing parties, the electorate is powerless to exert its influence.

A related vital requirement is for free competition between the parties. The voters must be able to hear diverse opinions and be able to make an uncoerced choice. . . . Nomination and campaigning must be available to the full range of candidates, and the means provided for transmitting their appeals to the electorate. . . .

Elections in the United States do largely meet the standards of meaningful popular decisions; true voter influence exists. The two parties compete freely with one another, and the extent of their competition is spreading to virtually all states. Access to the voters is open to diverse candidates, and no party or administration can control the means of communication. Suffrage is virtually universal, and voters have fairly simple choices to make for regular offices. In the overwhelming number of cases, voting is conducted honestly. . . .

---

the large cities where political parties had organized immigrant and ethnic populations. Reformers not only objected to this corruption, but they also opposed the growing political power of these urban populations and their leaders.

Personal registration imposed a new burden upon potential voters and altered the format of American elections. Under the registration systems adopted after 1890, it became the duty of individual voters to secure their own eligibility. This duty could prove to be a significant burden for potential voters. During a personal appearance before the registrar, individuals seeking to vote were (and are) required to furnish proof of identity, residence, and citizenship. While the inconvenience of registration varied from state to state, usually voters could register only during business hours on

Whatever the future may hold, present conditions in the United States do enable the voters to influence, but not control, the government. The evidence . . . does not confirm the most extravagant expectations of popular sovereignty. Neither are elections demonstrably dangerous or meaningless. Most basically, we have found the ballot to be an effective means for the protection of citizen interests. Elections in America ultimately provide only one, but the most vital, mandate.[1]

Reiter

Most of the major issues in American history have been resolved not by elections but by other historical forces. . . . Elections are not very good ways of expressing the policy views of the people who actually vote. Elections are even less effective as a means of carrying out the policy views of all citizens. . . .

Politics, we are encouraged to believe, occurs once a year in November, and for most adults it occurs only once every four years. We are able to discharge our highest civic function by taking a few minutes to go into a booth and flip a few levers once every four years. Although we are all free to engage in other political activities, such as collective action, writing to officials or working on campaigns, most adults are quite content to limit their political activity to that once-in-a-quadrennium lever flip. And if we think of voting as the crown jewel of our liberties, we will not think that citizenship requires anything else.

All in all, the message that elections sends us is to be passive about politics. Don't take action that involves any effort, don't unite with other citizens to achieve political goals, just respond to the choice that the ballot box gives us. In a strange way, then, elections condition us *away* from politics. A nation which defines its precious heritage in terms of political rights discourages its citizens from all but the *least* social, *least* public, and *least* political form of activity. This should raise the most profound questions for us. Why should we as a society discourage political activism? What is the real role that voting plays in our politics?[2]

[1]Gerald M. Pomper and Susan S. Lederman, *Elections in America: Control and Influence in Democratic Politics*, 2nd ed. (New York: Longman, 1980), pp. 223–25.
[2]Howard L. Reiter, *Parties and Elections in Corporate America* (New York: St. Martin's Press, 1987), pp. 1–3, 9.

weekdays. Many potential voters could not afford to lose a day's pay in order to register. Second, voters were usually required to register well before the next election, in some states up to several months earlier. Third, since most personal registration laws required a periodic purge of the elections rolls, ostensibly to keep them up-to-date, voters often had to re-register to maintain their eligibility. Thus, although personal registration requirements helped to diminish the widespread electoral corruption that accompanied a completely open voting process, they also made it much more difficult for citizens to participate in the electoral process.

Registration requirements particularly depress participation on the part of those with little education and low incomes, for two reasons. First, the simple obstacle of registering on weekdays during business hours is most difficult for working-class persons to overcome. Second, and more important, registration requires a greater degree of political involvement and interest than does the act of voting itself. To vote, a person need only be concerned with the particular election campaign at hand. Requiring individuals to register before the next election forces them to make a decision to participate on the basis of an abstract interest in the electoral process rather than a simple concern with a specific campaign. Such an abstract interest in electoral politics is largely a product of education. Those with relatively little education may become interested in political events because of a particular campaign, but by that time it may be too late to register. As a result, personal registration requirements not only diminish the size of the electorate but also tend to create an electorate that is, in the aggregate, better educated, higher in income and social status, and composed of fewer African Americans and other minorities than the citizenry as a whole. Presumably this is why elimination of personal registration requirements has not always been viewed favorably by some conservatives.[7]

Over the years, voter registration restrictions have been modified somewhat to make registration easier. In 1993, for example, Congress approved and President Clinton signed the "motor voter" bill to ease voter registration by allowing individuals to register when they applied for driver's licenses as well as in public assistance and military recruitment offices.[8] A similar bill

had been vetoed by President George Bush in 1992. Republicans objected to the bill because they feared it would increase registration by the poor and minority voters who, generally, tended to support the Democrats. Experience suggests, however, that *any* registration rules, however liberal, tend to depress voting on the part of the poor and uneducated.

Translating Voters' Choices into Electoral Outcomes

With the exception of America's personal registration requirements, contemporary governments generally do not try to limit the composition of their electorates. Instead, they prefer to allow everyone to vote and then to manipulate the outcome of the election. This is possible because there is no single or automatic way to decide the relationship between individual votes and electoral outcomes. There are any number of possible rules that can be used to determine how individual votes will be translated into collective electoral decisions. Two types of regulations are especially important: the rules that set the criteria for victory and the rules that define electoral districts.

THE CRITERIA FOR WINNING. In some nations to win a seat in the parliament or other representative body a candidate must receive a majority (50% + 1) of all the votes cast in the relevant district. This type of electoral system is called a *majority system* and was used in the primary elections of most southern states until recent years. Generally, majority systems have a provision for a second or "runoff" election among the two top candidates if the initial contest drew so many contestants that none received an absolute majority of the votes cast.

In other nations, candidates for office

[7] See Kevin Phillips and Paul H. Blackman, *Electoral Reform and Voter Participation* (Washington, DC: American Enterprise Institute, 1975).

[8] Helen Dewar, "'Motor Voter' Agreement is Reached," *Washington Post*, 28 April 1993, p. A6.

In Brief Box

WHO WINS?
TRANSLATING VOTERS' CHOICES INTO
ELECTORAL OUTCOMES

Majority System
Winner must receive a simple majority (50 percent plus one)
Example: formerly used in primary elections in the South

Plurality System
Winner is the candidate who receives the most votes, regardless of the percentage
Example: currently used in almost all general elections throughout the country

Proportional Representation
Winners are selected to a representative body in the proportion to the votes their
  party received
Example: used in New York City in the 1930s, resulting in several communist
  seats on the City Council

---

need not receive an absolute majority of the votes cast to win an election. Instead, victory is awarded to the candidate who receives the most votes in a given election regardless of the actual percentage of votes this represents. Thus, a candidate who receives 40 percent or 30 percent or 20 percent of the votes cast may win the contest so long as no rival receives more votes. This type of electoral process is called a *plurality system,* and it is the system used in almost all general elections in the United States.

Most European states employ a third form of electoral system, called *proportional representation.* Under proportional rules, competing political parties are awarded legislative seats roughly in proportion to their actual percentage of the popular votes cast. For example, a party that won 30 percent of the votes would receive roughly 30 percent of the seats in the parliament or other representative body. In the United States, proportional representation is used by many states in presidential primary elections. In these

primaries, candidates for the Democratic and Republican nominations are awarded convention delegates in rough proportion to the percentage of the popular vote they receive in the primary.

ELECTORAL DISTRICTS. Despite the use of proportional representation and the occasional use of majority voting systems, most electoral contests in the United States are decided on the basis of plurality rules.

Congressional district boundaries in the United States are redrawn by governors and state legislatures every ten years after the decennial census determines the number of House seats to which each state is entitled. Rather than seeking to manipulate the criteria for victory, American politicians have usually sought to influence electoral outcomes by manipulating the organization of electoral districts. This is called *gerrymandering* in honor of nineteenth-century Massachusetts Governor Elbridge Gerry, who was alleged to have designed a district in the

PROCESS BOX 9.1
Congressional Redistricting

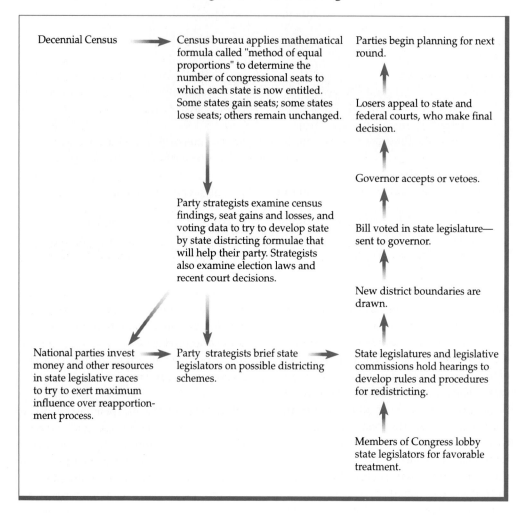

Decennial Census → Census bureau applies mathematical formula called "method of equal proportions" to determine the number of congressional seats to which each state is now entitled. Some states gain seats; some states lose seats; others remain unchanged.

Party strategists examine census findings, seat gains and losses, and voting data to try to develop state by state districting formulae that will help their party. Strategists also examine election laws and recent court decisions.

National parties invest money and other resources in state legislative races to try to exert maximum influence over reapportionment process.

Party strategists brief state legislators on possible districting schemes.

State legislatures and legislative commissions hold hearings to develop rules and procedures for redistricting.

Members of Congress lobby state legislators for favorable treatment.

New district boundaries are drawn.

Bill voted in state legislature—sent to governor.

Governor accepts or vetoes.

Losers appeal to state and federal courts, who make final decision.

Parties begin planning for next round.

shape of a salamander to promote his party's interests. The principle is a simple one. Different distributions of voters among districts produce different electoral outcomes; those in a position to control the arrangements of districts are also in a position to manipulate the results. For example, until recent years, gerrymandering to dilute the voting strength of racial minorities was employed by many state legislatures. One of the more common strategies involved redrawing congressional boundary lines in such a way as to divide and disperse a black population that would have otherwise constituted a majority within the original district.

This form of racial gerrymandering, sometimes called "cracking," was used in

Mississippi during the 1960s and 1970s to prevent the election of an African American congressman. Historically, the black population in Mississippi was clustered in the western half of the state along the Mississippi Delta. From 1882 until 1966, the delta was one congressional district. Although blacks constituted a clear majority within the district (66 percent in 1960), the continuing election of white congressmen was assured simply because blacks were *denied* the right to register and vote. With Congress's passage of the Voting Rights Act of 1965, however, the Mississippi state legislature moved swiftly to minimize the potential voting power of African Americans by redrawing congressional district lines in such a way as to fragment the African American population in the delta into four of the state's five congressional districts. Mississippi's gerrymandering scheme was preserved in the state's redistricting plans in 1972 and 1981 and helped to prevent the election of any African American representative until 1986, when Mike Espy became the first African American since Reconstruction to represent Mississippi in Congress.

In recent years, the federal government has encouraged what is sometimes called "benign gerrymandering," designed to increase minority representation in Congress. The 1982 amendments to the Voting Rights Act of 1965 foster the creation of legislative districts with predominantly African American or Hispanic American populations by requiring states, when possible, to draw district lines that take account of concentrations of African American and Hispanic American voters. These amendments were initially supported by Democrats who assumed that minority-controlled districts would guarantee the election of Democratic members of Congress. Republicans championed them hoping that if minority voters

were concentrated in their own districts, Republican prospects in other districts would be enhanced.[9] This practice is sometimes called "stacking."

The Supreme Court decision in 1993, in *Shaw* v. *Reno,* however, opened the way for challenges by white voters to the drawing of these districts. In the 5-to-4 majority opinion, Justice O'Connor wrote that if district boundaries were so "bizarre" as to be inexplicable on any ground other than an effort to ensure the election of minority group members to office, white voters would have reason to assert that they had been the victims of unconstitutional racial gerrymandering.[10]

Although governments do have the capacity to manipulate electoral outcomes, this capacity is not absolute. Electoral arrangements conceived to be illegitimate may prompt some segments of the electorate to seek other ways of participating in political life. Moreover, no electoral system that provides universal and equal suffrage can, by itself, long prevent an outcome favored by large popular majorities. Yet, faced with opposition short of an overwhelming majority, governments' ability to manipulate the translation of individual choices into collective decisions can be an important factor in preserving the established distribution of power.

Insulating Decision-Making Processes

Virtually all governments attempt at least partially to insulate decision-making processes from electoral intervention. The most obvious ways of doing this are confining

---

[9] Roberto Suro, "In Redistricting, New Rules and New Prizes," *New York Times,* 6 May 1990, sec. 4, p. 5.

[10] Shaw v. Reno, (1993); Linda Green House, "Court Questions Districts Drawn to Aid Minorities," *New York Times,* 29 June 1993, p. 1.

popular elections to only some governmental agencies, using various modes of indirect election, and setting lengthy terms of office. In the United States, the framers of the Constitution intended that only members of the House of Representatives would be subject to direct popular selection. The president and senators were to be indirectly elected for longer terms to allow them, as the *Federalist* put it, to avoid "an unqualified complaisance to every sudden breeze of passion, or to every transient impulse which the people may receive."[11]

Somewhat less obvious are the insulating effects of electoral arrangements that permit direct, and even frequent, popular election of public officials, but tend to fragment the impact of elections upon the government's composition. In the United States, for example, the constitutional provision of staggered terms of service in the Senate was designed to diminish the impact of shifts in electoral sentiment upon the Senate as an institution. Since only one-third of its members were to be selected at any one time, the composition of the institution would be partially protected from changes in electoral preferences.

The division of the nation into relatively small, geographically based constituencies for the purpose of selecting members of the House of Representatives was, in part, designed to have a similar effect. Representatives were to be chosen frequently. And although not prescribed by the Constitution, the fact that each was to be selected by a discrete constituency was thought by Madison and others to diminish the government's vulnerability to mass popular movements.

In a sense, the House of Representatives was compartmentalized in the same way that a submarine is divided into watertight sections to confine the impact of any damage to the vessel. First, by dividing the national electorate into small districts the importance of local issues would increase. Second, the salience of local issues would mean that a representative's electoral fortunes would be more nearly tied to factors peculiar to his or her own district than to national responses to issues. Third, given a geographical principle of representation, national groups would be somewhat fragmented while the formation of local forces that might or might not share common underlying attitudes would be encouraged. No matter how well-represented individual constituencies might be, the influence of voters on national policy questions would be fragmented.

Prior to the 1890s, voters cast ballots composed by the political parties. Each party printed its own ballots, listed only its own candidates for each office, and employed party workers to distribute its ballots at the polls. This ballot format virtually prevented split-ticket voting. Because only one party's candidates appeared on any ballot, it was very difficult for a voter to cast anything other than a straight party vote.

The advent of a new, neutral ballot represented a significant change in electoral procedure. The new ballot was prepared and administered by the state rather than the parties. Each ballot was identical and included the names of all candidates for office (see Figure 9.2). This ballot reform made it possible for voters to make their choices on the basis of the individual rather than the collective merits of a party's candidates. Because all candidates for the same office now appeared on the same ballot,

[11]Clinton Rossiter, ed., *The Federalist Papers* (New York: New American Library, 1961), No. 71, p. 432.

FIGURE 9.2 The Party-Column Ballot: General Election Ballot (November 1992)

Row	Office	A DEMOCRATIC	B REPUBLICAN	C CONSERVATIVE	D RIGHT TO LIFE	E LIBERAL	F LIBERTARIAN / I NATURAL LAW	G NO PARTY / J NEW ALLIANCE	H SWP SOCIALIST WORKERS
1	Electors for President and Vice-President of the United States / Vote once / Electores para Presidente y Vice-Presidente de los Estados Unidos / Vote solamente una vez	Bill Clinton AND Al Gore — DEMOCRATIC 1A	George Bush AND Dan Quayle — REPUBLICAN 1B	George Bush AND Dan Quayle — CONSERVATIVE 1C	George Bush AND Dan Quayle — RIGHT TO LIFE 1D	Bill Clinton AND Al Gore — LIBERAL 1E	Andre Marrou AND Nancy Lord — LIBERTARIAN 1F / John Hagelin AND Mike Tompkins — NATURAL LAW 1I / F LIBERTARIAN	Ross Perot AND James B. Stockdale — NO PARTY 1G / Lenora B. Fulani AND M. Elizabeth Munoz — NEW ALLIANCE 1J	James Mac Warren AND Estelle Debates — SOCIALIST WORKERS 1H
6	United States Senator / Vote for one / Senador de los Estados Unidos / Vote por uno	Robert Abrams DEMOCRATIC 6A	Alfonse M. D'Amato REPUBLICAN 6B	Alfonse M. D'Amato CONSERVATIVE 6C	Alfonse M. D'Amato RIGHT TO LIFE 6D	Robert Abrams LIBERAL 6E	Norma Segal LIBERTARIAN 6F / Stanley Nelson NATURAL LAW 6I	Mohammad T. Mehdi NEW ALLIANCE 6J	Ed Warren SOCIALIST WORKERS 6H
9	Justices of the Supreme Court / Jueces de la Corte Suprema / Vote for any six / Vote por seis	Steven W. Fisher DEMOCRATIC 9A	Thomas V. Polizzi REPUBLICAN 9B	Thomas V. Polizzi CONSERVATIVE 9C		Steven W. Fisher LIBERAL 9E			
10		Fred T. Santucci DEMOCRATIC 10A	Fred T. Santucci REPUBLICAN 10B	Fred T. Santucci CONSERVATIVE 10C		Fred T. Santucci LIBERAL 10E			
11		Simeon Golar DEMOCRATIC 11A	Richard J. Wagner REPUBLICAN 11B	Richard J. Wagner CONSERVATIVE 11C		Simeon Golar LIBERAL 11E			
12		Evelyn L. Braun DEMOCRATIC 12A	Joseph A. Suraci REPUBLICAN 12B	Evelyn L. Braun CONSERVATIVE 12C		Evelyn L. Braun LIBERAL 12E			
13		Richard Buchter DEMOCRATIC 13A	John G. Lopresto REPUBLICAN 13B	John G. Lopresto CONSERVATIVE 13C		Richard Buchter LIBERAL 13E			
14		Robert C. Kohm DEMOCRATIC 14A	Kerry J. Katsorhis REPUBLICAN 14B	Robert C. Kohm CONSERVATIVE 14C		Robert C. Kohm LIBERAL 14E			
15	Judge of the Civil Court (County) / Vote for any two / Juez de la Corte Civil (Condado) / Vote por dos	Darrell L. Gavrin DEMOCRATIC 15A		Paul Aronow CONSERVATIVE 15C		Darrell L. Gavrin LIBERAL 15E			
16		Frederick D. Schmidt DEMOCRATIC 16A		Frederick D. Schmidt CONSERVATIVE 16C	Frederick D. Schmidt RIGHT TO LIFE 16D				
17	Representative in Congress / Representante en Congreso / Vote for one - Vote por uno	Nydia M. Velazquez DEMOCRATIC 17A	Angel Diaz REPUBLICAN 17B	Angel Diaz CONSERVATIVE 17C	Angel Diaz RIGHT TO LIFE 17D	Ruben Franco LIBERAL 17E		Rafael Mendez NEW ALLIANCE 17J	
18	State Senator / Senador Estatal / Vote for one - Vote por uno	Emanuel R. Gold DEMOCRATIC 18A				Emanuel R. Gold LIBERAL 18E			
19	Member of Assembly / Miembro de la Asamblea / Vote for one - Vote por uno	Jeffrion L. Aubry DEMOCRATIC 19A				Jeffrion L. Aubry LIBERAL 19E			

Lot Q83

voters were no longer forced to choose a straight party ticket. This gave rise to the phenomenon of split-ticket voting in American elections.

Prior to the reform of the ballot, it was not uncommon for an entire incumbent administration to be swept from office and replaced by an entirely new set of officials. In the absence of a real possibility of split-ticket voting, any desire on the part of the electorate for change could be expressed only as a vote against all candidates of the party in power. Because of this, there always existed the possibility, particularly at the state and local levels, that an insurgent slate committed to policy change could be swept into power. The party ballot thus increased the potential impact of elections upon the governments' composition. Although this potential may not always have been realized, the party ballot at least increased the chance that electoral decisions could lead to policy changes. By contrast, because it permitted choice on the basis of candidates' individual appeals, ticket splitting led to increasingly divided partisan control of government.

Taken together, regulation of the electorate's composition, the translation of voters' choices into electoral decisions, and the impact of those decisions upon the government's composition allow those in power a measure of control over mass participation in political life. These techniques do not necessarily have the effect of diminishing citizens' capacity to influence their rulers' conduct. Rather, these techniques are generally used to *influence electoral influence.*

How Voters Decide

Thus far, we have focused on the election as an institution. But, of course, the election is also a process in which millions of individu-

als make decisions and choices that are beyond the government's control. Whatever the capacity of those in power to organize and structure the electoral process, it is these millions of individual decisions that ultimately determine electoral outcomes. Sooner or later the choices of voters weigh more heavily than the schemes of electoral engineers.

The Bases of Electoral Choice

Three types of factors influence voters' decisions at the polls: partisan loyalty, issue and policy concerns, and candidate characteristics.

PARTISAN LOYALTY. Many studies have shown that most Americans identify more or less strongly with one or the other of the two major political parties. Partisan loyalty was considerably stronger during the 1940s and 1950s than it is today. But even now most voters feel a certain sense of identification or kinship with the Democratic or Republican party. This sense of identification is often handed down from parents to children and is reinforced by social and cultural ties. Partisan identification predisposes voters in favor of their party's candidates and against those of the opposing party. At the level of the presidential contest, issues and candidate personalities may become very important, although even here many Americans supported George Bush or Michael Dukakis, Ronald Reagan or Walter Mondale, because of partisan loyalty. But partisanship is more likely to assert itself in the less visible races, where issues and the candidates are not as well known. State legislative races, for example, are often decided by voters' party ties. Once formed, voters' partisan loyalties seldom change. Voters tend to keep their party affiliations unless some crisis causes them to reexamine the bases of their loyalties and to conclude that they have not given their support to the appropriate party. During these relatively infrequent periods of electoral change, millions of voters can change their party ties. For example, at the beginning of the New Deal era between 1932 and 1936, millions of former Republicans transferred their allegiance to Franklin Roosevelt and the Democrats.

ISSUES. Issues and policy preferences are a second factor influencing voters' choices at the polls. Voters may cast their ballots for the candidate whose position on economic issues they believe to be closest to their own. Similarly, they may select the candidate who has what they believe to be the best record on foreign policy. Issues are more important in some races than others. If candidates actually "take issue" with one another, that is, articulate and publicize very different positions on important public questions, then voters are more likely to be able to identify and act upon whatever policy preferences they may have. In recent American history, the 1964 presidential election, pitting conservative Republican Barry Goldwater against liberal Democrat Lyndon Johnson, was one in which each candidate vigorously promoted a perspective on the role of government and shape of national policy very different from the one asserted by his opponent. Voters elected Johnson, basing their choices on the issues.

The 1980 and 1984 contests, won by Ronald Reagan, the most conservative American president of the postwar period, were very heavily issue oriented, with Reagan emphasizing tax policy, social policy, and foreign policy positions different from prior American governmental commitments. In response, voters in large numbers based their choices on issue and policy preferences. The 1992 election emphasized economic issues. Voters concerned with America's continuing economic recession and long-term economic prospects gave their support to Bill Clinton who called for an end to Reaganomics. Efforts by Bush to inject other issues, such as "family values," into the race proved generally unsuccessful.

The ability of voters to make choices on the bases of issue or policy preferences diminishes if competing candidates do not differ substantially or do not focus their campaigns on policy matters. Very often, candidates deliberately take the safe course and emphasize topics that will not be offensive to any voters. Thus, candidates often trumpet their opposition to corruption, crime, and inflation. Presumably, few voters favor these things. While it may be perfectly reasonable for candidates to take the safe course and remain as inoffensive as possible, this candidate strategy makes it extremely difficult for voters to make their issue or policy preferences the bases for their choices at the polls.

CANDIDATE CHARACTERISTICS. Candidates' personal attributes always influence voters' decisions. Some analysts claim that voters prefer tall candidates to short candidates, candidates with shorter names to candidates with longer names, and candidates with lighter hair to candidates with darker hair. Perhaps these rather frivolous criteria do play some role. But the more important candidate characteristics that affect voters' choices are race, ethnicity, religion, gender, geography, and social background. Voters presume that candidates with similar backgrounds to their own are likely to share their views and perspectives. Moreover, they may be proud to see someone of their ethnic, religious, or geographic background in a position of leadership. This is why, for many years, politicians sought to "balance the ticket," making certain that their party's ticket included members of as many important groups as possible. In 1988, for example, Democratic presidential candidate Michael Dukakis named Texas Senator Lloyd Bentsen as his running mate to balance the ticket with a conservative southerner. George Bush, in turn, selected Dan Quayle to appeal to younger voters and ultraconservatives.

Just as a candidate's personal characteristics may attract some voters, they may repel others. Many voters are prejudiced against candidates of certain ethnic, racial, or religious groups. And many voters—both men and women—continue to be reluctant to support the political candidacies of women, although this appears to be changing.

Voters also pay attention to candidates' personality characteristics, such as their "decisiveness," "honesty," and "vigor." In recent years, integrity has become a key election issue. During the 1992 campaign, George Bush accused Bill Clinton of seeking to mislead voters about his anti-Vietnam war activities and his efforts to avoid the draft during the 1960s. This, according to Bush, revealed that Clinton lacked the integrity required of a president. Clinton, in turn, accused Bush of resorting to mudslinging because of his poor standing in the polls—an indication of Bush's own character deficiencies.

All candidates seek, through polling and other mechanisms, to determine the best image to project to the electorate. At the same time, the communications media—television in particular—exercise a good deal of control over how voters perceive candidates. During the 1992 campaign, as

we shall see in Chapters 10 and 12, the candidates developed a number of techniques designed to take control of the image-making process away from the media. Among the chief instruments of this "spin control" was the candidate talk show appearance used very effectively by both Ross Perot and Bill Clinton. As we shall see, however, no candidate was fully able to circumvent media scrutiny.

Electoral Realignments

Elections are not only forms of political expression, they also have important consequences. Elections decide who will govern, which may have consequences for how the government behaves and what policy directions it pursues. In the United States, election outcomes have followed a fascinating pattern (see Figure 9.4). Typically, during the course of American political history, the national electoral arena has been dominated by one party for a period of roughly thirty years. At the conclusion of this period, the dominant party has been supplanted by a new party in what political scientists call a *critical electoral realignment*. The realignment is typically followed by a long period in which the new party is the dominant political force in the United States—not necessarily winning every election but generally maintaining control of the Congress and usually of the White House as well.[12]

Realigning Eras

Although there are some disputes among scholars about the precise timing of these

[12]See Walter Dean Burnham, *Critical Elections and the Mainsprings of American Electoral Politics* (New York: W. W. Norton, 1970). See also James L. Sundquist, *Dynamics of the Party System* (Washington, DC: Brookings Institution, 1983).

FIGURE 9.3
The Party Balance: Number of Institutions Controlled

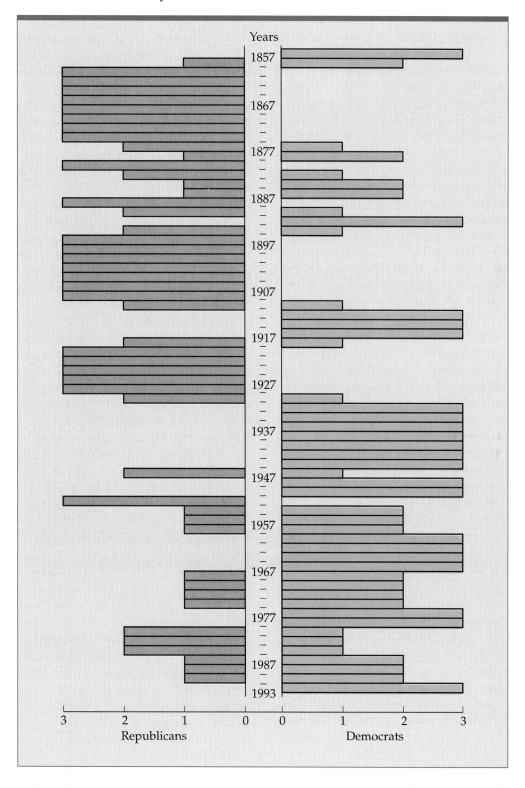

critical realignments, there is general agreement that at least five have occurred since the founding of the American Republic. The first took place around 1800 when the Jeffersonian Republicans defeated the Federalists and became the dominant force in American politics. The second realignment occurred around 1828 when the Jacksonian Democrats took control of the White House and the Congress. The third period of realignment centered on 1860. During this period, the newly founded Republican party led by Abraham Lincoln won power, in the process destroying the Whig party, which had been one of the nation's two major parties since the 1830s. During the fourth critical period, centered on the election of 1896, the Republicans reasserted their dominance of the national government, which had been weakening since the 1880s. The fifth realignment took place during the period 1932–1936 when the Democrats, led by Franklin Delano Roosevelt, took control of the White House and Congress and, despite sporadic interruptions, maintained control through the 1960s.

Historically, realignments occur when new issues combined with economic or political crises persuade large numbers of voters to reexamine their traditional partisan loyalties and permanently shift their support from one party to another. For example, during the 1850s, diverse regional, income, and business groups supported one of the two major parties, the Democrats or the Whigs, on the basis of their positions on various economic issues, such as internal improvements, the tariff, monetary policy, and banking. This economic alignment was shattered during the 1850s. The newly formed Republican party campaigned on the basis of opposition to slavery and, in particular, opposition to the expansion of slavery into the territories. The issues of slavery and sectionalism produced divisions within both the Democratic and the Whig parties, ultimately leading to the disappearance of the Whigs, and these issues compelled voters to reexamine their partisan allegiances. Many northern voters who had supported the Whigs or the Democrats on the basis of their economic stands shifted their support to the Republicans as slavery replaced tariffs and economic concerns as the central items on the nation's political agenda. Many southern Whigs shifted their support to the Democrats. The new sectional alignment of forces that emerged was solidified by the trauma of the Civil War and persisted almost to the turn of the century.

In 1896, this sectional alignment was at least partially supplanted by an alignment of political forces based on economic and cultural factors. During the economic crises of the 1880s and 1890s, the Democrats forged a coalition consisting of economically hard-pressed midwestern and southern farmers, as well as small-town and rural economic interests. These groups tended to be native-stock, fundamentalist Protestants. The Republicans, on the other hand, put together a coalition comprising most of the business community, industrial workers, and city dwellers. In the election of 1896, Republican candidate William McKinley, emphasizing business, industry, and urban interests, decisively defeated Democrat William Jennings Bryan, who spoke for sectional interests, farmers, and fundamentalism. Republican dominance lasted until 1932.

These periods of critical realignment are very important to understanding the relationship between elections and American governmental institutions and policies. Critics of the American political process frequently assert that it is very difficult for voting choices to be translated into programs and policies in the United States. Very often, it is true, elections result in one party controlling the presidency and the other the Congress. Frequently, policy initiatives taken by one elected branch of government are blocked by the other—or occasionally by the courts. Often, elections have no discernible consequences for the direction of public policy or the shape of governmental institutions.

Periods of critical realignment in American politics, however, have had extremely important institutional and policy results. Each period of realignment has represented a turning point in American politics. In effect, the choices made by the national electorate during these periods have helped to shape the course of American political history for a generation.[13]

Elections in America Today: Factional Struggle without Realignment

The importance of realignments in American political history has led analysts to search for evidence of contemporary realignments. Ronald Reagan's victory in 1980, followed by his landslide success in the 1984 presidential race, and a solid victory by Republican George Bush in the 1988 contest suggested to some observers that we had undergone another realignment and were entering a new Republican era in national politics.[14] However, Bush's defeat and the Democrats recapture of the White House in 1992 seemed to put an end to thoughts of Republican hegemony. To un-

derstand contemporary American electoral politics, though, we must look back to Roosevelt's New Deal realignment before moving forward to the Reagan, Bush, and Clinton eras.

THE NEW DEAL COALITION AND ITS DISRUPTION. Franklin Roosevelt's New Deal coalition was composed of unionized labor, members of urban ethnic groups, southerners, northern blacks, middle-class liberals, and, ultimately, important sectors of the American business community. Roosevelt and his successors won and maintained the support of these groups by building governmental institutions and enacting policies that served their needs and interests. For example, New Deal labor legislation confirmed the support of organized labor for the Democratic party; Roosevelt's welfare and social service programs won the loyalty of northern blacks and members of urban ethnic groups; southerners benefited from New Deal farm programs; middle-class liberals benefited from the expansion of white-collar employment in the public sector as well as from New Deal programs in areas such as education and the arts; segments of the business community benefited from New Deal support for free trade, and, later, from the expansion of industrial production in the World War II and postwar periods.[15]

This New Deal coalition dominated the government and politics of the United States until the 1960s, when it was shattered by conflicts over race relations, the Vietnam War, and the government's fiscal and regulatory policies. These conflicts drove apart the various groups that had made up the New Deal coalition and set the stage for new

---

[13]Ginsberg, *Consequences of Consent*, Chapter 4.

[14]For a fuller discussion, see Benjamin Ginsberg and Martin Shefter, "A Critical Realignment? The New Politics, the Reconstituted Right, and the Election of 1984," in *The Elections of 1984*, ed. Michael Nelson (Washington, DC: Congressional Quarterly Press, 1985).

[15]See Thomas Ferguson, "From Normalcy to New Deal: Industrial Structure, Party Competition and American Public Policy in the Great Depression," *International Organization* 38 (Winter 1984), pp. 42–94.

forces to attempt to reconstruct a governing coalition in the United States. Thus, today, middle-class liberals, organized labor, and blacks have vied for influence within the Democratic party, and have sought to use that party as a vehicle through which to secure power on the national level. However, segments of the business community, social and religious conservatives, upper-middle-class suburbanites, southern whites, and many northern blue-collar workers have united in a reconstituted coalition of the political Right within the Republican party.

Over the past twenty-six years, segments of the Democratic coalition have pursued a variety of electoral strategies. In 1968, liberal Democrats supported Eugene McCarthy's attempt to win the Democratic presidential nomination. In 1972, Democratic liberals forged an alliance with blacks that succeeded in securing the Democratic presidential nomination for George McGovern but was routed again in the general election by the Republicans. In 1976, liberals, in alliance with organized labor, played a key role in bringing about Jimmy Carter's presidential victory. This alliance between labor and liberals collapsed in 1980, when liberals spurned both Carter and Reagan and essentially boycotted the presidential contest—throwing away their votes in support of John Anderson's hopeless independent candidacy.

In 1984, Walter Mondale sought to build a strong and lasting alliance between liberals, blacks, and organized labor. Republicans, however, charged Mondale with pandering to "special interests" and routed him in the election. In 1988, Massachusetts Governor Michael Dukakis, seeking to win support from all elements of the party while not offending independents and Republicans, stressed the themes of competence and leadership and sought to eschew commitments on substantive programs. However, he too could not escape being depicted as a politician with commitments to constituencies and causes that could be served only at the expense of the taxpayer and middle America. And, once again, the Democrats lost the presidential contest.

REAGAN AND THE RECONSTITUTED RIGHT. Under the leadership of Ronald Reagan, the Reconstituted Right became the dominant force in American electoral politics in the 1980s. During the 1980 election campaign, Reagan fashioned a set of programs and policies designed to link the disparate forces on the political Right to one another and to his presidential campaign. First, Reagan promised middle-class suburbanites that he would trim social programs, cut taxes, and bring inflation under control—whatever the cost in terms of blue-collar employment. Second, Reagan promised social and religious conservatives that he would support "pro-family," anti-abortion, and school prayer legislation. Third, Reagan promised white southerners and other opponents of the civil rights revolution an end to federal support for affirmative action, minority quotas, and other programs designed to aid blacks. Fourth, Reagan promised American business a relaxation of the environmental rules and other forms of "new regulation" that liberals had succeeded in enacting during the 1970s. Finally, Reagan promised the defense industry greatly increased rates of military spending.

Under Reagan's leadership, the Republican party scored a decisive victory in the 1980 presidential election, won control of the Senate, and substantially increased its representation in the House. Once in office,

Reagan was able to begin fulfilling many of his campaign promises during his first term. The upper and upper-middle classes realized substantial savings from Reagan's tax reduction programs. Inflation was brought under control, although the cost of doing so was the deepest recession since the 1930s. Arms outlays increased dramatically. The federal regulatory climate became somewhat more favorable to business. The rate of increase in domestic social spending diminished. The federal government's efforts on behalf of minorities and the poor were reduced.[16]

Finally, under Reagan's auspices some legislation was enacted to promote school prayer, various federal agencies began to reduce their backing for abortion, and Reagan himself continued to offer moral support and encouragement to the various groups of social and religious conservatives who had championed his candidacy. As a result of what must be seen as a generally successful record of service to the coalition that elected him, Reagan increased his support among the forces that had initially placed him in office. In the 1984 election, Reagan's share of the vote rose within all of the major segments of the electorate that had backed him in 1980. This enabled Reagan to win 59 percent of the popular vote in 1984, and to carry forty-nine states.

The electoral dominance of Reagan's coalition seemed to be reaffirmed in 1988 with the victory of Reagan's vice president, George Bush. Although Bush and his running mate, Dan Quayle, were generally perceived to be weak campaigners, they were able to maintain the unity of the Reagan

coalition by castigating the Democrats for their liberalism. Thus, Bush won 54 percent of the popular vote and carried forty states. In the electoral college, Bush's margin was 426 to 112.

The 1992 Election: Shifting Alignments of Political Forces

Republican Disarray

By the end of George Bush's term in office, the Reagan coalition had begun to unravel. The two key elements in the electoral appeal of Reaganism had been prosperity at home and strength abroad. Reagan and his successor promised voters that by unleashing the energies of the free marketplace, without the damaging regulation imposed by Democrats, Republicans would bring a new era of prosperity to America. Moreover, Reagan and Bush promised to keep America strong. Only the Republican party, they argued, could be trusted to maintain American power in the face of the "evil empire" controlled by the Soviet Union. Reagan's programs of military buildup and economic stimulation appeared to fulfill both these pledges.

In 1992, these two key elements were gone. First, the nation had become mired in one of the longest economic downturns in recent decades. Second, the Soviet Union had collapsed, bringing an end to the Cold War and diminishing the threat of a nuclear holocaust.

Between 1989 and 1992, virtually every indicator of economic performance told the same sad story: rising unemployment, declining retail sales and corporate profitability, continuing penetration of American markets by foreign firms and the loss of

[16]See Lester Salamon and Michael Lund, eds., *The Reagan Presidency and the Governing of America* (Washington, DC: Urban Institute Press, 1985).

PROCESS BOX 9.2

How Presidential Campaigns Are Conducted—A Two-Year Cycle

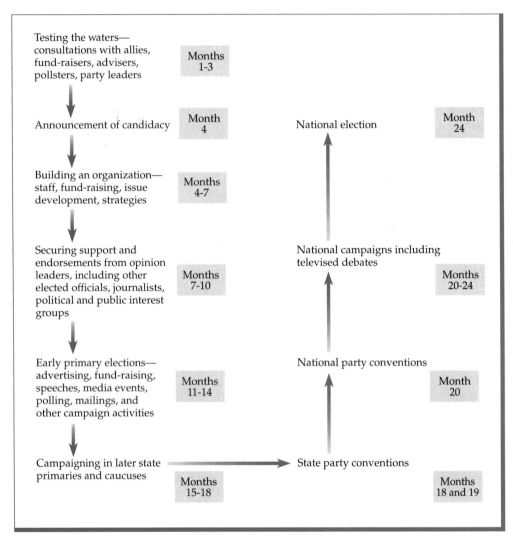

Testing the waters—consultations with allies, fund-raisers, advisers, pollsters, party leaders   Months 1-3

Announcement of candidacy   Month 4

Building an organization—staff, fund-raising, issue development, strategies   Months 4-7

Securing support and endorsements from opinion leaders, including other elected officials, journalists, political and public interest groups   Months 7-10

Early primary elections—advertising, fund-raising, speeches, media events, polling, mailings, and other campaign activities   Months 11-14

Campaigning in later state primaries and caucuses   Months 15-18

State party conventions   Months 18 and 19

National party conventions   Month 20

National campaigns including televised debates   Months 20-24

National election   Month 24

American jobs to foreigners, a sharp drop in real estate prices followed by a wave of bank collapses, and large numbers of business failures.

The poor performance of the American economy during his term in office eroded Bush's popularity and divided the Republi-

can coalition. First, business groups that had supported Republicans since the 1970s began to desert the GOP. During the 1970s, most businesses had perceived government as a threat, fearing that consumer and environmental legislation, which were supported by the Democrats, would be enormously costly and burdensome. Reagan's call for "deregulation" was a major source of the enthusiastic and virtually united support he received from the business community.

By 1992, however, economic hardship had divided the business community. Some business sectors, especially "big business" and the multinationals, continued to support Republican laissez-faire economics. Republican policies of free trade and unrestricted competition permitted the nation's largest firms to expand their manufacturing base abroad in countries where labor and production costs were cheap, while leaving the American market open to their finished products. These firms favored the North American Free Trade Agreement (NAFTA), negotiated by the Bush administration in 1992, because it would allow them to move much of their production to Mexico.

Small and medium-size firms, though, could not as easily move to Mexico or elsewhere to enjoy the benefits of free trade and cheap labor. These firms had been especially vehement opponents of regulation and thus were enthusiastic supporters of Reaganism in the 1970s. In the 1990s, however, new economic realities compelled them to seek governmental assistance rather than worry about the threat of excessive governmental regulation. In particular, firms facing severe foreign competition in the domestic and world markets sought government aid in the form of protection of their domestic markets coupled with vigorous government efforts to promote their exports. As a result, the political unity of American business brought about by Reagan was shattered and a major prop of the Republican coalition undermined.

Economic hardship also drove away the blue-collar support for the Republican coalition. Blue-collar voters had been tied to the Democratic party since the New Deal on the basis of the party's economic stands. During the 1980s, however, Reagan and Bush won the support of many of these voters in both the North and the South by persuading them to put their economic interests aside and to focus instead on their moral and patriotic concerns.

A major function of the Republican "social agenda" of opposition to abortion, support for prayer in the public schools, and unabashed patriotism was to woo blue-collar voters from the Democratic camp by persuading them to regard themselves as right-to-lifers and patriots rather than as workers. Similarly, Republican opposition to affirmative action and school busing was designed to appeal to blue-collar northerners as well as to traditionally Democratic southerners offended by their party's liberal positions on matters of race.

By 1992, however, the political value of the social agenda had diminished. Faced with massive layoffs in many of their industries, blue-collar voters could no longer afford the luxury of focusing on issues other than their economic interests. In a number of states, as a result, the racial issues of the 1980s lost their political potency.[17] Indeed, even patriotism gave way to economic concerns as the recession lengthened. This was why George Bush's incredible 91 percent approval rating following the Persian Gulf War fell as much as 50 points in less than one year as pocketbook issues replaced citizens' pride in American military prowess. During the 1980s and early 1990s, millions of working-class voters became unemployed or were forced to find lower-paying

[17]For a discussion of events in one state, see David Broder, "In North Carolina, Racially Coded Wedge Issues No Longer Dominate," *Washington Post*, 13 October 1992, p. A12.

jobs. These voters gradually deserted the Republican camp.

Though the constituency for the Republican social agenda had shrunk, the moral fervor of the groups most fiercely committed to those issues nonetheless grew. When right-to-life forces launched protests and sought to block the doors of abortion clinics across the nation, President Bush saw no choice but to strongly endorse the activities of these loyal Republicans. However, Bush's support of these groups hurt his standing among other suburban Republicans. The traditional Republican suburban upper-middle-class constituency had never been enthusiastic about the social agenda or about the sorts of people it had brought into the party. It had been prepared, however, to hold its collective nose so long as the social agenda brought political success and the Republican national leadership did not seem to be working very hard *actually* to bring about the criminalization of abortion, return prayer to the schools, and so forth. Ronald Reagan had been extremely adept at convincing right-to-lifers that he was on their side while reassuring his suburban upper-middle-class constituents that, however much he might talk about abortion, he did not actually plan to *do* anything about it.

Because Bush's political base on the Right was weaker than Reagan's, however, he felt compelled to do more to satisfy anti-abortion groups and other social conservatives. This led to a pattern of Supreme Court appointments and legislative initiatives that pleased social conservatives but offended upper-income suburban Republicans—the "country club set"—who had been the party's backbone. As the 1992 campaign approached, Bush suffered a considerable loss of support in this stratum that was only exacerbated by the prominent role assigned to social conservatives at the 1992 Republican convention.

Even more than their dismay over the conservative social agenda, economic hard times eroded Republican support among middle-class urban and suburban voters. Middle-class executives and professionals are usually fairly well insulated from the economic downturns that often devastate blue-collar workers, but the economic crises of the late 1980s and early 1990s had a major impact on them as well. The cumulative effect of the mergers and acquisitions of the 1980s, the failure of hundreds of banks, corporate restructuring and "downsizing," the massive shift of manufacturing operations out of the country, the decline of the securities industry, the collapse of the housing market, and the end of the defense boom meant at least the possibility of unemployment or income reduction for hundreds of thousands of white-collar, management, and professional employees. Even those whose jobs were secure saw their economic positions eroded by the sharply declining values of their homes.

Economic hard times gave middle-class voters another reason for alarm. One of the inevitable consequences of economic distress and unemployment is an increase in crime rates. During the late 1980s and early 1990s, crime rates throughout the United States soared. In 1980, middle-class taxpayers had responded favorably to Ronald Reagan's call for a cap on social spending coupled with a tough approach to crime. For twelve years, limits on domestic social spending were a cornerstone of the Republican program. In 1992, however, rising crime rates despite Republican "get tough" rhetoric allowed the Democrats to persuade many middle-class voters that the expansion of domestic social spending was a price that had to be paid for the preservation of social peace and public safety.

Thus, the decline of prosperity at home caused cracks in the Reagan coalition. Under the pressure of economic distress, groups that had been enthusiastic supporters of Reaganism in the early 1980s broke away from the GOP in 1992. To compound the Republican party's woes, the unity of its coalition was also undermined by the collapse of the Soviet Union and the end of the Cold War threat.

Strength abroad had been the second cornerstone of Reaganism. Reagan had defined the Soviet Union as an "evil empire" that threatened the security of the world. To confront the Soviets, the Reagan administration embarked on a massive arms buildup that raised American military spending to levels unprecedented for peacetime.

Whatever its strategic purposes, the Reaganite program of hard-line anticommunism and massive increases in arms spending had a number of domestic political functions. First, the Reaganite posture of at least rhetorical confrontation with the Soviet Union cemented the loyalty of political conservatives to the Reagan coalition and the Republican party. This posture also attracted the support of members of various ethnic groups that had reason either to oppose the U.S.S.R. or, as in the case of pro-Israel Jews, to favor increased American military outlays. Moreover, it helped the GOP to appeal to the patriotic sentiments of blue-collar voters who had traditionally supported the Democrats.

Second, the Reaganite military buildup was an enormous boon to the American defense industry and to those regions of the country—primarily the South and Southwest—where military construction was an important economic factor. During the 1980s, billions of dollars in new military contracts for items ranging from mundane uniforms and supplies to exotic antimissile defenses poured into the coffers of thousands of American corporations. At the same time, hundreds of thousands of workers benefited from high-paying jobs in the defense industry. This helped boost the prosperity of much of the Sunbelt and gave voters and industries in this region a strong reason to support the GOP.

Third, the military buildup represented an effort to assert the primacy of national security and international concerns over domestic issues. Since the New Deal, the Democratic party's political advantage had come in the arena of domestic policy. Under Reagan's leadership, the GOP sought to persuade voters that domestic concerns were secondary to the nation's vital security interests, which they claimed were severely threatened by the expansive Soviet empire. In the foreign policy arena, voters tended to have more confidence in Republican leadership. This tendency was reinforced during the Bush administration by the public's overwhelmingly favorable response to the president's handling of the Persian Gulf crises. The presence of a Soviet threat helped Republicans persuade voters to focus on foreign rather than on domestic policy and therefore to support the GOP.

In a similar vein, the Reaganite call for strengthening America's defenses provided a justification for limiting domestic social expenditures and programs. Domestic programs, and the federal, state, and quasi-public agencies that administered them, had become major elements of the organizational base of the national Democratic party. By asserting an overriding need to preserve the nation's security in a hostile world, the GOP was able to rationalize diverting funds from domestic to military programs and, in this way, to attack the Democratic party's institutional base. Thus, the Soviet threat not only permitted the Republicans to strengthen their own coalition but allowed them to attack their rivals' camp as well.

The collapse of the Soviet Union may have represented a victory for Republican foreign policy, but paradoxically it was a disaster for Republican domestic political strategy. As the Soviet Union weakened and, finally, dissolved, the rationale for a continuation of high levels of military spending disappeared, as did much of the justification for focusing on international rather than domestic problems and priorities. Industries and workers that had benefited from Republican military spending now began to look to the Democrats, whose call for massive investment in the American economic infrastructure held out the promise of a new array of government contracts to replace those lost by the ending of the Cold War.

At the same time, ethnic groups that had been drawn to the GOP by its anti-Soviet stance no longer had a strong reason to remain in the Republican camp. One group, Jewish Republicans, completely abandoned the GOP. The collapse of the Soviet Union had led the White House to conclude that it could now afford to loosen its ties to Arab nations. When American Jews protested this shift in U.S. policy, President Bush, during a televised news conference, appeared to question their patriotism. Despite the subsequent apologies, few Jewish Republicans returned to the fold.

Finally, especially when coupled with the poor performance of the American economy, the collapse of the Soviet Union made it impossible for the Republicans to continue to insist on the primacy of interna-

tional and security issues. Now that the threat of war had receded, Americans were freer than they had been in years to focus on problems at home. As a result, working-class voters who had been persuaded to support the GOP despite economic interests that had historically linked them to the Democrats now began to reassess their positions. Many patriots became workers once again.

Thus, the collapse of the Soviet Union undermined the second key element of the Republican coalition's political success. For twelve years, the Republicans had emphasized prosperity at home and strength abroad. Now, in 1992, the nation was not prosperous, and its unprecedented military strength seemed irrelevant.

As the loyalty of the forces brought into the Republican camp by Reaganite appeals began to wane, President Bush found himself increasingly dependent on a core Republican constituency of hard-line social and political conservatives. Political conservatives had been furious with Bush since 1991 when he broke his "Read my lips" pledge never to raise taxes, in order to reach a budget agreement with congressional Democrats. Bush angered these conservatives even further when he signed the 1991 Civil Rights Act and the Americans with Disabilities Act. The first was seen by conservatives as a "quotas" bill, while the second appeared to be opening the way to a torrent of litigation against business firms.

Bush calculated that he had to maintain his support on the political right in order to have any chance of re-election. For this reason, he gave conservatives, including his nemesis from the presidential primaries, Patrick Buchanan, a large role in the 1992 Republican National Convention, gave their views a prominent place in the Republican platform, and emphasized "family values" in his presidential campaign. All this helped to strengthen Bush's support on the Right. Unfortunately for Bush, his efforts to placate the Right led to unease among moderate Republicans whose support for the president was already wavering under the pressure of economic and world events.

Democratic Opportunity

These cracks in the Republican coalition provided the Democrats with their best opportunity in two decades to capture the White House. First, however, they had to put their own party's house in order. Since the early 1970s, Democratic candidates had been handicapped by problems of a liberal ideology and racial issues. The Democratic party's nominating process had produced candidates and platforms that were seen as too liberal by the general electorate. At the same time, the issue of race had divided the party. Democratic candidates depended heavily on African American voters and thus were compelled to appeal for their support. However, Democratic pledges and programs like affirmative action, designed to win the support of blacks, had the effect of alienating conservative working-class whites in the North and South whose votes the Democrats also needed. Race and a liberal ideology had helped undermine five Democratic candidacies since 1968. In 1992, however, the Democrats were able to handle both these problems successfully.

Since the electoral debacle of 1972, when Richard Nixon won a landslide victory over George McGovern, moderate Democrats had argued that the party needed to present a more centrist image if it hoped to be competitive in national elections. The major organizational vehicle for the centrists was the Democratic Leadership Council (DLC), an organization based in Washington and funded by business firms with ties to the Democratic party. Throughout the Reagan and Bush years, the DLC organized networks of state and local party officials and sought to develop political themes that could bring about a measure of party unity *and* appeal to the national electorate.[18]

In 1992, the DLC and its moderate allies were able to dominate the Democratic party's presidential nominating processes as well as its national convention. The party chose as its presidential and vice-presidential candidates Governor Bill Clinton and Senator Al Gore, both founding members of the DLC. The platform adopted at the party's national convention was widely perceived to be the most conservative in decades, stressing individual responsibility and private enterprise while implicitly criticizing welfare recipients. Though the platform mentioned the importance of protecting the rights of women, gays, and minorities, gone were the calls for expanded rights for criminals and welfare recipients that had provided Republicans with such convenient political targets in previous years.

Democrats sought to deal with their party's racial divisions by keeping black politicians and racial issues at arm's length and relying upon economic appeals to woo both working-class white and black voters. Democratic strategists calculated that black voters and politicians would have no choice but to support the Democratic ticket. Given the nation's economic woes, which afflicted blacks even more than whites, Democratic

[18]For a discussion, see Thomas Edsall, "The Democrats Pick a New Centerpiece," *Washington Post National Weekly Edition,* 24 August 1992, p. 14.

Pat Buchanan and Jerry Brown
The Politics of Insurgency

Presidential aspirants Pat Buchanan and Jerry Brown hoped to capitalize on their underdog status during the 1992 primaries in an effort to promote the issues that concerned them, and perhaps to knock off each party's front-runner.

Pat Buchanan challenged incumbent President George Bush in the Republican primaries with the hope of appealing to core Republican voters who viewed Bush as too liberal. An arch-conservative, Buchanan was trained as a journalist and worked as a speech writer for Presidents Nixon and Reagan. He served as Reagan's director of communications from 1985 to 1987. The contentious Buchanan became well known to viewers of such commentary, news, and discussion shows as "The McLaughlin Group," "Crossfire," and "The Capital Gang."

Buchanan turned his pit-bull style to the political arena in his run against Bush because of his belief that the president had abandoned the conservative legacy of Ronald Reagan. Buchanan advocated deep tax cuts, opposed the Persian Gulf War (he labeled Bush's "quest for global democracy" as "messianic globaloney"), and favored greater American isolationism in foreign policy. While Buchanan never posed a serious threat to Bush's renomination, his candidacy did serve to push Bush closer to the Republican's conservative base; it also overshadowed the presidential candidacy of former American Nazi and Ku Klux Klan leader David Duke.

In a similarly unorthodox style, former California Governor Edmund G. "Jerry" Brown entered the 1992 Democratic presidential contest with little prospect of victory. But

Pat Buchanan

leaders reasoned that they had no need to appeal explicitly for black support. This freed the party to seek the votes of conservative whites. One step in this direction was, of course, the creation of a ticket headed by two southerners. Democrats

hoped that the Clinton/Gore ticket would appeal directly to the southern white voters who once had been Democratic stalwarts but had made the Deep South a Republican bastion during the Reagan years.

Clinton went out of his way to assure

Brown, too, sought to promote concerns that he believed the mainstream nominees had neglected. Brown sought to appeal to the party's traditional liberal base, including union members, blacks, and environmentalists, in his "We the People" campaign. Ridiculed by some as "Governor Moonbeam" because of his unpredictable and unconventional political style (such as his study of Zen philosophy and the fact that his limousine when he was governor was a beat-up old compact car), Brown ran a shoestring campaign with few paid aides. He refused to accept campaign contributions over $100, and at every opportunity he advertised a toll-free number for those interested in contributing.

Brown argued strenuously for strict campaign contribution limits as well as for a major overhaul of the entire campaign finance process, term limits, a flat 13 percent tax on income, worker rights, and stricter environmental regulations. He also offered to make Jesse Jackson his vice-presidential running mate should he win the nomination. Despite a weak showing in the early primaries, Brown was able to stay in the race because of his economical campaign style and populist appeal, as reflected by his toll-free-number approach to fund-raising. By portraying himself as an outsider in the later primaries, Brown sought to undercut front-runner Bill Clinton and capitalize on the electorate's frustration with the political system, even though he admitted that as chair of the California state Democratic party from 1989 to 1991, he had raised tens of millions of dollars from the same wealthy special interests he was running against in 1992.

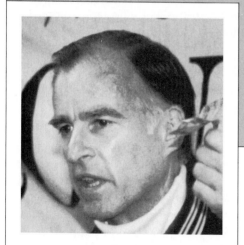

Jerry Brown

Both Buchanan and Brown pursued "outsider" campaigns, hoping to draw on their party's core bases. In the process, both reminded the front-runners that the party core constituents could not be ignored.

Source: Stephen J. Wayne, *The Road to the White House* (New York: St. Martin's Press, 1992).

conservative whites in both the North and the South that, unlike previous Democratic candidates, he would not cater to blacks. For example, Clinton was careful to avoid any association with America's most visible African American Democrat, Jesse Jackson. In a similar vein, Clinton seized an opportunity after the 1992 Los Angeles riots to sharply attack an African American rap singer, Sister Souljah, for her anti-white comments. Many African American Democrats were angry about the party's apparent shift to the Right on matters of race and threatened to withhold their backing in the general election. Jesse Jackson, for example, pointedly remarked, "It takes two wings to fly." There was, however, little that African American politicians could do, and, ultimately, Jackson and the others had no choice but to support the Clinton ticket.

Thus, Clinton became the first Democratic presidential candidate in two decades who was neither burdened by an excessively liberal image nor plagued by the party's racial division. With Democratic strategists believing they had stabilized the party's traditional southern, African American, and blue-collar base, Clinton and his allies moved to expand the Democratic coalition into Republican electoral territory— business and the middle class. For this purpose, the Democrats fashioned an economic message designed to appeal to business and the middle class without alienating the party's working-class constituency.

The centerpiece of the Democratic campaign was a call for the development of a multifaceted "national economic strategy." One major element of this strategy was support for free trade but with the proviso that America would act against nations deemed to be guilty of unfair trade practices or to have poor labor policies or deficient environmental programs.[19] A second element was increased government spending to support scientific research and development, as well as strong government backing for new technologies and industries, and tax credits for small and medium-size businesses. Third, the Democrats' economic strategy envisioned extensive retraining programs for workers to prepare them for jobs in the new, high-technology industries of the future. Fourth, the Democrats called for massive federal spending to rebuild America's industrial infrastructure. Finally, their 1992 national economic strategy promised expanded funding for education, health care, and other social services—to be paid for by tax increases on the wealthy— under the rubric of investment in the human-capital resources needed to improve America's competitive position in the world economy.

Taken as a whole, the Democrats' national economic strategy was a blueprint as much for political success as for economic recovery. Each element of their plan was calculated to appeal to the interests of traditional Democratic constituencies or to create a new coalition of forces that would strengthen the Democratic camp. Thus, most obviously, the pledge to invest heavily in research and new technologies, as well as in the modernization of America's infrastructure through such means as the creation of high-speed trains and electronic "information highways," was aimed at winning the support of firms in the computer, telecommunications, and aerospace industries threatened by cuts in defense spending and intense foreign competition. The executives of hundreds of high-tech firms responded to this Democratic initiative by announcing their support for Clinton.

Similarly, Democratic caveats on the issue of free trade were designed to reassure firms threatened by foreign competition, or by the competition of American firms utilizing cheap labor in Mexico under the new NAFTA agreement, that a Democratic administration would be sensitive to their needs. Democratic rhetoric suggested that especially troublesome foreigners or Mexi-

[19]Stuart Auerbach, "Bush, Clinton Differ on Government's Role," *Washington Post*, 8 October 1992, p. A23.

can transplants might be charged with unfair labor and trade practices, or even with environmental mismanagement, to protect the market share of American-based businesses.

Democratic support for limits on free trade were also designed to please organized labor, which feared a continuing loss of unionized jobs to foreign countries. Labor had reason, too, to support Democratic calls for infrastructural redevelopment (which would presumably provide public works jobs for unionized workers in a variety of industries) and job retraining programs. Through these initiatives, the Democrats hoped to rebuild their own economic infrastructure as well as the nation's. Under Franklin Roosevelt, the Democratic party had forged coalitions between industry and labor through regulatory, defense, and public employment programs that provided benefits for workers and their firms. These coalitions had been broken during the Reagan-Bush years with damaging consequences for the Democratic party's electoral prospects. With their new economic strategy, the Democrats hoped to reunite business and labor and tie both to the Democratic party.

Finally, the Democrats' national economic strategy identified a new rationale for traditional Democratic social programs and thus pointed the way toward an expansion of domestic social spending for the benefit of Democratic constituencies. The Reaganites had discredited Democratic social programs by charging that they represented transfers of income from the hardworking middle class to the unworthy poor. In 1992, the Democrats redefined social spending. No longer was social spending a transfer to the poor. Rather, it was now to be seen as an investment in resources needed to improve America's competitive position in the world.

This call obviously had enormous appeal not only for the nominal recipients of social services but, even more important, for the millions of public- and quasi-public-sector professionals in the human service, education, health care, mental health, and related fields who provided social services. In recent decades, these public-sector professionals came to be among the most vehement and important supporters of the Democrats and determined foes of the Republicans, who, of course, sought to limit domestic social spending.

With this national economic strategy, Clinton and the Democrats accomplished in 1992 what Reagan and the Republicans had achieved in 1980 when they formed a coalition with another political strategy presented as an economic theory—supply-side economics.

The Campaign

Against the backdrop of the continuing economic recession and Republican disarray, the Democrats' economic program and new posture of moderation on racial issues and ideology helped the Clinton/Gore ticket take a commanding lead in the polls in August 1992, after the Democratic National Convention. Unable to make effective use of economic issues because of the recession, or of the familiar Republican rallying cries of taxes, race, and regulation because of his own weak record in these areas, Bush fell back upon the theme of "family values" and attacks upon Clinton's character in his attempt to catch up in the polls. For three months, the nation was transfixed by the often bitter campaigning, the renewed candidacy of Ross Perot, and the presidential and vice-presidential debates before casting their vote on November 3.

The Republican ticket's difficulties became fully evident during the nationally televised presidential and vice-presidential debates in October. While the Democratic candidates focused on the nation's economic distress, constantly reminding voters of the need for programs and policies designed to improve the nation's economy, Bush and Quayle, for their part, had considerable difficulty articulating an affirmative message and were left to talk about character. Not surprisingly, the debates attracted few new voters to the Republican camp.

Complicating the debates, and the 1992 campaign more generally, was the peculiar candidacy of Ross Perot. During the spring of 1992, Perot had announced his intention to campaign as an independent presidential candidate if his name was placed on the ballot in every state. With more than a little help from a well-financed and well-organized Perot effort, Perot "volunteers" complied with Perot's stipulation, and his independent candidacy was launched.[20] Initially, Perot's blunt, no-nonsense, can-do style generated considerable enthusiasm among voters apparently tired of mainstream politicians. Perot made extremely effective use of television talk show and call-in programs such as "Larry King Live" to present himself as an ordinary American tired of the inability of the politicians to resolve the nation's many problems.

By mid-June, both major-party candidates began to assess the potential damage of a Perot candidacy. For their part, pundits began to discuss the possibility that, for the first time since 1824, an election might be thrown into the House of Representatives if a strong Perot showing prevented either major-party candidate from obtaining the electoral college majority needed to capture the White House.

On the last day of the Democratic National Convention, however, Perot surprised his supporters by withdrawing from the race. Perot never fully explained his decision, though many analysts believed he had grown irritated with the constant media scrutiny to which presidential candidates are subjected. Perot's decision to leave the race gave Clinton a boost. Perot had won the support of many disaffected Republicans not yet ready to back a Democrat. Having gotten their toes wet in the Perot camp, many of these voters were now ready to take the plunge and support Clinton. Perot thus served as a bridge for movements of voters from the Republican to the Democratic coalitions. Third-party and independent candidates often play this role.[21]

In the fall, however, Perot muddied the political waters once again by reentering the race, supposedly at the behest of the American people. Analysts initially greeted Perot's return with skepticism, believing that he could no longer have much impact on the election. However, Perot soon reestablished himself as a formidable figure, performing extremely well in the three presidential debates and again impressing voters as a plainspoken man of action. Following the debates, Perot presented his ideas and plans during dozens of talk show appearances and in a series of televised thirty- and sixty-minute infomercials, which drew substantial audiences. As Perot spent money freely (an estimated $60 million of his own funds), his standing in the

---

[20] Steven Holmes, "Grass-Roots Drive Shows Hand of Oz," *New York Times*, 30 September 1992, p. A20.

[21] See the discussion in Sundquist, *Dynamics of the Party System*, Chapter 2.

H. Ross Perot
Billionaire Populist

H. Ross Perot
(b. 1930)

During the 1992 presidential election, Texas businessman and billionaire H. Ross Perot alternately charmed and angered Americans with his plain-speaking, tough-talking, independent presidential candidacy.

Born in Texarkana, a town that straddles Texas and Arkansas, in 1930, Perot was raised in a home of modest means during the Depression era. After leaving the Navy in 1957, he worked for a fledgling computer company, IBM. In 1962, he formed his own company, modeled after IBM: Electronic Data Systems Corporation. Starting with $1,000, he built the company into a giant by the end of the 1960s and was soon a multimillionaire himself. His company's success rested primarily on a government program: processing Medicare claims in Texas for the federal Medicare program enacted in 1965. Some later accused Perot of having exercised undue influence to win the contract.

In the 1970s, Perot became heavily involved in the search for American soldiers missing in Southeast Asia, a concern he pursued for the next two decades. In 1979, he traveled personally and under cover to revolution-torn Iran to win the release of two of his employees. It was a move that underscored his personal courage to some and his recklessness to others.

On February 20, 1992, during an appearance on CNN's "Larry King Live," Perot was asked whether he would consider a run for the presidency. After much equivocation, he said he would if citizens put him on the ballot in all fifty states. Thus began the "Perot for President" movement, with financial support provided by Perot himself (who said that he was prepared to spend as much as

$200 million on the campaign if necessary). Perot unofficially launched his candidacy in June and proceeded to make the state of the economy and the ballooning federal deficit his primary issues. By this point, Perot was actually leading Republican incumbent George Bush and Democratic nominee Bill Clinton in some polls.

Yet with increased exposure came increased scrutiny. Critics accused Perot of being short-tempered, intolerant, and unwilling to listen to different points of view. These criticisms received support when Perot abruptly quit the race in mid-July. In still another unexpected move, Perot reentered the race in October, saying he was merely abiding the wishes of his supporters. Though many of his supporters were by now disenchanted, Perot's popular standing improved dramatically following his performance in all three national television debates. In late October, however, after accusing the Republicans of using various "dirty tricks" against him, none of which he could prove, his standing waned somewhat. He still won nearly 19 percent of the popular vote but no electoral votes.

Source: Lawrence Wright, "The Man from Texarcana," *New York Times Magazine,* 28 June, 1992.

polls rose, and pundits once again began to wonder whether the billionaire could affect the outcome of the election.

The Perot balloon, however, burst in late October. During an appearance on the CBS television program "60 Minutes," Perot asserted that his earlier decision to withdraw from the presidential campaign had been prompted by a Republican "dirty tricks" effort to somehow embarrass his daughter and spoil her wedding with a forged photograph. This strange claim was greeted by indignant Republican denials and general incredulity. Within two days, Perot withdrew the charge. This unusual episode led many voters to conclude that Perot was temperamentally unsuited for the White House. The Perot campaign's momentum waned.

On November 3, Perot captured nearly 19 percent of the popular vote. This was the best showing for an independent presidential bid since Theodore Roosevelt's Bull Moose candidacy in 1912. Perot, however, carried no states and appeared to draw support away from Clinton and Bush in roughly equal percentages. Thus, despite its sound and fury, the Perot campaign ultimately had little effect upon the outcome of the election.

More than anything else, the Perot episode revealed the weakness of America's two-party system. Many voters had grown so disenchanted with established politicians and parties, and so distrustful of their promises, that they were willing to consider electing an enigmatic and mercurial outsider to the nation's highest office. To many Americans, Perot seemed to be the savior on horseback who would somehow end the stalemate, corruption, and ineptitude plaguing the nation. Citizens, of course, look to such saviors when they lose confidence in the political process and even, perhaps, in democratic politics itself. The strength of the Perot candidacy was a symptom of popular disaffection. America's political leadership must take this disaffection seriously even as its most recent symptom goes away.

Democratic Triumph

After the long and arduous campaign, the result was almost anticlimactic. The Clinton/Gore ticket achieved a comfortable victory, winning 43 percent of the popular vote and 370 electoral votes. Bush and Quayle received 38 percent of the popular vote and only 168 electoral votes. Economic recession, the end of the Cold War, and the Democrats' newfound moderation on matters of race and ideology combined to oust the Republicans from the White House for the first time in twelve years.

According to national exit-poll results reported by the *Washington Post* immediately after the election, the single issue with the largest impact upon the election's outcome was the economy.[22] Nearly half of the voters surveyed cited jobs and the economy as their central concerns, and these voters supported the Democrats by a 2-to-1 margin. Among voters who felt that their own economic prospects were worsening, Clinton won by a 5-to-1 margin.

By contrast, Bush led Clinton by a 2-to-1 margin among voters citing the Republican theme of "family values" as an important issue. However, this major Republican focus was of concern to only one voter in seven. Similarly, against the backdrop of the end of the Cold War and the collapse of the Soviet Union, foreign policy no longer served as a major Republican rallying point.

[22] Thomas B. Edsall and E. J. Dionne, Jr., "Younger, Lower-Income Voters Spurn GOP," *Washington Post*, 4 November 1992, p. 1.

Voters concerned with foreign policy supported Bush by an overwhelming 9-to-1 margin. However, only one voter in twelve cited foreign policy as a major worry. Moreover, the once powerful Republican tax issue had completely lost its potency in the face of Bush's failure to adhere to his own pledge never to raise taxes. Only one voter in seven cited taxes as an important issue. Twenty percent of those surveyed said that Bush's failure to keep his promise on taxes was "very important."

At the same time, the Democrats' racial strategy was successful. Democratic strategists had opted to ignore blacks and to court conservative whites, calculating that the economic hard times left blacks no choice but to support the Clinton ticket. This calculation proved to be correct. Conservative white voters in the North and South responded positively to Clinton's well-publicized conflicts with Jesse Jackson and other Clinton gestures designed to distance himself from blacks. For their part, African American voters supported the Democratic ticket in overwhelming numbers, helping Clinton carry a number of southern states.

After twelve years, the political coalition formed by Ronald Reagan in 1980 had been shattered. The Republicans' bastions in the South and West had been breached. Many of the blue-collar "Reagan Democrats," lured to the GOP by social, patriotic, foreign policy, and racial issues, had returned to the Democratic fold. Even southern evangelicals—the prime targets for the GOP's family values campaign—were attracted to a Democratic ticket featuring two southern Baptists. At the same time, the GOP's core, upper-middle-class and business constituency could muster little enthusiasm for a Republican administration that had failed to hold the line on taxes and had allowed the economy to deteriorate, while devoting its energy and attention to abortion and other social issues. As a result, Clinton even outpolled Bush in the GOP's traditional suburban strongholds. Indeed, according to *New York Times* exit polls, among voters earning more than $75,000 a year, normally the nation's most rock-ribbed Republican group, Bush support fell from 62 percent in 1988 to a meager 48 percent in 1992.[23] Thus, on November 3, 1992, the nation elected a Democratic president. It was time for a change.

Congressional Elections

Neither side was fully pleased with the results of the 1992 congressional contest. In the Senate, the party balance remained unchanged. The Democrats continued to hold fifty-seven seats while the Republicans controlled forty-three. In the House of Representatives, the Republicans gained ten seats, leaving the Democrats with a 259-to-176 margin.

Thus, Democrats were disappointed because Clinton's victory in the presidential election did not translate into Democratic gains in Congress. In their euphoria following Clinton's victory, however, most Democrats predicted that the new Congress would work effectively with the Clinton administration. For their part, Republicans were sorry that the nation's dismay over congressional scandals and Americans' putative anti-incumbent mood did not result in more Republican victories. However, Republican congressional leaders breathed a sigh of relief that the collapse of the Bush campaign had not undermined their own positions.

Whatever its partisan makeup, the new Congress reflected a number of the changes

---

[23]"Portrait of the Electorate," *New York Times*, 5 November 1992, p. B9.

manifesting themselves in American society during the past decade. Most striking was the large number of women elected to the House and even to the Senate. Women had been mobilized for political action in the wake of the Clarence Thomas confirmation hearings. As a result, forty-seven women won election to the House of Representatives (compared with twenty-eight in the old House) and four to the Senate, where there were now six women. One of these women, Carol Moseley-Braun (Democrat-Illinois), became the first black woman elected to serve in the Senate. Two women now represented California: Dianne Feinstein and Barbara Boxer.

African American and Hispanic American representation in Congress also increased in 1992, the former from twenty-five to thirty-seven and the latter from eleven to eighteen. Four Asian Americans were elected to the House. One, Jay C. Kim, former Republican mayor of Diamond Bar, California, became the first Korean American elected to Congress. Increased minority voter registration coupled with the redrawing of congressional district boundaries to enhance minority groups' representation had achieved their purpose.

All in all, Americans elected 11 new senators and 110 new House members in 1992. This was the largest group of congressional freshmen since 1948, larger even than the classes entering with Lyndon Johnson's landslide victory in 1964 or in the post-Watergate 1974 election. Interestingly, though, this huge freshman class could not be said to represent a clear or consistent message from the electorate.

Did the electorate want a Congress that would support Bill Clinton? Perhaps, but 40 percent of the newcomers were Republicans. Was the electorate tired of politics as usual? Perhaps, but three-fourths of the newcomers had previous governmental experience. Did the electorate seek revenge on incumbents? After all, voters in fourteen states had approved congressional term-limit proposals. Nevertheless, most incumbents were re-elected. In the House, for example, 75 percent of those elected on November 3 were incumbents. Moreover, only sixteen of the newcomers actually defeated incumbents in the general election. The other ninety-four replaced incumbents who had retired, lost their districts in the decennial redrawing of district boundaries, or, in a few cases, were defeated in primaries. Viewed another way, 95 percent of the House incumbents running in the general election were successful. As usually happens, the electorate's biennial message to Washington was by no means loud and clear. It was left to the new Congress and the new administration to interpret the will of the people according to their own lights.

The Consequences of Consent

Voting choices and electoral outcomes can be extremely important in the United States. Yet, to observe that there can be relationships between voters' choices, leadership composition, and policy outputs is only to begin to understand the significance of democratic elections, rather than to exhaust the possibilities. Important as they are, voters' choices and electoral results may still be less consequential for government and politics than the simple fact of voting itself. The impact of electoral decisions upon the governmental process is, in some respects, analogous to the impact made upon organized religion by individuals' being able to worship at the church of their choice. The fact of worship can be more important than the particular choice. Similarly, the fact of mass electoral participation can be more significant than what or how the citizens decide once they participate. Thus, electoral participation has important consequences in that it socializes and institutionalizes political action.

First, democratic elections socialize political activity. Voting is not a natural or spontaneous phenomenon. It is an institutionalized form of mass political involvement. That individuals vote rather than engage in some other form of political behavior is a result of national policies that create the opportunity to vote and discourage other political activities relative to voting. Elections transform what might otherwise consist of sporadic, citizen-initiated acts into a routine public function. This transformation expands and democratizes mass political involvement. At the same time, however, elections help to preserve the government's stability by containing and channeling away potentially more disruptive or dangerous forms of mass political activity. By establishing formal avenues for mass participation and accustoming citizens to their use, government reduces the threat that volatile, unorganized involvement can pose to the established order.

Second, elections bolster the government's power and authority. Elections help to increase popular support for political leaders and for the regime itself. The formal opportunity to participate in elections serves to convince citizens that the government is responsive to their needs and wishes. Moreover, elections help to persuade citizens to obey. Electoral participation increases popular acceptance of taxes and military service upon which the government depends. Even if popular voting can influence the behavior of those in power, voting serves simultaneously as a form of co-optation. Elections—particularly democratic elections—substitute consent

for coercion as the foundation of governmental power.

Finally, elections institutionalize mass influence in politics. Democratic elections permit citizens to routinely select and depose public officials, and elections can serve to promote popular influence over officials' conduct. But however effective this electoral sanction may be, it is hardly the only means through which citizens can reward or punish public officials for their actions. Spontaneous or privately organized forms of political activity, or even the threat of their occurrence, can also induce those in power to heed the public's wishes. The alternative to democratic elections is not clearly and simply the absence of popular influence; it can be unregulated and unconstrained popular intervention into governmental processes. It is, indeed, often precisely because spontaneous forms of mass political activity can have too great an impact upon the actions of government that elections are introduced. Walter Lippmann, a journalist who helped to pioneer the idea of public opinion voicing itself through the press via the "Opinion/Editorial" page, once observed that "new numbers were enfranchised because they had power, and giving them the vote was the least disturbing way of letting them exercise their power."[24] The vote can provide the "least disturbing way" of allowing ordinary people to exercise power. If the people had been powerless to begin with, elections would never have been introduced.

Thus, although citizens can secure enormous benefits from their right to vote, government secures equally significant benefits from allowing them to do so.

---

[24]Walter Lippmann, *The Essential Lippmann*, ed. Clinton Rossiter and James Lare (New York: Random House, 1965), p. 12.

Time Line on Elections

EVENTS		INSTITUTIONAL DEVELOPMENTS
All electoral votes cast for Washington (1788)		Federalists in control of national government (1789–1800)
Thomas Jefferson elected president (1800)	**1800**	First electoral realignment—Jeffersonian Republicans defeat Federalists (1800)
Andrew Jackson elected president; beginning of party government (1828)		Second realignment—Jacksonian Democrats take control of White House and Congress (1828)
		Presidential nominating conventions introduced (1830s)
Whigs win; William Henry Harrison elected president (1840)		Whig party forms (1830s)
Lincoln elected (1860); South secedes (1860–1861)		Civil War realignment—Republican party founded (1856); Whig party destroyed (1860)
Civil War (1861–1865)		
Reconstruction (1865–1877)		Under Reconstruction Acts, blacks enfranchised in South (1867)
	1870	Fifteenth Amendment forbids states to deny voting rights based on race (1870)
Contested presidential election—Hayes v. Tilden (1876); Republican Rutherford Hayes elected by electoral vote of 185–184 (1877)		Hayes's election leads to end of Reconstruction; voting rights of South restored (1877)
		Southern blacks lose voting rights through poll taxes, literacy tests, grandfather clause (1870s–1890s)
		Progressive reforms—direct primaries, civil service reform, Australian ballot, registration requirements; voter participation drops sharply (1890s–1910s)
Republican William McKinley elected president (1896)		Realignment of 1896; Republican hegemony (1896–1932)
	1900	Seventeenth Amedment authorizes direct election of senators (1913)

EVENTS		INSTITUTIONAL DEVELOPMENTS
		Nineteenth Amendment gives women right to vote (1920)
Democrat Franklin D. Roosevelt elected president (1932)		Democratic realignment (1930s)
Democrat John F. Kennedy first Catholic elected president (1960)	**1960**	*Baker* v. *Carr*—Supreme Court declares doctrine of "one man, one vote" (1962); period of reapportionment (1960s)
		Voting Rights Act (1965)
Republican Richard Nixon elected president (1968)		Breakdown of Democratic New Deal coalition (1968)
Rise of black voting in the South (1970s)		Twenty-sixth Amendment lowers voting age to eighteen (1971)
Era of new campaign technology and PACS (1970s–1980s)		Federal Elections Campaign Act (1971)
Republican Ronald Reagan elected president (1980)	**1980**	New Republican era begins with election of Reagan (1980)
Geraldine Ferraro first woman on major party national ticket (1984)		Electoral stalemate; Democrats dominate Congress; Republicans control presidency (1986–1990)
Jesse Jackson first black candidate to become important presidential contender (1988)		
George Bush elected president (1988)		
Democrats regain control of Congress (1990)	**1990**	High levels of congressional party unity and partisan conflict as Democrats seek to strengthen control of government through ambitious program of economic, social, and political reform (1993)
Democrat Bill Clinton elected president; Democrats retain control of House and Senate (1992)		

Chapter Review

Allowing citizens to vote represents a calculated risk on the part of power holders. On the one hand, popular participation can generate consent and support for the government. On the other hand, the right to vote may give ordinary citizens more influence in the governmental process than political elites would like.

Voting is only one of the many possible types of political participation. The significance of voting is that it is an institutional and formal mode of political activity. Voting is organized and subsidized by the government. This makes voting both more limited and more democratic than other forms of participation.

All governments regulate voting to influence its effects. The most important forms of regulation include regulation of the electorate's composition, regulation of the translation of voters' choices into electoral outcomes, and insulation of policy-making processes from electoral intervention.

Voters' choices are based on partisanship, issues, and candidates' personalities. Which of these criteria will be most important varies over time and depends upon the factors that opposing candidates choose to emphasize in their campaigns.

Voters' choices have had particularly significant consequences during periods of critical electoral realignment. During these periods, which have occurred roughly every thirty years, new electoral coalitions have formed, new groups have come to power, and important institutional and policy changes have occurred. The last such critical period was associated with Franklin Roosevelt's New Deal.

Whatever voters decide, elections are important institutions because they socialize political activity, increase governmental authority, and institutionalize popular influence in political life.

For Further Reading

Andersen, Kristi. *The Creation of a Democratic Majority: 1928–1936.* Chicago: University of Chicago Press, 1979.

Black, Earl, and Merle Black. *The Vital South: How Presidents Are Elected.* Cambridge, MA: Harvard University Press, 1992.

Brady, David. *Critical Elections and Congressional Policymaking.* Stanford, CA: Stanford University Press, 1988.

Burnham, Walter D. *The Current Crisis in American Politics.* New York: Oxford University Press, 1982.

Carmines, Edward G., and James Stimson. *Issue Evolution: The Racial Transformation of American Politics.* Princeton: Princeton University Press, 1988.

Conway, M. Margaret. *Political Participation in the United States.* Washington, DC: Congressional Quarterly Press, 1985.

Dinkin, Robert J. *Campaigning in America: A History of Election Practices.* Westport, CT: Greenwood Press, 1989.

Ferguson, Thomas, and Joel Rogers. *Right Turn: The Decline of the Democrats and the Future of American Politics.* New York: Hill and Wang, 1986.

Fowler, Linda, and Robert D. McClure. *Political Ambition: Who Decides to Run for Congress.* New Haven: Yale University Press, 1989.

Ginsberg, Benjamin, and Martin Shefter. *Politics by Other Means: Institutional Conflict and the Declining Significance of Elections in America.* New York: Basic Books, 1990.

Jackson, Brooks. *Honest Graft: Big Money and the American Political Process.* New York: Alfred A. Knopf, 1988.

Jamieson, Kathleen H. *Eloquence in an Electronic Age: The Transformation of Political Speechmaking.* New York: Oxford University Press, 1988.

Nie, Norman, Sidney Verba, and John Petrocik. *The Changing American Voter.* Cambridge: Harvard University Press, 1979.

Niemi, Richard, and Herbert Weisberg. *Controversies in American Voting Behavior.* Washington, DC: Congressional Quarterly Press, 1984.

Norrander, Barbara. *Super Tuesday: Regional Politics and Presidential Primaries.* Lexington, KY: University of Kentucky Press, 1992.

Piven, Frances Fox, and Richard A. Cloward. *Why Americans Don't Vote.* New York: Pantheon, 1988.

Pohlmann, Marcus. *Black Politics in Conservative America.* New York: Longman, 1990.

Reed, Adolph. *The Jesse Jackson Phenomenon.* New Haven: Yale University Press, 1987.

Reichley, A. James, ed. *Elections American Style.* Washington, DC: Brookings Institution, 1987.

Sorauf, Frank. *Inside Campaign Finance: Myths and Realities.* New Haven, CT: Yale University Press, 1992.

Stanley, Harold. *Voter Mobilization and the Politics of Race: The South and Universal Suffrage, 1952–1984.* New York: Praeger, 1987.

Wilcox, Clyde. *God's Warriors: The Christian Right in Twentieth-Century America.* Baltimore: Johns Hopkins University Press, 1991.

10

POLITICAL PARTIES

We often refer to the United States as a nation with a "two-party system." By this we mean that in the United States the Democratic and Republican parties compete for office and power. Most Americans believe that party competition contributes to the health of the democratic process. Certainly, we are more than just a bit suspicious of those nations that claim to be ruled by their people but do not tolerate the existence of opposing parties.

The idea of party competition was not always accepted in the United States. In the early years of the Republic, parties were seen as threats to the social order. In his 1796 "Farewell Address," President George Washington warned his countrymen to shun partisan politics:

> Let me warn you in the most solemn manner against the baneful effects of the spirit of party generally. This spirit exists under different shapes in all government, more or less stifled, controlled, or repressed, but in those of the popular form it is seen in its greatest rankness and is truly their worst enemy.

Often, those in power viewed the formation of political parties by their opponents as acts of treason that merited severe punishment. Thus, in 1798, the Federalist party, which controlled the national government, in effect sought to outlaw its Jeffersonian Republican opponents through the infamous Alien and Sedition Acts, which, among other things, made it a crime to publish or say anything that might tend to defame or bring into disrepute either the president or the Congress (see Box 10.1). Under this law,

BOX 10.1
Alien and Sedition Acts: A Party's Attempt to Suppress the Opposition

In 1798 war seemed likely to break out between the United States and France. The overt purpose of the Alien and Sedition Acts was to protect the government against subversive activities by foreigners in the country—particularly the French. Their covert purpose, however, was to suppress Jefferson's and Madison's Republican party, which was rapidly gaining strength in its opposition to the Federalists.

The four pieces of legislation collectively referred to as the Alien and Sedition Acts are: (1) the Naturalization Act, passed June 18, 1798; (2) the Act Concerning Aliens, passed June 25, 1798; (3) the Act Respecting Alien Enemies, passed July 6, 1798; and (4) the Act for the Punishment of Certain Crimes (the Sedition Act), passed July 14, 1798.

The Alien Enemies Act never went into effect, because it was contingent on the declaration of war. The Alien Act, which gave the president power to order out of the country all aliens he considered a threat to national security, was never enforced. Nonetheless, it is believed to have been responsible for the departure of many of the French. Since most naturalized citizens became Republicans, this act may have functioned to diminish the number of potential Republicans. In extending the period of residence required for naturalization from five to fourteen years, the Naturalization Act was an obvious move to weaken the Republican party.

The Sedition Act had the most serious legal implications. It was designed to suppress critics of the administration by limiting their freedom of speech and of the press. It was used to indict approximately twenty-five persons. While fewer than half of those indicted were ever brought to trial, several prominent Republican journalists were convicted. By 1802 all but the Alien Enemies Act had either expired or been repealed.

---

twenty-five people—including several Republican newspaper editors—were arrested and subsequently convicted.[1]

Obviously, over the past two hundred years, our conception of political parties has changed considerably—from subversive organizations to bulwarks of democracy. In this chapter, we will examine the realities underlying these changing conceptions. First, we will evaluate America's two-party system, and assess the similarities and differences between the parties. Second, we will discuss the functions of the parties. Finally, we will address the significance and changing role of parties in American politics today.

[1]See Richard Hofstadter, *The Idea of a Party System* (Berkeley: University of California Press, 1969).

The Two-Party System in America

Political parties as they are known today developed along with the expansion of suffrage and can be understood only in the context of elections. The two are so intertwined that American parties actually take their shape from the electoral process. They were formed because there were elections to run. The shape of party organization in the United States has followed a simple rule: For every district where an election is held, there should be some kind of party unit.

Compared to political parties in Europe, parties in the United States have always seemed weak. They have no criteria for party membership—no cards for their members to carry, no obligatory participation in any activity, no notion of exclusiveness. And today, they seem weaker than ever: they inspire less loyalty and are less able to control nominations. Some people are even talking about a "crisis of political parties," as though party politics were being abandoned. But there continues to be at least some substance to party organizations in the United States.

Although George Washington deplored partisan politics, the two-party system emerged early in the history of the new Republic. Beginning with the Federalists and the Jeffersonian Republicans in the early 1800s, two major parties would continue to dominate national politics, although which particular two parties would change with the times and issues, culminating in today's Democrats and Republicans.

THE DEMOCRATS. When the Jeffersonian party splintered in 1824, Andrew Jackson emerged as the leader of one of its four factions. In 1830, Jackson's group became the Democratic party. This new party had the strongest national organization of its time and presented itself as the party of the common man. Jacksonians supported reductions in the price of public lands and a policy of cheaper money and credit. Laborers, immigrants, and settlers west of the Alleghenies were quickly attracted to it.

From 1828, when Jackson was elected president, to 1860, the Democratic party was the dominant force in American politics. For all but eight of those years, the Democrats held the White House. In addition, a Democratic majority controlled the Senate for twenty-six years and the House for twenty-four years during the same time period. Nineteenth-century Democrats emphasized the importance of interpreting the Constitution literally, upholding states' rights, and limiting federal spending.

In 1860, the issue of slavery split the Democrats along geographic lines. In the South, many Democrats served in the Confederate government. In the North, one faction of the party (the Copperheads) opposed the war and advocated negotiating a peace with the South. Thus, for years after the war, Republicans denounced the Democrats as the "party of treason."

The Democratic party was not fully able to regain its political strength until the Great Depression. In 1932, Democrat Franklin D. Roosevelt entered the White House. Subsequently, the Democrats won control of Congress as well. Roosevelt's New Deal coalition, composed of Catholics, Jews, African Americans, farmers, intellectuals, and members of organized labor, dominated American politics until the 1970s and served as the basis for the party's expansion of federal power and efforts to remedy social problems.

The Democrats were never fully united. In Congress, southern Democrats often aligned with Republicans in the so-called "conservative coalition" rather than with

How the U.S. Party System Evolved

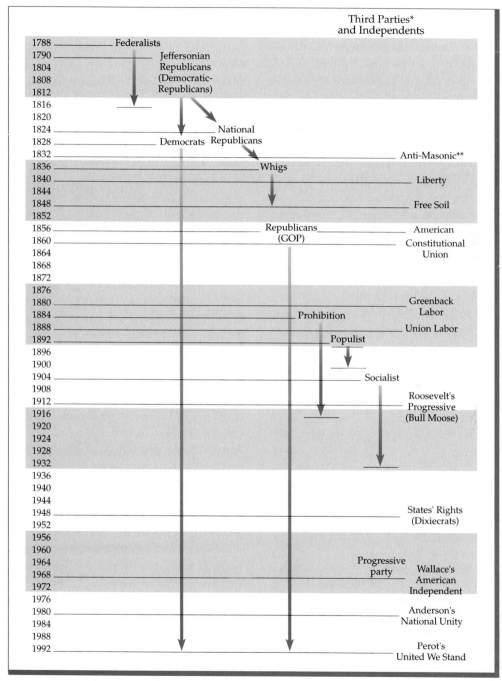

Third Parties*
and Independents

1788 — Federalists
1790 — Jeffersonian
1804 — Republicans
1808 — (Democratic-
1812 — Republicans)
1816
1820
1824 — National
1828 — Democrats Republicans
1832 — Anti-Masonic**
1836 — Whigs
1840 — Liberty
1844
1848 — Free Soil
1852
1856 — Republicans — American
1860 — (GOP) — Constitutional
1864 — Union
1868
1872
1876
1880 — Greenback
1884 — Prohibition — Labor
1888 — Union Labor
1892 — Populist
1896
1900
1904 — Socialist
1908
1912 — Roosevelt's
1916 — Progressive
1920 — (Bull Moose)
1924
1928
1932
1936
1940
1944
1948 — States' Rights
1952 — (Dixiecrats)
1956
1960
1964 — Progressive
1968 — party — Wallace's
1972 — American
1976 — Independent
1980 — Anderson's
1984 — National Unity
1988
1992 — Perot's
United We Stand

* Or in some cases, fourth party; most of these are one-term parties.
** The Anti-Masonics not only had the distinction of being the first third party, but it was also the first party to hold a national nominating convention and the first to announce a party platform.

members of their own party. But the Democratic party remained America's majority party, usually controlling both Congress and the White House, for nearly four decades after 1932. By the 1980s, the Democratic coalition faced serious problems. The once Solid South often voted for the Republicans, along with many blue-collar northern voters. On the other hand, the Democrats increased their strength among African American voters and women. At the present time, the Democrats continue to be the dominant force in Congress, even while the Republicans had an edge in presidential races. The Democrats also have a strong base in the bureaucracies of the federal government and the states, in labor unions, and in the not-for-profit sector of the economy. During the 1980s and 1990s, moderate Democrats were able to take control of the party nominating process and sought to broaden middle-class support for the Democrats. This helped the Democrats elect a president in 1992.

THE REPUBLICANS. The 1854 Kansas-Nebraska Act overturned the Missouri Compromise of 1820 and the Compromise of 1850, which had barred the expansion of slavery in the American territories. The Kansas-Nebraska Act gave each territory the right to decide whether or not to permit slavery. Opposition to this policy galvanized antislavery groups and led them to create a new party, the Republicans. It drew its membership from existing political groups—former Whigs, Know-Nothings, Free Soilers, and antislavery Democrats. In 1856, the party's first presidential candidate, John C. Fremont, won one-third of the popular vote and carried eleven states.

The early Republican platforms appealed to commercial as well as antislavery interests. The Republicans favored homesteading, internal improvements, the construction of a transcontinental railroad, and protective tariffs, as well as the containment of slavery. In 1858, the Republican party won control of the House; in 1860, the Republican presidential candidate, Abraham Lincoln, was victorious.

For almost seventy-five years after the North's victory in the Civil War, the Republicans were America's dominant political party. Between 1860 and 1932, Republicans occupied the White House for fifty-six years, controlled the Senate for sixty years, and the House for fifty. During these years, the Republicans came to be closely associated with big business. The party of Lincoln became the party of Wall Street.

The Great Depression, however, ended Republican supremacy. The voters held Republican President Herbert Hoover responsible for the economic catastrophe, and by 1936, the party's popularity was so low that Republicans won only eighty-nine seats in the House and seventeen in the Senate. The Republican presidential candidate, Governor Alfred M. Landon of Kansas, carried only two states. The Republicans won only four presidential elections between 1932 and 1980, and they controlled Congress for only four of those years (1947–1949 and 1953–1955).

The party has widened its appeal over the last four decades. Groups previously associated with the Democratic party—particularly blue-collar workers and southern Democrats—have been increasingly attracted to Republican presidential candidates (for example, Dwight D. Eisenhower, Richard Nixon, Ronald Reagan, and George Bush). Yet, Republicans generally have not done as well at the state and local levels and have had little chance of capturing a majority in either the House or Senate. The Watergate scandal of the Nixon administration was a setback in the party's efforts to increase its political power. In 1980, under the leadership of Ronald Reagan, the Republicans began to mount a new bid to become the nation's majority party, but the Iran-Contra scandal damaged Reagan's popularity. Reagan's successor, George Bush, was voted out of office in 1992 mainly in response to voters' concerns about the economy.

Similarities and Differences Today

One of the most familiar observations about American politics is that the two major parties try to be all things to all people and are therefore indistinguishable from each other. Data and experience give some support to this observation. The wide range of interests within the Democratic party today can be represented by liberals such as Mario Cuomo and Tom Harkin and by conservatives such as Howell Heflin. The 1992 Democratic presidential ticket consisted of two moderates, Bill Clinton and Al Gore, who appealed successfully for the votes of many conservative Democrats and moderate Republicans. A similar spectrum exists within the Republican party, as represented by liberals such as Mark Hatfield and conservatives like Newt Gingrich, although in the Reagan years liberal Republicans became something of an endangered species.

Parties in the United States are not programmatic or ideological, as they have sometimes been in England or in other parts of Europe. But this does not mean there are no differences between them. During the Reagan era, important differences emerged between the positions of Democratic and Republican party leaders on a number of key issues, and these differences are still apparent today. The national leadership of the Republican party supports maintaining high levels of military spending, cuts in social programs, tax relief for middle- and

upper-income voters, tax incentives to business, and the "social agenda" backed by members of conservative religious denominations.

The national Democratic leadership, on the other hand, supports expanded social welfare spending, cuts in military spending, increased regulation of business, and a variety of consumer and environmental programs. In 1990, for example, most Republicans supported President Bush's policies in the Persian Gulf, while most Democrats initially opposed the president's use of American military force against Iraq—at least until the president's policies succeeded. These differences reflect differences in philosophy as well as differences in the core constituencies to which the parties seek to appeal. The Democratic party at the national level seeks to unite organized labor, the poor, members of racial minorities, and liberal upper-middle-class professionals. The Republicans, by contrast, appeal to business, upper- and upper-middle-income groups in the private sector, and social conservatives.

Minor Parties

The United States is always said to have a two-party system, and Americans usually assume that only the candidates nominated by one of the two major parties have any chance of winning. Voters who would prefer a third-party candidate may feel compelled, nonetheless, to vote for the major-party candidate whom they regard as the "lesser of the two evils," to avoid wasting their vote in a futile gesture. Third-party candidates must struggle—usually without success—to overcome the perception that they cannot win. Thus, in 1992, many voters who favored Ross Perot gave their votes to George Bush or Bill Clinton on the presumption that Perot was not really electable.

DEBATING THE ISSUES

Party Politics in America: Are Three Parties Better than Two?

Since the start of the Republic, party politics has almost always been dominated by two large parties. Yet the parties have been persistently criticized for their sameness and monopoly on the political system. Political scientist Theodore J. Lowi argues that the two-party system is beyond repair and that a three- or multiparty system is our most constructive alternative. In a classic defense of two-partyism, Political parties expert E. E. Schattschneider argues that the present system suits an American public most comfortable with two large, diverse parties that emphasize compromise and moderation.

Lowi

Nothing about the present American party system warrants the respect it receives. Presidents need a party and have none. Voters need choices and continuity and rarely have either. Congress needs cohesion and has little. Although almost everyone recognizes that party organizations in the United States have all but disappeared . . . most people nevertheless assume that this is merely a momentary lapse and that the two-party system is the American way. But . . . it should be clear by now that big, modern, programmatic governments [like the U.S.] are not hospitable to two-party systems. . . . A two-party system simply cannot grapple with complex programmatic alternatives in a manner that is meaningful to large electorates. Modern programmatic governments do need political parties, just as much as traditional patronage governments needed them. It is not party systems but the two-party system in particular that no longer can suffice. No amount of tinkering by well-intentioned reformers can revive the two-party system. . . .

A multiparty system will seem alien on American soil only as long as the two-party system

As many scholars have pointed out, third-party prospects are also hampered by America's single-member-district plurality election system. In many other nations, several individuals can be elected to represent each legislative district. This is called a system of multimember districts. With this type of system, the candidates of weaker parties have a better chance of winning at least some seats. For their part, voters are less concerned about wasting ballots and usually more willing to support minor-party candidates.

Reinforcing the effects of the single-

member district, plurality voting rules (as was noted in Chapter 9) generally have the effect of setting what could be called a high threshold for victory. To win a plurality race, candidates usually must secure many more votes than they would need under most European systems of proportional representation. For example, to win an American plurality election in a single-member district where there are only two candidates, a politician must win more than 50 percent of the votes cast. To win a seat from a European multimember district under proportional rules, a candidate may

is taken as the only true, American way to govern. . . . The presence of other real parties with a real electoral base and a real presence in state legislatures, in Congress, and in the Electoral College, could clarify the policies, programs and the lines of accountability of the two major parties by reducing their need to appear to be all things to all people.[1]

Schattschneider

Does the fact that we have a two-party system make any difference? Most emphatically, it does! . . . What are the special qualities of American politics that result from the fact that we have a well-established two-party system?

First, the two-party system produces majorities automatically. Since there are only two major parties actually in the competition for power and these parties monopolize the vote, it is almost certain that one of them will get a majority. . . . The difficulty of assembling a majority is thus reduced very greatly. . . .

The second effect of the two-party system is the fact that it produces moderate parties. . . . The major party cannot afford to take an extreme stand, but neither is it condemned to futility . . . it is difficult to imagine anything more important than the tendency of the parties to avoid extreme policies. . . .

Minor party politicians, anxious to create new alternatives by breaking up the two-party system and trying to prove that the competition between the major parties is unreal, contend that the difference between the major parties is zero, while major party politicians have professed to see momentous alternatives between the great parties. . . . [But] the extravagant language of party orators, major and minor, deceives almost no one. . . . There seems to be ample moral authority in American civilization for a moderate party policy. The criticism most justly made of American major parties is not that they exhibit a tendency to be alike but rather that the moderate though significant differences between them are often too confused and ill defined to be readily understood.[2]

[1]Theodore J. Lowi, *The Personal President* (Ithaca, NY: Cornell University Press, 1985), pp. 203–4.
[2]E. E. Schattschneider, *Party Government* (New York: Holt, Rinehart, and Winston, 1942), pp. 84–93.

need to win only 15 or 20 percent of the votes cast. This high American threshold discourages minor parties and encourages the various political factions that might otherwise form minor parties to minimize their differences and remain within the major-party coalitions.

It would, nevertheless, be incorrect to assert (as some scholars have maintained) that America's single-member plurality election system is the major cause of our historical two-party pattern. All that can be said is that American election law depresses the number of parties likely to survive over long periods of time in the United States. There is nothing magical about two. Indeed, the single-member plurality system of election can also discourage second parties. After all, if one party consistently receives a large plurality of the vote, people may eventually come to see their vote *even for the second party* as a wasted effort. This is partly what happened to the Republican party in the Deep South before World War II.

Despite these obstacles, every presidential election brings out a host of minor-party hopefuls (see Table 10.1). Few survive until the next contest.

TABLE 10.1
PARTIES AND CANDIDATES IN 1992

In the 1992 presidential election, in addition to the Democratic and Republican nominees, twenty-one candidates appeared on the ballot in one or more states. Ross Perot came the closest to challenging the major-party candidates with nearly 19 percent of the popular vote. The remaining twenty candidates shared .79 percent of the votes cast with numerous write-ins. Many voters in 1992 told pollsters that they preferred "none of the above." However, in Nevada, where voters had an opportunity to mark this choice on their ballots, few actually did.

Candidate	Party	Vote Total	% of Vote
Bill Clinton	Democrat	44,908,233	42.95%
George Bush	Republican	39,102,282	37.40
Ross Perot	Independent	19,721,433	18.86
Andre Marrou	Libertarian	291,612	0.28
James "Bo" Gritz	Populist/Am. First	98,918	0.09
Lenora Fulani	New Alliance	73,248	0.07
Howard Phillips	U.S. Taxpayers	42,960	0.04
John Hagelin	Natural Law	37,137	0.03
Ron Daniels	Independent	27,396	0.02
Lyndon LaRouche	Independent	25,863	0.02
James Mac Warren	Socialist Workers	22,883	0.00
Drew Bradford	Independent	4,749	0.00
Jack Herer	Grass roots	3,875	0.00
Helen Halyard	Workers League	3,050	0.00
John Quinn Brisben	Socialist	2,909	0.00
John Yiamouyiannis	Independent	2,199	0.00
Delbert Ehlers	Independent	1,149	0.00
Jim Boren	Apathy	956	0.00
Earl Dodge	Prohibition	935	0.00
Eugene Hem	Third Party	405	0.00
Isabelle Masters	Looking Back Group	327	0.00
Robert J. Smith	American	292	0.00
Gloria Estella La Riva	Workers World	181	0.00
Write-in		177,207	0.17
None of the above	Nevada	2,537	0.00
TOTAL		104,552,736	100.00%

Source: *Washington Post*, 18 January, 1993.

Functions of the Parties

Parties perform a wide variety of functions. They are mainly involved in nominations and elections—providing the candidates for office, getting out the vote, and facilitating mass electoral choice. They also influence the institutions of government—providing the leadership and organization of the various congressional committees.

Nominations and Elections

Nomination means selecting one party candidate to run for each elective office. The nominating process can precede the election by many months, as it does when the many candidates for the presidency are eliminated from consideration through a grueling series of debates and state primaries until there is only one survivor in each party—the party's nominee. Nomination is the parties' most serious and difficult business. In the course of American political history, the parties have used three modes of nomination—the caucus, the convention, and the primary election (see In Brief Box).

THE CAUCUS. In the eighteenth and early nineteenth centuries, nominations were informal, without rules or regulations. Local party leaders would simply gather all the party activists, and they would agree on the person, usually from among themselves, who would be the candidate. The meetings where candidates were nominated were generally called *caucuses*. Informal nomination by caucus sufficed for the parties until

widespread complaints were made about cliques of local leaders or state legislators dominating all the nominations and leaving no place for the other party members who wanted to participate. Beginning in the 1830s, nominating conventions were proposed as a reform that would enable the mass membership of a party to express its will.

NOMINATION BY CONVENTION. A nominating convention is a formal caucus bound by a number of rules that govern participation and nominating procedures. Conventions are meetings of delegates elected by party members from the relevant county (county convention) or state (state convention). Delegates to each party's national convention (which nominates the party's presidential candidate) are chosen by party members on a state-by-state basis; there is no single national delegate selection process.

Historically, the great significance of the convention mode of nomination was its effect on the presidential selection process and on the presidency itself. For more than fifty years after America's founding, the

---

In Brief Box

THE NOMINATING PROCESS

Nomination by Caucus
Party leaders and active members gather informally to agree upon a candidate (common in the eighteenth and early nineteenth centuries)

Nomination by Convention
Party leaders and delegates chosen by party members meet formally to vote for the nomination (a more fomalized caucus that took shape in the 1830s)

Nomination by Primary Election
Every party member has a vote in an election that determines the nomination

Independent Candidates
Candidates must file a petition with a minimum number of signatures

nomination of presidential candidates was dominated by congressional caucuses, meetings of each party's congressional delegations which critics called "King Caucus." In the early 1830s, when the major parties adopted the national nominating convention, they broke the power of King Caucus. This helped to give the presidency a mass popular base. Nevertheless, reformers of the early twentieth century regarded nominating conventions as instruments of "boss rule." They proposed replacing conventions with primaries, which provide for direct choice by the voters at an election some weeks or months before the general election.

NOMINATION BY PRIMARY ELECTION.   In primary elections, party members select the party's nominees directly rather than selecting convention delegates who then select the nominees. Primaries are far from perfect replacements for conventions, since it is rare that more than 25 percent of the enrolled voters participate in them. Nevertheless, they are replacing conventions as the dominant method of nomination.[2] At the present time, only a small number of states, including Connecticut, Delaware, and Utah, provide for state conventions to nominate candidates for statewide offices, and even these states combine them with primaries whenever a substantial minority of delegates vote for one of the defeated aspirants.

Primary elections are of two types—closed and open. In a *closed primary*, participation is limited to individuals who have declared their affiliation by registering with the party. In an *open primary*, individuals declare their party affiliation on the actual

day of the primary election. To do so, they simply go the polling place and ask for the ballot of a particular party. The open primary allows each voter an opportunity to consider candidates and issues before deciding whether to participate and in which party's contest to participate. Open primaries, therefore, are less conducive than closed contests to strong political parties. But in either case, primaries are more open than conventions or caucuses to new issues and new types of candidates.

INDEPENDENT CANDIDATES. The types of nominating processes are summarized in the In Brief Box on page 301. The convention and primary methods are not the only ways that candidates can get on the ballot. State laws extend the right of *independent candidacy* to individuals who do not wish to be nominated by political parties or who are unable to secure a party nomination.

Although nomination by a political party is complicated, the independent route to the ballot is even more difficult. For almost all offices in all states, the law requires more signatures for independent nomination than for party designation. Table 10.2 shows some of the special difficulties of getting on the ballot as an independent candidate in New York State. The candidate for a party's nomination to Congress in New York must get 1,250 valid signatures within the congressional district, while the independent candidate must get 3,500 signatures.

The Parties' Influence on National Government

The ultimate test of the party system is its relationship to and influence on the institutions of government. Thus, it is important to examine the party system in relation to Congress and the president.

---

[2] For a discussion of some of the effects of primary elections, see Peter F. Galderisi and Benjamin Ginsberg, "Primary Elections and the Evanescence of Third Party Activity in the United States," in *Do Elections Matter?*, ed. Benjamin Ginsberg and Alan Stone (Armonk, NY: M. E. Sharpe, 1986), pp. 115–30.

TABLE 10.2
GETTING ON THE BALLOT IN NEW YORK STATE

Office Sought	Number of Signatures Required for Nominating Petitions	
	Party Designation	Independent Nomination
Governorship or other statewide office	20,000 or 5% of enrolled voters of party, whichever is less	20,000 or 5% of registered voters, whichever is less
Mayoralty of large city*	2,000	5% of last election vote for governor in city
County office*	1,500	1,500
City council	500	1,500
Congress	1,250	3,500
State senate	1,000	3,000
State assembly	500	1,500

* Outside the city of New York. For New York City, 5,000 signatures are required.
Source: New York State Political Calendar, 1988–1989 (Albany, NY: Fort Orange Press).
Adapted by permission.

THE PARTIES AND CONGRESS. Congress, in particular, depends more on the party system than is generally recognized. First, the speakership of the House is a party office. All the members of the House take part in the election of the Speaker. But the actual selection is made by the majority party. When the majority party caucus presents a nominee to the entire House, its choice is then invariably ratified in a straight party vote.

The committee system of both houses of Congress is also a product of the two-party system. Although the rules organizing committees and the rules defining the jurisdiction of each are adopted like ordinary legislation by the whole membership, all other features of the committees are shaped by parties. For example, each party is assigned a quota of members for each committee, depending upon the percentage of total seats held by the party. On the rare occasions when an independent or third-party candidate is elected, the leaders of the two parties must agree on whose quota this member's committee assignments will count against.

The assignment of individual members to committees is a party decision. Each party has a "committee on committees" to make such decisions. Permission to transfer from one committee to another is also a party decision. Moreover, advancement up the committee ladder toward the chair is a party decision. Since the late nineteenth century, most advancements have been automatic— based upon the length of continual service on the committee. This seniority system has existed only because of the support of the two parties, and each party can depart from it by a simple vote. During the 1970s, both parties reinstitued the practice of reviewing each chairmanship—voting anew every two years on whether each chair would be continued. Few chairs have actually been removed, but notice has been served that the seniority system is no longer automatic and has thereby reminded everyone that all committee assignments are party decisions. Thus, although party leaders no longer can control the votes of many members, the party system itself remains an important factor.

The continuing importance of parties in Congress became especially evident during the first months of the Clinton administration in 1993. Initially, congressional Democrats gave Clinton's economic proposals virtually unanimous support (see Chapter 5). The Democratic leadership was eager to contribute to a successful start by the first Democratic president in twelve years. Democratic unity, in turn, prompted an unprecedented display of unity among Republican members of Congress as well. In April 1993, Senate Republicans responded to what they saw as Democratic "steamroller" tactics by staging a filibuster against Clinton's proposed economic stimulus package.

By remaining united, the forty-three Republican senators (joined by one Democrat) prevented the Senate from voting on the Clinton proposal and ended any chance of its enactment. With the Republicans united, a Democratic effort to end the filibuster could muster only fifty-six of the sixty votes needed for cloture. Republicans were concerned less with the substance of Clinton's spending proposal (though they did regard it as unnecessary and wasteful) than with their own isolation and weakness in the face of growing Democratic strength and confidence.[3] They hoped that by blocking this Clinton initiative they could demonstrate that they were a force with which the president would have to reckon.[4] The party unity achieved during this early period had to be sustained in the face of constituency, interest group, and ideological pressures that often cut across party lines and oblige members of Congress to ignore their leaders' wishes. As a result, it was not surprising to see party unity weaken as the year went on. The Democrats were the first to crumble. In the June 1993 vote on Clinton's economic program, more than thirty House Democrats, including eleven subcommittee chairs, deserted their party to vote with the Republicans. Giving the forces working against party unity in Congress, it is sometimes surprising when either party retains any cohesion at all.

THE PARTIES AND ELECTION OF THE PRESIDENT: THE ELECTORAL COLLEGE. The Constitution is silent on the selection of qualified candidates for president. The framers probably assumed that there would be a "favorite son" from each of several states and that the qualifications of each would be well known to at least some of the more prominent and well-traveled people elsewhere. In November every four years, the voters—who would vote only for electors, not directly for president—would presumably choose as electors these prominent and well-traveled people, who would exercise proper collective judgment in their choice of the best person for president. This is why the electors as a group came to be called the *electoral college,* although the Constitution does not use the term and the electors never meet nationwide as a group.

The Twelfth Amendment provided that

[3]Adam Clymer, "Republican Redux: Filibustering in Senate, G.O.P. Strives to Make Itself a Force to Deal With," *New York Times,* 5 April 1993, p. A14

[4]David Broder, "Unity 'Doormat' Trips Democrats: Hill Republicans Turn Democrats' Hardball Tactics Into Rallying Point," *Washington Post,* 3 April 1993, p. 1.

the electors would meet in their respective states following their election in November and that they would cast separate ballots for president and vice-president. The name of each person receiving an electoral vote for president would be put on a list that would show the number of electoral votes cast for each. The lists would be sent to the Senate to be counted in a joint session of Congress. If no candidate received a majority of all electoral votes, the names of the top three candidates would be submitted to the House, where each state would be able to cast one vote, regardless of size. Whether a state's vote would be decided by a majority, plurality, or some other fraction of the state's delegates would be determined under rules established by the House. Thus, the general election was to be a nominating process, and the real election was to take place every four years in the House.

The last time the electoral college failed to produce a majority was in 1824, when four candidates, John Quincy Adams, Andrew Jackson, Henry Clay, and William H. Crawford, divided the electoral vote. The House of Representatives eventually chose Adams over the others. After 1824, however, the two major political parties began to dominate presidential politics to such an extent that by December of each election year only two candidates remained. This freed the parties and the candidates from having to plan their campaigns to culminate in Congress, and Congress very quickly ceased to dominate the presidential selection process.

Until the 1830s, the most important candidates for president were nominated by caucuses of members of Congress. But once the two major parties had practically eliminated the House's role in the final selection of candidates, they created a means outside Congress altogether for making the initial nominations. That means was the national

convention, which has given the president a popular base independent of Congress. Although the parties themselves have been weakened by the provisions in forty-seven states for selecting convention delegates by primaries, the two-party system still keeps Congress out of the selection process and keeps the presidency independent of Congress.

Although it has not functioned as the framers anticipated, the electoral college continues to be a part of the American presidential selection process. When Americans go to the polls on election day, they are technically not voting directly for presidential candidates, but rather are choosing among slates of electors selected by each state's party leadership. These electors are pledged, if elected, to support that party's presidential candidate. In each state, the slate that wins casts all the state's electoral votes for its party's candidate. Each state is entitled to a number of electoral votes equal to the state's senators and representatives combined for a total of 535 electoral votes for the fifty states.

In each state, the electors whose slate has won proceed to the state's capital on the Monday following the second Wednesday in December and formally cast their ballots. These are sent to Washington, tallied by the Congress in January, and the name of the winner is formally announced. On all but three occasions in American history, the electoral vote has simply ratified the nationwide popular vote. However, since electoral votes are won on a state-by-state basis, it is mathematically possible for a candidate who receives a nationwide popular plurality to fail to carry states whose electoral votes would add up to a majority. Thus, in 1876, Rutherford B. Hayes was the winner in the electoral college despite receiving fewer popular votes than his rival, Samuel Tilden. In 1888, Grover Cleveland received more popular votes than Benjamin Harrison but received fewer electoral votes.

The possibility that in some future election the electoral college will, once again, produce an outcome that is inconsistent with the popular vote has led to many calls for the abolition of this institution and the introduction of some form of direct popular election of the president. The 1992 Perot candidacy, at one point, opened the possibility of a discrepancy between the popular and electoral totals and even raised the specter of an election decided in the House of Representatives.

But efforts to introduce such a reform are usually blocked by political forces that believe they benefit from the present system. Minority groups that are influential in large urban states with many electoral votes feel that their voting strength would be diminished in a direct, nationwide, popular election. At the same time, some Republicans believe that their party's usual presidential strength in the South and West gives them a distinct advantage in the electoral college. There is little doubt, however, that an election resulting in a discrepancy between the electoral and popular outcomes would create irresistible political pressure to eliminate the electoral college and introduce direct popular election of the president.

Facilitation of Mass Electoral Choice

Parties facilitate mass electoral choice. As the late Harvard political scientist V. O. Key pointed out long ago, the persistence over time of competition between groups possessing a measure of identity and continuity is a necessary condition for electoral control.[5] Party identity increases the elector-

ate's capacity to recognize its options. Consistent party division organizes voters in a way necessary to sustain any popular influence in the governmental process. In the absence of party division, the voter is, in Key's words, confronted constantly by "new faces, new choices," and little basis exists for "effectuation of the popular will."[6]

Even more significant, however, is the fact that party organization is generally an essential ingredient for effective electoral competition by groups lacking substantial economic or institutional resources. Party building has typically been the strategy pursued by groups that must organize the collective energies of large numbers of individuals to counter their opponents' superior material means or institutional standing. Historically, disciplined and coherent party organizations were generally developed first by groups representing the political aspirations of the working classes. Parties, French political scientist Maurice Duverger notes, "are always more developed on the Left than on the Right because they are always more necessary on the Left than on the Right."[7]

In the United States, the first mass party was built by the Jeffersonians as a counterweight to the superior social, institutional, and economic resources of the incumbent Federalists. In a subsequent period of American history, the efforts of the Jacksonians to construct a coherent mass party organization were impelled by a similar set of circumstances. Only by organizing the power of numbers could the Jacksonian coalition hope to compete successfully against the superior resources that could be mobilized by its adversaries.

[5]V. O. Key, *Southern Politics* (New York: Random House, 1949), Chapter 14.

[6]Ibid.

[7]Maurice Duverger, *Political Parties* (New York: Wiley, 1954), p. 426.

The political success of party organizations forced their opponents to copy them in order to meet the challenge. It was, as Duverger points out, "contagion from the Left," that led politicians of the Center and Right to attempt to build strong party organizations.[8] These efforts were sometimes successful. In the United States during the 1830s, the Whig party, which was led by northeastern business interests, carefully copied the organizational techniques devised by the Jacksonians. The Whigs won control of the national government in 1840. But even when groups nearer the top of the social scale responded in kind to organizational efforts by their opponents, the effect nonetheless was to give lower-class groups an opportunity to compete on a more equal footing.

If no one is organized, middle- and upper-class factions almost inevitably have a substantial competitive edge over their lower-class rivals. But if both sides are organized, the net effect is still to erode the relative advantage of the well-off. Parties of the Right, moreover, were seldom actually able to equal the organizational coherence of the working-class opposition. As Duverger and others have observed, middle- and upper-class parties generally failed to construct organizations as effective as those built by their working-class foes, who typically commanded larger and more easily disciplined forces.

While political parties continue to be significant in the United States, the role of party organizations in electoral politics has clearly declined over the past three decades. This decline, and the partial replacement of the party by new forms of electoral technology, is one of the most important developments in twentieth-century American politics.

[8]Ibid., Chapter 1.

Weakening of Party Organization

Opposition to party politics was the basis for a number of the institutional reforms of the American political process at the turn of the twentieth century during the so-called Progressive Era. Many Progressive reformers were motivated by a sincere desire to rid politics of corruption and to improve the quality and efficiency of government in the United States. But simultaneously from the perspective of middle- and upper-class Progressives and the financial, commercial, and industrial elites with which they were often associated, the weakening or elimination of party organization would also mean that power could more readily be acquired and retained by the "best men"—those with wealth, position, and education.

The list of anti-party reforms of the Progressive Era is a familiar one. Ballot reform took away the parties' privilege of printing and distributing ballots and introduced the possibility of split-ticket voting. The introduction of nonpartisan local elections eroded grassroots party organization. The extension of "merit systems" for administrative appointments stripped party organizations of their vitally important access to patronage and thus reduced their ability to recruit workers. The development of the direct primary reduced party leaders' capacity to control candidate nominations. These reforms obviously did not destroy political parties as entities, but taken together they did substantially weaken party organizations in the United States.

After the turn of the century, the organizational strength of American political parties gradually diminished. Between the two world wars, organization remained the major tool available to contending electoral forces, but in most areas of the country the "reformed" state and local parties that survived the Progressive Era gradually lost their organizational vitality and coherence, and they became less effective campaign tools. While most areas of the nation continued to boast Democratic and Republican party groupings, reform meant the elimination of the permanent mass organizations that had been the parties' principal campaign weapons.

High-Tech Politics

As a result of Progressive reform, American party organizations entered the twentieth century with rickety substructures. As the use of civil service, primary elections, and other Progressive innovations spread, the strength of party organizations eroded. By the end of World War II, political scientists were already beginning to bemoan the absence of party discipline and "party responsibility" in the United States. This erosion of the parties' organizational strength set the stage for the introduction of new political techniques that represented radical departures from the campaign practices perfected during the nineteenth century. In place of manpower and organization, contending forces began to employ intricate electronic communications techniques to attract electoral support. This new political technology includes five basic elements.

1. *Polling.* Surveys of voter opinion provide the information that candidates and their staffs use to craft campaign strategies. Candidates use polls to select issues, to assess their own strengths and weaknesses as well as those of the opposition, to check voter response to the campaign, and to determine the degree to which various constituent groups are susceptible to campaign appeals. In recent years, pollsters have become central figures in most national campaigns. Indeed, Patrick Caddell, who polled for the 1976 Carter campaign, became part of Carter's inner circle of advisers and ultimately played a role in major policy decisions.[9] Virtually all contemporary campaigns for national and statewide office as well as many local campaigns make extensive use of opinion surveys. Republican pollsters were instrumental in persuading George Bush to select Dan Quayle as his running mate in 1988, arguing that their data showed Quayle to have strong appeal to the critically important "baby boom" group of voters in their thirties and forties.

2. *The broadcast media.* Extensive use of the electronic media, television in particular, has become the hallmark of the modern political campaign. One commonly used broadcast technique is the thirty- or sixty-second television spot advertisement that permits the candidate's message to be delivered to a target audience before uninterested or hostile viewers can psychologically, or physically, tune it out. Famous recent examples are George Bush's "Willie Horton" ad in the 1988 presidential campaign, which portrayed Michael Dukakis as soft on crime by showing a frightening close-up picture of Mr. Horton, a convicted felon who raped a woman while on a weekend furlough from a Massachusetts prison, and Lyndon Johnson's famous "daisy girl" ad in 1964, discussed in detail in Box 10.2.

Television spot ads and other media techniques are designed to establish candidate name identification, to create a favorable image of the candidate and a negative image of the opponent, to link the candidate with desirable groups in the community, and to communicate the candidate's stands

---

[9]Richard A. Joslyn, *Mass Media Elections* (New York: Random House, 1984).

BOX 10.2
The Daisy Girl

On September 7, 1964, NBC TV's "Monday Night at the Movies" was interrupted by what came to be one of the most famous and controversial political commercials ever shown on American television. In this ad, a little girl with long, light brown hair stood in a field picking daisy petals. As she pulled the petals, she counted 1-2-3, etc. As she counted, the voice of an announcer in the background counted backward, 10-9-8, and so on. As the counts continued, the announcer's voice became louder and the girl's voice more muted until the girl reached 10 and the announcer counted down to 0. At that point, a blinding nuclear explosion occurred destroying everything, with President Johnson saying, "These are the stakes. To make a world in which all of God's children can live or go into the dark. We must either love each other or we must die." The announcer then urged viewers to vote for President Johnson on November 3. The ad was cut after one use, but the use of short spots continued.

Source: Photo courtesy of the Lyndon Baines Johnson Library.

on selected issues. These spot ads can have an important electoral impact. Generally, media campaigns attempt to follow the guidelines indicated by a candidate's polls. Advertisements seek to tap a responsive chord with voters to reinforce existing loyalties.

The broadcast media are now so central to modern campaigns that most of a candidate's activities are tied to their media strategies.[10] For example, a sizable percentage of most candidates' newspaper ads are now used mainly to advertise radio and television appearances. Other candidate activities are designed expressly to stimulate television news coverage. For instance, incumbent senators running for re-election or

[10]Larry J. Sabato, *The Rise of Political Consultants* (New York: Basic Books, 1981).

for higher office almost always sponsor committee or subcommittee hearings to generate publicity. In recent years, Senate hearings on hunger, crime, health, and defense have been used mainly to attract television cameras.

The 1992 presidential election introduced three new media techniques: the talk show interview, the "electronic town hall" meeting, and the infomercial. Candidates used television and radio talk show and interview programs such as "Larry King Live," "Good Morning America," the "Rush Limbaugh" radio program, and even Arsenio Hall's late-night TV program to reach mass audiences. From the perspective of the candidates, these television and radio appearances offered excellent opportunities to appeal for the support of millions of potential voters. Because these are entertainment programs, viewers are perceived to be more relaxed and, hence, potentially more susceptible to candidates' appeals. Some programs allow listeners or viewers to call in, and this gives candidates a chance to demonstrate that they are responsive to ordinary people and sympathetic to their problems.

Similarly, the "town meeting" format gave a candidate the chance to appear in a hall with a group of ordinary citizens, answer their questions, and listen to their ideas. Bill Clinton felt that he was very effective in this format and insisted that one of the presidential debates be organized as a town meeting. After the election, Clinton hosted a series of televised meetings on the economy and promised to continue to make himself available to the public during his term in office. He and his aides viewed the town meeting as an excellent mechanism for bolstering public support.

Talk show appearances and town meetings, moreover, allowed candidates to avoid the twin problems usually associated with political use of the media—cost and filtering. Normally, candidates must spend hundreds of thousands—even millions—of dollars for the use of commercial television time, while press conferences and news program "sound bite" appearances left candidates at the mercy of media interpretations and possibly unfriendly editing. The talk show format gave candidates a free opportunity to present themselves and their ideas—often in the company of a congenial host—to millions of Americans without the media filtering or editorial revision that might undermine their presentations. For these reasons, in 1992, talk show appearances came to be the preferred candidate campaign vehicle. [11] The Larry King program became one of Ross Perot's major campaign vehicles, while George Bush made good use of a conservative radio host, Rush Limbaugh. Probably the most unusual talk show appearance of the campaign was Bill Clinton's saxophone solo on the Arsenio Hall show. Political pundits were divided on the electoral value of Clinton's performance. Music critics, however, all seemed to agree that Clinton should stick to politics.

In addition to making talk show appearances, independent candidate Ross Perot purchased several thirty-minute network television slots to present detailed expositions of his ideas and programs. In the early days of television, candidates often scheduled fifteen- and even thirty-minute presentations. This format, however, was abandoned because of its cost and because only a candidate's strongest supporters would take the time to watch such a long presentation. In essence, candidates were paying a great deal of money to preach to the already committed.

In recent years, changes in television cost

[11] See Howard Kurtz, "The Talk Show Campaign," *Washington Post*, 28 October 1992, p. 1.

structures have made thirty-minute slots available at reasonable prices. At any rate, from billionaire Perot's perspective, the several million dollars that his lengthy infomercials cost was certainly not prohibitive. After all, Perot was prepared to spend more than $60 million of his own money to finance his presidential bid. To the surprise of many analysts, Perot was able to attract large audiences for his detailed discussions of the nation's budget deficit and other economic topics. Perhaps the well-educated electorate of the 1990s is more willing than was the electorate of the 1950s to devote its time and attention to discourse and explanation. If so, we may see the thirty-second spot ad give way more and more to the thirty- or even sixty-minute infomercial in the years to come.

The most dramatic use of the electronic media in contemporary electoral politics is the televised debate. Televised presidential debates began with the 1960 Kennedy-Nixon clash. Today, candidates for many public offices hold debates during the weeks prior to the election. In 1992, the three leading presidential contenders, George Bush, Bill Clinton, and Ross Perot, debated on three occasions. Their respective running mates, Dan Quayle, Al Gore, and James Stockdale, met once. These presidential debates are held so late in the campaign season that they usually do not change many votes. Most viewers have already decided which candidate they will support and tend to use the debate to confirm their choice. Generally, viewers will perceive the candidate they already favor as the winner of the debate. This is especially true for viewers with strong partisan leanings. Republicans as a rule thought that George Bush was the stronger performer in the 1992 presidential debates, whereas Democrats were convinced that Bill Clinton was.

The debates do, however, allow candidates to reach the few viewers who have not fully made up their minds about the election. Moreover, the debates can enhance the credibility of lesser-known candidates. Thus, in 1960, little-known Senator Jack Kennedy was able to use a solid debate performance to become a credible (and eventually victorious) candidate in a race against his much better-known and experienced rival, Richard Nixon. In 1992, the presidential debates gave a major boost to the candidacy of Ross Perot. The opportunity to appear on an equal footing with the Democratic and Republican nominees and to show that he could—at the very least—hold his own against them gave Perot a chance to persuade uncommitted voters that he was a serious and credible candidate.

3. *Phone banks.* Through the broadcast media, candidates communicate with voters *en masse* and impersonally. Phone banks allow campaign workers to make personal contact with hundreds of thousands of voters. Personal contacts of this sort are thought to be extremely effective. Again, poll data serve to identify the groups that will be targeted for phone calls. Computers select phone numbers from areas in which members of these groups are concentrated. Staffs of paid or volunteer callers, using computer-assisted dialing systems and prepared scripts, then place calls to deliver the candidate's message. The targeted groups are generally those identified by polls as either uncommitted or weakly committed, as well as strong supporters of the candidate who are contacted simply to encourage them to vote.

Phone banks are used extensively in pivotal contests. Before the 1980 Iowa caucuses, for example, Democratic and Republican presidential hopefuls placed a total of more than three million phone calls to Iowa's 1.7 million registered voters. During the same year, former President Carter was reported to have personally placed between twenty and forty calls every night to homes in key primary and caucus states. On some New Hampshire blocks, a dozen or more residents eventually received telephone calls from the president.[12]

4. *Direct mail.* Direct mail serves both as a vehicle for communicating with voters and as a mechanism for raising funds. The first step in a direct mail campaign is the purchase or rental of a computerized mailing list of voters deemed to have some particular perspective or social characteristic. Often sets of magazine subscription lists or lists of donors to various causes are employed. For example, a candidate interested in reaching conservative voters might rent subscription lists from *National Review, Human Events,* and *Conservative Digest,* or a candidate interested in appealing to liberals might rent subscription lists from the *New York Review of Books* or the *New Republic.* Considerable fine-tuning is possible. After obtaining the appropriate mailing lists, candidates usually send pamphlets, letters, and brochures describing themselves and their views to voters believed to be sympathetic. Different types of mail appeals are made to different electoral subgroups.

In addition to use as a political advertising medium, direct mail has also become an important source of campaign funds. Computerized mailing lists permit campaign strategists to pinpoint individuals whose interests, background, and activities suggest that they may be potential donors to the campaign. Letters of solicitation are sent to these potential donors. Some of the money raised is then used to purchase additional mailing lists. Direct mail solicitation can be enormously effective.[13]

5. *Professional public relations.* Modern campaigns and the complex technology upon which they rely are typically directed by professional public relations consultants. Virtually all serious contenders for national and statewide office retain the services of professional campaign consultants. Increasingly, candidates for local office, too, have come to rely upon professional campaign managers. Consultants offer candidates the expertise necessary to conduct accurate opinion polls, produce television commercials, organize direct mail campaigns, and make use of sophisticated computer analyses. A "full-service" firm will arrange

> advertising campaigns for radio, television, and newspapers, including layout, timing, and the actual placing of advertisements; public relations and press services, including the organization of public meetings, preparation and distribution of press releases and statements, and detailed travel arrangements for the candidate; research and presentation of issues, including preparation of position papers, speech writing, and arranging for consultations between candidates and outside experts in appropriate areas of public policy; fundraising solicitations, both by mail and through testimonial dinners and other public events; public opinion sampling to test voter response to the campaign and voter attitudes on major issues; technical assistance on radio and television production, including the hiring of cameramen and recording studios for political films and broadcasts; campaign budgeting assistance designed to put campaign funds to the best possible use; use of data processing techniques to plan campaign strategy based on computer evaluations of thousands of bits of information; and mobilization of support through traditional door-to-door campaigns and telephone solicitation of voters.[14]

Several of the components of this "new" political technology were, of course, devel-

---

[12]Sabato, *Rise of Political Consultants,* p. 218.

[13]Ibid., p. 250.

[14]Joslyn, *Mass Media Elections,* p. 33.

oped long before World War II. Professional public relations firms first became involved in electoral politics in 1934, when the firm of Whittaker and Baxter helped to defeat novelist Upton Sinclair's Socialist candidacy in the California gubernatorial race by charging that Sinclair was a Communist. The firm was hired by California business interests. Primitive opinion polls were used in American elections as early as 1824, and relatively sophisticated surveys were employed extensively during the 1880s and 1890s.

After the Second World War, however, the introduction of television and the computer provided the mechanisms that became the electronic heart of the modern campaign. These electronic innovations coincided with a growing realization on the part of politicians and activists that the capacity of traditional party organizations to mobilize voters had greatly diminished. As this realization spread, a small number of candidates began to experiment with new campaign methods. The initial trickle of political techniques proved generally more effective than the more traditional campaign efforts that could be mounted by the now-debilitated party organizations.

In a number of well-publicized congressional, senatorial, and gubernatorial campaigns during the postwar years, candidates using the new campaign methods decisively defeated rivals who continued to rely on the older organizational techniques. The successful campaigns mounted by Richard Nixon, who relied on professional public relations in the 1948 California Senate race, and Jacob Javits, who made brilliant use of poll data in his 1948 New York congressional race, were very visible examples of the power of technology.

The number of technologically oriented campaigns increased greatly after 1971. The Federal Elections Campaign Act of that year prompted the creation of large numbers of political action committees (PACs) by a host of corporate and ideological groups. This development increased the availability of funds to political candidates—conservative candidates in particular—which meant in turn that the new technology could be used more extensively.

Initially, the new techniques were employed mainly by individual candidates who often made little or no effort to coordinate their campaigns with those of other political aspirants sharing the same party label. For this reason, campaigns employing the new technology sometimes came to be called "candidate-centered" efforts, as distinguished from the traditional party-coordinated campaign. Nothing about the new technology, however, precluded its use by political party leaders seeking to coordinate a number of campaigns. In recent years, party leaders, Republicans in particular, have learned to make good use of modern campaign technology. The difference between the old and new political methods is not that the latter is inherently candidate-centered while the former is strictly a party tool. The difference is, rather, a matter of the types of political resources upon which each method depends.

From Labor-Intensive to Capital-Intensive Politics

With the new political technique the party organization became less important, resulting in a shift from labor-intensive to capital-intensive campaigns. Campaign tasks once performed by masses of party workers and some cash now require fewer personnel but a great deal more money. The new political style depends on polls, computers, and other electronic paraphernalia. Of course, even when manpower and organization were the key electoral tools, money had considerable political significance. Nevertheless, during the nineteenth century, national political campaigns in the United States employed millions of workers. Indeed, as many as 2.5 million individuals were employed in political work during the 1880s.[15] The direct cost of campaigns, therefore, was relatively low. For example, in 1860, Abraham Lincoln spent only $100,000—which was approximately twice the amount spent by his chief opponent, Stephen Douglas.

Modern campaigns depend heavily on money. Each element of the new political technology is enormously expensive. A sixty-second spot announcement on prime-time network television costs hundreds of thousands of dollars each time it is aired. Opinion surveys can be quite expensive. Polling costs in a statewide race can easily reach or exceed the six-figure mark. Campaign consultants can charge substantial fees.

A direct mail campaign can eventually become an important source of funds but is very expensive to initiate. The inauguration of a serious national direct mail effort requires at least $1 million in "front end cash" to pay for mailing lists, brochures, letters, envelopes, and postage.[16] While the cost of televised debates is covered by the sponsoring organizations and the television stations and is thus free to the candidates, even debate preparation requires substantial staff work and research, and money.

It is the expense of the new technology that accounts for the enormous cost of recent American national elections. According to the nonpartisan Citizen's Research Foundation, an organization committed to campaign reform, total spending in the United States for all campaigning rose by 13 percent from 1956 to 1960 (from $155 million to $175 million) and by 14 percent between 1960 and 1964 (to $200 million). The increase grew to 50 percent between 1964 and 1968 (to $300 million), and another 42 percent increase occurred between 1968 an 1972 (to $425 million). Expenditures exceeded the half-billion-dollar mark ($540 million) in 1976, and the billion-dollar mark in 1988 and 1992.

In recent years, Congress has sought to regulate campaign finance. The Supreme Court, however, has limited the effect of this legislation by declaring unconstitutional any absolute limits on the freedom of individuals to spend their own money on campaigns.[17] The Federal Elections Campaign Act of 1971 imposed contribution limits and provided for full disclosure of all campaign receipts and expenditures (see Box 10.3).

In 1990 and 1991, congressional efforts to strengthen campaign finance rules were blocked by partisan conflicts, with each party only willing to support rules that it saw helping its own interests and hurting the opposition. Democrats, who benefit from incumbency, proposed public financing and spending limits that would thwart challengers. Republicans, who raise most of their money through direct mail, supported limits on the PAC spending upon which Democrats depend for nearly 25 percent of their campaign funds. Republicans, by contrast, depend upon PACs for only about 2 percent of their campaign funds.[18]

In 1993, President Clinton proposed a new set of campaign spending rules designed to limit the size of campaign contri-

---

[15] M. Ostrogorski, *Democracy and the Organization of Political Parties* (New York: Macmillan, 1902).

[16] Timothy Clark, "The RNC Prospers, the DNC Struggles as They Face the 1980 Election," *National Journal*, 27 October 1980, p. 1619.

[17] Buckley v. Valeo, 421, U.S. 1 (1976).

[18] *Congressional Quarterly Weekly Report*, 29 September 1990, p. 3089.

BOX 10.3
Federal Campaign Finance Regulation

Campaign Contributions

No individual may contribute more than $1,000 to any one candidate in any single election. Individuals may contribute as much as $20,000 to a national party commitee and up to $5,000 to a political action committee. Full disclosure is required by candidates of all contributions oveer $100. Candidates may not accept cash contributions over $100.

Political Action Committees

Any corporation, labor union, trade association or other organization may establish a political action committee (PAC). PACs must contribute to the campaigns of at least five different candidates and may contribute as much as $5,000 per candidate in any given election.

Presidential Elections

Candidates in presidential primaries may receive federal matching funds if they raise at least $5,000 in each of twenty states. The money raised must come in contributions of $250 and less. The amount raised by candidates in this way is matched by the federal government, dollar for dollar, up to a limit of $5 million. In the general election, major party candidates' campaigns are fully funded by the federal government. Candidates may spend no money beyond their federal funding. But independent groups may spend money on behalf of a candidate so long as their efforts are not directly tied to the official campaign. Minor-party candidates may be entitled to partial federal funding.

Federal Election Commission (FEC)

The six-member FEC supervises federal elections, collects and publicizes campaign finance records, and investigates violations of federal campaign finance law.

butions, to delimit campaign spending, and to provide congressional candidates with public funds to replace at least some of the private monies they are currently compelled to raise. His proposal would reduce the influence of business interests, thereby strengthening liberal, public interest groups that depend less on money to secure politi-

cal influence. In June 1993, the Senate passed a bill that contained some, but not all, of Clinton's proposals. The Senate bill contained provisions outlawing PAC contributions, introduced mechanisms for reducing campaign spending, and prohibited lobbyists from making contributions to senators they had lobbied within the preceding year. The bill provided only a limited role for public funding of campaigns. Designed to help incumbents rather than to serve only the interests of the Democratic party, the bill had some Republican support, whereas President Clinton's initial proposal had none.[19] Clinton's campaign finance reform plan is discussed more fully in Chapter 11.

Certainly "people power" is not irrelevant to modern political campaigns. Candidates continue to utilize the political services of tens of thousands of volunteer workers. Nevertheless, in the contemporary era, even the recruitment of volunteer campaign workers has become a matter of electronic technology. Employing a technique called "instant organization," paid telephone callers use phone banks to contact individuals in areas targeted by a computer (which they do when contacting potential voters, as we discussed before). Volunteer workers are recruited from among these individuals. A number of campaigns—Richard Nixon's 1968 presidential campaign was the first—have successfully used this technique.

The displacement of organizational methods by the new political technology has the most far-reaching implications for the balance of power among contending political groups. Labor-intensive organizational tactics allowed parties whose chief support came from groups nearer the bottom of the social scale to use the numerical superiority of their forces as a partial counterweight to the institutional and economic resources more readily available to the opposition. The capital-intensive technological format, by contrast, has given a major boost to the political fortunes of those whose supporters are better able to furnish the large sums needed to compete effectively.[20] Indeed, the new technology permits financial resources to be more effectively harnessed and exploited than was ever before possible.

In a political process lacking strong party organizations, the likelihood that groups that do not possess substantial economic or institutional resources can acquire some measure of power is severely diminished. Dominated by the new technology, electoral politics becomes a contest in which the wealthy and powerful have a decided advantage.

Is the Party Over?

Of course, the Democratic and Republican parties still exist. The contemporary parties, however, differ from their predecessors. In recent decades, the Democrats and Republicans have become entrenched in distinct segments of the national governmental apparatus. The Democrats have a hold on Congress, in federal social service, in labor and regulatory agencies, and in government bureaucracies and nonprofit organizations on the state and local levels that help administer national social programs. This entrenchment has its roots in Franklin D. Roosevelt's New Deal and Lyndon Johnson's Great Society programs that expanded the size and institutional capacities of the national government's domestic agencies. These developments have transformed the Democrats

---

[19] See Richard L. Berke, "Clinton Unveils Plan to Restrict PAC Influence," *New York Times,* 8 May 1993; and Helen Dewar and Kenneth Cooper, "Campaign Finance Bill Is Approved by Senate," *Washington Post,* 18 June 1993, p. A20.

[20] For discussions of the consequences, see Thomas Edsall, *The New Politics of Inequality* (New York: W. W. Norton, 1985). See also Thomas Edsall, "Both Parties Get the Campaign's Money—But the Boss Backs the GOP," *Washington Post National Weekly Edition,* 16 September 1986, p. 14; and Benjamin Ginsberg, "Money and Power: The New Political Economy of American Elections," in *The Political Economy,* ed. Thomas Ferguson and Joel Rogers (Armonk, NY: M.E. Sharpe, 1984).

PROCESS BOX 10.2
How to Run for Political Office

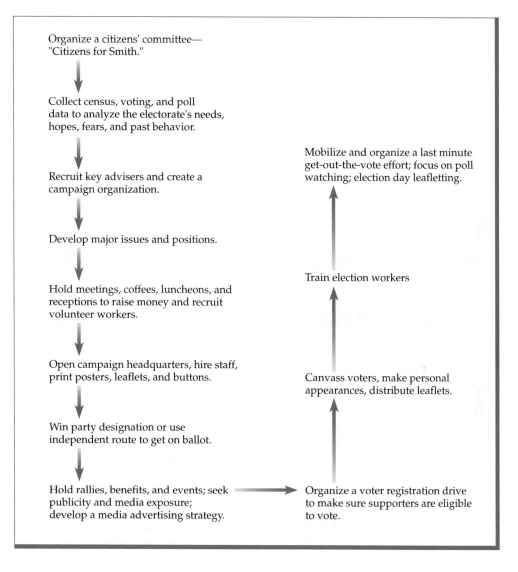

Organize a citizens' committee—
"Citizens for Smith."

Collect census, voting, and poll
data to analyze the electorate's needs,
hopes, fears, and past behavior.

Recruit key advisers and create a
campaign organization.

Develop major issues and positions.

Hold meetings, coffees, luncheons, and
receptions to raise money and recruit
volunteer workers.

Open campaign headquarters, hire staff,
print posters, leaflets, and buttons.

Win party designation or use
independent route to get on ballot.

Hold rallies, benefits, and events; seek
publicity and media exposure;
develop a media advertising strategy.

Mobilize and organize a last minute
get-out-the-vote effort; focus on poll
watching; election day leafletting.

Train election workers

Canvass voters, make personal
appearances, distribute leaflets.

Organize a voter registration drive
to make sure supporters are eligible
to vote.

from a political force based upon state and local party machines into one grounded in Congress and the domestic state.

In 1993, the Democrats sought to entrench themselves still further in the domestic state apparatus. The three chief vehicles for this effort were President Clinton's economic policy proposals, health care reform proposals, and political reform initiatives. Clinton's economic package entailed substantial tax increases and cuts in military spending. In this way, the administration hoped to make additional revenues available for Democratic social programs and agencies that had been starved for funding through twelve years of Republican rule.

Comparing the 1992 Republican and Democratic Platforms: Close on Economics, Distant on Social Issues

Political cynics often criticize America's political parties by saying that "there's not a dime's worth of difference between them." If this claim is true, it lends fuel to the fires of critics who say that the political parties have failed in their purpose of offering the voters a real choice. While there are indeed similarities, an examination of the party platforms from the 1992 presidential election reveals a few differences.

Both parties focused much attention on the role of government and economic issues. The Republican platform claimed proudly that it "cut taxes, reduced red tape, put people above bureaucracy. And . . . we vanquished the idea of the almighty state as the supervisor of our daily lives." The Democratic platform took a similar anti-government stand, noting the "anguish and the anger of the American people . . . directed . . . at Government itself," and calling for "a revolution in Government—to take power away from entrenched bureaucracies and narrow interests in Washington and put it back in the hands of ordinary people."

Both parties emphasized the need to create jobs. The Republicans stressed promoting economic growth to expand job opportunities. The Democrats took a similar tack by urging job creation in both the private and the public sector. Both parties addressed the problem of the federal budget deficit; the Republicans emphasized tax cuts to stimulate economic growth, while the Democrats stressed cuts in government spending levels.

Clinton's health care reform proposals promised to create an enormous new set of agencies and institutions that would permit Democrats to substantially expand their influence over an area representing nearly 15 percent of the domestic economy, while simultaneously attaching major constituency groups to the Democratic party.

Finally, Clinton proposed changes in campaign spending rules that would generally work to the advantage of liberal, public-interest groups and Democratic incumbents. He signed the "motor voter" bill, which potentially could bring larger numbers of mainly Democratic poor and minority voters to the polls. And he proposed reforms of the Hatch Act that would permit the heavily Democratic federal civil service to play a larger role in the political process.[21]

[21]Chuck Alston, "Democrats Flex New Muscle with Trio of Election Bills: Some Republicans Say That 'Motor Voter,' Campaign Finance and Hatch Act Bills Add Up to Permanent Power Grab," *Congressional Quarterly Weekly Report*, 20 March 1993, pp. 643–45.

The parties echoed similar themes on another spending issue—welfare. The Republicans claimed, "Today's welfare system is anti-work and anti-marriage." Departing from past platforms, the Democrats also adopted a strict tone: "Welfare should be a second chance, not a way of life. We want to break the cycle of welfare."

The greatest differences between the party platforms appeared in the realm of social issues. For example, the Republicans advocated a constitutional amendment prohibiting abortion under all circumstances, even including instances in which the life of the woman is at stake. (President Bush himself continued to favor abortion in such cases and in cases of rape or incest.) The Republican platform also opposed gay rights and birth control counseling; it favored school prayer, the construction of a barrier along the country's southern border to keep illegal immigrants out, and tuition tax credits for parents wishing to send their children to private and parochial schools.

In contrast, the Democrats supported abortion rights, including the enactment of protective national legislation. In addition, the platform also supported an end to the military's ban on gay soldiers and expanded health care and family planning efforts.

On the environment, the Republican platform emphasized development by saying, "Our public lands should not be arbitrarily locked up and put off limits to responsible

uses." The Democratic platform emphasized conservation: "We will protect our old-growth forests, preserve critical habitats . . . wetlands . . . soil, water, air, oppose new offshore oil drilling and mineral exploration." The Democrats expressed similar concerns about global warming, ozone depletion in the air, and biodiversity.

While both parties seemed to lean in the same more conservative direction in 1992, both still sought to emphasize their differences in order to woo voters.

Taken together, these proposals represented a bold effort to ensure continuing Democratic control of the government. Adoption of these proposals would solidify the Democratic party's institutional base in the bureaucracies of the executive branch while making it all the more difficult for Republicans to dislodge the Democrats through electoral methods.

The Republicans, in turn, have controlled the White House during the past quarter century, and still control the national security apparatus, sectors of the economy that benefit from military spending, and those segments of American society threatened by the welfare and regulatory state built by the Democrats. This was one of the major factors behind the efforts of the Reagan administration during the 1980s to increase levels of defense spending while reducing domestic social spending. In essence, Reagan sought to direct the flow of federal funds into agencies and institutions associated with the Republicans while reducing the flow of funds into those sectors of the government in which the Democrats were entrenched.

During the budget debates of the late 1980s and early 1990s, congressional Democrats sought to reverse this state of affairs by diminishing funding for the national security sector and increasing funding levels for the domestic social and regulatory sectors. Initially, Democratic efforts seemed to succeed. In the 1990 budget negotiations, congressional Democrats were able to defeat President Bush by producing a budget that opened the way for higher levels of social spending. Although the Persian Gulf War increased the popular standing and prestige of the national security sector, the collapse of the Soviet Union made it more difficult for Republicans to argue for the continuation of Cold War levels of military spending. Until the end of the Bush administration, proponents of defense spending were able to block demands for sharp cuts in the military. Once Democrats were in control of the White House, however, they made it clear that levels of defense spending would drop significantly.

To a considerable extent, this competitive entrenchment of Republicans and Democrats is a substitute for mass electoral mobilization as a means of securing power in the United States today. This is one reason why high levels of partisan conflict coexist with low rates of voter participation in contemporary American politics. To today's parties, traditional electoral politics is only one arena of political combat. In between elections, the Democrats and Republicans engage in institutional struggles with outcomes every bit as important as the verdict at the ballot box. We will discuss the impact of this situation in depth in Chapter 12.

Time Line on Political Parties

EVENTS	1800	INSTITUTIONAL DEVELOPMENTS
Parties form in Congress (1790s)		Washington peacefully assumes the presidency (1789)
Washington's Farewell Address warns against parties (1796) Republican Thomas Jefferson elected president (1800)		First party system—Federalists v. Republicans (1790s)
		Federalists try to retain power by Alien and Sedition Acts (1798) and by appointing "midnight judges" (1801)
Jefferson renominated by congressional caucus; re-elected by a landslide (1804)		Congressional caucuses nominate presidential candidates from each party (1804–1831)
Republican James Monroe re-elected president; no Federalist candidate; no caucuses called (1820)		Destruction of Federalists; period of one partyism; "era of good feelings" (1810s–1830s)

EVENTS		INSTITUTIONAL DEVELOPMENTS
		Republican party splinter into National Republicans (Adams) and Democratice Republicans (Jackson) (1824)
Democrat Andrew Jackson elected president, ushering in "era of common man" (1828)		Democrats use party rotation to replace National Republicans in government positions (1829)
National nominating conventions held by Democrats and National Republicans (1831)	**1830**	National nominating conventions replace caucuses as method of selecting presidential candidates from each party (1830s)
Whig presidential candidates lose to Democratic candidate Martin Van Buren (1840)		Second party system–Whig party forms in opposition to Jackson–Democrats v. Whigs (1830s–1850s)
Whig WilliamHenry Harrison elected president (1860)		Whigs gain presidency and majority in Congress; both parties organized down to the precinct level (1840)
Republican Abraham Lincoln elected president (1860)	**1850**	Third party system; destruction of Whigs; creation of Republicans— Democrats v. Republicans (1850s–1890s)
Civil War (1861–1865)		
Reconstruction (1865–1877)		
Republican William McKinley elected president; Democrats decimated (1896)	**1890**	Fourth party system; both the Democratic and Republican parties are rebuilt along new lines (1890s–1930s)
Era of groups and movements; millions of southern and eastern European immigrants arrive in U.S. (1870s–1890s)		Shrinking electorate; enactment of Progressive reforms, including registration laws, primary elections, the Australian ballot, and civil service reform; decline of party machines; emergence of many one-party states (1890s)
Democrat Franklin D. Roosevelt elected president (1932)	**1930**	Fifth party system; period of New Deal Democratic dominance (1930s–1960s)
Democratic convention—party badly damaged; Republican Richard Nixon elected president (1968)	**1960**	Disruption of New Deal coalition; decay of party organizations (1968)
		Federal Election Campaign Act regulates campaign finance (1971)

EVENTS		INSTITUTIONAL DEVELOPMENTS
Watergate scandal (1973–1974)		Introductionof new political techniques (1970s and 1980s)
Nixon resigns (1974)		
Republican Ronald Reagan elected president; Republican presidential ascendancy begins (1980)	**1980**	Efforts by Republicans to build a national party structure (1980s)
Republican George Bush elected president; Democrats continue to control House and Senate (1988 and 1990)	**1990**	Continuation of divided government, with Democrats controlling Congress and Republicans the White House (1980s–1992)
Partisan struggle over budget and Persian Gulf War (1990–1991)		
Democrat Bill Clinton elected president; Democrats retain control of House and Senate (1992)		High levels of congressional party unity and partisan conflict as Democrats seek to strengthen control of government through ambitious program of economic, social, and political reform

Chapter Review

Political parties seek to control government by controlling its personnel. Elections are their means to this end. Thus, parties take shape from the electoral process. The formal principle of party organization is this: For every district in which an election is held—from the entire nation to the local district, county, or precinct—there should be some kind of party unit.

The two-party system has dominated U.S. politics. Today, on individual issues, the two parties differ little from each other. In general, however, Democrats lean more to the Left on issues and Republicans more to the Right. Even though party affiliation means less to Americans than it once did, partisanship remains important. What

ticket splitting there is occurs mainly at the presidential level.

Third parties are short-lived for several reasons. They have limited electoral support, the tradition of the two-party system is strong, and a major party often adopts their platform. Single-member districts with two competing parties also discourage third parties.

Nominating and electing are the basic functions of parties. Originally nominations were made in party caucuses, and individuals who ran as independents had a difficult time getting on the ballot. In the 1830s, dissatisfaction with the cliquish caucuses led to nominating conventions. Although these ended the "King Caucus" that had nominated the presidential candidates, and thereby gave the presidency a popular base, they too proved unsatisfactory. Primaries have now more or less replaced the conventions. There are both closed and open primaries. Closed primaries are more supportive of strong political parties than open primaries. Contested primaries sap party strength and financial resources, but they nonetheless serve to resolve important social conflicts and recognize new interest groups. Winning by the top of a party ticket usually depends on the party regulars at the bottom getting out the vote. At all levels, the mass communications media are important. Mass mailings, too, are vital in campaigning. Thus, campaign funds are crucial to success.

Congress is organized around the two-party system. The House speakership is a party office. Parties determine the makeup of congressional committees, including their chairs, which are no longer based entirely on seniority.

In recent years, the role of parties in political campaigns has been partially supplanted by the use of new political technologies. These include the broadcast media, polling, professional public relations, phone banks, and direct mail fund-raising and advertising. These techniques are enormously expensive and have led to a shift from a labor-intensive to a capital-intensive politics. This shift works to the advantage of political forces representing the well-to-do. The parties currently have also entrenched themselves in government agencies and sectors of the national economy.

For Further Reading

Broder, David. *The Party's Over.* New York: Harper & Row, 1971.

Chambers, William N., and Walter Dean Burnham. *The American Party Systems: Stages of Political Development.* New York: Oxford University Press, 1975.

Cooper, Joseph, and Louis Maisel. *Political Parties: Development and Decay.* Beverly Hills, CA: Sage Publications, 1978.

Goldman, Ralph. *The National Party Chairmen and Committees: Factionalism at the Top.* Armonk, NY: M. E. Sharpe, 1990.

Herrnson, Paul S. *Party Campaigning in the 1980s.* Cambridge: Harvard University Press, 1988.

Hofstadter, Richard. *The Idea of a Party System: The Rise of Legitimate Opposition in the United States, 1780–1840.* Berkeley: University of California Press, 1970.

Kayden, Xandra, and Eddie Mahe, Jr. *The Party Goes On: The Persistence of the Two-Party System in the United States.* New York: Basic Books, 1985.

Lawson, Kay, and Peter Merkl. *When Parties Fail: Emerging Alternative Organizations.* Princeton: Princeton University Press, 1998.

LeBlanc, Hugh. *American Political Parties.* New York: St. Martin's Press, 1982.

Polsby, Nelson W. *Consequences of Party Reform.* New York: Oxford University Press, 1983.

Ranney, Austin. *Curing the Mischiefs of Faction.* Berkeley: University of California Press, 1975.

Sabato, Larry. *PAC Power.* New York: W. W. Norton, 1984.

Sabato, Larry. *The Rise of Political Consultants.* New York: Basic Books, 1971.

Shafer, Byron, ed. *Beyond Realignment: Interpreting American Electoral Eras.* Madison, WI: University of Wisconsin Press, 1991.

Smith, Eric R. *The Unchanging American Voter.* Berkeley: University of California Press, 1989.

Sorauf, Frank J. *Party Politics in America.* Boston: Little, Brown, 1984.

Sundquist, James. *Dynamics of the Party System.* Washington, DC: Brookings Institution, 1983.

Wattenberg, Martin. *The Decline of American Political Parties, 1952–1988.* Cambridge: Harvard University Press, 1989.

11

GROUPS AND INTERESTS

*A*mericans often worry about the problem of special interests. Many believe that organized groups, pursuing special agendas, dominate the governmental and policy-making process. Senator Edward Kennedy once said that Americans sometimes feel they have the "best Congress money can buy." Certainly, a good deal of what Americans see and read about their nation's politics seems to confirm this pessimistic view.

Thus, for example, during the 1992 national elections, more than four thousand special-interest groups contributed more than $230 million to Democratic and Republican candidates. Many of the largest contributions came from industries whose members have extensive dealings with the federal government. Securities and investment interests donated more than $11 million to national political candidates. Lawyers and lobbyists contributed more than $13 million. Oil and gas companies and insurance interests each contributed nearly $10 million. Real estate concerns gave about $6 million.

Does this sea of special-interest money affect the behavior of our legislators? The answer often seems to be that it does. Take the case of the so-called Keating Five. In 1990, the Senate Ethics Committee investigated five senators on their activities in behalf of Charles H. Keating, Jr., head of the American Continental Corporation, which at one time owned the failed Lincoln Savings and Loan Association. In preceding years, Keating and his associates had raised over $1.3 million for the campaign committees and political causes of Senators Alan Cranston (Democrat-California), Dennis DeConcini (Democrat-Arizona), John

Glenn (Democrat-Ohio), John McClain (Republican-Arizona), and Donald W. Riegle, Jr. (Democrat-Michigan). When the Lincoln Savings and Loan was collapsing in 1987, these senators met with federal regulators and allegedly "offered a deal" on behalf of Keating's company, asking for leniency in exchange for limiting high-risk investments. Two years later, the government filed a fraud and racketeering suit against Keating, and soon afterward the senators were accused of having used their influence to aid a corrupt contributor. This case was a clear indication to many citizens that a handsome campaign contribution brought special attention. Arizona political activists were so incensed that they organized an ultimately unsuccessful "recall drive" against both of their senators.[1] However, Alan Cranston retired from the Senate and John Glenn was almost defeated in 1992.

The framers of the American Constitution feared the power that could be wielded by organized interests. Yet, they believed that interest groups thrived because of freedom—the freedom that all Americans enjoyed to organize and express their views. To the framers, this problem presented a dilemma—indeed the dilemma of freedom versus power that is central to our text. If the government were given the power to regulate or in any way to forbid efforts by organized interests to interfere in the political process, the government would in effect have been given the power to suppress freedom. The solution to this dilemma was presented by James Madison.

. . . Take in a greater variety of parties and interest [and] you make it less probable that a majority of the whole will have a common motive to invade the rights of other citizens. . . . [Hence the advantage] enjoyed by a large over a small republic.[2]

According to the Madisonian theory, a good constitution encourages multitudes of interests so that no single interest can ever tyrannize the others. The basic assumption is that competition among interests will produce balance, with all the interests regulating each other.[3]

Certainly, there are tens of thousands of organized groups in the United States, ranging from civic associations to huge nationwide groups like the National Rifle Association, whose chief cause is opposition to gun registration, or Common Cause, a public interest group that advocates a variety of liberal political reforms. Despite the array of interest groups in American politics, however, we can be sure neither that all interests are represented nor that the results of this group competition are consistent with the common good. As we shall see, group politics is a political format that works more to the advantage of some types of interests than others.

In this chapter, we will examine some of the antecedents and consequences of interest group politics in the United States. First, we will seek to understand the character of the interests promoted by interest groups. Second, we will assess the growth of interest group activity in recent American political history, including the emergence of "public interest" groups. Finally, we will review and evaluate the strategies that competing groups use in their struggle for influence.

---

[1] *Congressional Quarterly Weekly Report*, 27 January 1990, pp. 211–16.

[2] Clinton Rossiter, ed., *The Federalist Papers* (New York: New American Library, 1961), No. 10, p. 83.

[3] Ibid.

Character of Interest Groups

Individuals form groups in order to increase the chance that their views will be heard and their interests treated favorably by the government. Interest groups are organized to influence governmental decisions. There are an enormous number of interest groups in the United States, and millions of Americans are members of one or more groups, at least to the extent of paying dues or attending an occasional meeting.

What Interests Are Represented

Interest groups come in as many shapes and sizes as the interests they represent. When most people think about interest groups, they immediately think of groups with a direct economic interest in governmental actions. These groups are generally supported by groups of producers or manufacturers in a particular economic sector. Examples of these types of groups include the National Petroleum Refiners Association and the American Farm Bureau Federation. At the same time that broadly representative groups like these are active in Washington, specific companies, like Shell Oil, International Business Machines, and General Motors may be active on certain issues that are of particular concern to them.

Labor organizations are equally active lobbyists. The AFL-CIO, the United Mine Workers, and the Teamsters are all groups that lobby on behalf of organized labor. In recent years, lobbies have arisen to further the interests of public employees, the most significant among these being the American Federation of State, County, and Municipal Employees.

Professional lobbies like the American Bar Association and the American Medical Association have been particularly success-ful in furthering their own interests in state and federal legislatures. Financial institutions, represented by organizations like the American Bankers Association and the National Savings & Loan League, although often less visible than other lobbies, also play an important role in shaping legislative policy.

Recent years have witnessed the growth of a powerful public interest lobby purporting to represent interests whose concerns are not likely to be addressed by traditional lobbies. These groups have been most visible in the consumer protection and environmental policy areas, although public interest groups cover a broad range of issues. The National Resources Defense Council, the Union of Concerned Scientists, and Common Cause are all examples of public interest groups.

The perceived need for representation on Capitol Hill has generated a public sector lobby in the past several years, including the National League of Cities and the "research" lobby. The latter group comprises think tanks and universities that have an interest in obtaining government funds for research and support, and it includes such prestigious institutions as Harvard University, the Brookings Institution, and the American Enterprise Institute. Indeed, many universities have expanded their lobbying efforts even as they have reduced faculty positions and course offerings.[4]

Organizational Components

Although there are many interest groups, most share certain key organizational components. First, all groups must attract and keep members. Usually, groups appeal to

---

[4]Betsy Wagner and David Bowermaster, "B.S. Economics," *Washington Monthly* (November 1992), pp. 19–22.

members not only by promoting political goals or policies they favor but also by providing them with direct economic or social benefits. Thus, for example, the American Association of Retired Persons (AARP), which promotes the interests of senior citizens, at the same time offers members a variety of insurance benefits and commercial discounts. Similarly, many groups whose goals are chiefly economic or political also seek to attract members through social interaction and good fellowship. Thus, the local chapters of many national groups provide their members with a congenial social environment while collecting dues that finance the national offices' political efforts.

Second, every group must build a financial structure capable of sustaining an organization and funding the group's activities. Most interest groups rely on annual membership dues and voluntary contributions from sympathizers. Many also sell some ancillary service to members, such as insurance and vacation tours. Third, every group must have a leadership and decision-making structure. For some groups, this structure is very simple. For others, it can be quite elaborate and involve hundreds of local chapters that are melded into a national apparatus. Finally, most groups include an agency that actually carries out the group's tasks. This may be a research organization, a public relations office, a lobbying office in Washington or a state capital.

One example of a successful interest group is the National Rifle Association (NRA). Founded in 1871, the NRA claims a membership of over three million. It employs a staff of 350 and manages an operating budget of $5.5 million. Organized ostensibly to "promote rifle, pistol and shotgun shooting, hunting, gun collecting, home firearm safety and wildlife conservation,"

the organization has been highly effective in recent decades in mobilizing its members to block any attempts to enact gun control measures, even though such measures are supported by 80 percent of the Americans surveyed in opinion polls. The NRA provides numerous benefits to its members, like sporting magazines and discounts on various types of equipment, and it is therefore adept in keeping its members enrolled and active. Though the general public may support gun control, this support is neither organized nor very intense. This allows the highly organized NRA to prevail though its views are those of a minority.

The Characteristics of Members

Membership in interest groups is not randomly distributed in the population. People with higher incomes, higher levels of education, and management or professional occupations are much more likely to become members of groups than those who occupy lower rungs on the socioeconomic ladder.[5] Well-educated, upper-income business and professional people are more likely to have the time and the money, and to have acquired through the educational process the concerns and skills, needed to play a role in a group or association. Moreover, for business and professional people, group membership may provide personal contacts and access to information that can help advance their careers. At the same time, of course, corporate entities—businesses and the like—usually have ample resources to form or participate in groups that seek to advance their causes.

The result is that interest group politics

[5]Kay Lehman Schlozman and John T. Tierney, *Organized Interests and American Democracy* (New York: Harper & Row, 1986), p. 60.

in the United States tends to have a very pronounced upper-class bias. Certainly, there are many interest groups and political associations that have a working-class or lower-class membership—labor organizations or welfare-rights organizations, for example—but the great majority of interest groups and their members are drawn from the middle and upper-middle classes. In general, the "interests" served by interest groups are the interests of society's "haves." Even when interest groups take opposing positions on issues and policies, the conflicting positions they espouse usually reflect divisions among upper-income strata rather than conflicts between the upper and lower classes.

In general, to obtain adequate political representation, forces from the bottom rungs of the socioeconomic ladder must be organized on the massive scale associated with political parties. Parties can organize and mobilize the collective energies of large numbers of people who, as individuals, may have very limited resources. Interest groups, on the other hand, generally organize smaller numbers of the better-to-do. Thus, the relative importance of political parties and interest groups in American politics has far-ranging implications for the distribution of political power in the United States. As we saw in Chapter 10, political parties have declined in influence in recent years. Interest groups, on the other hand, as we shall see shortly, have become much more numerous, active, and influential.

The Proliferation of Groups

Over the past twenty-five years, there has been an enormous increase both in the number of interest groups seeking to play a role

in the American political process and in the extent of their opportunity to influence that process. The explosion of interest group activity during the past quarter century has two basic origins: first, the expansion of the role of government during this period; and second, the coming of age of a new and dynamic set of political forces in the United States—a set of forces that have relied heavily on "public interest" groups to advance their causes.

Expansion of Government

Modern governments' extensive economic and social programs have powerful politicizing effects, often sparking the organization of new groups and interests. The activities of organized groups are usually viewed in terms of their effects upon governmental action. But interest group activity is often as much a consequence as an antecedent of governmental programs. Even when national policies are initially responses to the appeals of pressure groups, government involvement in any area can be a powerful stimulus for political organization and action by those whose interests are affected. A *New York Times* report, for example, noted that during the 1970s, expanded federal regulation of the automobile, oil, gas, education, and health care industries impelled each of these interests to increase its efforts substantially to influence the government's behavior. These efforts, in turn, had the effect of spurring the organization of other groups to augment or counter the activities of the first.[6]

Similarly, federal social programs have occasionally sparked political organization

[6]John Herbers, "Special Interests Gaining Power as Voter Disillusionment Grows," *New York Times,* 14 November 1978.

Ethel Andrus
The "Graying" of
American Politics

Ethel Andrus
(1885-1967)

During the early 1950s, Ethel Andrus, a retired high school principal, became active in the National Retired Teachers Association (NRTA). One of the major problems faced by NRTA members was the matter of health insurance. As elderly retirees, NRTA members found it difficult to obtain even minimal health insurance coverage at affordable rates. Yet, by very virtue of their age, NRTA members desperately needed such insurance. Andrus set about finding an insurance company that would provide NRTA members with adequate coverage at a more affordable group rate. In 1955, Andrus finally found an insurance broker, Leonard Davis, who saw the possibility of profitably insuring older people and persuaded an insurer to take a chance.

Then in 1958, partly at the urging of Davis, who wanted to expand his insurance business beyond the NRTA's membership, Andrus founded the American Association of Retired Persons (AARP). By this time Andrus was concerned with far more than insurance. Because Americans were living longer, there were many more Americans over the age of sixty-five than ever before. Yet, the elderly were not recognized as a group with distinct needs and problems—problems involving health, economics, adjusting to retirement, abuse, crime, and so forth.

Since its founding, AARP has moved beyond Andrus's conception. Today, the organization is among the most powerful lobbying groups in Washington. Through "telephone trees," AARP can mobilize a significant fraction of its 34 million members on behalf of issues of concern to the elderly. Recently, for example, AARP leadership in New Jersey moved to protest cuts in Medicare

spending. Using the telephone tree technique, the state AARP head called the state's eighteen district directors, who in turn phoned 130 chapter presidents. The chapter presidents called their assistants, who phoned members. Within a day, tens of thousands of AARP members were calling the offices of New Jersey's two senators, Bill Bradley and Frank Lautenberg, to demand that they oppose cuts in Medicare. AARP chapters in all fifty states were doing much the same thing.[*]

Few members of Congress are willing publicly to oppose AARP. Its members, most of whom are retired middle-income professionals, nearly all vote and have a great deal of time to write letters, attend rallies, and make their views known. Thus, AARP has compelled politicians to treat senior citizens and their political demands with great respect. This is not the sort of self-reliance that Andrus envisioned for senior citizens, but it is surely conducive to dignity. Andrus died in 1967, before the organization she founded reached its present level of membership and influence in Washington.

[*] Michael Weisskopf, "Shaking Telephone Tree at the Grass Roots: Huge Senior Citizens Lobby Answers Call to Fight Health Care Cuts," *Washington Post*, 11 June 1993, p. 1.

and action on the part of clientele groups seeking to influence the distribution of benefits and, in turn, the organization of groups opposed to the programs or their cost. In the same vein, federal programs and court decisions in such areas as abortion and school prayer were the stimuli for political action and organization by fundamentalist religious groups. Thus, the expansion of government in recent decades has also stimulated increased group activity and organization.

Even before President Clinton's task force on reforming the health care system had made a formal proposal, major lobbying campaigns were launched by hundreds of groups of physicians, the pharmaceutical industry, insurance companies, nursing groups, mental health professionals, and even chiropractors. Major insurance companies, organized as the Alliance for Managed Competition, enthusiastically supported what was generally seen as the president's preferred health care option. Smaller insurance companies, not surprisingly, sought to resist this effort by the giants to put them out of business. Their lobby group, called the Coalition for Health Insurance Choices, mounted a grassroots campaign against managed competition. At the same time, pharmaceutical manufacturers sponsored an advertising campaign designed to convince Americans that their health could not be maintained without a healthy prescription drug industry.[7] Each group claimed to speak for the public interest, although, curiously, each group's understanding of the public interest differed in some significant detail.

[7] Alissa J. Rubin, "Special Interests Stampede to Be Heard on Overhaul," *Congressional Quarterly Weekly Report,* 1 May 1993, pp. 1081–84; see also Howard Kurtz, "For Health Care Lobbies, a Major Ad Operation," *Washington Post,* 13 April 1993, p. D1.

New Politics Movement and Public Interest Groups

The second factor accounting for the explosion of interest group activity in recent years was the emergence of a new set of forces in American politics that can collectively be called the "New Politics movement."

The New Politics movement is a coalition of upper-middle-class professionals and intellectuals that formed during the 1960s in opposition to the Vietnam War and racial inequality. In more recent years, the forces of the New Politics have focused their attention on such issues as environmental protection, women's rights, and nuclear disarmament. This movement was spearheaded by young members of the upper middle class for whom the civil rights and antiwar movements were formative experiences, just as the Great Depression and World War II had been for their parents. The crusade against racial discrimination and the Vietnam War led these young men and women to become conscious of themselves, and to define themselves, as a political force in opposition to the public policies and politicians associated with the nation's postwar regime.

Members of the New Politics movement constructed or strengthened "public interest" groups, such as Common Cause, the Sierra Club, the Environmental Defense Fund, Physicians for Social Responsibility, the National Organization for Women, and the various organizations formed by consumer activist Ralph Nader. Through these groups, New Politics forces were able to influence the media, the Congress, and even the judiciary, and to enjoy a remarkable degree of success during the late 1960s and early 1970s in securing the enactment of policies they favored while undermining the powers and prerogatives of many members of the postwar governing coalition.

Ralph Nader
Father of the Consumer Movement

Ralph Nader
(b. 1934)

Perhaps the most startling fact about Ralph Nader's life of public service is that his profound impact on public policy has occurred despite the fact that he has never held public office.

Nader burst on the national scene at the age of thirty-two with the publication of *Unsafe at Any Speed*, a scathing indictment of the auto industry that criticized American carmakers for emphasizing profits and styling over safety and reliability. In the same year, Nader worked for enactment of the landmark National Traffic and Motor Vehicle Safety Act of 1966. This legislation set minimum safety standards for automobile design and construction, including such features as padded dashboards (unpadded dashes had produced brain damage injuries and decapitations) and collapsible steering columns (drivers were sometimes impaled on rigid columns).

Nader's activities have not been limited to auto safety, however. His investigations, and those of his associates, have encompassed such areas as gas pipeline safety standards, the condition of Native Americans, workplace safety, and food production standards. Nader no longer works alone. Investigations in these and other areas are carried on by several Nader-founded organizations, including the Center for the Study of Responsive Law, the Auto Safety Center, and the Public Interest Research Group. Nader and his associates are credited with the enactment of such key legislation as the Wholesome Meat Act of 1967, the Natu-

ral Gas Pipeline Safety Act of 1968, the Radiation Control for Health and Safety Act of 1968, the Coal Mine Health and Safety Act of 1969, and the Comprehensive Occupational Safety and Health Act of 1970.

Considered the father of the consumer movement, Nader himself is concerned with limiting what he sees as overweening corporate power. Nader argues that some corporate executives belong in jail for defrauding consumers, poisoning the food and water supply, and willfully manufacturing unsafe products. Nader's organizations are funded by book sales, lecture fees, private donations, and foundation grants. The personal habits of this Harvard-trained lawyer are spartan. Nader works long hours, does not own a car, and lives in a modest residence.

One consumer expert noted that Nader "has done more as a private citizen for our country and its people than most public officials do in a lifetime." Nader critics might disagree. They would certainly agree, however, that Nader has been a potent force in national politics.

Source: Ralph Nader, *Unsafe at Any Speed: The Designed-in Dangers of the American Automobile* (New York: Grossman Publishers, 1966).

New Politics activists also played a major role in securing the enactment of environmental, consumer, and occupational health and safety legislation. This represented a dramatic change in the thrust of federal regulatory policy, whose primary function previously had been to restrict price competition in regulated industries, enabling firms in these industries to reap handsome profits and to pay above-market wages to their employees. In addition, environmental and community activists defeated numerous public works projects and, along with anti-nuclear activists, they have played an important role in restricting the growth of the multi-billion-dollar nuclear power industry.

Environmental and consumer legislation in particular opened up avenues for participation by public interest groups in the political process. Turning frequently to the courts to enforce their assertions, public interest groups were frequently able to halt federally funded projects that they found objectionable.

New Politics groups sought to distinguish themselves from other interest groups—business groups, in particular—by styling themselves "public interest" organizations to suggest that they served the general good rather than their own selfish interest. These groups' claims to represent *only* the public interest should be viewed with caution, however. Quite often, goals that are said to be in the general or public interest are also or indeed primarily in the particular interest of those who espouse them. For example, environmental controls and consumer regulations not only serve a general interest in air and water quality and public safety, they also represent a way of attacking and weakening the New Politics movement's political rivals, especially big business and organized labor, by imposing restrictions on the manner in which goods can be produced, on capital investment, and on the flow of federal resources to these interests.

Private groups have also succeeded in cloaking their particular interests in the mantle of the public interest by allying themselves with public interest groups. One recent example is the case of cable television re-regulation. In 1987, Congress freed the television cable industry from local government price regulation. The result was a 61 percent increase in cable rates over the next three years. Public interest groups, led by the Consumer Federation of America (CFA), lobbied for the enactment of federal regulations governing cable prices and policies. Their efforts, however, were defeated by the cable industry.

In 1991, consumer groups formed an alliance with the National Association of Broadcasters (NAB)—the powerful lobby group representing the television networks and local television stations. The NAB promised to support cable re-regulation in exchange for CFA support for a statutory provision that would require cable companies to pay local television stations for permission to transmit their programs. CBS President Laurence Tisch said that this provision would be worth one billion dollars to the broadcast industry. The NAB, in turn, mobilized the support of organized labor. Labor was willing to back the broadcasters because most television stations are unionized while most cable companies are not. For his part, Gene Kimmelman, legislative director of the CFA, called the alliance with broadcasters "a deal with the devil that was not a bad deal."[8]

---

[8]Mike Mills, "Bush Asks for a Sign of Loyalty; Congress Changes the Channel," *Congressional Quarterly Weekly Report*, 10 October 1992, pp. 3147–49.

In 1992, the alliance of consumer groups, broadcasters, and organized labor was able to overcome the lobbying power of the cable owners to secure the enactment of a bill re-regulating the cable industry and providing potentially enormous financial benefits to the broadcast industry. President Bush, however, responded to the cable owners and vetoed the bill. After a fierce battle, the cable television bill became the only one of Bush's forty-six vetoes to be overridden by Congress. The "deal with the devil" between public and private interests had prevailed.

This example underscores the often ambiguous character of claims that a policy serves the public interest. Whose interests truly prevailed in the case of cable television re-regulation? Who will ultimately provide the additional funds that will now flow into the coffers of the broadcast industry? The public interest is a concept that should be used cautiously. Claims that a group and its programs only serve some abstract public interest must always be viewed with a healthy measure of skepticism.[9]

Strategies: The Quest for Political Power

As we saw, people form interest groups in order to improve the probability that they and their interests will be heard and treated favorably by the government. The quest for political influence or power takes many forms, but among the most frequently used strategies are: going public, lobbying, estab-

lishing access to key decision makers, using the courts, and going partisan. These strategies do not exhaust all the possibilities, but they paint a broad picture of groups competing for power through the maximum utilization of their resources.

Going Public

Going public is a strategy that attempts to mobilize the widest and most favorable climate of opinion. Many groups consider it imperative to maintain this climate at all times, even when they have no issue to fight about. An increased use of this kind of strategy is usually associated with modern advertising. As early as the 1930s, political analysts were distinguishing between the "old lobby" of direct group representation before Congress and the "new lobby" of public relations professionals addressing the public at large to reach Congress.[10]

One of the best-known ways of going public is the use of institutional advertising. A casual scanning of important mass circulation magazines and newspapers will provide numerous examples of expensive and well-designed ads by the major oil companies, automobile and steel companies, other large corporations, and trade associations. The ads show how much these organizations are doing for the country, for the protection of the environment, or for the defense of the American way of life. Their purpose is to create and maintain a strongly positive association between the organization and the community at large in the hope that these favorable feelings can be drawn on as needed for specific political campaigns later on.

[9]See Benjamin Ginsberg, *The Captive Public* (New York: Basic Books, 1986), Chapter 4. See also David Vogel, "The Public Interest Movement and the American Reform Tradition," *Political Science Quarterly* 95 (Winter 1980), pp. 607–27.

[10]E. Pendleton Herring, *Group Representation before Congress* (New York: McGraw-Hill, 1936).

Cesar Chavez and Pat Robertson
Grassroots Populism

Grassroots politics takes many forms in America. One could scarcely find two more different grassroots activists than Cesar Chavez and Pat Robertson.

Cesar Chavez was the son of migrant farmers who harvested crops in Arizona and California. Chavez had long dreamed of organizing migrant workers, who typically labored under the most oppressive and exploitative circumstances. In 1962, he began to organize California grape pickers. In 1966, his group merged with another to form the United Farm Workers Organizing Committee. Shortly after the merger, they won their first big victory: wine grape growers recognized the UFWOC as the official bargaining agent for the workers. Renamed the United Farm Workers (UFW) in 1973, the organization attracted national attention, calling for boycotts on lettuce, grapes, and other produce as a means of forcing growers to make concessions concerning migrant worker safety, wages, and working conditions.

Chavez abhorred violence, finding success in nonviolent grassroots tactics such as picketing, marches, boycotts, fasting, and other legal direct-action methods borrowed from other movement leaders like Mahatma Gandhi and Martin Luther King, Jr. Chavez and his group won some important victories by turning national attention to the plight of migrant workers whose labors brought fresh produce to the rest of the country. In the 1980s, the UFW lost some organizing struggles to the Teamsters Union. Yet Chavez continued to exert key influence, engaging, for example, in a protracted fast in 1988 to draw attention to the use of pesticides considered harmful to both farm workers and consumers. The years of fasting took their toll, however, and Chavez died from heart failure in 1993.

Television evangelist turned presidential candidate Gordon M. "Pat" Robertson applied his own grassroots approach to Republican party politics in the 1980s and 1990s. The son of a United States senator, Pat Robertson

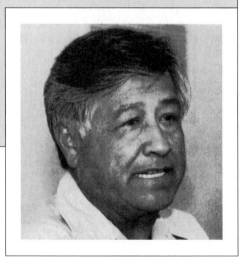

Cesar Chavez

Another form of going public is the grassroots lobbying campaign. In such a campaign, a lobby group mobilizes its members and their families throughout the country to write to their representatives in support of the group's position. For example, in 1993, lobbyists for the Nissan Motor Company sought to organize a "grassroots"

at first turned his back on politics to start his own ministry. In the early 1970s, Robertson took over a run-down television station in Virginia in order to "claim it for the Lord." Within a decade, he had built a television ministry that reached about 30 million homes on the Christian Broadcast Network (CBN) and grossed $200 million per year. Robertson's face became well known because of his television program "The 700 Club." Robertson's electronic grassroots support provided the basis for his move into national politics.

In 1987, Robertson announced that he would seek the Republican nomination for the presidency. Few considered his candidacy serious at first, but once again Robertson demonstrated what the *New York Times* called "awesome organizing ability." Emphasizing family values in his speeches, Robertson activated thousands of fundamentalist Christians, many of whom had never before been involved in politics. In the early party primaries and caucuses, where personal involvement counts the most, Robertson's supporters raised money from small donors and turned out for caucuses and primary elections. To the surprise of most pundits, Robertson finished second in the 1988 Iowa caucuses, and scored well in several primaries.

Yet much of what Robertson said aroused suspicion, including his assertions that only Christians and Jews were fit to govern and that both God and Satan had spoken directly to him, and that the world would end soon. He was labeled as quick-tempered and intolerant by critics, and in the long run his campaign faded. Despite his controversial views, Robertson has remained an important force in the Republican party, serving as a keynote speaker at its 1992 national convention. Robertson's fundamentalist Christian organizing tactics have subsequently spread to other Christian political organizations seeking to win local political races around the country.

As the accomplishments of both Chavez and Robertson illustrate, an individual or movement that can demonstrate its ability to rally significant numbers of motivated citizens to attract national attention or raise money can win important political concessions. Even in the modern media age, grassroots politics matters.

Source: Mark P. Petracca, ed., *The Politics of Interests* (Boulder: Westview Press, 1992).

Pat Robertson

effort to prevent President Clinton from raising tariffs on imported "mini-vans," including Nissan's Pathfinder model. Nissan's twelve hundred dealers across the nation, as well as the dealers' employees and family members, were urged to dial a toll-free number that would automatically generate a prepared mailgram opposing the tariff to the president and each of the dealers' senators. The mailgram warned that the proposed tariff increase would hurt middle-class auto purchasers and small business men like the dealer himself.[11]

Among the most effective users of the grassroots lobby effort in contemporary American politics is the religious Right. Networks of evangelical churches have the capacity to generate hundreds of thousands of letters and phone calls to Congress and the White House. For example, the religious Right was outraged when President Clinton announced soon after taking office that he planned to end the military's ban on the recruitment of homosexual soldiers. The Reverend Jerry Falwell, an Evangelist leader, called upon viewers of his television program to dial a 900 number that would add their names to a petition urging Clinton to retain the ban on gays in the military. Within a few hours, 24,000 persons had called to support the petition.[12]

Lobbying

The First Amendment to the Constitution provides for the right to "petition the Government for a redress of grievances." But as early as the 1870s, "lobbying" became the common term for petitioning—and it is an accurate one. Petitioning cannot take place on the floor of the House or Senate. Therefore, petitioners must confront members of Congress in the lobbies, giving rise to the term "lobbying."

The Federal Regulation of Lobbying Act defines a lobbyist as "any person who shall engage himself for pay or any consideration for the purpose of attempting to influence the passage or defeat of any legislation to the Congress of the United States." Each lobbyist must register with the clerk of the House and the secretary of the Senate.

Lobbyists badger and buttonhole legislators, administrators, and committee staff members with facts about pertinent issues and facts or claims about public support of them.[13] Lobbyists can serve a useful purpose in the legislative and administrative process by providing this kind of information. In 1978, during debate on a bill to expand the requirement for lobbying disclosures, Democratic Senators Edward Kennedy of Massachusetts and Dick Clark of Iowa joined with Republican Senator Robert Stafford of Vermont to issue the following statement: "Government without lobbying could not function. The flow of information to Congress and to every federal agency is a vital part of our democratic system."[14] But they also added that there is a darker side to lobbying—one that requires regulation. The "Keating Five" scandal is a good example of this dark side.

The business of lobbying is uneven and unstable. Some groups send their own loyal members to Washington to lobby for them. These representatives usually possess a lot of knowledge about a particular issue and the group's position on it, but they have little knowledge about or experience in Washington or national politics. They tend not to remain in Washington beyond the campaign for their issue.

Other groups, including foreign governments, hire lobbyists with a considerable

[11]Michael Weisskopf and Steven Mufson, "Lobbyists in Full Swing on Tax Plan," *Washington Post,* 17 February 1993, p. 1.

[12]Michael Weisskopf, "Energized by Pulpit or Passion, the Public Is Calling," *Washington Post,* 1 February 1993, p. 1.

[13]For discussions of lobbying, see Allan J. Cigler and Burdett A. Loomis, eds., *Interest Group Politics* (Washington, DC: Congressional Quarterly Press, 1983). See also Jeffrey M. Berry, *Lobbying for the People* (Princeton: Princeton University Press, 1977).

[14]"The Swarming Lobbyists," *Time,* 7 August 1978, p. 15.

PROCESS BOX 11.1
How Interest Groups Influence Congress

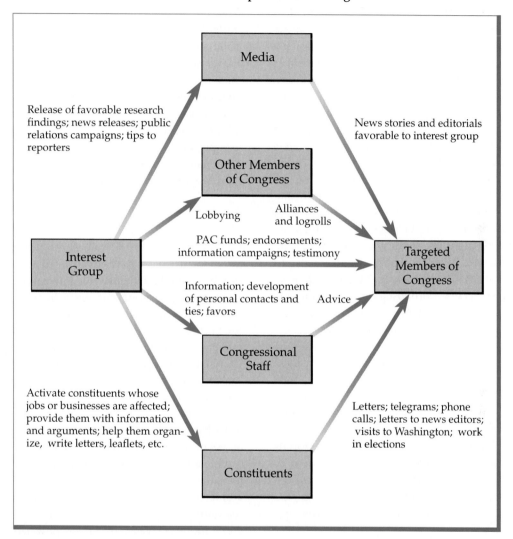

Media

Release of favorable research
findings; news releases; public
relations campaigns; tips to
reporters

News stories and editorials
favorable to interest group

Other Members
of Congress

Lobbying   Alliances
            and logrolls

PAC funds; endorsements;
information campaigns; testimony

Interest
Group

Targeted
Members of
Congress

Information; development
of personal contacts and   Advice
ties; favors

Congressional
Staff

Activate constituents whose
jobs or businesses are affected;
provide them with information
and arguments; help them organize, write letters, leaflets, etc.

Letters; telegrams; phone
calls; letters to news editors;
visits to Washington; work
in elections

Constituents

amount of Washington wisdom. These professional lobbyists, who live in the Washington area, are either lawyers or former members of Congress or of government agencies. They seek to maintain close relationships with government agencies, members of Congress, and congressional staffers. These relationships often create misgivings about lobbying. During the past several years, for example, the Mexican government and major Mexican corporations have employed a large number of former U.S. government officials to lobby on behalf of the North American Free Trade Agreement (NAFTA).

Before his inauguration, Bill Clinton imposed stringent restrictions on future lobbying by members of his transition team. During the 1992 presidential campaign, Ross Perot had charged that both the Clinton and the Bush staffs included many professional lobbyists. One member of the Bush staff, as Perot noted, had often been employed as a lobbyist by Japanese firms. Perot suggested that it was inappropriate for someone who might be characterized as the agent of a foreign government to be involved in a presidential campaign. In May 1993, Clinton proposed tough new conflict-of-interest rules for members of his own and subsequent administrations that would limit future lobbying by government officials.[15] Among his proposals was one that prohibited deductions for lobbying costs as legitimate business expenses. This would, in effect, make it more costly for firms to employ lobbyists on behalf of their concerns. Not surprisingly, this proposal was bitterly resented by the lobbying industry which saw it as a mortal threat to its own business interests. How did lobbying firms respond? By lobbying, of course. The American League of Lobbyists, a trade group representing the lobbying industry, quickly mobilized its members to conduct a vigorous campaign to defeat the proposal. One worried Washington lobbyist, however, observed, "This seems so self-serving, you wonder who is going to listen to us anyway."[16]

The lobby industry in Washington is growing. At least eighteen hundred associations employing more than forty thousand persons are located in Washington. New groups are moving in all the time, relocating from Los Angeles, Chicago, and other important cities. More than two thousand individuals are registered with Congress as lobbyists, and many local observers estimate that the actual number of people engaged in important lobbying (part-time or full-time) is closer to fifteen thousand. In addition to the various unions, commodity groups, and trade associations, the important business corporations keep their own representatives in Washington.

Gaining Access

Lobbying is an effort by outsiders to exert influence on Congress or government agencies by providing them with information about issues, support, and even threats of retaliation. Access is actual involvement in the decision-making process. It may be the outcome of long years of lobbying, but it should not be confused with lobbying. If lobbying has to do with "influence on" a government, access has to do with "influence within" it. Many interest groups resort to lobbying because they have insufficient access or insufficient time to develop it.

One interesting example of a group that had access but lost it and turned to lobbying and later to a strategy of "going public" is the dairy farmers. Through the 1960s, the dairy industry was part of the powerful coalition of agricultural interests that had full access to the Congress and to the Department of Agriculture. During the 1960s, a series of disputes broke out between the dairy farmers and the producers of corn, grain, and other agricultural commodities over commodities prices. Dairy farmers, whose cows consume grain, prefer low commodities prices while grain producers obviously prefer to receive high prices. The

---

[15]Jacob Weisberg, "Springtime for Lobbyists," *New Republic,* 1 February 1993, pp. 33–41.

[16]Michael Weisskopf, "Lobbyists Rally Around Their Own Cause: Clinton Move to Eliminate Tax Break Sparks Intense Hill Campaign," *Washington Post,* 14 May 1993, p. A16.

commodities producers won the battle, and Congress raised commodities prices, in part at the expense of the dairy farmers. In the 1970s, the dairy farmers left the agriculture coalition, set up their own lobby and political action groups, and became heavily involved in public relations campaigns and both congressional and presidential elections. The dairy farmers encountered a number of difficulties in pursuing their new "outsider" strategies. Indeed, the political fortunes of the dairy operations were badly hurt when they were accused of making illegal contributions to President Nixon's reelection campaign in 1972.

Access is usually a result of time and effort spent cultivating a position within the inner councils of government. This method of gaining access often requires the sacrifice of short-run influence. For example, many of the most important organized commodity interests in agriculture devote far more time and resources cultivating the staff and trustees of state agriculture schools and county agents back home than buttonholing members of Congress or bureaucrats in Washington.

Figure 11.1 is a sketch of some of the most important access patterns in recent American political history. Each pattern is almost literally a triangular shape, with one point in an executive branch program, another point in a Senate or House legislative committee or subcommittee, and a third point in some highly stable and well-organized interest group. The points in the triangular relationship are mutually supporting; they count as access only if they last over a long period of time. For example, access to a legislative committee or subcommittee requires that at least one member of it support the interest group in question. This member also must have built up considerable seniority in Congress. An interest cannot feel comfortable about its access to Congress until it has one or more of its "own" people with ten or more years of continuous service on the relevant committee or subcommittee.

A very important example of access politics in action is the military-industrial complex—a notion put forth by President Eisenhower in his farewell address in January 1961. The military-industrial complex is a pattern of relationships among manufacturers, the Defense Department, and Congress that has emerged out of America's vast peacetime involvement in international military and economic affairs. More than four years before Eisenhower's farewell address, the House Armed Services Committee conducted a survey of the postmilitary careers of retired armed forces officers above the rank of major. The survey disclosed that more than 1,400 officers, including 261 at the rank of general or its equivalent in the navy, had left the armed forces directly for employment by one of the hundred leading defense contractors.[17] This same pattern was at the heart of the military procurement scandal that rocked the Reagan administration in 1988 when the news media and congressional investigators revealed that some defense contractors had systematically overcharged the Pentagon for military hardware and supplies.

During the Reagan and Bush administrations, the military-industrial complex became more closely linked to the Republican White House than to the Democratic Congress. Indeed, Republicans in the executive branch saw the military-industrial complex as an institutional base that could serve the Republican party in much the same way

---

[17]U.S. Congress, House of Representatives, *Report of the Subcommittee for Special Investigations of the Committee on Armed Services*, 96th Congress, 1st session (Washington, DC: Government Printing Office, 1960), p. 7.

FIGURE 11.1
The Iron Triangle in Defense
The emergence of an Iron Triangle was apparent very early in the relations of defense contractors and the federal government. Defense contractors are powerful actors in shaping defense policy, acting in concert with defense subcommittees in Congress and executive agencies concerned with defense.

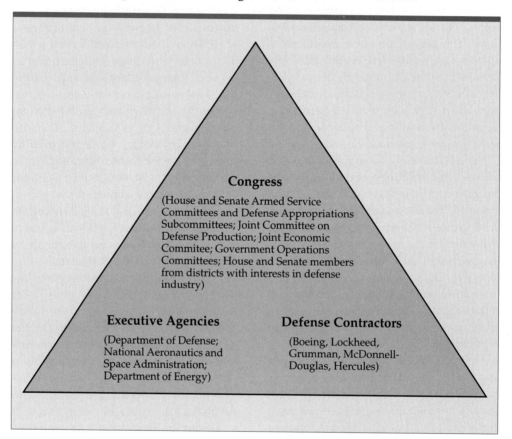

Congress

(House and Senate Armed Service Committees and Defense Appropriations Subcommittees; Joint Committee on Defense Production; Joint Economic Commitee; Government Operations Committees; House and Senate members from districts with interests in defense industry)

Executive Agencies

(Department of Defense; National Aeronautics and Space Administration; Department of Energy)

Defense Contractors

(Boeing, Lockheed, Grumman, McDonnell-Douglas, Hercules)

that the welfare and regulatory agencies of the domestic state served the Democrats. Thus, military and defense agencies, linked to industries and regions of the country that benefited economically from high levels of defense spending, could enhance Republi-can political strength in the same way that domestic agencies, their clients in the public and not-for-profit sectors, and the benefici-aries of domestic spending programs strengthened the Democrats.

Between 1988 and 1990, the military-industrial complex was weakened by procurement scandals, budget cuts, and cost overruns that led to the cancellation of weapons projects such as the Navy's new, multi-billion-dollar A-12 bomber. However, the successful performance of American military forces, and, especially, of the technologically sophisticated new weapons systems used in the Persian Gulf War of 1991 provided an enormous boost for the political prestige of the entire national security sector and weakened opposition to continued high levels of military spending. Televised accounts of the success of "smart bombs," cruise missiles, the radar-evading "stealth" fighter, and antimissile defenses such as the "Patriot" system silenced congressional and other critics who had argued for years that the military-industrial complex built costly weapons that did not function properly. Nevertheless, the political and economic collapse of the Soviet Union eliminated the major military threat to the United States and thus the justification for further high levels of spending. As the Clinton administration began to cut defense outlays to reduce the nation's budget deficit and free more funds for domestic programs, the military-industrial complex found itself gradually losing influence.[18]

Access to centers of power in Washington can also be secured through the services of certain important Washington lawyers and lobbyists. These individuals can, for a fee, provide access to key members of Congress and to the White House. "Influence peddling" is the negative term for this sale or rental of access that goes on openly in Washington. Commerce Secretary Ron Brown, for example, was an important Washington lawyer-lobbyist, earning nearly one million dollars annually for his services to corporate clients and foreign governments, before joining the government. Brown's ties to a variety of corporate interests raised many questions about President Clinton's wisdom in appointing him—questions that Brown and his supporters angrily rebutted.[19]

Former Defense Secretary Clark Clifford provides another important recent example. After leaving the government, Clifford became one of the most important lawyers and lobbyists in Washington. In 1992, however, he was indicted by a federal grand jury for his role in the illegal takeover of Washington's First American Bank by a foreign banking corporation, the Luxembourg-based Bank of Credit and Commerce International (BCCI). Clifford was charged with lying to bank regulators about BCCI's control of First American. A number of lobbyists and politicians have figured in the Justice Department's probe of fraud, illegal laundering of drug money, and bribery by BCCI. In 1993, Senator Orrin Hatch (Republican-Utah), who had defended the bank on the Senate floor even after bank officers pleaded guilty to federal money-laundering charges, came under investigation for his links to BCCI.[20]

Using the Courts (Litigation)

Interest groups sometimes turn to litigation when they lack access or when their satis-

---

[18]Thomas Ricks, "With Cold War Over, The Military-Industrial Complex is Dissolving," *Wall Street Journal*, 20 May 1993, p. 1.

[19]William Raspberry, "Why Did Ron Brown Become a Target?" *Washington Post*, 20 January 1993, p. A21.

[20]Sharon Walsh, "Hatch's Links to BCCI Are Probed, Sources Say," *Washington Post*, 20 January 1993, p. A12.

In Brief Box

INTEREST GROUP STRATEGIES

Going Public
Especially via advertising; also through boycotts, strikes, rallies, marches, and sit-ins, generating positive news coverage

Lobbying
Influencing the passage or defeat of legislation
Three types of lobbyists:
Amateur—loyal members of a group seeking passage of legislation that is currently under scrutiny
Paid—often lawyers or professionals without a personal interest in the legislation who are not lobbyists full-time
Staff—employed by a specific interest group full-time for the express purpose of influencing or drafting legislation

Access
Development of close ties to decision makers on Capitol Hill

Litigation
Taking action through the courts, usually in one of three ways:
Filing suit against a specific government agency or program
Financing suits brought against the government by individuals
Filing companion briefs as *amicus curiae* (friend of the court) to existing court cases

Partisan Politics
Giving financial support to a particular party or candidate
Congress passed the Federal Election Campaign Act of 1971 to try to regulate this practice by limiting the amount of funding interest groups can contribute to campaigns

Bribery
There are no reliable data on the incidence of bribery and corruption, but scandals like Abscam raise doubts about governmental ethics

---

faction with government in general or with a specific government program is running low and they feel they have insufficient influence to change the situation. They can use the courts to affect public policy in at least three ways: (1) by bringing suit directly on behalf of the group itself, (2) by financing suits brought by individuals, or (3) by filing a companion brief as *amicus curiae* (literally "friend of the court") to an existing court case.

Among the most significant modern illustrations of the use of the courts as a strategy for political influence are those that accompanied the "sexual revolution" of the 1960s and the emergence of the movement for women's rights. Beginning in the mid-sixties, a series of cases were brought into the federal courts in an effort to force definition of a right to privacy in sexual matters. The case began with a challenge to state restrictions on obtaining contraceptives for nonmedical purposes, a challenge that was effectively made in *Griswold v. Connecticut*, where the Supreme Court held that states could neither prohibit the dissemination of information about nor prohibit the actual use of contraceptives by married couples. That case was soon followed by *Eisenstadt v. Baird*, in which the Court held that the states could not prohibit the use of contraceptives by single persons any more than they could prohibit their use by married couples. One year later, the Court held, in the 1973 case of *Roe v. Wade*, that states could not impose an absolute ban on voluntary abortions. Each of these cases, as well as others, was part of the Court's enunciation of a constitutional doctrine of privacy.[21]

The 1973 abortion case sparked a controversy that brought conservatives to the fore on a national level. These conservative groups made extensive use of the courts to whittle away the scope of the privacy doctrine. They obtained rulings, for example, that prohibit the use of federal funds to pay for voluntary abortions. And in 1989, right-to-life groups used a strategy of litigation that significantly undermined the *Roe v. Wade* decision in the case of *Webster v. Reproductive Health Services* (see Chapter 4), which restored the right of states to place restrictions on abortion.[22]

Another extremely significant set of contemporary illustrations of the use of the courts as a strategy for political influence

are those found in the history of the NAACP. The most important of these court cases was, of course, *Brown v. Board of Education of Topeka,* in which the U.S. Supreme Court held that legal segregation of the schools was unconstitutional.[23]

Business groups are also frequent users of the courts because of the number of government programs applied to them. Litigation involving large businesses is most mountainous in such areas as taxation, antitrust, interstate transportation, patents, and product quality and standardization.

Groups will also sometimes seek legislation designed to help them secure their aims through litigation. During the 1970s, for example, Congress fashioned legislation meant to make it easier for environmental and consumer groups to use the courts. Several regulatory statutes, such as the 1973 Endangered Species Act, contained "citizen suit" provisions, in effect, giving environmental groups the right to bring suits challenging the decisions of executive agencies and the actions of business firms in environmental cases even if the groups bringing suit were not being directly harmed by the governmental or private action in question. Such suits, moreover, could be financed by the expedient of "fee shifting"—that is, environmental or consumer groups could pay for successful suits by collecting legal fees and expenses from their opponents.

In its decision in the 1992 case of *Lujan* v. *Defenders of Wildlife* (see Chapter 9), the Supreme Court seemed to question the constitutionality of citizen suit provisions. Justice Scalia indicated that such provisions violated Article III of the U.S. Constitution, which limits the jurisdiction of the federal

[21]Griswold v. Connecticut, 381 U.S. 479 (1965). Eisenstadt v. Baird, 405 U.S. 438 (1972). Roe v. Wade, 410 U.S. 113 (1973).

[22]Webster v. Reproductive Health Services, 109 S.Ct. 3040 (1989).

[23]Brown v. Board of Education of Topeka, 347 U.S. 483 (1954).

courts to actual cases and controversies.[24] This means that only persons directly affected by a case can bring it before the court. If the Court continues to take this position, the capacity of public interest groups to employ a strategy of litigation will be diminished. Congress, however, has continued to write legislation designed to assist groups in achieving their aims through litigation.

An important recent product of this relationship between legislation and litigation is the 1990 Americans with Disabilities Act (ADA), which took full effect in July 1992. The act resulted from the lobbying efforts of a host of public interest and advocacy groups and is aimed at allowing individuals with hearing, sight, or mobility impairments to participate fully in American life. Under the terms of this significant piece of legislation, businesses, private organizations, and local governmental agencies were required to make certain that their administrative procedures and physical plants did not needlessly deprive individuals with physical or emotional disabilities of access to the use of their facilities, or of employment and other opportunities.

Subsequently, the 1991 Civil Rights Act granted disabled individuals who believed that their rights under the ADA had been violated the right to sue for compensatory and punitive damages, as well as the right to demand a jury trial. In other words, this *legislation* encouraged individuals with disabilities to make use of *litigation* to secure their new rights and press their interests.

Hundreds of legal complaints were immediately filed. An advocacy group, the Disability Rights Litigation and Defense Fund, trained five thousand "barrier busters" to look for violators of the act and to file lawsuits. Federal officials estimated that the ADA would generate approximately fifteen thousand discrimination cases every year—an estimate the act's critics consider much too low.[25]

Electoral Politics

Many groups seek to make use of electoral politics as a route to political influence. By far the most common electoral strategy employed by interest groups is that of giving financial support to the parties or to particular candidates. But such support can easily cross the threshold into outright bribery. Therefore, Congress has occasionally made an effort to regulate this strategy. A recent effort was the Federal Election Campaign Act of 1971 (as amended in 1974). This act limits campaign contributions and requires that each candidate or campaign committee itemize the full name and address, occupation, and principal business of each person who contributes more than $100. These provisions have been effective up to a point, considering the rather large number of embarrassments, indictments, resignations, and criminal convictions in the aftermath of the Watergate scandal.

The Watergate scandal, itself, was triggered by the illegal entry of Republican workers into the office of the Democratic National Committee in the Watergate apartment building. But an investigation quickly revealed numerous violations of campaign finance laws involving millions of dollars in unregistered cash from corporate executives to President Nixon's re-election com-

---

[24]Lujan v. Defenders of Wildlife, 112 S.Ct. (1992); see also Linda Greenhouse, "Court Limits Legal Standing in Suits," *New York Times*, 13 June 1992, p. 12.

[25]See "Disabling America," *Wall Street Journal*, 24 July 1992, p. A10. See also Gary Becker, "How the Disabilities Act Will Cripple Business," *Business Week*, 14 September 1992, p. 14.

TABLE 11.1
PAC SPENDING

Years	Contributions
1977–1978 (est.)	$ 77,800,000
1979–1980	131,153,384
1981–1982	190,173,539
1983–1984	266,822,476
1985–1986	339,954,416
1987–1988	364,201,275
1989–1990	372,100,000
1991–1992 (est.)	409,310,000

Source: Federal Election Commission.

mittee. Many of these revelations were made by the famous Ervin committee, whose official name and jurisdiction was the Senate Select Committee to Investigate the 1972 Presidential Campaign Activities.

Reaction to Watergate produced further legislation on campaign finance in 1974 and 1976, but the effect has been to restrict individual rather than interest group campaign activity. Individuals may now contribute no more than $1,000 to any candidate for federal office in any primary or general election. A political action committee (PAC), however, can contribute $5,000, provided it contributes to at least five different federal candidates each year. Beyond this, the laws permit corporations, unions, and other interest groups to form PACs and to pay the costs of soliciting funds from private citizens for the PACs.

Electoral spending by interest groups has been increasing steadily despite the flurry of reform following Watergate. Table 11.1 presents a dramatic picture of the growth of PACs as the source of campaign contributions. The dollar amounts for each year indicate the growth in electoral spending. The number of PACs has also increased significantly—from 480 in 1972 to more than 4,000 in 1992 (see Table 11.2). Although

TABLE 11.2
POLITICAL ACTION COMMITTEE GROWTH: 1974–1992

As of:	Corporate	Labor	Trade	Non-connected	Cooperative	Corp. w/o stock	Total
12/31/74	89	201	318				608
12/31/78	785	217	453	162	12	24	1,653
12/31/80	1,206	297	576	376	42	56	2,551
12/31/84	1,682	394	698	1,053	52	130	4,009
12/31/86	1,744	384	745	1,077	56	151	4,157
12/31/92	1,735	347	770	1,145	56	142	4,195

Source: Federal Election Commission.

DEBATING THE ISSUES

PACs and Politics

*T*he attempt to reform campaign finance laws in the early 1970s had an unintended effect: It prompted an explosion in the number and influence of Political Action Committees (PACs), organizations formed by corporations, unions, trade associations, and other entities to raise and distribute campaign contributions. Numbering now in the thousands, PACs are perfectly legal, yet are often condemned for corrupting the political process and providing incumbents with even more political advantages. (PACs rarely contribute to challengers since they have little chance of defeating incumbents.)

Campaign finance expert Herbert Alexander defends PACs, arguing that the case against them is exaggerated. Public interest activist Fred Wertheimer summarizes the objections to PACs.

Alexander

Seen in historical perspective, political action committees represent a functional system for political fundraising that developed, albeit unintentionally, from efforts to reform the political process. PACs represent an expression of an issue politics that resulted from attempts to remedy a sometimes unresponsive political system. And they represent an institutionalization of the campaign fund solicitation process that developed from the enactment of reform legislation intended to increase the number of small contributors. . . . PAC supporters . . . should question the unarticulated assumptions at the basis of much anti-PAC criticism. Money is not simply a necessary evil in the political process. By itself money is neutral. . . . There is nothing inherently immoral or corrupting about corporate or labor contributions of money. . . . All campaign contributions are not attempts to gain special favors. . . . Money is not the sole, and often not even the most important, political resource. . . . Curbing interest group contributions will not free legislators of the dilemma of choosing between electoral necessity and legislative duty. . . . A direct dialogue between candidates and individual

the reform legislation of the early and mid-1970s attempted to reduce the influence of special interests over elections, the effect has been almost the exact opposite. Opportunities for legally influencing campaigns are now widespread.

Given the enormous costs of television commercials, polls, computers, and other elements of the new political technology

(see Chapter 10), most politicians are eager to receive PAC contributions and are at least willing to give a friendly hearing to the needs and interests of contributors. It is probably not the case that most politicians simply sell their services to the interests that fund their campaigns. But there is considerable evidence to support the contention that interest groups' campaign contributions do

voters without interest group influence is not possible in a representative democracy. . . . The freedom to join in common cause with other citizens remains indispensable to our democratic system. The pursuit of self-interest is . . . a condition, not a problem.[1]

Wertheimer

The growth of PACs and the increased importance of PAC money have had a negative effect on two different parts of the political process—congressional elections and congressional decision making. First, PAC money tends to make congressional campaigns less competitive because of the overwhelming advantage enjoyed by incumbents in PAC fund-raising. The ratio of PAC contributions to incumbents over challengers in 1984 House races was 4.6 to 1.0; in the Senate, incumbents in 1984 enjoyed a 3.0 to 1.0 advantage in PAC receipts [comparable ratios hold for subsequent elections]. . . . The advantage enjoyed by incumbents is true for all kinds of PAC giving—for contributions by labor groups, corporate PACs, and trade and membership PACs. . . .

Second, there is a growing awareness that PAC money makes a difference in the legislative process, a difference that is inimical to our democracy. PAC dollars are given by special interest groups to gain special access and special influence in Washington. Most often PAC contributions are made with a legislative purpose in mind. . . .

Common Cause and others have produced a number of studies that show a relationship between PAC contributions and legislative behavior. The examples run the gamut of legislative decisions. . . .

PAC gifts do not guarantee votes or support. PACs do not always win. But PAC contributions do provide donors with critical access and influence; they do affect legislative decisions and are increasingly dominating and paralyzing the legislative process.[2]

[1]Herbert Alexander, "The Case for PACs." Public Affairs Council monograph (Washington, DC: 1983).
[2]Fred Wertheimer, "Campaign Finance Reform: The Unfinished Agenda," *The Annals of the American Academy of Political and Social Science* 486 (July 1986), pp. 92–93.

influence the overall pattern of political behavior in Congress and the state legislatures.[26]

A recent lawsuit, for example, brought to

[26]See Benjamin Ginsberg and John Green, "The Best Congress Money Can Buy," in *Do Elections Matter?*, ed. Benjamin Ginsberg and Alan Stone (Armonk, NY: M.E. Sharpe, 1986).

light documents recording the activities of the General Electric Company's political action committee over a ten-year period. The PAC made hundreds of thousands of dollars in donations to congressional and senatorial campaigns for individuals who were or could be "helpful" to the company. One House member was given money because company officials felt that his help in protecting a $20 million GE project "alone justifies supporting him."[27]

In May 1993, President Clinton introduced a set of proposals designed to diminish the impact of private contributions in political campaigns. Under his proposals, congressional candidates could have voluntarily agreed to spending limits that would have, in turn, entitled them to public campaign funds. Contributions by individuals to political parties also would have been limited and contributions by PACs to campaigns curtailed.[28] Beyond its direct implications for members of Congress, Clinton's plan would have also restricted the influence of business firms and wealthy individuals who rely on making campaign contributions to promote their political interests. The beneficiaries would have been the various public interest groups, tied to the Democratic party, that rely more on litigation, grass-roots lobbying, and electoral activism than on money to promote their interests. Primarily for this reason, Republicans strongly opposed Clinton's reform efforts.

Financial support is not the only way that organized groups seek influence through electoral politics. Sometimes, activism can be even more important than campaign contributions. In recent years, for example, both opponents and proponents of abortion rights have been extremely active in national and local elections, providing political candidates with numerous campaign workers and activists. The willingness of pro- and anti-abortion groups to work vig-

orously in election campaigns helps to explain why the issue is far more important politically than its salience in public opinion polls might suggest.

In 1992, activists on both sides campaigned hard for the election of congressional candidates who supported their positions. In House races, abortion rights activists, organized in groups such as the Planned Parenthood Federation and Voters for Choice, helped secure the election of a number of sympathetic new legislators. Some observers calculated that backers of abortion rights gained as many as twenty votes in the House of Representatives. At the same time, opponents of abortion, led by the National Right to Life Committee, were pleased to see Georgia Democratic Senator Wyche Fowler defeated in a special runoff election by Republican Paul Coverdell. Fowler, a consistent supporter of abortion rights, had been vehemently opposed by anti-abortion forces.

Of course, abortion rights groups were especially pleased by the defeat of George Bush and the victory of Bill Clinton in the 1992 presidential contest. Since the late 1970s, Republican presidential strategy had involved opposition to abortion as a way of attracting the allegiance of conservative Catholics and fundamentalist Protestants. To this end, President Bush had supported legislative restrictions on abortion, endeavored to appoint federal judges known to be unfriendly to abortion, and signed a number of executive orders limiting abortion. These included the so-called gag rule, prohibiting abortion counseling in federally funded family planning clinics. President Clinton, who had been strongly supported by abortion rights forces, moved quickly to rescind the gag rule and other anti-abortion executive orders of the Bush era. With Clin-

[27]Charles Babcock, "GE Files Offer Rare View of What PACs Seek to Buy on Capitol Hill," *Washington Post*, 1 June 1993, P. A10.

[28]Richard L. Berke, "Clinton Unveils Plan to Restrict PAC Influence," *New York Times*, 8 May 1993, p. 1.

ton in office, abortion rights groups pressed for the enactment of a "Freedom of Choice Act," that would outlaw most state restrictions on abortion.[29]

Groups and Interests— The Dilemma

James Madison wrote that "liberty is to faction what air is to fire."[30] By this he meant that the organization and proliferation of interests was inevitable in a free society. To seek to place limits on the organization of interests, in Madison's view, would be to limit liberty itself. Madison believed that interests should be permitted to regulate themselves by competing with one another. So long as competition among interests was free, open, and vigorous, there would be some balance of power among them and none would be able to dominate the political or governmental process.

There is considerable competition among organized groups in the United States. As we saw, cable television interests were recently defeated by an alliance of television networks and consumer groups after a fierce battle. Similarly, pro- and anti-abortion forces continue to be locked in a bitter struggle. Nevertheless, interest group politics is not as free of bias as Madisonian theory might suggest. Though the weak and poor do occasionally become organized to assert their rights, interest group politics is generally a form of political competition in which the wealthy and powerful are best able to engage.

Moreover, though groups sometimes organize to promote broad public concerns, interest groups more often represent relatively narrow, selfish interests. Small, self-interested groups are organized much more easily than large and more diffuse collectivities are. For one thing, the members of a relatively small group—say, bankers or hunting enthusiasts—are usually able to recognize their shared interests and the need to pursue them in the political arena. Members of large and more diffuse groups—say, consumers or potential victims of firearms—often find it difficult to recognize their shared interests or the need to engage in collective action to achieve them.[31] This is why causes presented as public interests by their proponents often turn out, upon examination, to be private interests wrapped in a public mantle.

Thus, we have a dilemma to which there is no ideal answer. To regulate interest group politics is, as Madison warned, to limit freedom and to expand governmental power. Not to regulate interest group politics, on the other hand, may be to ignore justice. Those who believe that there are simple solutions to the problems of political life would do well to ponder this problem.

[29]Julie Rovner, "Mixed Results on Both Sides Keep Spotlight on Abortion," *Congressional Quarterly Weekly Report,* 7 November 1992, pp. 3591–92.

[30]Rossiter, ed., *The Federalist Papers,* No. 10, p. 78.

[31]Mancur Olson, Jr., *The Logic of Collective Action* (Cambridge: Harvard University Press, 1971).

Time Line on Interest Groups

EVENTS		INSTITUTIONAL DEVELOPMENTS
Early trade associations and unions formed (1820s and 1830s)		Term "lobbyist" is first used (1830)
Citizen groups and movements form—temperance (1820s), antislavery (1810–1830), women (1848), abolition (1850s)	1850	Local regulations restricting or forbidding manufacture and sale of alcohol (1830–1860); several states pass laws granting women control over their property (1839–1860s)
Civil War (1861–1865)		Lobbying is recognized in law and practice (1870s)
Development of agricultural groups, including the Grange (1860s–1870s)		Grangers successfully lobby for passage of "Granger laws" to regulate rates charged by railroads and warehouses (1870s)
American Federation of Labor (AFL) formed (1886)	1880	Beginnings of labor and unemployment laws (1880s)
Farmers' Alliances and Populists (1880s–1890s)		Election of candidates pledged to farmers (1890s)
Middle-class Progressive movement and trade associations (1890s)		Laws for direct primary, voter registration, regulation of business (1890s–1910s)
Growth of movement for women's suffrage (1890s)		Women's suffrage granted by Wyo., Colo., Utah, Idaho (1890s)
Renewal of women's movements—temperance (1890s) and suffrage (1914)	1900	
World War I (1914–1919)		Prohibition (Eighteenth) Amendment ratified (1919)
Teapot Dome scandal (1924)		
Growth of trade associations (1920s)		Nineteenth Amendment gives women the vote (1920)
		Corrupt practices legislation passed; lobbying registration legislation (1920s)

EVENTS		INSTITUTIONAL DEVELOPMENTS
American Farm Bureau Federation (1920); farm bloc (1920s)		Farm bloc lobbies for farmers (1921–1923)
CIO is formed (1938)		Wagner National Labor Relations Act (1935)
U.S. enters W.W. II (1941–1945)	**1940**	Federal Regulation of Lobbying Act (1946)
Postwar wave of strikes in key industries (1945–1946)		Taft-Hartley Act places limits on unions (1947)
AFL and CIO merge (1955)	**1950**	
Senate hearings into labor racketeering (1950s)		Landrum-Griffin Act to control union corruption (1959)
Civil rights movement—boycotts, sit-ins, vote drives (1957), March on Washington (1963)		Passage of Civil Rights Acts of 1957, 1960, 1964, Voting Rights Act of 1965 (1960s)
National Organization of Women (NOW) formed (1966)		
Vietnam War: antiwar movement (1965–1973)	**1970**	End of draft (1971)
Watergate scandal (1972–1974)		Campaign spending legislation leads to PACs (1970s)
		Roe v. *Wade* (1973)
Pro-life and pro-choice groups emerge (post-1973)		
Public interest groups formed (1970s–1980s)		Consumer, environmental, health, and safety legislation (1970s)
Moral Majority formed (late 1970s)		Ethics in Government Act (1978)
		PACs help to elect conservative candidates (1980s)
Pentagon procurement scandal (1988)		
		Further regulation of lobbying (1980s)
The Keating Five investigation (1990–1991)	**1990**	Clinton proposals to restrict lobbying activities (1993)
Intense efforts by interest groups to influence Clinton health care and economic proposals (1993)		Expanded use of new technologies for grassroots lobby efforts (1993)

Chapter Review

Efforts by organized groups to influence government and policy are becoming an increasingly important part of American politics. The expansion of government over the past several decades has fueled an expansion of interest group activity. In recent years upper-middle-class Americans have organized public interest groups to vie with more specialized interests. All groups use a number of strategies to gain power.

Going public is an effort to mobilize the widest and most favorable climate of opinion. Advertising is a common technique in this strategy.

Lobbying is the act of petitioning legislators. Lobbyists—individuals who receive some form of compensation for lobbying—are required to register in the House and Senate. In spite of an undeserved reputation for corruption, they serve a useful function, providing members of Congress with a vital flow of information.

Access is participation in government. Groups with access have less need for lobbying. Most groups build up access over time through great effort. They work years to get their members into positions of influence on congressional committees.

Litigation sometimes serves interest groups when other strategies fail. Groups may bring suit on their own behalf, finance suits brought by individuals, or file *amicus curiae* briefs.

Groups engage in electoral politics either by embracing one of the major parties, usually through financial support or through a nonpartisan strategy. Interest groups' campaign contributions now seem to be flowing into the coffers of candidates at a faster rate than ever before.

For Further Reading

Cigler, Alan J., and Burdett A. Loomis. *Interest Group Politics.* Washington, DC: Congressional Quarterly Press, 1983.

Day, Christine. *What Older Americans Think: Interest Groups and Aging Policy.* Princeton: Princeton University Press, 1990.

Goldfield, Michael. *The Decline of Organized Labor in the United States.* Chicago: University of Chicago Press, 1987.

Hansen, John Mark. *Gaining Access: Congress and the Farm Lobby, 1919–1981.* Chicago: University of Chicago Press, 1991.

Lowi, Theodore J. *The End of Liberalism.* New York: W. W. Norton, 1979.

McFarland, Andrew S. *Common Cause: Lobbying in the Public Interest.* Chatham, NJ: Chatham House, 1984.

Milbrath, Lester W. *Environmentalists: Van-guard for a New Society.* Albany: State University of New York Press, 1984.

Moe, Terry M. *The Organization of Interests.* Chicago: University of Chicago Press, 1980.

Olsen, Mancur, Jr. *The Logic of Collective Action: Public Goods and the Theory of Groups.* Cambridge: Harvard University Press, 1971.

Paige, Connie. *The Right to Lifers.* New York: Summit, 1983.

Petracca, Mark, ed. *The Politics of Interests: Interest Groups Transformed.* Boulder: Westview, 1992.

Pope, Jacqueline. *Biting the Hand That Feeds Them: Women on Welfare at the Grass Roots Level.* New York: Praeger, 1989.

Sabato, Larry. *PAC Power: Inside the World of Political Action Committees.* New York: W. W. Norton, 1984.

Schlozman, Kay Lehman, and John T. Tierney. *Organized Interests and American Democracy.* New York: Harper & Row, 1986.

Staggenborg, Suzanne. *The Pro-Choice Movement: Organization and Activism in the Abortion Conflict.* New York: Oxford University Press, 1991.

Stockman, David. *The Triumph of Politics.* New York: Harper & Row, 1986.

Truman, David. *The Governmental Process: Political Interests and Public Opinion.* New York: Alfred A. Knopf, 1951.

Vogel, David. *Fluctuating Fortunes.* New York: Basic Books, 1989.

12

POLITICS AND GOVERNMENT: THE PROBLEM WITH THE PROCESS

*O*ver the preceding five chapters, we analyzed the disparate pieces of America's political process. We examined elections and political parties, evaluated the role of public opinion, and weighed the place of the media and interest groups in the workings of the American political system. Process can be meaningful in and of itself—witness the significance that many Americans attach to the right to participate in their government. Nevertheless, we study the American political process mainly because we believe that it has important consequences for American government and policy.

Having examined these parts of the contemporary American political process, let's try to step back and assess their impact on the institutions, policies, and governance of the United States. Unfortunately, as we shall see, in a number of important respects, America's current political process undermines our government's capacity to govern.

Can the Government Govern?

As we approach the twenty-first century, America faces many problems. Our capacity to compete successfully in world markets against other major industrial nations, most notably Japan and Germany, is open to question. America no longer seems able to provide enough jobs or an adequate standard of living for all of its citizens. Our dependence on foreign sources of energy is growing once again.

Now that America is the world's largest debtor, its economy and economic policy are increasingly vulnerable to the wishes of foreign bondholders.[1] America's educational system is widely viewed as deserving failing marks. Millions of Americans lack adequate housing or health care. American cities are plagued by crime and drugs.

In such areas as health care, housing, crime, and education, the U.S. government has seemed unable to formulate or implement effective programs and policies. In other areas, the government, itself, is the cause of the nation's problems. For example, the long-term strength of the American economy is threatened by the $4 trillion national debt that is the fiscal legacy of the Reagan and Bush presidencies. Despite a general realization that the debt problem must be brought under control by some combination of tax increases and spending cuts, America's political leadership has been, thus far, incapable of swallowing the bitter medicine of fiscal discipline.

Shortly after entering office, President Clinton introduced a package of tax increases and spending cuts nominally designed to reduce the federal deficit by hundreds of millions of dollars. Many of the so-called cuts in spending, proclaimed by the president, however, turned out to be changes in accounting procedures or unspecified "administrative savings" rather than actual reductions in federal outlays.[2] Even in some areas where real cuts were planned, such as in allocations for agricul-tural programs, congressional supporters of the interests affected were able to compel the president to restore the expenditures he had proposed eliminating.[3] Many experts doubted that the president's plans would actually result in substantial deficit reductions.[4] An excellent recent volume of essays published by Washington's prestigious Brookings Institution was aptly entitled *Can the Government Govern?* The short answer to this complex question was a very clear "No!"[5]

One major reason for our present quandary is that over the past several decades an unhealthy and fundamentally undemocratic political process has developed in the United States. The framers of the Constitution believed that a strong government rested most securely upon a broad and active popular base. "I would raise the federal pyramid to a considerable altitude," said Pennsylvania delegate James Wilson. "Therefore, I would give it as broad a base as possible." As we saw in Chapter 1, concern for the new government's power and stability was a main reason that the framers established representative institutions and permitted political participation on the part of ordinary citizens. For much of U.S. history, the "federal pyramid," indeed, rested upon a relatively broad base of vigorous—often tumultuous—popular participation, with most major issues debated, fought, and ultimately resolved in the electoral arena. America's democratic politics, in turn, provided political leaders with a base of sup-

---

[1] Douglas R. Sease and Constance Mitchell, "World's Bond Buyers Gain Huge Influence over U.S. Fiscal Plans," *Wall Street Journal*, 6 November 1992, p. 1.

[2] See Robert J. Samuelson, "Not-So-Serious Spending Cuts," *Washington Post*, 25 February 1993, p. A23.

[3] Eric Pianan and David Hilzenrath, "Budget Negotiators Soften Spending Cuts, Tax Rises," *Washington Post*, 1 April 1993, p. A6.

[4] See Allan Meltzer, "The Worst Kind of Short-Term Thinking," *Wall Street Journal*, 22 February 1993, p. A10.

[5] John Chubb and Paul Peterson, eds., *Can the Government Govern?* (Washington, DC): Brookings Institution, 1989).

port from which to develop and implement programs, contend with powerful entrenched interests, and during times of crisis, such as the Civil War and World War II, ask their countrymen for the exertions and sacrifices needed in order for the nation to survive. As the framers had intended, democratic politics protected citizens' liberties *and* helped promote governance.

In recent decades, however, as noted in Chapter 9, popular participation in American political life has declined sharply. Despite a much ballyhooed increase in voter turnout, only 55 percent of eligible Americans bothered to vote in the 1992 presidential election. At the same time, the political parties that once mobilized voters and imparted a measure of unity to the scattered pieces of the American governmental structure have decayed (see Chapter 10), making it very difficult, if not impossible, to create a coherent government through the American electoral process.

Both reflecting and reinforcing these changes in the character of elections, the contending political forces in the United States have come to rely heavily on forms of political conflict that neither require nor encourage much in the way of citizen involvement. In recent years, many of the most important national political struggles have been fought largely outside the electoral arena rather than through competitive electoral contests. In fact, in contemporary America, electoral results themselves have at times been negated or reversed by political forces that were not satisfied with the outcomes.

America's contemporary political process—characterized by low voter turnout, weak parties, and the rise of a "politics by other means"—has narrowed the base upon which the "federal pyramid" rests and is the source of many of our government's present problems. As we shall see in this chapter, this political process is increasingly undemocratic, fragments political power, and fails to provide elected officials with the strong and stable political base they need to govern effectively. Most important, America's contemporary political patterns undermine the ability of elected officials to bring about or even to take account of the public good.

Let us now look critically at the pieces of America's political process and then consider their implications for our government's capacity to govern. We will first consider the declining importance of popular voting and the rise of new forms of political conflict in the United States. Second, we will see how these new forms of conflict undermine governance. Finally, we will attempt to ascertain why there are no easy solutions for America's current political problems. In particular, we will see why, despite their claims to the contrary, major political forces in the United States today are not interested in the one course of action that might restore the government's capacity to govern—the revitalization of the electoral process.

The Decline of Voting and the Rise of "Politics by Other Means"

For most of U.S. history, elections were the main arenas of political combat. In recent years, however, elections have become less effective as ways of resolving political conflicts in the United States. Today's political struggles are frequently waged elsewhere, and crucial policy choices tend to be made outside the electoral realm. Rather than engage voters directly, contending political forces rely on such weapons of institutional combat as congressional investigations, media revelations, and judicial proceedings. In contemporary America, even electoral success fails to confer the capacity to govern, and political forces, even if they lose at the polls or do not even compete in the electoral arena, have been able to exercise considerable power.

Several trends in contemporary American political life bring sharply into focus the declining significance of the electoral arena. American elections in recent decades have been characterized by strikingly low levels of voter turnout and by a decline of political competition. Since 1900, turnout in national elections has declined by 25 percentage points. In the 1992 presidential election, only 55.9 percent of the eligible electorate went to the polls, and in the 1990 midterm congressional elections, voter turnout was a mere 33 percent. In other Western democracies, turnout normally exceeds 80 percent.

The extent to which genuine competition takes place in the electoral arena has also declined sharply in recent decades—especially in congressional races, which tend to be dominated by incumbents who are able to use the resources of their office to turn back any opponents who present themselves. In 1986, 1988, and 1990, 98 percent of the incumbents who sought another term were victorious.

In the 1992 general election, despite media claims of an anti-incumbent "mood" in the country, and despite nationwide redistricting, about 95 percent of those incumbents seeking re-election were successful. According to one estimate, there was effectively no opposition in more than three hundred House races.[6] The unusually large size

[6]See Charles Babcock, "In Donating $230 Million, Interests Favored Bush, Hill Democrats," *Washington Post*, 23 October 1992, p. A19.

of the 1992 freshman congressional class was due more to retirements and deaths among incumbents than to their defeat at the polls. Only sixteen incumbent members of Congress were actually defeated in the 1992 general election. Many modern-day congressional races are decided by more than a twenty-point margin; frequently, incumbents face no electoral challenge whatsoever.

Politics outside the Electoral Arena

As competition in the electoral arena has declined, the significance of other forms of political combat has risen. Contemporary political struggles have come increasingly to involve the criminal justice system and the courts, the national security apparatus, and the mass media. Let us look at the political role played by each of these non-electoral institutions.

CRIMINAL INDICTMENTS. One important substitute for competition in the electoral arena is the growing political use of a powerful non-electoral weapon—the criminal justice system. Between the early 1970s and the present, there was more than a tenfold increase in the number of indictments brought by federal prosecutors against national, state, and local officials. The data given in Figure 12.1 actually understate the extent to which public officials have been subjected to criminal proceedings in recent years, because they do not include those political figures (such as Ronald Reagan's attorney general, Edwin Meese, and former Democratic House Speaker Jim Wright) who were targets of investigations that did not result in indictments.

Many of the individuals indicted have been lower-level civil servants, but large numbers have been prominent political fig-

FIGURE 12.1

Federal Indictments and Convictions of Public Officials, 1970–1990*

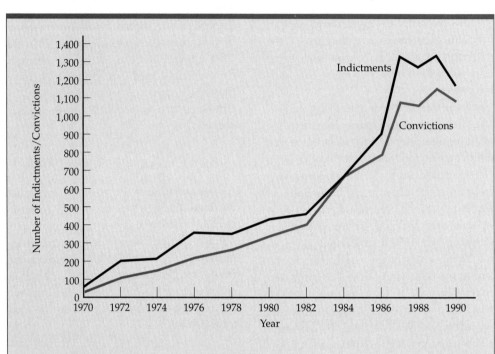

* Reporting procedures were modified in 1983, so pre- and post-1983 data are not strictly comparable.
Source: Annual reports of the U.S. Department of Justice, Public Integrity Section, 1971–1988; *Statistical Abstract of the United States* (Washington, DC: GOP, 1992), p. 195, Ed.

ures—among them more than a dozen members of Congress, several federal judges, and numerous state and local officials. Some of these indictments were initiated by Republican administrations, and their targets were primarily Democrats. At the same time, a substantial number of high-ranking Republicans in the executive branch—including former Defense Secretary Caspar Weinberger, former Assistant Secretary of State Elliott Abrams, presidential aides Michael Deaver and Lyn Nofziger, and, of course, national security official Oliver North—were the targets of criminal prosecutions stemming from allegations or investigations initiated by Democrats. Weinberger and Abrams, along with several other figures in the Iran-Contra case, were pardoned by President George Bush in December 1992, just before he left office. In justifying the pardons, Bush charged that Democrats were attempting to criminalize policy differences.

There is no particular reason to believe that the level of political corruption or abuse of power in America actually increased tenfold over the past two decades; although it could be argued that this sharp rise reflects a heightened level of public concern about governmental misconduct. However, both the issue of government ethics and the growing use of criminal sanctions against public officials have been, as we shall see, closely linked to struggles for political power in the United States. In the aftermath of Watergate, institutions such as the office of special counsel were established and processes for ethics investigations created to investigate allegations of unethical conduct on the part of public figures. Since then political forces have increasingly sought to make use of these mechanisms to discredit their opponents. When scores of investigators, accountants, and lawyers are deployed to scrutinize the conduct of a John Tower, a Jim Wright, or a Caspar Weinberger, it is all but certain that something questionable will be found. The creation of these investigative processes, more than changes in the public's tolerance for government misconduct, explains why public officials are increasingly being charged with ethical and criminal violations.

THE JUDICIARY. The growing use of criminal indictments as a partisan weapon has helped enhance the political importance of the judiciary. The prominence of the courts has been heightened by the sharp increase in the number of major policy issues that have been fought and decided in the judicial realm rather than in the arena of electoral politics.[7] The federal judiciary has become the main institution for resolving struggles over such issues as race relations and abortion, and it has also come to play a more significant role in deciding questions of social welfare and economic policy.[8] The number of suits brought by civil rights, environmental, feminist, and other liberal groups seeking to advance their policy goals increased dramatically during the 1970s and 1980s—reflecting the willingness and ability of these groups to fight their battles in the judicial arena. For example, as Figure 12.2 indicates, the number of civil rights cases brought in federal courts doubled during this period. After the emergence of a conservative majority on the Supreme Court in 1989, forces on the political Right began to use litigation to implement their own policy agenda. The growing political importance of the federal judiciary explains why Supreme Court confirmation battles, such as the struggle over the Clarence Thomas nomination, came to be so bitterly fought during the Reagan and Bush administrations.[9]

THE NATIONAL SECURITY APPARATUS. One of the best-documented examples of the use of the national security apparatus as a political weapon is the substantial expansion in the number of domestic counterintelligence operations directed against groups opposed to the policies of the executive branch during the 1960s and early 1970s. Such actions included wiretaps, surveillance, and efforts to disrupt the activities of the groups.[10] During the 1970s, congressional opposition brought a halt to these

---

[7]Jeremy Rabkin, *Judicial Compulsions* (New York: Basic Books, 1989).

[8]Martin Shapiro, "The Supreme Court's 'Return' to Economic Regulation," *Studies in American Political Development* 1 (1986); pp. 91–142.

[9]Martin Shefter, "Institutional Conflict over Presidential Appointments: The Case of Clarence Thomas," *PS: Political Science & Politics* 25, no. 4 (December 1992), pp. 676–78.

[10]William Keller, *The Liberals and J. Edgar Hoover* (Princeton: Princeton University Press, 1989), Chapter 5.

FIGURE 12.2
Civil Rights Cases Brought in Federal Courts

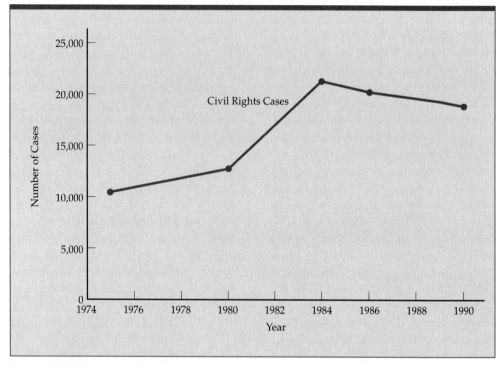

Source: *Statistical Abstract of the United States* (Washington, DC: 1988, 1989, 1992).

counterintelligence efforts; however, recent revelations indicate that in the 1980s, the FBI placed under surveillance groups opposing the Reagan administration's policies in Central America. His administration also relied on the national security apparatus to circumvent and undercut congressional opposition to its policies.

THE MEDIA. Another institution whose political significance has increased dramatically is the mass media. With the decline of political parties, politicians have become almost totally dependent on the media to reach their constituents, but this dependence has made politicians extremely vulnerable to attack by and through the media. At the same time, the development of techniques of investigative reporting and critical journalism, as we saw in Chapter 8, provided the modern news media with powerful weapons to use in political struggles.

The national media enhanced their autonomy and political power by aggressively investigating, publicizing, and exposing instances of official misconduct.[11]

[11]Samuel P. Huntington, *American Politics: The Promise of Disharmony* (Cambridge: Harvard University Press, 1981), pp. 203–10.

Conservative forces during the Nixon and Reagan years responded to media criticism by denouncing the press as biased and seeking to curb it. However, members of Congress and groups opposed to conservative presidential policies benefited from the growing influence of the press and, as noted in Chapter 8, were prepared to defend it when it came under attack.

Revelation, Investigation, Prosecution

Taken together, the expanded political roles of the national news media and the federal judiciary has given rise to a major new weapon of political combat—revelation, investigation, and prosecution. The acronym for this, RIP, forms a fitting political epitaph for the public officials who have become its targets. The RIP weaponry was initially forged by opponents of the Nixon administration in their struggles with the White House, and through the Reagan years it was used primarily by congressional Democrats to attack their foes in the executive branch. In the 1980s, however, Republicans also began to wield the RIP weapon.

In 1972, after his re-election, President Nixon undertook to expand executive power at the expense of Congress by impounding funds appropriated for domestic programs and reorganizing executive agencies without legislative authorization. In addition, the White House established the so-called "plumbers" squad of former intelligence agents and mercenaries to plug leaks of information to Congress and the press, and (its opponents claimed) it sought to undermine the legitimacy of the federal judiciary by appointing unqualified justices to the Supreme Court. The administration's adversaries also charged that it tried to limit Congress's influence over foreign policy by keeping vital information from it, most notably, the "secret bombing" of Cambodia in 1973.

At the same time, Nixon sought to curtail the influence of the national news media. His administration brought suit against the *New York Times* in an effort to block publication of the Pentagon Papers and threatened, using the pretext of promoting ideological diversity, to compel the national television networks to sell the local stations they owned. The president's opponents denounced the administration's actions as abuses of power—which they surely were—and launched a full-scale assault upon Richard Nixon in the Watergate controversy.

The Watergate attack began with a series of revelations in the *Washington Post* linking the White House to a break-in at the Watergate Hotel headquarters of the Democratic National Committee. The *Post*'s reporters were quickly joined by scores of investigative journalists from the *New York Times, Newsweek, Time,* and the television networks.

As revelations of misdeeds by the Nixon White House proliferated, the administration's opponents in Congress demanded a full legislative investigation. In response, the Senate created a special committee, chaired by Senator Sam Ervin, to investigate White House misconduct in the 1972 presidential election. Investigators for the Ervin committee uncovered numerous questionable activities on the part of Nixon's aides, and these were revealed to the public during a series of dramatic, nationally televised hearings.

Evidence of criminal activity unearthed by the Ervin committee led to congressional pressure for the appointment of a special prosecutor. Ultimately, a large number of

The RIP Process

New appointment is proposed by the White House.

OPPONENTS	SUPPORTERS

Opponents of the appointment do an extensive background check, trying to find any negative information that may exist.

Supporters martial evidence: the nominee's experience, judgment, knowledge, etc.

Negative information discovered about the appointee is made public through leaks, rumors, and disclosures to reporters, TV news programs, and other media outlets.

Positive information is disseminated through the media: public statements in support of nominee, etc., picked up by newspapers, TV news programs, and news magazines.

In order to follow up on the leaks, the media do further investigations and the process picks up momentum, often resulting in additional negative information.

Supporters seek to refute damaging information by providing additional positive evidence and challenging media investigations and negative allegations.

Congressional hearings

Hostile questioning due to negative information in the media.

More negative information is uncovered and publicized by the media as momentum peaks.

Supporters are gradually silenced by momentum of negative information.

Supporters drop away, when accusations aimed at nominee prove to be accurate, particularly if the nominee has broken the law.

Nominee withdraws or is defeated.

high-ranking administration officials were indicted, convicted, and imprisoned. Impeachment proceedings were initiated against President Nixon, himself and when evidence linking him directly to the cover-up of the Watergate burglary was found, he was forced to resign from office. Thus, with the help of the RIP weaponry, the Nixon administration's antagonists achieved a total victory in their conflict with the president. Although no subsequent president has been driven from office, opponents of presidential administrations have since used the RIP process to attack and weaken their foes in the executive branch.

The RIP process became institutionalized when Congress adopted the 1978 Ethics in Government Act, which established procedures facilitating the appointment of special prosecutors to deal with allegations of wrongdoing in the executive branch. The act also defined as criminal several forms of influence peddling in which executive officials had traditionally engaged, such as lobbying former associates after leaving office. (Such activities are also traditional on Capitol Hill, but Congress chose not to impose the restrictions embodied in the act upon its own members and staff.) Basically, Congress created new crimes that executive branch officials could be charged with.

The extent to which the RIP process has come to be a routine feature of American politics became evident during the Iran-Contra conflict when Democrats charged that the Reagan administration had covertly sold arms to Iran and used the proceeds to provide illegal funding for Nicaraguan Contra forces, in violation of the Boland Amendment which prohibited such help. After the diversion of funds to the Contras was revealed, it was universally assumed that Congress should conduct televised hearings and the judiciary should appoint an independent counsel to investigate the officials involved in the episode. Yet this procedure is really quite remarkable: The RIP process has criminalized ordinary policy differences. Officials who in other democracies would merely be compelled to resign from office are now threatened with criminal prosecution in the United States.

Revelations and investigations of misconduct by public figures have become an important vehicle for political competition in the United States. The primary means through which liberal political forces attacked the White House and mobilized support for themselves during the Reagan administration were the investigations of EPA administrator Anne Burford Gorsuch, Attorney General Edwin Meese, and Supreme Court nominee Robert Bork, as well as the hearings on the Iran-Contra affair.

During the early months of the Bush presidency, partisan warfare chiefly took the form of allegations of misconduct lodged by Democrats and Republicans against one another. Senate Democrats were able to block John Tower's confirmation as secretary of defense with charges that his record of alcohol abuse and sexual impropriety and his ties to defense contractors rendered him unfit to head the Defense Department. Republicans then drove Democratic House Speaker Jim Wright from office with accusations of financial misdeeds, including allegations that Wright and his wife had received large sums of money from a real estate developer and had used inflated royalties from a book contract as a cover for exceeding the limits in congressional rules on outside income. At roughly the same time, charges of improper loans and investments compelled Democratic House whip Tony Coelho to resign.

Anita F. Hill
Sexual Harassment
Becomes an Issue

Anita F. Hill
(b. 1956)

One of the most highly visible political struggles in recent years, involving the incendiary issues of race, sex, and ideology, occurred far away from the American voting booth. At the center of the controversy was a little-known law professor from the University of Oklahoma, Anita Hill.

The initial confirmation hearings of Supreme Court nominee Clarence Thomas proceeded uneventfully in the late summer of 1991. Before the committee could make a formal recommendation to the Senate, however, news leaked out that they had a deposition from a woman who had worked under Thomas at the Department of Education and the Equal Employment Opportunity Commission (EEOC) in the 1980s. In the deposition, Anita Hill—a Yale-trained lawyer, like Thomas—claimed she had been sexually harassed by Thomas over a period of years.

When news of these charges leaked out, public pressure forced the committee to reopen the hearings. Hill's critics sought to discredit her testimony, suggesting that she was in fact a scorned woman who had unsuccessfully pursued Thomas. They also questioned why, if the allegations were true, Hill maintained a professional relationship with Thomas for several years without reporting the incidents or simply leaving. Hill responded that she was intimidated, fearful, and in need of the job. She said that she had respected the work Thomas had done at EEOC and simply did not consider reporting the advances. While some questioned Hill's honesty, her responses were consistent with the way women have typically responded to sexual harassment in the workplace.

Thomas hotly and categorically denied the accusations, claiming that he was being subjected to a "high-tech lynching." Both Thomas and Hill produced witnesses who supported their testimony, but Hill's credibility was hurt by the fact that no eyewitness ever heard or observed the alleged sexual advances. In a close vote, the Judiciary Committee recommended Thomas's confirmation to the Senate. The Senate subsequently approved Thomas by the narrowest ratification margin in history, 52 to 48.

The consequences of the hearings extended far beyond the Senate. The controversy provoked intense discussion and debate throughout the country. Greater attention and awareness was focused on the issue of sexual harassment.

No final resolution to the conflicting stories emerged. Polls taken months after the incident indicated that more Americans believed Hill than they did Thomas. Yet Hill sought no special celebrity, and she returned to her teaching job in Oklahoma.

Congressional Democrats responded with allegations that Wright's chief accuser, Republican House whip Newt Gingrich, also reaped improper profits from a book contract and engaged in dubious campaign fund-raising activities. Subsequently, House Democrats launched an investigation of Republican misuse of funds in the Department of Housing and Urban Development under former secretary Samuel Pierce.

Later, House Republicans called upon Democratic Representative Barney Frank to resign after embarrassing accounts of his personal life appeared in the press. In 1991, Democrats savaged Bush's Supreme Court nominee, Clarence Thomas, with sexual harassment charges while Republicans attacked the House Democratic leadership with charges of mismanaging the House bank and post office. In 1992, Democrats called for an investigation of the Bush administration's dealings with Iraq prior to the 1991 Persian Gulf War. They also demanded that a special counsel be appointed to examine charges that the Bush administration had improperly intervened in a case involving the Atlanta branch of Italy's Banca Nazionale del Lavoro (BNL), a bank charged with having provided illegal loans to Iraq during that nation's war with Iran.[12]

Divided Government: 1968–1992

The use of non-electoral means of political combat became more widely used during the 1980s and 1990s as a result of two decades of divided government. Since 1968 the Republicans have won all but two presiden-

tial elections, while the Democrats have dominated congressional races. As a result, rather than pinning its hopes on defeating its opponent in the electoral arena, each party sought to strengthen the institution it thought it could be sure of controlling while undermining the one associated with the enemy.

The Republicans reacted to their inability to win control of Congress by seeking to enhance the powers of the White House relative to the legislative branch. As previously mentioned, President Nixon impounded billions of dollars already appropriated by Congress and attempted, through various reorganization schemes, to bring executive agencies under closer White House control while severing their ties to the House and Senate. Presidents Reagan and Bush tolerated budget deficits of unprecedented magnitude in part because these deficits precluded new congressional spending; they also sought to increase presidential authority over executive agencies and diminish congressional authority by centralizing control over administrative rule making in the Office of Management and Budget. In addition, Reagan undertook to circumvent the legislative restrictions on presidential conduct embodied in the War Powers Act by sending American military forces abroad without congressional approval.

The Democrats, as we saw in Chapter 5, responded to the Republican presidential advantage by seeking to strengthen Congress while reducing the powers and prerogatives of the presidency—in sharp contrast to their behavior from the 1930s to the 1960s, when the Democratic party enjoyed an advantage in presidential elections. In the 1970s, Congress greatly enlarged its committee and subcommittee staffs, thus enabling the House and Senate to monitor

---

[12]George Lardner, Jr., "House Democrats Seek Independent Counsel to Probe Handling of BNL Case," *Washington Post*, 16 October 1992, p. A17.

Ronald Reagan and Bill Clinton
Redefining the Role of Government

Debate over the size, scope, and power of the federal government dominated the American political agenda in the 1980s and 1990s. Ronald Reagan swept into office in 1980 in large part on the promise to reduce government. Yet twelve years after Reagan's election, Bill Clinton won the presidency based on his pledge to mobilize the resources of government to attack pressing domestic problems.

Ronald Reagan's career in politics extended back to his days as an actor, when he was elected president of the Screen Actors Guild in 1947. He began his political life as a Democrat but formally switched to the Republican party in 1962. He became an ardent supporter of conservative Republican Barry Goldwater's unsuccessful bid for the presidency in 1964. Two years later Reagan was elected governor of California, a position he held for eight years. In 1976, Reagan narrowly lost the Republican nomination to incumbent Gerald Ford. Four years later, he captured the nomination and the presidency on a crest of conservative enthusiasm for less government and stronger national defense spending, defeating beleaguered incumbent Jimmy Carter.

In his inaugural address, Reagan stated unequivocally that "government is not the solution to our problem; government is the problem." During his first term in office, Reagan won major revisions in fiscal policy and brought about the enormous increases in military spending that he sought. During his second term, however, most of Reagan's legislative efforts were blocked by Congress and his administration ended under the cloud of the Iran-Contra scandal. Whether viewed as successful or not, the Reagan administration redefined the American political agenda to one in which more would have to be done with less.

Although considered by many to be a supporter of big-government spending, Bill Clinton sought to adapt to the post–Reagan era of

Ronald Reagan

and supervise closely the activities of executive agencies. Through the 1974 Budget and Impoundment Act, Congress increased its control over fiscal policy. It also enacted a number of statutory restrictions on presidential authority in the realm of foreign policy during the 1970s, including the Foreign Commitments Resolution and the

limited government by redefining the Democratic party while still drawing on the party's tradition of activism. Clinton's humble Arkansas roots belied his grand ambitions. A Rhodes scholar and graduate of Yale Law School, Clinton set his sights early on a political career. He became the nation's youngest governor when first elected in 1978. After an unexpected defeat in 1980, Clinton came back two years later to recapture the office, which he held until assuming the presidency.

Despite early political setbacks, Clinton proved to be a tenacious and durable campaigner for the 1992 presidential nomination. By the time he won the Democratic nomination, he stood even with his two rivals, George Bush and Ross Perot. From the end of the Democratic convention to election day, Clinton never trailed in the polls. Sensing that the mood of the country called for governmental leadership to address such pressing domestic problems as economic decline, revamping the nation's creaking health care system, and improving America's competitiveness, Clinton promised in his inaugural address to "resolve to make our Government a place for what Franklin Roosevelt called bold, persistent experimentation."

Once in office, Clinton introduced an ambitious package of proposals, including tax and spending increases, changes in America's health care system, and reform of campaign finance and lobbying practices. His proposals were initially greeted with enthusiasm by the media, the public, and members of his own party in Congress. Within several months, however, Clinton faced intense opposition from the Republicans, large segments of the media, and even from key congressional Democrats. Analysts asked whether Clinton's difficulties resulted from the president's own errors or whether they reflected some of the more systemic problems faced by America's government today. Is government the problem as Reagan suggests or the solution as Clinton contends? The debate continues. . . .

Source: John Chubb and Paul Peterson, eds., *Can Government Govern?* (Washington, DC: Brookings Institution, 1989).

Bill Clinton

Arms Export Control Act. Finally, congressional investigations, often conducted in conjunction with media exposés and judicial proceedings were effective in constraining executive power. The most important example is the Iran-Contra affair, which represented the culmination of two decades of struggle over foreign policy.

No More Division?

Bill Clinton's victory in the 1992 presidential election, coupled with continued Democratic control of Congress, has at least temporarily ended America's experiment with divided partisan control of the national government. However, it remains to be seen whether this will bring an end to the politics of RIP. There is no reason to believe it will. Clinton had campaigned as a centrist, or "New Democrat," but he and his supporters represented only one faction of the Democratic party. Given America's disjointed and decayed party structure they have little or no capacity to control or discipline the other factions. Indeed, during the last Democratic administration, the presidency of Jimmy Carter, liberal Democrats who were dissatisfied with the president's handling of environmental, consumer, and economic policies launched fierce RIP attacks against members of the president's staff.

Thus, it was hardly a surprise when factional conflicts broke out in the Democratic camp immediately after the 1992 election.[13] Nor was it surprising that even before Clinton's inauguration, the president-elect's cabinet appointees came under RIP attack. Clinton's commerce secretary designate, Ron Brown, was assailed for vigorously soliciting corporate and interest group contributions for an inaugural affair in his honor. Brown quickly canceled the event and was able to weather the storm because the host of Democratic politicians for whom he had raised funds over the years rallied to his defense.[14]

At the same time, Clinton's first choice for attorney general, Zoë Baird, was attacked for employing as household workers a Peruvian couple who had entered the United States illegally and for not securing appropriate documentation or making Social Security payments for them. Baird made a large payment retroactively and paid a fine. Nevertheless, after two days of hostile questioning by members of the Senate Judiciary Committee and a deluge of letters and phone calls to members of Congress by individuals and groups protesting the nomination, Baird asked the president to withdraw her name. Clinton, eager to contain the damage from what came to be called the "dannygate" affair, hardly bothered to defend his nominee and quickly rescinded the appointment.[15]

The campaign against Baird, according to some observers, was organized and orchestrated not by Republicans but by Democratic liberals. Consumer advocate Ralph Nader and other liberals objected to Baird's background as a corporate lawyer and to her past support for tort law reforms that would restrict citizen suits (see Chapter 7).[16] Some Republicans cheerfully joined the attack, happy to have an opportunity to give Clinton a black eye during his first week in office.

Immediately after his inauguration, Clinton attempted to bolster his support among the powerful liberal forces in the party by adopting a more liberal stance on domestic social spending, as well as on gay

[13]See Thomas B. Edsall, "Cracks in the Clinton Coalition," *Washington Post*, 8 November 1992, p. C1. See also Elizabeth Drew, "The White House's New New Dealers," ibid.

[14]Paul Barrett and David Rogers, "Senate Support for Zoë Baird is Precarious," *Wall Street Journal*, 22 January 1993, p. A3.

[15]Ruth Marcus and David Broder, "President Takes Blame for Rushing Baird Selection," *Washington Post*, 23 January 1993, p. A1.

[16]Michael Isikoff and Ruth Marcus, "As Support for Baird Erodes, Senators Call for Withdrawal," *Washington Post*, 22 January 1993, p. 1. See also Seymour Martin Lipset, "Roosevelt Redux for the Democrats," *Wall Street Journal*, 21 January 1993, p. A14.

rights, abortion, minority representation, and other causes championed by the Democratic Left. Campaign promises such as welfare reform and the "middle-class tax cut," backed by the centrists, were forgotten. Clinton and his team believed it had been Carter's failure to reach out to the party's liberal wing after campaigning as a moderate that had led to the collapse of his presidency twelve years earlier.[17] But in shifting to the left, Clinton was also echoing one of George Bush's tactics. Bush, a centrist, had felt compelled to try to maintain the allegiance of forces on his party's right wing by championing their views on abortion and other social issues.

By moving to the right, of course, Bush had alienated moderate Republicans. In a similar way, as he sought to accommodate liberal forces, Clinton risked losing the support of Democrats from other parts of the political spectrum. Liberals insisted that the president's health care reform package include a guarantee of funding for abortions for all women. This enraged conservatives, who then vowed to oppose the entire plan.[18] His effort to end the military's ban on gay personnel engendered intense opposition within the armed services and among conservative and even moderate Democrats. Democratic opposition was led by the powerful chair of the Senate Armed Service Committee, Senator Sam Nunn of Georgia. His efforts to conciliate liberals by expanding domestic spending programs led to a revolt among conservative and moderate Democrats, who demanded the imposition

of caps on the growth of entitlement programs such as Medicare.[19]

The Senate's Democratic leadership became increasingly concerned that the administration's difficulties would, if unchecked, lead to a total collapse that could hurt Democratic senators and House members up for re-election in 1994. To prevent a complete disaster, Democratic Senate leaders took charge of the budget package in the Finance committee, and suggested that the president confine himself to enunciating broad principles while leaving it to Congress to develop the "details" of legislation.[20]

Clinton then surprised politicians in both parties by appointing David Gergen, who had formerly been a key adviser to three Republican presidents including Ronald Reagan, to the newly created position of presidential "counselor." The president hoped Gergen would reassure moderates and conservatives that the administration was moving back to the political center. While some politicians and commentators praised the Gergen appointment, for the most part, both the liberal and conservative camps charged Clinton (and Gergen) with deceit and opportunism. Liberals were dismayed that Clinton would give a key White House position to an individual who had played a central role in selling Ronald Reagan's program to the nation.[21]

Debate over the Gergen appointment had hardly ended when Clinton sparked a new controversy, when, again seeking to pla-

[17]Fred Barnes, "Back to Basics," *New Republic,* 17 May 1993, pp. 16–18. See also Michael Kelly, "New Democrats Say Clinton Has Veered Left and Left Them," *New York Times,* 23 May 1993, p. 20. See also Adam Clymer, "Single-Minded President," *New York Times,* 4 April 1993, p. 1.

[18]Dana Priest, "Health Plan Threatened by Abortion Coverage," *Washington Post,* 19 May 1993, p. 1.

[19]Eric Pianin, "Hill Democrats Press for Entitlement Caps," *Washington Post,* 18 May 1993, p. 1.

[20]David Broder, "Democrats Worrying: Clinton's Problems Raise Fears for 1994," *Washington Post,* 9 June 1993, p. 1. See also Ann Devroy and Eric Pianin, "Clinton Yields on Energy Tax," *Washington Post,* 9 June 1993, p. 1.

[21]See Ruth Marcus, "Clinton's New Spin Doctor Has Left a Trail of Blunt Diagnoses," *Washington Post,* 31 May 1993, p. A4; and "A History of Gergenism," *New York Times,* 2 June 1993, p. A18.

cate conservative and moderate Democrats, he withdrew his nomination of Lani Guinier, an African American law professor at the University of Pennsylvania, to head the civil rights division of the Justice Department.

Conservatives had strongly opposed the Guinier nomination and had mounted an RIP attack against her by writing press releases, reports, and op-ed pieces characterizing her as an extremist. In the course of the Guinier nomination battle, her critics acknowledged that they were seeking to make use of the same techniques used so successfully by liberal forces over the preceding years. "There's no question," one critic said, "that in terms of tactics, the playbook was written by the left and we're playing by the rules of the game established over the last twelve years."[22]

Clinton initially accused Guinier's opponents of painting a misleading picture of her views. But once the president concluded that a battle over the nomination was certain to alienate the conservatives and moderates he was now trying to court, Clinton abandoned the effort. Clinton's decision to withdraw the nomination was based on a political calculation similar to the one that led to his attacks on Jesse Jackson and rap singer Sister Souljah during his campaign. The president concluded that, although they would be angered by his actions, African Americans and their liberal political allies ultimately would have no choice but to continue to support his administration. Whereas if he continued to alienate conservative Democrats, he would undermine his chances of winning their approval for his economic, health care, and political reform proposals.[23]

In the end, the president's handling of the Guinier nomination proved divisive and costly. As in the hiring of Gergen, Clinton's efforts to satisfy moderates and conservatives deeply offended liberal Democrats while doing little to placate the party's other wing. Civil rights leaders denounced the president for failing to even allow Guinier an opportunity to present her case to the Senate Judiciary Committee, which would have had to confirm the appointment. Conservatives, for their part, expressed disdain for the president's "waffling" and condemned him as an individual whose "only core principle is to bend to the strongest political force."[24]

THE MEDIA'S MESSAGE. In addition to the problems he faced from interest group opposition, partisan antagonism, and factional struggle in his own party, Clinton also found himself under attack from the national news media. As has often been noted, many of America's most prominent journalists tend to identify themselves as liberal Democrats, and many had implicitly or explicitly supported Clinton during the 1992 campaign. During his first two months in office, President Clinton continued to have considerable media support. After his initial budget proposals were accepted by Congress, he was hailed as a political genius. A few weeks later, however, the media began to adopt a considerably more critical stance. In the wake of the Republican senatorial filibuster that defeated Clinton's proposed economic stimulus package, many commentators concluded that Clinton was not experienced enough to manage the congressional process. After his first one hundred days in office, the president was accused of having lost his focus, of a lack of organiza-

---

[22]Michael Isikoff, "Power Behind the Thrown Nominee: Activist with Score to Settle," *Washington Post*, 6 June 1993, p. A11.

[23]Ruth Marcus, "Clinton Withdraws Nomination of Guinier," *Washington Post*, 4 June 1993, p. 1.

[24]Paul A. Gigot, "Guinier Is Going, No, She's Staying, No, Going . . . ," *Wall Street Journal*, 4 June 1993, p. A14.

tion, and of trying to do too many things at once.[25]

Why did the president's relationship with the national media sour so quickly? There are essentially two reasons. First, as discussed in Chapter 13, the power of the news media in the United States is, in large measure, linked to the media's capacity to investigate and criticize. Investigative reporting and adversarial journalism are techniques that enhance the power and status of the media relative to other American political and social institutions. For this reason, any administration can expect a certain amount of critical coverage.

Second, the president and members of his staff responded to media criticism in ways that were guaranteed to antagonize journalists and generate even more hostility. For example, to avoid media questions, the president spurned press conferences in favor of "town meetings" with the public. Members of his staff helpfully observed that the president did not need the media and could reach "over their heads" to the American public. In a similar vein, large sections of the White House press office were declared "off-limits" to reporters who then resented what they saw as another effort to block their access to legitimate news.

Once David Gergen joined the White House staff, he sought to develop a better relationship with the national media. He scheduled a White House cook-out for reporters, removed restrictions on media access to presidential press aides, and sought to schedule several traditional presidential press conferences to give journalists the opportunity they had been demanding to question the president. But the first of these news conferences ended rather badly. Clinton had just nominated Judge Ruth Bader Ginsburg to the U.S. Supreme Court, filling the vacancy created by Justice Byron White's pending retirement. Asked a question that seemed to imply criticism of his selection process, the president gave an angry response and stalked off, refusing to take any more questions.[26] (See Box 12.1.)

What came to be known as the "one-question news conference" drew angry responses from the national media. The next day, the nation's two most influential newspapers, the *New York Times* and the *Washington Post*, both published editorials praising Judge Ginsburg but sharply criticizing the White House for its selection process. The *Times* castigated the president for "an intemperate response to a reporter's question about his erratic selection process."[27] In its news coverage, the *Post* ridiculed the selection process as erratic and ultimately based on the president's personal rapport with the nominee—"personal karma," the *Post* called it—rather than reasoned judgment.[28]

Later that week, the White House scheduled a prime time press conference. The president hoped to use reporters' questions to review his administration's achievements. Two of the three national networks, however, refused to carry the news conference. Network executives saw the conference as simply another effort by David Gergen to manipulate the news.[29]

---

[25] See, for example, Thomas B. Edsall, "Clinton Loses Focus—and Time," *Washington Post*, 2 May 1993, p. C1. But see also Jeffrey Birnbaum, "Resentful of Negative Coverage, Clinton Spurns the Media, but He May Need to Woo Them Back," *Wall Street Journal*, 15 April 1993, p. A16.

[26] Howard Kurtz, "One Question Too Many For Clinton," *Washington Post*, 15 June 1993, p. A13.

[27] See "Mr. Clinton Picks a Justice," *New York Times*, 15 June 1993, p. A26.

[28] Ann Devroy and Ruth Marcus, "After 87 Days, Tortuous Selection Process Came Down to Karma," *Washington Post*, 15 June 1993, p. A11; and "Judge Ginsburg's Nomination . . . And Getting There," *Washington Post*, 15 June 1993, p. A20.

[29] See Gwen Ifill, "Clinton, in Prime Time, Spurned by Two Networks," *New York Times*, 18 June 1993, p. A18.

BOX 12.1
"The Ginsburg Nomination:
The One-Question News Conference"

*A*fter remarks by Supreme Court nominee Ruth Bader Ginsburg, President Clinton took a question from Brit Hume of ABC News. The news conference opened and closed with this exchange:

Q: "Mr. President, the result of the Guinier nomination, sir, and your apparent focus on Judge Breyer, and your turn, late it seems, to Judge Ginsburg may have created an impression, perhaps unfair, of a certain zigzag quality in the decision-making process here. I wonder, sir, if you could kind of walk us through it and perhaps disabuse us of any notion we might have along those lines. Thank you."

A: "I have long since given up the thought that I could disabuse some of you of turning any substantive decision into anything but a political process. How you could ask a question like that after the statement she just made is beyond me.
"Goodbye. Thank you."

Sources: Cable News Network; news reports.

Reprinted from the *Washington Post*, 15 June 1993.

Can Democratic Politics Function without Voters?

During the political struggles of the past decades, politicians sought to undermine the instituion associated with their foes, disgrace one another on national television, force their competitors to resign from office, and in a number of cases, send their opponents to prison. Remarkably, one tactic that has not been so widely used is the mobilization of the electorate. Of course, Democrats and Republicans have contested each other and continued to contest each other in national elections. Voter turnout even inched up in 1992. However, neither side has made much effort to mobilize new voters, to create strong local party organizations, or in general, to make full use of the electoral arena to defeat its enemies.

The 1993 "Motor-Voter" Act is, at best, a very hesitant step in the direction of expanded voter participation. The act requires all states to allow voters to register by mail when they renew their driver's licenses (twenty-eight states already have similar mail-in procedures) and provides for the placement of voter registration forms in motor vehicle, public assistance, and military recruitment offices. This type of passive approach to registration still places the burden of action on the individual citizen and is not likely to result in many new registrants, especially among the poor and uneducated. Mobilization requires more than the distribution of forms.[30]

It is certainly not true that politicians don't know how to mobilize new voters and expand electoral competition. Voter mobilization is hardly a mysterious process. It entails an investment of funds and organizational effort to actively register voters and bring them to the polls on election day. Occasionally, politicians demonstrate that they *do* know how to mobilize voters if they have a strong enough incentive. For example, a massive get-out-the-vote effort by Democrats to defeat neo-Nazi David Duke in the 1991 Louisiana Democratic gubernatorial primary led to a voter turnout of over 80 percent of those eligible—twice the normal turnout level for a Louisiana primary.

How extraordinary, then, that politicians who will stop at nothing in their efforts to

"RIP" the opposition stop short of attempting to expand the electorate to overwhelm their foes in competitive elections. Why is this?

A large part of the answer to this question is that the decline of political party organizations over the past several decades strengthened politicians in both camps who were linked with and supported by the middle and upper-middle classes. Recall from Chapter 10 that party organization is an especially important instrument for enhancing the political influence of groups at the bottom of the social hierarchy—groups whose major political resource is numbers. Parties allowed politicians to organize the energies of large numbers of individuals from the lower classes to counter the superior financial and institutional resources available to those from the middle and upper classes.

The decline of party organization that resulted, in large measure, from the efforts of upper- and middle-class "reformers," over the years, undermined politicians such as union officials and Democratic and Republican "machine" leaders who had a stake in popular mobilization, while strengthening politicians with an upper-middle- or upper-class base. Recall the effects of registration laws, the elimination of patronage practices, and so forth, discussed in Chapter 11. As a result of these reforms, today's Democratic and Republican parties are dominated by different segments of the American upper-middle class. For the most part, contemporary Republicans speak for business and professionals from the private sector, while Democratic politicians and political activists are drawn from and speak for upper-middle-class professionals in the public and not-for-profit sector.

Both sides give lip service to the idea of fuller popular participation in political life. Politicians and their upper-middle-class

---

[30]For an excellent discussion see Steven J. Rosenstone and John Mark Hansen, *Mobilization, Participation and Democracy in America* (New York: Macmillan, 1993), Chapter 8.

constituents in both camps, however, have access to a variety of different political resources—the news media, the courts, universities, and interest groups, to say nothing of substantial financial resources. As a result, neither side has much need for or interest in political tactics that might, in effect, stir up trouble from below. Both sides prefer to compete for power without engaging in full-scale popular mobilization. This is a political process whose class bias is so obvious and egregious that, if it continues, Americans may have to begin adding a qualifier when they describe their politics as democratic. Perhaps the terms "semi-democratic," "quasi-democratic," or "neo-democratic" are in order to describe a political process in which ordinary voters have as little influence as they do in contemporary America.

Politics and Governance

The failure of political leaders to organize and mobilize strong popular bases leaves them weak and vulnerable to the institutions and interests, including the mass media, upon which they are now so dependent. Party politicians had stable, organized, popular followings that could be counted upon when their leaders came under fire. As Chicago's longtime machine mayor, Richard J. Daley, once said in response to media attacks, "When you've got the people behind you, you don't need the media. . . . The media can kiss my ———!" Contemporary politicians seldom have well-organized popular followings. Lacking such a base of support, they seldom can afford Mayor Daley's indifference to his media image.

Contemporary American politics undermine governance in four ways. First, elec-

tions today fail to accomplish what must be the primary task of any leadership selection process: they fail to determine *who will govern*. An election should award the winners with the power to govern. Only in this way can popular consent be linked to effective governance. Under the fragmented system bequeathed to us by the Constitution's framers, seldom at any point in American history have all the levers of power been grasped by a unified and disciplined party or group.

Today, however, with the decay of America's political party organizations, this fragmentation has increased sharply. There are many victorious cliques and factions with little unity among them. During the Bush presidency, fragmentation and division led to a pattern of "gridlock" in which little or nothing could be accomplished in Washington. Deep factional divisions within the Democratic party, as we have seen, posed severe problems for the Clinton administration within the first few months of office, producing a paralysis not too different from the infamous gridlock of the Bush years.

As we saw in Chapter 5, a number of conservative Democrats joined with the Republican opposition to oppose Clinton on issues ranging from the budget to the question of allowing gays in the military. Clinton was forced to change his proposals to accommodate this opposition within his own party. The budget eventually enacted by Congress and signed into law by the president in August 1993 bore little resemblance to Clinton's initial proposals. Congressional opponents forced Clinton to abandon his campaign promise to provide middle-class tax relief as well as the bulk of his package of social and economic "investments." One journalist, sympathetic to Clinton's original goals, called the budget a "far cry" from Clinton's original proposals and hardly a long-term solution to the nation's problems.[31]

In addition to factional opposition, Clinton's efforts were hampered by the fact that many congressional Democrats have become "soloists," willing to give the administration their support only in exchange for some set of tangible benefits for themselves and the interests they represent. In the absence of party organizations and mechanisms for enforcing party discipline, there is little to prevent legislators from demanding what amounts to immediate political payoffs in exchange for their support on important pieces of legislation. The result is that all legislation effectively becomes special-interest legislation filled with loopholes and special benefits. For example, the 1993 budget contains provisions requiring that cigarettes manufactured in the U.S. contain 75 percent domestically grown tobacco. This provision was inserted at the behest of Senator Wendell Ford of Kentucky for the benefit of his state's tobacco farmers. Similarly, Democratic Representative James Bilbray of Nevada agreed to support the budget only after securing a tax credit designed to offset the Social Security taxes paid on employees' tips by restaurant owners—an important constituency group in his district. Texas Democrat Solomon Ortiz traded his support of the president's budget for an enlarged share of defense conversion funds for his district. The list goes on and on.[32] No wonder columnist David Broder called the resulting budget a "pastiche of conflicting goals."[33] One Clinton administration official conceded that because the

budget was "driven by politics not policy," it was "not the greatest package ever."[34]

Long-standing institutional rivalries also work to thwart governance. For example, the Senate's Democratic leadership was no more willing to give fellow Democrat Clinton the line-item veto power he requested than they had been to accede to similar requests from Republican presidents.

Second, contemporary governments are weak and unstable. Elected officials subjected to RIP attacks often find that their poll standing (today's substitute for an organized popular base) can evaporate overnight and their capacity to govern disappear with it. Thus, the Nixon administration was paralyzed for three years by the Watergate affair and the Reagan White House for two years by the Iran-Contra affair. Congress was nearly immobilized for a year by the Tower-Wright-Coelho-Frank imbroglio and for another year by the post office scandal. This is hardly a recipe for a strong government to solve America's long-term deficit and trade problems.

Third, because they lack a firm popular base, politicians seldom have the capacity to confront entrenched economic or political interest groups even when the public interest seems clear. For example, early in the Bush administration, the Treasury Department's plan for resolving the crisis in the savings and loan (S & L) industry involved the imposition of a fee on S & L deposits. This idea was adamantly rejected by the industry and met overwhelming resistance on Capitol Hill, where thrift institutions enjoyed a good deal of influence. The administration was compelled to disown the Treasury plan and proposed, instead, a plan in

---

[31]David Broder, "Some Victory," *Washington Post*, 10 August 1993, p. A15.

[32]David Rogers and John Harwood, "No Reasonable Offer Refused as Administration Bargained to Nail Down Deficit Package in House," *Wall Street Journal*, 6 August 1983, p. A12.

[33]Broder, "Some Victory."

[34]Hobart Rowan, "It's Not Much of a Budget," *Washington Post*, 12 August 1993, p. A27.

DEBATING THE ISSUES

Is America Declining?

*T*he end of the Cold War has resulted in important changes in the relationships among nations. While America seemed to emerge triumphantly from the eclipse of communism in the former Soviet Union and elsewhere, many have viewed America's changing role in the world as being in decline.

Foreign policy expert Edward N. Luttwak summarizes the concerns of many who fear that the United States is losing its economic competitive edge, to the point where we may one day resemble nations of the developing world, struggling to keep our economic heads above water. Newspaper editor Robert L. Bartley argues that the gloom-and-doomers ignore or distort the evidence indicating America's continued strength and resilience.

Luttwak

When will the United States become a third-world country? One estimate would place the date as close as the year 2020. A more optimistic projection might add another ten or fifteen years. Either way, if present trends simply continue, all but a small minority of Americans will be impoverished soon enough, left to yearn hopelessly for the lost golden age of American prosperity. . . .

The relentless erosion of the entire economic base of American society is revealed by undisputed statistics. . . . During the last 20 years—half a working lifetime—American "non-farm, non-supervisory" employees actually earned slightly less, year by year. As a matter of fact, by 1990 their real earnings . . . had regressed to the 1965 level. Will they regress further . . . to the 1955 level by the year 2000? It seems distinctly possible. . . .

Who are these poor unfortunates whose real earnings have been declining since 1965? Are they perhaps some small and peculiar minority? Not so . . . they numbered 74,888,000, or just over 81 percent of all non-farm employees—that is, more than eight out of ten of all Americans who are not self-employed, from corporate executives earning hundreds or even thousands of dollars per hour, to those working at the minimum wage.

---

which general tax revenues would finance the bulk of the cost of the $166 billion bailout. In this way, a powerful interest, the savings and loan industry, was able to shift the burden of a major federal initiative designed for the industry's own benefit from itself to the general public. Moreover, to mask the impact that the bailout would have on the nation's budget deficit, it was largely financed through "off-budget" procedures—a ploy that over time adds billions of dollars to the cost of the bailout.

In a similar vein, after his election in 1992, President Clinton felt compelled to reassure the nation's business community and powerful banking and financial interests that his administration would be receptive to their needs. This was a major reason that Clin-

Far from being a minority whose fate cannot affect the base of American society, then, they *are* the base of American society. . . .

How can the entire structure of American affluence and advancement from luxurious living to scientific laboratories *not* decline when the vast majority of all working Americans are earning less and less? And how can the U.S. not slide toward third world conditions if this absolute decline continues while in both Western Europe and East Asia real earnings continue to increase?[1]

Bartley

To the ordinary, everyday senses of mankind, America has not declined, it has prevailed. Its foe of two generations has collapsed and now even seeks to adopt American institutions of democracy and market economics.

Though to people who use their eyes and ears it is obvious that American influence in the world is on the rise, we have not been able to put the notion of decline behind us. For a segment of American opinion refuses to use its eyes and ears. Instead, proponents of decline confuse themselves with statistics they do not understand, or in some cases willingly distort. They invoke jingoism by turning international trade into some kind of combat, instead of a series of mutually beneficial arrangements among consenting adults. . . .

. . . Our dilemma is that all of us living in the 1990s have been taught from the cradle not to believe in dreams. We are cynical about politicians, and they live down to our expectations. . . . Instead of the promise of world cooperation led by the United States, we have the gloomy apostles of decline, alarmed because goods and capital move across lines someone drew on maps, trying to manufacture conflict out of the peaceful and mutually beneficial intercourse among peoples.

The last time the will of the West was tested, it rose to the challenge. In particular, the American electorate understood that the threat was Soviet Communism, not the military-industrial complex. With the more subtle test of a litany of decline coming out of Cambridge, Detroit, and Washington, there will again be confusion and apparent close calls, but in the end the delusion will not sell. Indeed, given any sort of intellectual and political leadership to frame the challenge, the American nation will rise to the rich opportunity before it.[2]

[1]Edward N. Luttwak, "Is America on the Way Down? Yes," *Commentary*, March 1992, pp. 15, 21.
[2]Robert L. Bartley, "Is America on the Way Down? No," *Commentary*, March 1992, pp. 22, 27.

ton—who had campaigned as a staunch opponent of business-as-usual in Washington—named Democratic National Committee chair Ron Brown to be his secretary of Commerce and Texas Democratic Senator Lloyd Bentsen to the post of secretary of the Treasury. Brown was a veteran Washington corporate lobbyist well known to the business community. Bentsen, as chair of the Senate Finance Committee, was noted for his close and cordial relationship with banking, finance, insurance, and real estate interests.[35] President Clinton was no more eager

[35]Jill Abramson and John Harwood, "Some Say Likely Choice of Bentsen, the Insider, for Treasury Post Could Send the Wrong Signals," *Wall Street Journal*, 9 December 1992, p. A26.

than his predecessor to confront these interests. Later, to secure the enactment of his tax proposals, Clinton felt compelled to give major tax concessions to a variety of interests including aluminum producers, real estate developers, multinational corporations, and the energy industry.[36]

Finally, the enhanced political power of non-electoral institutions means that the question of who will *not* govern is unlikely to be resolved in the electoral arena. The most important function of an election is to determine who will govern. At the same time, elections must also deprive the losing party of the power to prevent the winning party from governing effectively. Today, elections not only fail to determine who will govern but also do not definitively determine *who will not exercise power*. Given the political potency of non-electoral modes of political struggle, electoral defeat does not deprive the losing party of the power to undermine the programs and policies of the winner. Indeed, as we have seen, electoral verdicts can now be reversed outside the electoral arena.

As a result, even as the "winners" in the American electoral process do not acquire firm control of the government, so the "losers" are not deprived of power. Instead, "winners" and "losers" typically engage in a continuing struggle, which often distracts them from real national problems. For example, in 1991 and 1992, official Washington seemed much more concerned with several thousand dollars in bounced congressional checks than with several hundred billion dollars in debts.

More important, however, this struggle compels politicians to pay greater heed to the implications of policies for their domestic political battles than for collective national purposes. The Reagan and Bush administrations' tolerance of enormous budget deficits and their program of deregulation provide examples of this phenomenon. One important reason why Republican administrations were prepared to accept the economic risks of unprecedented deficits is the constraint these deficits imposed on congressional power. Similarly, the Republicans pressed for deregulation in part because the constellations of interests surrounding many regulatory policies are important Democratic bastions. This sort of political gamesmanship caused the administration to overlook potential costs and risks of their policies. The relaxation of regulatory restraints on financial institutions permitted many S & Ls to shift from their traditional role as home mortgage lenders into potentially more lucrative but dangerously speculative areas. We all now know the results.

Their concern for their institutional and political advantage can also affect the way officials respond to the initiatives of their opponents. For example, congressional Democrats regularly voted for lower levels of military spending than the two Republican administrations proposed, not because they were less committed to the nation's defense, but because the defense establishment has been an important institutional bastion of the Republicans. This reason also played a part in Democratic opposition to the 1991 Persian Gulf War.

Similarly, despite the continuing problem of America's huge budget deficit, the Clinton administration has been committed to increases in federal domestic spending. Like Reagan's and Bush's reasons for defense spending, domestic social spending is politically necessary for the Clinton administration, whatever the long-term economic

---

[36]David Hilzenrath, "Bentsen Signals White House's Willingness to Deal," *Washington Post*, 17 May 1993, p. A4.

risks it may entail. Indeed, despite his reputation as a "policy wonk," Clinton quickly found that it was virtually impossible to focus on questions of policy effectiveness. Purely political considerations frequently had to come first.[37] In contemporary America, political struggle is constant, leaving little room for consideration of long-term public interests.

Electoral Mobilization and Governmental Power

What can be done to restore our government's capacity to govern? The most important implication of the political patterns we have observed is that good government is unlikely to result from an unhealthy politics. Rejuvenation of America's governmental capabilities would first and foremost require the revitalization of America's political process. In particular, we would need to revive the nation's crumbling electoral institutions.

Of course, the relationship between political patterns and governmental effectiveness is complex. Practices that severely undermine governmental capacities in some settings may not in others—witness the ability of Japan to thrive despite widespread political corruption in its government. But, political patterns sometimes emerge that seriously inhibit governments from pursuing collective purposes. For example, in Israel during the late 1980s, electoral stalemate between the Labor and Likud parties paralyzed the government. This stalemate prevented the government from responding ef-

fectively to the uprisings in the occupied territories and to diplomatic initiatives by the Palestine Liberation Organization, thereby threatening the close relationship with the United States, which is necessary for Israel's very survival.

Similar examples can be found in American history. In the United States during the early 1930s, prevailing party and factional conflict led the government to pursue policies that exacerbated rather than relieved the Depression. A notable example is the Smoot-Hawley Tariff of 1930. Congressional logrolling practices of the 1930s led to the adoption of the highest tariffs in American history. This provoked foreign retaliation, precipitated a virtual collapse of international trade, and helped turn what could have been an ordinary cyclical downturn into the most severe economic crisis of the modern era. Even more striking than the events of the early 1930s are those preceding the Civil War. Political paralysis and partisan deadlock during the James Buchanan administration prevented the government from responding to its own dismemberment as southern states seceded from the Union.

Historically, efforts to overcome political patterns that undermine governmental effectiveness have taken one of two forms in the United States: political demobilization or mobilization. Political demobilization involves attempts to free government from "political interference" by insulating decision-making processes, restricting political participation, or both. Mobilization consists of efforts by one or another contender for power to overcome political stalemate and governmental paralysis by bringing new voters into the electorate and strengthening their political base sufficiently to confront and prevail over entrenched social and economic interests.

[37] See Jeffrey H. Birnbaum and Michael K. Frisby, "Clinton's Zigzags between Politics and Policy Explain Some Problems of His First 100 Days," *Wall Street Journal*, 29 April 1993, p. A16.

Demobilization and insulation were the paths followed by institutional reformers in the United States during the Progressive era. The Progressives, who spoke for a predominantly middle-class constituency, sought to cope with the problems of turn-of-the-century America by strengthening the institutions of national, state, and local government. Progressives undertook to strengthen executive institutions by promoting civil service reform, creating regulatory commissions staffed by experts, and transferring fiscal and administrative responsibilities from elected to appointed officials.[38] In addition, asserting that the intrusion of partisan considerations undermined governmental efficiency, the Progressives attacked state and local party organizations. They sponsored legislative investigations of ties between party leaders and businessmen as well as the criminal prosecution of politicians they deemed to be corrupt. The Progressives also supported the enactment of personal registration requirements for voting that served to reduce turnout among the poorly educated, immigrant, nonwhite, and working-class voters who had provided the various party organizations with their mass base.[39]

In the short run, the Progressive strategy of administrative reform did help improve the functioning of government in the United States. Government agencies penetrated by parties and rife with patronage are not well suited to performing the functions of a modern state. However, politicians are not in a position to prevail over entrenched social and economic forces when they lack the support of an extensive and well-organized mass constituency. In the long run, the Progressive strategy of insulation and demobilization weakened American government relative to powerful interests in society and helped produce the low rates of voter turnout that ultimately contributed to political stalemate in the United States today.

The second strategy—political mobilization—was used most effectively in the United States by the administrations of Abraham Lincoln and Franklin D. Roosevelt. To fight the Civil War and break the power of Southern slaveholders, the Lincoln administration vastly expanded the scope of the American national state. It raised an enormous army and created a national system of taxation, a national currency, and a national debt. The extraordinary mobilization of the electorate that brought the Republicans to power in 1860 enabled them to raise more than two million troops, to sell more than $2 billion in bonds to finance the military effort, and to rally popular support for the war. The higher levels of party organization and political mobilization in the North than in the South, as much as the superiority of Northern industry, help explain the triumph of the Union cause in the Civil War.[40]

In a similar vein, the Roosevelt administration permanently transformed the American institutional landscape, creating the modern welfare and regulatory state.[41] The support that the administration mobilized through party organizations and labor unions helped it contend with opposition to its programs both inside and outside the

---

[38]Stephen Skowronek, *Building a New American State* (New York: Cambridge University Press, 1982).

[39]Frances Fox Piven and Richard A. Cloward, *Why Americans Don't Vote* (New York: Pantheon, 1988), Chapter 3.

[40]Eric McKitrick, "Party Politics and the Union and Confederate War Efforts," in *The American Party Systems,* ed. by William N. Chambers and Walter Dean Burnham (New York: Oxford University Press, 1967), pp. 117–51.

[41]See the essays in Margaret Weir, Ann Orloff, and Theda Skocpol, eds., *The Politics of Social Policy in the United States* (Princeton: Princeton University Press, 1988).

institutions of government. A marked increase in voter turnout, a realignment of some existing blocs of voters, and a revitalized Democratic party apparatus provided Roosevelt with the enormous majorities in the electoral college and Congress that allowed him to secure the enactment of his New Deal programs.[42] Worker mobilization through unions and strikes forced businessmen to accept the new pattern of industrial relations the administration was seeking to establish.[43]

Electoral Mobilization in Contemporary Politics

The dangers facing the United States in the 1990s may not be as immediate as those it confronted on the eve of the Civil War or in the aftermath of the 1929 stock market crash. Nevertheless, America's political processes impede governmental responses to the challenges of today.

What could strengthen America's government? The answer lies in the realm of electoral organization and mobilization. As political scientists have been arguing for decades, stronger political parties could potentially diminish our electoral and governmental fragmentation and produce governments with greater unity and collective purpose than is currently possible.

A bit of party discipline might go a long way toward enhancing the government's capacity to govern. A bit of party unity, moreover, might go a long way toward giving elected officials the strength to withstand attacks by their opposition. Parties could

certainly be strengthened through changes in campaign-funding rules, nominating rules, and ballot laws that might give party leaders greater control over campaign funds and candidate nominations. Unfortunately, one element of President Clinton's campaign finance reform package would have just the opposite effect. Clinton proposed prohibiting the use of so-called "soft money" (money contributed to the parties rather than to the candidates) in federal campaigns. Under present federal law, there is no restriction on the amount that wealthy individuals and interests can contribute to parties for voter registration, grass-roots organizing, and other partisan activities not directly linked to a particular candidate's campaign efforts.

Critics charge that soft-money contributions allow wealthy donors unfair influence in the political process and, perhaps, this potential does exist. However, soft money also provides the national and state parties with the means to engage in voter registration and turn-out drives and to strengthen state and local party organizations. These are goals that should be encouraged rather than thwarted.[44]

Unfortunately, today's independent politicians have little stake in subjecting themselves to party control. Why, for example, should the currently autonomous members of Congress or of the state legislatures accept party control of nominations or campaign spending? The benefits of reforming the electoral system might accrue to the nation, but the costs would be borne by the very individuals who would have to agree

---

[42]Kristi Andersen, *The Creation of a Democratic Majority, 1928–1936* (Chicago: University of Chicago Press, 1979).

[43]David Plotke, "The Wagner Act, Again: Politics and Labor, 1935–37," *Studies in American Political Development* 3 (1988), pp. 105–56.

[44]See Beth Donovan, "Much-Maligned 'Soft Money' Is Precious to Both Parties: Clinton Wants to Ban Its Use in Federal Campaigns; Scholars Say it Assists Grass-Roots Growth," *Congressional Quarterly Weekly Report,* 15 May 1993, pp. 1195–1200.

In Brief Box

CAN THE GOVERNMENT GOVERN?

Over the past several decades, an undemocratic political process has developed in the United States, as popular participation in American political life has declined. With the decay of political parties, it has become more difficult to create an effective government capable of dealing with the economic and social issues affecting the nation. The existing political forces have come to rely heavily on forms of political conflict that neither require nor encourage much in the way of citizen involvement. We now have a government run by a "politics by other means."

Forms of "politics by other means"
1) Increasing number of criminal indictments against national, state, and local officials
2) Federal judiciary's central role in resolving struggles over major issues such as race relations, abortion, and social welfare, and economic policy
3) The use of the national security apparatus, for example the FBI, against groups opposed to the policies of the executive branch
4) Politicians' almost total dependence on the media to reach their constituents
5) RIP—Expansion of the political roles of the national news media and the federal judiciary has given rise to the new weapon of revelation, investigation, and prosecution

How does "politics by other means" undermine governance?
1) Deprives election winners of the power to govern
2) Subjects elected officials to the whims of public opinion
3) Prevents officials from confronting entrenched economic and political interest groups
4) Election losers are not deprived political power
5) Politicians are compelled to pay greater attention to domestic political battles rather than to the nation's pressing needs

What can be done?
We can try to revive the nation's crumbling electoral institutions through the mobilization of the electorate. It is unlikely, however, that either the Republican or Democratic party will attempt this because of the risks involved that potentially threaten their present political power and influence. As long as America's nonelectoral political patterns persist, the nation will continue to pay the price of its undemocratic politics.

---

to any package of reforms. In the nineteenth century, Progressives were able to undermine political parties precisely because they found elected representatives eager to free themselves from party discipline. Today's legislators are not eager to bind themselves again with the shackles their predecessors worked so hard to remove.

As for voter mobilization, were one of America's political parties to mobilize and forge organizational links to new voters, it might put itself in a position to prevail over entrenched interests and powerful social forces for the sake of achieving collective national purposes. Under such circumstances, the most debilitating feature of the contemporary American policy-making process—the government's lack of a firm base of support—might be contained.

For the Democrats, a strategy of mobilization presumably would involve a serious effort—going far beyond the Motor Voter Act—to bring into the electorate the tens of millions of working-class and poor Americans who at present stand entirely outside the political process. Figure 12.3 illustrates the large and long-standing differences in American voting-participation rates associated with race, education, and employment. Bringing citizens who currently do not vote into the Democratic party would probably require an organizational and programmatic focus on economic issues that unites poor, working-, and lower-middle-class voters and overcomes the racial and cultural issues that divide them.

Though it is generally assumed that only the Democrats could benefit from any substantial expansion of the electorate, it is important to note that mobilization is a strategy that the Republicans could employ as well.[45] Indeed, in the late 1970s and early 1980s, it was the GOP, through its alliance with conservative evangelicals, that made the more concerted effort to bring new voters into the electorate. Their efforts were limited, however and, thus, so was the party's ability to construct a base of support for conservatism large enough to pose a challenge to Democratic congressional hegemony.

By contrast, Europe's great conservative mobilizers of the nineteenth century, Otto von Bismarck and Benjamin Disraeli, brought millions of new working-class voters into the electorate and constructed extensive party organizations to link them securely to the conservative cause. By sponsoring factory and social legislation, moreover, they appealed to these voters on the basis of their long-term economic concerns, not simply their religious and nationalistic passions. Their counterpart in the United States, Abraham Lincoln, proceeded along similar lines. Nineteenth-century Republican electoral mobilization entailed the construction of party organizations throughout the North and relied on economic appeals as much as on the issues of slavery and union. The most important Republican slogan in 1860, after all, was "Vote yourself a farm, vote yourself a tariff." As these examples suggest, its position as the more conservative of the two major parties does not preclude the contemporary GOP from organizing a broad popular base for itself.

It is not likely, however, that either the Democrats or the Republicans will be willing to embark on the path of full-scale political mobilization. The politicians who have risen to the top in contemporary America learned their skills and succeeded in a low-voter-mobilization environment. And the weapons of political combat that have become central in American politics contribute to maintaining such an environment. When they rely mainly on these weapons to compete with one another, politicians provide voters with little opportunity or reason to participate in politics. Indeed, they give voters new reasons to refrain from participating.

Conversely, politicians competing for the support of a highly mobilized electorate would have to deal with questions of con-

[45]James DeNardo, "Turnout and the Vote: The Joke's on the Democrats," *American Political Science Review* 70 (June 1980), pp. 406–20.

FIGURE 12.3
Percentage Reporting They Voted

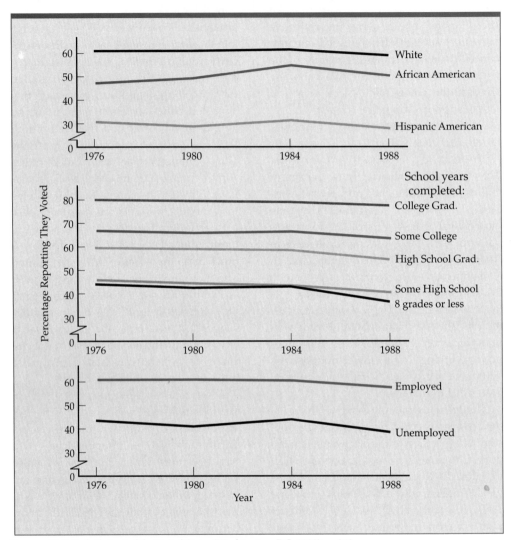

Source: *Statistical Abstract of the United States* (Washington, DC: 1993), p. 269.

cern to tens of millions of voters and would find it impossible to focus on the issues of personal impropriety that loom so large in American politics today. Nor would they find themselves so vulnerable to such

charges. In 1944, for example, when Republicans charged that Franklin Roosevelt had used government property for his personal benefit by sending a U.S. Navy destroyer to retrieve a pet he had left behind on the

Aleutian Islands, the president ridiculed them for attacking "my little dog, Fala."[46] FDR's links to a mass constituency were too strong to be threatened by the GOP charges, and therefore he was in a position to dismiss them with a derisive quip. Lacking such support, elected officials today are much more vulnerable to any allegations of personal impropriety.

In contrast to the immediate gains that politicians can realize today by resorting to revelations and investigations to drive opponents from office, the path of voter mobilization would entail major risks for both parties. For the Republicans, expansion of the electorate could threaten an influx of poor voters, who wouldn't seem likely to be supporters of the GOP. As for the Democrats, whatever the potential benefits to the party as a whole, an influx of millions of new voters would create serious uncertainties for current office holders at the local,

state, and congressional levels. Moreover, various interests allied with the Democrats—notably upper-middle-class environmentalists, public interest lawyers, antinuclear activists, and the like—could not be confident of retaining their influence in a more fully mobilized electoral environment. Finally, though it is seldom openly admitted, the truth is that many members of both the liberal and the conservative camps are wary of fuller popular participation in American politics. Conservatives fear blacks, and liberals often have disdain for working- and lower-middle-class whites.

As long as these conditions persist, the path of electoral mobilization will not be taken. America's non-electoral political patterns, governmental incapacities, and economic difficulties will endure, and America will continue to pay the price of its undemocratic politics. This price is a government that cannot govern—surely a price the nation cannot afford to pay as it confronts the economic and social problems of the twenty-first century.

[46]John P. Diggins, *The Proud Decades: America in War and Peace, 1941–1960* (New York: W.W. Norton, 1988), p. 21.

Time Line on Politics and Goverment

EVENTS		INSTITUTIONAL DEVELOPMENTS
		Long-term decline in voter turnout begins (1890)
	1900	
McCarthy hearings (1950s)	**1950**	
	1960	Decay of political party organizations (1960s)
		Rise of activist and adversarial media (1968)

EVENTS		INSTITUTIONAL DEVELOPMENTS
	1970	
Watergate hearings (1973–1974)		Legislative limits on presidential power; War Powers Resolution (1973); Budget and Impoundment Control Act (1974); Ethics in Government Act (1978)
Iran–Contra affair (1986)	**1980**	Reagan's deficits impose budgetary limits on Congress; period of intense conflict between legislative and executive branches (1980–1992)
Tower, Wright, Coelho and Frank revelations (1989)		
Clarence Thomas hearings (1990)	**1990**	
House post office and bank scandals (1992)		
Nannygate; Travelgate (1993)		Democratic control of both branches doesn't end gridlock (1993)

Chapter Review

As we approach the twenty-first century, America faces many problems. In such areas as health care, housing, crime, and education the U.S. government has been unable to formulate or implement effective programs or policies. In other areas, it is the government, itself, that seems to be the cause of the nation's difficulties. For example, the long-term strength of the American economy is threatened by the $4 trillion debt that is the fiscal legacy of the Reagan and Bush presidencies.

One major reason for our present dilemma is that an unhealthy and fundamentally undemocratic political process has developed in the United States over the past several decades. For much of American his-

tory, government rested on a relatively broad base of vigorous—often tumultuous—popular participation, with most major issues being debated, fought, and ultimately resolved in the electoral arena. America's democratic politics, in turn, provided political leaders with a base of support from which to develop and implement programs, contend with powerful, entrenched interests, and during times of crisis such as the Civil War and World War II, ask their countrymen for the exertions and sacrifices needed in order for the nation to survive.

In recent decades, however, popular participation in American political life has declined sharply. Despite a much ballyhooed increase in voter turnout in the 1992 presidential election, only 55 percent of eligible Americans bothered to vote. At the same time, the political parties that once mobilized voters and imparted a measure of unity to the scattered pieces of the American governmental structure have decayed, making it very difficult, if not impossible, to create a coherent government through the American electoral process.

Both reflecting and reinforcing these changes in the electoral process, contending political forces in the United States have come to rely heavily on forms of political conflict that neither require nor encourage much citizen involvement. In recent years, many of the most important national political struggles have been largely fought outside the electoral arena rather than through competitive electoral contests.

America's contemporary political process, characterized by low voter turnout, weak parties, and the rise of a "politics by other means," is the source of many of our government's present problems. This process is increasingly undemocratic, fragments political power, and fails to provide elected officials with the strong and stable political base needed to govern effectively. Most important, this process undermines the ability of elected officials to bring about, or even to take account of, the public good.

For Further Reading

Birnbaum, Jeffrey. *The Lobbyists* (New York: Times Books, 1992).

Calleo, David. *The Bankrupting of America* (New York: William Morrow, 1992).

Dionne, Jr., E.J. *Why Americans Hate Politics* (New York: Simon & Schuster, 1991).

Draper, Theodore. *A Very Thin Line: The Iran-Contra Affairs* (New York: Simon & Schuster, 1991).

Friedman, Benjamin. *Day of Reckoning: The Consequences of American Economic Policy Under Reagan and After* (New York: Random House, 1988).

Jackson, Brooks. *Honest Graft: Big Money and the American Political Process* (Washington, DC: Farragut Publishing, 1990 rev. ed.).

Johnson, Haynes. *Sleepwalking Through History* (New York: W. W. Norton, 1991).

Kernell, Samuel, ed. *Parallel Politics: Economic Policymaking in Japan and the United States* (Washington, DC: Brookings Institution, 1991).

Kurtz, Howard. *Media Circus* (New York: Times Books, 1993).

Kutler, Stanley. *The Wars of Watergate* (New York: W. W. Norton, 1990).

Phillips, Kevin. *Boiling Point: Democrats, Republicans and the Decline of Middle-Class Prosperity* (New York: Random House, 1993).

Rosenstone, Steven, and John Mark Hansen. *Mobilization, Participation and Democracy in America* (New York: Macmillan, 1993).

Sundquist, James L. *Constitutional Reform and Effective Government* (Washington, DC: Brookings Institution, 1992, rev. ed.).

Weaver, R. Kent, and Bert Rockman, eds. *Do Institutions Matter?* (Washington, DC: Brookings Institution, 1993).

13

INTRODUCTION TO PUBLIC POLICY

*T*ry as we may to have a system of limited government, where freedom and control are balanced, control must be the first priority. Without public order—that is, a predictable and relatively safe society—our freedom would not count for much.

The most deliberate form of government control we call "public policy." *Public policy* is an officially expressed intention backed by a sanction, and that sanction can be a reward or a punishment. A public policy may also be called a law, a rule, a statute, an edict, a regulation, an order. Today, "public policy" is the preferred term, probably because it conveys more of an impression of flexibility and compassion than other terms. But citizens, especially students of political science, should never forget that "policy" and "police" have common origins. Both derive from *polis* and *polity*, which refer to the political community, and "political community" is another, more positive term for public order. A public policy is thus composed of two parts—(1) one or more goals; and (2) some kind of a sanction. The first has to do with the purposes of government. The second is concerned with the means of achieving those purposes. Governments adopt many policies to pursue many goals, which is why Congress is so busy all the time. In contrast, there are very few types of sanctions to provide government with the means of fulfilling those purposes. We call these sanctions "techniques of control" to indicate the coercive aspect of policy. We deal with these in the first section of this chapter precisely because there are so few of them. The second section of this chapter will discuss some examples of actual policy goals that are served by these techniques of control.

Techniques of Control

Techniques of control are to policy makers roughly what tools are to a carpenter. There are a limited number of techniques; there is a logic or an orderliness to each of them; and there is an accumulation of experience that helps us know if a certain technique is likely to work. There is no unanimous agreement on technique, just as carpenters will disagree about the best tool for a task. But we offer here a workable elementary handbook of techniques that will be useful for analyzing all policies.

The Chapter 13 In Brief Box on page 392 lists important techniques of control available to policy makers. They are grouped into three categories—promotional, regulatory, and redistributive policies. In this section, the specifics of each will be discussed and explained. Each category of policy is associated with a different kind of politics. In other words, since these techniques are different ways of using government, each type is likely to develop a distinctive pattern of power.

Promotional Techniques

Promotional techniques are the carrots of public policy. Their purpose is to encourage people to do something they might not otherwise do, or to get people to do more of what they are already doing. Sometimes the purpose is merely to compensate people for something done in the past. As the Chapter 13 In Brief Box demonstrates, promotional techniques can be classified into at least three separate types—subsidies, contracts, and licenses.

SUBSIDIES. Subsidies are simply government grants of cash, goods, services, or land. Although subsidies are often denounced as "giveaways," they have played a fundamental role in the history of government in the United States. As we discussed in Chapter 3, subsidies were the dominant form of public policy of both the national government and the state and local governments throughout the nineteenth century. The first planning document ever written for the national government, Alexander Hamilton's *Report on Manufactures,* was based almost entirely on Hamilton's assumption that American industry could be encouraged by federal subsidies and that these were not only desirable but constitutional.

The thrust of Hamilton's plan was not lost on later policy makers. Subsidies in the form of land grants were given to farmers and to railroad companies to encourage western settlement. Substantial cash subsidies have traditionally been given to commercial shipbuilders to help build the commercial fleet and to guarantee the use of the ships as military personnel carriers in time of war.

Subsidies have always been a technique favored by politicians because subsidies can be treated as "benefits" that can be spread widely in response to many demands that might otherwise produce profound political conflict. Subsidies can, in other words, be used to buy off the opposition.

So widespread is the use of the subsidy technique in government that it takes encyclopedias to keep track of them all. Indeed, for a number of years, one company published an annual *Encyclopedia of U.S. Government Benefits*, a thousand-page guide to benefits

> for every American—from all walks of life. . . . [R]ight now, there are thousands of other American Taxpayers who are missing out on valuable Government Services, simply because they do not know about them. . . . Start your own business. . . . Take an extra vacation. . . . Here are all the opportunities your tax dollars have made possible.[1]

Another secret of the popularity of subsidies is that those who receive the benefits do not perceive the controls inherent in them. In the first place, most of the resources available for subsidies come from taxation. (In the nineteenth century, there was a lot of public land to distribute, but that is no longer the case.) Second, the effect of any subsidy has to be measured in terms of what people *would be doing* if the subsidy had not been available. For example, many thousands of people settled in lands west of the Mississippi only because land subsidies were available. Hundreds of research laboratories exist in universities and corporations only because certain types of research subsidies from the government are available. And finally, once subsidies exist, the threat of their removal becomes a very significant technique of control.

CONTRACTING. Like any corporation, a government agency must purchase goods and services by contract. The law requires open bidding for a substantial proportion of these contracts because government contracts are extremely valuable to businesses in the private sector and because the opportunities for abuse are great. But contracting is more than a method of buying goods and services. Contracting is also an important technique of policy because government agencies are often authorized to use their contracting power as a means of encouraging corporations to improve themselves, as a means of helping to build up whole sectors of the economy, and as a means of encouraging certain desirable goals or behavior, such as equal employment opportunity.

For example, the infant airline industry of the 1930s was nurtured by the national government's lucrative contracts to carry airmail. A more recent example is the use of contracting to encourage industries, universities, and others to engage in research and development (R & D). The biggest recent government contract for R & D was the Superconducting Super Collider, whose estimated cost in 1994 was over $10 billion.

The power of contracting is of great significance for administrations like those of Reagan and Bush because of their commitment to "privatization." When a president says he wants to restore as much government as possible to the private sector, he may seek to terminate a government program and leave the activity to private companies to pick up. That would be true privatization. But in most instances, true privatization is neither sought nor achieved. Instead, the government program is transferred to a private company to provide the service *under a contract with the government,* paid for by the government, and supervised by a government agency. In this case, privatization is only a euphemism. Government by contract has been around

---

[1] Roy A. Grisham and Paul McConaughty, eds., *Encyclopedia of U.S. Government Benefits* (Union City, NJ: William H. Wise, 1972). The quote is taken from the dust jacket. A comparable guide published by the *New York Times* is called *Federal Aid for Cities and Towns* (New York: Quadrangle Books, 1972). It contains 1,312 pages of federal government benefits that cities and towns, rather than individuals, can apply for.

for a long time and has always been seen by business as a major source of economic opportunity.

LICENSING. A license is a privilege granted by a government to do something that it otherwise considers to be illegal. For example, state laws make medical practice and taxi driving without a license illegal. The states then create a board of doctors and a "hack bureau" to grant licenses respectively for the practice of medicine and for the operation of a cab for hire to all persons who have met the particular qualifications specified in the statute or by the agency. Licensing was used by kings to grant privileges to the favored few. Gourmet products in France still carry reference to the original license granted by a French monarch in the nineteenth century. It may mean nothing today except as a symbol of tradition and longevity. But it meant life or death to the company when the bottling of mineral water or the packaging of the cheese was illegal without the king's permission. Today in modern industrial societies licensing has also proved to be an effective technique. Like subsidies and contracting, licensing has two sides. One is the giveaway side, making the license a desirable object of patronage. The other side of licensing is the control or regulatory side.

Regulatory Techniques

If promotional techniques are the carrots of public policy, *regulatory techniques* can be considered the sticks. Regulation comes in several forms, but every regulatory technique shares a common trait—direct government control of conduct. The conduct may be regulated because people feel it is harmful to others, or threatens to be, such as drunk driving or false advertising. Or the conduct may be regulated because people think it's just plain immoral, whether it is harming anybody or not, such as prostitution, gambling, or drinking. Because there are many forms of regulation, we have subdivided them here: (1) police regulation, through civil and criminal penalties, (2) administrative regulation, and (3) regulatory taxation.

POLICE REGULATION. "Police regulation" is not a technical term, but we use it for this category because these techniques come closest to the traditional exercise of "police power." After a person's arrest and conviction, these techniques are administered by courts and, where necessary, penal institutions. They are regulatory techniques.

Civil penalties usually refer to fines or some other form of material restitution (such as public service) as a sanction for violating civil laws or such common law principles as negligence. Civil penalties can range from the $5 fine for a parking violation to a more onerous penalty for late payment of income taxes or to the much more onerous penalties for violating the antitrust laws against unfair competition or the environmental protection laws against pollution. *Criminal penalties* usually refer to imprisonment but can also involve heavy fines and the loss of certain civil rights and liberties, such as the right to vote or the freedom of speech.

ADMINISTRATIVE REGULATION. Police regulation addresses conduct considered immoral. In order to eliminate such conduct, strict laws have been passed and severe sanctions enacted. But what about conduct that is not considered morally wrong but has harmful consequences? There is, for example, nothing morally wrong with radio or television broadcasting. But broadcast-

---

In Brief Box

GOVERNMENT TECHNIQUES OF PUBLIC CONTROL

Types of Techniques	Techniques	Definitions and Examples
Promotional techniques	Subsidies and grants of cash, land, etc.	"Patronage" is the promotion of private activity through what recipients consider "benefits" (example: in the nineteenth century the government encouraged westward settlement by granting land to those who went west)
	Contracting	Agreements with individuals or firms in the "private sector" to purchase goods or services
	Licensing	Unconditional permission to do something that is otherwise illegal (franchise, permit)
Regulatory techniques	Criminal penalties	Heavy fines or imprisonment Loss of citizenship
	Civil penalties	Less onerous fines, probation, exposure, restitution
	Administrative regulation	Setting interest rates, maintaining standards of health, investigating and publicizing wrongdoing
	Subsidies, contracting, and licensing	Regulatory techniques when certain conditions are attached (example: the government refuses to award a contract to firms that show no evidence of affirmative action in hiring)
	Regulatory taxation	Taxes that keep consumption or production down (liquor, gas, cigarette taxes)
	Expropriation	"Eminent domain" is the power to take private property for public use
Redistributive techniques	Fiscal use of taxes	Altering the distribution of money by changing taxes or tax rules
	Fiscal use of budgeting	Deficit spending to pump money into the economy when it needs a boost; creating a budget surplus through taxes to discourage consumption in inflationary times
	Fiscal use of credit and interest (monetary techniques)	Changing interest rates affect both demand for money and consumption. When rates are low it is easy to borrow and thus invest and consume

ing on a particular frequency or channel is regulated by government because disorder would amount to virtual chaos if everybody could broadcast on any frequency at any time.

This kind of conduct is thought of less as *policed* conduct and more as *regulated* conduct. When conduct is said to be regulated, the purpose is rarely to eliminate the conduct but rather to influence it toward more appropriate channels, toward more appropriate locations, or toward certain qualified types of persons, all for the purpose of minimizing injuries or inconveniences. This type of regulated conduct is sometimes called **administrative regulation** because the controls are given over to administrative agencies rather than to the police. Each regulatory agency in the executive branch has extensive powers to keep a sector of the economy under surveillance and also has powers to make rules dealing with the behavior of individual companies and people. But these administrative agencies have fewer powers of punishment than the police and the courts have, and the administrative agencies generally rely on the courts to issue orders enforcing the rules and decisions made by the agencies.

Sometimes a government will adopt administrative regulation if an economic activity is considered so important that it is not to be entrusted to competition among several companies in the private sector. This is the rationale for the regulation of local or regional power companies. A single company, traditionally called a "utility," is given an exclusive license (or franchise) to offer these services, but since the one company is made a legal monopoly and is protected from competition by other companies, the government gives an administrative agency the power to "regulate" the quality of the services rendered, the rates charged for those services, and the margin of profit the company is permitted to make.

At other times, administrative regulation is the chosen technique because the legislature decides that the economy needs protection from itself—that is, it may set up a regulatory agency to protect companies from destructive or predatory competition, on the assumption that economic competition is not always its own solution. This is the rationale behind the Federal Trade Commission, which has the responsibility of watching over such practices as price discrimination or pooling agreements between two or more companies when their purpose is to eliminate competitors.

Subsidies, licensing, and contracting are listed a second time in the In Brief Box because, although these techniques can be used strictly as promotional policies, they can also be used as techniques of administrative regulation. It all depends on whether the law sets serious conditions on eligibility for the subsidy, license, or contract. To put it another way, the threat of losing a valuable subsidy, license, or contract can be used by the government as a sanction to improve compliance with the goals of regulation. For example, the threat of removal of the subsidies called "federal aid to education" has had a very significant influence on the willingness of schools to cooperate in the desegregation of their student bodies and faculties. For another example, social welfare subsidies (benefits) can be lowered to encourage or force people to take low-paying jobs, or they can be increased to placate people when they are engaging in political protest.[2]

---

[2]For an evaluation of the policy of withholding subsidies to carry out desegregation laws, see Gary Orfield, *Must We Bus?* (Washington, DC: Brookings Institution, 1978). For an evaluation of the use of subsidies to encourage work or to calm political unrest, see Frances Fox Piven and Richard Cloward, *Regulating the Poor: The Functions of Public Welfare* (New York: Random House, 1971).

DEBATING THE ISSUES

Regulation: Governmental Scalpel or Blunt Instrument?

Regulation has long been a key tool employed by government to advance public safety and welfare. Yet the rise of government regulation has also spawned intense criticism that such regulation has been more harmful than helpful. Editor Barry Crickmer argues against governmental regulatory efforts on the grounds that they are costly and ineffective. Political scientist Susan Tolchin and journalist Martin Tolchin argue that government regulation is unfairly blamed by big business for a variety of ills, and that regulation is in fact essential for the good of modern society.

Crickmer

Federal regulation is often called inflationary, irritating, costly, and even farcical. But that's not the worst that can be said of it. The worst is that it isn't working.

The development, methodology, philosophy, and results of federal intervention in the marketplace fit Sir Ernest Benn's definition of politics as "the art of looking for trouble, finding it everywhere, diagnosing it wrongly, and applying unsuitable remedies."

For all the billions of dollars the regulatory agencies have spent and the billions more they have caused to be spent, there is surprisingly little evidence that the world is any better off than it would have been without federal tinkering. . . .

The question is, why? Why has the direct and indirect expenditure of more than $100 billion a year on federal regulation failed to produce results commensurate with the effort? Or in some cases, any positive results at all?

Is the federal government trying to do the impossible? Or is it trying to do the possible in an impossible way? The answer is probably a little of both.

Many of the newer regulatory programs were ill-conceived and ill-considered. Typically, each got started after a single-interest pressure group succeeded in creating a wave of hysteria over an alleged crisis.

When this happens, most members of Congress quickly jump on the reform bandwagon. Those who don't may get crushed under its wheels. . . .

The news media—especially television—build pressure for quick fixes because they tend

---

An important social goal for which regulatory licensing has been a standard technique is the prevention of unqualified persons from practicing medicine. That power can, of course, be abused, as when medical licenses are issued merely to hold down the number of physicians so that they can charge higher fees. Other examples of regulatory licensing range from the allocation of channels for television companies, to the issuing of licenses for the export of wheat or to operate an automobile or restaurant, to the issuing of permits to hunt or fish in season.

Like subsidies and licensing, government contracting can be an entirely different

to focus on problems that can be presented dramatically, rather than on the comparatively dry analyses of possible solutions. . . .

In the words of [former] Washington Gov. Dixie Lee Ray, a former federal regulatory herself: "The reality is that zero defects in products plus zero pollution plus zero risk on the job is equivalent to maximum growth of government plus zero economic growth plus runaway inflation. That's what we have."[1]

Tolchin and Tolchin

Regulation has become the national whipping boy. . . . The American automobile industry blamed its precipitous decline, not on its high prices, oversized cars, or shoddy products, but on the raft of government regulations intended to improve the safety and fuel efficiency of the vehicles and perhaps make them more marketable. . . .

By the late 1970s, complaints of excessive regulation had become management's all-purpose cop-out. Were profits too low? Blame regulation. Were prices too high? Blame regulation. Were inadequate funds and manpower earmarked for research and development? Blame regulation for sapping both funds and manpower. Was American industry unable to compete with foreign competitors? Blame regulation.

In a highly technological society such as ours, the need for increased regulation is manifest. It is inconceivable to think of "lessening the regulatory burden," as some put it, at a time when private industry has the power to alter our genes, invade our privacy, and destroy our environment. A single industrial accident . . . is capable of taking a huge toll in human life and suffering. Only the government has the power to create and enforce the social regulations that protect citizens from the awesome consequences of technology run amuck. Only the government has the ability to raise the national debate above the "balance sheet" perspective of American industry. This is not to dismiss the many socially conscious businessmen who are concerned with the public interest, but, unfortunately, they do not represent the political leadership of the business community. After all, the "bottom line" for business is making a profit, not improving the quality of the environment or the work place. Its primary obligation is to its shareholders, not to the community at large.[2]

[1]Barry Crickmer, "Regulation: How Much Is Enough?" *Nation's Business,* March 1980, pp. 26–33.
[2]Susan Tolchin and Martin Tolchin, *Dismantling America* (New York: Houghton Mifflin, 1983), pp. 3–5.

kind of technique of control when the contract or its denial is used as a reward or punishment to gain obedience in a regulatory program. For example, Kennedy and Johnson initiated the widespread use of executive orders, administered by the Office of Federal Contract Compliance in the Department of Labor, to prohibit racial discrimination by firms receiving government contracts.[3] The value of these contracts to many private corporations was so great that

[3]For an evaluation of Kennedy's use of this kind of executive power, see Carl M. Brauer, *John F. Kennedy and the Second Reconstruction* (New York: Columbia University Press, 1977), especially Chapter 3.

they were quite willing to alter if not elimi-nate racial discrimination in employment practices if that was the only way to qualify to bid for government contracts. Nowadays, it is common to see on employment ads the statement "We are an equal opportunity employer."

REGULATORY TAXATION. Taxation is gener-ally understood to be a fiscal technique, and it will be discussed as such below. But in many instances, the primary purpose of the tax is not to raise revenue but to discourage or eliminate an activity altogether by mak-ing it too expensive for most people. For example, since the end of Prohibition, al-though there has been no penalty for the production or sale of alcoholic beverages, the alcohol industry is not free from regula-tion. First, all alcoholic beverages have to be licensed, allowing only those companies that are "bonded" to put their product on the market. Beyond that, federal and state taxes on alcohol are made disproportion-ately high, on the theory that, in addition to the revenue gained, less alcohol will be con-sumed. For the same reasons, there was for many years a heavy tax on colored marga-rine, imposed through the lobbying efforts of the dairy industry, which sought to pro-tect its market against the artificial spread.[4]

We may be seeing a great deal more regu-lation by taxation for at least the following reasons. First, it is a kind of hidden regula-tion, acceptable to people who in principle are against regulation. Second, it permits a certain amount of choice. For example, a heavy tax on gasoline or on smokestack and chemical industries (called an "effluent tax") will encourage drivers and these com-panies to regulate their own activities by permitting them to decide how much pollu-tion they can afford. Third, advocates of regulatory taxation believe it to be more efficient than other forms of regulation, re-quiring less bureaucracy and less supervi-sion.

EXPROPRIATION. *Expropriation*—seizing pri-vate property for a public use—is a widely used technique of control in the United States, especially in land-use regulation. Al-most all public works, from highways to parks to government office buildings, in-volve the forceful taking of some private property in order to assemble sufficient land and the correct distribution of land for the necessary construction. The vast Inter-state Highway Program required expro-priation of thousands of narrow strips of private land. "Urban redevelopment" pro-jects often require city governments to use the powers of seizure in the service of pri-vate developers, who actually build the ur-ban projects on the land that would be far too expensive if purchased on the open mar-ket. Private utilities that supply electricity and gas to individual subscribers are given powers to take private property whenever a new facility or a right-of-way is needed.

We generally call the power to expropri-ate *eminent domain*.[5] The Fifth Amendment of the U.S. Constitution surrounds this expro-priation power with important safeguards against abuse, so that government agencies

---

[4]For many years, margarine was sold in white, one-pound blocks, resembling lard, and was very unappetizing. An envelope of yellow food coloring accompanied the package, so that the consumer could take the trouble to make the margarine look a bit more like butter.

[5]For an evaluation of the politics of eminent domain, see Theodore Lowi and Benjamin Ginsberg, *Poliscide* (New York: Macmillan, 1976), especially Chapters 11 and 12, writ-ten by Julia and Thomas Vitullo-Martin.

in the United States are not permitted to use that power except through a strict due process and they must offer "fair market value" for the land sought. Another form of expropriation is forcing individuals to work for a public purpose—for example, drafting people for service in the armed forces.

Redistributive Techniques

Redistributive techniques are usually of two types—fiscal and monetary—but they have a common purpose, to control people by manipulating the entire economy rather than by regulating people directly. As observed earlier, regulatory techniques focus upon individual conduct. The regulatory rule may be written to apply to the whole economy. For example: "Walking on the grass is not permitted," or "Membership in a union may not be used to deny employment, nor may a worker be fired for promoting union membership." Nevertheless, the regulation focuses on individual strollers or individual employers who might walk on the grass or discriminate against a trade union member. In contrast, techniques are redistributive if they seek to control conduct more indirectly by altering the conditions of conduct or manipulating the environment of conduct.

FISCAL TECHNIQUES. Fiscal techniques of control are the government's taxing and spending powers. Personal and corporate income taxes, which raise most government revenues, are the most prominent examples. While the direct purpose of an income tax is to raise revenue, each approach to taxation has a different impact on the economy, and government can plan for that impact. For example, although the main reason given for increasing the Social Security tax (which

is an income tax) was to keep Social Security solvent, a big reason for it in the minds of many legislators was that it would reduce inflation by shrinking the amount of money people could spend on goods and services.

President Clinton's commitment in his 1992 campaign for a "middle-class" tax cut was motivated by the goal of encouraging economic growth through increased consumption. Soon after the election, upon learning that the deficit was far larger than had earlier been reported, he had to break his promise of such a tax cut. Nevertheless, the idea of a middle-class tax cut is still an example of a fiscal policy aimed at increased consumption, because of the theory that people in middle-income brackets will tend to spend a high proportion of unexpected earnings or windfalls, rather than saving or investing them.

MONETARY TECHNIQUES. Monetary techniques also seek to influence conduct by manipulating the entire economy through the supply or availability of money. The Federal Reserve Board (the Fed) can adopt what is called a "hard money policy" by increasing the interest rate it charges member banks (called the "discount rate"). In 1980, when inflation was at a historic high, the Fed permitted interest rates to reach a high of nearly 20 percent in an attempt to rein it in. During the 1991 recession, however, the Fed permitted interest rates to drop well below 10 percent, hoping this would encourage people to borrow more to buy houses, etc. Another monetary policy is one of increasing or decreasing the "reserve requirement," which sets the actual proportion of deposited money that a bank must keep "on demand" as it makes all the rest of the deposits available as new loans. A third important technique used by the Fed is

PROCESS BOX 13.1
The Federal Dollar
Where It Comes From, Where It Goes, and How (Fiscal Year 1993)

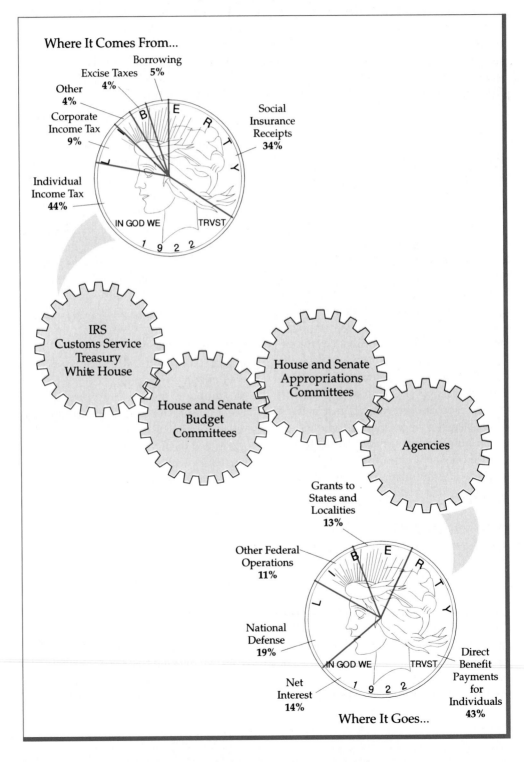

Where It Comes From...

Borrowing 5%

Excise Taxes 4%

Other 4%

Corporate Income Tax 9%

Individual Income Tax 44%

Social Insurance Receipts 34%

IN GOD WE TRVST

1 9 2 2

IRS
Customs Service
Treasury
White House

House and Senate Budget Committees

House and Senate Appropriations Committees

Agencies

Grants to States and Localities 13%

Other Federal Operations 11%

National Defense 19%

Net Interest 14%

IN GOD WE TRVST

1 9 2 2

Direct Benefit Payments for Individuals 43%

Where It Goes...

"open market operations"—the buying and selling of Treasury securities to absorb excess dollars or to release more dollars into the economy.

SPENDING POWER AS FISCAL POLICY. Perhaps the most important redistributive technique of all is the most familiar one—"spending power"—which is a combination of subsidies and contracts. These techniques can be used for policy goals far beyond the goods and services bought and the individual conduct regulated.

One of the most important examples of the national government's use of purchasing power as a fiscal or redistributive technique is found in another of the everyday activities of the Federal Reserve Board. The Fed goes into the "open market" to buy and sell government bonds in order to increase or decrease the amount of money in circulation. By doing so, the Fed can raise or lower the prices paid for goods and the interest rate paid on loans.

Substantive Uses of the Policies

The Welfare State as Fiscal and Social Policy

Government involvement in the relief of poverty and dependency was insignificant until the twentieth century because of our antipathy to government and because of our confidence that all of the deserving poor could be cared for by private efforts alone. This traditional approach crumbled in 1929 in the wake of the Depression when some misfortune befell nearly everyone. Americans finally confronted the fact that poverty and dependency would be the result of imperfections of the economic system itself.

Americans held to their distinction between the deserving and undeserving poor but significantly altered these standards regarding who was deserving and who was not. And once the idea of an imperfect system was established, a large-scale public approach became practical not only to alleviate poverty but to redistribute wealth and to manipulate economic activity through fiscal policy.

The architects of the original Social Security system in the 1930s were probably well aware that a large welfare system can be good *fiscal* policy. When the economy is declining and more people are losing their jobs or are retiring early, welfare payments go up automatically, thus maintaining consumer demand and making the "downside" of the business cycle shorter and shallower. Conversely, during periods of full employment or high levels of government spending, when inflationary pressures can mount, welfare taxes take an extra bite out of consumer dollars, tending to dampen inflation, flattening the "upside" of the economy.

However, the authors of Social Security were more aware of the *social* policy significance of the welfare state. They recognized that a large proportion of the unemployment, dependency, and misery of the 1930s was due to the imperfections of a large, industrial society and occurred through no fault of the victims of these imperfections. They also recognized that opportunities to achieve security, let alone prosperity, were unevenly distributed in our society. This helps explain how the original Social Security laws came to be called—both by supporters and by critics—the welfare state. The 1935 Social Security Act provided for two separate categories of welfare—*contributory* and *noncontributory*. Table 13.1 is an outline of the key programs in each of these categories.

TABLE 13.1
PUBLIC WELFARE PROGRAMS

Type of Program	Statutory Basis	Year Enacted	Number of Recipients in 1992 (in Millions)	Federal Outlays in 1992 (in Billions of Dollars)
Contributory (Insurance) System				
Old Age, Survivors and Disability Insurance	Social Security Act (SSA), Title II	1935	39.8	$280.6
Medicare	SSA Title XVIII	1965	34.2	$118.6
Unemployment compensation	SSA Title III	1935	8.6	$36.7
Noncontributory (Public Assistance) System				
Medicaid	SSA Title XIX	1965	25.3	$72.5
Food stamps	Food Stamp Act	1964	21.5	$22.7
Aid to Families with Dependent Children	SSA Title IV	1935	11.5	$14.5
Supplemental Security Income (cash assistance for aged, blind, disabled)	SSA Title XVI	1974	5.0	$19.8
Housing assistance to low-income families	National Housing Act	1937	2.5	$19.4
School Lunch Program	National School Lunch Act	1946	24.0	$6.3
Training and employment program	Job Training Partnership Act	1982	1.2	$5.8

Source: Office of Management and Budget, *The Budget of the United States Government, Fiscal Year 1993* (Washington, DC: Government Printing Office, 1993), pp. 107, 161–62; Bureau of the Census, *Statistical Abstract of the United States, 1992*, 112th ed. (Washington, DC: Government Printing Office, 1992), pp. 318–19, 356.

CONTRIBUTORY PROGRAMS. Contributory programs are financed by taxation, which can be called "forced savings." These programs are what most people have in mind when they refer to Social Security or social insurance. Under the original old-age insurance program, the employer and the employee were each required to pay equal amounts, which in 1937 were set at 1 percent of the first $3,000 of wages, to be deducted from the paycheck of each employee and matched by the same amount from the employer. This percentage increased over the years, so that the total contribution is now 7.65 percent but subdivided as follows: 6.20 percent on the first $55,500 for the Social Security benefits and an additional 1.45 percent on the first $130,200 for Medicare.[6]

[6] Although on paper the employer is taxed, this is all part of "forced savings," because in reality the employer's contribution is nothing more than a mandatory wage or salary increase that the employee never sees or touches before it goes into the trust fund held exclusively for the contributory programs.

Social Security is a rather conservative approach to welfare. In effect, the Social Security (FICA) tax is a message that people cannot be trusted to save voluntarily in order to take care of their own needs. But in another sense, it is quite radical. Social Security is not real insurance; workers' contributions do not accumulate in a personal account like an annuity. Consequently, contributors do not receive benefits in proportion to their own contributions, and this means that there is a redistribution of wealth occurring. In brief, contributory Social Security mildly redistributes wealth from higher- to lower-income people, and it quite significantly redistributes wealth from young to old people and from younger workers to older retirees.

NONCONTRIBUTORY PROGRAMS.   Non-contributory programs are also known as public assistance programs. Historically, the two most important ones are aid to the aged, blind, and disabled—now grouped together as Supplemental Security Income (SSI)—and Aid to Families with Dependent Children (AFDC). Both programs are "means tested," requiring the applicant to show some definite need for assistance and an inability to provide for it.

Over the years, coverage has expanded and benefits have been increased in both contributory and noncontributory programs and through cash and in-kind benefits. Congress increased Social Security benefits every two or three years during the 1950s and 1960s. The biggest single expansion in contributory programs since 1935 was the establishment in 1965 of Medicare, which provides substantial medical services to elderly persons who are already eligible to receive old-age, survivors, and disability insurance under the original Social

Security system. In 1972, Congress decided to end the grind of biennial legislation by establishing "indexing," whereby benefits paid out under contributory programs would be tied to the Cost of Living Index (COLA, also called the Consumer Price Index), so that benefits would increase automatically as the cost of living rose. But, of course, Social Security taxes (contributions) also increased after almost every benefit increase. This made Social Security, in the words of one observer, "a politically ideal program. It bridged partisan conflict by providing liberal benefits under conservative financial auspices."[7]

The noncontributory public assistance categories also made their most significant advances during the 1960s. The largest single category of expansion was the establishment in 1965 of Medicaid, which extended medical services to all low-income persons who had already established eligibility through "means testing" under AFDC.

The expansion of all types of benefits and the expansion of the number of persons eligible to receive them added tremendously to the costs of noncontributory welfare programs. Meanwhile, important demographic changes were adding costs to the contributory programs and at the same time were reducing the amount of revenue raised by Social Security taxes. The most important demographic change was an increase in the number of elderly Americans relative to the number of individuals in the work force. Between the 1950s and the 1980s, the ratio between the two dropped from a high of eighteen workers for every one retired eligi-

[7]Edward J. Harpham, "Fiscal Crisis and the Politics of Social Security Reform," in *The Attack on the Welfare State*, ed. Anthony Champagne and Edward Harpham (Prospect Heights, IL: Waveland Press, 1984), p. 13.

PROCESS BOX 13.2
The Web of Benefits and Controls for a Welfare Mother

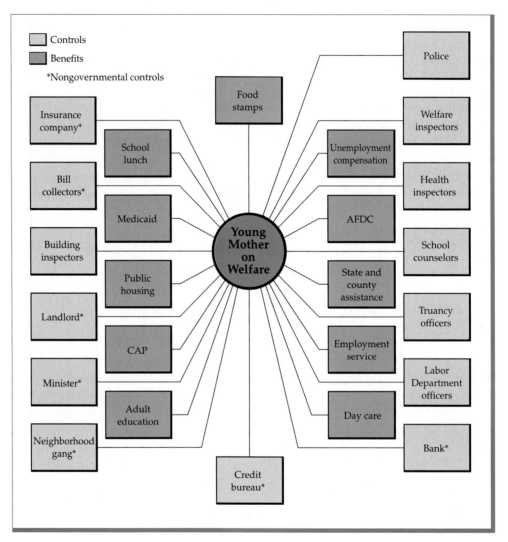

ble beneficiary to four workers for every retired eligible beneficiary.[8] This obviously added greatly to the gap between welfare contributions and welfare obligations, which in 1973 was defined as a "fiscal crisis."

Consensus gradually formed for a long-term solution, and in 1977 Congress adopted a series of tax increases extending over thirteen years, the final one taking effect January 1, 1990. Thus, during the 1980s,

[8]From *Social Security Bulletins,* quoted in Gary Freeman and Paul Adams, "The Politics of Social Security," in *The Political Economy of Public Policy,* ed. Alan Stone and Edward Harpham (Beverly Hills, CA: Sage Publications, 1982), p. 245.

instead of a deficit, the Social Security Trust Fund began producing surpluses. In 1989, the Social Security surplus—contributions received in excess of benefits paid out—reached over $50 billion. The annual surplus was projected to go up to $200 billion by the year 2002. Around the year 2020 the ratio of retirees to workers will require a drawing down of the surpluses. But by then, there will only be IOUs and not cash in the trust fund. Why? To avoid raising income and sales taxes, the Bush and Reagan administrations borrowed from the Social Security Trust Fund by selling it U.S. bonds—essentially IOUs. This could compromise the Social Security system in the future by producing high inflation, which hurts the elderly, who are on fixed incomes, most of all.

President Clinton was elected on a platform of "putting people first," but deficit realities significantly revised the meaning of his promise. His most positive proposal was for an increase in 1994 in the Earned Income Tax Credit (EITC), by which working households with children can file through their income tax returns for an income supplement if their annual earned incomes were below $20,000. But it was almost certain to fail because it involved too much revenue loss during a period of deficit reduction. Clinton's 1993–1994 agenda for Congress also included reductions rather than increases in Social Security retirement benefits—raising taxes on benefits received and freezing or capping cost of living (COLA) increases. Even more conservatively, President Clinton also favored strengthening the enforcement of child-support laws and tying welfare benefits closer to work, or "workfare," requirements. This was all part of his effort to call on all classes of Americans to share the burden of deficit reduction while at the same time trying to confirm as strongly as possible the proposition that the welfare state is here to stay.

Imperfections in the Society: Changing the Rules of Inequality

A capitalist employer will always prefer the most efficient worker at the lowest price and will want to fire or refuse to hire the least efficient. How, then, do we account for the fact that a disproportionate number of African Americans, Hispanic Americans, women, and other minorities are found in poverty in America?[9] This has to be explained by the *social rules* that are shaped by the personal prejudices of individuals and the traditions of communities. Employers may share in these prejudices, but that would be a departure from rational economic behavior. As long as prejudice exists, there will be biases in the composition of the poverty class, unless public policies—that is, regulatory policies—intervene.

As observed in Chapter 4, equal protection of the laws might have been established and implemented by the courts alone. But after a decade of frustration, the courts and Congress ultimately came to the conclusion that the task of changing the social rules would require legislative and administrative, as well as judicial, action. Table 13.2 provides an overview of the efforts by Congress to make equal protection of the laws a reality. Three civil rights acts were passed during the first decade after the 1954 Supreme Court decision in *Brown v. Board of*

[9] John Schwarz and Thomas Volgy have carefully documented their findings that, at the beginning of the 1990s, 7.4 percent of all fully employed workers lived beneath the level of economic self-sufficiency. They also reported that 10.2 percent of white female heads of households and 21.8 percent of black female heads of households were in the same situation. Even with education through high school, 13.1 percent of the white women and 25.7 percent of the black women who headed their households, *fully employed*, lived beneath economic self-sufficiency. Thus, merely "getting a job" is not necessarily the appropriate answer. John E. Schwarz and Thomas J. Volgy, *The Forgotten Americans: Thirty Million Working Poor in the Land of Opportunity.* (New York: W. W. Norton, 1992), pp. 68–80.

TABLE 13.2
KEY PROVISIONS OF FEDERAL CIVIL RIGHTS LAWS (1957–1978)

Civil Rights Act of 1957	Established the Commission on Civil Rights to monitor civil rights progress. Elevated the importance of the Civil Rights Division of the Department of Justice, headed by an assistant attorney general. Made it a federal crime to attempt to intimidate a voter or to prevent a person from voting.
Civil Rights Act of 1960	Increased the sanction against obstruction of voting or of court orders enforcing the vote. Established federal power to appoint referees to register voters wherever a "pattern or practice" of discrimination was found and declared by a federal court.
Equal Pay Act of 1963	Banned wage discrimination on the basis of sex in jobs requiring equal skill, effort, and responsibility. Exceptions involved employee pay differentials based on factors other than sex, such as merit or seniority.
Civil Rights Act of 1964	*Voting:* Title I made a sixth-grade education (in English) a presumption to literacy.
	Public accommodations: Title II barred discrimination in any commercial lodging of more than five rooms for transient guests and in any service station, restaurant, theater, or commercial conveyance. The complainant could bring suit or the attorney general could take the initiative if he or she saw a "pattern or practice" of discrimination.
	Public schools: Title IV empowered the attorney general to sue for desegregation whenever a segregation complaint was found meritorious. Title VI authorized the withholding of federal aid to segregated schools.
	Private employment: Title VII outlawed discrimination in a variety of employment practices on the basis of race, religion, and sex (sex added for the first time in areas other than wage discrimination). Established the Equal Employment Opportunity Commission (EEOC) to enforce the law but required it to defer enforcement to state or local agencies for sixty days following each complaint.
Civil Rights Act of 1965	*Voting rights only:* Empowered the attorney general, with the Civil Service Commission, to appoint voting examiners to replace local registrars wherever he or she found fewer than 50 percent of the persons of voting age had voted in the 1964 presidential election and to suspend all literacy tests where they were used as a tool of discrimination.

Education. But these acts were of only marginal importance. The first two, in 1957 and 1960, established that the Fourteenth Amendment of the Constitution, adopted almost a century earlier, could no longer be ignored, particularly in regard to voting. The third, the Equal Pay Act of 1963, was more important, but it was concerned with women in the public sector and consequently did not touch the question of racial discrimination or discrimination in the private sector.

By far the most important piece of legislation passed by Congress was the Civil Rights Act of 1964. It not only put some teeth in the voting rights provisions of the 1957

Civil Rights Act of 1968	*Open housing:* Made it a crime to refuse to sell or rent a dwelling on the basis of race or religion, if a bona fide offer had been made, or to discriminate in advertising or in the terms and conditions of sale or rental. Administered by the Department of Housing and Urban Development, but the burden of proof is on the complainant, who must seek local remedies first, where they exist.
Amendments of 1970 to Voting Rights Act	Extended 1965 act and included some districts in northern states.
Equal Employment Opportunity Act of 1972	Increased coverage of the Civil Rights Act of 1964 to include public-sector employees. Gave EEOC authority to bring suit against persons engaging in "pattern or practice" of employment discrimination.
Amendments of 1975 to Voting Rights Act	Extended 1965 act and broadened antidiscrimination measures to include protection for language minorities (e.g., Hispanics, Native Americans).
Amendments of 1978 to Civil Rights Act of 1964	Prohibited discrimination in employment on the basis of pregnancy or related disabilities. Required that pregnancy or related medical conditions be treated as disabilities eligible for medical and liability insurance.
Amendments of 1982 to Voting Rights Act	Extended 1965 act and strengthened antidiscrimination measures by requiring only proof of *effect* of discrimination, not *intent* to discriminate.
Americans with Disabilities Act of 1990	Extended to people with disabilities; protection from discrimination in employment and public accommodations similar to those given to women and racial, religious, and ethnic minorities by the 1964 Civil Rights Act. Required that public transportation systems, other public services, and telecommunications systems be accessible to those with disabilities.
Civil Rights Act of 1991	Reversed several Court decisions, beginning with *Wards Cove* (1989), that had made it harder for women and minorities to seek compensation for job discrimination. It put back on the employer the "burden of proof" to show that a discriminatory policy was a business necessity.

and 1960 acts but also went far beyond voting to attack discrimination in public accommodations, segregation in the schools, and, at long last, the discriminatory conduct of employers in hiring, promoting, and laying off their employees. Discrimination against women was also included, extending the important 1963 provisions. The 1964 act seemed bold at the time, revolutionary to some, but it was enacted ten years after the Supreme Court had declared racial discrimination "inherently unequal" under the Fifth and Fourteenth Amendments. And it was enacted after blacks had demonstrated time after time that discrimination was no longer acceptable. The choice in 1964 was not between congressional action or inaction but between legal action or expanded violence.

The 1964 legislation declared discrimination by private employers and state governments (school boards, etc.) illegal, then went even further to provide for administrative agencies to help the courts implement these laws. Title IV of the 1964 act, for example, authorized the executive branch, through the Justice Department, to implement federal court orders to desegregate schools, and to do so without having to wait for individual parents to bring complaints. Title VI vastly strengthened the role of the executive branch and the credibility of court orders by providing that federal grants-in-aid to state and local governments for education be withheld from any school system practicing racial segregation.

In the decade following the 1964 Civil Rights Act, the Justice Department brought legal action against more than 500 school districts. During the same period, administrative agencies filed actions against 600 school districts, threatening to suspend federal aid to education unless real desegregation steps were taken. At the same time, the federal government filed more than 400 antidiscrimination suits in federal courts against hotels, restaurants, taverns, gas stations, and other "public accommodations" under title II.[10]

Title VII, the fair employment title of the 1964 act, declared job discrimination illegal. This title covered all employers of more than fifteen employees, all governmental agencies, and also trade unions. Some of the powers to enforce fair employment practices were delegated to the Justice Depart-

ment's Civil Rights Division and others to a new agency created in the 1964 act, the Equal Employment Opportunity Commission (EEOC). It is also important to note the use here of another "technique of control" identified earlier in this chapter—by executive order, these agencies had the power of the national government to revoke public contracts for goods and services and to refuse to engage in contracts for goods and services to any private company that could not guarantee that its rules for hiring, promotion, and firing were nondiscriminatory.[11]

Affirmative Action

Unfortunately, the civil rights laws were best designed for middle-class victims, because they had the education, the self-esteem, and the resources to pursue their grievances through law and politics. But as they succeeded, they moved away not only from lower-paying jobs but also from segregated neighborhoods, and they deprived their former neighbors of their example and their leadership, underscoring the plight of those who remained.[12] "Affirmative action" seemed to be the answer.

Most affirmative action comes not from new legislation but from more vigorous and positive interpretations of existing legislation arising out of feelings on the part of many that positive actions are necessary to

---

[10] For a review of these suits, see Richard Kluger, *Simple Justice* (New York: Random House, 1975), p. 759 and Chapters 25 and 26.

[11] Although 1964 was the most important year for civil rights law, it was not the only important year. In 1965, Congress significantly strengthened legislation protecting voting rights. For a comprehensive analysis and evaluation of the Voting Rights Act, see Bernard Grofman and Chandler Davidson, eds., *Controversies in Minority Voting—The Voting Rights Act in Perspective* (Washington, DC: Brookings Institution, 1992).

[12] William Julius Wilson, *The Truly Disadvantaged* (Chicago: University of Chicago Press, 1987).

overcome the long years of discrimination. President Johnson put the case emotionally in 1965: "You do not take a person who, for years, has been hobbled by chains . . . and then say you are free to compete with all the others, and still just believe that you have been completely fair."[13] Consequently, one of the first affirmative action programs was President Johnson's War on Poverty, begun in 1964. The aim was to help people in underprivileged and ghetto neighborhoods form organizations with a leadership that could speak for the people in those neighborhoods. The ultimate goal of these "Community Action Programs" was to provide more assistance and at the same time teach the poor how to organize to compete more effectively in political as well as economic life.

The War on Poverty has been subjected to a good deal of valid criticism. But there is no denying that some of the various redistributive programs that Congress included as part of the War on Poverty did reach poor neighborhoods. Job Corps and food stamps did have a positive effect on the overall level of poverty. Head Start did redistribute educational opportunities for individuals in those neighborhoods. And the Community Action Programs did in fact bring political experience and leadership skills to unprecedented numbers of black and other minority residents of poor and hitherto isolated neighborhoods.[14]

Affirmative action also took the form of efforts by the agencies in the Department of Health, Education, and Welfare to shift their focus from "desegregation" to "integration." Federal agencies—sometimes with court orders and sometimes without them—required school districts to present plans for busing children across district lines, for pairing schools, for closing certain schools, and for redistributing faculties as well as students, under pain of loss of grants-in-aid from the federal government. The guidelines issued for such plans literally constituted preferential treatment to compensate for past discrimination.

Affirmative action was also initiated in the area of employment opportunity. The Equal Employment Opportunity Commission often has required plans whereby employers must attempt to increase the number of their minority employees, and the Office of Federal Contract Compliance in the Department of Labor has used the threat of contract revocation for the same purpose.

The constitutionality of some of these affirmative action policies has been upheld.[15] But criticism mounted during the 1970s, especially against affirmative action, which, the critics argued, was a form of reverse discrimination that installed unqualified people in jobs and lowered efficiency without improving opportunity. In this context, Ronald Reagan became "the

---

[13]From Lyndon B. Johnson, *The Vantage Point* (New York: Holt, Rinehart and Winston, 1971), p. 166.

[14]For a criticism of the administrative methods used, see Theodore J. Lowi, *The End of Liberalism* (New York: W. W. Norton, 1979), Chapter 8. For a very positive account of the amount of money spent and the impact made, see John Schwarz, *America's Hidden Success* (New York: W. W. Norton, 1988), pp. 34–50.

[15]For example, Fullilove v. Klutznick, 448 U.S. 448 (1980). Here the Supreme Court upheld the "minority business enterprise" (MBE) provisions of the Public Works Employment Act of 1977, an affirmative action policy which required that 10 percent of federal funds granted for local public works projects must be used to procure services or supplies from businesses owned by minority group members. Although the Court was split in two or three directions, yielding no absolutely clear majority opinion, the decision did sustain the statute, upholding the objectives of the MBE as within Congress's power. For a discussion of the case, see Paul Brest and Sanford Levinson, *Processes of Constitutional Decision Making* (Boston: Little, Brown, 1983), pp. 541, 547. *Fullilove* was reaffirmed on June 8, 1990, in Metro Broadcasting v. FCC, 110 S.Ct. 2997 (1990).

W. E. B. DuBois and Booker T. Washington: Competing Paths to Equality

*T*wo of the most important founders of the modern civil rights movement shared the same goal—equality for African Americans—but differed markedly on how best to achieve that goal.

William Edward Burghardt (better known as W. E. B.) DuBois, born in Massachusetts in 1868, entered the academic world via Fisk University and Harvard University, where his doctoral dissertation on the slave trade was the first volume published in the Harvard Historical Studies series. DuBois taught at many universities, wrote numerous books, and founded the National Association for the Advancement of Colored People (NAACP).

Booker T. Washington was born a Virginia slave in 1856. After the Civil War, Washington worked in coal mines and salt furnaces. In 1872, he was admitted to the Hampton Institute, an industrial school for blacks. Five years later he became a teacher there. In 1881, Washington established and headed the Tuskegee Institute in Alabama, a school modeled on Hampton that emphasized vocational trades for blacks, including farming, carpentry, mechanical skills, and teaching. Eventually, Washington became a prominent political figure, and an adviser to Presidents Theodore Roosevelt and William H. Taft.

DuBois's philosophy of race relations emphasized the importance of black self-sufficiency and excellence, urging cultivation of a "talented tenth" that could excel and lead other blacks. And as early as 1903, he predicted that "the problem of the twentieth century is the problem of the color line." Washington, on the other hand, espoused the view that blacks

W. E. B. DuBois

first president in the post-World War II period to reverse this trend of an increasingly active government role in . . . redressing the consequences of past discrimination."[16]

[16]D. Lee Bawden and John L. Palmer, "Social Policy," in *The Reagan Record*, ed. John L. Palmer and Isabel Sawhill (Cambridge: Ballinger Publishing, 1984), p. 201.

The budgets and staff of key civil rights agencies were cut to the bone.[17] Busing was opposed. Government cases against school segregation, housing discrimination, and job discrimination dropped to a fraction of the cases brought under previous admini-

[17]Ibid., pp. 204–5.

should seek "through compromise, an emergence into an economic, social, and cultural stability never quite equal to the white man's." This philosophy led Washington to state that blacks were better off by getting practical vocational education than by seeking college training. DuBois did not reject the need for vocational education, but he took sharp issue with Washington's willingness to accept an inferior and segregated status for blacks.

Not surprisingly, Washington's views found wider acceptance among white Americans, which won him influence among the nation's political leaders. Washington also promoted his views through his financial control of various black newspapers. Washington avoided any endorsement of controversial political causes, although he did funnel money secretly to support lawsuits to fight discrimination in the courts. Toward the end of his life, his influence declined, as the views of organizations such as the NAACP acquired greater respect.

DuBois never backed down from his advocacy of political and social equality. For many years, he worked for the NAACP and edited its publication called *The Crisis*. In 1950, he unsuccessfully ran for U.S. senator from New York on the American Labor party ticket. Disillusioned with American party politics, DuBois joined the Communist party and traveled extensively in China and the Soviet Union. In 1961, the aged man moved to Ghana, to direct the writing of the *Encyclopedia Africana*.

Both DuBois and Washington believed that their philosophies would ultimately help eradicate inequality. The course chosen by DuBois, however, more closely foreshadowed the civil rights struggles of years to come.

Sources: Booker T. Washington, *Up from Slavery* (New York: Corner House, 1971; orig. published in 1901); W. E. B. DuBois, *The Souls of Black Folk* (New York: Signet Classics, 1969; orig. published in 1903).

Booker T. Washington

strations.[18] And although federal court decisions have upheld the use of statistics on the "effect" of discrimination as a basis for Justice Department initiatives in filing "pattern and practice" suits to open opportunities for minorities, the Justice Department under President Reagan virtually terminated such suits, focusing instead on individual cases where intent to discriminate could be proven.[19]

President Bush continued in the Reagan direction. He vetoed the Civil Rights Act of

[18]Ibid., p. 206.

[19]Ibid.

1990 as a "quota bill" (although he accepted essentially the same bill in 1991). Most important, though, he "relentlessly" appointed known social conservatives to the federal courts "with the same energy that Ronald Reagan did."[20] And his single appointment to the Supreme Court, Clarence Thomas, to replace civil rights advocate Thurgood Marshall, had been an opponent of anything that had to do with affirmative action.

Since the Supreme Court has not declared affirmative action unconstitutional, many opportunities remain for civil rights groups to pursue new policies as well as to get more sympathetic agencies created. Although some African American commentators have argued that affirmative action programs will be counterproductive, most civil rights leaders and their organizations continue to support affirmative action programs as absolutely essential.[21] The issue can be understood as a struggle to change the rules determining who shall be poor, because poverty is almost surely the status to which people are doomed if they get no assistance to break out of the circle of poverty.

[20] An observation by Nan Aron of the liberal Alliance for Justice, quoted in Ruth Marcus, "Using the Bench to Bolster a Conservative Team," *Washington Post National Weekly Edition*, 25 February–3 March 1991, p. 31.

[21] For the "anti" side, see Thomas Sowell, *Preferential Policies—An International Perspective* (New York: William Morrow, 1990). For the pro side, see Charles Willie, *Caste and Class Controversy on Race and Poverty—Round Two of the Willie-Wilson Debate*, 2nd ed. (Dix Hills, NY: General Hall Inc., Publishers, 1989). See also Anne Costain, "The Women's Lobby: Impact of a Movement on Congress," in *Interest Group Politics*, ed. Alan Cigler and Burdette Loomis (Washington, DC: Congressional Quarterly Press, 1983), pp. 191–216.

Time Line on Public Policy

EVENTS	1800	INSTITUTIONAL DEVELOPMENTS
Alexander Hamilton's *Report on Manufactures* present the first comprehensive statement of the policies necessary for American economic development (1791)		Regulatory policies reserved to the states–policies controlling property, land use, education, morality, marriage, criminal conduct (1790s–1990s)
		Promotional policies used by national government to encourage national commerce: tariffs (1792); land grants, internal improvements, shipping subsidies, etc. (1800s)
Territorial expansion, western settlement (1800s)		
Civil War (1861–1865)		
		Reconstruction; military occupation of South; return to normal promotional policies (1870s)

EVENTS		INSTITUTIONAL DEVELOPMENTS
Growth and mechanization of industry; formation of corporations; commercialization of agriculture (1860s–1890s)		National government adopts first regulatory policies—Interstate Commerce Act (1887), Sherman Antitrust Act (1890)
Abuses of workers and farmers; unionization; progressive reform movement (1880s–1890s)		
	1900	Supreme Court declares income tax unconstitutional (1895); Sixteenth Amendment provides for income tax (1913)
Airplane, automobile, electrification, and mass production create another "industrial revolution" (1900s–1920s)		Federal Trade Act (1914); Federal Reserve System (1913)
World War I (1914–1919)		Mobilization of entire economy for war
Stock market crash (1929); Great Depression (1929–1933)	**1930**	Demobilization and return to status quo (1920s)
Franklin Roosevelt elected and initiates the New Deal (1932)		New Deal policies: bank rescue, relief for unemployed, many new regulatory agencies, agriculture relief policies, Social Security Act, National Labor Relations Act (1933–1936)
U.S. enters World War II; total mobilization of society and economy (1941–1945)	**1940**	
Postwar demobilization; strikes; fear of inflation and depression		GI Bill of Rights for educational and vocational training (1944); National School Lunch Program (1946); housing policies; Council of Economic Advisers and commitment to "full employment planning" (1946–1947)
Civil Rights Movement (1950s and 1960s)	**1950**	*Brown* v. *Board of Education*—Court rules against school segregation (1954)

EVENTS		INSTITUTIONAL DEVELOPMENTS
Soviets launch Sputnik (1957)		First federal aid to education—National Defense Education Act (1958)
Growth of government (1960s); Kennedy assassinated; Johnson assumes presidency (1963)	**1960**	Equal pay for women (1963); Civil Rights Act establishes EEOC (1964); Food Stamp Act (1964); Elementary and Secondary School Act (1965); Voting Rights Act, Medicare and Medicaid (1965); War on Poverty (1964–1968)
Vietnam War and "confidence gap" (1965–1973)	**1970**	Indexing of welfare benefits (1972); Supplemental Security Income (SSI)(1974)
Richard Nixon elected (1968); administrative reorganization (1968–1974)		
Energy crisis; rise of "stagflations" (1973)		EEOC strengthened, especially for women (1972)
Reaction begins against regulation (1978–1980)	**1980**	Deregulation of securities (1975), railroads (1976 and 1980), airlines (1978–1981), banking (1980), motor carriers (1980)
Ronald Reagan elected (1980)		Executive Order 12291 mandates presidential oversight of all regulatory proposals (1981)
Public reaction against social policies as well as regulation (1980s)		Cuts in health and housing programs (1981–1984)
		Historic tax cuts (1981)
		Deregulation through executive management (1980s)
		Welfare, health, and housing appropriations begin to increase (1986–1988)
George Bush elected (1988)		Tax Reform Act (1986); Gramm-Rudman Act fails to stem growing deficits

EVENTS		INSTITUTIONAL DEVELOPMENTS
Public sentiment for some reregulation begins to mount (1990)	**1990**	"No new taxes" pledge broken (1991); continuity with Reagan domestic policies remains strong
		Bush vetoes extensively but accepts Clean Air Act (1990) and Americans with Disabilities Act (1991), and favors abortion regulation (1989–1992)
Clinton election supported by many industries demanding "more government" (1992)		Clinton deregulates morality (gays in the military, abortion counseling) and supports moderate economic regulation (1993)

Chapter Review

Madison set the tone for this chapter in *The Federalist*, No. 51, in three sentences of prose that have more the character of poetry:

> Justice is the end of government,
> It is the end of civil society.
> It ever has been and ever will be pursued
> Until it be obtained,
> Or until liberty be lost in the pursuit.

Our economic system is the most productive ever developed, but it is not perfect—and many policies have been adopted over the years to deal with imperfections. The first section of this chapter provided an introduction to the "techniques of control" that all policies embody. Policy is the purposive and deliberate aspect of government in action. But if policy is to come anywhere near obtaining its stated goal (clean air, stable prices, equal employment opportunity), it must be backed up by some kind of sanction—the ability to reward or punish—coupled with some ability to administer or implement those sanctions. The "techniques of control" were presented in three categories—promotional techniques, regulatory techniques, and redistributive techniques. These three techniques are found in the multitude of actual policies adopted by legislatures and implemented by administrative agencies. Good policy analysis consists largely of identifying the techniques of control and choosing the policies that seek to manipulate "the economy as a system." Redistributive techniques usually come in the form of (1) monetary policies, which are concerned with control of banks, currency, and credit; (2) fiscal policies, which have to do with taxing and spending; and (3) welfare policies, which have the dual purpose of stabilizing the economy while providing a safety net for dependent and poor people.

The final section looked at imperfections in our society and how public policies have succeeded or failed in dealing with these imperfections, particularly in the distribution of opportunities. Although the welfare state itself has a great deal to do with the distribution of opportunities, this section was concerned with civil rights. An important distinction was made between policies concerning the elimination of discrimination versus policies concerning "affirmative action" aimed at overcoming and compensating for the results of discrimination in the past. Considerable progress has been made in the former but little in the latter. Civil rights laws have been helpful to women and members of minority groups who were already in the middle class of Americans. But their success in taking advantage of the civil rights laws served to increase the distance between themselves and the lower-income members of the same groups. Affirmative action policies are aimed precisely at the groups left behind, but these policies have produced a great deal of controversy. The struggle over the effort to bring solutions to these groups of people, and the controversy over the permissibility of quotas will influence the agenda of public policy well into the next century.

For Further Reading

Bullock, Charles, III, and Charles M. Lamb. *Implementation of Civil Rights Policy.* Monterey, CA: Brooks/Cole, 1984.

Chubb, John, and Paul Peterson, eds. *Can the Government Govern?* Washington, DC: Brookings Institution, 1988.

Derthick, Martha. *Agency under Stress: The Social Security Administration in American Government.* Washington, DC: Brookings Institution, 1990.

Foreman, Christopher. *Signals from the Hill: Congressional Oversight and the Challenge of Social Regulation.* New Haven: Yale University Press, 1988.

Forer, Lois G. *Criminals and Victims—A Trial Judge Reflects on Crime and Punishment.* New York: W. W. Norton, 1980.

Greider, William. *Secrets of the Temple: How the Federal Reserve Runs the Country.* New York: Simon and Schuster, 1987.

Gutmann, Amy. *Democracy and the Welfare State.* Princeton: Princeton University Press, 1988.

Heilbroner, Robert. *The Nature and Logic of Capitalism.* New York: W. W. Norton, 1985.

Lemann, Nicholas. *The Promised Land: The Great Black Migration and How It Shaped America.* New York: Alfred A. Knopf, 1991.

Lenno, Rhonda F. *Class Struggle and the New Deal: Industrial Labor, Industrial Capital and the State.* Lawrence: University of Kansas Press, 1988.

Levi, Margaret. *Of Rule and Revenue.* Berkeley: University of California Press, 1988.

Marmor, Theodore R., Jerry L. Mashaw, and Phillip L. Harvey. *America's Misunderstood Welfare State.* New York: Basic Books, 1990.

Paul, Ellen. *Equity and the Gender: The Comparable Worth Debate.* New Brunswick, NJ: Transaction, 1989.

Piven, Frances Fox, and Richard A. Cloward. *Regulating the Poor.* New York: Pantheon, 1971.

Rubin, Irene S. *The Politics of Public Budgeting—Getting and Spending, Borrowing and Balancing.* Chatham, NJ: Chatham House, 1990.

Sanders, M. Elizabeth. *The Regulation of Natural Gas.* Philadelphia: Temple University Press, 1981.

Sawhill, Isabel. *Challenge to Leadership—Eco-*

nomic and Social Issues for the Next Decade. Washington, DC: Urban Institute Press, 1988.

Stone, Alan. *Wrong Number: The Break Up of AT&T.* New York: Basic Books, 1989.

Tatalovich, Raymond, and Byron Daynes, eds. *Social Regulatory Policy: Moral Controversies in American Politics.* Boulder, CO: Westview Press, 1988.

Vogel, David. *Fluctuating Fortunes: The Political Power of Business in America.* New York: Basic Books, 1989.

Weir, Margaret, Ann Orloff, and Theda Skocpol. *The Politics of Social Policy in the United States.* Princeton: Princeton University Press, 1988.

14

FOREIGN POLICY AND WORLD POLITICS

*E*ver since Franklin Roosevelt's dramatic "Hundred Days" in 1933, there has by tradition been a "honeymoon period," during which presidents address America's needs and Congress is expected to cooperate in a bipartisan spirit. Yet, for most presidents, the honeymoon is short, if there is one at all. The interruption in the happy marriage is usually foreign policy.

When President Bush assumed office on January 20, 1989, he proclaimed his commitment to a "kinder, gentler" society and gave America his plans for education, the drug epidemic, the plight of the disabled, and the "peace dividend." But within days of his inauguration, President Bush was off to the Far East, and he returned to a series of crises ranging from Nicaragua to NATO, from Khomeini's death to the collapse of the Berlin Wall. Even the good news of the end of the Cold War did not permit President Bush to turn to domestic policy.

President Clinton was by background and temperament a domestic president, and he marched into Washington with a bulging domestic portfolio. Yet within hours of his election in November, he discovered how sensitive foreign affairs can be. Having supported political asylum for Haiti's immigrants during his campaign, his election produced a whirlwind of boatbuilding on the island. Clinton was forced to reverse his stand before Florida became flooded with immigrants. It must have reminded him how easily foreign policy can trump domestic policy.

Then President-elect Clinton felt obliged to give Bush's decision to send troops to Somalia an enthusiastic endorsement. There was also the agonizing dissolution of Yugoslavia and the question of whether America would have to follow the Somalia precedent with humanitarian aid and, quite possibly, military involvement in Bosnia. Then again, there was the instability of the Yeltsin regime and the possibility of Russia's collapse—potentially far more violent than Yugoslavia's.

Most American presidents have been domestic politicians who set out to make their place in the history books through domestic policy achievements. Despite their limited experience with foreign affairs, all postwar presidents have been confronted with major foreign policy issues as soon as they took the oath of office. They had to spend inordinate amounts of time on foreign policy throughout their tenure, and most of their legacy, for better and for worse, is in foreign policy.

This chapter will explore American foreign policy, the changing attitudes of presidents and other Americans toward world politics, and the place of America in world affairs. Although modern presidents cannot escape the demands of foreign policy and world politics, this has not always been the case in our nation's history, as we shall see in this chapter.

This chapter will begin with the world of nation-states and why nation-states present such a serious challenge to each other. From there, we trace out the history of America's place in the world of nation-states and how that history has influenced our contemporary foreign policies. Then we identify and evaluate the six basic instruments of American foreign policy. The last section of the chapter looks at actual roles we have attempted to play in world affairs.

The Setting: A World of Nation-States

A nation is a population of individuals bound to each other by a common past, a common language, or other cultural ties that draw them together and distinguish them from other peoples. When such a nation has sufficient self-consciousness to organize itself also into a political entity, it is generally referred to as a nation-state. But why form a nation-state? As Hans Morgenthau, one of the most eminent students of the nation-state noted, "The most elementary function of the nation-state is the defense of the life of its citizens and of their civilization. A political organization that is no longer able to defend these values . . . must yield, either through peaceful transformation or violent destruction, to one capable of that defense."[1]

For at least two centuries, nation-states have effectively defended their populations; and the attraction to forming nation-states does not seem to have waned as a third century approaches. There were 54 nation-states at the beginning of the twentieth century. In 1945, when the United Nations (U.N.) was founded, there were 67, of which 51 were U.N. charter members. In 1979, 153 nation-states were recognized members of the United Nations. In 1991, seven new nation-states were added, and in 1992, eleven more were formed and imme-

[1]Hans J. Morgenthau, *The Purpose of American Politics* (New York: Alfred A. Knopf, 1960), pp. 169–70.

diately given diplomatic recognition and U.N. membership status, bringing the total to 177.[2] (One former nation-state—the Republic of China, or Taiwan—was divested of membership.) Most of these new member states had been republics within the former Soviet Union, but others had been republics of Yugoslavia. In January 1993, one more nation-state was formed, when Czechoslovakia was split into the Czech Republic and Slovakia bringing the total now to 178. More are sure to come in the near future.

But why does the principle of the nation-state tend to draw nations into war? As people form themselves into nation-states as a means of defense, they become unified only by isolating themselves from other nations. By doing so, each nation deprives itself of information about the motives and interests of other nations. Modern means of transportation and communication have made the world smaller but not better acquainted. Mutual ignorance has tended to breed hostility because each nation-state conducts its foreign policy on the assumption that every country will pursue its interests at the expense of others.

The national purpose or national interest of the nation-state is said to be the maintenance of its *sovereignty.* Sovereignty can be defined as respect by other nations for the claim by a government that it has conquered its territory and is the sole authority over its population.

Obviously, no nation-state is completely sovereign. In 1973, even the most powerful nation-states were brutally reminded of the fragility of their sovereignty when the Organization of Petroleum Exporting Countries (OPEC) adopted a common foreign policy to control the price of oil on the world market, and the price of oil soared. The fragility of sovereignty was shown when Iraq occupied Kuwait in 1990 and then had its own sovereignty violated by a large U.N. military force.

Obviously, sovereignty is something a country possesses as a matter of degree. At one end of the sovereignty continuum are the small and weak nation-states, commonly referred to as "satellites," because their own claim to sovereignty depends upon some powerful neighbor. At the other end of the continuum are those nation-states called the "powers," the "superpowers," and the "imperial powers." They have the resources to conduct their own foreign policy and to defend the sovereignty of one or more satellites.

In the middle of the continuum are middle-size states that are ungraciously called "client" states. These states have the capacity to carry out their own foreign policy most of the time, but their sovereignty in the long run still depends upon the interests of one or more of the major powers.[3]

The power of a nation-state can be measured roughly according to the number and size of its satellites and clients. By that standard, the United States is the greatest of the superpowers, but it is not the only one. For most of this century, the Soviet Union was virtually America's equal. And if the Russian republic can stabilize itself, it will probably return to some kind of superpower status early in the next century. The People's Republic of China is becoming a superpower. Japan has already become a

---

[2]*The Statesmen's Yearbook* (London: Macmillan, varying years).

[3]At least one nation-state in the middle of the continuum, Switzerland, is not a client state. Switzerland's sovereignty is well guarded by most other states in order to maintain at least one country where diplomacy and business can take place no matter how chaotic international relations may be. But most of the nation-states in this middle category are best understood as "client" states.

superpower, even though it has no armed forces with international capacity. This may be a new phenomenon—an economic superpower. In that context, the oil-rich Arab states can achieve superpower status if they can maintain unity. And we may see another economic superpower if the multistate European Community becomes an integrated economic system.

Regardless of the status of each nation-state, all tend, in their foreign policies, to assume what some experts have called "the worst plausible case." In other words, each nation-state has to assume that its sovereignty is ultimately at risk of being encroached upon by one or more other nation-states. Just when they begin to relax their foreign policies, some dissatisfied dictator or neighbor will perceive it as an opportunity to threaten their sovereignty or rule.

This chapter has no solution to the many foreign policy issues nation-states confront. Nonetheless, because the conduct of foreign policy is so complex and because there are particular problems facing a democracy, such as the United States, as it formulates and puts into effect particular foreign policies, a well-balanced analysis of foreign policy problems is essential. Such an analysis must treat at least three dimensions of foreign policy, which will make up the three main sections of this chapter:

1. *Values.* What does the United States want? What are its national interests, if any? What counts as success?

2. *Instruments.* What tools are available for the conduct of foreign policy? What institutions, administrative arrangements, statutes, and programs have been established in order to enable the government to pursue our national interests?

3. *Roles.* How does the United States behave in world politics? Are its roles consistent with its values?

The Values in American Foreign Policy

When President Washington was preparing to leave office in 1796, he crafted with great care, and with the help of Hamilton and Madison, a farewell address that is one of the most memorable documents written by a government official or politician in all of American history. We have already had occasion to look at a portion of Washington's farewell address, because in it he gave some stern warnings against political parties. But Washington's greater concern was to warn the nation against foreign influence:

> History and experience prove that foreign influence is one of the most baneful foes of republican government. . . . The great rule of conduct for us in regard to foreign nations is, in extending our commercial relations to have with them as little *political* connection as possible. So far as we have already formed engagements let them be fulfilled with perfect good faith. Here let us stop. . . . There can be no greater error than to expect or calculate upon real favors from nation to nation. . . . Trust to temporary alliances for extraordinary emergencies, [but in all other instances] steer clear of permanent alliances with any portion of the foreign world. . . . Such an attachment of a small or weak toward a great and powerful nation dooms the former to be the satellite of the latter. [Emphasis in original.][4]

With the exception of a few leaders like Thomas Jefferson and Thomas Paine, who were eager to take sides with the French against all others, Washington was prob-

[4] A full version of the text of the farewell address, along with a discussion of the contribution to it made by Hamilton and Madison, will be found in Daniel J. Boorstin, ed., *An American Primer* (Chicago: University of Chicago Press, 1966), vol. 1, pp. 192–210. This editing is by Richard B. Morris.

ably expressing sentiments shared by most Americans. In fact, during most of the nineteenth century, American foreign policy was to a large extent no foreign policy. But Americans were never isolationist if isolationism means the refusal to have any associations with the outside world. Americans were eager for trade and for the treaties and contracts facilitating trade. Americans were also expansionists, but their vision of expansionism was limited to filling up the American continent only.

Three familiar historical factors help explain why Washington's sentiments became our tradition and the source of our foreign policy values. The first was the deep anti-statist ideology shared by most Americans in the nineteenth century, and on into the twentieth century. The second factor was federalism. The third was the United States's position in the world as a client state. Most nineteenth-century Americans recognized that if the United States became entangled in foreign affairs, national power would naturally grow at the expense of the states, and so would the presidency at the expense of Congress. Why? Because foreign policy meant having a professional diplomatic corps, professional armed forces with a general staff—and secrets. This meant professionalism, elitism, and remoteness from citizens. Being a client state gave us the luxury of being able to keep our foreign policy to a minimum. Maintaining American sovereignty was in the interest of the European powers.

Legacy of the Traditional System

Two identifiable legacies flowed from the long tradition based on antistatism, federalism, and client status. One is the *intermingling* of domestic and foreign policy institutions. The second is *unilateralism*—America's willingness to go it alone. Each of these will reveal a great deal about the values behind today's conduct of foreign policy.

INTERMINGLING OF DOMESTIC AND FOREIGN POLICY. Because the major European powers once policed the world, American political leaders could treat foreign policy as a mere extension of domestic policy. The tariff is the best example. A tax on one category of imported goods as a favor to interests in one section of the country would directly cause friction elsewhere in the country. But the demands of those adversely affected could be met without directly compromising the original tariff, by adding a tariff to *still other goods* that would placate those who were complaining about the original tariff. In this manner, Congress was continually adding and adjusting tariffs on more and more classes of commodities.

An important aspect of the intermingling of domestic and foreign affairs was amateurism. Americans refused to develop a tradition of a separate foreign service composed of professional people who spent much of their adult lives in foreign countries, learning foreign languages, absorbing foreign cultures, and developing a sympathy for foreign points of view. Instead, we have tended to be highly suspicious of any American diplomat or entrepreneur who attempts to speak sympathetically of any such foreign viewpoints.[5] No systematic progress was made to create a professional diplomatic corps until after the passage of the Foreign Service Act of 1946.

UNILATERALISM. Unilateralism, not isolationism, was the American posture toward the world. Isolationism means to try to cut

---

[5] E. E. Schattschneider, *Politics, Pressures and the Tariff* (Englewood Cliffs, NJ: Prentice-Hall, 1935).

off contacts with the outside, to be a self-suf-
ficient fortress. We were never isolationist.
Unilateralism means to "go it alone."
Americans have always been more likely to
rally round the president in support of direct action rather than for a sustained, diplomatic involvement.

The Great Leap—Thirty Years Later

The traditional era of U.S. foreign policy
came to an end with World War I for several
important reasons. First, the "balance of
power" system[6] that had kept the major
European powers from world war for 100
years had collapsed.[7] In fact, the great powers themselves had collapsed internally.
The most devastating of all wars up to that
time had laid waste their economies, their
empires, and, in most cases, their political
systems. Second, the United States was no
longer a client state but in fact one of the
great powers. Third, as shown in earlier
chapters, the United States was soon to shed
its traditional domestic system of federalism with its national government of almost
pure promotional policy. Thus, virtually all
the conditions that contributed to the traditional system of American foreign policy
had disappeared. *Yet, there was no discernible
change in America's approach to foreign policy
in the period between World War I and World
War II.* After World War I, as one foreign
policy analyst put it, "the United States
withdrew once more into its insularity.
Since America was unwilling to use its

power, that power, for purposes of foreign
policy, did not really exist."[8]

The Great Leap in foreign policy was
finally made thirty years after conditions
demanded it and only then after another
world war, to which America's post-World
War I behavior had undoubtedly contributed. This is not said with the intent merely
to criticize—for who knows how different
the world would have been if America had
been more engaged in world affairs during
the interwar years. The observation is made
to emphasize the strength of the traditional
pattern, so strong as to resist change in the
face of compelling conditions.

Pressure for a new tradition came into
direct conflict with the old. The new tradition required foreign entanglements; the old
tradition feared them deeply. The new tradition required diplomacy; the old dis-
trusted it. The new tradition required acceptance of antagonistic political systems; the
old embraced democracy and was aloof
from all else.

The main instruments of foreign policy
in the new, post-World War II tradition can
also be seen as five case studies in the balancing of the old tradition against the demands for a new tradition. Each is a dramatic illustration of how traditional values
shaped the instruments we would use to
fashion our new place in the world as the
leading imperial power.

The Instruments of Modern American Foreign Policy

Just as we spoke of the techniques of control
backing domestic policy, we speak here of
instruments of foreign policy. Like a tool or

[6]"Balance of power" is the primary foreign policy role played by the major European powers during the nineteenth century, and it is a role available to the United States in contemporary foreign affairs, a role occasionally adopted but not on a world scale. This is the third of the four roles identified and discussed below.

[7]The best analysis of what he calls the "100 years' peace" will be found in Karl Polanyi, *The Great Transformation* (New York: Rinehart, 1944; Beacon paperback edition, 1957), pp. 5ff.

[8]John G. Stoessinger, *Crusaders and Pragmatists—Movers of Modern American Foreign Policy* (New York: W. W. Norton, 1985), pp. 21, 34.

technique, an instrument is neutral, capable of serving many goals. There have been many instruments of American foreign policy, and we can deal here only with those instruments we deem to be most important in the modern epoch: diplomacy, the United Nations, the international monetary structure, economic aid, collective security, and military deterrence. Each will be evaluated for its utility in the conduct of American foreign policy, and each will be assessed in light of the history and development of American values.

Diplomacy

We begin this treatment of instruments with diplomacy because it is the instrument to which all other instruments must be subordinated, although they seldom are. Diplomacy is the representation of a government to other foreign governments. Its purpose is to promote national values or interests by peaceful means. According to Hans Morgenthau, "A diplomacy that ends in war has failed in its primary objective."[9]

The first effort to create a modern foreign service was made by the Rogers Act of 1924. But it took World War II and the Foreign Service Act of 1946 to forge the foreign service into a fully professional diplomatic corps.

Diplomacy, by its very nature, is overshadowed by spectacular international events, dramatic initiatives, and meetings among heads of state or their direct personal representatives. Traditional American distrust of diplomacy continues today, albeit in weaker form. Impatience with or downright distrust of diplomacy has been built not only into all the other instruments of foreign policy but also into the modern presidential

system itself.[10] So much personal responsibility has been heaped upon the presidency that it is difficult for presidents to entrust any of their authority or responsibility in foreign policy to professional diplomats stuck away in the State Department and other bureaucracies. And the American practice of appointing political friends and party fund-raisers to major ambassadorial positions does not inspire trust. During his first year in office, President Bush named 87 ambassadorial appointees, 48 of whom were important political contributors. Thus, 57 percent of Bush's appointments were political, compared with 37 percent by both Carter and Reagan at equivalent points in their respective terms. President Clinton was slower in making his appointments, filling a mere dozen ambassadorial posts during his first seven months in office. But his list of nominees and potential nominees also included a large proportion of friends and campaign contributors.[11]

As discouraging as it is to foreign service careerists to have political hacks appointed over their heads, it is probably less discouraging than the less-noticed practice of temporarily removing diplomats from a foreign policy issue as soon as relations with a particular country begin to heat up, pulling the issue upstairs to the secretary of state or into the White House.

The United Nations

The utility of the United Nations to the United States as an instrument of foreign policy can too easily be underestimated. During the first decade or more after its

[9]Hans Morgenthau, *Politics among Nations*, 2nd ed. (New York: Knopf, 1956), p. 505.

[10]See Chapter 6 and Theodore Lowi, *The Personal President—Power Invested, Promise Unfulfilled* (Ithaca: Cornell University Press, 1985), pp. 167–69.

[11]Elaine Sciolino, "Some Friends Fret as Clinton Is Slow in Choosing Envoys," *New York Times*, 3 June 1993, p. 1.

founding in 1945, the United Nations was literally a direct servant of American interests. The most spectacular example of the United States's use of the United Nations as an instrument of American foreign policy was the official U.N. authorization and sponsorship of intervention in Korea with an international "peacekeeping force" in 1950. Thanks to the Soviet boycott of the United Nations at that time, depriving the U.S.S.R. of its ability to use its veto in the Security Council of the U.N., the United States was able to conduct the Korean War under the auspices of the United Nations.

The United States provided 40 percent of the U.N. budget in 1946 (its first full year of operation) and 28.8 percent of the billion-dollar U.N. budget of 1992.[12] Many Americans feel the United Nations does not give good value for the investment. But any evaluation of the United Nations must take into account the purpose for which the United States sought to create it: *power without diplomacy.* After World War II, when the United States could no longer remain aloof from foreign policy, the goal was to use our power to create an international structure that could be run with a minimum of regular diplomatic involvement—so that Americans could return to their normal domestic pursuits. As one constitutional scholar characterized our founding in 1787, so we could

say of our effort to found the United Nations—we sought to create "a machine that would go of itself."[13]

The U.N. may have gained a new lease on life in the post–Cold War era first with its performance in the Gulf War and then with its role in Somalia. Although President Bush's immediate reaction to Iraq's invasion of Kuwait was unilateral, he quickly turned to the U.N. for sponsorship. The U.N. General Assembly initially adopted resolutions condemning the invasion and approving the full blockade of Iraq. Once the blockade was seen as having failed to achieve the unconditional withdrawal demanded by the U.N., the General Assembly adopted further resolutions authorizing the twenty-nine-nation coalition to use force if, by January 15, 1991, the resolutions were not observed. The Gulf War victory was a genuine U.N. victory. The cost of the operation was estimated at $61.1 billion. First authorized by the U.S. Congress, actual U.S. outlays were offset by pledges from the other participants—the largest shares coming from Saudi Arabia ($15.6 billion), Kuwait ($16 billion), Japan ($10 billion), and Germany ($6.5 billion). Final U.S. costs were estimated at a maximum of $8 billion.[14]

Whether the U.N. can maintain its central position in future border and trade disputes, demands for self-determination, and other provocations to war depends entirely upon the character of each dispute.

The Gulf War was a special case because it was a clear case of invasion of one country by another that also threatened the control

---

[12] In 1992, the Russian Federation contributed 9.4 percent; Germany, 8.0 percent; Japan, 11.9 percent; France, 5.7 percent; and Great Britain, 4.7 percent. The official U.N. budget of about a billion dollars is down significantly from the maximum $1.8 billion of 1988–1989. But these figures are not indicative of the U.N. scale of operation, because they do not include U.S. and other contributions to specific U.N. operations and organizations. The following are examples of U.S. contributions (based on the 1990 budget): peacekeeping, $104 million; inter-American Organizations, $103 million; U.N. Children's Fund, $64 million; U.N. development program, $105 million; world food program, $163 million. See *The 1993 Information Please Almanac,* (Boston: Houghton Mifflin, 1992), pp. 65 and 297–98.

[13] Michael Kammen, *A Machine That Would Go of Itself—The Constitution in American Culture* (New York: Alfred A. Knopf, 1986).

[14] There is in fact an ongoing dispute over a "surplus" of at least $2.2 billion, on the basis of which Japan and others are expecting a bit of a rebate. *Report of the Secretary of Defense to the President and Congress* (Washington, DC: Government Printing Office February 1992), p. 26.

George Kennan and Henry Kissinger
Architects of American Foreign Policy

*T*wo of the most important and influential figures in American foreign policy never held elective office. Known more for their intellect than for their use of political power, both George Kennan and Henry Kissinger developed powerful paradigms for the conduct of American foreign policy.

George Kennan, a career foreign service officer and expert on the Soviet Union, has spent many years studying Soviet language and politics. While serving as second-in-command at the American embassy in Moscow at the end of World War II, Kennan was asked for advice about postwar Soviet intentions from policy makers in Washington. His response was an 8,000-word telegram in which he attacked America's spirit of cooperation with the Soviets. Kennan believed that the U.S.S.R. viewed the world as divided into two camps, socialist and capitalist, and that in such a "bipolar" world there could be no peaceful coexistence. Therefore, the United States had two choices: (1) resist Soviet efforts to undermine the Western coalition or (2) buy time until the Soviet Union changed from within.

This telegram became the blueprint for America's postwar policy in what has been labeled the Cold War. Fearing he had succeeded too well, however, Kennan published an article a year later in the journal *Foreign Affairs* under the pseudonym Mr. X, in which he argued that the U.S.S.R. was not out to dominate the world. Rather, he asserted, the Soviets wanted a ring of sympathetic nations around their country as a buffer against future attacks (remembering that over the centuries the Soviets had been attacked and devastated numerous times by invading armies). Kennan's conclusion to his article literally became American policy for the next two decades: "The main element of any United States policy toward the Soviet Union must be that of a long-term patient but firm and vigilant *containment* of Russian expansive tendencies" (emphasis added).

George Kennan

of oil, which is of vital interest to the industrial countries of the world. But in the case of Somalia, while the conflict violated the world's conscience, it did not threaten vital national interests outside the country's re-

gion. The United States had propped up Somalia's government for years for purely Cold War purposes, but abandoned its dictatorial regime in 1990 and left it to a chaotic civil war—with many war lords, tribal lead-

Like Kennan's, Henry Kissinger's path to foreign policy grew from intellect and experience. As a Harvard Ph.D. and professor, Kissinger wrote extensively in the 1950s and 1960s on American-Soviet policy and the role of nuclear weapons. Impressed with his ideas, foreign policy experts in the Eisenhower, Kennedy, and Johnson administrations sought Kissinger's advice as a so-called defense intellectual. In 1969, Kissinger was selected by newly elected President Richard Nixon to serve as his national security adviser. Together, Nixon and Kissinger changed the shape of U.S. foreign policy. While taking a hard line on the Vietnam War, Kissinger orchestrated Nixon's historic trips to China and the Soviet Union in 1972, ushering in an era of "detente" between the superpowers. He was also instrumental in reaching an important agreement with the Soviets to limit nuclear arms, known as SALT I (the Strategic Arms Limitation Treaty). Kissinger sought to implement his long-standing belief in "power politics"—namely, that the only international relations that really matter are those between the world's big and powerful nations, and that the problems of smaller nations are best viewed in terms of how they affect the superpowers. While this philosophy was helpful in guiding improved U.S.-Soviet relations, it contributed to mistakes in Vietnam.

Through a combination of intellect and an unexcelled talent for bureaucratic politics, Kissinger dominated foreign policy making during the Nixon and Ford administrations (he was named secretary of state in 1973). After Ford's defeat in 1976, Kissinger began a consulting firm that helped provide access to top governmental and corporate leaders for his clients, which have included China and other nations. In contrast, George Kennan withdrew from public life, in part because of his disenchantment with the course of foreign policy in the 1950s and 1960s. As a scholar and researcher affiliated with the Institute for Advanced Study, School of Historical Study, in Princeton, Kennan continued to garner respect for his intellect and perspectives on the policy he had helped create.

Source: Fred Kaplan, *The Wizards of Armageddon* (New York: Simon and Schuster, 1983).

Henry Kissinger

ers, and gangs of marauding youths. Late in 1992 thousands of American soldiers under U.N. sponsorship were dispatched with almost no advance public preparation for a limited military intervention to make the country safe enough for humanitarian aid. One expert on diplomatic affairs characterized the operation as the affirmation of an important principle (and possibly a new U.N. precedent): "Once a country utterly loses its ability to govern itself, it also loses its claim to sovereignty and should become a ward of the United Nations."[15]

Somalia has been called a "war of conscience," and it was the first in which U.N. troops were used more for humanitarian purposes. The second became Bosnia, where Bosnian Serb and Croat troops were ejecting Muslims to prevent establishment of an independent state of Bosnia and Herzegovena. Throughout 1993, U.N. troops were employed as peacekeepers in an effort to maintain "safe havens" for Muslims, while diplomats searched for a peaceful solution.

Both of these interventions show the promise and the limits of the U.N. as an instrument of foreign policy in the post–Cold War era. Although the United States can no longer control U.N. decisions as it could in the U.N.'s early days, the U.N. continues to function as a useful instrument of American foreign policy.

The International Monetary Structure

Fear of a repeat of the economic devastation that followed World War I brought the United States together with its allies (except the U.S.S.R.) to Bretton Woods, New Hampshire, in 1944 to create a new international economic structure for the postwar world. The result was actually two institutions, the International Bank for Reconstruction and Development (the World Bank) and the International Monetary Fund (IMF).

The World Bank was set up to finance long-term capital. Leading nations took on the obligation of contributing funds to enable the World Bank to make loans to capital-hungry countries. (The U.S. quota has been about one-third of the total.)

The IMF was set up to provide for the short-term flow of money. After the war the dollar, instead of gold, was the chief means by which the currencies of one country would be "changed into" currencies of another country for purposes of making international transactions. To permit debtor countries with no international balances to make purchases and investments, the IMF was set up to lend dollars or other appropriate currencies to needy member countries to help them overcome temporary trade deficits. For many years after World War II, the IMF, along with U.S. foreign aid, in effect constituted the only international medium of exchange.

The collapse of the U.S.S.R. and the eagerness shown by the newly independent members of the former Communist bloc to join the free market have been acclaimed as the triumph of capitalism. And this may be only a modest exaggeration.

During the past decade, the IMF returned to a position of enhanced importance through its efforts to reform some of the largest debtor nations, particularly those in the Third World, to bring them more fully into the global capitalist economy. The power of the IMF to set conditions on the loans it makes and to work with major private banks to refinance ("roll over") existing debt seems to have had a positive effect. For example, on August 20, 1982, Mexico announced that it would quit trying to repay its international debt, for the time being. This also meant no more borrowing. Exactly ten years later, in August of 1992, "the Latin American debt saga [was], more or less, over. . . . Nowhere are the celebrations of life after debt bigger than on Wall Street. The re-emerging markets of Latin America had

---

[15]Strobe Talbott, "America Abroad," *Time,* 14 December 1992, p. 35.

TABLE 14.1

THE WORLD'S LEADING DEBTOR NATIONS IN 1990 (IN BILLIONS OF DOLLARS)

Nation	Debt	Nation	Debt
United States	3,233	Morocco	24
Brazil	108	Yugoslavia	21
Mexico	94	Peru	19
Argentina	63	Chile	18
Nigeria	36	Colombia	17
Philippines	27	Côte d'Ivoire	16
Venezuela	26	Ecuador	12

Sources: U.S. figure: *The World Almanac and Book of Facts, 1993* (New York: World Almanac, 1992), p. 128. All other figures are from OECD, *Financing and External Debt of Developing Countries, 1991* (Paris, 1992).

become hot business."[16] This modest but substantial reentry of Latin American countries into the world market is not due altogether to efforts of the IMF or the World Bank. But they helped pave the way for a trickle, then a flow, if not a flood, of Wall Street investment in Mexico and other countries.

Russia and thirteen other former Soviet republics were invited to join the IMF and the World Bank with the expectation of receiving $10.5 billion from these two agencies, primarily for a rouble-stabilization fund. Each republic will get a permanent IMF representative, and the IMF is increasing its staff by at least 10 percent to provide expertise to cope with the problems of these emerging capitalist economies.[17]

Economic Aid

Commitment to rebuilding war-torn countries came as early as commitment to the basic postwar international monetary structure. This is the way President Franklin Roosevelt put the case in a press conference in November 1942, less than one year after we entered the war:

> Sure, we are going to rehabilitate [other nations after the war]. Why? . . . Not only from the humanitarian point of view . . . but from the view point of our own pocketbooks, and our safety from future war.[18]

The particular form and timing for enacting American foreign aid was heavily influenced by Great Britain's sudden decision in 1947 that it would no longer be able to maintain its commitments to Greece and Turkey. (Full proof that America would now have to *have* clients rather than *be* one.) Within three weeks of that announcement, President Truman recommended a $400 million direct aid program for Greece and Turkey, and by mid-May of 1947 Congress approved it. Since President Truman had placed the Greece-Turkey action within the larger context of a commitment to help rebuild and defend all countries the world over, wher-

[16]"Falling in Love Again," *The Economist*, 22 August 1992, p. 63.

[17]"IMF: Sleeve-Rolling Time," *The Economist*, May 2, 1992, pp. 98–99.

[18]Quoted in John Lewis Gaddis, *The United States and the Origin of the Cold War, 1941–1947*, p. 21.

ever the leadership wished to develop democratic systems or to ward off communism, the Greek-Turkish aid was followed quickly by the historically unprecedented program that came to be known as the Marshall Plan, named in honor of Secretary of State (and former five-star general) George C. Marshall.[19]

The Marshall Plan—officially known as the European Recovery Plan (ERP)—was essential for the rebuilding of war-torn Europe. By 1952, the United States had spent over $34 billion for the relief, reconstruction, and economic recovery of Western Europe. The emphasis was shifted in 1951, with passage of the Mutual Security Act, to building up European military capacity. Of the $48 billion appropriated between 1952 and 1961, over half went for military assistance, the rest for continuing economic aid. Over those years, the geographic emphasis also shifted, toward South Korea, Taiwan, the Philippines, Vietnam, Iran, Greece, and Turkey—that is, toward the rim of communism. In the 1960s, the emphasis shifted once again, toward what became known as the Third World. From 1962 to 1975, over $100 billion was sent, mainly to Latin America for economic assistance. Other countries of Africa and Asia were also brought in.[20]

Many critics have argued that foreign aid is really aid for political and economic elites, not for the people. Although this is to a large extent true, it needs to be understood in a broader context. If a country's leaders oppose distributing food or any other form of assistance to its people, there is little the United States, or any aid organization, can do, short of terminating the assistance. Goods have to be exchanged across national borders before they can reach the people who need them. Needy people would probably be worse off if we cut off aid altogether. The lines of international communication must be kept open. That is why diplomacy exists, and foreign aid can facilitate diplomacy just as diplomacy is needed to help get foreign aid where it is most needed.

An important criticism of U.S. foreign aid policy is that it has not been tied closely enough to U.S. diplomacy. The original Marshall Plan was set up as an independent program outside the State Department and had its own separate missions in each participating country. "ERP became a Second State Department."[21] This did not change until the program was reorganized as the Agency for International Development (AID) in the early 1960s and became part of the State Department. Meanwhile, the Defense Department always had principal jurisdiction over that substantial proportion of economic aid that went to military assistance. The Department of Agriculture has administered the commodity aid programs, such as Food for Peace. Each department has in effect been able to conduct its own foreign policy, leaving many foreign diplomats to ask, "Who's in charge here?"

That brings us back to the history of our efforts to balance traditional values with the modern needs of world leadership. Economic assistance is an instrument of American foreign policy, but it has been less effective than it might have been, because of the inability of American politics to overcome its traditional opposition to foreign entanglements and build a unified foreign policy—something that the older nation-states

---

[19]The best account of the decision and its purposes will be found in Joseph Jones, *The Fifteen Weeks* (New York: Viking, 1955).

[20]Robert A. Pastor, *Congress and the Politics of U.S. Foreign Economic Policy* (Berkeley: University of California Press, 1980), pp. 256–80.

[21]Quoted in Lowi, *The End of Liberalism*, p. 162.

In Brief Box

INSTRUMENTS OF FOREIGN POLICY

Diplomacy
The representation of a government to other foreign governments
Designed to promote national values or interests by peaceful means, mainly talk

United Nations
International peacekeeping structure created by the United States in the 1940s as a response to World War II (originally a goal set by President Woodrow Wilson after World War I)
Often used as a tool to further the aims of American foreign policy (Korean War, Persian Gulf War)

International Monetary Structure
Formation of the World Bank (International Bank for Reconstruction and Development) and the International Monetary Fund (IMF) in response to economic devastation following World War II
World Bank set up to make long-term loans to countries for capital investment
IMF to provide for short-term flows of money to facilitate trade (fund made up of gold and currencies of each member country)

Economic Aid
The first economic assistance plan of any importance was the Marshall Plan or European Recovery Plan set up to rebuild Europe after World War II
Economic assistance has no doubt been a cornerstone in American foreign policy toward Third World countries, especially during the 1960s and early 1970s when the United States sent over $100 billion to Latin America to thwart the advance of communism

Collective Security
Mutual defense alliances set up after World War II
Agreement that an attack against a member country would be considered as an attack against all member countries
The first treaty calling for a mutual security alliance was Rio Treaty (OAS) between United States and various Central and South American countries, Mexico, and Haiti. Other examples are NATO, ANZUS, SEATO

Military Deterrence
Mobilization of troops during peacetime combined with a willingness to expand defense budget
The "balance of terror" or Mutually Assured Destruction (MAD) between superpowers during the Cold War
Post-Cold War continuation of race in technical innovation and arms sales

would call a foreign ministry. We have undoubtedly made progress, but foreigners still often wonder who is in charge.

Collective Security

In 1947, most Americans hoped that the United States could meet its world obligations through the United Nations and economic structures alone. But most foreign policy makers recognized that it was a vain hope even as they were permitting and encouraging Americans to believe it. They had anticipated the need for military entanglements at the time of the drafting of the original U.N. Charter by insisting upon language that recognized the right of all nations to provide for their mutual defense independently of the United Nations. And almost immediately after enactment of the Marshall Plan, the White House and a parade of State and Defense officials followed up with an urgent request to the Senate to ratify and to Congress to finance mutual defense alliances.

At first quite reluctant to approve treaties providing for national security alliances, the Senate ultimately agreed with the executive branch. As shown in Table 14.2, the first collective security agreement was the Rio Treaty (ratified by the Senate in September 1947), which created the Organization of American States (OAS). This was the model treaty, anticipating all succeeding collective security treaties by providing that an armed attack against any of its members "shall be considered as an attack against all the American States," including the United States. But since OAS involved only the Western Hemisphere, a more significant break with U.S. tradition against peacetime entanglements came with the North Atlantic Treaty (signed in April 1949), which cre-

ated the North Atlantic Treaty Organization (NATO). ANZUS, a treaty tying Australia and New Zealand to the United States was signed in September 1951. Three years later, the Southeast Asia Treaty created the Southeast Asia Treaty Organization (SEATO).

In addition to these ***multilateral collective security treaties,*** the United States entered into a number of ***bilateral treaties***—treaties between two countries. The important ones are shown in Table 14.3. President Carter's reestablishment of full diplomatic relations with the People's Republic of China required cancellation of the treaty with the Republic of China (Taiwan). All other treaties continue in force. As one author observed, the United States has been a *producer* of security while most of its allies have been *consumers* of security.[22] Figure 14.1 demonstrates that the United States has consistently devoted at least 6 percent of its gross national product (GNP) to defense, growing toward 7 percent during the 1980s, while NATO allies spend around 4 percent of their respective GNPs and Japan spends about 1 percent.

This pattern has continued in the post–Cold War era, and its best illustration is in the Persian Gulf War, where the United States provided the initiative, the leadership, and most of the armed forces, even though the allies were obliged to reimburse us for over 90 percent of the cost.

It is difficult to evaluate collective security and its treaties, because the purpose of collective security as an instrument of foreign policy is prevention, and success of this kind has to be measured according to what did *not* happen. The critics have argued that our collective security treaties posed a threat of encirclement to the U.S.S.R., forc-

[22]George Quester, *The Continuing Problem of International Politics* (Hinsdale, IL: Dryden Press, 1974), p. 229.

TABLE 14.2
U.S. COLLECTIVE SECURITY (MULTILATERAL) TREATIES

Treaty	Date Signed	Members	
Rio Treaty (OAS)[a]	September 2, 1947	Argentina	Guatemala
		Bolivia	Haiti
Treaty Terms: An armed attack against any American State "shall be considered as an attack against all the American States," and each one "undertakes to assist in meeting the attack."		Brazil	Honduras
		Chile	Mexico
		Colombia	Nicaragua
		Costa Rica	Panama
		Cuba[b]	Paraguay
		Dominican Republic	Peru
			United States
		Ecuador	Uruguay
		El Salvador	Venezuela
North Atlantic Treaty (NATO)[c]	April 4, 1949	Belgium	Luxembourg
		Canada	Netherlands
		Denmark	Norway
Treaty Terms: "The parties agree that an armed attack against one or more of them in Europe or North America shall be considered an attack against them all; and each party [will take such action as deemed necessary]."		France[d]	Portugal
		Germany[e]	Spain
		Greece[f]	Turkey[f]
		Iceland	United Kingdom
		Italy	United States
ANZUS Treaty[g]	September 1, 1951	Australia	
		New Zealand	
Treaty Terms: Each party recognizes that "an armed attack in the Pacific Area on any of the parties would be dangerous to its own peace and safety," and agrees that it will act "to meet the common danger. . . ."		United States	
Southeast Asia Treaty (SEATO)[h]	September 8, 1954	Australia	Philippines
		France	Thailand
		New Zealand	United Kingdom
Treaty Terms: Each party "recognizes that aggression . . . against any of the parties . . . would endanger its own peace and safety," and each will "in that event act to meet the common danger . . ."		Pakistan	United States

[a]The Organization of American States (OAS), called for by the Rio Treaty, was established in April 1948, and includes the Caribbean states: Antigua and Barbuda, Bahamas, Barbados, Dominica, Grenada, Jamaica, St. Christopher and Nevis, St. Lucia, St. Vincent and the Grenadines, Suriname, Trinidad, and Tobago.
[b]Suspended from the OAS in 1962.
[c]The North Atlantic Treaty Organization (NATO) was established in September 1950.
[d]Withdrew forces by 1967 but remains a NATO member.
[e]The Federal Republic of Germany joined in 1954 and maintained its membership, joined by East Germany, as a new united Germany in 1990.　　　　[f]Joined in 1951.
[g]Abbreviation made up of the first letters of the names of the member nations.
[h]The Southeast Asia Treaty Organization (SEATO) was established in September 1954.
Sources: Paul Y. Hammond and John Morton Blum, *The Cold War Years: American Foreign Policy since 1945,* p. 256. Copyright © 1969 by Harcourt Brace Jovanovich, Inc., rearranged and printed with the permission of the publisher. Updated from U.S. Department of State, *Treaties in Force,* 1989 (Washington, DC: Government Printing Office, 1989).

TABLE 14.3
BILATERAL TREATIES BETWEEN THE UNITED STATES AND INDIVIDUAL NATIONS

Treaty	Date Signed	Members
Philippine Treaty	August 30, 1951	Philippines United States

Treaty Terms
Each party recognizes that an "armed attack in the Pacific Area on either of the parties would be dangerous to its own peace and safety," and each party agrees that it will act "to meet the common dangers in accordance with its constitutional processes."

Treaty	Date Signed	Members
Republic of Korea Treaty	October 1, 1953	Republic of Korea United States

Treaty Terms
Each party recognizes that "an armed attack in the Pacific Area on either of the parties . . . would be dangerous to its own peace and safety," and each party agrees to "act to meet the common danger in accordance with its constitutional processes."

Treaty	Date Signed	Members
Republic of China Treaty*	December 2, 1954	Republic of China United States

Treaty Terms
Each party recognizes that "an armed attack in the West Pacific Area directed against the territories of either of the parties would be dangerous to its own peace and safety" and that each would "act to meet the common danger in accordance with its constitutional process. (The territory of the Republic of China is defined as "Taiwan and the Pescadores.")

Treaty	Date Signed	Members
Japanese Treaty†	January 19, 1960	Japan United States

Treaty Terms
Each party recognizes that "an armed attack against either party in the territories under the administration of Japan would be dangerous to its own peace and safety," and each party would "act to meet the common danger in accordance with its own constitutional provisions and processes."

Treaty	Date Signed	Members
Spanish Treaty	January 24, 1979	Spain United States

Treaty Terms
Each party is ready to prepare plans for action to be taken "in case of an attack against Spain or the United States in the context of a general attack against the West."

* The treaty was abrogated on January 1, 1980; but Congress in 1979 had passed a law (not written in the form of a defense agreement) requiring the United States "to maintain the capacity to resist any resort to force. . . that would jeopardize the security of Taiwan."
† Replaced the bilateral security treaty of 1951.

Sources: Paul Y. Hammond and John Morton Blum, *The Cold War Years: American Foreign Policy since 1945*, p. 256. Copyright © 1969 by Harcourt Brace Jovanovich, Inc., rearranged and printed with the permission of the publisher. Updated primarily from U.S. Department of States, Treaties in Force, 1979 (Washington, DC: Government Printing Office, 1979), pp. 3031–33.

FIGURE 14.1

Total Defense Spending
(As a Percentage of Gross National Product)

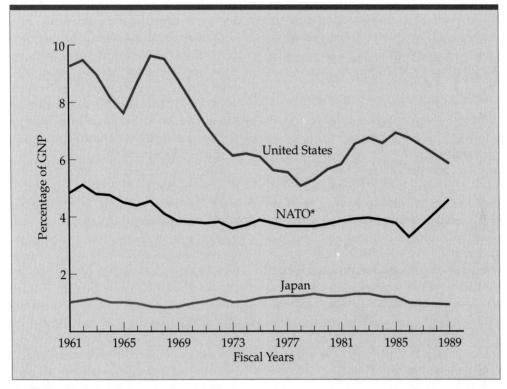

* Excluding the United States.
Source: U.S. Senate, Hearings before the Committee on the Budget, "Concurrent Resolution on the Budget for Fiscal Year 1989 (Washington, DC: Government Printing Office, 1988), p. 138.

ing it to produce its own collective security, particularly in the Warsaw Pact.[23] Nevertheless, no one can deny the counterargument that the world enjoyed more than forty-five years without world war.

Both arguments are now obsolete. The Cold War as we knew it is over. The Warsaw

Pact was formally terminated in 1991, East and West Germany were united, and the newly unified Germany elected to maintain membership in NATO, with the blessing of the Soviet Union. The end of the Cold War and of the Warsaw Pact produced an "identity crisis" in NATO and among its members, including the United States.

NATO and the other mutual security organizations throughout the world are likely to survive in the post-Cold War era. But these organizations are going to be less like

[23]The Warsaw Pact was signed in 1955 by the U.S.S.R., the German Democratic Republic (East Germany), Poland, Hungary, Czechoslovakia, Romania, Bulgaria, and Albania. Albania later dropped out.

military alliances and more like economic associations to advance technology, reduce trade barriers, and protect the world environment. Another form of collective security may well have emerged from the 1991 Persian Gulf War, with nations forming temporary coalitions under U.N. sponsorship to check a particularly aggressive nation.

Military Deterrence

For the first century and a half of its existence as an independent republic, the United States held strongly to a "Minuteman" theory of defense: Maintain a small corps of professional officers, a few flagships, and a small contingent of marines; leave the rest of defense to the state militias. In case of war, mobilize as quickly as possible, taking advantage of the country's immense size and its separation from Europe to gain time to mobilize. The United States applied this policy as recently as post-World War I and was beginning to apply it after World War II, until the new policy of preparedness won out. The cycle of demobilization-remobilization was broken. With preparedness as the goal, peacetime defense expenditures grew steadily.

However, the size of the defense budget has not been central to the consideration of deterrence as an instrument of foreign policy. Whether arms expenditures are motivated by a bilateral struggle between the United States and the Soviet Union or by a confrontation with a multiplicity of potential aggressors, as appears to be the situation for the 1990s, the goal is not military dominance as such but *deterrence from any attack at all.* The Iraqi invasion of Kuwait proved that whatever had deterred the Soviet Union from aggression was not necessarily translatable into post-Cold War conflicts.

The victory against Iraq may lead to technologies and policies of deterrence more appropriate to the post-Cold War world. But deterrence is still the name of the game, and the resumption and escalation of arms sales throughout the world, and especially in the Middle East since the Gulf War, suggests that the United States and other powers will have a real struggle to make deterrence work. There continues to be a kind of "arms race," but that race continues to be not for quantitative but for technologically qualitative superiority.

For over a century after Napoleon brought to the world the first mass citizen armies, military capacity in the Western world was measured quantitatively. Technology was, of course, always important. Technological superiority helped to make possible the domination of the Western powers over their non-Western colonies and the domination of small U.S. armed contingents over the American Indians. But it was probably not until World War II that technology became the key to the military's value as an instrument of foreign policy. From then on, the technological tail began to wag the military dog. And it is not merely a question of adding technology by giving each soldier an automatic weapon and an electronic communications device. Technology means a policy of planned technological innovation.

Probably the most important outcome of the Persian Gulf War, especially from the military point of view, is that most of this expensive technology worked as well as its supporters had claimed. This will likely enhance the credibility of using military technology as the primary deterrent in the world.

The policy of planned technological innovation is called research and development (R & D). R & D is certainly not limited to national defense. American industries spend billions of dollars on R & D annually, and many nonmilitary agencies of the federal government engage in some R & D. But nowhere is R & D such a high priority as in the modern American military establishment. The U.S. government and private industry together are spending about $150 billion a year on R & D "covering everything from mapping the human genome to exploring the frontiers of physics. That is about 3 percent of America's gross domestic product, and about the same percentage that Japan and Germany spend." But there the similarity ends. Germany and Japan devote almost all of their R & D to civilian projects; the United States spends about 40 percent of its R & D on military projects. This came to nearly $60 billion in 1992, up from over $45 billion in 1988 and around $13 billion in 1980.[24]

There is an additional "hidden" R & D military budget in the private manufacture of military hardware. It is difficult to determine just where R & D ends and manufacturing begins; nevertheless, it is certain that R & D takes a significant bite of each private defense production contract.

The end of the Cold War raised public expectations for a "peace dividend" at last, after nearly a decade of the largest peacetime defense budget increases in U.S. history. Many defense experts, liberal and conservative, feared what they called a budget "free-fall" not only because deterrence was still needed but also because severe and abrupt cuts could endanger private industry in many friendly foreign countries as well as in the United States.

The Persian Gulf War brought both points dramatically into focus. First, the Iraqi invasion of Kuwait revealed the size, strength, and advanced modern technological base not only of the Iraqi armed forces but of other countries, Arab and non-Arab, including the capability, then or soon, to make atomic weapons and other weapons of massive destructive power. Moreover, the demand for more-advanced weaponry was intensifying. The decisive victory of the United States and its allies in the Gulf War, far from discouraging the international arms trade, gave it fresh impetus. Following the Gulf War victory, *Newsweek* reported that "industry reps quickly realized that foreign customers would now be beating a path to their doors, seeking to buy the winning weaponry." The Soviet Union had led the list of major world arms sellers, and Russia and several other republics of the former Soviet Union have continued to make international arms sales, particularly since now there are "no ideological limitations" in the competition for customers.[25] The United States now probably leads the list of military weapons exporters, followed by France, Great Britain, and China. Note that these countries are also the five permanent members of the U.N. Security Council. The biggest buyers of military hardware are India, Japan, Saudi Arabia, and Syria. Iraq, second only to India before the Gulf War (and a major U.S. customer), will surely return as an important buyer if restrictions are lifted. Thus, some shrinkage of defense expenditure has been desirable but both

[24]The R & D budget totals include the following agencies: Department of Defense, Department of Energy (military related), and the National Aeronautics and Space Administration (NASA). See *Statistical Abstract*, 1900, pp. 331, 584. Of the $49.7 billion R & D budget in 1989, $2.5 billion was from the Department of Energy, $4.8 billion was from the Department of Defense, and $5.4 billion was from NASA. The above quotation and the 1992 figures come from Michael Lubell, "Getting the Right Mix on R&D," *New York Times*, 27 December 1992, sec. 3, p. 11.

[25]"Arms for Sale," *Newsweek*, 8 April 1991, pp. 22–27.

PROCESS BOX 14.1
How the F-16 Is Produced
The International Relations of Defense

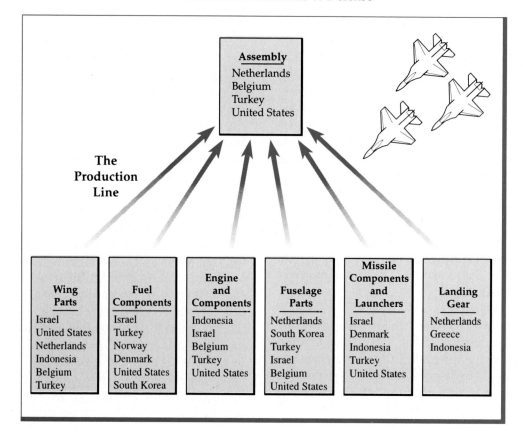

Democrats and Republicans agree that this reduction must be guided by the continuing need to maintain U.S. and allied credibility as a deterrent to post–Cold War arms races.

As to the second point, domestic pressures join international demands to fuel post–Cold War defense spending. Each cut in military production and each closing of a military base or plant means a significant loss of jobs. Moreover, conversion of defense industries to domestic uses cannot be done by the United States alone. Process Box 14.1 conveys a dramatic picture of the "international relations" of the production of one single weapons system, the F-16 fighter airplane.

All of this suggests that the threat of the arms race and international conflicts persist even in the post–Cold War era. It also suggests that the United States is an important part of the problem as well as the most essential part of the solution. The only real hope for a significant reduction in the international demand for arms will come from changes in the general political and economic environment. But such changes do not happen spontaneously. On the international level, genuine reduction in the demand for arms will require diplomacy; try as we might, power without diplomacy can never be a permanent solution. And this must in turn be accompanied by economic growth, not only in the United States but everywhere.

Roles Nations Play

Although each president has hundreds of small foreign fires to fight and can choose the instruments of policy in each particular situation, his primary foreign policy problem is choosing an overall *role* for the country in foreign affairs. Roles help us to define a situation in order to control the element of surprise in international relations. Surprise is in fact the most dangerous aspect of international relations, especially in a world made small and fragile by "smart weapons" technology.

Choosing a Role

The problem of choosing a role can be understood by identifying a limited number of roles actually played by nation-states in the past. Four such roles will be drawn from history—the Napoleonic, the Holy Alliance, the balance-of-power, and the economic expansionist roles. Although the definitions will be exaggerations of the real world, they do capture in broad outline the basic choices available.

THE NAPOLEONIC ROLE. The Napoleonic role takes its name from the role played by post-revolutionary France under Napoleon.

The French at that time felt not only that their new democratic system of government was the best on earth but that France would not be safe until the system was adopted universally. If this meant intervention into the internal affairs of France's neighbors, and if that meant warlike reactions, then so be it. President Woodrow Wilson expressed a similar viewpoint when he supported our declaration of war in 1917 by his argument that "the world must be made safe for democracy." Obviously such a position can be adopted by any powerful nation as a rationalization for intervening at its convenience in the internal affairs of another country. But it can also be sincerely espoused, and in the United States it has from time to time enjoyed broad popular consensus. We played the Napoleonic role most recently in ousting Philippine dictator Ferdinand Marcos (February 1986), Panamanian leader Manuel Noriega (December 1989), and the Sandinista government of Nicaragua (February 1990).

THE HOLY ALLIANCE ROLE. The concept of the Holy Alliance emerged out of the defeat of Napoleon and the agreement by the leaders of Great Britain, Russia, Austria, and Prussia to preserve the social order against *all* revolution, including democratic revolution, at whatever cost. (Post-Napoleonic France also joined it.) The Holy Alliance system made use of every kind of political instrument available—including political suppression, espionage, sabotage, and outright military intervention—to keep existing governments in power. The Holy Alliance role is comparable to the Napoleonic role in that each operates on the assumption that intervention into the internal affairs of other countries is justified for the maintenance of peace. But Napoleonic intervention is motivated by fear of dictatorship, and it

Colin Powell
Soldier-Diplomat

Colin Powell followed one of the few available career paths open to blacks in the years after World War II—military service. Powell graduated at the top of his ROTC class in 1958. After receiving his commission, he served two tours of duty in Vietnam, and was injured and decorated both times.

In 1971, he was accepted into the highly competitive White House Fellowship program. Powell returned to active military service in 1973, which included a tour in Korea, where he served as a battalion commander. He also served in the Carter administration as assistant to the deputy secretary of defense. In 1983, Powell was again called to serve in the Department of Defense (DOD), under President Reagan's defense secretary Caspar Weinberger. In that position, Powell became one of only five DOD officials informed of the covert effort to sell weapons to Iran in the scheme later labeled the Iran-Contra Affair. Yet Powell was one of the few individuals involved to emerge unscathed, because he had questioned the legality of the arms transfer before the investigation began, and had been forthright in his testimony before Congress.

In June 1986 Powell returned to his preferred profession, active military service, in Germany. Six months later, Frank Carlucci, who had been appointed Reagan's national security adviser, asked Powell to return to Washington to serve as his deputy. Powell declined several times, but reluctantly agreed after a direct request from Reagan. In this capacity, Powell oversaw the reorganization of the National Security Council called for by the Tower commission.

Colin Powell
(b. 1937)

In November 1987, Carlucci was named secretary of defense, and Powell became national security adviser. In that position, Powell won praise for coordinating implementation of the terms of the recently signed Intermediate-Range Nuclear Forces (INF) Treaty with the Soviet Union. In 1989, President Bush nominated General Powell to be chairman of the Joint Chiefs of Staff, a position that perhaps best matches Powell's desire to remain in military service with his highly regarded ability to deal with Washington politics. In this position, Powell directed allied forces in the brief but militarily successful war with Iraq in early 1991. The swift victory, highlighted by a brilliantly conceived flanking encirclement of static Iraqi fortifications in the February ground assault, only served to further polish Powell's image. (Powell had rejected an earlier plan calling for a frontal assault against Iraqi positions.)

While he incurred the ire of some in the Bush administration for repeating his early doubts about the wisdom of the military campaign, most people have praised Powell's handling of the war.

Source: Bob Woodward, *The Commanders* (New York: Simon and Schuster, 1991).

can accept and even encourage revolution. In contrast, Holy Alliance intervention is antagonistic to political change *as such,* even when this means supporting a dictatorship.[26] Because the Holy Alliance role became more important after the Cold War ended, illustrations of this role will be given later in the chapter.

THE BALANCE-OF-POWER ROLE. This role is basically an effort by the major powers to play off against each other so that no great power or combination of great and lesser powers can impose conditions on the others. The most relevant example is found in the nineteenth century, especially the latter half. The feature of the balance-of-power role that is most distinct from the two previously identified roles is that this role accepts the political system of each country, asking no questions except whether the country will join an alliance and will use its resources to ensure that each country will respect the borders and interests of all the others.[27]

THE ECONOMIC EXPANSIONIST ROLE. This role, also called the capitalist role, shares with the balance-of-power role the attitude that the political system or ideology of a country is irrelevant; the only question is whether a country has anything to buy or sell and whether its entrepreneurs, corporations, and government agencies will honor their contracts. Governments and their ar-

mies are occasionally drawn into economic expansionist relationships in order to establish, reopen, or expand trade relationships, and to keep the lines of commerce open. But the role is political. The point can be made that the economic expansionist role was the role consistently played by the United States in Latin and Central America until the Cold War (perhaps in the 1960s and beyond) pushed us toward the Holy Alliance role in most of those countries.

However, like arms control, economic expansion does not happen spontaneously. In the past, economic expansion owed a great deal to military backing, because contracts do not enforce themselves, trade deficits are not paid automatically, and new regimes don't always honor the commitments made by regimes they replace. The only way to expand economic relationships is through diplomacy.

Roles for America Today

Although "making the world safe for democracy" was a popular expression of World War I, it was taken more seriously after World War II, when at last the United States was willing to play a more sustained part in foreign affairs. The Napoleonic role was most suited to our view of the postwar world. To create the world's ruling regimes in our own image would indeed give us the opportunity to return to our private pursuits, for if all or even most of the world's countries were governed by democratic constitutions, there would be no war since no democracy would ever attack another democracy—or so we assumed. The emergence of the Soviet Union as a superpower was the overwhelming influence on American foreign policy thinking in the post-

[26] For a thorough and instructive exposition of the original Holy Alliance pattern, see Paul M. Kennedy, *The Rise and Fall of the Great Powers* (New York: Random House, 1987), pp. 159–60. And for a comparison of the Holy Alliance role with the "balance of power," to be discussed next, see Polanyi, *The Great Transformation,* pp. 5–11 and 259–62.

[27] Felix Gilbert et al., *The Norton History of Modern Europe* (New York: W. W. Norton, 1971), pp. 1222–24.

American Foreign Policy: Self-Interest or Idealism?

With the end of the Cold War and the breakup of the Soviet Union, many foreign policy experts are reassessing America's role in the world community. Some argue that it is time to focus our attention and resources more directly on our own problems and needs. Others argue that this is no time for the United States to abandon its world leadership role.

Economist Alan Tonelson defends what he labels an "interest-based" foreign policy for America. Such a position emphasizes placing American needs first and advocates foreign interventions only when they serve our interest. Foreign policy specialist Joshua Muravchik, on the other hand, rejects the realist view of Tonelson and others; he maintains that America has both a right and an obligation to extend democratic values around the world.

Tonelson

The United States cannot hope to achieve the desired level of security and prosperity by underwriting the security and prosperity of countries all over the world, and by enforcing whatever global norms of economic and political behavior this ambition requires. . . . It must therefore distinguish between what it must do that is absolutely essential for achieving this more modest set of objectives and those things it might do that are not essential. It must, in other words, begin to think in terms not of the whole world's well-being but rather of purely national interests. . . .

. . . An interest-based U.S. foreign policy would firmly subordinate international activism and the drive for world leadership to domestic concerns. Indeed, it would spring from new and more realistic ideas about what can be expected of a country's official foreign policy in the first place. . . . An interest-based approach would also reject the idea that meeting a set of global responsibilities can be the lodestar of U.S. foreign policy. . . . An interest-based foreign policy would acknowledge that the citizens of a democracy have every right to choose whatever foreign policy they please. . . .

World War II era. The distribution of power in the world was "bipolar," and Americans saw the world separated in two, with an "Iron Curtain" dividing the Communist world from the free world. Immediately after the war, the American foreign policy goal had been "pro-democracy," a Napoleonic role dominated by the Marshall Plan and the genuine hope for a democratic world. This quickly shifted toward a Holy Alliance role, with "containment" as our primary foreign policy criterion.[28] Containment was fundamentally a Holy Alliance concept. According to foreign policy expert Richard Barnet, during the 1950s and 1960s,

[28]The original theory of containment was articulated by former ambassador and scholar George Kennan in a famous article published under the pseudonym Mr. X, "The Sources of Soviet Conduct," *Foreign Affairs* 25 (1947), p. 556.

The new foreign policy certainly would not preclude acting on principle. But it would greatly de-emphasize conforming to abstract standards of behavior. In fact, the new foreign policy would shy away from any overarching strategy of or conceptual approach to international relations. . . . Its only rule of thumb would be "whatever works" to preserve or enhance America's security and prosperity. . . .[1]

Muravchik

Although many state actions aim to defend interests, many do not. Some are motivated by altruism. The United States rushes to aid to the victims of flood, famine, or other catastrophe wherever these occur for no motive other than human sympathy. Several other countries do the same. Various states offer asylum to the persecuted, provide good offices for the mediation of distant disputes, and even contribute troops to international peacekeeping forces, all for reasons that are essentially humanitarian. . . . The realists are left with the argument that it is wrong to foist our ways—that is, democracy—on others. In saying this the realists suddenly are arguing in moral terms. Their point, however, entails a logical fallacy. The reason it is wrong to impose something on others, presumably, is because it violates their will. But absent democracy, how can their will be known? Moreover, why care about violating people's will unless one begins with the democratic premise that popular will ought to be sovereign?

This argument implies that people prefer to be ruled by an indigenous dictator than to be liberated through foreign influence. The realists will have a hard time explaining this to the people of Panama who danced in the streets when U.S. invaders ousted dictator Manuel Noriega. . . .

The examples of Panama, Japan, Germany, the Dominican Republic, and Grenada notwithstanding, to foist democracy on others does not ordinarily mean to impose it by force. Nor does it mean to seek carbon copies of American institutions. . . . If individuals are obliged to abide by certain moral rules, can they be exempted from those rules when they act collectively with others in the name of the nation?[2]

[1]Alan Tonelson, "What Is the National Interest?" *The Atlantic,* July 1991, pp. 37, 39.
[2]Joshua Muravchik, *Exporting Democracy: Fulfilling America's Destiny* (Washington, DC: AEI Press, 1991), pp. 25, 34–36.

"the United States used its military or paramilitary power on an average of once every eighteen months either to prevent a government deemed undesirable from coming to power or to overthrow a revolutionary or reformist government considered inimical to America's interests."[29] Although Barnet

[29]Richard Barnet, "Reflections," *New Yorker,* 9 March 1987, p. 82.

did not refer to Holy Alliance, his description fits the model perfectly.

During the 1970s, the United States played the Holy Alliance role less frequently, not so much because of the outcome of the Vietnam War as because of the emergence of a multipolar world. In 1972, the United States accepted the People's Republic of China as the government of mainland China and broke forever its pure bipolar Cold War view of world power distribution. Other powers became politically important as well, including Japan, the European Economic Community (EC), India, and, depending on their own resolve, the countries making up the organization of Petroleum Exporting Countries (OPEC). The United States experimented with all four of the previously identified roles, depending on which was appropriate to a specific region of the world. In the Middle East, we tended to play an almost classic balance-of-power role, by appearing sometimes cool in our relations with Israel and by playing off one Arab country against another. President Nixon introduced balance-of-power considerations in the Far East by "playing the China card." In other parts of the world, particularly in Latin America, we tended to hold to the Holy Alliance role.

This multipolar phase lasted until 1989, when the Soviet Union collapsed and the Cold War ended. Soon thereafter the Warsaw Pact collapsed too, ending armed confrontation in Europe. With almost equal suddenness, armed suppression of minorities within Russia and Eastern Europe was relaxed, and the popular demand for "self-determination" produced several new nation-states and the demand for still more. On the one hand, it is indeed good to witness the reemergence of some twenty-five major nationalities after anywhere from forty-five to seventy-five years of suppression. On the other hand, policy makers with a sense of history are aware that this new world order bears a strong resemblance to the world of 1914. It was known then as Balkanization. Balkanization meant nationhood and self-determination. But it also meant war. The Soviet Union after World War I, and Yugoslavia after World War II, kept more than twenty-five nationalities from making war against each other for several decades until 1989. The world was caught unprepared for the dangers of a new disorder that the reemergence of these nationalities produced.

It should also be emphasized that the demand for nationhood has been emerging with new vigor in many other parts of the world—the Middle East, south and southeast Asia, South Africa. Perhaps this is *world Balkanization*. We should not overlook the reemergence of the spirit of nationhood among ethnic minorities in Canada and the United States.

GLOBALIZATION OF MARKETS. The collapse of the Cold War unleashed another dynamic factor, the globalization of markets; one could call it the globalization of capitalism. This is good news, but it has its problematic side because the free market can disrupt nationhood. Although globalization of markets is enormously productive, countries like to enjoy its benefits while attempting at the same time to prevent international economic influences from affecting local jobs, local families, and established class and tribal relationships.

This struggle between capitalism and nationhood produces a new kind of bipolarity in the world. The old world order was shaped by *external bipolarity*—of West versus East. This seems to have been replaced by *internal bipolarity,* wherein each country is struggling to make its own hard policy choices to preserve its cultural uniqueness while competing effectively in the global marketplace. The question is, What are the implications of internal bipolarity for the role or roles America is going to have to play in the post–Cold War world?

At first glance, it appears that America finally got what it wanted—a world that would run itself well enough without need for much U.S. foreign policy at all. But we have obviously been betrayed by events. U.S. foreign policy roles and priorities have not been shuffled very much, if at all. In fact, the Holy Alliance role seems to be more prominent than ever. There is, of course, one big difference—the absence of the Soviet Union and the current willingness of Russia to support rather than oppose American policies. During the Cold War era, the purpose of the Holy Alliance role was to keep regimes in power *as long as they did not espouse Soviet foreign policy goals.* In the post–Cold War world, the purpose of the Holy Alliance role is still to keep regimes in power, but only as long as they maintain general stability, keep their nationalities contained within their own borders, and encourage their economies to attain some level of participation in the global market.

Perhaps the first indication of post–Cold War American foreign policy conduct was President Bush's conciliatory approach to the dictatorial regime of the People's Republic of China following its brutal military suppression of the democratic student movement in Tiananmen Square in June 1989. Not only did the dictator Deng Xiaoping receive America's most ardent public embrace; China received our coveted "most favored nation" status despite repeated efforts by Congress to deny it until China reformed itself.[30] President Clinton continued this approach, again renewing China's "most favored nation" status in 1993, but with a promise to review it carefully after a year to be sure that political reform in China warranted another renewal.

Iraq offers probably the most meaningful example because our approach to Iraq's invasion of Kuwait was a genuine "concert of nations" approach. The concert in this case was the twenty-nine-nation alliance, under U.N. sponsorship, to remove Iraq's army from Kuwait. After the victory, President Bush initially took a Napoleonic position, urging the people of Iraq to "take matters into their own hands" and to force Hussein to "step aside." But once the uprisings began, President Bush backed away, thus revealing that the real intent had been to leave the existing military and party dictatorship in power, with or without Hussein.

Another indication of our post–Cold War role is the new arms race—that is, the international market in military products—and the growing importance of the Holy Alliance role in America's effort to produce a "new world order." The primary incentive in the international sale of military products is to keep our own defense industry alive and prosperous in the face of domestic defense budget cuts. We remain the biggest producer and exporter of advanced weaponry, but many other countries manufacture military materials, and a tremendous proportion of their military goods are for export. These countries are Brazil (over 80 percent for export); Italy (62 percent); Israel (47 percent); Spain (41 percent); the United Kingdom (40 percent); and Sweden (24 percent).[31] This means that each of these economies has a heavy stake in the international arms market. It also means that the United States and Russia in particular have a double stake in its maintenance, because they profit not only from their own exports but from royalties they earn on the exports of the other countries since most of the weapons and weapons components these smaller countries manufacture are *under license from the United States and Russia.*[32] Until 1991, Iraq

---

[30]The 1974 Trade Act provides that nonmarket—namely, Communist—countries will not receive the trade concessions enjoyed by our best customers unless the president waives the restriction.

[31]See U.S. Congress, Office of Technology Assessment, *Global Arms Trade* (Washington, DC: Government Printing Office, June 1991).

[32]The license is a sale to a foreign company by, for example, a U.S. company, of the right to manufacture one of its products. This is subject to approval by the Departments of Defense and State.

was the biggest importer of military goods. Between 1983 and 1988, the U.S. Arms Control and Disarmament Agency could identify $40 billion worth of arms bought by Iraq on the international market. And Iraq will almost certainly return in the near future to major status as a purchaser. Meanwhile, the largest importers are Saudi Arabia ($26 billion imported during the same five years), India ($15 billion during same period), Syria ($13 billion), and Iran ($12 billion). There were many other big-ticket importers.[33]

Why are these countries buying so much advanced military material? In some instances there are actual arms races. Just as the United States and the Soviet Union used weaponry as a deterrent against each other, so smaller but neighboring countries use their weaponry as a deterrent against one another. The value of weapons importation for these countries can be seen in the regular use the United States and the United Nations make of restrictions and embargoes on weapons as sanctions against misbehaving countries.

Another reason is that many of the most despotic regimes view a big military presence as an essential means of maintaining control of their own population. And all too often, the United States has cooperated in this aspect of the arms trade, even encouraging it, as part of our worldwide Holy Alliance role. Supporting existing regimes was a key aspect of the original Holy Alliance of the nineteenth century and remains a key aspect of it in the post–Cold War world today. The United States will never wholly approve of despotic regimes and is rarely even comfortable with benevolent but undemocratic ones. But we find ourselves supporting distasteful regimes be-cause we like world stability more than we dislike undemocratic regimes. And this attitude makes the Holy Alliance role a lot easier to play, because it is an attitude with which our European allies are historically comfortable.

A Holy Alliance role, however, will never relieve the United States of the need for diplomacy. In fact, diplomacy becomes all the more important because despotic regimes eventually fail and in the process attempt to thrust their problems on their neighbors. The dissolution of Yugoslavia and the inability of a concert of nations to stop the genocidal ethnic struggle there testify to the limits of the Holy Alliance role. This is not to argue that war is never justifiable or that peace can always be achieved by talk among professional diplomats or purchased by compromise or appeasement. It is only to argue that there are severe limits on how often a country like the United States can engage in Holy Alliances. When leaders in a democracy like ours engage in unilateral or multilateral direct action, with or without military force, they must have overwhelming justification. In all instances, the political should dominate the military. That is what diplomacy is all about. In 1952, the distinguished military career of General Douglas MacArthur was abruptly terminated when President Truman dismissed him for insubordination. At issue was MacArthur's unwillingness to allow the military in Korea to be subordinated to the politicians and the diplomats. His argument was "In war, there is no substitute for victory."[34] But he was overlooking the prior question and therefore missed the very point that should guide any foreign policy: Is there a substitute for war?

[33]See U.S. Congress, Office of Technology Assessment, *Global Arms Trade*, pp. 4-7.

[34]Address to a joint session of Congress, 9 April, 1951.

Time Line on Foreign Policy

EVENTS		INSTITUTIONAL DEVELOPMENTS
Treaties with Britain and Spain establish recognition of U.S. sovereignty (1795)		U.S. attempts to steer clear of foreign alliances; pursues neutrality policy (1790s)
Louisiana Purchase from France (1803)	**1800**	
War of 1812, despite American attempts to maintain neutrality (1812)		Monroe Doctrine to prevent further European colonization in Western Hemisphere (1823)
War with Mexico, ending in Mexico's giving up claim to Texas and ceding California and New Mexico to U.S. (1846–1848)		Manifest Destiny doctrine leads to war with Mexico (1840s); Mexican War first successful defensive war (1846–1848)
Civil War (1861–1865)	**1860**	
U.S. purchases Alaska from Russia; Midway Islands annexed (1867)		Unilateralism prevails (1870s–1890s)
First Inter-American Conference between U.S. and Latin American nations (1889–1890)		Reciprocal agreements between U.S. and Latin American nations (1890)
Spanish-American War; treaty leads to U.S. annexation of Puerto Rico, Guam, Philippines; Hawaii annexed (1898)		U.S. concern with world markets after closing of American frontier (1890s)
World War I (1914–1919)	**1900**	U.S. does not join the League of Nations (1919)
Unprecedented inflation and political instability in Germany (1920s)		Rogers Act recognizes foreign service officers as part of government career system (1924)
U.S. enters World War II (1941–1945)		U.N. established (1945)
Bretton Woods Conference (1944)		Foreign Service Act creates a professional diplomatic corps (1946)

EVENTS		INSTITUTIONAL DEVELOPMENTS
Soviets have A-bomb (1949)		Cold War and containment—Truman Doctrine (1947); Marshall Plan (1947); Rio Treaty creating OAS (1947); NATO (1949); Mutual Security (1951); SEATO (1954)
Korean War (1950–1953)	**1950**	
U.S. intervenes in Iran (1953); in Guatemala (1954)		
Soviets launch Sputnik (1957); First U.S. satellite (1958)		U.S. and Soviets race to the moon (1957–1969)
Bay of Pigs Invasion (1961); Cuban Missile Crisis (1962)	**1960**	U.S. and Soviets face off in Cuba (1962)
		Nuclear Test-Ban Treaty (1963)
U.S. builds up troops in Vietnam (1965–1973)		Détente between U.S. and Soviet Union (1970s)
Nixon visits China (1972)		U.S.-Soviet Trade Agreement (1972)
Arab Oil Embargo (1973–1974)		End of U.S. military draft (1973)
		Termination of Bretton Woods System (1973)
U.S. intervenes in Chile (1974)		
Camp David Summit (1978)		Panama Canal Treaty (1978)
U.S. formally recognizes China (1979)		
Iranian hostage crisis (1979–1981)	**1980**	SALT II Agreement (1979–1981)
		SALT II repudiated (1981)
		SDI ("Star Wars") commitment (1980s)
Grenada invasion (1983)		Policy of covert action in Latin America (1980s)
First Reagan–Gorbachev Summit (1985)		
Iran–Contra affair (1986–1987)		INF Treaty (1988)
Panama invaded (1989)		
Collapse of Soviet system; Berlin Wall comes down (1989)		NATO/Warsaw Pact withdrawal begins (1989)

EVENTS		INSTITUTIONAL DEVELOPMENTS
Germany reunified; *perestroika* in trouble (1990)	**1990**	Eastern Europe tries capitalism (1990)
War in Persian Gulf (1991)		Efforts to cut defense spending; formation of 29-nation coalition under U.N. auspices to conduct blockade and invasion of Iraq (1990–1991)
Communist rule in U.S.S.R. and Yugoslavia ends (1991)		
UN-sponsored humanitarian intervention in Somalia (1992)		Clinton-Yeltsin summit cements U.S.-Russian ties (1993)
Crisis in Bosnia (1993)		Clinton favors collective approach rather than leadership role in Bosnia, but acts unilaterally against Iraq and takes lead in G7 talks (1993)

Chapter Review

This chapter began with a definition of the United States as a nation-state in a world of nation-states, whose ignorance of each other breeds distrust and hostility. The purpose of foreign policy is to defend national sovereignty against other nation-states that are conducting their foreign policy for the same purpose. The chapter was then divided into three sections, each devoted to one of the fundamental dimensions of foreign policy: values, instruments, and roles.

The first section, on values, traced out the history of American values that had a particular relevance to American perspectives on the outside world. We found that the American fear of a big national state applied to foreign as well as domestic governmental powers. The founders and the active public of the founding period all recognized that foreign policy was special, that the national government had special powers in its dealings with foreigners, and that presidential supremacy was justified in the conduct of foreign affairs. The only way to avoid the big national government and presidential supremacy was to avoid the foreign entanglements that made foreign policy, diplomacy, secrecy, and presidential discretion necessary. Americans held on to their "antistatist" tradition until World War II, long after world conditions cried out for American involvement. And even as we became involved in world affairs, we held on tightly to the legacies of 150 years of tradition: the *intermingling* of domestic and foreign policy institutions, and *unilateralism*, the tendency to "go it alone" when confronted with foreign conflicts.

The second section looked at the instruments—that is, the tools—of American foreign policy. These are the basic statutes and the institutions by which foreign policy has been conducted since World War II thrust us into international engagements. Each of these instruments was presented: diplomacy, the United Nations, the international monetary structure, economic aid, collective security, and military deterrence. Although Republicans and Democrats look at the world somewhat differently, and although each president has tried to impose a distinctive flavor of his own on foreign policy, they have all made use of these basic instruments, and that has given foreign policies a certain continuity. When Congress created these instruments after World War II, the old tradition was still so strong that it moved Congress to try its best to create instruments that would do their international work with a minimum of diplomacy—a minimum of the human element. This is what we called power without diplomacy.

The third section concentrated on the role or roles the president and Congress have sought to play in the world. To help simplify the tremendous variety of tactics and strategies that foreign policy leaders can select, we narrowed the field down to four categories of roles nations play, suggesting that there is a certain amount of consistency and stability in the conduct of a nation-state in its dealings with other nation-states. These were labeled according to actual roles that diplomatic historians have identified in the history of major Western nation-states: the Napoleonic, Holy Alliance, balance-of-power, and economic expansionist roles.

The final section attempted to identify and assess the role of the United States in the post–Cold War era, essentially the Holy Alliance role. But whatever its advantages may be, the Holy Alliance approach will never allow the United States to conduct foreign policy without diplomacy. We are tied inextricably to the perils and ambiguities of international relationships, and diplomacy is still the monarch of all available instruments of foreign policy.

For Further Reading

Bundy, McGeorge. *Danger and Survival: Choices about the Bomb in the First Fifty Years.* New York: Random House, 1989.

Feldman, Lily Gardner. *The Special Relationship between West Germany and Israel.* Boston and London: George Allen & Unwin, 1984.

Ferrell, Robert H. *American Diplomacy: The 20th Century.* New York: W. W. Norton, 1988.

Fukuyama, Francis. "The End of History?" *The National Interest,* Summer 1988.

Gilpin, Robert. *The Political Economy of International Relations.* Princeton: Princeton University Press, 1987.

Graubard, Stephen R., ed., "The Exit from Communism." *Daedalus,* Spring 1992.

Hilsman, Roger. *The Politics of Policymaking in Defense and Foreign Affairs.* Englewood Cliffs, NJ: Prentice-Hall, 1987.

Kennan, George F. *Around the Cragged Hill—A Personal and Political Philosophy.* New York: W. W. Norton, 1993.

Kennedy, Paul. *The Rise and Fall of the Great Powers: Economic Change and Military Conflict from 1500 to 2000.* New York: Random House, 1987.

LeFeber, Walter. *The American Age: United States Foreign Policy at Home and Abroad since 1750.* New York: W. W. Norton, 1989.

Macchiarola, Frank J., and Robert B. Oxnam, eds. *The China Challenge: American Policies in East Asia.* New York: Academy of Political Science, 1991.

Nau, Henry. *The Myth of America's Decline:*

Leading the World Economy into the 1990s. New York: Oxford University Press, 1990.

Shazan, Naomi. *Negotiating the Non-Negotiable: Jerusalem in the Framework of an Israeli-Palastinian Settlement.* Cambridge: American Academy of Arts and Sciences, March 1991.

Stein, Arthur. *Why Nations Cooperate: Circumstance and Choice in International Relations.* Ithaca: Cornell University Press, 1990.

U.S. Congress. *Report of the Congressional Committees Investigating the Iran-Contra Affair.* New York: Random House, 1988.

Wallace, William. *The Transformation of Western Europe.* London: Royal Institute of International Affairs, 1990.

Wessell, Nils H., ed. *The New Europe: Revolution in East-West Relations.* New York: Academy of Political Science, 1991.

15

THE STATE OF THE UNION

*I*n the autumn of 1989, the world began to change dramatically. Today we hear talk of a new world order, but in late 1989 we could see nothing but world disorder—a disorder both threatening and hopeful. Was the world, as well as America, in decline, or was America, as well as the world, a phoenix rising from the ashes?

An important and hopeful element of the new world disorder was the collapse of the Soviet empire. As the Berlin Wall tumbled down, the Iron Curtain was raised, revealing the Soviet military in retreat and the Soviet Union's East European satellites drifting out of orbit. Then, in 1991, the failed coup against Gorbachev weakened what was left of the central government and gave the Baltic states, as well as several other republics, a chance to achieve their independence. The people of all these newly independent countries were expressing the hopes and desires that define for Americans "the pursuit of happiness." New constitutions were written, new governments were formed, and everywhere dramatic signs of economic freedom emerged. These new states looked to the West for their political and economic models.

America the Beacon

In the late 1980s, a book entitled *The Rise and Fall of the Great Powers* explained why a decline of American influence in the world was all but inevitable. Within five years, however, not only had America reemerged as the world's preeminent military power but, perhaps more than ever, American democracy had become an example—a beacon—to the new nations of the world.

Despite America's many problems, there is much about the American democratic system that *is* worthy of emulation. Americans have not always been outstanding theorists of democracy, but, for 200 years, they have been among its foremost practitioners and have developed noteworthy ideas, institutions, and practices.

Foremost among these is the idea of constitutionalism. There are many good constitutions but only one principle of constitutionalism: to choose among instruments of government and then to set those choices slightly above majority rule and outside the immediate control of the people who are in power at a given moment in time. By this means, a people can set limits on the power of government and at the same time set limits on themselves.

Another American governmental institution worthy of emulation is our system of competing political parties. This is absolutely necessary for the American political system and for every system that wishes to maintain democracy. A *two*-party system is not sacred. What is necessary is some kind of competitive party system, one in which the parties enjoy control over the nomination and election process, and one in which the parties have the resources to mobilize voters without (and despite) government sponsorship. This is the best way to ensure democratic accountability and popular participation.

The part of the American model most eligible for literal imitation is our provision in the Constitution for civil liberties and civil rights. But this must be properly understood. A mere listing of liberties and rights—"parchment guarantees"—is not enough. As we stressed so often in the text, the sphere of civil liberties and civil rights grows out of provisions and traditions that give individual citizens a specific cause of action if they feel their rights have been denied, and courts and other institutions that provide access to government for individual citizens and possess the power to act, utilizing a known set of enforceable remedies.

Freedom and Power

While the world is watching us, we must never cease watching ourselves—to make certain that America's democratic system continues to be worthy of emulation. In particular, we must make certain that, as a nation, we never forget that the chief problem or contradiction upon which our government is built is the problem of political freedom and governmental power. At what point does the power that we grant the government begin to pose a threat to our freedom and well-being? Can we indefinitely use government to improve our lot or does the government's power become more dangerous the more it grows?

During the first century of our own nation's history, Americans were profoundly distrustful of government. Our forebears were convinced that governmental power always posed a threat to their liberties. Given a choice, nineteenth-century Americans preferred freedom to government, and they were willing to forgo some of the benefits of government to ensure the preservation of liberty. In this spirit, they constructed and maintained a system of government whose powers were severely circumscribed. Federalism divided power between the state and the national governments and limited the scope of the national government's activities. Within the national structure, the principle of separation of powers dispersed authority among the three branches of government and between the two houses of Congress, thus using each institution to check and limit the powers of the others. The Constitution and the Bill of Rights placed restrictions on the range of governmental activity, prohibiting actions deemed to violate the fundamental liberties of the people. These limits and restraints meant that the national government was not as useful a servant as it might have been. For example, its capacity to promote the development of the economy was limited. It had little ability to provide assistance to the poor and needy. Even its capacity to provide for the common defense was limited.

During the course of the twentieth century, however, Americans constructed a larger and more powerful governmental apparatus—one capable of providing far more in the way of services and benefits than the institution they had inherited. By the close of the twentieth century, as we have seen, our national government has come to provide a vast array of services to Americans from every walk of life. The brief list of beneficiaries of federal programs given in Chapter 1 could be expanded for hundreds of pages.

It is difficult to deny that through these programs, and many others, Americans benefit from the activities and services of "big government." Opinion polls suggest that, despite some hostility to taxes, most Americans continue to support an extensive role for the national government. In fact, most would like government to do more rather than less in a variety of areas.

Of course, to make it possible for our

government to provide the services we want, we have been forced to relax some of the constraints that bound and limited governmental actions. As we saw earlier, in order to give the national government more power to act, the restraints of federalism were weakened and the national government was allowed to exercise economic and police powers previously reserved to the states. To make the national government capable of more vigorous and decisive action both at home and abroad, a more powerful presidency and an enormous administrative bureaucracy were created and the separation of powers was weakened. To make it possible for the national government to provide the economic and social programs we desire, we have eagerly sought to justify governmental intervention in every area of our economy and society. Indeed , to face the challenges of the modern era, we may have no choice but to increase the strength and efficiency of our government and, so, provide it with an even greater capacity to intervene in our lives.

But despite the erosion of the restraints on governmental power, few Americans have perceived the growth of government over the past half century as posing a sustained threat to their liberties. As we saw in Chapter 1, the once-liberal theory that led Americans to agree with Jefferson that the best government was the one that governed least came to be supplanted by a democratic theory of state power. This democratic theory held that the contradiction between freedom and government could be resolved by strengthening democratic controls on government, and as long as the people controlled the government, what did it matter if government became more powerful? After all, if the government was simply the servant of the people, then its power was nothing more than its ability to serve them, and limits on its power were, in effect, limits on the citizens themselves.

Thus far, we *have* managed to have both a more powerful government and considerable freedom. Indeed, in many ways, Americans enjoy greater freedom now than ever before. Recall that judicial interpretations in recent years have expanded the scope of free speech, strengthened freedom of assembly, introduced a right to privacy, and limited the power of the police and prosecutors in dealing with criminal defendants. At the same time, the courts and Congress have strengthened the civil rights not only of African Americans but of *all* Americans. We are undeniably enjoying both the blessings of freedom and the benefits of government. But the success we have achieved should not lead us to believe that there is no problem at all. There *is* a contradiction between freedom and governmental power, and this contradiction is not eliminated by democratic control of government.

The Conditions for Democracy

Virtually everywhere in the world democratic controls seem to be associated with political liberty. Generally speaking, the same nations that possess democratic political institutions are also the most likely to respect basic civil liberties. For example, in one recent survey that sought to rank all nominally independent nations on a 1 (most free) to 7 (least free) scale on the basis of citizens' civil rights and liberties, all eighteen nations in the "most free" group were democracies. No nation that had a competitive electoral process ranked below the sec-

ond scale position on civil liberties.[1] In another study, freedom of the press was found to be "complete" in thirty-three of forty nations with competitive electoral systems, while only six of thirty-six electorally uncompetitive nations could boast a completely free press.[2]

Such associations, however, do not tell the whole story. The history of the relationship between liberty and democratic practices suggests that democratic institutions are usually the result of rather than the cause of freedom. The citizens of the democracies are not free because they possess democratic controls; rather, they exercise democratic controls because they are free. A measure of liberty is a necessary precondition for the functioning of democratic processes. Governmental interference with speech, assembly, association, and the press precludes open and competitive politics.[3]

More fundamentally, democratic institutions are most likely to emerge and flourish where the public already possesses some freedom from governmental control. As we saw in Chapters 1 and 9, democratic elections are often introduced when governments are unable to compel the people's acquiescence. In a sense, elections are inaugurated in order to persuade a reluctant populace to surrender at least some of its freedom and allow itself to be governed. Thus, in the United States, the introduction of democratic institutions, as well as the adoption of formal constitutional guaran-

[1] Raymond O. Gastil et al., *Freedom in the World: Political Rights and Civil Liberties* (New York: Freedom House, 1979).

[2] Arthur S. Banks and Robert B. Textor, *A Cross-Polity Survey* (Cambridge: MIT Press, 1963).

[3] See Madison's discussion in *The Federalist Papers*, No. 10, ed. Clinton Rossiter (New York: New American Library, 1937). See also Carl Cohen, *Democracy* (Athens: University of Georgia Press, 1971), Chapter 10.

tees of civil liberties, was in part prompted by the fact that the citizenry was free—born free, as Alexis de Tocqueville observed—and had the desire to remain so. Even several of the framers of the Constitution who were hostile to the principle of democracy nevertheless urged the adoption of democratic governmental forms on the grounds that the populace would otherwise refuse to accept the new government. John Dickinson, a prominent and well-to-do delegate from Delaware, asserted that limited monarchy was superior to any republican form of government. Unfortunately, however, limited monarchy was out of the question because of the "spirit of the times."[4] Similarly, senior Virginia delegate George Mason concluded that "notwithstanding the oppression and injustice experienced among us from democracy, the genius of the people is in favor of it, and the genius of the people must be consulted."[5] Subsequently, as we saw, the Constitution's proponents agreed to add the formal guarantees of civil liberties embodied in the Bill of Rights only when it appeared that the Constitution might otherwise not be ratified.[6] In effect, the public had to be persuaded to permit itself to be governed because it was, in fact, free to choose otherwise. Given the absence of a national military force and the virtually universal distribution of firearms and training in their use, the populace could not easily have been compelled to accept a government it did not desire.

In general, democratic political practices are most likely to emerge and prosper in "free societies"—societies in which politically relevant resources are distributed outside the control of the central government. The importance of the distribution of military force is clear. When at some critical historical juncture rulers lacked the necessary force to govern, they tended to become much more concerned with citizens' rights.

Other resources are probably of even greater importance to the maintenance of freedom. An active private press coupled with a literate population, as in America, can, with information about government activities, stimulate resistance to those in power.[7] Broadly distributed reservoirs of private financial resources often help the formation of opposition. We are fortunate in the United States to possess a democratic form of government, but it is not a substitute for—and could not exist for long without—a significant measure of popular freedom.

One of the great problems facing the people in the new nations today is the development of personal freedom and independent resources on a scale sufficient to defend them from governmental power and to keep that power respectful of individuals. During forty-five years of Communist rule in Eastern Europe and the Soviet Union, governments did not redistribute wealth from the rich to the poor but actually redistributed resources from all the people to the government itself. This means that, for the near future, property, education, skill, and all the other resources that make for personal autonomy are too narrowly distributed to provide fertile ground for democratic processes. In other words, as a

[4]Max Farrand, ed., *The Records of the Federal Convention of 1787* (New Haven: Yale University Press, 1966), vol. 1, p. 86.

[5]Ibid., p. 101.

[6]Forrest McDonald, *The Formation of the American Republic* (Baltimore, MD: Penguin, 1965), Chapter 8.

[7]See Richard Hofstadter, *The Idea of a Party System* (Berkeley: University of California Press, 1969), Chapter 3.

prerequisite to freedom, these governments must cooperate in the distribution and redistribution of resources to the people so that they have a stake in the new order and the ability to sustain some control over their governments. Will the new governments of Eastern Europe, and the former territories of the Soviet Union, be willing to do this?

Freedom or Power?

In the United States, constitutionally mandated controls on government offer some measure of protection for civil liberties and civil rights. The availability of governmental controls, however, if based on democratic processes, tends eventually to persuade citizens that they may enjoy the benefits of the state's power without risk to their freedom. Why, after all, should it be necessary to limit a servant's capacity to serve?

Unfortunately, despite democratic processes controlling government, individual freedom and governmental power inevitably conflict. This conflict does not necessarily mean deliberate and overt governmental efforts to abridge liberties. Typically, the erosion of citizens' liberties in the democracies is a more subtle, insidious, and often unforeseen result of routine administrative processes. As we saw earlier, federal agencies such as the Interstate Commerce Commission, the Civil Aeronautics Board, and the Federal Trade Commission have considerable control over who may enter the occupations and businesses that they regulate. The Food and Drug Administration has a good deal to say about what we may eat. The Federal Communications Commission has a measure of influence over what Americans see and hear over the airwaves. The Internal Revenue Service, in the mundane course of collecting taxes, makes decisions about what is and is not a religion, what is or is not political activity, whether given forms of education are or are not socially desirable, what types of philanthropy serve the public interest, and what sorts of information it should acquire about every citizen. The administration of tax policy is among the most intrusive activities of the federal government. Thus, congressional tax legislation and IRS regulations can have a critical effect upon every individual's business decisions, marital plans, childbirth and child-rearing decisions, vacation plans, and medical care. And housing policies, educational policies, and welfare programs, which are often directed by agencies given broad, discretionary mandates by Congress, affect the most minute details of citizens' lives.

Despite the availability of democratic institutions, Americans cannot expect to use the government's power without surrendering at least some of their freedom. This is the dark side of government. A government capable of solving our problems and maintaining America's place in the world is also a government capable of threatening our cherished liberties.

More than 150 years ago, Alexis de Tocqueville prophesied that Americans would someday become so convinced that they controlled the government that they would be willing to surrender their liberty to it. This would leave them, he warned, holding the ends of their own chains. For now, we possess both the blessing of freedom and the service of government. Let us hope we can keep them.

For Further Reading

Arendt, Hannah. *The Human Condition.* Chicago: University of Chicago Press, 1958.

Cnudde, Charles F., and Deane E. Neubauer. *Empirical Democratic Theory.* Chicago: Markham, 1969.

Laski, Harold. *Liberty in the Modern State.* London: Faber and Faber, 1930.

Locke, John. *The Second Treatise of Government.* Indianapolis: Bobbs-Merrill, 1972.

Love, Nancy S., ed. *Dogmas and Dreams: Political Ideologies in the Modern World.* Chatham, NJ: Chatham House, 1991.

McIlwain, Charles H. *Constitutionalism, Ancient and Modern.* Ithaca: Cornell University Press, 1947.

Mannheim, Karl. *Man and Society in an Age of Reconstruction.* London: Kegan Paul, Trench, Trubner and Co., 1940.

Mathiopoulos, Marjarita. *History and Progress: In Search of the European and American Mind.* New York: Praeger, 1989.

Mill, James. *An Essay on Government.* Cambridge, England: Cambridge University Press, 1937.

Mill, John Stewart. *On Liberty.* New York: W. W. Norton, 1975.

Schumpeter, Joseph A. *Capitalism, Socialism and Democracy.* New York: Harper & Row, 1950.

Shklar, Judith N. *American Citizenship—The Quest for Inclusion.* Cambridge: Harvard University Press, 1990.

Thompson, Dennis P. *The Democratic Citizen.* Cambridge, England: Cambridge University Press, 1970.

APPENDIX

THE DECLARATION OF INDEPENDENCE

In Congress, July 4, 1776

When in the course of human events, it becomes necessary for one people to dissolve the political bands which have connected them with another, and to assume the Powers of the earth, the separate and equal station to which the Laws of Nature and of Nature's God entitle them, a decent respect to the opinions of mankind requires that they should declare the causes which impel them to the separation.

We hold these truths to be self-evident, that all men are created equal, that they are endowed by their Creator with certain unalienable rights, that among these are Life, Liberty, and the pursuit of Happiness. That to secure these rights, Governments are instituted among Men, deriving their just powers from the consent of the governed. That whenever any Form of Government becomes destructive of these ends, it is the Right of the People to alter or to abolish it, and to institute new Government, laying its foundation on such principles and organizing its powers in such form, as to them shall seem most likely to effect their Safety and Happiness. Prudence, indeed, will dictate that Governments long established should not be changed for light and transient causes; and accordingly all experience hath shown, that mankind are more disposed to suffer, while evils are sufferable, than to right themselves by abolishing the forms to which they are accustomed. But when a long train of abuses and usurpations, pursuing invariably the same Object evinces a design to reduce them under absolute Despotism, it is their right, it is their duty, to throw off such Government, and to provide new Guards for their future security.— Such has been the patient sufferance of these Colonies; and such is now the necessity which constrains them to alter their former Systems of Government. The history of the present King of Great Britain is a history of repeated injuries and usurpations, all having in direct object the establishment of an absolute Tyranny over these States. To prove this, let Facts be submitted to a candid world.

He has refused his Assent to Laws, the most wholesome and necessary for the public good.

He has forbidden his Governors to pass Laws of immediate and pressing importance, unless suspended in their operation till his Assent should be obtained; and when so suspended, he has utterly neglected to attend to them.

He has refused to pass other Laws for the accommodation of large districts of people, unless those people would relinquish the right of Representation in the Legislature, a right inestimable to them and formidable to tyrants only.

He has called together legislative bodies at places unusual, uncomfortable, and distant from the depository of their public Records, for the sole purpose of fatiguing them into compliance with his measures.

He has dissolved Representative Houses repeatedly, for opposing with manly firmness his invasions on the rights of the people.

He has refused for a long time, after such dissolutions, to cause others to be elected; whereby the Legislative powers, incapable of Annihilation, have returned to the People at large for their exercise; the State remaining in the mean time exposed to all dangers of invasion from without, and convulsions within.

He has endeavored to prevent the population of these States; for that purpose obstructing the Laws of Naturalization of Foreigners; refusing to pass others to encourage their migrations hither, and raising the conditions of new Appropriations of Lands.

He has obstructed the Administration of Justice, by refusing his Assent to Laws for establishing Judiciary powers.

He has made Judges dependent on his Will alone, for the tenure of their offices, and the amount and payment of their salaries.

He has erected a multitude of New Offices, and sent hither swarms of Officers to harass our People, and eat out their substance.

He has kept among us, in times of peace, Standing Armies without the Consent of our legislature.

He has affected to render the Military independent of and superior to the Civil Power.

He has combined with others to subject us to a jurisdiction foreign to our constitution, and unacknowledged by our laws; giving his Assent to their Acts of pretended Legislation:

For quartering large bodies of armed troops among us:

For protecting them, by a mock Trial, from Punishment for any Murders which they should commit on the Inhabitants of these States:

For cutting off our Trade with all parts of the world:

For imposing taxes on us without our Consent:

For depriving us of many cases, of the benefits of Trial by jury:

For transporting us beyond Seas to be tried for pretended offences:

For abolishing the free System of English Laws in a neighboring Province, establishing therein an Arbitrary government, and enlarging its Boundaries so as to render it at once an example and fit instrument for introducing the same absolute rule into these Colonies:

For taking away our Charters, abolishing our most valuable Laws, and altering fundamentally the Forms of our Governments:

For suspending our own Legislatures, and declaring themselves invested with Power to legislate for us in all cases whatsoever.

He has abdicated Government here, by declaring us out of his Protection and waging War against us.

He has plundered our seas, ravaged our Coasts, burnt our towns, and destroyed the lives of our people.

He is at this time transporting large armies of foreign mercenaries to compleat the works of death, desolation, and tyranny, already begun with circumstances of Cruelty & perfidy scarcely paralleled in the most barbarous ages, and totally unworthy the Head of a civilized nation.

He has constrained our fellow Citizens taken Captive on the high Seas to bear Arms against their Country, to become the executioners of their friends and Brethren, or to fall themselves by their Hands.

He has excited domestic insurrections amongst us, and has endeavored to bring on the inhabitants of our frontiers, the merciless Indian Savages, whose known rule of warfare, is an undistinguished destruction of all ages, sexes, and conditions.

In every stage of these Oppressions We have Petitioned for Redress in the most humble terms: Our repeated Petitions have been answered only by repeated injury. A Prince, whose character is thus marked by every act which may define a Tyrant, is unfit to be the ruler of a free people.

Nor have We been wanting in attention to our British brethren. We have warned them from time to time of attempts by their legislature to extend an unwarrantable jurisdiction over us. We have reminded them of the circumstances of our emigration and settlement here. We have appealed to their native justice and magnanimity, and we have conjured them by the ties of our common kindred to disavow these usurpations, which, would inevitably interrupt our connections and correspondence. They too must have been deaf to the voice of justice and of consanguinity. We must, therefore, acquiesce in the necessity, which denounces our Separation, and hold them, as we hold the rest of mankind, Enemies in War, in Peace Friends.

WE, THEREFORE, the Representatives of the UNITED STATES OF AMERICA, in General Congress, Assembled, appealing to the Supreme Judge of the world for the rectitude of our intentions, do, in the Name, and by Authority of the good People of these Colonies, solemnly publish and declare, That these United Colonies are, and of Right ought to be FREE AND INDEPENDENT STATES; that they are Absolved from all Allegiance to the British Crown, and that all political connection between them and the State of Great Britain, is and ought to be totally dissolved; and that as Free and Independent States, they have full Power to levy War, conclude Peace, contract Alliances, establish Commerce, and to do all other Acts and Things which Independent States may of right do. And for the support of this Declaration, with a firm reliance on the Protection of Divine Providence, we mutually pledge to each other our Lives, our Fortunes, and our sacred Honor.

The foregoing Declaration was, by order of Congress, engrossed, and signed by the following members:

John Hancock
NEW HAMPSHIRE
Josiah Bartlett
William Whipple
Matthew Thornton

MASSACHUSETTS BAY
Samuel Adams
John Adams
Robert Treat Paine
Elbridge Gerry

RHODE ISLAND
Stephen Hopkins
William Ellery

CONNECTICUT
Roger Sherman
Samuel Huntington
William Williams
Oliver Wolcott

NEW YORK
William Floyd
Philip Livingston
Francis Lewis
Lewis Morris

NEW JERSEY
Richard Stockton
John Witherspoon
Francis Hopkinson
John Hart
Abraham Clark

PENNSYLVANIA
Robert Morris
Benjamin Rush
Benjamin Franklin
John Morton
George Clymer
James Smith
George Taylor
James Wilson
George Ross

DELAWARE
Caesar Rodney
George Read
Thomas M'Kean

MARYLAND
Samuel Chase
William Paca
Thomas Stone
Charles Carroll,
of Carrollton

VIRGINIA
George Wythe
Richard Henry Lee
Thomas Jefferson
Benjamin Harrison
Thomas Nelson, Jr.
Francis Lightfoot Lee
Carter Braxton

NORTH CAROLINA
William Hooper
Joseph Hewes
John Penn

SOUTH CAROLINA
Edward Rutledge
Thomas Heyward, Jr.
Thomas Lynch, Jr.
Arthur Middleton

GEORGIA
Button Gwinnett
Lyman Hall
George Walton

Resolved, That copies of the Declaration be sent to the several assemblies, conventions, and committees, or councils of safety, and to the several commanding officers of the continental troops; that it be proclaimed in each of the United States, at the head of the army.

THE CONSTITUTION OF THE UNITED STATES OF AMERICA

Annotated with references to the Federalist Papers

Federalist Paper Number and Author

[PREAMBLE]

We the People of the United States, in Order to form a more perfect Union, establish Justice, insure domestic Tranquility, provide for the common defence, promote the general Welfare, and secure the Blessings of Liberty to ourselves and our Posterity, do ordain and establish this Constitution for the United States of America.

84 (Hamilton)

Article I

Section 1

[LEGISLATIVE POWERS]

10, 45 (Madison)

All legislative Powers herein granted shall be vested in a Congress of the United States, which shall consist of a Senate and House of Representatives.

Section 2

[HOUSE OF REPRESENTATIVES, HOW CONSTITUTED, POWER OF IMPEACHMENT]

39 (Madison)
45 (Madison)
52–53, 57 (Madison)

The House of Representatives shall be composed of Members chosen every second Year by the People of the several States, and the Electors in each State

52 (Madison), 60 (Hamilton)

shall have the Qualifications requisite for Electors of the most numerous Branch of the State Legislature.

No Person shall be a Representative who shall not have attained to the Age of twenty-five Years, and been seven Years a Citizen of the United States, and who shall not, when elected, be an inhabitant of that State in which he shall be chosen.

54 (Madison)

Representatives and *direct Taxes*[1] shall be apportioned among the several States which may be included within this Union, according to their respective Numbers, *which shall be determined by adding to the whole Number of free Persons, including those bound to Service for a Term of Years, and excluding Indi-*

54 (Madison)

ans not taxed, three-fifths of all other Persons.[2] The actual Enumeration shall be

58 (Madison)

made within three Years after the first Meeting of the Congress of the United States, and within every subsequent

---

[1] Modified by Sixteenth Amendment.

[2] Modified by Fourteenth Amendment.

Term of ten Years, in such Manner as they shall by Law direct. The Number of Representatives shall not exceed one for every thirty Thousand, but each State shall have at Least one Representative; *and until such enumeration shall be made, the State of New Hampshire shall be entitled to chuse three, Massachusetts eight, Rhode-Island and Providence Plantations one, Connecticut five, New-York six, New Jersey four, Pennsylvania eight, Delaware one, Maryland six. Virginia ten, North Carolina five, South Carolina five, and Georgia three.*[3]

55–56
(Madison)

When vacancies happen in the Representation from any State, the Executive Authority thereof shall issue Writs of Election to fill such Vacancies.

79
(Hamilton)

The House of Representatives shall chuse their Speaker and other Officers; and shall have the sole Power of Impeachment.

Section 3
[THE SENATE, HOW CONSTITUTED, IMPEACHMENT TRIALS]

39, 45
(Madison),
60
(Hamilton),

The Senate of the United States shall be composed of two Senators from each State, *chosen by the Legislature thereof,*[4] for six Years; and each Senator shall have one Vote.

62–63
(Madison)
59
(Hamilton)

Immediately after they shall be assembled in Consequence of the first Election, they shall be divided as equally as may be into three Classes. The Seats of the Senators of the first Class shall be vacated at the Expiration of the second Year, of the second Class at the Expiration of the fourth Year, and of the third Class at the Expiration of the sixth Year, so that one third may be chosen every second Year: *and if vacancies happen by Resignation, or otherwise, during the Recess of the Legislature of any State, the Executive thereof may make tem-*

68
(Hamilton)

porary Appointments until the next Meeting of the Legislature, which shall then fill such Vacancies.[5]

62
(Hamilton),

No person shall be a Senator who shall not have attained to the Age of thirty Years, and been nine Years a Citizen of the United States, and who shall not, when elected, be an Inhabitant of that State for which he shall be chosen.

The Vice-President of the United States shall be President of the Senate, but shall have no Vote, unless they be equally divided.

The Senate shall chuse their other Officers, and also a President pro tempore, in the Absence of the Vice-President, or when he shall exercise the Office of President of the United States.

39
(Madison),
65–67, 79
(Hamilton)
65
(Hamilton)

The Senate shall have the sole Power to try all Impeachments. When sitting for that Purpose, they shall be on Oath or Affirmation. When the President of the United States is tried, the Chief Justice shall preside: And no Person shall be convicted without the Concurrence of two-thirds of the Members present.

84
(Hamilton)

Judgment in Cases of Impeachment shall not extend further than to removal from Office, and disqualification to hold and enjoy any Office of honor, Trust or Profit under the United States: but the Party convicted shall nevertheless be liable and subject to Indictment, Trial, Judgment and Punishment, according to Law.

Section 4
[ELECTION OF SENATORS AND REPRESENTATIVES]

59–61
(Hamilton)

The Times, Places and Manner of holding Elections for Senators and Representatives, shall be prescribed in each State by the Legislature thereof;

[3] Temporary provision.

[4] Modified by Seventeenth Amendment.

[5] Ibid.

but the Congress may at any time by Law make or alter such Regulations, except as to the Places of chusing Senators.

The Congress shall assemble at least once in every Year, and such Meeting shall be on the first Monday in December, unless they shall by Law appoint a different Day.[6]

Section 5

[QUORUM, JOURNALS, MEETINGS, ADJOURNMENTS]

Each House shall be the Judge of the Elections, Returns and Qualifications of its own Members, and a Majority of each shall constitute a Quorum to do Business; but a smaller Number may adjourn from day to day, and may be authorized to compel the Attendance of absent Members, in such Manner, and under the Penalties as each House may provide.

Each House may determine the Rules of its Proceedings, punish its Members for disorderly Behavior, and, with the Concurrence of two-thirds, expel a Member.

Each House shall keep a Journal of its Proceedings, and from time to time publish the same, excepting such Parts as may in their Judgment require Secrecy; and the Yeas and Nays of the Members of either House on any question shall, at the Desire of one-fifth of the present, be entered on the Journal.

Neither House, during the Session of Congress, shall, without the Consent of the other, adjourn for more than three days, nor to any other Place than that in which the two Houses shall be sitting.

Section 6

[COMPENSATION, PRIVILEGES, DISABILITIES]

The Senators and Representatives shall receive a Compensation for their

Services, to be ascertained by Law, and paid out of the Treasury of the United States. They shall in all Cases, except Treason, Felony and Breach of the Peace, be privileged from Arrest during their Attendance at the Session of their respective Houses, and in going to and returning from the same; and for any Speech or Debate in either House, they shall not be questioned in any other Place.

55 (Madison), 76 (Hamilton)

No Senator or Representative shall, during the time for which he was elected, be appointed to any civil Office under the authority of the United States, which shall have been created, or the Emoluments whereof shall have been encreased during such time; and no Person holding any Office under the United States, shall be a Member of either House during his Continuance in Office.

Section 7

[PROCEDURE IN PASSING BILLS AND RESOLUTIONS]

66 (Hamilton)

All Bills for raising Revenue shall originate in the House of Representatives; but the Senate may propose or concur with Amendments as on other Bills.

69, 73 (Hamilton)

Every Bill which shall have passed the House of Representatives and the Senate, shall, before it become a Law, be presented to the President of the United States; if he approve he shall sign it, but if not he shall return it, with his Objections to that House in which it shall have originated, who shall enter the Objections at large on their Journal, and proceed to reconsider it. If after such Reconsideration two-thirds of that House shall agree to pass the Bill, it shall be sent, together with the Objections, to the other House, by which it shall likewise be reconsidered, and if approved by two-thirds of that House it shall become a Law. But in all such Cases the Votes of both Houses shall

---

[6] Modified by Twentieth Amendment.

be determined by Yeas and Nays, and the Names of the Persons voting for and against the Bill shall be entered on the Journal of each House respectively. If any Bill shall not be returned by the President within ten Days (Sundays excepted) after it shall have been presented to him, the Same shall be a Law, in like Manner as if he had signed it, unless the Congress by their Adjournment prevent its Return, in which Case it shall not be a Law.

69, 73 (Hamilton)

Every Order, Resolution, or Vote to which the Concurrence of the Senate and House of Representatives may be necessary (except on a question of Adjournment) shall be presented to the President of the United States; and before the Same shall take Effect, shall be approved by him, or being disapproved by him, shall be repassed by two-thirds of the Senate and House of Representatives, according to the Rules and Limitations prescribed in the Case of a Bill.

Section 8
[POWERS OF CONGRESS]

The Congress shall have Power

30–36 (Hamilton),

41 (Madison)

56 (Madison)

To lay and collect Taxes, Duties, Imposts and Excises, to pay the Debts and provide for the common Defence and general Welfare of the United States; but all Duties, Imposts and excises shall be uniform throughout the United States;

42, 45, 56 (Madison)

To borrow Money on the Credit of the United States;

To regulate Commerce with foreign Nations, and among the several States, and with the Indian Tribes;

32 (Hamilton),

42 (Madison)

To establish an uniform Rule of Naturalization, and uniform Laws on the subject of Bankruptcies throughout the United States;

42 (Madison)

To coin Money, regulate the Value thereof, and of foreign Coin, and fix the Standard of Weights and Measures;

42 (Madison)

To provide for the Punishment of counterfeiting the Securities and current Coin of the United States;

42 (Madison)

To establish Post Offices and post Roads;

43 (Madison)

To promote the Progress of Science and useful Arts, by securing for limited Times to Authors and Inventors the exclusive Right to their respective Writings and Discoveries;

81 (Hamilton) 42 (Madison)

To constitute Tribunals inferior to the supreme Court;

To define and Punish Piracies and Felonies committed on the high Seas, and Offences against the Law of Nations;

41 (Madison)

To declare War, grant Letters of Marque and Reprisal, and make Rules concerning Captures on Land and Water;

23, 24, 26 (Hamilton),

To raise and support Armies, but no Appropriation of Money to that Use shall be for a longer Term than two Years;

41 (Madison)

To provide and maintain a Navy;

To make Rules for the Government and Regulation of the land and naval forces;

29 (Hamilton)

To provide for calling for the Militia to execute the Laws of the Union, suppress Insurrections and repel Invasions;

29 (Hamilton),

56 (Madison)

To provide for organizing, arming, and disciplining, the Militia, and for governing such Part of them as may be employed in the Service of the United States, reserving to the States respectively, the Appointment of the Officers, and the Authority of training the Militia according to the discipline prescribed by Congress;

32 (Hamilton),

43 (Madison) 43 (Madison)

To exercise exclusive Legislation in all Cases whatsoever, over such District (not exceeding ten Miles square) as may, by Cession of particular States, and the Acceptance of Congress, become the Seat of the Government of the United States, and to exercise like Authority over all Places purchased by the Consent of the Legislature of the State in which the Same shall be, for the Erection of Forts, Magazines, Arsenals, dock-Yards, and other needful Buildings;—And

29, 33 (Hamilton) 44 (Madison)   To make all Laws which shall be necessary and proper for carrying into Execution the foregoing Powers, and all other Powers vested by this Constitution in the Government of the United States, or in any Department or Officer thereof.

Section 9

[SOME RESTRICTIONS ON FEDERAL POWER]

42 (Madison)   *The Migration or Importation of such Persons as any of the States now existing shall think proper to admit, shall not be prohibited by the Congress prior to the Year one thousand eight hundred and eight, but a Tax or Duty may be imposed on such Importation, not exceeding ten dollars for each Person.*[7]

83, 84 (Hamilton)   The privilege of the Writ of *Habeas Corpus* shall not be suspended, unless when in Cases of Rebellion or Invasion the public Safety may require it.

84 (Hamilton)   No Bill of Attainder or ex post facto Law shall be passed.

No Capitation, or other direct, Tax shall be laid, unless in Proportion to the Census or Enumeration herein before directed to be taken.[8]

No Tax or Duty shall be laid on Articles exported from any State.

32 (Hamilton)   No Preference shall be given by any Regulation of Commerce or Revenue to the Ports of one State over those of another; nor shall vessels bound to, or from, one State, by obliged to enter, clear, or pay Duties in another.

No Money shall be drawn from the Treasury, but in Consequence of Appropriations made by Law; and a regular Statement and Account of the Receipts and Expenditures of all public Money shall be published from time to time.

39 (Madison), 84 (Hamilton)   No Title of Nobility shall be granted by the United States: And no Person holding any Office of Profit or Trust under them, shall, without the Consent of the Congress, accept of any present, Emolument, Office or Title, of any kind whatever, from any King, Prince, or foreign State.

Section 10

[RESTRICTIONS UPON POWERS OF STATES]

33 (Hamilton), 44 (Madison)   No State shall enter into any Treaty, Alliance, or Confederation; grant Letters of Marque and Reprisal; coin Money; emit Bills of Credit; make any Thing but gold and silver Coin a Tender in Payment of Debts; pass any Bill of Attainder, ex post facto Law, or Law impairing the Obligation of Contracts, or grant any Title of Nobility.

32 (Hamilton), 44 (Madison)   No State shall, without the Consent of the Congress, lay any Imposts or Duties on Imports or Exports, except what may be absolutely necessary for executing its inspection Laws: and the net Produce of all Duties and Imposts, laid by any State on Imports or Exports, shall be for the Use of the Treasury of the United States; and all such Laws shall be subject to the Revision and Control of the Congress.

No State shall, without the Consent of Congress, lay any Duty of Tonnage, keep Troops, or Ships of War in time of Peace, enter into any Agreement or Compact with another State, or with a foreign Power, or engage in War, unless actually invaded, or in such imminent Danger as will not admit of Delay.

Article II

Section 1

[EXECUTIVE POWER, ELECTION, QUALIFICATIONS OF THE PRESIDENT]

---

[7] Temporary provision.

[8] Modified by Sixteenth Amendment.

39
(Madison),
70, 71, 84
(Hamilton)
69, 71
(Hamilton)
39, 45
(Madison),
68, 77
(Hamilton)

The executive Power shall be vested in a President of the United States of America. *He shall hold his Office during the Term of four years and, together with the Vice-President, chosen for the same Term, be elected, as follows:*[9]

Each State shall appoint, in such Manner as the Legislature thereof may direct, a Number of Electors, equal to the whole Number of Senators and Representatives to which the State may be entitled in the Congress: but no Senator or Representative, or Person holding an Office of Trust or Profit under the United States, shall be appointed an Elector.

66
(Hamilton)

The electors shall meet in their respective States, and vote by ballot for two Persons, of whom one at least shall not be an Inhabitant of the same State with themselves. And they shall make a List of all the Persons voted for, and of the Number of Votes for each; which List they shall sign and certify, and transmit sealed to the Seat of the Government of the United States, directed to the President of the Senate. The President of the Senate shall, in the Presence of the Senate and House of Representatives, open all the Certificates, and the Votes shall then be counted. The Person having the greatest Number of Votes shall be the President, if such Number be a Majority of the whole Number of Electors appointed; and if there be more than one who have such Majority and have an equal Number of Votes, then the House of Representatives shall immediately chuse by Ballot one of them for President; and if no person have a Majority, then from the five highest on the List the said House shall in like manner chuse the President. But in chusing the President, the Votes shall be taken by States, the Representation from each State having one Vote; A quorom for this Purpose shall consist of a Member or Members from two-thirds of the States, and a Majority of all the

States shall be necessary to a Choice. In every Case, after the Choice of the President, the person having the greatest Number of Votes of the Electors shall be the Vice-President. But if there should remain two or more who have equal vote, the Senate shall chuse from them by Ballot the Vice-President.[10]

The Congress may determine the Time of chusing the Electors, and the Day on which they shall give their Votes; which Day shall be the same throughout the United State.

64 (Jay)

No Person except a natural born citizen, or a Citizen of the United States, at the time of the Adoption of this Constitution, shall be eligible to that Office who shall not have attained to the Age of thirty-five Years, and been fourteen Years a Resident within the United States.

In Case of the Removal of the President from Office, or his Death, Resignation, or Inability to discharge the Powers and Duties of the said Office, the same shall devolve on the Vice-President, declaring what Officer shall then act as President, and such Officer shall act accordingly, until the Disablility be removed, or a President shall be elected.

73, 79
(Hamilton)

The President shall, at stated Times, receive for his Services, a compensation, which shall neither be encreased nor diminished during the Period for which he shall have been elected, and he shall not receive within that Period any other Emolument from the United States, or any of them.

Before he enter on the Execution of his Office, he shall take the following Oath of Affirmation:—"I do solemnly swear (or affirm) that I will faithfulexecute the Office of President of the United States, and will to the best of my Ability, preserve, protect and defend the Constitution of the United States."

[9] Number of terms limited to two by Twenty-second Amendment.

[10] Modified by Twelfth and Twentieth Amendments.

Section 2

[POWERS OF THE PRESIDENT]

69, 74
(Hamilton)

74
(Hamilton)

69
(Hamilton)
74
(Hamilton)
42
(Madison),
64 *Jay),
66
(Hamilton)
42
(Madison),
66, 69,
76, 77
(Hamilton)

The President shall be Commander in Chief of the Army and Navy of the United States, and of the Militia of the several States, when called into the actual Service of the United States; he may require the Opinion, in writing, of the principal Officer in each of the executive Departments, upon any Subject relating to the Duties of their respective Offices, and he shall have Power to grant Reprieves and Pardons for Offences against the United States, except in Cases of Impeachment.

He shall have Power, by and with the Advice and Consent of the Senate, to make Treaties, provided two-thirds of the Senators present concur; and he shall nominate, and by and with the Advice and Consent of the Senate, shall appoint Ambassadors, other public Ministers and Consuls, Judges of the Supreme Court, and all other Officers of the United States, whose Appointments are not herein otherwise provided for, and which shall be established by Law: but the Congress may by Law vest the Appointment of such inferior Officers, as they think proper, in the President alone, in the Courts of Law, or in the Heads of Departments.

67, 76
(Hamilton)

The President shall have Power to fill up all Vacancies that may happen during the Recess of the Senate, by granting Commissions which shall expire at the End of their next Session.

Section 3

[POWERS AND DUTIES OF THE PRESIDENT]

77
(Hamilton)
69, 77
(Hamilton)
77
(Hamilton)
69, 77
(Hamilton)
42
(Madison),

He shall from time to time give to the Congress Information of the State of the Union, and recommend to their Consideration such Measures as he shall judge necessary and expedient; he may, on extraordinary Occasions, convene both Houses, or either of them,

69, 77
(Hamilton)
78
(Hamilton)

and in Case of Disagreement between them, with Respect to the Time of Adjournment, he may adjourn them to such Time as he shall think proper; he shall receive Ambassadors and other public Ministers; he shall take Care that the Laws be faithfully executed, and shall Commission all the Officers of the United States.

Section 4

[IMPEACHMENT]

39
(Madison),
69
(Hamilton)

The President, Vice-President and all civil Officers of the United States shall be removed from Office on Impeachment for, and Conviction of, Treason, Bribery, or other high Crimes and Misdemeanors.

Article III

Section 1

[JUDICIAL POWER, TENURE OF OFFICE]

81, 82
(Hamilton)
65
(Hamilton)
78, 79
(Hamilton)

The judicial Power of the United States, shall be vested in one supreme Court, and in such inferior Courts as the Congress may from time to time ordain and establish. The Judges, both of the supreme and inferior Courts, shall hold their Offices during good Behavior, and shall, at stated Times, receive for their Services, a Compensation, which shall not be diminished during their Continuance in Office.

Section 2

[JURISDICTION]

80
(Hamilton)

The judicial Power shall extend to all Cases, in Law and Equity, arising under this Constitution, the Laws of the United States, and Treaties made, or which shall be made, under their Authority;—to all Cases affecting Ambassadors, other public Ministers and Consuls;—to all Cases of admiralty and maritime Jurisdiction;—to Controversies to which the United States shall be a party;—to Controversies between two or more States;—*between a State and Citizens of another State;*—between Citizens of different States,—between Citizens of the same State claiming Lands under Gra between a State, or the Citizens thereof, *and foreign States, Citizens or Subjects.*[11]

81
(Hamilton)

In all Cases affecting Ambassadors, other public Ministers and Consuls, and those in which a State shall be Party, the supreme Court shall have original Jurisdiction. In all the other Cases before mentioned, the supreme Court shall have appellate Jurisdiction, both as to Law and Fact, with such Exceptions, and under such Regulations as Congress shall make.

83, 84
(Hamilton)

The Trial of all Crimes, except in Cases of Impeachment, shall be by Jury; and such Trial shall be held in the State where the said Crimes shall have been committed; but when not committed within any State, the Trial shall be at such Place or Places as the Congress may by Law have directed.

Section 3
[TREASON, PROOF, AND PUNISHMENT]

43
(Madison),
84
(Hamilton)

Treason against the United States, shall consist only in levying War against them, or in adhering to their Enemies, giving them Aid and Comfort. No Person shall be convicted of Treason unless on the Testimony of two Witnesses to the same overt Act, or on Confession in open Court.

43
(Madison),
84
(Hamilton)

The Congress shall have Power to declare the Punishment of Treason, but no Attainder of Treason shall work Corruption of Blood, or Forfeiture except during the Life of the Person attained.

Article IV

Section 1
[FAITH AND CREDIT AMONG STATES]

42
(Madison)

Full Faith and Credit shall be given in each State to the public Acts, Records, and judicial Proceedings of every other State. And the Congress may by general Laws prescribe the Manner in which such Acts, Records and Proceedings shall be proved, and the Effect thereof.

Section 2
[PRIVILEGES AND IMMUNITIES, FUGITIVES]

80
(Hamilton)

The Citizens of each State shall be entitled to all Privileges and Immunities of Citizens in the several States.

A person charged in any State with Treason, Felony or other Crime, who shall flee from Justice, and be found in another State, shall on Demand of the executive Authority of the State from which he fled, be delivered up to be removed to the State having Jurisdiction of the Crime.

No person held to Service or Labour in one State, under the Laws thereof, escaping into another, shall, in Consequence of any Law or Regulation therein, be discharged from such Service or Labour, but shall be delivered up on Claim of the Party to whom such Service or Labour may be due.[12]

Section 3
[ADMISSION OF NEW STATES]

43
(Madison)

New States may be admitted by the Congress into this Union; but no new State shall be formed or erected within the Jurisdiction of any other State; nor any State be formed by the Junction of two or more States, or Parts of States, without the Consent of the Legislatures of the States concerned as well as of the Congress.

---

[11] Modified by Eleventh Amendment.

[12] Repealed by the Thirteenth Amendment.

43
(Madison)

The Congress shall have Power to dispose of and make all needful Rules and Regulations respecting the Territory or other Property belonging to the United States; and nothing in this Constitution shall be so construed as to Prejudice any Claims of the United States, or of any particular State.

Section 4

[GUARANTEE OF REPUBLICAN GOVERNMENT]

39, 43
(Madison)

The United States shall guarantee to every State in this Union a Republican Form of Government, and shall protect each of them against Invasion; and on Application of the Legislature, or of the Executive (when the Legislature cannot be convened) against domestic Violence.

Article V

[AMENDMENT OF THE CONSTITUTION]

39, 43
(Madison)
85
(Hamilton)

The Congress, whenever two-thirds of both Houses shall deem it necessary, shall propose Amendments to this Constitution, or, on the Application of the Legislatures of two-thirds of the several States, shall call a Convention for proposing Amendments, which, in either Case, shall be valid to all Intents and Purposes, as Part of this Constitution, when ratified by the Legislatures of three-fourths of the several States, or by Conventions in three-fourths thereof, as the one or the other Mode of Ratification may be proposed by the Congress; *Provided that no Amendment which may be made prior to the Year One thousand eight hundred and eight shall in any Manner affect the first and fourth*

43
(Madison)

Clauses in the Ninth Section of the first Article;[13] and that no State, without its Consent, shall be deprived of its equal Suffrage in the Senate.

Article VI

[DEBTS, SUPREMACY, OATH]

43
(Madison)

All Debts contracted and Engagements entered into, before the Adoption of this Constitution, shall be as valid against the United States under this Constitution, as under the Confederation.

27, 33
(Hamilton),
39, 44

This Constitution, and the Laws of the United States which shall be made in Pursuance thereof; and all Treaties made, or which shall be made, under the Authority of the United States, shall be the supreme Law of the Land; and the Judges in every State shall be bound thereby, any Thing in the Constitution or Laws of any State to the Contrary notwithstanding.

27
(Hamilton),
44

The Senators and Representatives before mentioned, and the Members of the several State Legislatures, and all executive and judicial Officers, both of the United States and of the several States, shall be bound by Oath or Affirmation, to support this Constitution; but no religious Test shall be required as a Qualification to any Office or public Trust under the United States.

Article VII

[RATIFICATION AND ESTABLISHMENT]

39, 40, 43
(Madison)

The Ratification of the Conventions of nine States, shall be sufficient for the Establishment of this Constitution between the States so ratifying the Same.[14]

Done in Convention by the Unanimous Consent of the States present the Seventeenth Day of September in the Year of our Lord one thousand seven hundred and Eighty seven and of the Independence of the United States of

---

[13] Temporary provision.

[14] The Constitution was submitted on September 17, 1787, by the Constitutional Convention, was ratified by the conventions of several states at various dates up to May 29, 1790, and became effective on March 4, 1789.

America the Twelfth. *In Witness wherefore We have hereunto subscribed our Names, G:*⁰ WASHINGTON— *Presidt, and Deputy from Virginia*

New Hampshire	JOHN LANGDON
	NICHOLAS GILMAN
Massachusetts	NATHANIEL GORHAM
	RUFUS KING
Connecticut	WM SAML JOHNSON
	ROGER SHERMAN
New York	ALEXANDER HAMILTON
New Jersey	WIL: LIVINGSTON
	DAVID BREARLY
	WM PATERSON
	JONA: DAYTON
Pennsylvania	B FRANKLIN
	THOMAS MIFFLIN
	ROBT MORRIS
	GEO. CLYMER

	THOS. FITZSIMONS
	JARED INGERSOLL
	JAMES WILSON
	GOUV MORRIS
Delaware	GEO READ
	GUNNING BEDFOR JUN
	JOHN DICKINSON
	RICHARD BASSETT
	JACO: BROOM
Maryland	JAMES MCHENRY
	DAN OF ST. THOS. JENIFER
	DANL CARROLL
Virginia	JOHN BLAIR—
	JAMES MADISON JR.
North Carolina	WM BLOUNT
	RICHD DOBBS SPAIGHT
	HU WILLIAMSON
South Carolina	J. RUTLEDGE
	CHARLES COTESWORTH PINCKNEY
	PIERCE BUTLER
Georgia	WILLIAM FEW
	ABR BALDWIN

AMENDMENTS TO THE CONSTITUTION

*Proposed by Congress and Ratified
by the Legislatures of the Several States,
Pursuant to Article V of the Original Constitution.*

Amendments I–X, known as the Bill of Rights, were proposed by Congress on September 25, 1789, and ratified on December 15, 1791. Federalist Papers comments, mainly in opposition to a Bill of Rights, can be found in #84 (Hamilton).

Amendment I

[FREEDOM OF RELIGION, OF SPEECH, AND OF THE PRESS]

Congress shall make no law respecting an establishment of religion, or prohibiting the free exercise thereof; or abridging the freedom of speech, or of the press; or the right of the people peaceably to assemble, and to petition the Government for a redress of grievances.

Amendment II

[RIGHT TO KEEP AND BEAR ARMS]

A well regulated Militia, being necessary to the security of a free State, the right of the people to keep and bear Arms, shall not be infringed.

Amendment III

[QUARTERING OF SOLDIERS]

No Soldier shall, in time of peace be quartered in any house, without the consent of the Owner, nor in time of war, but in a manner to be prescribed by law.

Amendment IV

[SECURITY FROM UNWARRANTABLE SEARCH AND SEIZURE]

The right of the people to be secure in their persons, houses, papers, and effects, against unreasonable searches and seizures, shall not be violated, and no Warrants shall issue, but upon probable cause, supported by Oath or affirmation, and particularly describing the place to be searched, and the persons or things to be seized.

Amendment V

[RIGHTS OF ACCUSED PERSONS IN CRIMINAL PROCEEDINGS]

No person shall be held to answer for a capital, or otherwise infamous crime, unless on a presentment or indictment of a Grand Jury, except in cases arising in the land or naval forces, or in the

Militia, when in actual service in time of War or in public danger; nor shall any person be subject for the same offence to be twice put in jeopardy of life or limb; nor shall be compelled in any Criminal Case to be a witness against himself, nor be deprived of life, liberty, or property, without due process of law; nor shall private property be taken for public use, without just compensation.

Amendment VI

[RIGHT TO SPEEDY TRIAL, WITNESSES, ETC.]

In all criminal prosecutions, the accused shall enjoy the right to a speedy and public trial, by an impartial jury of the State and district wherein the crime shall have been committed, which district shall have been previously ascertained by law, and to be informed of the nature and cause of the accusation; to be confronted with the witnesses against him; to have compulsory process for obtaining Witnesses in his favor, and to have the Assistance of Counsel for his defence.

Amendment VII

[TRIAL BY JURY IN CIVIL CASES]

In suits at common law, where the value in controversy shall exceed twenty dollars, the right of trial by jury shall be preserved, and no fact tried by a jury shall be otherwise re-examined in any Court of the United States, than according to the rules of the common law.

Amendment VIII

[BAILS, FINES, PUNISHMENTS]

Excessive bail shall not be required, nor excessive fines imposed, nor cruel and unusual punishments inflicted.

Amendment IX

[RESERVATION OF RIGHTS OF PEOPLE]

The enumeration in the Constitution, of certain rights, shall not be construed to deny or disparage others retained by the people.

Amendment X

[POWERS RESERVED TO STATES OR PEOPLE]

The powers not delegated to the United States by the Constitution, nor prohibited by it to the States, are reserved to the States respectively, or to the people.

Amendment XI

[*Proposed by Congress on March 4, 1794; declared ratified on January 8, 1798.*]
[RESTRICTION OF JUDICIAL POWER]

The Judicial power of the United States shall not be construed to extend to any suit in law or equity, commenced or prosecuted against one of the United States by Citizens of another State, or by Citizens or Subjects of any Foreign State.

Amendment XII

[*Proposed by Congress on December 9, 1803; declared ratified on September 25, 1804.*]
[ELECTION OF PRESIDENT AND VICE-PRESIDENT]

The Electors shall meet in their respective states, and vote by ballot for President and Vice-President, one of whom, at least, shall not be an inhabitant of the same state with themselves; they shall name in their ballots the person voted for as President, and in distinct ballots the person voted for as Vice-President, and they shall make distinct lists of all persons voted for as President, and of all persons voted for as Vice-President, and of the number of votes for each, which lists they shall sign and certify, and transmit sealed to the seat of the government of the United States, directed to the President of the Senate;—The President of the Senate shall, in presence of the Senate and House of Representatives, open all the certificates and the votes shall then be counted;—The person having the greatest number of votes for President, shall be the President, if such number be a majority of the whole number of Electors appointed; and if no person have such majority, then from the persons having the highest numbers not exceeding three on the list of those voted for as President, the House of Representatives shall choose immediately, by ballot, the President. But in choosing the President, the votes shall be taken by states, the representation from each state having one vote; a quorum for this purpose shall consist of a member or members from two-thirds of the states, and a majority of all states shall be necessary to a choice. And if the House of Representatives shall not choose a President whenever the right of choice shall devolve upon them, before the fourth day of March next following, then the Vice-President, shall act as President, as in the case of the death or other constitutional disability of the President. The person having the greatest number of votes as Vice-President, shall be the Vice-President, if such a number be a majority of the whole number of Electors appointed, and if no person have a majority, then from the two highest numbers on the list, the Senate shall choose the Vice-President; a quorum for the purpose shall consist of two-thirds of the whole number of Senators, and a majority of the whole number shall be necessary to a choice. But no person constitutionally ineligible to the office of President shall be eligible to that of Vice-President of the United States.

Amendment XIII

[*Proposed by Congress on January 31, 1865; declared ratified on December 18, 1865.*]

Section 1
[ABOLITION OF SLAVERY]

Neither slavery nor involuntary servitude, except as a punishment for crime whereof the party shall have been duly convicted, shall exist within the United States, or any place subject to their jurisdiction.

Section 2
[POWER TO ENFORCE THIS ARTICLE]

Congress shall have power to enforce this article by appropriate legislation.

Amendment XIV

[*Proposed by Congress on June 13, 1866, declared ratified on July 28, 1868.*]

Section 1
[CITIZENSHIP RIGHTS NOT TO BE ABRIDGED BY STATES]

All persons born or naturalized in the United States, and subject to the jurisdiction thereof, are citizens of the United States and of the State wherein they reside. No State shall make or enforce any law which shall abridge the privileges or immunities of citizens of the United States; nor shall any State deprive any person of life, liberty, or property, without due process of law; nor deny to any person within its jurisdiction the equal protection of the laws.

Section 2
[APPORTIONMENT OF REPRESENTATIVES IN CONGRESS]

Representatives shall be apportioned among the several States according to their respective numbers, counting the whole number of persons in each State, excluding Indians not taxed. But when the right to vote at any election for the choice of electors for President and Vice-President of the United States, Representatives in Congress, the Executive and Judicial officers of a State, or the members of the Legislature thereof, is denied to any of the male inhabitants of such State, being twenty-one years of age, and citizens of the United States, or in any way abridged, except for participation in rebellion, or other crime, the basis of representation therein shall be reduced in the proportion which the number of such male citizens shall bear to the whole number of male citizens twenty-one years of age in such State.

Section 3
[PERSONS DISQUALIFIED FROM HOLDING OFFICE]

No person shall be a Senator or Representative in Congress, or elector of President and Vice-President, or hold any office, civil or military, under the United States, or under any State, who, having previously taken an oath, as a member of Congress, or as an officer of the United States, or as a member of any State legislature, or as an executive or judicial officer of any State, to support the Constitution of the United States, shall have engaged in insurrection or rebellion against the same, or given aid or comfort to the enemies thereof. But Congress may by a vote of two-thirds of each House, remove such disability.

Section 4
[WHAT PUBLIC DEBTS ARE VALID]

The validity of the public debt of the United States, authorized by law, including debts incurred for payment of pensions and bounties for services in suppressing insurrection or rebellion, shall not be questioned. But neither the United States nor any State shall assume or pay any debt or obligation incurred in aid of insurrection or rebellion against the United States, or any claim for the loss or emancipation of any slave; but all such debts, obligations and claims shall be held illegal and void.

Section 5
[POWER TO ENFORCE THIS ARTICLE]

The Congress shall have power to enforce, by appropriate legislation, the provisions of this article.

Amendment XV

[*Proposed by Congress on February 26, 1869; declared ratified on March 30, 1870.*]

Section 1
[NEGRO SUFFRAGE]

The right of citizens of the United States to vote shall not be denied or abridged by the United States or by any State on account of race, color, or previous condition of servitude.

Section 2
[POWER TO ENFORCE THIS ARTICLE]

The Congress shall have power to enforce this article by appropriate legislation.

Amendment XVI

[*Proposed by Congress on July 12, 1909; declared ratified on February 25, 1913.*]
[AUTHORIZING INCOME TAXES]

The Congress shall have power to lay and collect taxes on incomes, from whatever source derived, without apportionment among the several States, and without regard to any census or enumeration.

Amendment XVII

[*Proposed by Congress on May 13, 1912; declared ratified on May 31, 1913.*]
[POPULAR ELECTION OF SENATORS]

The Senate of the United States shall be composed of two Senators from each State, elected by the people thereof, for six years; and each Senator shall have one vote. The electors in each State shall have the qualifications requisite for electors of the most numerous branch of the State Legislature.

When vacancies happen in the representation of any State in the Senate, the executive authority of such State shall issue writs of election to fill such vacancies: Provided, That the Legislature of any State may empower the executive thereof to make temporary appointment until the people fill the vacancies by election as the Legislature may direct.

This amendment shall not be so construed as to affect the election or term of any Senator chosen before it becomes valid as part of the Constitution.

Amendment XVIII

[*Proposed by Congress December 18, 1917; declared ratified on January 29, 1919.*]

Section 1
[NATIONAL LIQUOR PROHIBITION]

After one year from the ratification of this article the manufacture, sale, or transportation of intoxicating liquors within, the importation thereof into, or the exportation thereof from the United States and all territory subject to the jurisdiction thereof for beverage purposes is hereby prohibited.

Section 2
[POWER TO ENFORCE THIS ARTICLE]

The Congress and the several states shall have concurrent power to enforce this article by appropriate legislation.

Section 3
[RATIFICATION WITHIN SEVEN YEARS]

This article shall be inoperative unless it shall have been ratified as an amendment to the Constitution by the legislatures of the several states, as provided in the Constitution, within seven years from the date of the submission hereof to the states by the Congress.[1]

Amendment XIX

[*Proposed by Congress on June 4, 1919; declared ratified on August 26, 1920.*]

[WOMAN SUFFRAGE]

The right of the citizens of the United States to vote shall not be denied or abridged by the United States or by any state on account of sex.

Congress shall have power, by appropriate legislation, to enforce this article by appropriate legislation.

Amendment XX

[*Proposed by Congress on March 2, 1932; declared ratified on February 6, 1933.*]

Section 1
[TERMS OF OFFICE]

The terms of the President and Vice-President shall end at noon on the 20th day of January, and the terms of the Senators and Representatives at noon on the 3rd day of January, of the years in which such terms would have ended if this article had not been ratified; and the terms of their successors shall then begin.

Section 2
[TIME OF CONVENING CONGRESS]

The Congress shall assemble at least once in every year, and such meeting shall begin at noon on the 3rd day of January, unless they shall by law appoint a different day.

Section 3
[DEATH OF PRESIDENT-ELECT]

If, at the time fixed for the beginning of the term of the President, the President-elect shall have died, the Vice-President-elect shall become President. If a President shall not have been chosen before the time fixed for the beginning of his term, or if the President-elect shall have failed to qualify, then the Vice-President-elect shall act as President until a President shall have qualified; and the Congress may by law provide for the case wherein neither a President-elect nor a Vice-President-elect shall have qualified, declaring who shall then act as President, or the manner in which one who is to act shall be selected, and such person shall act accordingly until a President or Vice-President shall have qualified.

Section 4
[ELECTION OF THE PRESIDENT]

The Congress may by law provide for the case of the death of any of the persons from whom the House of Representatives may choose a President whenever the right of choice shall have devolved upon them, and for the case of the death of any of the persons from whom the Senate may choose a Vice-President whenever the right of choice shall have devolved upon them.

Section 5
[AMENDMENT TAKES EFFECT]

Sections 1 and 2 shall take effect on the 15th day of October following ratification of this article.

Section 6
[RATIFICATION WITHIN SEVEN YEARS]

This article shall be inoperative unless it shall have been ratified as an amendment to the Constitution by the legislatures of three-fourths of the several States within seven years from the date of its submission.

Amendment XXI

[*Proposed by Congress on February 20, 1933; declared ratified on December 5, 1933.*]

Section 1
[NATIONAL LIQUOR PROHIBITION REPEALED]

The eighteenth article of amendment to the Constitution of the United States is hereby repealed.

---

[15] Repealed by the Twenty-first Amendment.

Section 2
[TRANSPORTATION OF LIQUOR INTO "DRY" STATES]

The transportation or importation into any State, Territory, or Possession of the United States for delivery or use therein of intoxicating liquors, in violation of the laws thereof, is hereby prohibited.

Section 3
[RATIFICATION WITHIN SEVEN YEARS]

This article shall be inoperative unless it shall have been ratified as an amendment to the Constitution by conventions in the several States, as provided in the Constitution, within seven years from the date of the submission hereof to the States by the Congress.

Amendment XXII

[*Proposed by Congress on March 21, 1947; declared ratified on February 26, 1951.*]

Section 1
[TENURE OF PRESIDENT LIMITED]

No person shall be elected to the office of President more than twice, and no person who has held the office of President or acted as President for more than two years of a term to which some other person was elected President shall be elected to the Office of the President more than once. But this Article shall not apply to any person holding the office of President when this Article was proposed by the Congress, and shall not prevent any person who may be holding the office of President, or acting as President, during the term within which this Article becomes operative from holding the office of President or acting as President during the remainder of such term.

Section 2
[RATIFICATION WITHIN SEVEN YEARS]

This Article shall be inoperative unless it shall have been ratified as an amendment to the Constitution by the legislatures of three-fourths of the several states within seven years from the date of its submission to the States by the Congress.

Amendment XXIII

[*Proposed by Congress on June 21, 1960; declared ratified on March 29, 1961.*]

Section 1
[ELECTORAL COLLEGE VOTES FOR THE DISTRICT OF COLUMBIA]

The District constituting the seat of Government of the United States shall appoint in such manner as the Congress may direct:

A number of electors of President and Vice-President equal to the whole number of Senators and Representatives in Congress to which the District would be entitled if it were a State, but in no event more than the least populous State; they shall be in addition to those appointed by the States, but they shall be considered, for the purposes of the election of President and Vice-President, to be electors appointed by a State; and they shall meet in the District and perform such duties as provided by the twelfth article of amendment.

Section 2
[POWER TO ENFORCE THIS ARTICLE]

The Congress shall have power to enforce this article by appropriate legislation.

Amendment XXIV

[*Proposed by Congress on August 27, 1963; declared ratified on January 23, 1964.*]

Section 1
[ANTI-POLL TAX]

The right of citizens of the United States to vote in any primary or other election for President or Vice-President, for electors for President or Vice-President, or for Senator or Representative of Congress, shall not be denied or abridged by the United States or any State by reasons of failure to pay any poll tax or other tax.

Section 2
[POWER TO ENFORCE THIS ARTICLE]

The Congress shall have power to enforce this article by appropriate legislation.

Amendment XXV

[Proposed by Congress on July 7, 1965; declared ratified on February 10, 1967.]

Section 1
[VICE-PRESIDENT TO BECOME PRESIDENT]

In case of the removal of the President from office or his death or resignation, the Vice-President shall become President.

Section 2
[CHOICE OF A NEW VICE-PRESIDENT]

Whenever there is a vacancy in the office of the Vice-President, the President shall nominate a Vice-President who shall take the office upon confirmation by a majority vote of both houses of Congress.

Section 3
[PRESIDENT MAY DECLARE OWN DISABILITY]

Whenever the President transmits to the President pro tempore of the Senate and the Speaker of the House of Representatives his written declaration that he is unable to discharge the powers and duties of his office, and until he transmits to them a written declaration to the contrary, such powers and duties shall be discharged by the Vice-President as Acting President.

Section 4
[ALTERNATIVE PROCEDURES TO DECLARE AND TO END PRESIDENTIAL DISABILITY]

Whenever the Vice-President and a majority of either the principal officers of the executive departments, or of such other body as Congress may by law provide, transmit to the President pro tempore of the Senate and the Speaker of the House of Representatives their written declaration that the President is unable to discharge the powers and duties of his office, the Vice-President shall immediately assume the powers and duties of the office as Acting President.

Thereafter, when the President transmits to the President pro tempore of the Senate and the Speaker of the House of Representatives his written declaration that no inability exists, he shall resume the powers and duties of his office unless the Vice-President and a majority of either the principal officers of the executive departments, or of such other body as Congress may by law provide, transmit within four days to the President pro tempore of the Senate and the Speaker of the House of Representatives their written declaration that the President is unable to discharge the powers and duties of his office. Thereupon Congress shall decide the issue, assembling within 48 hours for that purpose if not in session. If the Congress, within 21 days after receipt of the latter written declaration, or, if Congress is not in session, within 21 days after Congress is required to assemble, determines by two-thirds vote of both houses that the President is unable to discharge the powers and duties of his office, the Vice-President shall continue to discharge the same as Acting President; otherwise, the President shall resume the powers and duties of his office.

Amendment XXVI

[Proposed by Congress on March 23, 1971; declared ratified on June 30, 1971.]

Section 1
[EIGHTEEN-YEAR-OLD VOTE]

The right of citizens of the United States, who are eighteen years of age or older, to vote shall not be denied or abridged by the United States or by any State on account of age.

Section 2
[POWER TO ENFORCE THIS ARTICLE]

The Congress shall have power to enforce this article by appropriate legislation.

Amendment XXVII

[Proposed by Congress on September 25, 1789; ratified on May 7, 1992.]

[CONGRESSIONAL PAY RAISES]

No law varying the compensation for the services of the Senators and Representatives shall take effect until an election of Representatives shall have intervened.

THE FEDERALIST PAPERS

No. 10: Madison

Among the numerous advantages promised by a well-constructed Union, none deserves to be more accurately developed than its tendency to break and control the violence of faction. The friend of popular governments never finds himself so much alarmed for their character and fate as when he contemplates their propensity to this dangerous vice. He will not fail, therefore, to set a due value on any plan which, without violating the principles to which he is attached, provides a proper cure for it. The instability, injustice, and confusion introduced into the public councils have, in truth, been the mortal diseases under which popular governments have everywhere perished, as they continue to be the favorite and fruitful topics from which the adversaries to liberty derive their most specious declamations. The valuable improvements made by the American constitutions on the popular models, both ancient and modern, cannot certainly be too much admired; but it would be an unwarrantable partiality to contend that they have as effectually obviated the danger on this side, as was wished and expected. Complaints are everywhere heard from our most considerate and virtuous citizens, equally the friends of public and private faith and of public and personal liberty, that our governments are too unstable, that the public good is disregarded in the conflicts of rival parties, and that measures are too often decided, not according to the rules of justice and the rights of the minor party, but by the superior force of an interested and overbearing majority. However anxiously we may wish that these complaints had no foundation, the evidence of known facts will not permit us to deny that they are in some degree true. It will be found, indeed, on a candid review of our situation, that some of the distresses under which we labor have been erroneously charged on the operation of our governments; but it will be found, at the same time, that other causes will not alone account for many of our heaviest misfortunes; and, particularly, for that prevailing and increasing distrust of public engagements and alarm for private rights which are echoed from one end of the continent to the other. These must be chiefly, if not wholly, effects of the unsteadiness and injustice with which a factious spirit has tainted our public administration.

By a faction I understand a number of citizens, whether amounting to a majority or minority of the whole, who are united and actuated by some common impulse of passion, or of interest, adverse to the rights of other citizens, or to the permanent and aggregate interests of the community.

There are two methods of curing the mischiefs of faction: the one, by removing its causes; the other, by controlling its effects.

There are again two methods of removing the causes of faction: the one, by destroying the liberty which is essential to its existence; the other, by giving to every citizen the same opinions, the same passions, and the same interests.

It could never be more truly said than of the first remedy that it was worse than the disease. Liberty is to faction what air is to fire, an aliment without which it instantly expires. But it could not be a less folly to abolish liberty, which is essential to political life, because it nourishes faction than it would be to wish the annihilation of air, which is essential to animal life, because it imparts to fire its destructive agency.

The second expedient is an impracticable as the first would be unwise. As long as the reason of man continues fallible, and he is at liberty to exercise it, different opinions will be formed. As long as the connection subsists between his reason and his self-love, his opinions and his passions will have a reciprocal influence on each other; and the former will be objects to which the latter will attach themselves. The diversity in the faculties of men, from which the rights of property originate, is not less an insuperable obstacle to a uniformity of interests. The protection of these faculties is the first object of government. From the protection of different and unequal faculties of acquiring property, the possession of different degrees and kinds of property immediately results; and from the influence of these on the sentiments and views of the respective proprietors ensues a division of the society into different interests and parties.

The latent causes of faction are thus sown in the nature of man; and we see them everywhere brought into different degrees of activity, according to the different circumstances of civil society. A zeal for different opinions concerning religion, concerning government, and many other points, as well of speculation as of practice; an attachment to different leaders ambitiously contending for pre-eminence and power; or to persons of other descriptions whose fortunes have been interesting to the human passions, have, in turn, divided mankind into parties, inflamed them with mutual animosity, and rendered them much more disposed to vex and oppress each other than to co-operate for their common good. So strong is this propensity of mankind to fall into mutual animosities that where no substantial occasion presents itself the most frivolous and fanciful distinctions have been sufficient to kindle their unfriendly passions and excite their most violent conflicts. But the most common and durable source of factions has been the various and unequal distribution of property. Those who hold and those who are without property have ever formed distinct interests in society. Those who are creditors, and those who are debtors, fall under a like discrimination. A landed interest, a manufacturing interest, a mercantile interest, a moneyed interest, with many lesser interests, grow up of necessity in civilized nations, and divide them into different classes, actuated by different sentiments and views. The regulation of these various and interfering interests forms the principal task of modern legislation and involves the spirit of party and faction in the necessary and ordinary operations of government.

No man is allowed to be judge in his own cause, because his interest would certainly bias his judgment and, not improbably, corrupt his integrity. With equal, nay with greater reason, a body of men are unfit to be both judges and parties at the same time; yet what are many of the most important acts of legislation but so many judicial determinations, not indeed concerning the rights of single persons, but concerning the rights of large bodies of citizens? And what are the different classes of legislators but advocates and parties to the causes which they determine? Is a law proposed concerning private debts? It is a question to which the creditors are parties on one side and the debtors on the other. Justice ought to hold the balance between them. Yet the parties are, and must be, themselves the judges; and the most numerous party, or in other words, the most powerful faction must be expected to prevail. Shall domestic manufacturers be encouraged, and in what degree, by restrictions on foreign manufacturers? are questions which would be differently decided by the landed and the manufacturing classes, and probably by neither with a sole regard to justice and the public good. The apportionment of taxes on the various descriptions of property is an act which seems to require the most exact impartiality; yet there is, perhaps, no legislative act in which greater opportunity and temptation are given to a predominant party to trample on the rules of justice. Every shilling with which they overburden the inferior number is a shilling saved to their own pockets.

It is in vain to say that enlightened statesmen will be able to adjust these clashing interests and render them all subservient to the public good. Enlightened statesmen will not always be at the helm. Nor, in many cases, can such an adjustment be made at all without taking into view indirect and remote considerations, which will rarely prevail over the immediate interest which one party may find in disregarding the rights of another or the good of the whole.

The inference to which we are brought is that the *causes* of faction cannot be removed and that relief is only to be sought in the means of controlling its *effects*.

If a faction consists of less than a majority, relief is supplied by the republican principle, which enables the majority to defeat its sinister views by regular vote. It may clog the administration, it may convulse the society; but it will be unable to execute and mask its violence under the forms of the Constitution. When a majority is included in a faction, the form of popular government, on the other hand, enables it to sacrifice to its ruling passion or interest both the public good and the rights of other citizens. To secure the public good and private rights against the danger of such a faction, and at the same time to preserve the spirit and the form of popular government, is then the great object to which our inquiries are directed. Let me add that it is the great desideratum by which alone this form of government can be rescued from the opprobrium under which it has so long labored and be recommended to the esteem and adoption of mankind.

By what means is this object attainable? Evidently by one of two only. Either the existence of the same passion or interest in a majority at the same time must be prevented, or the majority, having such coexistent passion or interest, must be rendered, by their number and local situation, unable to concert and carry into effect schemes of oppression. If the impulse and the opportunity be suffered to coincide, we well know that neither moral nor religious motives can be relied on as an adequate control. They are not found to be such on the injustice and violence of individuals,

and lose their efficacy in proportion to the number combined together, that is, in proportion as their efficacy becomes needful.

From this view of the subject it may be concluded that a pure democracy, by which I mean a society consisting of a small number of citizens, who assemble and administer the government in person, can admit of no cure for the mischiefs of faction. A common passion or interest will, in almost every case, be felt by a majority of the whole; a communication and concert results from the form of government itself; and there is nothing to check the inducements to sacrifice the weaker party or an obnoxious individual. Hence it is that such democracies have ever been spectacles of turbulence and contention; have ever been found incompatible with personal security or the rights of property; and have in general been as short in their lives as they have been violent in their deaths. Theoretic politicians, who have patronized this species of government, have erroneously supposed that by reducing mankind to a perfect equality in their political rights, they would at the same time be perfectly equalized and assimilated in their possessions, their opinions, and their passions.

A republic, by which I mean a government in which the scheme of representation takes place, opens a different prospect and promises the cure for which we are seeking. Let us examine the points in which it varies from pure democracy, and we shall comprehend both the nature of the cure and the efficacy which it must derive from the Union.

The two great points of difference between a democracy and a republic are: first, the delegation of the government, in the latter, to a small number of citizens elected by the rest; secondly, the greater number of citizens and greater sphere of country over which the latter may be extended.

The effect of the first difference is, on the one hand, to refine and enlarge the public views by passing them through the medium of a chosen body of citizens, whose wisdom may best discern the true interest of their country and whose patriotism and love of justice will be least likely to sacrifice it to temporary or partial considerations. Under such a regulation it may well happen that the public voice, pronounced by the representatives of the people, will be more consonant to the public good than if pronounced by the people themselves, convened for the purpose. On the other hand, the effect may be inverted. Men of factious tempers, of local prejudices, or of sinister designs, may, by intrigue, by corruption, or by other means, first obtain the suffrages, and then betray the interests of the people. The question resulting is, whether small or extensive republics are most favorable to the election of proper guardians of the public weal; and it is clearly decided in favor of the latter by two obvious considerations.

In the first place it is to be remarked that however small the republic may be the representatives must be raised to a certain number in order to guard against the cabals of a few; and that however large it may be they must be limited to a certain number in order to guard against the confusion of a multitude. Hence, the number of representatives in the two cases not being in proportion to that of the constituents, and being proportionally greatest in the small republic, it follows that if the proportion of fit characters be not less in the large than in the small republic, the former will present a greater option, and consequently a greater probability of a fit choice.

In the next place, as each representative will be chosen by a greater number of citizens in the large than in the small republic, it will be more difficult for unworthy candidates to practise with success the vicious arts by which elections are too often carried; and the suffrages of the people being more free, will be more likely to center on men who possess the most attractive merit and the most diffusive and established characters.

It must be confessed that in this, as in most other cases, there is a mean, on both sides of which inconveniencies will be found to lie. By enlarging too much the number of electors, you render the representative too little acquainted with all their local circumstances and lesser interests; as by reducing it too much, you render him unduly attached to these, and too little fit to comprehend and pursue great and national objects. The federal Constitution forms a happy combination in this respect; the great and aggregate interests being referred to the national, the local and particular to the State legislatures.

The other point of difference is the greater number of citizens and extent of territory which may be brought within the compass of republican than of democratic government; and it is this circumstance principally which renders factious combinations less to be dreaded in the former than in the latter. The smaller the society, the fewer probably will be the distinct parties and interests composing it; the fewer the distinct parties and interests, the more frequently will a majority be found of the same party; and the smaller the number of individuals composing a majority, and the smaller the compass within which they are placed, the more easily will they concert and execute their plans of oppression. Extend the sphere and you take in a greater variety of parties and interests; you make it less probable that a majority of the whole will have a common motive to invade the rights of other citizens; or if such a common motive exists, it will be more difficult for all who feel it to discover their own strength and to act in unison with each other. Besides other impediments, it may be remarked that, where there is a consciousness of unjust or dishonorable purposes, communication is always checked by distrust in proportion to the number whose concurrence is necessary.

Hence, it clearly appears that the same advantage which a republic has over a democracy in controlling the effects of faction is enjoyed by a large over a small republic—is enjoyed by the Union over the States composing it. Does this advantage consist in the substitution of representatives whose enlightened views and virtuous sentiments render them superior to local prejudices and to schemes of injustice? It will not be denied that the representation of the Union will be most likely to possess these requisite endowments. Does it consist in the greater security afforded by a greater variety of parties, against the event of any one party being able to outnumber and oppress the rest? In an equal degree does the increased variety of parties comprised within the Union increase this security? Does it, in fine, consist in the greater obstacles opposed to the concert and accomplishment of the secret wishes of an unjust and interested majority? Here again the extent of the Union gives it the most palpable advantage.

The influence of factious leaders may kindle a flame within their particular States but will be unable to spread a general conflagration through the other States. A religious sect may degenerate into a political faction in a part of the Confederacy; but the variety of sects dispersed over the entire face of it must secure the national councils against any danger from that source. A rage for paper money, for an abolition of debts, for an equal division of property, or for any other improper or wicked project, will be less apt to pervade the whole body of the Union than a particular member of it, in the same proportion as such a malady is more likely to taint a particular county or district than an entire State.

In the extent and proper structure of the Union, therefore, we behold a republican remedy for the diseases most incident to republican government. And according to the degree of pleasure and pride we feel in being republicans ought to be our zeal in cherishing the spirit and supporting the character of federalist.   PUBLIUS

No. 51: Madison

To what expedient, then, shall we finally resort, for maintaining in practice the necessary partition of power among the several departments as laid down in the Constitution? The only answer that can be given is that as all these exterior provisions are found to be inadequate the defect must be supplied, by so contriving the interior structure of the government as that its several constituent parts may, by their mutual relations, be the means of keeping each other in their proper places. Without presuming to undertake a full development of this important idea I will hazard a few general observations which may perhaps place it in a clearer light, and enable us to form a more correct judgment of the principles and structure of the government planned by the convention.

In order to lay a due foundation for that separate and distinct exercise of the different powers of government, which to a certain extent is admitted on all hands to be essential to the preservation of liberty, it is evident that each department should have a will of its own; and consequently should be so constituted that the members of each should have as little agency as possible in the appointment of the members of the others. Were this principle rigorously adhered to, it would require that all the appointments for the supreme executive, legislative, and judiciary magistracies should be drawn from the same fountain of authority, the people, through channels having no communication whatever with one another. Perhaps such a plan of constructing the several departments would be less difficult in practice than it may in contemplation appear. Some difficulties, however, and some additional expense would attend the execution of it. Some deviations, therefore, from the principle must be admitted. In the constitution of the judiciary department in particular, it might be inexpedient to insist rigorously on the principle: first, because peculiar qualifications being essential in the members, the primary consideration ought to be to select that mode of choice which best secures these qualifications; second, because the permanent tenure by which the appointments are held in that department must soon destroy all sense of dependence on the authority conferring them.

It is equally evident that the members of each department should be as little dependent as possible on those of the others for the emoluments annexed to their offices. Were the executive magistrate, or the judges, not independent of the legislature in this particular, their independence in every other would be merely nominal.

But the great security against a gradual concentration of the several powers in the same department consists in giving to those who administer each department the necessary constitutional means and personal motives to resist encroachments of the others. The provision for defense must in this, as in all other cases, be made commensurate to the danger of attack. Ambition must be made to counteract ambition. The interest of the man must be connected with the constitutional rights of the place. It may be a reflection on human nature that such devices should be necessary to control the abuses of government. But what is government itself but the greatest of all reflections on human nature? If men were angels, no government would be necessary. If angels were to govern men, neither external nor internal controls on government would be necessary. In framing a government which is to be administered by men over men, the great difficulty lies in this: you must first enable the government to control the governed; and in the next place oblige it to control itself. A dependence on the people is, no doubt, the primary control on the government; but experience has taught mankind the necessity of auxiliary precautions.

This policy of supplying, by opposite and rival interests, the defect of better motives, might be traced through the whole system of human affairs, private as well as public. We see it particularly displayed in all the subordinate distributions of power, where the constant aim is to divide and arrange the several offices in such a manner as that each may be a check on the other—that the private interest of every individual may be a sentinel over the public rights. These inventions of prudence cannot be less requisite in the distribution of the supreme powers of the State.

But it is not possible to give to each department an equal power of self-defense. In republican government, the legislative authority necessarily predominates. The remedy for this inconveniency is to divide the legislature into different branches; and to render them, by different modes of election and different principles of action, as little connected with each other as the nature of their common functions and their common dependence on the society will admit. It may even be necessary to guard against dangerous encroachments by still further precautions. As the weight of the legislative authority requires that it should be thus divided, the weakness of the executive may require, on the other hand, that it should be fortified. An absolute negative on the legislature appears, at first view, to be the natural defense with which the executive magistrate should be armed. But perhaps it would be neither altogether safe nor alone sufficient. On ordinary occasions it might not be exerted with the requi-

site firmness, and on extraordinary occasions it might be perfidiously abused. May not this defect of an absolute negative be supplied by some qualified connection between this weaker branch of the stronger department, by which the latter may be led to support the constitutional rights of the former, without being too much detached from the rights of its own department?

If the principles on which these observations are founded be just, as I persuade myself they are, and they be applied as a criterion to the several State constitutions, and to the federal Constitution, it will be found that if the latter does not perfectly correspond with them, the former are infinitely less able to bear such a test.

There are, moreover, two considerations particularly applicable to the federal system of America, which place that system in a very interesting point of view.

First. In a single republic, all the power surrendered by the people is submitted to the administration of a single government; and the usurpations are guarded against by a division of the government into distinct and separate departments. In the compound republic of America, the power surrendered by the people is first divided between two distinct governments, and then the portion allotted to each subdivided among distinct and separate departments. Hence a double security arises to the rights of the people. The different governments will control each other, at the same time that each will be controlled by itself.

Second. It is of great importance in a republic not only to guard the society against the oppression of its rulers, but to guard one part of the society against the injustice of the other part. Different interests necessarily exist in different classes of citizens. If a majority be united by a common interest, the rights of the minority will be insecure. There are but two methods of providing against this evil: the one by creating a will in the community independent of the majority— that is, of the society itself; the other, by comprehending in the society so many separate descriptions of citizens as will render an unjust combination of a majority of the whole very improbable, if not impracticable. The first method prevails in all governments possessing an hereditary or self-appointed authority. This, at best, is but a precarious security; because a power independent of the society may as well espouse the unjust views of the major as the rightful interests of the minor party, and may possibly be turned against both parties. The second method will be exemplified in the federal republic of the United States. Whilst all authority in it will be derived from and dependent on the society, the society itself will be broken into so many parts, interests and classes of citizens, that the rights of individuals, or of the minority, will be in little danger from interested combinations of the majority. In a free government the security for civil rights must be the same as that for religious rights. It consists in the one case in the multiplicity of interests, and in the other in the multiplicity of sects. The degree of security in both cases will depend on the number of interests and sects; and this may be presumed to depend on the extent of country and number of people comprehended under the same government. This view of the subject must particularly recommend a proper federal system to all the sincere and considerate friends of republican government, since it shows that in exact proportion as the territory of the Union may be formed into more circumscribed Confederacies, or States, oppressive combinations of a majority will be facilitated; the best security, under the republican forms, for the rights of every class of citizen, will be diminished; and consequently the stability and independence of some member of the government, the only other security, must be proportionally increased. Justice is the end of government. It is the end of civil society. It ever has been and ever will be pursued until it be obtained, or until liberty be lost in the pursuit. In a society under the forms of which the stronger faction can readily unite and oppress the weaker, anarchy may as truly be said to reign as in a state of nature, where the weaker individual is not secured against the violence of the stronger; and as, in the latter state, even the stronger individuals are prompted, by the uncertainty of their condition, to submit to a government which may protect the weak as well as themselves; so, in the former state, will the more powerful factions or parties be gradually induced, by a like motive, to wish for a government which will protect all parties, the weaker as well as the more powerful. It can be little doubted that if the State of Rhode Island was separated from the Confederacy and left to itself, the insecurity of rights under the popular form of government within such narrow limits would be displayed by such reiterated oppressions of factious majorities that some power altogether independent of the people would soon be called for by the voice of the very factions whose misrule had proved the necessity of it. In the extended republic of the United States, and among the great variety of interests, parties, and sects which it embraces, a coalition of a majority of the whole society could seldom take place on any other principles than those of justice and the general good; whilst there being thus less danger to a minor from the will of a major party, there must be less pretext, also, to provide for the security of the former, by introducing into the government a will not dependent on the latter, or, in other words, a will independent of the society itself. It is no less certain than it is important, notwithstanding the contrary opinions which have been entertained, that the larger the society, provided it lie within a practicable sphere, the more duly capable it will be of self-government. And happily for the *republican cause,* the practicable sphere may be carried to a very great extent by a judicious modification and mixture of the *federal principle.* Publius

GLOSSARY OF TERMS

absolutism A system of government in which the sovereign has unlimited powers; despotism.

administrative legislation Rules made by regulatory agencies and commissions.

affirmative action A policy or program designed to redress historic injustices committed against racial minorities and other specified groups by making special efforts to provide members of these groups with access to educational and employment opportunities.

agency representation The type of representation by which representatives are held accountable to their constituents if they fail to represent them properly; that is, constituents have the power to hire and fire their representative. This is the incentive for good representation when the personal backgrounds, views, and interests of the representative differ from their constituents.

Aid to Families of Dependent Children (AFDC) The largest federal cash transfer program (as distinguished from assistance in kind). Federal funds, administered by the states, for children living with parents or relatives who fall below state standards of need.

amicus curiae "Friend of the court"; individuals or groups who are not parties to a lawsuit but who seek to assist the court in reaching a decision by presenting additional briefs.

appropriation The amounts approved by Congress in statutes (bills) that each unit or agency of government can spend.

area sampling A polling technique used for large cities, states, or the whole nation, when a high level of accuracy is desired. The population is broken down into small, homogeneous units, such as counties; then several units are randomly selected to serve as the sample.

Articles of Confederation America's first written constitution. Adopted by the Continental Congress in 1777, the Articles of Confederation and Perpetual Union were the formal basis for America's national government until 1789 when they were supplanted by the Constitution.

Australian ballot An electoral format that presents the names of all the candidates for any given office on the same ballot. Introduced at the turn of the century, the Australian ballot replaced the partisan ballot and facilitated split-ticket voting.

authoritarian government A system of rule in which the government recognizes no formal limits but may, nevertheless, be restrained by the power of other social institutions.

authorization The process by which Congress enacts or rejects proposed statutes (bills) embodying the positive laws of government.

autocracy A form of government in which a single individual—a king, queen, or dictator—rules.

automatic stabilizers A category of public policy, largely fiscal and monetary, that automatically works against inflationary and deflationary tendencies in the economy.

balance of payments   Name for the "bottom line" in international trade. An excess of imports over exports is called "the international debt," which in the United States has been growing at a rate of over $100 billion per year.

balance of power   A system of political alignments by which stability can be achieved.

balance-of-power role   The strategy whereby many countries form alliances with one or more other countries in order to counterbalance the behavior of other, usually more powerful nation-states.

bandwagon effect   A situation wherein reports of voter or delegate opinion can influence the actual outcome of an election or a nominating convention.

bellwether districts   Towns or districts that are microcosms of the whole population or that have been found to be good predictors of electoral outcomes.

bicameralism   Having a legislative assembly composed of two chambers or houses; opposite of unicameralism.

bilateral treaty   Treaty made between two nations; contrast with multilateral treaty.

bill of attainder   A legislative act which inflicts guilt and punishment without a judicial hearing or trial, it is proscribed by Article I, Section 10, of the Constitution.

bill of information   Official opinion of a government prosecutor or district attorney that there is sufficient evidence of a crime to bring a case to trial; in some places the equivalent of an indictment by a grand jury.

Bill of Rights   The first ten amendments to the U.S. Constitution, ratified in 1791, they ensure certain rights and liberties to the people.

binding primary   Primary election in which the candidates for election as delegates to a presidential nominating convention pledge themselves to a certain candidate and are bound to vote for that person until released from the obligation.

bipartisan foreign policy   Based on the assumption that "politics stops at the water's edge," this is a strategy pursued by most presidents since World War II to coopt the opposition party leaders in order to minimize the amount of public criticism and the leakage of confidential information for political purposes.

bipartisanship   Close cooperation between two parties; usually an effort by the two major parties in Congress to cooperate with the president in making foreign policy.

bureaucracy   The complex structure of offices, tasks, rules, and principles of organization that are employed by all large-scale institutions to coordinate the work of their personnel effectively.

cabinet   The secretaries, or chief administrators, of the major departments of the federal government. Cabinet secretaries are appointed by the president with the consent of the Senate.

Calendar Wednesday   A procedure in the House whereby a committee chairman can bypass the Rules Committee and bring proposed legislation directly to the floor for consideration.

capitalism   The economic system in which most of the means of production and distribution are privately owned and operated for profit.

categoric grants-in-aid   Grants by Congress to states and localities, with the condition that expenditures be limited to a problem or group specified in the law.

caucus   A normally closed meeting of a political or legislative group to select candidates, plan strategy, or make decisions regarding legislative matters.

certificate of convenience and necessity
Permission granted by a regulatory agency to an individual or group to conduct a particular type of business; license.

checks and balances   Mechanisms through which each branch of government is able to participate in and influence the activities of the other branches. Major examples include the presidential veto power over congressional legislation, the power of the Senate to approve presidential appointments, and judicial review of congressional enactments.

citizenship   The duties, rights, and privileges of being a citizen of a political unit.

civil disobedience   A form of direct action politics that involves the refusal to obey civil laws considered unjust. This is usually a nonviolent or passive resistance.

civil law   A system of jurisprudence, including private law and governmental actions, to settle disputes that do not involve criminal penalties.

civil liberties   Areas of personal freedom with which governments are constrained from interfering.

civil penalties   Regulatory techniques in which fines or another form of material restitution is imposed for violating civil laws or common law principles, such as negligence.

civil rights   Legal or moral claims that citizens are entitled to make upon the government.

clientele agencies   Departments or bureaus of government whose mission is to promote, serve, or represent a particular interest.

client state   A nation-state whose foreign policy is subordinated to that of another nation.

closed primary   A primary election in which voters can participate in the nomination of candidates, but only of the party in which they are enrolled for a period of time prior to primary day.

closed rule   Provision by the House Rules Committee limiting or prohibiting the introduction of amendments during debate.

closed shop   A contract between an employer and a union in which the employer agrees to hire no worker who is not a bona fide member of that union. This was outlawed by the Taft-Hartley Act of 1947.

cloture rule   Rule allowing a majority or two-thirds or three-fifths of the members in a legislative body to set a time limit on debate over a given bill.

coattail effect   Result of voters casting their ballot for president or governor and "automatically" voting for the remainder of the party's ticket.

collective bargaining   Negotiation between an employer and a union whose right to negotiate has been established by the vote of the employees; closely tied to the right to strike in case the bargaining process breaks down.

commerce power   Power of Congress to regulate trade among the states and with foreign countries.

common law   Law common to the realm in An-glo-Saxon history; judge-made law based on the precedents of previous lower court decisions.

concurrent power   Authority possessed by both state and national governments, such as the power to levy taxes.

confederation   League of independent states.

congressional veto   Legislative veto; a statutory arrangement under which Congress delegates power to an agency but requires the agency to submit its plans to Congress or to one of its committees for approval. See *legislative veto*.

conscription   Compulsory military service, usually for a prescribed period or for the duration of a war; "the draft."

conservative   Today this term refers to those who generally support the social and economic status quo and are suspicious of efforts to introduce new political formulae and economic arrangements. The belief that a large and powerful government poses a threat to citizens' freedoms.

constituency   The district comprising the area from which an official is elected.

constituent policy   Policies or programs that focus on the internal structure or operation of governmental agencies.

constitutionalism   An approach to legitimacy in which the rulers give up a certain amount of power in return for their right to utilize the remaining powers.

constitutional government   A system of rule in which formal and effective limits are placed on the powers of the government.

contracting power   The power of government to set conditions on companies seeking to sell goods or services to government agencies.

contract model   A theory asserting that governments originate from general agreements among members of the public about the necessity of dealing with common problems.

contributory programs   Social programs financed in whole or in part by taxation or other mandatory contributions by their present or future recipients. The most important example is Social Security, which is financed by a payroll tax.

control agencies   Agencies that have the power to intervene in the private sphere to regulate the conduct of individuals, groups, or corporations.

cooperative federalism   A type of federalism existing since the New Deal era in which grants-in-aid have been used strategically to encourage states and localities (without commanding them) to pursue nationally defined goals. Also known as intergovernmental cooperation.

cooptation   Strategy of bringing an individual into a group by joint action of the members of that group, usually in order to reduce or eliminate the individual's opposition.

correlational analysis   Analysis of two or more items that involve a mutual relationship; effort to determine the degree of relative correspondence between two sets of data.

coup d'état   Sudden, forcible overthrow of a government.

criminal law   The branch of law that deals with disputes or actions involving criminal penalties (as opposed to civil law), it regulates the conduct of individuals, defines crimes, and provides punishment for criminal acts.

criminal penalties   Regulatory techniques in which imprisonment or heavy fines and the loss of certain civil rights and liberties are imposed.

critical electoral realignment   The point in history when a new party supplants the ruling party, becoming in turn the dominant political force. In the United States, this has tended to occur roughly every 30 years.

debt limit   Ceiling established by Congress upon the total amount of debt the government can accumulate. Can be changed by Congress as need requires.

debt service   Interest paid on the public debt; an "uncontrollable" budget item because the amount is determined by general interest rates.

de facto segregation   Racial segregation that is not a direct result of law or government policy but is, instead, a reflection of residential patterns, income distributions, or other social factors.

deficit financing   Usually refers to deficits that are deliberately incurred as part of an effort to fight off a deflationary phase of the business cycle. Deficits are financed by borrowing.

de jure segregation   Racial segregation that is a direct result of law or official policy.

delegated powers   Constitutional powers as-signed to one governmental agency that are exercised by another agency with the express permission of the first.

democratic government   A system of rule that permits citizens to play a significant part in the governmental process, usually through the selection of key public officials.

deregulation   A policy of reducing or eliminating regulatory restraints on the conduct of individuals or private institutions.

direct action   A form of politics that uses informal channels to attempt to force rulers into a new course of action, such as violent politics or civil disobedience.

discharge petition   Procedure of the House whereby an absolute majority of the members can force a bill out of committee when the committee itself has refused to report it out for consideration.

discount rate   The interest rate charged by the Federal Reserve when commercial banks borrow in order to expand their lending operations. An effective tool of monetary policy.

double jeopardy   Trial more than once for the same crime. The Constitution guarantees that no one shall be subjected to double jeopardy.

dual federalism   The system of government that prevailed in the United States from 1789 to 1937 in which most fundamental governmental powers were shared between the federal and state governments.

due process   The right of every citizen against arbitrary action by national or state governments.

economic expansionist role   The strategy often pursued by many capitalist countries to adopt foreign policies that will maximize the success of domestic corporations in their dealings with other countries.

elastic clause   See *necessary and proper clause.*

electoral college   The presidential electors from each state who meet in their respective state capitals after the popular election to cast ballots for president and vice president.

electorate   All of the eligible voters in a legally designated area.

elite   Those people at the top who exercise a major influence on decision making.

eminent domain The right of government to take private property for public use, with reasonable compensation awarded for the property.

entitlement Eligibility for benefits by virtue of a category of benefits defined by law. Category can only be changed by legislation. Deprivation of individual benefits can be determined only through due process in court.

environmental impact statement Since 1969, all federal agencies must file a statement demonstrating that a new program or project will not have a net negative impact on the human or physical environment.

equal time rule The requirement that broadcasters provide candidates for the same political office an equal opportunity to communicate their messages to the public.

equality of opportunity A universally shared American ideal that all have the freedom to use whatever talents and wealth they have to reach their fullest potential.

equity Judicial process providing a remedy to a dispute where common law does not apply.

exclusive power Power belonging exclusively to and exercised only by the national or state government.

executive agreement An agreement between the president and another country which has the force of a treaty but does not require the Senate's "advice and consent."

executive privilege The claim that confidential communications between a president and close advisers should not be revealed without the consent of the president.

ex post facto law "After the fact" law; law that is retroactive and that has an adverse effect on someone accused of a crime. Under Article I, Sections 9 and 10, of the Constitution, neither the state nor the national government can enact such laws; this provision does not apply, however, to civil laws.

expressed power The notion that the Constitution grants to the federal government only those powers specifically named in its text.

expropriation Confiscation of property with or without compensation.

extraction-coercion cycle A process of state-building in which governments use military force to extract money and other resources from the populace. These resources are then used to enhance the government's military power, which is used to extract more resources, and so on.

faction Group of people with common interests, usually in opposition to the aims or principles of a larger group or the public.

fairness doctrine A Federal Communications Commission requirement for broadcasters who air programs on controversial issues to provide time for opposing views.

federalism System of government in which power is divided by a constitution between a central government and regional governments.

Federal Reserve System (Fed) Consisting of twelve Federal Reserve Banks, the Fed facilitates exchanges of cash, checks, and credit; it regulates member banks; and it uses monetary policies to fight inflation and deflation.

filibuster A tactic used by members of the Senate to prevent action on legislation they oppose by continuously holding the floor and speaking until the majority backs down. Once given the floor, Senators have unlimited time to speak, and it requires a vote of three-fifths of the Senate to end the filibuster.

first-strike capability The number and power of nuclear weapons, plus delivery, that it would take to attack a major power with such extensive success that it would wipe out the capacity of the enemy to retaliate.

fiscal year The yearly accounting period, which for the national government is October 1–September 30. The actual fiscal year is designated by the year in which it ends.

fiscal policy Use of taxing, monetary, and spending powers to manipulate the economy.

food stamps The largest in-kind welfare program, administered by the Department of Agriculture, providing coupons to individuals and families who satisfy a "needs test;" the food stamps can be exchanged for food at most grocery stores.

franchise The right to vote; see *license, suffrage*.

full faith and credit clause   Article IV, Section 1, of the Constitution provides that each state must accord the same respect to the laws and judicial decisions of other states that it accords to its own.

gerrymandering   Apportionment of voters in districts in such a way as to give unfair advantage to one political party.

government   Institutions and procedures through which a territory and its people are ruled.

grants-in-aid   Programs through which Congress provides money to state and local governments on the condition that the funds be employed for purposes defined by the federal government.

Great Compromise   Agreement reached at the Constitutional Convention of 1787 that gave each state an equal number of senators regardless of its population, but linked representation in the House of Representatives to population.

Gross National Product (GNP)   An index of the total output of goods and services. A very imperfect measure of prosperity, productivity, inflation, deflation, but its regular publication influences business conditions as well as reflecting them.

habeas corpus   A court order demanding that the individual in custody be brought into court and shown the cause for detention. *Habeas corpus* is guaranteed by the Constitution and can be suspended only in cases of rebellion or invasion.

haphazard sampling   A type of sampling of public opinion which is an unsystematic choice of respondents.

Holy Alliance role   A strategy pursued by a superpower to prevent any change in the existing distribution of power among nation-states, even if this requires intervention into the internal affairs of the country in order to keep an authoritarian ruler from being overthrown.

home rule   Power delegated by the state to a local unit of government to manage its own affairs.

homesteading   A national policy that permits people to gain ownership of property by occupying public or unclaimed lands, living on the land for a specified period of time, and making certain minimal improvements on that land. Also known as squatting.

ideology   The combined doctrines, assertions, and intentions of a social or political group that justify its behavior.

illusion of central tendency   The assumption that opinions are "normally distributed"—that responses to opinion questions are heavily distributed toward the center, as in a bell-shaped curve.

illusion of saliency   Impression conveyed by polls that something is important to the public when actually it is not.

impoundment   Efforts by presidents to thwart congressional programs that they cannot otherwise defeat by refusing to spend the funds that Congress has appropriated for them. Congress placed limits on impoundment in the Budget and Impoundment Control Act of 1974.

independent agencies   Agencies set up by Congress to be independent of direct presidential authority. Congress usually accomplishes this by providing the head or heads of the agency with a set term of office rather than allowing their removal at the pleasure of the president.

indexing   Periodic adjustments of welfare payments, wages, or taxes, tied to the cost of living.

indirect election   Provision for election of an official where the voters first select the delegates or "electors," who are in turn charged with making the final choice. The presidential election is an indirect election.

injunction   A court order requiring an individual or organization either to cease or to undertake some form of action to prevent a future injury or to achieve some desirable state of affairs.

in-kind benefits   Goods and services provided to needy individuals and families by the federal government, as contrasted with cash benefits. The largest in-kind federal welfare program is food stamps.

iron triangle   Name assigned by political scientists to the stable and cooperative relationships that often develop between a congressional committee or subcommittee, an administrative agency, and one or more supportive interest groups. Not all of these relationships are triangular, but the iron triangle is perhaps the most typical.

item veto   The power to veto specific provisions of a bill. Although some state governors possess this power, the President of the United States does not, and must accept or veto a bill in its entirety.

jingoism   Extreme or militant devotion to one's country.

Johnson rule   Senate rule, adopted while Lyndon Johnson was majority leader, providing that no senator could receive an assignment to a second major committee until all senators had received consideration for a major committee assignment.

judicial review   Power of the courts to declare actions of the legislative and executive branches invalid or unconstitutional. The Supreme Court asserted this power in *Marbury* v. *Madison*.

Kitchen Cabinet   An informal group of advisers to whom the president turns for counsel and guidance. Members of the official cabinet may or may not also be members of the Kitchen Cabinet.

laissez-faire   An economic theory first advanced by Adam Smith, it calls for a "hands off" policy by government toward the economy, in an effort to leave business enterprises free to act in their own self-interest.

legiscide   The diminution of congressional power through the enactment of statutes granting virtually unlimited discretion to the executive branch.

legislative clearance   The power given to the president to require all agencies of the executive branch to submit to him through the budget director all requests for new legislation along with estimates of their budgetary needs.

legislative intent   The supposed real meaning of a statute as it can be interpreted from the legislative history of the bill.

legislative supremacy   The preeminent position assigned to the Congress by the Constitution.

legislative veto   A provision in a statute permitting Congress (or a congressional committee) to review and approve actions undertaken by the executive under authority of the statute. Although the U.S. Supreme Court held the legislative veto unconstitutional in the 1983 case of *Immigration and Naturalization Service* v. *Chadha*, Congress continues to enact legislation incorporating such a veto.

legitimacy   Popular acceptance of a government and its decisions.

liberal   A liberal today generally supports political and social reform; extensive governmental intervention in the economy; the expansion of federal social services; more vigorous efforts on behalf of the poor, minorities, and women; and greater concern for consumers and the environment.

license   Permission to engage in some activity that is otherwise illegal, such as hunting or practicing medicine. Synonymous with franchise, permit, certificate of convenience and necessity.

line agency   Department, bureau, or other unit of administration whose primary mission requires it to deal directly with the public; contrast with staff or overhead agency.

lobbying   Strategy by which organized interests seek to influence the passage of legislation by exerting direct pressure on members of the legislature.

logrolling   A legislative practice wherein reciprocal agreements are made between legislators, usually in voting for or against a bill. In contrast to bargaining, parties to logrolling have nothing in common but their desire to exchange support.

macroeconomic techniques   Economic policies designed to control the economy through taxing and spending (fiscal policy) and manipulation of the supply of money and credit (monetary policy).

majority leader   The elected leader of the party holding a majority of the seats in the House of Representatives or in the Senate. In the House, the majority leader is subordinate in the party hierarchy to the Speaker.

majority rule   Rule by at least one vote more than half of those voting.

majority system   A type of electoral system in which, to win a seat in the parliament or other representative body, a candidate must receive a majority of all the votes cast in the relevant district.

marketplace of ideas   The public forum in which beliefs and ideas are exchanged and compete.

Marxism   The system of thought developed by Karl Marx, it is predicated upon a history of class struggle between those who control production and distribution (the owners) and the workers, culminating in the overthrow of the owners, the redistribution of wealth and power, and the "withering away of the state."

Medicaid   A federally financed, state-operated program for medical services to low-income people. Eligibility tied largely to AFDC.

Medicare   National health insurance for the elderly and for the disabled.

military-industrial complex   A concept coined by President Eisenhower in his farewell address, in which he was referring to the threats to American democracy that may arise from too close a friendship between major corporations in the defense industry and the Pentagon. This is one example of the larger political phenomenon of the "iron triangle."

minority leader   The elected leader of the party holding less than a majority of the seats in the House or Senate.

Miranda rule   Principles developed by the Supreme Court in the 1966 case of *Miranda* v. *Arizona* requiring that persons under arrest be informed of their legal rights, including their right to counsel, prior to police interrogation.

monetary techniques   Efforts to regulate the economy through manipulation of the supply of money and credit. America's most powerful institution in the area of monetary policy is the Federal Reserve Board.

monopoly   The existence of a single firm in a market that divides all the goods and services of that market. Absence of competition.

multilateral treaty   A treaty among more than two nations.

multiple-member constituency   Electorate that selects all candidates at large from the whole district; each voter is given the number of votes equivalent to the number of seats to be filled.

multiple-member district   See *multiple-member constituency*.

multiplier effect   A fiscal policy permitting member banks to borrow money from the Federal Reserve System. Member banks put a certain percentage of this loan, the reserve requirement, into reserves, and make the remainder available for credit to customers. As this process continues, as long as each loan becomes a deposit in a bank within the system, the original loan from the Fed is multiplied dramatically. The Fed profoundly influences the economy by raising or lowering the reserve requirement.

Napoleonic role   Strategy pursued by a powerful nation to prevent aggressive actions against themselves by improving the internal state of affairs of a particular country, even if this means encouraging revolution in that country. Based on the assumption that countries with comparable political systems will never go to war against each other.

nationalism   The widely held belief that the people who occupy the same territory have something in common, that the nation is a single community.

nationalization   Government acquisition of a private enterprise that will then be operated as a government agency. Can take place either by confiscation or by eminent domain.

national supremacy   A principle, rooted in Article VI of the Constitution, which asserts that national law is superior to all other law.

nation-state   A political entity consisting of a people with some common cultural experience (nation) who also share a common political authority (state), recognized by other sovereignties (nation-states).

necessary and proper clause   Article I, Section

8, of the Constitution, it enumerates the powers of Congress and provides Congress with the authority to make all laws "necessary and proper" to carry them out; also referred to as the "elastic clause."

nomination The process through which political parties select their candidates for election to public office.

nuclear freeze A popular policy in the early 1980s to stop the testing, production, and deployment of nuclear weapons, leaving all sides with whatever capacity they had at the moment of the freeze. This became less attractive after the success of disarmament negotiations between President Reagan and Premier Gorbachev.

oligarchy A form of government in which a small group of landowners, military officers, or wealthy merchants controls most of the governing decisions.

oligopoly The existence of two or more competing firms in a given market, where price competition is usually avoided because they know that they would all lose from such competition. Rather, competition is usually through other forms, such as advertising, innovation, and obsolescence.

open market operations A Federal Open Market Committee of the Fed buys and sells government securities, etc., to help finance government operations and to loosen or tighten the total amount of credit circulating in the economy.

open primary A primary election in which the voter can wait until the day of the primary to choose which party to enroll in to select candidates for the general election: see *closed primary.*

ordinance The legislative act of a local legislature or municipal commission. Puts the force of law under city charter but is a lower order of law than a statute of the national or state legislature.

overhead agency A department, bureau, or other unit of administration whose primary mission is to regulate the activities of other agencies; it generally has no direct authority over the public. Contrast with line or auxiliary agency.

oversight The effort by Congress, through hearings, investigations and other techniques, to exercise control over the activities of executive agencies.

parity (farm) Price of selected farm products, partially guaranteed by government purchases and acreage allotments, to help farmers maintain purchasing power equal to a previous base period of good years.

partisanship Loyalty to a particular political party.

party vote A roll-call vote in the House or Senate in which at least 90 percent of the members of one party take a particular position and are opposed by at least 90 percent of the members of the other party. Party votes are rare today, although they were fairly common in the nineteenth century.

patriotism Love of one's country; loyalty to one's country.

patronage The resources available to higher officials, usually opportunities to make partisan appointments to offices and to confer grants, licenses, or special favors to supporters.

per curiam Decision by an appellate court, without a written opinion, that refuses to review the decision of a lower court; amounts to a reaffirmation of the lower court's opinion.

petition Right granted by the First Amendment to citizens to inform representatives of their opinions and to make pleas before government agencies.

plaintiff The individual or organization who brings a complaint in court.

plebiscite A direct vote by the electorate on an issue presented to them by a government.

pluralism The theory that all interests are and should be free to compete for influence in the government. The outcome of this competition is compromise and moderation.

pluralist politics Politics in which political elites actively compete for leadership, voters choose from among these elites, and new elites can emerge in quest of leadership.

plurality rule Victory to the individual who gets the most votes in an election, not necessarily a majority of votes cast.

police power Power reserved to the state to

regulate the health, safety, and morals of its citizens.

policy of redistribution An objective of the graduated income tax—to raise revenue in such a way as to reduce the disparities of wealth between the lowest and the highest income brackets.

political socialization Induction of individuals into the political culture; learning how to accept authority; learning what is legitimate and what is not.

polity A society with an organized government; the "political system."

poll tax A state-imposed tax upon the voters as a prerequisite to registration, it was rendered unconstitutional in national elections by the Twenty-fourth Amendment and in state elections by the Supreme Court in 1966.

populism A late 1870s political and social movement of western and southern farmers that protested eastern business interests.

pork-barrel legislation Appropriations made by legislative bodies for local projects that are often not needed but that are created so that local representatives can carry their home district in the next election.

positive law Law made in and by legislatures self-consciously to fit an occasion; contrast with divine law, natural law, judge-made law.

power elite The group that is said to make the most important decisions in a particular community.

power-without-diplomacy Post-World War II foreign policy in which the goal was to use American power to create an international structure that could be run with a minimum of regular diplomatic involvement.

precedents Prior cases whose principles are used by judges as the bases for their decisions in present cases.

preferential primary Primary election in which the elected delegates to a convention are instructed, but not bound, to vote specifically for the presidential candidate preferred by the voters on a separate part of the ballot.

prior restraint An effort by a governmental agency to block the publication of material it deems libelous or harmful in some other way. In the United States, the courts forbid prior restraint except under the most extraordinary circumstances; censorship.

private bill A proposal in Congress to provide a specific person with some kind of relief, such as a special exemption from immigration quotas.

private law A system of jurisprudence designed to settle disputes between citizens who prefer the courts to the use of personal force.

privileges and immunities clause Article IV of the Constitution, it provides that the citizens of any one state are guaranteed the "privileges and immunities" of every other state, as though they were citizens of that state.

probability sampling A method used by pollsters to select a sample in which every individual in the population has a known (usually equal) probability of being selected as a respondent so that the correct weight can be given to all segments of the population.

procedural due process The Supreme Court's efforts to forbid any procedure that shocks the conscience or that makes impossible a fair judicial system. See *due process.*

progressive/regressive taxes A judgment made by students of taxation about whether a particular tax hits the upper brackets more heavily (progressive) or the lower brackets (regressive) more heavily.

promotional agencies See *clientele agencies.*

promotional techniques A technique of control that encourages people to do something they might not otherwise do, or continue an action or behavior. There are three types; subsidies, contracts, and licenses.

proportional representation A multiple-member district system that allows each political party representation in proportion to its percentage of the vote.

public assistance program A noncontributory social program providing assistance for the aged, poor, or disabled. Major examples include Aid to Families with Dependent Children (AFDC), and Supplemental Security Income (SSI).

public corporation An agency set up by a government but permitted to finance its own operations by charging for its services or by selling bonds.

public law   Cases in private law, civil law, or criminal law in which one party to the dispute argues that a license is unfair, a law is inequitable or unconstitutional, or an agency has acted unfairly, violated a procedure, or gone beyond its jurisdiction.

public policy   A governmental law, rule, statute, or edict that expresses the government's goals and provides for rewards and punishments to promote their attainment.

quorum   The minimum number of members of a deliberative body who must be present in order to conduct business.

quota sampling   A type of sampling of public opinion which is used by most commercial polls. Respondents are selected whose characteristics closely match those of the general population along several significant dimensions, such as geographic region, sex, age, and race.

random sample polling   Polls in which respondents are chosen mathematically, at random, with every effort made to avoid bias in the construction of the sample.

rate regulation   Power delegated by the legislature to any regulatory agencies to set ceilings on how much railroads and other "common carriers" can charge for their services, based upon the best available estimates of a "fair return" on investments.

realigning eras   Periods during which major groups in the electorate shift their political party affiliations. Realigning eras have often been associated with long-term shifts in partisan control of the government and with major changes in public policy. One of the most important realigning eras was the period of the New Deal in the 1930s when President Franklin Roosevelt led the Democrats to a position of power that they have still not entirely relinquished.

reapportionment   The redrawing of election districts and the redistribution of legislative representatives due to shifts in population.

referendum   The practice of referring a measure proposed or passed by a legislature to the vote of the electorate for approval or rejection.

regulation   A particular use of government power, a "technique of control" in which the government adopts rules imposing restrictions on the conduct of private citizens.

regulation of entry   The purpose of licensing; permission to enter a trade or market. For example, medical licensing boards determine whether a person holding the MD degree can engage in the practice of medicine, or the FCC decides to permit a radio station to commence operation.

regulatory agencies   Departments, bureaus, or independent agencies whose primary mission is to eliminate or restrict certain behaviors defined as being evil in themselves or evil in their consequences.

regulatory tax   A tax whose primary purpose is not to raise revenue but to influence conduct—e.g., a heavy tax on gasoline to discourage recreational driving.

regulatory techniques   Techniques that government uses to control the conduct of the people.

redistribution   A particular use of government power, a "technique of control" in which the government adopts rules defining categories of individuals for purposes of conferring benefits or taking income or property.

representative democracy   A system of government that provides the populace with the opportunity to make the government responsive to its views through the selection of representatives, who, in turn, play a significant role in governmental decision making.

reserve requirement   The amount of liquid assets and ready cash that banks are required to hold to meet depositors' demands for their money. Ratio revolves above and below 20 percent of all deposits, with the rest being available for new loans.

revenue acts   Acts of Congress providing the means of raising the revenues needed by the government. The Constitution requires that all such bills originate in the House.

revenue sharing   A scheme to allocate national resources to the states according to a population and income formula.

revolution A complete or drastic change of government and the rules by which government is conducted.

revolutionary politics A form of politics that rejects the existing system of government entirely and attempts to replace it with a different organizational structure and a different ruling group.

right of rebuttal A Federal Communications Commission regulation giving individuals the right to have the opportunity to respond to personal attacks made on a radio or TV broadcast.

roll-call vote Each legislator's yes or no vote is recorded as the clerk calls the names of the members alphabetically.

satellites Nation-states that are militarily, economically, and politically subordinate to other nations.

second-strike capacity The number and power of nuclear weapons, plus delivery, that would be available after a first strike to wipe out the attacker. This is a measure of the "deterrent effect" of nuclear power.

select committee A legislative committee established for a limited period of time and for a special purpose; not a standing committee.

selective polling A sample drawn deliberately to reconstruct meaningful distributions of an entire constituency; not a random sample.

seniority Priority or status ranking given to an individual on the basis of length of continuous service in an organization.

separation of powers The division of governmental power among several institutions that must cooperate in decision making.

service agencies Departments or other bureaus whose primary mission is to promote the interests of dependent persons or to deal with their problems.

single-member constituency An electorate that is allowed to elect only one representative from each district; the normal method of representation in the United States.

single-member district See *single-member constituency.*

sociological representation A type of representation in which representatives have the same racial, ethnic, religious, or educational backgrounds as their constituents. It is based on the principle that if two individuals are similar in background, character, interests, and perspectives, then one could correctly represent the other's views.

sovereignty Supreme and independent political authority.

Speaker of the House The chief presiding officer of the House of Representatives. The Speaker is elected at the beginning of every Congress on a straight party vote. The Speaker is the most important party and House leader, and can influence the legislative agenda, the fate of individual pieces of legislation, and members' positions within the House.

special counsel A prosecutor appointed under the terms of the Ethics in Government Act to investigate criminal misconduct by members of the executive branch.

split-ticket voting The practice of casting ballots for the candidates of at least two different political parties in the same election. Voters who support only one party's candidates are said to vote a straight party ticket.

staff agency An agency responsible for maintaining the bureaucracy, with responsibilities such as purchasing, budgeting, personnel management, planning.

standing The right of an individual or organization to initiate a court case.

standing committee A regular legislative committee that considers legislation within its designated subject area; the basic unit of deliberation in the House and Senate.

stare decisis Literally "let the decision stand." A previous decision by a court applies as a precedent in similar cases until that decision is overruled.

state A community that claims the monopoly of legitimate use of physical force within a given territory; the ultimate political authority; sovereign.

statute A law enacted by a state legislature or by Congress.

Strategic Defense Initiative (SDI, or Star Wars) A plan developed by the Reagan administration to construct a sophisticated system that would protect the United States against nuclear missile attack. Opponents forced the Reagan and Bush administrations substantially to scale back the initial, extremely expensive and ambitious plan.

subsidies Governmental grants of cash or other valuable commodities such as land to individuals or organizations. Subsidies can be used to promote activities desired by the government, to reward political support, or to buy off political opposition.

substantive due process A judicial doctrine used by the appellate courts, primarily before 1937, to strike down economic legislation the courts felt was arbitrary or unreasonable.

supremacy clause Article VI of the Constitution, which states that laws passed by the national government and all treaties are the supreme laws of the land and superior to all laws adopted by any state or any subdivision.

suffrage The right to vote; see also *franchise*.

Supplemental Security Income (SSI) A program providing a minimum monthly income to people who pass a "needs test" and who are sixty-five years or older, blind, or disabled. Financed from general revenues rather than from Social Security Contributions.

systematic sampling A method used in probability sampling to ensure that every individual in the population has a known probability of being chosen as a respondent. For example, by choosing every ninth name from a list.

Three-Fifths Compromise Agreement reached at the Constitutional Convention of 1787 which stipulated that for purposes of the apportionment of congressional seats, every slave would be counted as three-fifths of a person.

ticket balancing Strategy of party leaders to nominate candidates from each of the major ethnic, racial, and religious affiliations.

ticket splitting The practice of voting for candidates of different parties on the same ballot.

totalitarian government A system of rule in which the government recognizes no formal limits on its power and seeks to absorb or eliminate other social institutions that might challenge it.

treaty A formal agreement between sovereign nations to create or restrict rights and responsibilities. In the U.S. all treaties must be approved by a two-thirds vote in the Senate. See also *executive agreement.*

trust A method of avoiding competition in which two or more companies assign voting rights or actual stock to a common board of trustees to control marketing and other policies. A popular misuse of the term is to describe a single large corporation that dominates a particular market and pursues monopolistic pricing policies.

turnout The percentage of eligible individuals who actually vote.

tyranny Oppressive and unjust government that employs cruel and unjust use of power and authority.

uncontrollables A term applied to budgetary items that are beyond the control of budgetary committees and can only be controlled by substantive legislative action by Congress itself. Some uncontrollables are actually beyond the power of the Congress, because the terms of payment are set in contracts, such as interest on the debt.

unilateralism A foreign policy that seeks to avoid international alliances, entanglements, and permanent commitments in favor of independence, neutrality, and freedom of action.

urban renewal An important urban policy of the national government during the 1950s in which large categories of grants-in-aid were made available to cities on condition that they develop plans for removing slums and for restoring property to more valuable uses, including new housing as well as new structures for business and civic affairs.

vested interests Fixed or established interests; interests not varying with changing conditions; privileges respected or accepted by others.

veto The president's constitutional power to turn down acts of Congress. A presidential veto may be overridden by a two-thirds vote of each house of Congress.

whip system   Primarily a communications network in each house of Congress, whips take polls of the membership in order to learn their intentions on specific legislative issues and to assist the majority and minority leaders in various tasks.

withholding tax   Deduction by employers of a specified percentage of all wages, paid to the government in advance to guarantee payment of taxes.

writ of *certiorari*   A decision concurred in by at least four of the nine Supreme Court justices to review a decision of a lower court; from the Latin "to make more certain."

GLOSSARY OF COURT CASES

Abrams v. *United States* (1919) The Supreme Court upheld the convictions of five Bolshevik sympathizers under the Espionage Act which made it an offense to intend interference in the war with Germany. Although the defendants actually opposed American intervention in the Russian Revolution, the Court imputed to them the knowledge that their actions would necessarily inpede the war effort against Germany.

Argersinger v. *Hamlin* (1972) The Court extended the right to counsel for those accused of misdemeanors.

Arizona v. *Fulminante* (1991) A bare majority of the Rehnquist Court held that coerced confessions may be used at trial if it could be shown that other evidence was also used to support a guilty verdict. But, the Court also held that in this case, the admission of a coerced confession was not "harmless error" and remanded the case for a new trial.

Associated Press v. *National Labor Relations Board* (1937) A case resulting from New Deal legislation in which the Court ceased trying to restrict the national government from regulating local conditions. Here, the Court held that the labor relations of newspapers and press associations were also subject to the Labor Relations Act.

Baker v. *Carr* (1962) The Court held that the issue of malapportionment of election districts raised a justiciable claim under the Equal Protection Clause of the Fourteenth Amendment. The effect of the case was to force the reapportionment of nearly all federal, state, and local election districts nationwide.

Barron v. *Baltimore* (1833) This was one of the most significant cases ever handed down by the Court. Chief Justice John Marshall confirmed the concept of "dual citizenship," in that, each American is separately a citizen of the national government and of the state government. This meant that the Bill of Rights applied only nationally, and not to state or local laws. The consequences of this ruling were felt well into the twentieth century.

Benton v. *Maryland* (1969) The Court ruled that double jeopardy was a right incorporated in the Fourteenth Amendment as a restriction on the states.

Berkey Photo Inc. v. *Eastman Kodak Co.* (1979) In a reminder of the limited place of juries within the judicial system, an appellate judge upheld a trial judge's decision to reduce a $120 million jury verdict award to $87 million, and further "remitted" the award to $900,000.

Berman v. *Parker* (1954) In this case, which involved a government effort to clear slum properties in the nation's capital to make way for new housing, the Court held that the government had a very broad constitutional sanction, under the concept of "eminent domain," to declare that the public interest required the taking of land from a private owner.

Board of Education of Oklahoma City **v.** *Dowell* **(1991)** This case, which restricted the use of court-ordered busing to achieve school integration, gave an early indication of the attitude of the new Bush Court.

Bolling **v.** *Sharpe* **(1954)** This case, which did not directly involve the Fourteenth Amendment because the District of Columbia is not a state, confronted the Court on the grounds that segregation is inherently unequal. Its victory in effect was "incorporation in reverse," with equal protection moving from the Fourteenth Amendment to become part of the Bill of Rights.

Bowers **v.** *Hardwick* **(1986)** In this case, the Supreme Court upheld a Georgia statute prohibiting sodomy, by ruling that the constitutional right of privacy protected the traditional family unit but not the conduct between homosexuals when that conduct offended "traditional Judeo-Christian values."

Bowsher **v.** *Synar* **(1986)** This was the second of two cases since 1937 in which the Court invalidated an act of Congress on constitutional grounds. In this case, the Court struck down the Gramm-Rudman Act mandating a balanced federal budget, ruling that it was unconstitutional to grant the comptroller general "executive" powers.

Brandenburg **v.** *Ohio* **(1969)** The Court overturned an Ohio statute forbidding any person from urging criminal acts as a means of inducing political reform or from joining any association that advocated such activities, on the grounds that the statute punished "mere advocacy" and therefore violated the free speech provisions of the federal Constitution.

Brown **v.** *Allen* **(1952)** This case demonstrates how extremely difficult it is for state legislatures or Congress to summon up the majorities necessary to react against a Supreme Court decision. Justice Robert Jackson commented that "The Court is not final because it is infallible; the Court is infallible because it is final."

Brown **v.** *Board of Education of Topeka, Kansas* **(1954)** The Supreme Court struck down the "separate but equal" doctrine as fundamentally unequal. This case eliminated state power to use race as a criterion of discrimination in law and

provided the national government with the power to intervene by exercising strict regulatory policies against discriminatory actions.

Brown **v.** *Board of Education of Topeka, Kansas* **(*Brown II*) (1955)** One year after *Brown* the Court issued a mandate for state and local boards to proceed "with all deliberate speed" to desegregate schools.

Buckley **v.** *Valeo* **(1976)** The Supreme Court limited congressional attempts to regulate campaign financing by declaring unconstitutional any absolute limits on the freedom of individuals to spend their own money on campaigns.

Cable Network News **v.** *Noriega* **(1990)** The doctrine of "no prior restraint" was weakened when the Supreme Court held that the Cable Network News could be restrained from broadcasting supposedly illegally obtained tapes of conversations between former Panamanian leader Manuel Noriega and his lawyer until the trial court had listened to the tapes and had determined whether such a broadcast would violate Noriega's right to a fair trial.

Chicago, Burlington, and Quincy Railroad Company **v.** *Chicago* **(1897)** This case effectively overruled *Barron* by affirming that the due process clause of the Fourteenth Amendment did prohibit states from taking property for a public use without just compensation.

Citizens to Preserve Overton Park, Inc. **v.** *Volpe* **(1971)** Beginning with the Supreme Court's decision in this case, the federal courts allowed countless challenges to federal agency actions under the National Environmental Policy Act (NEPA), brought by public interest groups asserting that the agencies had failed to consider the adverse effects of their actions upon the environment as required by NEPA.

City of Richmond **v.** *J. A. Croson Co.* **(1989)** In this case the Supreme Court held that minority set-aside programs would have to redress specific instances of identified discrimination in order to avoid violating the rights of whites.

The Civil Rights Cases **(1883)** The Court struck down the Civil Rights Act of 1875, which attempted to protect blacks from discriminatory treatment by proprietors of public facilities. It ruled that the Fourteenth Amendment applied only to discriminatory actions by state officials and did not apply to discrimination against blacks by private individuals.

Coleman **v.** *Thompson* **(1991)**   In this case, the Supreme Court cut away further at the rights of an accused in holding that a defendant does not have a constitutional right to counsel on appeal from a state habeas trial court judgement.

Cooper **v.** *Aaron* **(1958)**   In this historic case, the Supreme Court required that Little Rock, Arkansas, desegregate its public schools by immediately complying with a lower court's order, and warned that it is "emphatically the province and duty of the judicial department to say what the law is."

Dartmouth College **v.** *Woodward* **(1819)**   In this case the Supreme Court held that one who converts the property of another in good faith is entitled to an allowance for those improvements.

Doe **v.** *Bolton* **(1973)**   Decided along with *Roe*, this case extended the decision in *Roe* by striking down state requirements that abortions be performed in licensed hospitals; that abortions be approved beforehand by a hospital committee; and that two physicians concur in the abortion decision.

Dred Scott **v.** *Sandford* **(1857)**   This was the infamous case in which Chief Justice Roger Taney wrote that blacks were not citizens; that they "were never thought of or spoken of except as property." In a vain attempt to settle the slavery issue, which was threatening to tear the country apart, the Court went further to rule that the Missouri Compromise was unconstitutional, and Congress could not bar slavery from the territories. This ruling probably hastened the onset of the Civil War.

Duke Power Co. **v.** *Carolina Environmental Study* **(1978)**   The Supreme Court dealt anti-nuclear power activists a significant blow by upholding a federal statute limiting liability for damages accruing from nuclear power plant accidents.

Duncan **v.** *Louisiana* **(1968)**   The Court established the right to trial by jury in state criminal cases where the accused faces a serious charge and sentencing.

Edwards **v.** *California* **(1941)**   In an important case arising out of the Depression, the Court struck down a California law prohibiting any person from knowingly bringing nonresident indigents into the state, ruling that the measure had been designed in part to limit interstate competition for jobs.

Eisenstadt **v.** *Baird* **(1972)**   The Court struck down state laws prohibiting the use of contraceptives by unmarried persons.

Engel **v.** *Vitale* **(1962)**   In interpreting the separation of church and state doctrine, the Court ruled that organized prayer in the public schools was unconstitutional.

Escobedo **v.** *Illinois* **(1964)**   The Supreme Court expanded the rights of an accused in this case by giving suspects the right to remain silent and the right to have counsel present during questioning.

Frontiero **v.** *Richardson* **(1973)**   The Court rendered an important decision relating to the economic status of women when it held that the armed services could not deny married women fringe benefits, such as housing allowances and health care, that were automatically granted to married men.

Fullilove **v.** *Klutznick* **(1980)**   The Court upheld the Public Works Employment Act of 1977, which required that at least 10 percent of federal funds for federal public works contracts be awarded to minority-owned businesses to remedy past discriminatory barriers, even if there was no evidence of deliberate discrimination by individual contractors.

Garcia **v.** *San Antonio Metropolitan Transit Authority* **(1985)**   The question of whether the national government had the right to regulate state and local businesses was again raised in this case. The Court ruled that the national government had the right to apply minimum-wage and overtime standards to state and local government employees. This case overturned *National League of Cities* v. *Usery* (1976).

G. E. **v.** *Gilbert* **(1976)**   In this case, the Court found no legislative requirement that pregnancy leaves be treated identically to other disability leaves. Congress effectively reversed the Court's decision by amending Title VII of the 1964 Civil Rights Act to require employers to provide benefits for pregnancy leaves similar to those for other temporary disability leaves.

Gibbons v. *Ogden* (1824)   An early major case establishing the supremacy of the national government in all matters affecting interstate commerce, in which John Marshall broadly defined what Article I, Section 8, meant by "commerce among the several states." He affirmed that the federal government alone could regulate trade, travel, and navigation between the states.

Gideon v. *Wainwright* (1963)   The Warren Court overruled an earlier case (*Betts* 1942) and established that "any person haled into court, who is too poor to have a lawyer, cannot be assured a fair trial unless counsel is provided for him."

Gitlow v. *New York* (1925)   The Court ruled that the freedom of speech is "among the fundamental personal rights and 'liberties' protected by the due process clause of the Fourteenth Amendment from impairment by the states."

Griffin v. *Prince Edward County School Board* (1964)   The Supreme Court forced all the schools in Prince Edward County to reopen after they had been closed for five years to avoid desegregation.

Griggs v. *Duke Power Company* (1971)   The Court held that although the statistical evidence did not prove intentional discrimination, and although the hiring requirements were race-neutral in appearance, their effects were sufficient to shift the burden of justification to the employer to show that his requirements were a "business necessity" that bore "a demonstrable relationship to successful performance."

Griswold v. *Connecticut* (1965)   The Court ruled that the right to privacy included the right to marital privacy and struck down state laws restricting married persons' use of contraceptives and the circulation of birth control information.

Hague v. *Committee for Industrial Organization* (CIO) (1939)   The Court extended the concept of a public forum to include public streets and meeting halls and incorporated the freedom of assembly into the list of rights held to be fundamental and therefore binding on the states as well as on the national government.

Hammer v. *Dagenhart* (1918)   The Court ruled unconstitutional the 1916 laws that banned goods made by children from interstate commerce. This was overturned in 1941 in *U. S.* v. *Darby.*

Harris v. *New York* (1971)   In a ruling that limited the *Miranda* ruling, the Burger Court held that although a statement was inadmissible because of failure to give the Miranda warning, it could be used to impeach the defendant's testimony if the defendant took the stand.

Herring v. *State* (1904)   In this perjury case, the Georgia Supreme Court declared that if the Fourth Amendment right to privacy means anything, it means that, "before Georgia can prosecute its citizens for making choices about the most intimate aspects of their lives, it must do more than assert that the choice they have made is an 'abominable crime not fit to be named among Christians.'"

Hodgson v. *Minnesota* (1990)   In this case the Supreme Court upheld a Minnesota statute requiring parental notification before an abortion could be performed on a woman under the age of eighteen.

Humphrey's Executor v. *United States* (1935)   The Court in this case made a distinction between "purely executive" officials—whom the president could remove at his discretion—and officials with "quasi-judicial and quasi-legislative" duties—who could be removed only for reasons specified by Congress. This decision limited the president's removal powers.

Immigration and Naturalization Services (INS) v. *Chada* (1983)   This was the first of two cases since 1937 in which the Court invalidated an act of Congress on constitutional grounds. In this case the Court declared the legislative veto unconstitutional.

In re Agent Orange Product Liability Litigation (1983)   In this case, a federal judge in New York certified Vietnam War veterans as a class with standing to sue a manufacturer of herbicides for damages allegedly incurred from exposure to the defendants' product while they were in Vietnam.

***In re Debs* (1895)**   The Supreme Court upheld President Cleveland's power to obtain an injunction against the Pullman Strike, even in the absence of any statutory warrant, on the grounds that "the wrongs complained of by the President were such . . . as affect the public at large."

***In re Neagle* (1890)**   The Supreme Court held that the protection of a federal judge was a reasonable extension of the president's constitutional power to "take care that the laws be faithfully executed."

***In re Oliver* (1948)**   The Court incorporated the right to a public trial in the Fourteenth Amendment as a restriction on the states.

***Katz* v. *United States* (1967)**   In repudiation of the *Olmstead* doctrine, the Supreme Court declared that the Fourth Amendment "protects people, not places," and held that electronic surveillance conducted outside the judicial process, whether or not it involves trespass, is *per se* unreasonable.

***Katzenbach* v. *McClung* (1964)**   The Court gave an extremely broad definition to "interstate commerce" so as to allow Congress the constitutional authority to cover discrimination by virtually any local employer. Although the Court agreed that this case involved a strictly intrastate restaurant, they found a sufficient connection to interstate commerce resulting from the restaurant's acquisition of food and supplies so as to hold that racial discrimination at such an establishment would "impose commercial burdens of national magnitude upon interstate commerce."

***Kirchberg* v. *Fenesta* (1973)**   In a continuing effort to abolish gender lines in the law, the court invalidated Louisiana's "head and master" rule that gave married men the sole right to dispose of property held jointly by both spouses.

***Lee* v. *Weisman* (1992)**   A bare majority of the court ruled that prayers during a pulic school graduation cermony amounted to a "state-sponsored and state-directed religious exercise" in violation of the First Amendment.

***Lochner* v. *New York* (1905)**   Seeking to protect business from government regulation, the court invalidated a New York state law regulating the sanitary conditions and hours of labor of bakers on the gorounds that the law interfered with liberty of contract.

***Loving* v. *Virginia* (1967)**   The Court invalidated a Virginia statute prohibiting interracial marriages, on the grounds that the statute violated guarantees of due process and equal protection contained in the Fourteenth Amendment of the Constitution.

***Lucas* v. *South Carolina Coastal Council* (1992)**   The Court remanded this case to the state courts to determine whether the owner of a beachfront property had suffered economic loss by a zoning restriction aimed at preserving the beach and sand dunes. The Court's ruling recognized that a property owner is entitled to just compensation when a government's regulations diminish the value of private property, just as in an eminent domain proceeding.

***Lujan* v. *Defenders of Wildlife* (1992)**   The Court restricted the concept of standing by requiring that a party bringing suit against a government policy show that the policy is likely to cause them direct and imminent injury.

***McGrain* v. *Dougherty* (1927)**   The Court unanimously affirmed Congress's power to compel a private individual to testify in its investigations and hearings, but it also required that the congressional committee show that its questions served a legislative purpose before compelling a witness to answer.

***Malloy* v. *Hogan* (1964)**   The Court ruled that the right of a person to remain silent and not incriminate himself applied to the states as well as to the federal government. This decision incorporated the Fifth Amendment into the Fourteenth Amendment.

***Mapp* v. *Ohio* (1961)**   The Court held that evidence obtained in violation of the Fourth Amedment ban on unreasonable searches and seizures would be excluded from trial.

***Marbury* v. *Madison* (1803)**   This was the landmark case in which Chief Justice Marshall established that the Court had the right to rule on the constitutionality of federal and state laws, although judicial review was not explicitly granted by the Constitution.

Martin v. *Hunter's Lessee* (1816) In this case, the Supreme Cout confirmed its congressionally conferred power to review and reverse state constitutions and laws whenever they are clearly in conflict with the U.S. Constitution, federal laws, or treaties.

Martin v. *Wilks* (1989) The Supreme Court further eased the way for employers to prefer white males when it held that any affirmative action program already approved by federal courts could be subsequently challenged by white males who alleged that the program discriminated against them.

Masson v. *New Yorker* (1991) The Supreme Court held that a successful libel claim must prove that an allegedly libelous author and/or publisher acted with requisite knowledge of falsity or reckless disregard as to truth or falsity in publishing the allegedly libelous material.

McCulloch v. *Maryland* (1819) This was the first and most important case favoring national control of the economy over state control. In his ruling, John Marshall established the "implied powers" doctrine enabling Congress to use the "necessary and proper" clause of Article I, Section 8 to interpret its delegated powers. This case also concluded that, when state law and federal law were in conflict, national law took precedence.

Metro Broadcasting v. *FCC* (1990) In one of its few efforts to continue some affirmative action programs, the Rehnquist Court upheld two federal programs aimed at increasing minority ownership of broadcast licenses on the grounds that they serve the important governmental objective of broadcast diversity, and they are substantially related to the achievement of that objective.

Milliken v. *Bradley* (1974) The Supreme Court severely restricted the *Swann* ruling when it determined in this case that only cities found guilty of deliberate and *de jure* segregation (segregation in law) would have to desegregate their schools. This ruling exempted most northern states and cities from busing because school segregation in northern cities is generally *de facto* segregation (segregation in fact) that follows

from segregated housing and other forms of private discrimination.

Morrison v. *Olson* (1988) The Supreme Court upheld the constitutionality of the special prosecutor law, which allows the attorney general to recommend that a panel of federal judges appoint an independent counsel to investigate alleged wrongdoing by officials of the executive branch.

Muskrat v. *United States* (1911) The Court held that the case before it must be a real controversy, with two adversarial parties; if one side is a straw man, the adversarial system cannot work.

Myers v. *United States* (1926) The Court upheld a broad interpretation of the president's power to remove executive officers whom he had appointed, despite restrictions imposed by Congress. (Later limited by *Humphrey's* 1935).

NAACP v. *Alabama ex rel. Patterson* (1958) The Court recognized the right to "privacy in one's association" in its ruling protecting the NAACP from the state of Alabama using its membership list.

NAACP v. *Button* (1963) The state of Virginia sued the NAACP in an attempt to restrict or eliminate its efforts to influence the pattern of cases by soliciting legal business in which they were not parties and had no pecuniary right or liability. The Supreme Court held that this strategy was protected by the First and Fourteenth Amendments, just as other forms of speech and petition are protected.

National Labor Relations Board v. *Jones & Laughlin Steel Corporation* (1937) In a case involving New Deal legislation, the Court reversed its earlier rulings on "interstate commerce" and redefined it to permit the national government to regulate local economic and social conditions.

National League of Cities v. *Usery* (1976) Although in this case the Court invalidated a congressional act applying wage and hour regulations to state and local governments, it reversed its decision nine years later in *Garcia* v. *San Antonio Metropolitan Transit Authority* (1985).

Near v. *Minnesota* (1931) In this landmark case, which established the doctrine of "no prior restraint," the Court held that, except under extraordinary circumstances, the First Amendment prohibits government agencies from seeking to prevent newspapers or magazines from printing whatever they wish.

New York Times **v.** *Sullivan* **(1964)** In this case, the Supreme Court held that to be deemed libelous, a story about a public official not only had to be untrue, but had to result from "actual malice" or "reckless disregard" for the truth. In practice, this standard of proof is nearly impossible to reach.

New York Times **v.** *United States* **(1971)** In this case, the so-called *Pentagon Papers* case, the Supreme Court ruled that the government could not block publication of secret Defense Department documents that had been furnished to the *New York Times* by a liberal opponent of the Vietnam War who had obtained the documents illegally.

New York **v.** *Quarles* **(1984)** The Supreme Court made a significant cutback in the area of criminal procedure when it ruled that statements obtained in violation of the *Miranda* requirements are admissible when those statements are responses to police questions asked out of concern for public safety.

Nix **v.** *Williams* **(1984)** The Court held in this case that unlawfully obtained evidence is admissible at trial if it ultimately or inevitably would have been discovered by lawful means.

Ohio **v.** *Akron Center for Reproductive Health* **(1990)** The Supreme Court upheld a state law requiring parental notification before an abortion could be performed on a woman under the age of eighteen.

Olmstead **v.** *United States* **(1928)** The Supreme Court first confronted the issue of electronic surveillance in this case, which involved the wiretapping of a gang of rum-runners. The Court concluded that the Fourth Amendment was not applicable, because there had been no trespass of a constitutionally protected area nor a seizure of a physical object.

Palko **v.** *Connecticut* **(1937)** The Court decided that double jeopardy was not a provision of the Bill of Rights protected at the state level. This was not reversed until 1969 in *Benton* v. *Maryland*.

Panama Refining Company **v.** *Ryan* **(1935)** The Court ruled against a section of the National Industrial Recovery Act, a New Deal statute, as being an invalid delegation of legislative power to the executive branch.

Payne **v.** *Tennessee* **(1991)** The Supreme Court overruled some earlier decisions in holding that the Eighth Amendment does not erect a *per se* bar prohibiting a capital sentencing jury from considering "victim impact" evidence relating to the victim's personal characteristics and the emotional impact of the murder on the victim's family, nor does it preclude a prosecutor from arguing such evidence at a capital sentencing hearing.

Penry **v.** *Lynaugh* **(1989)** In this case the Supreme Court eased restrictions on the use of capital punishment by allowing states to execute mentally retarded murderers.

Planned Parenthood of Southeastern Pennsylvania **v.** *Casey* **(1992)** Abandoning *Roe's* assertion of a woman's "fundamental right" to choose abortion, a bare majority of the Court redefined it as a "limited or qualified" right subject to regulation by the states, so long as the states do not impose an "undue burden" on women. Specifically, the Court upheld portions of Pennsylvania's strict abortion law which included the requirement of parental notification for minors and a twenty-four hour waiting period.

Plessy **v.** *Ferguson* **(1896)** The Court, in this now infamous case, held that the Fourteenth Amendment's "equal protection of the laws" was not violated by racial distinction as long as the "separate" facilities were "equal."

Plyler **v.** *Doe* **(1982)** The Supreme Court invalidated on equal-protection grounds a Texas statute that withheld state funds from local school districts for the education of children who were illegal aliens and that further authorized the local school districts to deny enrollment to such children.

Pollock **v.** *Farmers' Loan and Trust Company* **(1895)** In this case involving the unconstitutionality of an income tax of 2 percent on all incomes over $4,000, the Supreme Court declared that any direct tax as such must be apportioned in order to be valid.

Red Lion Broadcasting v. FCC (1969)   In upholding the fairness doctrine in this case, the Court differentiated between the broadcast media and the print media in regards to the First Amendment. The Court ruled that "a license permits broadcasting, but the licensee has no constitutional right to be the one who holds the license or to monopolize a radio frequency to the exclusion of his fellow citizens."

Reed v. Reed (1971)   In this case, which made gender lines in the law illegitimate for the first time, the Supreme Court invalidated an Idaho probate statute that required courts to give preference to males over females as administrators of estates.

Regents of the University of California v. Bakke (1978)   This case addressed the issue of qualification versus minority preference. The Court held that universities could continue to take minority status into consideration because a "diverse student body" contributing to a "robust exchange of ideas" is a "constitutionally permissible goal" on which a race-conscious university admissions program may be predicated.

Roe v. Wade (1973)   This is the famous case that rendered unconstitutional all state laws making abortion a crime, ruling that the states could not interfere in a woman's "right to privacy" and her right to choose to terminate a pregnancy.

Rust v. Sullivan (1991)   In the case, the Court upheld regulations of the Department of Health and Human Services that prohibited the use of Title X family planning funds for abortion counseling, referral, or activities advocating abortion as a method of family planning.

Schechter Poultry Co. v. United States (1935)   The Court declared the National Industrial Recovery Act of 1933 unconstitutional on the grounds that Congress had delegated legislative power to the executive branch without sufficient standards or guidelines for presidential discretion.

Schuttlesworth v. Birmingham Board of Education (1958)   This decision upheld a "pupil placement" plan purporting to assign pupils on various bases, with no mention of race. This case interpreted *Brown* v. *Board of Education* to mean that school districts must stop explicit racial discrimination but were under no obligation to take positive steps to desegregate.

Scott v. Illinois (1979)   The Burger Court narrowed the virtually absolute right of defendants to legal counsel by identifying circumstances under which counsel need not necessarily be present.

Shelley v. Kraemer (1948)   In this case, the Supreme Court ruled against the widespread practice of "restrictive covenants," declaring that although private persons could sign such covenants, they could not be judicially enforced since the Fourteenth Amendment prohibits any organ of the state, including the courts, from denying equal protection of its laws.

Sierra Club v. Morton (1972)   To have standing is to be the proper person to bring suit, and the basic requirement for standing is to show injury to oneself. In this case, the Court expanded the definition of injury from simply personal and/or economic harm to include such values as "aesthetic and environmental well being."

The Slaughterhouse Cases (1873)   The Court ruled that the federal government was under no obligation to protect the "privileges and immunities" of citizens of a particular state against arbitrary action by that state's government. This was similar to the *Barron* case, except it was thought that the Fourteenth Amendment would now incorporate the Bill of Rights, applying it to the states. The Court however ruled that the Fourteenth Amendment was to "protect Negroes as a class" and had nothing to do with individual liberties.

Smith v. Allwright (1944)   The Supreme Court struck down the southern practice of "white primaries," which legally excluded blacks from participation in the nominating process. The Court recognized that primaries could no longer be regarded as the private affairs of parties because parties were an integral aspect of the electoral process, and thus became an "agency of the State" prohibited from discriminating against blacks within the meaning of the Fifteenth Amendment.

Stanford v. Kentucky (1989)   The Supreme Court again eased restrictions on capital punishment by allowing states to execute murderers who were as young as sixteen at the time of the crime.

Stanley v. Georgia **(1969)** In reversing a conviction based on a Georgia statute, the Supreme Court held that mere private possession of obscene materials could not be made a crime even if the actual material itself was unprotected by the First and Fourteenth amendments.

Steward Machine Company v. Davis **(1937)** A case resulting from New Deal legislation in which the Court upheld the Social Security Act of 1935.

Stone v. Powell **(1976)** In this case, the Supreme Court ruled that where the state courts have concluded that an accused's Fourth Amendment rights had not been violated, federal courts should not exercise *habeas corpus* jurisdiction to review those findings.

Swann v. Charlotte-Mecklenberg Board of Education **(1971)** This case involved the most important judicial extension of civil rights in education after 1954. The Court held that state-imposed desegregation could be brought about by "busing," and under certain limited circumstances even racial quotas could be used as the "starting point in shaping a remedy to correct past constitutional violations."

Sweatt v. Painter **(1950)** The Court ruled in favor of a black student who refused to go to the Texas law school for blacks, arguing that it was inferior to the state school for whites. Although the Court still did not confront the "separate but equal" rule in this case, it did question whether any segregated facility could be equal.

TVA v. Hill **(1978)** In a significant case, the Court held that the Endangered Species Act made it an unqualified duty for governmental agencies to refrain from taking actions that would harm threatened or endangered species. Congress amended the act to allow agencies to weigh the costs of protecting a species against the benefits to be gained from proceeding with certain kinds of projects.

United States v. Curtiss-Wright Export Co. **(1936)** In this case the Court held that Congress may delegate a degree of discretion to the president in foreign affairs that might violate the separation of powers if it were in a domestic arena.

United States v. Darby Lumber Company **(1941)** The Court ruled that Congress could set minimum wage and hour requirements under the Fair Labor and Standards Act of 1938. This case invalidated *Hammer v. Dagenhart* (1918).

United States v. Harris **(1971)** Restricting the *Mapp* ruling somewhat, this case ruled that technical violations of search and seizure ought not to be used to free known criminals.

United States v. Leon **(1984)** In a further deterioration of the rights of an accused, the Supreme Court held that evidence obtained in reasonable reliance on a defective search warrant is admissible at trial.

United States v. Nixon **(1974)** The Court declared unconstitutional President Nixon's refusal to surrender subpoenaed tapes as evidence in a criminal prosecution. The Court argued that executive privilege did not extend to data in presidential files or tapes bearing upon criminal prosecution.

United States v. Pink **(1942)** The Court ruled that executive agreements have the same legal status as treaties, despite the fact that they do not require the "advice and consent" of the Senate.

United States v. S.C.R.A.P. **(1973)** In this case, the Court further defined issues of standing by holding that to have standing an individual must be among those injured and must show specific, personal, and substantial harm.

United Steel Workers v. Weber **(1979)** In rejecting the claim of a white employee who had been denied a place in a training program in which half the spots were reserved for black employees, the Supreme Court claimed that Title VII of the Civil Rights Act of 1964 did not apply to affirmative action programs voluntarily established by private companies.

Wabash, St. Louis and Pacific Railway Company v. Illinois **(1886)** The Supreme Court struck down a state law prohibiting rate discrimination by a railroad, arguing that the route of an interstate railroad could not be subdivided into its separate state segments for purposes of regulation. In response to the need for some form of regulation, Congress passed the Interstate Commerce Act of 1887, creating the Interstate Commerce Commission (ICC), the first federal administrative agency.

Wards Cove **v.** *Atonio* **(1989)**   The Court held that the burden of proof of unlawful discrimination should be shifted from the defendant (the employer) to the plaintiff (the person claiming to be the victim of discrimination).

Webster **v.** *Reproductive Health Services* **(1989)** In upholding a Missouri law that restricted the use of public medical facilities for abortion, the Court opened the way for states to again limit the availability of abortions.

West Coast Hotel Company **v.** *Parrish* **(1937)** The Court upheld Washington state's minimum wage law, reversing its previous conservative rulings that had narrowly interpreted the right of contract and limited the right of states to enact social and economic regulation.

Wickard **v.** *Filburn* **(1942)**   In this case, the Supreme Court established the "cumulative effect" principle. The Court held that Congress could control a farmer's production of wheat for home consumption because the cumulative effect of home consumption of wheat by many farmers might reasonably be thought to alter the supply-and-demand relationships of the interstate commodity market.

Worcester **v.** *Georgia* **(1832)**   The Court ruled that states could not pass laws affecting federally recognized Indian nations, and therefore Georgia had no right to trespass on the Cherokee's lands without their assent. To which President Andrew Jackson is reported to have replied, "John Marshall has made his decision, now let him enforce it."

Youngstown Sheet and Tube Co. **v.** *Sawyer* **(1952)** This case is also known as the *Steel Seizure* case. During the Korean War, when the United Steelworkers threatened to go on strike, President Truman seized the mills and placed them under military operation. He argued he had inherent power to prevent a strike that would interfere with the war. The Court ruled against him, however, saying that presidential powers must be authorized by statute and did not come from anything inherent in the presidency.

Acknowledgments

CHAPTER 2
Page 18 Bettmann Archive; **page 21** Courtesy of the New York Historical Society, New York City; **page 32** Bettmann Archive; **page 33** Bettmann Archive.

CHAPTER 3
Page 51 Missouri Historical Society; **page 62** Reuters/Bettmann; **page 63** Lang Communications.

CHAPTER 4
Page 74 UPI/Bettmann Newsphotos; **page 78** Bettmann Archive; **page 79** UPI/Bettmann Newsphotos; **page 86** Warder Collection.

CHAPTER 5
Page 102 Courtesy of Tom Foley; **page 103** Courtesy of Newt Gingrich; **page 109** Black Star; **page 124** Courtesy of Carol Mosley-Braun.

CHAPTER 6
Page 143 Courtesy of Culver Pictures, Inc.; **page 164** Reuters/Bettmann; **page 165** Courtesy of White House, Vice President's Office.

CHAPTER 7
Page 198 Warder Collection; **page 206** Warder Collection; **page 207** UPI/Bettmann Newsphotos.

CHAPTER 8
Page 228 UPI/Bettmann Newsphotos; **page 229** AP/Wide World Photos.

CHAPTER 9
Page 278 Reuters/Bettmann Newsphotos; **page 279** Reuters/Bettmann Newsphotos; **page 283** UPI/Bettmann Newsphotos.

CHAPTER 10
Page 318 and 319 (c) 1993 Joe Dator and the Cartoon Bank, Inc.

CHAPTER 11
Page 329 Courtesy of the American Association of Retired Persons; **page 331** UPI/Bettmann Newsphotos; **page 334** AP/Wide World Photos; **page 335** AP/Wide World Photos.

CHAPTER 12
Page 364 UPI/Bettmann Newsphotos; **page 366** Courtesy of the White House; **page 367** Courtesy of the White House.

CHAPTER 13
Page 408 Warder Collection; **page 409** Warder Collection.

CHAPTER 14
Page 424 AP/Wide World Photos; **page 425** Warder Collection; **page 438** AP/Wide World Photos.

INDEX

ABC News, 372
abortion, 222, 270, 271, 273, 274, 330, 348–49, 359, 369, 382
   Burger court and, 77, 190, 208, 343
   Rehnquist court and, 80–81, 197, 208, 343
   right-to-life movement and, 208, 225, 226, 343
Abraham, Henry, 94, 212
Abrams, Elliott, 358
Abramson, Jill, 377*n*
Abramson, Paul R., 219*n*
Ada v. *Guam Society of Obstetricians and Gynecologists,* 190
Adams, Abigail, 21
Adams, Brock, 109
Adams, John, 19, 21, 165, 191
Adams, John Quincy, 21, 305
Adams, Paul, 402*n*
Adams, Samuel, 15–18
administrative regulation, 391–96
advertising:
   by interest groups, 333
   by political parties, 308–9, 314
AFDC (Aid to Families with Dependent Children), 401
affirmative action, 88–91, 270, 271, 273, 406–10, 414
Afghanistan, 224
AFL-CIO, 326
Africa, foreign aid to, 428
age discrimination, 81
Agency for International Development (AID), U.S., 428
Agnew, Spiro, 234
Agriculture Department, U.S., 338, 428
Aid to Families with Dependent Children (AFDC), 401
AIM (American Indian Movement), 74
airline industry, 390
Alabama, 77
alcohol industry, 396
Alexander, Herbert, 346–47
Alien and Sedition Acts (1798), 9, 292–93
Alliance for Managed Competition, 330
Alston, Chuck, 318*n*
American Association of Retired Persons, 327, 329
American Bankers Association, 326

American Bar Association, 326
American Continental Corporation, 324
American Enterprise Institute, 227, 326
American Farm Bureau Federation, 326
American Federation of State, County, and Municipal Employees, 326
American Indian Movement (AIM), 74
American Labor party, 409
American Medical Association, 326
American Revolution:
   first casualties of, 16
   and limits to government, 8
   political background to, 14–19
Americans with Disabilities Act (1990), 209, 344, 405
amicus curiae briefs, 202, 342, 352
amnesty, presidential power of, 142–44
Amtrak, 2
Andersen, Kristi, 290, 381*n*
Andrus, Ethel, 329
Antifederalists, 32–33, 34
Anton, Thomas, 67
ANZUS Treaty (1951), 430
apartheid, 221, 222
appeal, writs of, 192, 194, 195
appeals courts, federal:
   annual caseload of, 186, 188
   judicial circuits of, 188–89
   lawmaking and, 194
   regulatory agencies heard by, 188
   role of, 186, 212
   Supreme Court and, 56
Arab nations, 419, 442
Arendt, Hannah, 456
Argersinger v. *Hamlin,* 77*n*
Arizona, 325
Arkansas, 85, 235, 367
Armey, Richard, 101
Arms Control and Disarmament Agency, U.S., 444
Arms Export Control Act, 366–67
arms sales, 435–37, 443–44
Armstrong, Scott, 87*n*
Army, U.S., 18–19
Arnold, Peri E., 180

Arnold, R. Douglas, 138
Aron, Nan, 410*n*
Articles of Confederation and Perpetual Union, 30, 31,
   40
   "comity clauses" of, 29
   congressional powers defined by, 17–19
   Constitutional Convention and, 20, 34
   "excessive democracy" in, 25, 36
   as first constitution, 17, 36
   weakness of, 10–11, 19–20, 38
artisans, 15
Asher, Herbert, 250
Asia, 428
Aspin, Les, 134, 155
attorney general, 155, 156
Attucks, Crispus, 16
Atwater, Lee, 172, 229
Auerbach, Stuart, 280*n*
Austin, Erik, 255*n*
Australia, 430
authoritarian governments, 6, 7
autocracy, 6
automobile industry, 331
Auto Safety Center, 331

B-2 "stealth" bomber, 119
Babcock, Charles, 348*n*, 357*n*
"baby boomers," 308
Baer, Judith A., 94
Bailyn, Bernard, 37
Baird, Zoë, 368
Baker, James A., III, 163
Baker, Liva, 196*n*
Baker, Ross K., 138
Baker v. *Carr*, 80*n*
Bakke, Allan, 89
Balanced Budget and Emergency Deficit Control
   (Gramm-Rudman-Hollings) Act (1985), 151*n*,
   160
balance-of-power foreign policy role, 421, 437, 439,
   442, 448
ballots, party vs. neutral, 262–64, 263, 307
Banca Nazionale del Lavoro, 365
Bank of Credit and Commerce International (BCCI),
   341
Bank of the United States, 26
banks, 274, 376–77
   Depression-era run on, 3
   federal chartering of, 26, 43
Banks, Arthur S., 453*n*
Banks, Dennis, 74
Barker, Lucius J., 169*n*
Barnes, Fred, 369*n*
Barnet, Richard, 441*n*
Barrett, Paul M., 197*n*, 368*n*
Barron v. *Baltimore*, 70–73, 75–76, 94
Bartley, Robert L., 376–77
Bawden, D. Lee, 408*n*, 409*n*
BCCI (Bank of Credit and Commerce International),
   431
Beard, Charles, 22–23, 37
Becker, Carl, 17*n*, 37

Becker, Gary, 344*n*
Belej, Peter, 57*n*
Belgium, 254
Beltz, Herman, 95
Bendix, Reinhard, 13
"benign gerrymandering," 261
Bennett, W. Lance, 250
Bensel, Richard, 67
Bentsen, Lloyd, 134, 155, 163, 377
Berger, Raoul, 67
Berke, Richard L., 199*n*, 316*n*, 348*n*
Berlin Wall, collapse of, 172, 416, 450
Berman v. *Parker*, 185
Bernstein, Carl, 233*n*
Berry, Jeffrey M., 336*n*
BIA (Bureau of Indian Affairs), 74
bicameralism, 23, 25, 28, 100–101
Bickel, Alexander, 202*n*, 212
Bilbray, James, 375
Bill of Rights, 25, 31, 33, 34, 57, 68–95, 452
   adoption of, 33, 68, 454
   analysis of, 60, 70
   civil liberties in, 68–81
   civil rights in, 69, 71*n*, 81–91
   early opposition to, 32–33
   Fourteenth Amendment's nationalization of, 71,
      73–76, 80, 81, 93–94
   state rights and, 71–73, 75
Binder, Leonard, 13
Binion, Gayle, 80*n*
Birmingham, Ala., 87*n*, 90*n*
Birnbaum, Jeffrey, 371*n*, 379*n*, 387
birth control, 77, 319, 343
Biskupic, Joan, 197*n*, 199*n*
Blackman, Paul H., 258*n*
Blackmun, Harry, 76, 81, 201
blacks, 88–89, 99, 129, 206–7, 273, 286, 370, 385
   Congressional Caucus of, 114
   Democratic party and, 269, 270, 277–80, 285
   as interest group, 169
   in Senate, 286
   voting rights of, 24, 25, 82, 85, 87, 120, 260–61
   see also civil rights; civil rights movement
Blasi, Vincent, 212
Blow, Henry, 51
Board of Customs Commission, 16
Board of Education of Oklahoma City v. *Dowell*, 87*n*
Boland Amendment, 363
Bolivia, 144*n*
Bolling v. *Sharpe*, 84*n*
"boll weevils" (Democratic Forum), 114
Bonior, David, 101
Bork, Robert, 123, 204–5, 363
Bosnia, 417, 426
Boston, Mass., 14, 205–6
Boston Tea Party, 15–17, 18
bourgeoisie, 8, 9
Bowers v. *Hardwick*, 201
Bowman, Ann O'M., 67
Bowsher v. *Synar*, 151*n*, 160*n*
Boxer, Barbara, 99, 286
Brady, David, 290
Braestrup, Peter, 250

Brandeis, Louis D., 200
Brauer, Carl M., 395*n*
Brazil, 443
Brest, Paul, 80*n*, 85*n*, 407*n*
Brigham, John, 95
Broder, David, 107*n*, 155, 167*n*, 273*n*, 304*n*, 323, 368*n*, 369*n*, 375
Brookings Institution, 326, 355
Brown, Dee A., 74*n*
Brown, Jerry, 278–79
Brown, Linda, 84
Brown, Oliver, 84
Brown, Ron, 341, 368, 377
Brown v. *Allen,* 189*n*
Brown v. *Board of Education of Topeka,* 73, 82, 84, 85, 87, 94, 206, 207, 343
Bryan, William Jennings, 268
Bryner, Gary, 180, 212
Buchanan, James, 51, 379
Buchanan, Patrick, 278–79
Buckley v. *Valeo,* 314*n*
"buck stops here" sign, 145
Budget and Impoundment Control Act (1974), 113, 130, 146*n*, 160, 366
budget deficit, 131, 134, 160, 161, 318, 355, 365, 378, 386, 403
budget director, 160, 162, 176
budget process, 130–31, 161, 369
Bud Shuster Byway, 127
Bullock, Charles, III, 414
Bundy, McGeorge, 448
bureaucracy, 172–78
    characteristics of, 173
    Congress and, 176–78
    president and, 173–76, 180
    size of, 12, 172–73, 174–75
Bureau of Indian Affairs (BIA), 74
Bureau of the Budget, 166, 176
Burger, Warren, 76–81
Burger court, 77–80, 190, 208, 343
Burnham, James, 138
Burnham, Walter Dean, 254*n*, 266*n*, 290, 323
Bush, George, 50, 59, 134, 144, 166, 224, 235, 238, 369, 438, 443
    ambassadorial appointments by, 422
    budget director and, 160, 162
    budget problems and, 131, 355, 365, 378, 386
    civil rights legislation and, 189, 409–10
    domestic inaction of, 162
    domestic vs. foreign policy record of, 416
    election of, 3, 162–63, 269, 271, 296
    in election of 1992, 164, 216, 271, 273–77, 278, 281, 282, 284, 297, 310, 311, 319, 338, 348, 387
    on equality of opportunity, 220
    Iran-Contra affair and, 142–44, 358
    Joint Chiefs of Staff and, 159
    Persian Gulf War and, 131–33, 172, 216, 238, 320, 423
    press conferences held by, 167
    public opinion of, 171, 172, 216, 228
    Quayle and, 164, 271, 308
    Supreme Court appointments by, 197, 199, 206, 208, 274, 410
    veto power used by, 121, 333

as vice-president, 140, 163
    White House staff of, 157
    "Willie Horton" ad and, 308
Bush administration, 123, 138, 238, 339, 355, 359, 363, 365, 374, 375, 390, 403
business cycle, 399
busing, school desegregation and, 87, 120, 246, 273, 407
Butterfield, Fox, 226*n*
Byrd, Robert C., 120

cabinet, presidential, 154–57, 174–75, 180
Caddell, Patrick, 308
calendars, congressional, 115–16
California, 99, 313, 366
California/Davis Medical School, University of, 90
"California Mafia," 157
Calleo, David, 387
Calmes, Jacqueline, 120*n*
Cambodia, Nixon's secret bombing of, 361
Campaign Finance Act (1974), 130
Canada, 235
Cannon, John, 9*n*
capitalism, state property and trespass law origins of, 42
Carlucci, Frank, 438
Carmines, Edward G., 290
Carp, Robert, 213
Carter, Jimmy, 142, 308, 312, 366, 368, 369, 422, 430
    election of, 162, 163, 270
    media and, 167
    party support for, 168
    Sandinistas recognized by, 144
    White House Staff of, 157
Carter, Stephen L., 88, 89
Carter administration, 125, 130, 155, 158, 238, 438
Carville, James, 228–29
case (controversy), in rules of access, 190
Case Act (1972), 125
Catholics, 225, 226
Catton, Bruce, 51*n*, 228–29
caucuses, 101, 113–14, 137, 143, 301, 322–23
cause of action, 64
CBN (Christian Broadcasting Network), 226, 335
CBS, 224–25, 235, 332
censorship, 224
Center for the Study of Responsive Law, 331
Central America, 380
Central Intelligence Agency (CIA), 123, 142, 175
certiorari, writs of, 192, 194, 195, 200
Chamber of Commerce, 227
Chambers, William N., 323
Champagne, Anthony, 401*n*
Chavez, Cesar, 334–35
checks and balances, 31–32, 52, 53, 134
Cherokee tribe, 203
Chicago, Burlington and Quincy Railroad Company v. *Chicago,* 72*n*
China, People's Republic of, 144, 418, 430, 435, 441, 443
Christian Broadcasting Network (CBN), 226, 335
Christopher, Warren, 155
Chubb, John, 414, 355*n*, 367*n*

CIA (Central Intelligence Agency), 123, 142, 175
Cigler, Allan J., 336*n*, 352, 410
cities:
    grants-in-aid to, 47
    growth of, 9
    home rule of, 46
citizenship, 218
    "diversity of," 186, 211
    dual, 70–71, 94
    single national, 71
Citizen's Research Foundation, 314
City of Richmond v. *J.A. Croson Co.,* 90*n*
Civil Aeronautics Board, 455
civil law, 183, 391
civil liberties, 68–81, 220–21, 451, 453
    civil rights compared with, 69, 93–94
    definition of, 68, 93
    due process clause and, 69
    Fourteenth Amendment and, 71–73
    Supreme Court stances on, 72–73, 76–81
civil rights, 81–91, 197, 220–21, 359, 360, 370, 451,
    453
    civil liberties compared with, 69, 93–94
    equal protection clause and, 69
    Fourteenth Amendment and, 71*n*
    as governmental obligations, 69
    "group," 91
Civil Rights Act (1875), 81*n*, 82
Civil Rights Act (1957), 404
Civil Rights Act (1960), 404
Civil Rights Act (1964), 46*n*
    Title I, 404
    Title II, 87*n*, 404, 406
    Title IV, 404, 406
    Title VI, 406
    Title VII, 87–88, 404, 406
Civil Rights Act (1965), 404
Civil Rights Act (1968), 75, 405
Civil Rights Act (1990) (vetoed), 409–10
Civil Rights Act (1991), 90–91, 189, 344, 405, 410
Civil Rights Cases, 81*n*
Civil Rights Commission, 87
civil rights movement, 119, 120
    cause and effect in, 83
    King and, 86
    media's importance in, 230
Civil War, U.S., 43, 51, 71, 120, 268,356, 379, 380, 386
Clark, Dick, 336
Clark, Janet, 124*n*
Clark, Russel G., 207
Clark, Timothy, 314*n*
class action suits, 190, 205
class conflict, 9, 373–74, 385
Clay, Henry, 305
Clean Air Act (1963), 113
Clem, Alan L., 138
Cleveland, Grover, 305–6
"client" states, 418, 420
Clifford, Clark, 341
Clinton, Bill, 4, 91, 134, 144, 160, 163–65, 166, 176,
    219–20, 335, 336
    abortion rights and, 348–49
    appointments by, 154, 155, 157, 341, 368, 369–70,
        371, 372, 422

    budget and, 162, 166, 317, 341, 355, 369, 370, 374,
        375, 378–79
    economic program of, 304, 317, 355, 367, 369, 403
    economic stimulus package of, 106–8, 119, 304, 370
    in election of 1992, 79, 228–29, 235, 245, 266,
        277–85, 297, 338, 348, 367, 368, 403
    foreign policy and, 416–17, 443
    gays in the military and, 368–69, 374
    governmental philosophy of, 366–67
    health care and, 317–18, 330, 367, 369, 370
    legislative program of, 102, 104, 169, 317–18, 367,
        368–71
    and line-item veto, 134, 375
    media and, 167, 225, 235, 238, 310, 311, 370–71, 374
    political reform and, 314–16, 317, 318, 338, 348, 367,
        370, 381
    public opinion and, 216–17, 225, 228, 233–34, 311
    as strong President, 140, 154, 155
    and Supreme Court, 81, 91, 199, 371, 372
    vice-president and, 163, 165
    White House staff of, 157–58
Clinton, George, 32–33, 34
Clinton administration, 63, 134, 138, 285, 368–71
closed primaries, 302, 323
"closed rule," 115
cloture rules, 120, 138
Cloward, Richard A., 291, 380*n,* 393*n*, 414
Clubb, Jerome, 255*n*
Clymer, Adam, 108, 304, 369*n*
CNN, 235
Cnudde, Charles F., 456
Coalition for Health Insurance Choices, 330
Coal Mine Health and Safety Act (1969), 331
Coelho, Tony, 363
Coffey, Linda, 78
Cohen, Carl, 453*n*
Cohler, Anne M., 37
collective bargaining, 44
"comity clauses," 29, 36
commerce, 30
    constitutional regulation of, 28, 43
    interstate vs. intrastate, 40, 43–46, 73, 87, 151
Committee on Public Information (CPI), 224
Committee on the Constitutional System, 54–55
committees, *see* congressional committees; House
        committees; Senate committees; *specific*
        committees
"committee veto," 125
Common Cause, 227, 325, 326, 330, 347
common law, 183, 185, 186
communications technology, 218–19
Communist party, 409
Community Action Programs, 407
Comprehensive Occupational Safety and Health Act
    (1970), 331
Concerned Senators for the Arts, 114
Congress, U.S., 12, 20, 85, 94, 98–139, 208–9, 224,
        285–86, 341, 361, 378, 443
    affirmative action and, 90–91
    appropriations power of, 52
    in Articles of Confederation, 17–19, 25
    bicameralism of, 22–23, 25, 28, 100–101
    budget process and, 119–21, 130–31, 161, 374
    bureaucracy and, 176–78

calendars of, 115–16
caucuses of, 101, 113–14, 137
commerce and, 44–46
Connecticut compromise and, 22–24
in Constitution, 25–26, 98
constitutional amendments and, 57, 58–59, 60
debate rules of, 116–17, 120
Democratic control of, 3, 115, 168, 268, 269, 285, 294–97, 316–19, 365, 368, 383
Depression-era legislation passed by, 3
diversity in membership of, 98–99
and election of president, 305
electoral realignments and, 266–69
First Amendment as limit on, 60, 70
floor access in, 110
grants-in-aid from, 47–50
hearings and investigations by, 122–23, 177, 357, 358, 359
interest groups and, 329, 330, 337, 347–48
judicial review of, 191
legislative clearance and, 166
legislative process in, 98–101, 112–13, 114–21, 137–38
lower courts created by, 29
military-industrial complex and, 339–41
in 1988 and 1990 elections, 3
oversight and, 122–23, 177
party leadership in, 101–4, 381
Persian Gulf War and, 131–33, 238
presidential power balance with, 55–56, 98, 121, 129–35, 138, 141, 143, 144–45, 149–51, 361, 363, 365–67, 378
procedural rules of, 115, 116, 137
redistricting of, 261
staff agencies of, 113
staff system of, 112–13, 137
Supreme Court decisions overturned by, 189
term limits for, 132–33
veto overrides and, 28, 121, 125–26, 146
war powers of, 18, 26, 130
weapons of control of, 122
see also House of Representatives, U.S.; Senate, U.S.
Congressional Black Caucus, 114
Congressional Budget Office (CBO), 113, 130
Congressional Caucus for Women's Issues, 114
congressional committees, 119, 137–38, 149, 323, 365–66
assignments to, 102–4, 108–10
deliberation by, 114–15
direct government and, 125
oversight and, 122–23
system of, 111–12, 303–4
see also House committees; Senate committees
Congressional Government (Wilson), 149
Congressional Quarterly, 120*n*, 127*n*, 138, 145*n*, 168*n*, 314*n*, 318*n*, 325*n*, 330*n*, 332*n*, 336*n*, 349*n*
Congressional Record, 113*n*
Congressional Research Service, 113
Connecticut, 20, 34, 302
Connecticut (Great) Compromise, 22–24
conscription, 6, 16
Conservative Digest, 312
conservatives, 164, 197, 271, 274, 276–77, 285, 361, 366, 369, 383, 385

affirmative action and, 91
liberals compared with, 221–23, 250
publications read by, 312
public opinion and, 225–26
resurgence of, 223, 270–71, 335, 336, 359
voter registration requirements and, 258
Constitution, U.S., 15, 24–36, 452
Article I, 25–28, 36, 43, 44, 52, 60, 73, 98, 101, 149
Article II, 27, 28, 36, 141–42, 145, 146
Article III, 27, 29, 36, 60, 189, 208–9, 343–44
Article IV, 27, 29–30, 36, 145
Article V, 27, 30–31, 36
Article VI, 27, 30, 36, 192
Article VII, 27, 31, 36
"comity clauses" of, 29, 36
Congress in, 25–26, 98, 134
as contract, 39
doctrine of expressed power in, 26
First Revolution of, 46, 73
framers' aims in, 22–23, 25, 26, 28, 29, 36, 40–41, 42, 52, 149, 204–5, 246, 262, 325, 355–56, 374
judiciary in, 25, 27, 29, 36, 183
"necessary and proper" clause of, 26, 43
president in, 28, 36, 141–49, 180
ratification of, 31, 33–34, 36
Second Revolution of, 46, 73–76
state governments' power in, 26, 28
"strict construction" of, 76
Supreme Court in, 29, 189
vice–president in, 162
see also Bill of Rights
constitutional amendments, 26, 30–31, 36, 39, 56–64
First, 60, 69, 70, 73, 75, 80*n*, 94, 336
Second, 60, 69, 70
Third, 60, 70
Fourth, 60, 70, 76
Fifth, 60, 69, 70, 72, 73, 196, 396–97, 405
Sixth, 60, 69, 70, 73*n*, 196
Seventh, 60, 70
Eighth, 60, 70
Ninth, 70, 75
Tenth, 70, 75
Eleventh, 61
Twelfth, 304–5
Thirteenth, 30, 57, 62, 63, 89
Fourteenth, *see* Fourteenth Amendment
Fifteenth, 57, 89
Sixteenth, 62, 63
Seventeenth, 25, 52
Eighteenth, 58, 67
Twenty-first, 58
Twenty-seventh, 57
see also Bill of Rights
Constitutional Convention, 20–24, 28, 31, 32, 34–35
constitutional government, 6, 7, 8, 451
Consumer Federation of America, 332
consumer movement, 331, 332–33, 343
Consumer Price (Cost of Living) Index, 401, 403
containment of Soviet Union, 424
Continental Congress, First, 17
Continental Congress, Second, 17, 19
contraceptives, 77, 343
contracting, 390–91, 393, 394–96
Contras, 131

contributory negligence, 183
controversy (case), in rules of access, 190
conventions, nomination by, 301–2, 305
Conway, M. Margaret, 290
Cook, Timothy, 250
Cooper, Joseph, 323
cooperative federalism, 49
Cooper v. *Aaron, 85n*
Copperheads, 294
corporate tax, 6
Corwin, Edward S., 141*n*, 180
Costain, Anne, 410*n*
Cost of Living (Consumer Price) Index, 401, 403
counsel, right to, 77
Court of Appeals, 56; *see also* appeals courts, federal
Court of Claims, U.S., 188
courts, *see* federal courts; judiciary; state courts;
        specific courts
Coverdell, Paul, 348
"cracking," 260–61
Cranston, Alan, 127, 324, 325
Crawford, William H., 305
creative federalism, 50
credit, federal government and, 3
Creel, George, 224
criminal defendants, procedural rights of, 76, 197, 246
criminal indictments, 357–59, 363, 382
criminal law, 42, 183, 391
Crisis, 409
Cronin, Thomas E., 158*n*
Crovitz, L. Gordon, 67
C-Span, 103, 110
currency, 28, 44
Curtiss-Wright Export Corp., U.S. v., 144
Customs Court, U.S., 188
Czechoslovakia, 144, 418
Czech Republic, 418

Dahl, Robert A., 13, 203*n*
dairy industry, 338–39, 394–96
"daisy girl" ad, 308, 309
Daley, Richard J., 374
Darcy, R., 124*n*
Darman, Richard, 162, 176
Daschle, Tom, 108
Davidson, Chandler, 406*n*
Davidson, Roger, 138
Davis, James W., 125*n*
Davis, Leonard, 329
Davis, Sue, 213
Day, Christine, 352
Day After, The, 226
Daynes, Byron, 52*n*, 415
Deaver, Michael, 358
Debs, Eugene V., 224
debt, national, 355, 427
Declaration of Independence, 17, 21, 36
declaratory judgment, 190
DeConcini, Dennis, 127, 324–25
Deering, Christopher, 139
defendants, definition of, 183
Defenders of Wildlife, 208
Defense Department, U.S., 339, 363, 428, 435*n*, 443*n*

defense industry, 339–41
defense spending, 10, 271, 274, 275, 317, 320, 378, 430,
        433–37
Delaware, 20, 34, 84, 302
delegated powers, 141, 152, 176
democracy:
    bourgeois opposition to, 8–9
    bureaucracy and, 172–78
    common belief in, 219
    conditions for, 439–41, 453–55
    constitutional, 8, 451
    definition of, 8
    "excessive," 25, 34, 36
    representative, 4
    without voters, 372–74
Democratic Forum ("boll weevils"), 114
Democratic Leadership Council (DLC), 277
Democratic National Committee, 225
Democratic party, 101–4, 112, 131, 132–33, 150, 155,
        216, 304, 340, 357–85, 436
    campaign financing and, 245, 314, 324
    Congress controlled by, 3, 115, 134, 168, 268,
        294–97, 316–19, 365, 383
    congressional redistricting and, 261
    discipline in, 375, 381
    electoral realignments and, 268–69
    filibusters by, 120
    history of, 294–96
    interest group support of, 169, 277, 348, 375,
        376–78
    New Deal coalition and, 269–70, 273, 294
    New Deal era strengthening of, 265
    in 1988 election, 271
    in 1992 election, 274–75, 277–86, 300
    Republican Party compared with, 105–8, 245, 297,
        319–20, 322, 372–74
    southern faction of, 294–96
    Steering and Policy Committee of, 102–3, 303, 108,
        112
Democratic Study Group, 102, 114
DeNardo, James, 383*n*
Deng Xiaoping, 443
Derthick, Martha, 46*n*, 414
Desert Shield, Desert Storm, *see* Persian Gulf War
Devroy, Ann, 225*n*, 236*n*, 369*n*, 371*n*
Dewar, Helen, 119*n*, 258*n*
Dickinson, John, 454
dictatorships, 217
Dinkin, Robert J., 290
Dionne, E. J., 4*n*, 284*n*, 387
diplomacy, 420, 422, 429, 437, 439, 444, 448
direct committee government, 125
direct mail soliciting, 312, 314, 323
district courts, federal, 186–88, 212
District of Columbia, 42, 61, 84, 188
"diversity of citizenship," 186
Divine, Robert A., 16*n*
divine right of kings, 17
Dixon, Alan, 124
DLC (Democratic Leadership Council), 277
Dodd, Lawrence, 138, 160*n*, 177*n*
Dole, Robert, 104
dollar, U.S., 426
Domestic Council, 155

Dominican Republic, 441
Donovan, Beth, 110*n*, 381*n*
double jeopardy, 69, 73
Douglas, Stephen, 240, 314
Douglas, William O., 200
Dowd, Ann Reilly, 157*n*
draft, military, 6, 16
Draper, Theodore, 387
dual citizenship, 70–71
"dual federalism," 40, 49
DuBois, W.E.B., 408–9
due process, 64, 69, 72, 94
Dukakis, Michael, 163, 270, 308
Duke, David, 278, 373
Duncan v. *Louisiana,* 73*n*
Duverger, Maurice, 306–7
Dye, Thomas R., 46*n,* 67

Earned Income Tax Credit, 403
Eastern Europe, 253
  economic and social reform in, 442, 454–55
East India Company, 15, 17
economic expansionist foreign policy role, 437, 439,
    448
economy, U.S., 277, 280–81, 284, 317, 318, 359, 367,
    368, 376–77, 382, 385, 386
Edsall, Thomas Byrne, 284*n*, 316*n*, 368*n*, 371*n*
education, 355, 386
  desegregation and, 73, 82–88, 146, 206–8, 343, 393,
    406, 407–8
  federal student loans for, 2
Edwards, George, III, 167*n*, 181
EEOC (Equal Employment Opportunity Commis-
    sion), 207, 364, 406, 407
"effluent tax," 396
Eisenhower, Dwight D., 134, 142, 146, 167–68, 296, 339
Eisenstadt v. *Baird,* 77*n*, 343
Eisenstein, James, 213
Eisenstein, Zillah, 95
Elazar, Daniel, 67
Elder, Janet, 244*n*
Elder, Shirley, 139
election of 1800, 268
election of 1824, 143, 305
election of 1828, 143, 268, 294
election of 1832, 143
election of 1840, 307
election of 1858, 296
election of 1860, 268, 294, 296, 314, 380
election of 1876, 305
election of 1888, 305–6
election of 1896, 268
election of 1932, 268, 294
election of 1934, 313
election of 1936, 296
election of 1948, 243, 313
election of 1952, 243
election of 1954, 168
election of 1956, 168, 236, 243
election of 1958, 168
election of 1960, 162, 163, 242, 243, 311
election of 1964, 163, 243, 265, 286
election of 1966, 168
election of 1968, 76, 163, 196, 231, 242, 243, 270, 316

election of 1972, 230, 243, 270, 277, 339, 361
election of 1974, 286
election of 1976, 162, 163, 242, 243, 270, 308
election of 1980, 3, 162, 163, 265, 269, 270, 285, 311
election of 1984, 3, 234, 243, 265, 269, 271, 347
election of 1986, 357
election of 1988, 163, 269, 271, 357
  Bush's "Willie Horton" ad and, 308
  candidate comparison in, 163
  congressional-presidential split in, 3
  public opinion polls and, 243
election of 1990, 297, 357
election of 1991, 373
election of 1992, 3, 91, 98–99, 134, 199, 216, 269,
    271–87, 297
  Congressional, 109, 124, 285–86, 357
  funding of, 324
  issues in, 132, 266, 277–81
  margin of victory, 163–65, 284, 285, 300
  media and, 238–39, 266, 282, 284, 310–11
  parties and candidates in, 300
  voter turnout, 356, 357, 373, 387
election of 1994, 369
elections, 453
  accountability promoted by, 252
  ballot types used in, 262–64, 263, 307
  bases of electoral choice in, 264–66
  campaign spending in, 313–16, 317, 318
  candidate characteristics and, 262–64
  choices manipulated in, 254, 258–61
  decision-making process insulated from, 254,
    261–64
  decline of voting in, 356–57, 372–74, 386–87
  electoral composition and, 254–58
  governmental impact of, 286–87
  issue and policy concerns in, 264, 265
  mass political influence institutionalized by, 287
  media and, 231–34
  partisan loyalty in, 264–65
  party realignments and, 266–71
  political activity socialized by, 287
  popular influence facilitated by, 3, 12–13, 252
  presidential primary, *see* primary elections
  public opinion poll predictions of, 242, 243, 250
  realigning eras and, 266–69
  registration systems for, 255–58
  regulation of, 253–64
  runoff, 258
  true role of, 256–57
  two-year cycle of, 272
  voter mobilization for, 372–74, 379–85, 387
  voter turnout levels in, 254, 255, 384
electoral college, 25, 28, 52, 142, 282, 304–6
electoral districts, 80, 259–61, 298
electoral systems, 258–59, 356
  majority, 258, 259
  plurality, 259, 298–99
  proportional representation, 259
"electronic town hall," 310
Emerson, John, 51
Emily's List, 109
eminent domain, 72, 185, 396–97
employment, discrimination in, 85, 87–88, 403–6, 408–9
en banc, 186, 189

Encyclopedia Africana, 409n
Encyclopedia of U.S. Government Benefits, 390
Endangered Species Act (1973), 130, 208, 343
Energy Department, U.S., 435n
Engel v. Vitale, 59n, 80n
Environmental Defense Fund, 330
Environmental Protection Agency (EPA), 363
EOP (Executive Office of the President), 158–62, 166, 176
Epstein, Richard, 69n
Equal Employment Opportunity Act (1972), 405
Equal Employment Opportunity Commission (EEOC), 207, 364, 406, 407
Equal Pay Act (1963), 404
equal protection clause, 69, 81–82, 84n, 85, 94
Equal Rights Amendment (ERA), 59, 62–63
equity cases, 185
Erikson, Robert S., 250
Ervin, Sam, 361
Espionage Law, 224
Espy, Mike, 134, 261
Ethics in Government Act (1978), 56, 363
Europe, *see* Eastern Europe; Western Europe
European Community, 419, 442
European Recovery (Marshall) Plan, 428, 430
excise tax, 6
exclusionary rule, 76
exclusive powers, 28
execution, stays of, 189, 200
executive agreements, 125, 144–45
executive branch, 39, 56, 140–81
    checks and balances and, 53
    in Constitution, 28
    limits on, 59–60, 70
    see also president
Executive Office of the President (EOP), 158–62, 166, 176
executive orders, 395, 406
expressed power, doctrine of, 26
expropriation, 396–97

F-16 fighter, 436
FAA (Federal Aviation Administration), 2
Falwell, Jerry, 336
farmers, 9, 15, 20, 389
Farrand, Max, 31n, 35n, 37, 57n, 454n
Faubus, Orval, 85, 146
Faulkner, Robert K., 213
Faux, Marian, 79n
FEC (Federal Election Commission), 229–30, 315
"federal aid to education," 393
Federal Aviation Administration (FAA), 2
Federal Bureau of Investigation (FBI), 142, 175, 196, 360
federal courts, 182–213
    annual caseload of, 186
    categories of cases heard by, 186, 211
    lower, 186–88
    organization of, 187, 212
    traditional limitations on, 202–3
    see also appeals courts, federal; district courts, federal; judiciary; Supreme Court, U.S.
Federal Election Commission (FEC), 229–30, 315

Federal Elections Campaign Act (1971), 313, 314, 342, 344
Federal Housing Administration (FHA), 2
federalism, 31, 38–50, 66, 150, 420, 451–52
    cooperative, 49
    creative, 50
    definition of, 39
    "dual," 40, 49
    framers' intentions and, 31–32, 39
    "new," 50
    state differences fostered by, 40
Federalist Papers, The, 17n, 32, 34, 50n, 57n, 149, 262, 325n, 349n, 453n
Federalist party, 9, 26, 32–33, 34, 268, 292, 294, 306
"federal pyramid," 355–56
Federal Regulation of Lobbying Act (1946), 336
Federal Reserve Board, 151n, 397–99
Federal Trade Act (1914), 151n
Federal Trade Commission, 188, 393, 455
Feinstein, Dianne, 99, 286
Feldman, Lily Gardner, 448
felonies, right to counsel and, 77
Fenno, Richard, Jr., 104n, 138
Ferguson, Thomas, 169n, 269n, 290
Ferraro, Geraldine, 162, 234
Ferrell, Robert H., 448
Fesler, James W., 177n, 181
FHA (Federal Housing Administration), 2
FICA (Social Security) tax, 401
Field, Stephen, 188–89
filibusters, 117–19, 120, 121, 138, 304, 370
Fiorina, Morris, 138
"fireside chats," 167, 236, 237
fiscal redistributive techniques, 397, 413–14
Fisher, Louis, 56n, 138
flag-burning amendment, 59
Fleming, Roy B., 213
Florio, Jim, 229
Foley, Tom, 57, 101, 102–3
Food and Drug Administration, 455
Food for Peace, 428
food stamps, 407
Ford, Gerald, 142, 168, 234
Ford, Wendell, 375
Ford administration, 130
Foreign Affairs, 424
foreign aid, 427–30
Foreign Commitments Resolution, 366
foreign policy, 129, 416–49
    balance-of-power role and, 437, 439, 442, 448
    collective security treaties and, 430–34
    diplomacy and, 422, 429
    domestic policy and, 420, 447
    economic aid and, 427–30
    economic expansionist role and, 437, 439, 448
    executive agreements and, 125
    Holy Alliance role and, 437–39, 440–44, 448
    instruments of, 419, 421–37, 447, 448
    international monetary structure and, 426–27, 429
    market globalization and, 442–44
    military deterrence and, 434–37
    Napoleonic role and, 437, 439, 440, 443, 448
    national roles and, 419, 437–44
    roles for America and, 439–44

U.N. and, 422–26, 429
unilateralism in, 420–21, 447
values in, 419–21, 447
between World Wars I and II, 421, 447
Foreign Service Act (1946), 420, 422
Foreman, Christopher, 138, 414
Forer, Lois G., 95, 414
Fortune, 157*n*
Fourteenth Amendment, 57, 89, 404, 405
adoption of, 62, 94
Bill of Rights incorporated into, 72, 73–75, 94
Bill of Rights nationalized by, 71, 73–75, 94
due process clause of, 64, 69, 72, 94
equal protection clause of, 69, 81–82, 84*n*, 85, 94
federal vs. state power and, 62
group rights as basis of, 91
privacy and, 78
Fowler, Linda, 138, 290
Fowler, Wyche, 348
Fox, Harrison W., 113*n*
France, 30, 254, 293, 391, 423*n*, 435
Frank, Barney, 365
Frankfurter, Felix, 200
Franklin, Benjamin, 17
Franklin, Grace A., 181
Frederickson, H. George, 181
freedom:
from arbitrary search and seizure, 8
of assembly, 8, 73, 453
common belief in, 219
of conscience, 8
governmental power and, 4, 10–11, 12–13,
451–55
interest groups and, 325, 349
of press, 73
of speech, 8, 72, 75, 453
"free enterprise," 44
Freeman, Gary, 402*n*
Free Soil party, 51, 296
Fremont, John C., 296
French Revolution, 10
Friedman, Benjamin, 387
Friedman, Lawrence, 81*n*
Friendly, Fred W., 95
Friends of the Earth, 227
Frisby, Michael K., 225*n*, 379*n*
Fry, Bryan R., 181
Fukuyama, Francis, 448
Fulbright, J. William, 237
full faith and credit clause, 29, 36
Fullilove v. *Klutznick,* 90*n*, 407*n*
Fulton, Robert, 43
Fund, John H., 132–33

Gaddis, John Lewis, 427*n*
Galderisi, Peter F., 302*n*
Gallup, George, 250
Gallup Polls, 241, 242, 243
GAO (General Accounting Office), 113, 160
Garcia v. *San Antonio Metropolitan Transit Authority,*
151*n*
Garfinkle, Adam, 226*n*
Garrity, W. Arthur, 205–6
Garrow, David J., 95, 230*n*

Gastil, Raymond O., 453*n*
"gender gap," 221
General Accounting Office (GAO), 113, 160
General Electric, 347–48
General Motors, 326
Genêt, Edmond, 144
George, John, 219*n*, 251
Georgia, 22, 24, 34, 203
"Georgia Mafia," 157
Gephardt, Richard, 101
Gergen, David, 369–70, 371
German Democratic Republic (East Germany), 433
Germany, Federal Republic of (West Germany), 423*n*
Germany, Nazi, 244
Germany, reunified, 172, 354, 423, 433, 435, 441
Gerry, Elbridge, 259–60
gerrymandering, 259–60, 261
Gibbons v. *Ogden,* 43–44
G.I. Bill, 2
Gigot, Paul A., 370*n*
Gilbert, Felix, 439
Gilpin, Robert, 448
Gingrich, Newt, 101, 102–3, 110, 365
Ginsberg, Benjamin, 67, 169*n*, 208*n*, 222*n*, 246*n*, 250,
253*n*, 269*n*, 290, 302*n*, 316*n*, 333*n*, 347*n*, 396*n*
Ginsburg, Douglas, 123
Ginsburg, Ruth Bader, 81, 199, 371, 372
Gitlin, Todd, 230*n*
Gitlow v. *New York,* 72*n*
Glenn, John, 127, 325
gold, 426
Goldfield, Michael, 352
Goldman, Sheldon, 213
Goldwater, Barry, 62, 265, 366
Goosetree, Robert E., 146*n*
Gorbachev, Mikhail S., 450
Gore, Albert, 108, 163, 164–65, 225, 277, 278, 281, 311
Gorsuch, Anne, 363
government:
alternative forms of, 4, 6–7
components of, 4
electoral effect on, 286–87
freedom and, *see* freedom, governmental power and
legitimacy of, 38–39
limits on, 8–9, 10–11, 64
meaning and character of, 4
means of coercion and, 6
political parties' influence on, 302–6
public opinion shaped by, 12, 217, 224–25, 250
revenue collecting by, 4, 6
state, *see* state governments
unitary, 40, 42
government, U.S.:
activities of, 5, 40–43
in Articles of Confederation, 17–20
commerce and, 40, 43–46
as "commercial republic," 41–42
direct influence on state and local governments by,
47
divided (1968–1992), 365–67
domestic violence and, 30
electoral mobilization and, 379–85
exclusive powers of, 28
founding of, 14–37

government, U.S. (*continued*)
  grants-in-aid from, 47–50
  growth of, 3, 42, 43
  as largest employer, 3
  legislative epoch of, 149–51
  new challenges for, 354–56
  people's relationship with, 2–4, 12–13
  revenue sharing and, 50
  state governments and, 11, 25, 26, 28, 31–32,
    34–35, 36, 40, 47–50, 61–62
  suppression by, 9
governmental lobbies, 326
Government Organization Manual, U.S., 202
Graber, Doris, 250
Gramm-Rudman-Hollings (Balanced Budget and
    Emergency Deficit Control) Act (1985), 151*n*,
    160
grand juries, 73, 77
Grant, Ruth W., 13
grants-in-aid, 47–50
Graubard, Stephen R., 448
Great Britain, 19, 30, 244, 423*n*, 427, 435, 437, 443
Great (Connecticut) Compromise, 22–24
Great Society, 316, 394–95, 407
Greece, 427–28
Green, John, 347*n*
Greenhouse, Linda, 208*n*, 344*n*
Greider, William, 414
Grenada, U.S. invasion of, 131, 441
Griffin v. *Prince Edward County School Board*, 85*n*
Griggs v. *Duke Power Company*, 88*n*, 90
Grinstein, Gerald, 113
Griswold v. *Connecticut*, 77*n*, 343
Grodzins, Morton, 49*n*, 67
Grofman, Bernard, 406*n*
Grove, Lloyd, 108
Guinier, Lani, 370
gun control, 246, 327
Gunther, Gerald, 191*n*
Gutmann, Amy, 414

habeas corpus, writs of, 26–28, 192, 194, 195, 200
Haiti, 416–17
Hall, Arsenio, 310
Hamilton, Alexander, 9, 10, 11, 28, 32, 33, 34, 389, 419
Hamilton, Charles V., 213
Hammond, Susan W., 113*n*
Hansen, John Mark, 352, 373*n*, 387
Harbison, Winfred A., 95
Harpham, Edward J., 401*n*, 402*n*
Harris, U.S. v., 76*n*
Harrison, Benjamin, 306
Harris Polls, 242, 243
Hartz, Louis, 13, 220*n*
Harvard University, 326
Harvey, Phillip L., 414
Harwood, John, 375*n*, 377*n*
Haskins, George L., 213
Hatch, Orrin, 341
Hatch Act, 318
Hatfield, Mark, 127
Hawgood, John A., 254*n*
Hayes, Rutherford B., 305
Health, Education and Welfare Department, U.S., 407

health care, 317, 318, 330, 355, 367, 369, 386
health insurance, 231, 329, 330
Heart of Atlanta Motel v. *U.S.*, 46*n*
Heclo, Hugh, 181
Heilbroner, Robert, 414
Henry, Patrick, 34
Hentoff, Nat, 95
Herbers, John, 328*n*
Heritage Foundation, 227
Herring, E. Pendleton, 333*n*
Herrnson, Paul S., 323
Hess, Stephen, 232, 233
Higgs, Robert, 13
Hill, Anita, 124, 364
Hill, Larry B., 181
Hilsman, Roger, 448
Hilzenrath, David, 355*n*, 378*n*
Hodgson, Godfrey, 169*n*
Hofstadter, Richard, 9*n*, 293*n*, 323, 454*n*
Holloway, Harry, 219*n*, 251
Holmes, Oliver Wendell, 200
Holmes, Steven, 227*n*, 282*n*
Holy Alliance foreign policy role, 437–39, 440–44, 448
home rule, 46
homosexuals, rights of, 201, 277, 319, 368–69, 374
Hoover, Herbert, 296
Hoover Institution, 227
Horowitz, Donald, 205*n*
Horton, Willie, 308
House committees:
  Agriculture, 102, 104
  Appropriations, 111, 121, 123, 130, 160, 177
  Armed Services, 155, 339
  Budget, 130
  Government Operations, 177
  Intelligence, 123
  Rules, 111, 115, 116, 138
  Un-American Activities, 123
  Ways and Means, 104, 130, 160
House of Commons (Great Britain), 17
House of Representatives, U.S., 142, 143, 282, 285–86,
    306, 365, 369
  calendars of, 115
  compartmentalization of, 262
  Connecticut Compromise and, 22
  direct election of, 11, 25, 52, 262
  line-item veto and, 134
  members' salaries in, 99
  party discipline in, 105–7, 110
  party leadership in, 101–4
  revenue bills and, 25
  Senate compared with, 100–101, 119
  Speaker of, 101–3, 110, 112, 116, 137, 303, 323
  term of office in, 25
  Three-fifths Compromise and, 24
housing, discrimination and segregation in, 82, 85,
    408–9
Housing and Urban Development Department, U.S.,
    365
Human Events, 312
Hume, Brit, 372
Humphrey's Executor v. *United States*, 145*n*
Huntington, Samuel P., 13, 43*n*, 129*n*, 360*n*
Hussein, Saddam, 443

Hyde, Henry, 103
Hyneman, Charles, 172*n*

IBM, 326
ICC (Interstate Commerce Commission), 188, 455
Idelson, Holly, 108
Ifill, Gwen, 371*n*
Illinois, 124
"illumination," 253
IMF (International Monetary Fund), 426, 429
immigration, 218
Immigration and Naturalization Service v. *Chadha,* 125
impeachment, 28, 141*n*, 363
impoundment, 130, 146*n*
income tax, 6, 63–64, 131, 270, 271, 276, 285, 317, 318, 397
independent candidates, 301, 302, 303
"indexing," 401
India, 435, 444
Indiana, 164
Indians, American, 18, 74, 75, 88–89, 203, 331
individual rights, 39
Industrial Revolution, 9
INF (Intermediate-Range Nuclear Forces) Treaty (1987), 438
inflation, 270, 271
influence, political, definition of, 7
"infomercials," 235, 282, 310, 311
injury, Supreme Court's definition of, 190
"instant organization," 316
"institutional presidency," 158
intelligence agencies, U.S., 142
interest groups, 324–53, 374
    access gained by, 338–41, 342, 352
    bribery by, 342
    class bias of, 327–28
    freedom and, 325, 349
    governmental expansion and, 328–30
    litigation by, 341–44, 352
    local vs. national, 100–101
    New Politics movement and, 330–33
    organizational components of, 326–27
    partisan politics and, 342, 344–49
    political strategies of, 333–49, 352
    presidents supported by, 169
    proliferation of, 328–33
    public opinion shaped by, 225–30
    public strategies of, 333–36, 342, 349, 352
    range of, 326
    see also lobbyists; political action committees
interest rates, 397
Interior Department, U.S., 208
Intermediate-Range Nuclear Forces (INF) Treaty (1987), 438
"internal improvements," 41
Internal Revenue Code, 188
Internal Revenue Service (IRS), 455
International Bank for Reconstruction and Development (World Bank), 426–27, 429
International Monetary Fund (IMF), 426, 429
International Workers of the World (IWW), 224
Interstate Commerce Act (1887), 151*n*
Interstate Commerce Commission (ICC), 188, 455

Interstate Highway Program, 2, 396
Iowa, 311
Iran, 428, 444
Iran-Contra affair, 56, 122, 131, 144, 148, 176, 297, 358, 363, 367, 438
Iraq, Persian Gulf War and, 131–32, 172, 216, 365, 418, 423, 434, 435, 443–44
"Irish Mafia," 157
IRS (Internal Revenue Service), 455
Isikoff, Michael, 368*n*, 370*n*
isolationism, 420–21
Israel, 275, 379, 442, 443
Italy, 443
IWW (International Workers of the World), 224

Jackson, Andrew, 52, 143, 150, 203, 294, 305
Jackson, Brooks, 235, 290, 387
Jackson, Jesse, 279, 380, 385, 370
Jackson, Robert H., 189, 200
Jacksonians, 307
Jacobson, Gary, 109*n*, 139
Jahnige, Thomas P., 213
Jamieson, Kathleen H., 290
Japan, 354, 379, 418–19, 423*n*, 430, 435, 441
Javits, Jacob, 313
Jay, John, 32, 34
JCOS (Joint Chiefs of Staff), 159, 438
Jefferson, Thomas, 150, 419
    "best government" saying of, 3, 452
    on Bill of Rights, 68
    Declaration of Independence written by, 17
    Federalist opposition to, 9, 292
    on limited government, 10–11
    women in politics opposed by, 21
Jeffersonian Republicans, 9, 268, 292, 294, 306
Jensen, Merrill, 19*n*
Job Corps, 407
Johnson, Andrew, 142
Johnson, Haynes, 387
Johnson, Herbert A., 213
Johnson, Lyndon B., 308, 309, 316, 394, 395
    affirmative action inaugurated by, 90, 407
    election of, 163, 265, 286
    JFK and, 162
    media's relationship with, 167, 231, 234
    party support for, 168
    public opinion polls used by, 241
    War on Poverty of, 316, 394–95, 407
Johnson administration, 50, 129, 230
Joint Chiefs of Staff (JCOS), 159, 438
Jones, Joseph, 428
Joslyn, Richard A., 251, 308*n*, 312*n*
judges, justices:
    dissenting opinions by, 199–200, 212
    in district courts, 188
    lifetime appointments of, 27, 29
    opinion writing by, 199–200, 212
    presidential appointment of, 29, 199, 203; *see also specific presidents*
    "riding circuit" by, 188–89
    role of, 185
    stays of execution reviewed by, 189
"judicial activism," 79–80, 196, 209

judicial process, 183–86
judicial review, 189–95
    and administration of justice, 192–94
    of Congress, 191
    definition of, 29, 189
    lawmaking and, 194
    of state actions, 192
    of statutes, 54–55
    Supreme Court power of, 29, 36, 52–55, 189–91
judiciary, 19, 39, 52–55, 182–213, 330, 357, 359, 361,
    367, 382
    in Bill of Rights, 60
    checks and balances and, 53
    in Constitution, 25, 27, 29, 36, 183
    jurisdiction of, 186–89
    limits on, 59–60, 70
    see also federal courts; Supreme Court, U.S.
Judiciary Act (1789), 192
juries:
    grand, 73, 77
    integration of, 85, 87
    role of, 185–86, 211–12
    in Sixth Amendment, 69
Justice Department, U.S., 56, 341, 406, 409

Kagay, Michael, 244*n*
Kammen, Michael, 423*n*
Kansas, 84
Kansas City, Mo., 207
Kansas-Nebraska Act (1854), 296
Kaplan, Fred, 425*n*
Katz, Jeffrey, 114
Katzenbach v. *McClung*, 46*n*, 87*n*
Kayden, Xandra, 323
Kearns, Doris, 181
Kearny, Richard, 67
Keating, Charles, 127, 324, 325
"Keating Five," 127, 324–25, 336
Kefauver, Estes, 236
Keller, Morton, 13
Keller, William, 359
Kelley, E. Wood, 67
Kelly, Alfred, 75*n*, 77*n*, 85*n*, 95
Kelly, Michael, 369*n*
Kennan, George F., 424–25, 440*n*, 448
Kennedy, Anthony, 197, 199
Kennedy, Edward, 324, 336
Kennedy, John F., 155, 170, 237, 240, 311, 395
    election of, 163
    "Irish Mafia" of, 157
    LBJ and, 162
    party support for, 168
    press conferences of, 167, 236
Kennedy, Paul, 439*n*, 448
Kernell, Samuel, 387
Kesler, Charles R., 132–33
Kettl, Donald F., 67, 177*n*, 181
Key, V. O., 306
Kim, Jay C., 286
Kimmelman, Gene, 332
King, Larry, 310
King, Martin Luther, Jr., 86
Kinsley, Michael, 239

Kissinger, Henry A., 159, 425
"Kitchen Cabinet," presidential, 157
Kluger, Richard, 84*n*, 207*n*, 406*n*
Know-Nothing party, 296
Korea, Republic of (South), 428
Korean War, 6, 423
Krauss, Clifford, 104*n*
Kurtz, Howard, 234, 238, 310*n*, 330*n*, 371*n*, 387
Kutler, Stanley, 387
Kuwait, Persian Gulf War and, 131–32, 172, 418, 423,
    434, 435, 443

Labor Department, U.S., 395, 407
labor unions, 151, 269, 270, 273, 280, 281, 322, 326, 373,
    381
Lamb, Charles M., 414
landed gentry, 9
land grants, 47, 390
Landon, Alfred M., 296
Lardner, George, Jr., 365*n*
Laski, Harold, 456
Lasswell, Harold, 7*n*
Latin America, 426–27, 428, 439, 442
law, types of, 183–85
Lawson, Kay, 323
Lebanon, 131
LeBlanc, Hugh, 323
Lederman, Susan S., 256–57
Lee, Marcia, 59*n*
Lee, Richard Henry, 34
Lee v. *Weisman*, 197
LeFeber, Walter, 448
legislative branch:
    checks and balances and, 39, 53
    supremacy of, 52
    see also Congress, U.S.
legislative clearance, 166
legislative process, 98–101, 112–13, 114–21, 137–38
Leloup, Lance T., 139
Lemann, Nicholas, 414
Lenno, Rhonda F., 414
Levi, Margaret, 414
Levinson, Sanford, 80*n*, 85*n*, 407*n*
Levy, Leonard, 95, 204–5
Lewis, Anthony, 95
Lewis, Jerry, 101
liberals, 359, 368, 369, 370, 385
    affirmative action and, 91
    conservatives compared with, 221–23, 250, 361
    1988 election and, 271
    1992 election and, 277, 280
    publications read by, 312
    public opinion and, 225–26
Library of Congress, 197
Libya, U.S. bombing of, 131
licensing, 391, 393
Light, Paul, 139
Limbaugh, Rush, 310
limits, 452
    on Congress, 59–60, 70
    on executive branch, 59–60, 70
    on federal government, 8, 64
    on judiciary, 59–60, 70

procedural, 69, 94
substantive, 69, 94
Lincoln, Abraham, 52, 150, 240, 268, 296, 314, 380, 383
Lincoln Savings and Loan Association, 324
line-item veto, 134, 375
Lippmann, Walter, 251, 287
Lipset, Seymour M., 251
literacy tests, 120, 254
Little Rock, Ark., 85, 146
Livingston, Robert, 17
lobbyists, 112, 129, 326, 334–38, 342, 352, 363
local government, state governments' creation of,
    46–47
Locander, Robert, 167*n*
Lochner v. *New York*, 44*n*
Locke, John, 456
logrolling, 111
London, 253
Loomis, Burdett A., 336*n*, 352, 410*n*
Louisiana, 80–81*n*, 82, 373
Love, Nancy S., 456
Lowi, Theodore J., 157*n*, 169*n*, 181, 298–99, 352, 396*n*,
    407*n*, 422*n*, 428*n*
"Loyal Opposition," 9
Lujan v. *Defenders of Wildlife*, 208–9, 343, 344*n*
Lukas, J. Anthony, 87*n*
Lund, Michael, 271*n*
Luttbeg, Norman, 250
Luttwak, Edward N., 376–77
lynching, 120
Lynn, Naomi B., 181

MacArthur, Douglas, 444
McCarthy, Eugene, 231, 270
McCarthy, Joseph, 134, 236
Macchiarola, Frank J., 448
McClain, John, 325
McClure, Robert D., 138, 290
McCorvey, Norma, 78–79
McCulloch v. *Maryland*, 26, 43, 44
McDonald, Forrest, 37, 454*n*
McFarland, Andrew S., 352
McGovern, George, 270, 277
McGrain v. *Dougherty*, 123*n*
McIlwain, Charles H., 456
McKay, David, 181
McKinley, William, 268
McKitrick, Eric, 380*n*
McLarty, Thomas, 157
Madison, James, 20, 24, 32–33, 34, 50, 57, 150, 191, 205,
    262, 325, 349, 413, 419, 453*n*
Magnuson, Warren, 113
Mahe, Eddie, Jr., 323
Main, Jackson Turner, 15*n*
Maisel, Louis, 323
Malbin, Michael W., 113*n*, 139
Mann, Thomas E., 244*n*
Mannheim, Karl, 456
Mansbridge, Jane, 59*n*
Mapp v. *Ohio*, 76
Marbury, William, 191
Marbury v. *Madison*, 54*n*, 191
Marcos, Ferdinand, 437

Marcus, George E., 251
Marcus, Ruth, 119*n*, 225*n*, 368*n*, 369*n*, 370*n*, 371*n*, 410*n*
margarine, regulatory tax on, 396
Margolis, Michael, 251
market globalization, 354, 367, 442–44
marketplace of ideas, 217–23
    agreement and disagreement in, 220–21
    common fundamental values in, 219–20
    contemporary state of, 219–23
    origins of, 217–19
Mark Hatfield Marine Science Center, 127
Marmor, Theodore R., 414
Marshall, John, 26, 43–44, 54, 70, 191, 203
Marshall, Thurgood, 88–89, 197, 201, 206–7, 410
Marshall (European Recovery) Plan, 428, 430
Martin, Lynn, 235
Martin v. *Hunter's Lessee*, 192*n*
Martin v. *Wilks*, 90*n*
Maryland, 24, 26
Mashaw, Jerry L., 414
Mason, George, 57*n*, 454
Massachusetts, 16, 17, 18, 20, 23, 34, 259–60
Mass Transportation Act (1964), 113
Matalin, Mary, 228–29
Mathiopoulos, Marjarita, 456
Mauser, Gary A., 251
Mayhew, David R., 139
Means, Russell, 74
media, 330, 360–61, 374
    events shaped by, 230
    investigative reporting by, 236–40, 357, 360–61, 367,
        370–71
    manipulation of news by, 240
    political parties' use of, 234–36, 308–12, 314
    presidents' relationship with, 166–67, 231–34,
        236–40
    public opinion and, 217, 230–40, 250
    sources of power of, 230–34, 250
    story preparation process in, 239
Medicaid, 401
medical practice, licensing of, 394
Medicare, 2, 329, 369, 394, 401
Meese, Edwin, 357, 363
Melnick, R. Shep, 213
Meltzer, Allan, 355*n*
Memphis, Tenn., 86
merchant class, of New England, 15–17, 19, 24, 30
Merkl, Peter, 323
Mexico, 235, 273, 280, 337, 426
Meyer, Michael J., 69*n*
Mezey, Susan G., 213
Mfume, Kweisi, 114
Michel, Robert, 101
Michigan, 57
middle class, 8–9
"midnight judges," 191
Milbrath, Lester W., 352
Mildred and Claude Pepper Foundation, 127
military:
    blacks in, 82
    homosexuals in, 369, 374
military deterrence, as foreign policy, 271, 274–76,
    434–37
military-industrial complex, 339–41

Mill, James, 456
Mill, John Stuart, 456
Mills, Mike, 332*n*
minimum wage, 151*n*
Minnesota, 80*n,* 162
Minow, Martha, 69*n,* 95
"Minuteman" theory of defense, 434
Miranda, Ernesto, 196
Miranda v. *Arizona,* 76–77, 196
Miranda warning, 76, 77, 196
misdemeanors, right to counsel and, 77
Mississippi, 261
Missouri, 82
Missouri Compromise, 51, 296
Missouri ex rel. Gaines v. *Canada,* 82*n*
Missouri Law School, University of, 82
Missouri v. *Jenkins,* 206–7
Mitchell, Constance, 355*n*
Mitchell, George, 104
Moe, Terry M., 352
Mondale, Walter, 162, 270
monetary redistributive techniques, 397–99, 413–14
monopolies, 43
Montesquieu, 31
Montgomery, Ala., 86
Montgomery Improvement Association, 86
Moore, Barrington, 13
Moore v. *Ogilvie,* 190
mootness, 190
Moran v. *McDonough,* 206*n*
Morgan, Robert, 113
Morgenthau, Hans, 417, 422
Morin, Richard, 244*n,* 245*n*
Morrison v. *Olson,* 56*n*
mortgages, 3
Moseley-Braun, Carol, 124, 286
Mosher, Frederic C., 181
"Motor-Voter" Act (1993), 373, 383
Mozambique, 224
Muravchik, Joshua, 440–41
Murley, John A., 59*n*
Murphy, Walter F., 192*n,* 203*n*
Murray, Patty, 109
Mushroom Caucus, 114
Muskie, Edmund, 234
Muskrat v. *United States,* 190
Mutual Security Act (1951), 428
Myers v. *United States,* 145*n*

NAACP (National Association for the Advancement
    of Colored People), 77, 206, 343, 408, 409
NAACP v. *Alabama ex rel. Patterson,* 77*n*
NAB (National Association of Broadcasters), 332
Nacos, Brigitte L., 251
Nader, Ralph, 330, 331, 368
NAFTA (North American Free Trade Agreement),
    235, 273, 280, 337
Napoleonic foreign policy role, 437, 439, 440, 443, 448
Nardulli, Peter F., 213
Nathan, Richard, 181
National Aeronautics and Space Administration
    (NASA), 435*n*

National Association for the Advancement of Colored
    People (NAACP), 77, 206, 343, 408, 409
National Association of Broadcasters (NAB), 332
National Economic Council, 155
National Guard, U.S., 85, 146
National Industrial Recovery Act (1933), 144*n,* 152*n*
National Institutes of Health, 2
National Labor Relations (Wagner) Act (1935), 151
National Labor Relations Board (NLRB), 151, 188
National Labor Relations Board v. *Jones & Laughlin Steel
    Company,* 46*n,* 73*n,* 151
National League of Cities, 326
National League of Cities v. *Usery,* 151*n*
National Opinion Research Center, 244
National Organization for Women, 63, 227, 330
National Petroleum Refiners Association, 326
National Retired Teachers Association, 329
National Review, 312
National Rifle Association, 325, 327
National Right to Life Committee, 348
National Savings Loan League, 326
National Security Agency (NSA), 142
National Security Council (NSC), 142, 155, 158–59, 438
National Security Staff, 176
national security structure, 357, 359–60
National Traffic and Motor Vehicle Safety Act (1966),
    331
National Women's Political Caucus, 109
nation-states, 9–10, 40, 417–19, 447, 448
Native Americans, 18, 74, 75, 88–89, 203, 331
NATO (North Atlantic Treaty Organization), 416, 430
Natural Gas Pipeline Safety Act (1968), 331
Natural Resources Defense Council, 326
Nau, Henry, 448
Navy, U.S., 341
NBC, 235, 240, 309
Neagle case, 141, 144, 188–89
Near v. *Minnesota,* 73*n*
Neely, Richard, 213
negligence, contributory, 183
Nelson, Michael, 145*n*
Neubauer, Deane E., 456
Neuman, W. Russell, 251
Neustadt, Richard E., 31*n,* 52*n,* 148*n,* 181
New Deal, 203, 273, 275, 290, 316
    coalition in, 169, 269–70, 294
    federal government's expansion and, 44, 151–52,180
    party loyalty switch in, 265, 269
"new" federalism, 50
New Hampshire, 23, 34, 312
Newhouse, John, 163*n*
New Jersey, 20, 21, 34, 57
New Jersey Plan, 22
New Politics movement, 330–33
New Republic, 312, 338*n*
newspapers, 309
Newsweek, 361, 435
New York, 20, 23, 34, 162, 302, 303, 313
New Yorker, 163*n*
New York Post, 231
New York Review of Books, 312
New York Times, 199*n,* 208*n,* 230, 237, 261*n,* 285*n,* 328,
    335, 344*n,* 348*n,* 361, 371, 422*n*

New York v. *Quarles,* 201
New Zealand, 430
Nicaragua, 131, 176, 224, 363, 416, 437
Nie, Norman, 253, 290
Niemi, Richard, 290
Nissan Motor Company, 335–36
Nixon, Richard M., 163, 168, 196, 277, 311, 313, 316,
    339, 361, 363, 425
  China recognized by, 144, 425, 442
  filibustering against policies of, 120
  Ford's pardon of, 142
  impoundment and, 130, 365
  media and, 234
  OMB and, 176
  Supreme Court appointments of, 76
  Watergate scandal and, 167, 230, 296, 345, 361, 363
Nixon, U.S. v., 55*n*
Nixon administration, 134, 157, 158–59, 230, 238,
    296–97, 361, 363, 375
NLRB (National Labor Relations Board), 151, 188
Nobel Prize, 86
Nofziger, Lyn, 358
nomination process, 301, 322–23
Noriega, Manuel, 172, 437, 441
North, Oliver, 358
North American Free Trade Agreement (NAFTA),
    235, 273, 280, 337
North Atlantic Treaty (1949), 430
North Atlantic Treaty Organization (NATO), 416, 430
North Carolina, 20, 24, 34
NSA (National Security Agency), 142
NSC, *see* National Security Council
nuclear freeze movement, 225, 226
Nunn, Sam, 238, 369

OAS (Organization of American States), 430–31
O'Brien, David M., 80, 213
O'Connor, Sandra Day, 197, 199, 261
Office of Federal Contract Compliance, 395, 407
Office of Management and Budget (OMB), 130,
    159–62, 166, 176, 180, 365
Office of Technology Assessment, 113
Ohio, 80*n*
oil crisis (1973), 418
Oleszek, Walter, J., 139
oligarchy, 6
Oliver case, 73*n*
Ollie's Barbecue, 87*n*
Olsen, Mancur, Jr., 349*n*, 352
OMB, *see* Office of Management and Budget
Omnibus Crime Control and Safe Streets Act (1968),
    196
O'Neill, Michael J., 232–33
O'Neill, Thomas "Tip," 102
OPEC (Organization of Petroleum Exporting Coun-
    tries), 418, 442
"open market operations," 399
open primaries, 302, 323
"open rule," 115
Operation Rescue, 78–79
Oppenheimer, Bruce J., 138, 160*n*

opportunity, equality of, 219–20
Orfield, Gary, 87*n*, 393*n*
Organization of American States (OAS), 430–31
Organization of Petroleum Exporting Countries
    (OPEC), 418, 442
organized crime, 236
Orloff, Ann, 380, 415
Ornstein, Norman, 139, 177*n*
Orren, Gary, 244*n*
Ortiz, Solomon, 375
Ostrogorski, M., 314*n*
Otten, Alan, 235*n*
oversight, congressional, 122–23, 177
Oxnam, Robert B., 448

PACs, *see* political action committees
Page, Benjamin I., 246*n*
Paige, Connie, 226*n*, 352
Paine, Thomas, 419
Palko v. *Connecticut,* 73*n*
Palley, Howard, 67
Palley, Marian Lief, 67
Palmer, John L., 408*n*, 409*n*
Palmer, R. R., 37
Panama, U.S. invasion of, 172, 437, 441
Panama Refining Company v. *Ryan,* 152*n*
Panetta, Leon, 134, 162
Paraguay, 144*n*
pardons, presidential, 142–44
Parent, William A., 69*n*
parliaments, 8
party committees, 102–4
party votes, 105, 107
Pastor, Robert A., 428*n*
Patent and Trademark Office, U.S., 188
Paterson, William, 22
patronage, 126–29, 154, 236
Paul, Ellen, 414
PBS, 235
Peabody, Robert L., 139
"peace dividend," 435
Peele, Gillian, 226*n*
Penno, Richard F., 165*n*
Pennsylvania, 19, 20, 34, 80
Pentagon Papers, 361
Pepper, Claude, 127
per curiam rejections, 202
Perot, Ross, 3, 231, 232–33, 281–84, 297, 300, 306, 338,
    367
  political organization of, 227–30, 282
  program of, 164, 282
  use of media by, 167, 231, 232–33, 235, 266, 282, 283,
    310, 311
Persian Gulf War, 164, 172, 216, 225, 238, 275, 278, 320,
    365, 378, 430, 434, 435, 438
  events of, 131–32
  Holy Alliance role and, 443
  military technology used in, 341
Pertschuk, Michael, 113
Peterson, Paul, 67, 355*n*, 367*n*, 414
Petracca, Mark P., 335*n*, 352

Petrocik, John, 290
Pfiffner, James, 181
Philippines, 428, 437
Phillips, Kevin, 258*n*, 387
phone banks, 311–12, 316
Physicians for Social Responsibility, 227, 330
Pianan, Eric, 355*n*, 369*n*
Pierce, Samuel, 365
Piereson, James, 251
Pink, U.S. v., 125*n*, 144
Piven, Frances Fox, 291, 393*n*, 380*n*, 414
plaintiffs, definition of, 183
Planned Parenthood Federation, 348
Planned Parenthood of Southeastern Pennsylvania v.
    Casey, 79, 197
planters, southern, 15, 17, 19, 24
Plessy v. *Ferguson*, 82
Plotke, David, 381*n*
Poage, Robert, 102
"pocket veto," 121
Pohlmann, Marcus, 291
Polanyi, Karl, 421*n*, 439*n*
police, 151, 452
    civil liberties and power of, 76–77
    regulation of, 391
political action committees (PACs), 313, 314, 315,
        345–48
political demobilization, 379–80
political mobilization, 379, 380–81, 383
political parties, 101–11, 137–38, 149, 240, 292–93,
        381–85, 451
    campaign spending by, 313–16
    class and, 306–7
    committees and, 102–4
    decline of, 284, 294, 298–99, 307–20, 356, 373,
        374–75, 387
    development of, 52, 294–99, 306–7
    direct mail soliciting by, 312, 314, 323
    discipline of, 104–11, 381
    early opposition to, 292, 294
    electoral choice and, 256, 306–7
    electoral realignment and, 266–71
    functions of, 300–307
    fund-raising by, 312, 313, 323
    governmental influence of, 302–6
    House and Senate leadership structure of, 101–4
    interest groups and, 342, 344–49, 374–79, 385, 386
    media used by, 234–36, 308–12, 314
    minor, 297–300
    modern technology and, 308–13
    nomination process and, 301, 322–23
    phone banks used by, 311–12, 316
    president's support from, 111, 167–69
    Progressive era reform and, 307–8
    public opinion polls used by, 308
    public relations used by, 312–13
    voter loyalty to, 264–65
    see also specific parties
political process, 354, 356, 379, 381, 386
politics:
    "by other means," 356–72, 382
    definition of, 7
    governance and, 354–87
    popular influence expanded through, 9–11

public participation in, 253
    without voters, 372–74
    see also elections
polls and surveys, 240–45, 308, 375
poll taxes, 120, 254
Polsby, Nelson W., 181, 323
Pomper, Gerald M., 229, 256–57
Pope, Jacqueline, 352
pork barrel, 126–27
Powell, Colin, 159, 438
Powell, Lewis, 76
power:
    definition of, 7
    as end vs. means, 4
    powers vs., 148
powers:
    delegated, 141, 152, 176
    exclusive, 28
    expressed, 26
    police, 76–77, 151
    power vs., 148
    presidential, *see* president
    see also separation of powers
prayer in school, 59, 80
precedents in common law, 183
president, 140–81
    appointment powers of, 123
    bills signed by, 114
    bureaucracy and, 173–76, 180
    cabinet and, 154–57, 174–75, 180
    congressional power balance with, 50, 55–56, 98,
        121, 129–35, 138, 141, 143, 144–45, 149–51, 361,
        363, 365–67, 378
    in Constitution, 28, 36, 141–48, 180
    diplomatic powers of, 144–45, 180
    electoral realignments and, 267, 268–69
    executive agreements by, 125, 144–45
    Executive Office of, 158–62, 166, 176
    executive power of, 145, 148–49
    formal resources of power of, 154–63, 180
    as head of government, 145–48
    as head of state, 142–45
    impeachment of, 28, 141*n*
    impoundment power of, 130, 146*n*
    indirect election of, 25, 28, 52, 142, 262, 304–6
    informal resources of power of, 163–72, 180
    initiative and, 165–66
    "inner cabinet" of, 153, 156
    interest group support of, 169
    judicial powers of, 142–44, 180
    "Kitchen Cabinet" of, 157
    legislative clearance and, 166
    in legislative epoch, 149–51
    legislative power of, 145, 146
    mandate of, 163–65
    media's relationship with, 166–67, 231–34, 236–40
    military powers of, 142, 144, 145–48, 180
    national convention system and, 52, 150
    New Deal's expansion of role of, 44–46, 151–52
    party support of, 111, 167–69
    press conferences and, 166–67, 236
    public opinion and, 169–72, 170, 171
    public opinion polls used by, 241
    "special assistants" to, 157, 175

strength of, 25, 52, 56, 148–52
treaty-making power of, 123–25
veto power of, 28, 121, 125–26, 134, 146–48, 333
vice-president's relationship with
    White House staff and, 157–58, 175, 180
see also specific presidents
President's Committee on Administrative Management, 173–74
President's Committee on Civil Rights, 82
press, freedom of, 73
Price, David, 139, 160*n*
Priest, Dana, 225*n*, 369*n*
primary elections, 323
    media coverage of, 231, 234
    nomination by, 301, 302
    proportional representation electoral system used in, 259
privacy, right to, 76, 77–80, 343, 453
private bills, 127–29
"privatization," 390
privileges and immunities, 29, 36
procedural limits, 69, 94
Progressivism, 255–56, 307–8, 380, 382
Prohibition, 58, 62–63, 67
property, government seizure of, 69, 72
property law, 42
prosecutorial power, civil liberties and, 76
Protestants, 225, 226
Public Affairs Council, 227
Public Interest Research Group, 331
public law, 185
public opinion, 12, 216–17
    governmental policy and, 246–47, 250
    governmental shaping of, 12, 217, 224–25, 250
    and marketplace of ideas, 217–23
    measurement of, 217, 240–45
    media and, 217, 230–40, 250
    politicians' uncertainty about, 245–46
    presidents and, 169–72, 170, 171, 216–17
    private groups' shaping of, 225–30
    surveys and, 241–45
public policy, 388–415
    control techniques in, 389–99, 413
    definition of, 388
    inequality in, 403–10
    promotional control techniques in, 389–91, 392, 413
    redistributive policies in, 389, 392, 397–99, 413–14
    regulatory control techniques in, 389, 391–97, 413
public relations, political parties' use of, 312–13
"Publius," 34
Puerto Rico, 188
"pupil placement" laws, 85, 85*n*

Quayle, J. Danforth, 163, 164–65, 271, 282, 308, 311
Queenan, Joe, 227
Quester, George, 430*n*
quotas, racial, 90, 270, 271, 410

Rabe, Barry, 67
Rabkin, Jeremy, 67, 359*n*
racial discrimination:
    affirmative action and, 89–91, 270, 406–10, 414
    state governments and, 82–84, 85

see also blacks; civil rights; civil rights movement; segregation
railroads, 389
Randall, Richard S., 95
Randolph, Edmund, 20
Ranney, Austin, 323
Raspberry, William, 341*n*
Reagan, Ronald, 50, 59, 134, 140, 157, 160, 163, 166, 171, 172, 224, 226, 271, 273, 275, 297, 369, 422
    budget deficit and, 355, 365, 378, 386
    Bush and, 162–63, 281
    civil rights and, 407–10
    election of, 265, 269, 270–71, 285
    governmental philosophy of, 3–4, 366–67
    media and, 167, 234
    Reconstituted Right and, 270–71, 278
    Supreme Court appointments by, 197, 199, 274
    as "Teflon president," 234
Reagan administration, 49, 50, 123, 138, 157, 206–7, 238, 319–20, 339, 355, 359, 361, 363, 390, 403, 438
    Iran-Contra affair and, 56, 122, 131, 297, 360, 363, 366, 375
recessions, 271–77, 397
"reconciliation bill," 121
Reconstituted Right, Reagan and, 270–71
Reconstruction, 120
Rector, Robert, 394–95
Reed, Adolph, 291
Reed, Esther DeBerdt, 21
Reed, Stanley, 200
Regents of the University of California v. *Bakke,* 89*n,* 90
regulatory agencies, 188
regulatory policy, 209, 271, 378, 380
    techniques of, 391–97
regulatory taxation, 391, 396
Rehnquist, William, 56, 76, 80, 87, 90*n*
Rehnquist court, 76, 80–81, 206–8, 343
Reichley, A. James, 291
Reiter, Howard L., 256–57
Religious Right, 164, 271, 285, 345, 383
Reno, Janet, 155
Report on Manufactures (Hamilton), 389
representation, principle of, 39
representative democracy, 4
Republican party, 4, 59, 62, 112, 115, 121, 126, 150, 162–63, 168, 226, 270, 299, 304, 313, 348, 357–85, 436
    as big business party, 296
    campaign financing and, 245, 314, 324
    Committee on Committees of, 103, 303
    congressional redistricting and, 261
    conservative Democrats aligned with, 294–96
    Democratic Party compared with, 105–8, 245, 297, 319–20, 322, 372–74
    electoral college supported by, 306
    electoral realignments and, 268–69
    filibusters by, 119, 120, 304
    history of, 296–97
    interest group support of, 169, 348, 375–76
    Jeffersonian, 9, 268, 292, 294, 306
    military-industrial complex and, 339–40
    in 1992 election, 271–77, 281–86, 300
    presidency controlled by, 134, 296, 319, 365

Republican party (*continued*)
  weakening of, in New Deal era, 265
Republican Wednesday Group, 114
research and development contracting, 280, 390,
    434–35
"research" lobby, 326
restraints, *see* limits
"restrictive covenants," 82
retirement, compulsory, 81
revelation, investigation, prosecution (RIP), 361–65,
    368, 370, 373, 375
revenue sharing, 50
Revolutionary War, *see* American Revolution
Rhode Island, 19, 25, 31, 34
Ricks, Thomas, 341*n*
Riegle, Donald W., Jr., 127, 325
Rieselbach, Leroy, 139
rights:
  as cause of action, 64
  to counsel, 77
  individual, 39
  to privacy, 76, 77–80
  see also Bill of Rights; civil rights
right-to-life movement, 225, 226, 343; *see also* abortion
Rio Treaty (1947), 430, 431
riots, as political participation, 253
RIP, *see* revelation, investigation, prosecution
Ripley, Randall B., 139, 181
Rise and Fall of the Great Powers, The (Kennedy), 450
Robertson, Pat, 334–35
Robinson, Donald L., 24*n*, 67
Roche, John P., 22, 23
Rockman, Bert, 387
Roe v. *Wade*, 59, 77, 78–79, 80, 81, 190, 197, 343
Rogers, David, 368*n*, 375*n*
Rogers, Joel, 290
Rogers Act (1924), 422
Rokkan, Stein, 254*n*
Roosevelt, Franklin D., 144, 169, 240, 265, 268, 269,
    281, 294, 316, 384–85, 427
  "court packing" plan of, 203
  "fireside chats" and press conferences of, 167, 236,
    237
  presidential role expanded by, 129, 144, 151, 367,
    380–81
  White House staff of, 157, 158
  see also New Deal
Roosevelt, Theodore, 148–49, 231, 236, 284
Roper, Burns W., 244*n*
Roper Polls, 241, 242, 243
Rosenstone, Steven J., 373*n*, 387
Rossiter, Clinton, 13*n*, 50*n*, 57*n*, 262*n*, 325*n*, 349*n*, 453*n*
Rovner, Julie, 349*n*
Rowan, Hobart, 375*n*
"royalists," 15, 19
Rubin, Alissa J., 330*n*
Rubin, Eva, 213
Rubin, Irene S., 181, 414
Russian Republic, 418, 427, 435, 442, 443

Sabato, Larry, 309*n*, 312*n*, 323, 352
St. Louis Globe-Democrat, 236
St. Mary's Honor Center vs. *Hicks*, 91*n*

Salamon, Lester, 271*n*
SALT I (Strategic Arms Limitation Talks), 425
Samuelson, Robert J., 355*n*
Sanders, M. Elizabeth, 414
Sandinistas, 144
"satellite" countries, 418
Saudi Arabia, 172, 423, 435, 444
Savage, David G., 56*n*, 76*n*
savings and loan scandal, 375, 378
Sawhill, Isabel, 414
SBA (Small Business Administration), 2
Scalia, Antonin, 197, 208–9
Schattschneider, E. E., 298–99, 420*n*
Schechter Poultry Corp. v. *United States*, 152*n*
Schick, Allen, 139
Schlafly, Phyllis, 62–63
Schlesinger, Arthur, Jr., 54, 55, 143*n*, 144*n*
Schlozman, Kay Lehman, 327*n*, 353
Schneider, William, 251
school desegregation, 73, 82–88, 146, 206–8, 343, 393,
    406, 407–8
schools, prayer in, 59, 80, 197, 271, 273, 330
Schott, Richard, 177*n*
Schumpeter, Joseph A., 13, 456
Schwartz, Bernard, 87*n*
Schwartz, John E., 394–95, 403*n*, 407*n*
Scigliano, Robert, 202*n*, 213
Sciolino, Elaine, 422*n*
SCLC (Southern Christian Leadership Conference), 86
Scott, Dred, 51
searches and seizures, 73, 76–77
Sease, Douglas R., 355*n*
SEATO (Southeast Asia Treaty Organization), 430
secretary of defense, 155, 156
secretary of state, 155, 156, 422
secretary of the treasury, 155, 156
Securities and Exchange Commission (SEC), 188
segregation, 230
  de facto, 84–85, 87, 91
  de jure, 84–85, 91
  "separate but equal" doctrine and, 82–84
  state power of, 73
Seib, Gerald F., 225*n*
self-incrimination, 73
"Selling of the Pentagon, The," 224–25
Senate, U.S., 109, 124, 129, 285–86, 310, 364, 369
  calendars of, 115
  Connecticut Compromise and, 23
  direct vs. indirect election of, 25, 52, 100, 262
  filibusters in, 117–18, 120, 121, 138, 370
  House of Representatives compared with,
    100–101, 119
  line-item veto and, 134, 375
  party leadership in, 101–4, 106
  presidential appointments and, 29, 123, 145
  president of, 101, 104, 116
  special powers of, 123–25
  term of office in, 25, 100, 262
  treaty ratification power of, 25, 28, 122, 123–25
Senate committees:
  Appropriations, 111, 121, 123, 130, 160, 177
  Armed Services, 369
  Budget, 130
  Commerce, 113

Ethics, 127, 324
Finance, 130, 160, 369, 377
Government Operations, 177
Intelligence, 123
Judiciary, 364, 370
Select Committee to Investigate the 1972 Presidential Campaign Activities (Ervin Committee), 345, 361–63
senior citizens, as interest group, 327, 329
Senior Executive Service, 154
"separate but equal" doctrine, 82–84
separation of powers, 31, 38–39, 50–56, 149, 208–9, 452
  checks and balances in, 31–32, 52, 53, 134
  mixed regime produced by, 31
  problems with, 54–55
  reasoning behind, 50
sequestration, 160
Shapiro, Robert Y., 204*n*, 246*n*, 359*n*
Shaw v. *Reno,* 261
Shays, Daniel, 20
Shays's Rebellion, 10, 20
Shazan, Naomi, 449
Shefter, Martin, 67, 222*n*, 269*n*, 290, 359*n*
Shelby, Richard, 108, 119
Shelley v. *Kraemer,* 82*n*
Shell Oil, 326
Sherman, Roger, 17
Sherman Antitrust Act (1890), 44*n*, 151*n*
Shklar, Judith N., 456
shopkeepers, 15
Shuster, Bud, 127
Shuttlesworth v. *Birmingham Board of Education,* 85*n*
Sierra Club, 227, 330
Sierra Club v. *Morton,* 190
Silberman, Charles, 95
Silent Scream, The, 226
Silverstein, Mark, 95, 208*n*
Sinclair, Barbara, 139
Sinclair, Upton, 313
Skocpol, Theda, 13, 380*n*, 415
Skowronek, Stephen, 380*n*
Slaughterhouse Cases, 71*n*, 81*n*, 91*n*
slavery, slaves, 71, 120, 268, 294
  state property law and, 42, 51
  territorial expansion of, 296
  Thirteenth Amendment and, 30, 63
  Three-fifths Compromise and, 23–24
Slovakia, 418
Small Business Administration (SBA), 2
Smith, Eric R., 323
Smith, Steven S., 139
Smith v. *Allwright,* 82*n*, 200
Smoot-Hawley Tariff (1930), 379
social insurance tax, 6, 400
Socialist party, 224, 313
Social Security, 2, 160, 329, 397, 394, 399, 400–403
Social Security Act (1935), 399
Social Security (FICA) tax, 401
Social Security Trust Fund, 403
solicitor general, Supreme Court and, 197, 200–202, 212
Somalia, 140, 417, 423, 424–26
Sorauf, Frank J., 323
Souter, David, 197, 199

South Africa, Republic of, 221, 222
South Carolina, 23, 24, 34, 80*n*, 84
Southeast Asia Treaty (1954), 430
Southeast Asia Treaty Organization (SEATO), 430
Southeastern Pennsylvania v. *Casey,* 80*n*
Southern Christian Leadership Conference (SCLC), 86
sovereignty, 418
Soviet Union, 7, 9, 144, 275, 284, 376, 435, 442, 443, 454–55
  collapse of, 144, 172, 271, 276, 284, 376, 418, 426, 433, 442, 450
  containment policy and, 424, 439–40
  U.N. and, 423
Sowell, Thomas, 410*n*
Spain, 443
Speaker of the House, 101–3, 110, 112, 116, 137, 303, 323
"special assistants," presidential, 157, 175
"special masters," 192
special prosecutor, 359, 361, 363, 365
speech, freedom of, 8, 72, 75, 453
spending power, 397, 399
Spirit of the Laws, The (Montesquieu), 31
Spitzer, Robert, 52*n*
Springfield Republican, 236
SSI (Supplemental Security Income), 401
Stafford, Robert, 336
Staggenborg, Suzanne, 353
Stalin, Joseph, 7
Stamp Act (1765), 14
standing, rules of, 190, 204
Stanley, Harold, 291
stare decisis, 183
state courts, 183, 186, 187
State Department, U.S., 422, 428, 443*n*
state governments:
  in Articles of Confederation, 17–19
  in Bill of Rights, 70–73, 75
  in Constitution, 26, 28
  federal government and, 11, 25, 26, 28, 31–32, 34–35, 36, 40, 47–50, 61–62
  as fundamental governing bodies, 40–43, 46
  in legal disputes, 192, 194
  local governments created by, 46–47
  party loyalty and, 264
  racial discrimination and, 82–84, 85
  revenue sharing and, 50
  Supreme Court decisions overturned by, 189–91
  taxation of federal agencies by, 26
  traditional activities of, 40–43
states:
  admission of, 30
  comity (reciprocity) among, 29, 36
  constitutional amendments and, 58–59
  differences among, 40
statutes, judicial review of, 54–55
Steel Caucus, 114
Steffens, Lincoln, 231
Stein, Arthur, 449
Steinem, Gloria, 62–63
Steiner, Gilbert, 59*n*
Stenholm, Charles, 107
Steward Machine Co. v. *Davis,* 46*n*
Stidham, Ronald, 213

Stimson, James, 290
Stockdale, James, 311
Stockman, David, 176, 353
stock market crash (1929), 3
Stoessinger, John G., 421*n*
Stone, Alan, 302*n*, 402*n*, 415
Stone, Geoffrey, 69*n*
Stone, Harlan F., 200
Storing, Herbert, 37
Strahan, Randall, 139
Strategic Arms Limitation Treaty (SALT I), 425
Strayer, Joseph R., 13
student loans, 2
subsidies, 389–90, 393
substantive limits, 69, 94
Sullivan, John L., 251
Sundquist, James L., 139, 266*n*, 282*n*, 323, 387
Sunstein, Cass, 69*n*, 95
Sununu, John, 157
Superconducting Super Collider, 390
"superpower" countries, 418
Supplemental Security Income (SSI), 401
supremacy clause, 30, 192
Supreme Court, U.S., 26, 59, 314, 359
    affirmative action and, 90, 91, 407*n*, 410
    annual caseload of, 186
    under Burger, 76–81, 190, 208, 343
    Bush's appointments to, 79, 199, 208, 410
    citizen suits and, 343
    civil liberties and, 72–73, 76–81
    civil rights legislation and, 81*n*, 82–84, 85–87
    Clinton's appointments to, 81, 199, 371, 372
    congressional and state overturning of decisions
        by, 189–91
    in Constitution, 29, 189
    on delegated powers, 56, 152*n*
    dissenting opinions in, 199–200, 212
    in Dred Scott case, 51
    dual citizenship confirmed by, 70–71
    on eminent domain, 72, 185
    on executive agreements, 125
    in federal vs. state issues, 43–48, 151
    Fourteenth Amendment cases and, 71–73, 75–76, 81,
        91
    full dress review by, 186
    on Gramm-Rudman-Hollings Act, 160
    as "imperial judiciary," 80
    individual justices as influence on, 197–201
    influences on, 197–202
    injury defined by, 190
    interstate commerce redefined by, 40, 73
    "judicial activism" and, 79–80, 196
    judicial revolutions and, 203–9
    legal path to, 193, 195
    lifetime appointments to, 27, 29
    Nixon's appointments to, 76, 361
    opinion writing in, 199–200, 212
    original jurisdiction of, 192, 195
    pattern of cases and, 197, 202
    politics and, 202–9
    on presidential powers, 144–45
    Reagan's appointments to, 79, 123, 199
    under Rehnquist, 76, 80–81, 206–8, 343
    Roosevelt's "court packing" plan for, 203
    rules of access to, 190, 204
    solicitor general and, 197, 200–202, 212
    "strict construction" of Constitution by, 76
    vetoes declared unconstitutional by, 125–26
    under Warren, 73, 76, 77, 80, 81, 196
    see also judicial review
Suro, Roberto, 261*n*
surveys and polls, 240–45, 308
Swann v. *Charlotte-Mecklenburg Board of Education*, 87*n*
Sweatt v. *Painter*, 82*n*
Sweden, 443
Switzerland, 418*n*
Syria, 435, 444

Taft, William Howard, 148–49
Taiwan, 418, 428, 430
Talbott, Strobe, 426*n*
talk shows, 310
Taney, Roger, 51
tariffs, 41, 420
Tatalovich, Raymond, 52*n*, 415
Tax Court, U.S., 188
taxes, 8, 16, 26
    distribution of benefits vs. burdens of, 6
    1989 totals of, 6
    "without representation," 8, 14
    see also specific taxes
Teamsters, 326
Tedin, Kent, 250
television, 308–11, 312, 314, 332–33, 361, 371
tenBroek, Jacobus, 205
Tennessee, 143, 165
term limits, 132–33
territorial courts, federal, 188
territories, 30, 42
Terry, Randall, 78–79
Testament, 226
Tet offensive, 234
Texas, 78, 162
Texas Law School, University of, 82
Textor, Robert B., 453*n*
Thernstrom, Abigail M., 95
think tanks, 326
third-party candidates, 297–300, 303, 322
Third World, 4, 428
Thomas, Clarence, 124, 206–7, 286, 359, 364, 365, 410
Thompson, Dennis L., 212
Thompson, Dennis P., 456
Thornburgh, Richard, 228
Three-fifths Compromise, 23–24
Thurow, Sarah, 95
Tiananmen Square, 443
Tierney, John T., 327*n*, 353
Tilden, Samuel, 305
Tilly, Charles, 4*n*, 13
Time, 336*n*, 361
Tisch, Lawrence, 332
Tocqueville, Alexis de, 13, 454, 455
Tonelson, Alan, 440–41
Topeka, Kans., 84
To Secure These Rights, 82
totalitarian governments, 7
Tower, John, 123, 363

Tower Commission, 438
Townshend Acts (1767), 16, 18
trade, 15, 18–19
Trade Act (1974), 443*n*
Traugott, Michael, 245*n*
Travel and Tourism Caucus, 114
Treasury Department, U.S., 166, 175
treaties:
    collective security, 429, 430–34
    executive agreements compared with, 125, 144–45
    presidential negotiation of, 28, 123–25
    Senate's power of ratification of, 25, 28, 122, 123–25
    supremacy clause and, 30, 36
Treaty of Versailles (1919), 120
trials:
    annual number of, 182
    Fifth Amendment and, 69
    Sixth Amendment and, 69, 73*n*
Tribe, Lawrence, 213
Truman, David, 353
Truman, Harry S., 82, 111, 145, 427, 444
Tulis, Jeffrey, 150*n*
Turkey, 427–28
Tuskegee Institute, 408

"unalienable rights," 17
unemployment, 16, 271, 273, 354
unilateralism, 420–21, 447
Union of Concerned Scientists, 326
unitary governments, 40, 42
United Farm Workers of America, 334
United Farm Workers Organizing Committee, 334
United Mine Workers, 326
United Nations (U.N.), 417–18, 435
    Bosnia and, 426
    foreign policy role of, 422–26, 429, 444
    Persian Gulf War and, 132, 423–24, 434, 443
    Somalia and, 140, 423, 424–26
United States Code, 145*n*
United States v. *Curtiss-Wright Export Corp.*, 144
United States v. *Harris*, 76*n*
United States v. *Nixon*, 55*n*
United States v. *Pink*, 125*n*, 144
United Steelworkers v. *Weber*, 90*n*
United We Stand America, 227–30, 282
universities, as interest group, 326
Unsafe at Any Speed (Nader), 331
Utah, 302
utilities companies, 393

Verba, Sidney, 253, 290
Veteran's Administration Hospitals, 2
veto power, 28, 121, 125–26, 134, 146–48, 333
vice-president:
    in Constitution, 162
    as NSC member, 155
    president's relationship with, 162–63
    as Senate's president, 101, 162
Vietnam, Republic of (South), 428
Vietnam War, 120, 167, 269, 330, 425, 441
    draft and, 6, 142
    media and, 224–25, 230, 231, 234, 236–38

secret executive agreements and, 125
Virginia, 20, 23, 24, 34, 84
Virginia Plan, 20–22, 32
Vogel, David, 227*n*, 333*n*, 353, 415
Volgy, Thomas, 403*n*
Voters for Choice, 348
voting rights, 61
    of blacks, 24, 25, 82, 85, 87, 120, 260–61
    history of, 254–58
    of women, 21, 25, 254
Voting Rights Act (1965), 120, 261, 405

Wade, Henry, 78
wage, minimum, 151*n*
Wagner (National Labor Relations) Act (1935), 151
Walker, Samuel, 37
Wallace, William, 449
Wall Street Journal, 197*n*, 341*n*, 344*n*
Walsh, Lawrence E., 131
Walsh, Sharon, 341*n*
Ward's Cove v. *Atonio*, 90
War on Poverty, 316, 394–95, 407
War Powers Resolution (1973), 130, 365
warrants, search and seizure and, 73, 76–77
Warren, Earl, 73, 76, 77, 196, 205
Warsaw Pact (1955), 433, 442
Washington, 109
Washington, Booker T., 408–9
Washington, D.C., marches on, 86
Washington, George, 144, 292, 294, 419–20
Washington Post, 230, 237, 238, 273, 284, 300*n*, 330*n*, 336*n*, 338*n*, 341*n*, 348*n*, 361, 371
Watergate scandal, 56, 146*n*, 148, 167, 230, 286, 296, 344–45, 359, 361, 375
Wattenberg, Martin, 323
Wayne, Stephen J., 297*n*
weapons of control, congressional, 122
Weaver, R. Kent, 387
Weber, Eugen, 8*n*
Weber, Max, 13
Webster v. *Reproductive Health Services*, 77, 80*n*, 343
Weddington, Sarah, 78
Weinberger, Caspar, 144, 358, 438
Weir, Margaret, 380, 415
Weisberg, Herbert, 290
Weisberg, Jacob, 338*n*
Weiser, Benjamin, 197
Weisskopf, Michael, 329*n*, 336*n*, 338*n*
Welch, Susan, 124*n*
welfare state, 46, 319, 380
    contributory programs and, 399–401
    as fiscal and social policy, 319, 394–95, 399–403, 414
    non-contributory programs and, 399, 401–3
Wertheimer, Fred, 346–47
Wessell, Nils H., 449
Western Europe, 19, 253
    governmental evolution in, 8–11
    unitary governments in, 40
    voting rights in, 254
Whig party, 268, 296, 307
whips, 104, 110, 137
White, Byron, 81, 197, 199, 371
White House staff, 157–58, 175, 180

"white primaries," 82
Whittaker and Baxter, 313
Wholesome Meat Act (1967), 331
Wiener v. *United States,* 145*n*
Wildavsky, Aaron, 181
Willbern, York, 46*n*
Williams, Joan, 86*n*
Williamson, Richard, 124
Willie, Charles, 410*n*
Wills, Garry, 37
Wilson, James, 355
Wilson, James Q., 181
Wilson, William Julius, 406*n*
Wilson, Woodrow, 120, 149, 151*n*, 224, 236, 437
Wines, Michael, 119*n*
Wofford, Harris, 228
Wolfe, Christopher, 213
Wollheim, Richard, 3*n*
women, 99, 109, 129
    "gender gap" and, 221
    1992 election and, 277, 286
    pre-Revolution activism of, 21
    rights of, 76, 77–80, 88–89, 342, 359, 364, 405
    voting rights of, 21, 25, 254

Wong, Kenneth K., 67
Wood, Gordon S., 37
Woods, Harriet, 109
Woodward, Bob, 87*n*, 197*n*, 438*n*
Worcester v. *Georgia,* 203*n*
working class, 9, 15
World Balkanization, 442
World Bank (International Bank for Reconstruction
    and Development), 426–27, 429
World War I, 6, 120, 224, 421, 437
World War II, 6, 241, 356, 386, 434
Wright, Deil S., 67
Wright, Jim, 102, 103, 110, 357, 363, 365
Wright, Lawrence, 283*n*
writs, 192–94, 195
    of *habeas corpus,* 26–28, 192, 194, 195, 200
Wyoming, 57

Yarmolinsky, Adam, 146*n*
Yeltsin, Boris, 417
Youngstown Sheet Tube Co. v. *Sawyer,* 55*n*
Yugoslavia, 144, 417, 418, 442, 444
"yuppies," 129